PEARSON EDEXCEL INTERNATIONAL GCSE (9–1)

SCIENCE SINGLE AWARD

Student Book

BIOLOGY
Phil Bradfield
Steve Potter

CHEMISTRY
Jim Clark
Steve Owen
Rachel Yu

PHYSICS
Brian Arnold
Penny Johnson
Steve Woolley

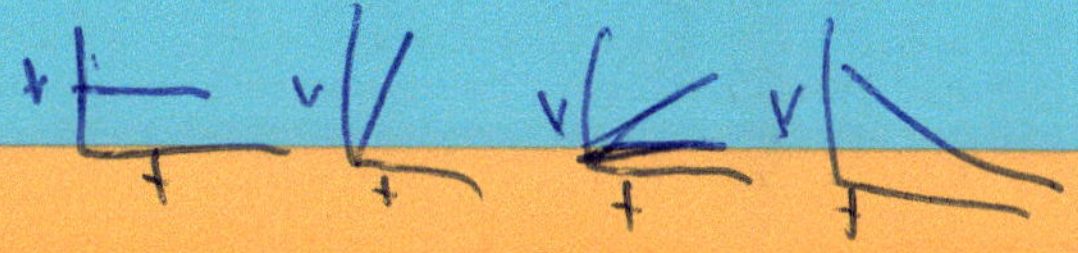

gradient = speed

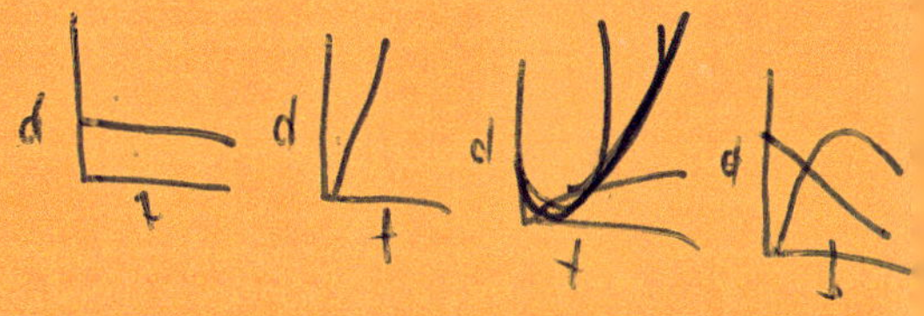

acceleration = $\frac{v-u}{t}$

average speed / velocity-time graph = $\frac{v+u}{2}$

IAN ANDREEV

ITY

Ilower Gcfe.

distance / velocity time graph
= calculate the area

gradient / velocity time graph
= $\frac{v-u}{2}$

gradient / distance time graph
= $\frac{d}{t}$

$v = \frac{s}{t}$ $s = v \times t$ $t = \frac{s}{v}$

Published by Pearson Education Limited, 80 Strand, London, WC2R 0RL.

www.pearsonglobalschools.com

Copies of official specifications for all Edexcel qualifications may be found on the website: https://qualifications.pearson.com

Text © Pearson Education Limited 2020
Development edited by Kate Blackham, Katharine Godfrey-Smith and Deborah Webb
Copy edited by Tim Jackson
Proofread by Rebecca Ramsden
Indexed by Judith Reading
Designed by © Pearson Education Limited 2020
Typeset by © SPi Global
Original illustrations © Pearson Education Limited 2020
Illustrated by © SPi Global
Cover design by © Pearson Education Limited 2020
Cover images: Front: **Alamy Images:** PLG/Alamy Stock Photo
Inside front cover: **Shutterstock.com:** Dmitry Lobanov

The rights of Brian Arnold, Phil Bradfield, Jim Clark, Penny Johnson, Steve Owen, Steve Potter, Steve Woolley and Rachel Yu to be identified as authors of this work have been asserted by them in accordance with the Copyright, Designs and Patents Act 1988.

First published 2020

23 22
10 9 8 7

British Library Cataloguing in Publication Data
A catalogue record for this book is available from the British Library

ISBN 9781292306216

Copyright notice
All rights reserved. No part of this publication may be reproduced in any form or by any means (including photocopying or storing it in any medium by electronic means and whether or not transiently or incidentally to some other use of this publication) without the written permission of the copyright owner, except in accordance with the provisions of the Copyright, Designs and Patents Act 1988 or under the terms of a licence issued by the Copyright Licensing Agency, 5th Floor, Shackleton House, 4 Battlebridge Lane, London, SE1 2HX (www.cla.co.uk). Applications for the copyright owner's written permission should be addressed to the publisher.

Printed in the UK by Ashford Press Ltd

Endorsement Statement
In order to ensure that this resource offers high-quality support for the associated Pearson qualification, it has been through a review process by the awarding body. This process confirms that this resource fully covers the teaching and learning content of the specification or part of a specification at which it is aimed. It also confirms that it demonstrates an appropriate balance between the development of subject skills, knowledge and understanding, in addition to preparation for assessment.

Endorsement does not cover any guidance on assessment activities or processes (e.g. practice questions or advice on how to answer assessment questions), included in the resource nor does it prescribe any particular approach to the teaching or delivery of a related course.

While the publishers have made every attempt to ensure that advice on the qualification and its assessment is accurate, the official specification and associated assessment guidance materials are the only authoritative source of information and should always be referred to for definitive guidance.
Pearson examiners have not contributed to any sections in this resource relevant to examination papers for which they have responsibility.

Examiners will not use endorsed resources as a source of material for any assessment set by Pearson. Endorsement of a resource does not mean that the resource is required to achieve this Pearson qualification, nor does it mean that it is the only suitable material available to support the qualification, and any resource lists produced by the awarding body shall include this and other appropriate resources.

Acknowledgements
We are grateful to the following for permission to reproduce copyright material:

(Key: b-bottom; c-centre; l-left; r-right; t-top)

123RF GB LIMITED: Ron Zmiri/123RF 101TL, Molekuul/123RF 175C, Frogtravel/123RF 178, Sittiporn Kheawkham/123RF 211, Avilog/123RF 214, Scanrail/123RF 274, Jozsef Szasz-Fabian/123RF 300TR, Melinda Nagy/123RF 308, Leung Cho Pan/123RF 324, Choneschones/123RF 326T, Homestudio/123RF 332B, Anyka/123RF 424, Cristimatei/123RF 444T; **Alamy Images:** Rachel Husband/Alamy Stock Photo 4TL, Hayley Evans/Alamy Stock Photo 4TR, Nathan Allred/Alamy Stock Photo 4B, IanDagnall Computing/Alamy Stock Photo 5TC, JLImages/Alamy Stock Photo 6T, Guenther/Blickwinkel/Alamy Stock Photo 7TL, Nigel Cattlin/Alamy Stock Photo 9BL, NaturimBild/Blickwinkel/Alamy Stock Photo 15TL, Fox/Blickwinkel/Alamy Stock Photo 15 CL, Guenther/Blickwinkel/Alamy Stock Photo 15 CR, Fox/Blickwinkel/Alamy Stock Photo 15TR, Greg Dale/National Geographic Image Collection/Alamy Stock Photo 64, Ernie Janes/Alamy Stock Photo 72, Flpa/Alamy Stock Photo 83T, FineArt/Alamy Stock Photo 91, Naturfoto-Online/Alamy Stock Photo 93, Jim West/Alamy Stock Photo 100, Jan Wlodarczyk/Alamy Stock Photo 101TR, Sergey Nivens/Alamy Stock Photo 118, Peter Anderson (c) Dorling Kindersley/Alamy stock Photo 5, World History Archive/Alamy Stock Photo 158, Trevor Chriss/Alamy Stock Photo 176, Nikos Pavlakis/Alamy Stock Photo 206TR, Monty Rakusen/Image Source/Alamy Stock Photo 214TL, David Taylor/Alamy Stock Photo 221, Bud Force/Aurora Open RF/Cavan Images/Alamy Stock Photo 278, Nasa Photo/Alamy Stock Photo 294, Nick Greening/Alamy Stock Photo 295TL, Michele Burgess/Alamy Stock Photo 295TR, Vladimir Galkin/Alamy Stock Photo 300TC, Charles Stirling/Alamy Stock Photo 308TL, Scott Ramsey/Alamy Stock Photo 308TR, Linda Richards/Alamy Stock Photo 311TR, U.S. Navy/Age fotostock/Alamy Stock Photo 314, Granger Historical Picture Archive/Granger, NYC/Alamy Stock Photo 319, Trevor Chriss/Alamy Stock Photo 325TR, Pixel shepherd/Alamy Stock Photo 325BL, Studioshots/Alamy Stock Photo 326, Cultura RM/IE245/Alamy Stock Photo 334, Sciencephotos/Alamy Stock Photo 338, Philipus/Alamy Stock Photo 339, Andrew Michael/Alamy Stock Photo 345T, Sciencephotos/Alamy Stock Photo 350, Chris Rose/Alamy Stock Photo 356TR, PjrStudio/Alamy Stock Photo 356BL, ImagineThat/Alamy Stock Photo 357, Authentic Creations/Alamy Stock Photo 365CL, Radoslav Radev/Alamy Stock Photo 365BL, Henry Westheim Photography/Alamy Stock Photo 373TL, Sean Pavone/Alamy Stock Photo 373TR, Pictorial Press Ltd/Alamy Stock Photo 379, Ian Dagnall/Alamy Stock Photo 384C, Jeff Rotman/Alamy Stock Photo 391TC, Wave Royalty Free,Inc/Design Pics Inc/Alamy Stock Photo 391TR, Emmanuel Lacoste/Alamy Stock Photo 392T, Interfoto/Personalities/Alamy Stock Photo 393, The Natural History Museum/Alamy Stock Photo 395, Pictorial Press Ltd/Alamy Stock Photo 396T, Paul ridsdale pictures/Alamy Stock Photo 406, Samart boonyang/Alamy Stock Photo 408, Pictorial Press Ltd/Alamy Stock Photo 414, Ange/Alamy Stock Photo 429, Pulsar Imagens/Alamy Stock Photo 431BL, Art Directors&Trip/Alamy Stock Photo 441, Horizon International Images Limited/Alamy Stock Photo 443, Richard Wainscoat/Alamy Stock Photo 444, Nasa/Alamy Stock Photo 446, Andrew Michael/Alamy Stock Photo FM(006); **Fotolia:** Kateryna_Kon/Fotolia 22, Kateryna_Kon/Fotolia 83, Grinchh/Fotolia 145, Arpad Nagy-Bagoly/Fotolia 284, Troninphoto/Fotolia 312TR, ArtushFoto/Fotolia 317, Ktsdesign/Fotolia 352, Schankz/Fotolia 392B; **GETTY IMAGES INCORPORATED:** Muditha Madushan/ EyeEm/ Getty Images 2, Klaus Vedfelt/Digital Vision/Getty Images 14, Science Photo Library - H. BOND/NASA/ESA/STScI/Brand X Pictures/Getty Images 134, Maxim Grigoryev/TASS/Getty images 188, PaulFleet/iStock/Getty Images Plus/Getty Images 232, YinYang/E+/Getty Images 311, Frantic00/Getty Images 312, Peter Turnley/Corbis Historical/Getty Images 314TL, Robert Sullivan/Afp/Getty Images 356, Scott Eells/Bloomberg/Getty Images 359, Carlos Herrera/Icon Sportswire/Corbis/Getty Images 373, Science & Society Picture Library/Getty Images 384B; **Maritime & Coastguard Agency:** Maritime & Coastguard Agency 355T; **NASA:** NASA 391; **Nature Picture Library:** Nature Production/Nature Picture Library 251T; **Pearson Education Ltd:** Trevor Clifford/Pearson Education Ltd 30, Jules Selmes/Pearson Education Ltd 329, Oxford Designers & Illustrators Ltd/Pearson Education Ltd 288, Studio 8/Pearson Education Ltd 331, Gareth Boden/Pearson Education Ltd 338TL; **Science Photo Library Ltd:** Stephen Ausmus/US Department Of Agriculture/Science Photo Library 5TL, Power and Syred/Science Photo Library 5BL, Dorling Kindersley/Uig/Science Photo Library 6, Sinclair Stammers/Science Photo Library 7TC, Dr.Gopal Murti/Science Photo Library 7TR, Lee D. Simon/Science Photo Library 9BC, Biomedical Image Unit ,SouthHampton General hospital/Science Photo Library 17, Dr.Gopal Murti/Science Photo Library 18, John Durham/Science Photo Library 21, Science Photo Library 22TL,Martyn F. Chillmaid/Science Photo Library 22CL, Martyn F. Chillmaid/Science Photo Library 22C,Andrew Lambert Photography/Science Photo Library 30, Susumu Nishinaga/Science Photo Library 31TL, Steve Gschmeissner/Science Photo Library 31TR, JC Revy, ISM/Science Photo Library 32, Science Photo Library 36T, Biophoto Associates/Science Photo Library 36B, Ralphs Hutchings, Visuals Unlimited/Science Photo Library 51T, Nibsc/Science Photo Library 51B, Science Photo Library 60, Animated Healthcare Ltd/Science Photo Library 73, Omikron/Science Photo Library 74T, Andrew Lambert Photography/Science Photo Library 74B, National Library of Medicine/Science PhotoLibrary 90, Natural History Museum, London/Science Photo Library 92BR, Natural History Museum, London/Science Photo Library 92BL, Martyn F. Chillmaid/Science Photo Library 103, David Parker/Science Photo Library 119TR, Volker Steger/Science Photo Library 127, Dr Brad Mogan /Visuals Unlimited/Science Photo Library 129, GustoImages/Science Photo Library 138, Andrew Lambert Photography/Science Photo Library 148, Mikkel Juul Jensen/Science Photo Library 170, Charles D. Winters/Science Photo Library 330, Martyn F Chillmaid/Science Photo Library 189, Martyn F Chillmaid/Science Photo Library 191, Martyn F Chillmaid/Science Photo Library 192, Andrew Lambert Photography/Science Photo Library 196T, Editorial Image/Science Photo Library 196B, Charles D Winters/Science Photo Library 353, Andrew Lambert Photography/Science Photo Library 202, Martyn F Chillmaid/Science Photo Library 203, Martyn F Chillmaid/Science Photo Library 209, Giphotostock/Science Photo Library 215, Giphotostock/Science Photo Library 216, Crown Copyright/Health and Safety Laboratory/Science Photo Library 219, MARTYN F. CHILLMAID / SCIENCE PHOTO LIBRARY 220, Martyn F Chillmaid/Science Photo Library 221T, David Taylor/Science Photo Library 221BL1, Science Photo Library 221BC, GiphotoStock/Science Photo Library 221BR1, Science Photo Library 221BR2, Andrew Lambert Photography/Science Photo Library 222, Martyn F Chillmaid/Science Photo Library 231, Phil Degginger/Science Photo Library 233, Martyn F Chillmaid/Science Photo Library 238, GiphotoStock/Science Photo Library 244, Dorling Kindersley/Uig/Science Photo Library 248,Science Photo Library 251, Carol and Mike Werner/Science Photo Library 262, Lea Paterson/Science Photo Library 263, Martyn F. Chillmaid/Science Photo Library 282, Martyn F Chillmaid/Science Photo Library 284TL, Volker Steger/Science Photo Library 284TR, Andrew Lambert Photography/Science Photo Library 303, Cordelia Molloy/Science Photo Library 309C,

(Continues on page 464)

COURSE STRUCTURE

BIOLOGY

UNIT 1: THE NATURE AND VARIETY OF LIVING ORGANISMS — 2
1 THE CHARACTERISTICS OF LIVING ORGANISMS AND THEIR VARIETY — 3

UNIT 2: STRUCTURE AND FUNCTION IN LIVING ORGANISMS — 14
2 LEVELS OF ORGANISATION AND CELL STRUCTURE — 15
3 BIOLOGICAL MOLECULES — 20
4 MOVEMENT OF SUBSTANCES INTO AND OUT OF CELLS — 28
5 NUTRITION — 34
6 RESPIRATION — 47
7 GAS EXCHANGE — 50
8 TRANSPORT — 56

UNIT 3: REPRODUCTION AND INHERITANCE — 72
9 REPRODUCTION — 73
10 INHERITANCE — 81

UNIT 4: ECOLOGY AND THE ENVIRONMENT — 100
11 THE ORGANISM IN THE ENVIRONMENT — 101
12 FEEDING RELATIONSHIPS AND CYCLES WITHIN ECOSYSTEMS — 107

UNIT 5: USE OF BIOLOGICAL RESOURCES — 118
13 FOOD PRODUCTION — 119
14 GENETIC MODIFICATION (GENETIC ENGINEERING) — 125

CHEMISTRY

UNIT 1: PRINCIPLES OF CHEMISTRY — 134
1 STATES OF MATTER — 135
2 ELEMENTS, COMPOUNDS AND MIXTURES — 142
3 ATOMIC STRUCTURE — 151
4 THE PERIODIC TABLE — 158
5 CHEMICAL FORMULAE AND EQUATIONS — 162
6 IONIC BONDING — 170
7 COVALENT BONDING — 178

UNIT 2: INORGANIC CHEMISTRY — 188
8 GROUP 1 (ALKALI METALS): LITHIUM, SODIUM AND POTASSIUM — 189
9 GROUP 7 (HALOGENS): CHLORINE, BROMINE AND IODINE — 196
10 GASES IN THE ATMOSPHERE — 199
11 REACTIVITY SERIES — 206
12 ACIDS AND ALKALIS — 214
13 CHEMICAL TESTS — 219

UNIT 3: PHYSICAL CHEMISTRY — 230
14 ENERGETICS — 231
15 RATES OF REACTION — 244

UNIT 4: ORGANIC CHEMISTRY — 262
16 INTRODUCTION TO ORGANIC CHEMISTRY — 263
17 CRUDE OIL — 267
18 ALKANES — 274
19 ALKENES — 280
20 SYNTHETIC POLYMERS — 284

COURSE STRUCTURE	iv
ABOUT THIS BOOK	vi
ASSESSMENT OVERVIEW	viii

BIOLOGY

UNIT 1	2
UNIT 2	14
UNIT 3	72
UNIT 4	100
UNIT 5	118

CHEMISTRY

UNIT 1	134
UNIT 2	188
UNIT 3	230
UNIT 4	262

PHYSICS

UNIT 1	294
UNIT 2	324
UNIT 3	344
UNIT 4	372
UNIT 5	390
UNIT 6	402
UNIT 7	414
UNIT 8	440
APPENDIX A: PERIODIC TABLE	452
APPENDIX B: COMMAND WORDS	453
INDEX	454

ON THE EBOOK

APPENDIX C: PHYSICAL FORMULAE

APPENDIX D: PHYSICAL QUANTITIES

APPENDIX E: EXPERIMENTAL AND INVESTIGATIVE SKILLS

BIOLOGY GLOSSARY

CHEMISTRY GLOSSARY

PHYSICS GLOSSARY

BIOLOGY ANSWERS

CHEMISTRY ANSWERS

PHYSICS ANSWERS

PHYSICS

UNIT 1: FORCES AND MOTION — 294
1. MOVEMENT AND POSITION — 295
2. FORCES AND SHAPE — 308
3. FORCES AND MOVEMENT — 314

UNIT 2: ELECTRICITY — 324
4. MAINS ELECTRICITY — 325
5. CURRENT AND VOLTAGE IN CIRCUITS — 328
6. ELECTRICAL RESISTANCE — 334

UNIT 3: WAVES — 344
7. PROPERTIES OF WAVES — 345
8. THE ELECTROMAGNETIC SPECTRUM — 352
9. LIGHT AND SOUND WAVES — 359

UNIT 4: ENERGY RESOURCES AND ENERGY TRANSFER — 372
10. ENERGY TRANSFERS — 373
11. WORK AND POWER — 379

UNIT 5: SOLIDS, LIQUIDS AND GASES — 390
12. PRESSURE — 391
13. SOLIDS, LIQUIDS AND GASES — 395

UNIT 6: MAGNETISM AND ELECTROMAGNETISM — 402
14. MAGNETISM AND ELECTROMAGNETISM — 403
15. ELECTRIC MOTORS — 408

UNIT 7: RADIOACTIVITY AND PARTICLES — 414
16. ATOMS AND RADIOACTIVITY — 415
17. RADIATION AND HALF-LIFE — 422
18. APPLICATIONS OF RADIOACTIVITY — 427
19. FISSION AND FUSION — 433

UNIT 8: ASTROPHYSICS — 440
20. MOTION IN THE UNIVERSE — 441
21. STELLAR EVOLUTION — 446

ABOUT THIS BOOK

This book is written for students following the Edexcel International GCSE (9–1) Science Single Award specification. You will need to study all of the content in this book for your examinations, apart from content in Extension boxes.

The units of this book reflect specification topics. Each unit contains concise explanations and worked examples, plus numerous exercises that will help you build up confidence. The book also describes the methods for carrying out all of the required practicals.

Science-specific terminology for each topic is highlighted in the text and definitions are provided in the glossaries on the eBook. A list of command words at the back of this book will help you to learn the language you will need in your examinations and understand better how to answer different types of question. Answers and extra appendices are provided on the eBook, which you can access using the scratch-off code on the inside cover of this book.

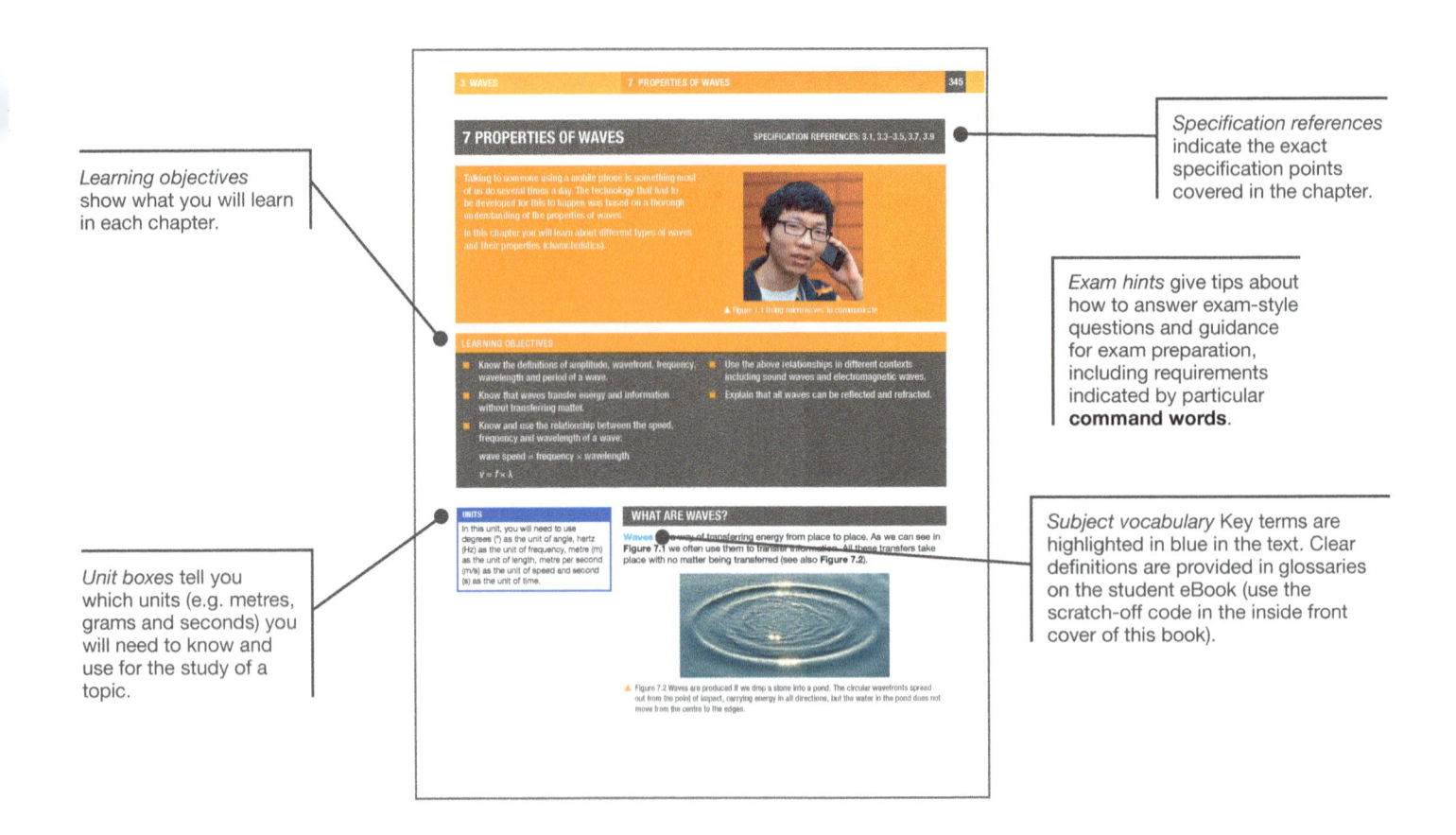

Learning objectives show what you will learn in each chapter.

Unit boxes tell you which units (e.g. metres, grams and seconds) you will need to know and use for the study of a topic.

Specification references indicate the exact specification points covered in the chapter.

Exam hints give tips about how to answer exam-style questions and guidance for exam preparation, including requirements indicated by particular **command words**.

Subject vocabulary Key terms are highlighted in blue in the text. Clear definitions are provided in glossaries on the student eBook (use the scratch-off code in the inside front cover of this book).

ABOUT THIS BOOK

Did you know? Interesting facts help you remember the key concepts.

Activity boxes describe the methods for carrying out all of the practicals you will need to know for your examination.

Extension boxes include content that you will not need to revise for your examination because it is not included in the IG Single Award specification. However, content covered will help to extend your understanding of the topic.

Questions indicate which key *transferable skills* you will need to practise in answering the question, so you can see which skills you are developing. These skills are an important basis for key academic qualities, and will also be valuable for further study and in the workplace. You can find details of these skills on the Edexcel qualification website under 'teaching and learning resources'.

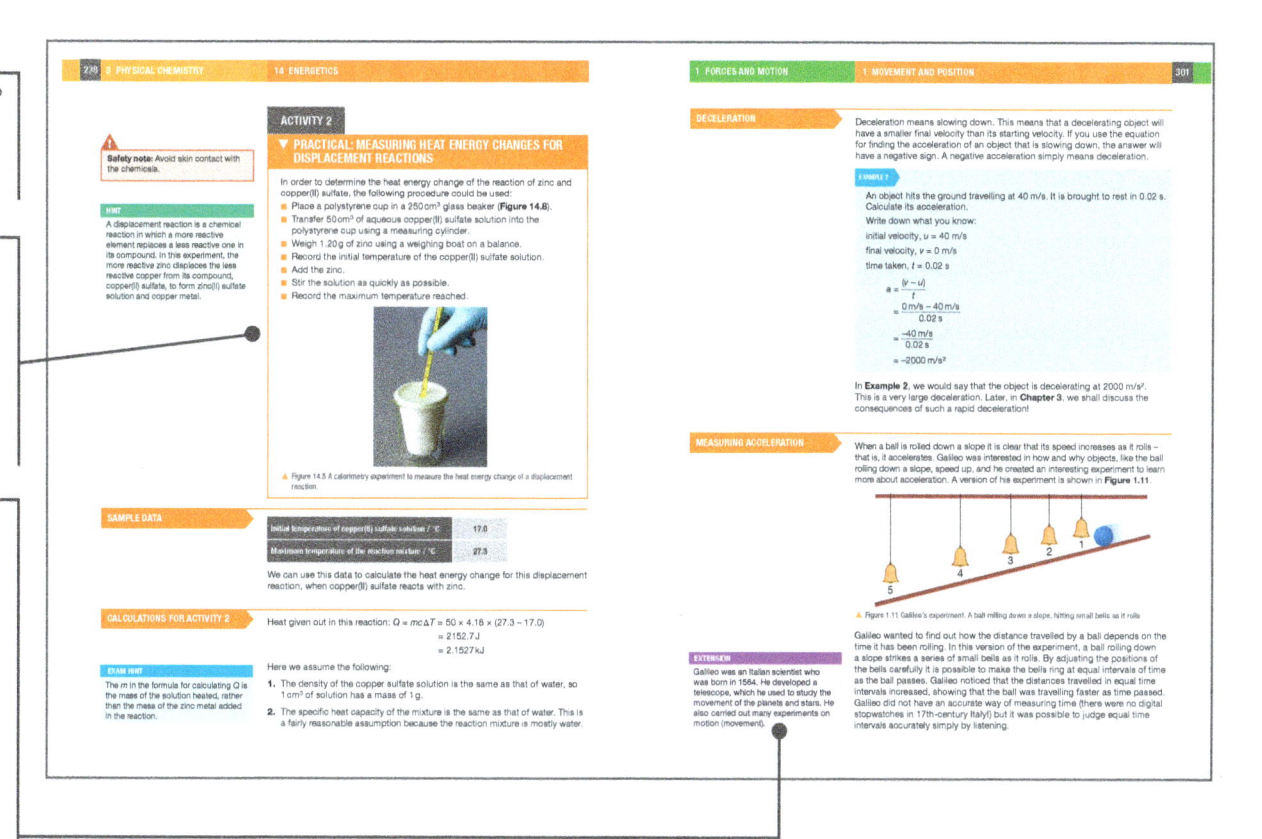

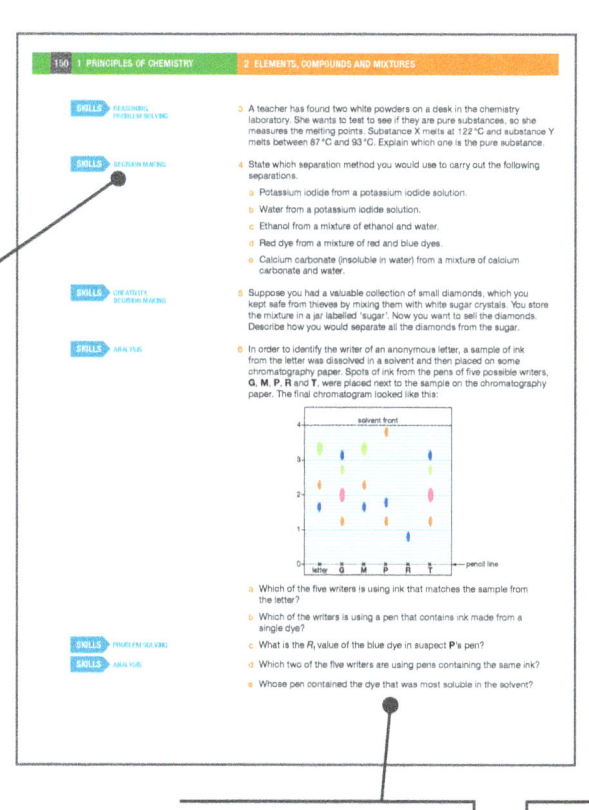

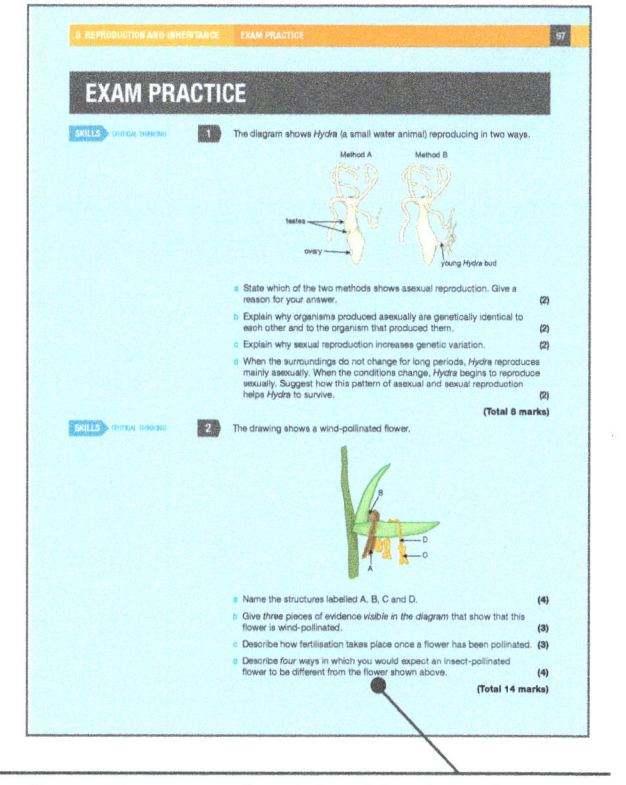

Chapter questions test your knowledge of the topic in that chapter.

Exam practice questions test your knowledge of the whole unit and provide quick, effective feedback on your progress as well as giving you practice in answering questions in an exam style format (e.g. use of command words, breakdown of marks and structure of questions).

ASSESSMENT OVERVIEW

The following tables give an overview of the assessment for this course.

We recommend that you study this information closely to help ensure that you are fully prepared for this course and know exactly what to expect in the assessment.

BIOLOGY PAPER 1	SPECIFICATION	PERCENTAGE	MARK	TIME	AVAILABILITY
Written examination paper Paper code 4SS0/1B Externally set and assessed by Edexcel	Science Single Award	33.3%	60	1 hour 10 minutes	January and June examination series First assessment June 2019

CHEMISTRY PAPER 1	SPECIFICATION	PERCENTAGE	MARK	TIME	AVAILABILITY
Written examination paper Paper code 4SS0/1C Externally set and assessed by Edexcel	Science Single Award	33.3%	60	1 hour 10 minutes	January and June examination series First assessment June 2019

PHYSICS PAPER 1	SPECIFICATION	PERCENTAGE	MARK	TIME	AVAILABILITY
Written examination paper Paper code 4SS0/1P Externally set and assessed by Edexcel	Science Single Award	33.3%	60	1 hour 10 minutes	January and June examination series First assessment June 2019

ASSESSMENT OBJECTIVES AND WEIGHTINGS

ASSESSMENT OBJECTIVE	DESCRIPTION	% IN INTERNATIONAL GCSE
AO1	Knowledge and understanding of science	38%–42%
AO2	Application of knowledge and understanding, analysis and evaluation of science	38%–42%
AO3	Experimental skills, analysis and evaluation of data and methods in science	19%–21%

EXPERIMENTAL SKILLS

In the assessment of experimental skills, students may be tested on their ability to:

- solve problems set in a practical context
- apply scientific knowledge and understanding in questions with a practical context
- devise and plan investigations, using scientific knowledge and understanding when selecting appropriate techniques
- demonstrate or describe appropriate experimental and investigative methods, including safe and skilful practical techniques
- make observations and measurements with appropriate precision, record these methodically and present them in appropriate ways
- identify independent, dependent and control variables
- use scientific knowledge and understanding to analyse and interpret data to draw conclusions from experimental activities that are consistent with the evidence
- communicate the findings from experimental activities, using appropriate technical language, relevant calculations and graphs
- assess the reliability of an experimental activity
- evaluate data and methods taking into account factors that affect accuracy and validity.

CALCULATORS

Students are permitted to take a suitable calculator into the examinations. Calculators with QWERTY keyboards or that can retrieve text or formulae will not be permitted.

BIOLOGY UNIT 1
THE NATURE AND VARIETY OF LIVING ORGANISMS

Any living thing, whether it is an animal, a plant or a bacterium, is called an organism. There is an enormous variety of organisms. Unit 1 looks at the similarities and differences between living things and how we put them into groups based on the features that they show. All organisms are made of microscopic 'building blocks' called cells. You will find out a little about cells in this unit, but you will learn much more about them in Unit 2.

1 THE CHARACTERISTICS OF LIVING ORGANISMS AND THEIR VARIETY

SPECIFICATION REFERENCES: 1.1–1.4

'Characteristics' are features which allow us to recognise something for what it is. We recognise that an object is a car by its body, wheels, engine and seats. These are the characteristics of a car. Characteristics also allow us to tell the difference between things. For example the characteristics of a bus are different from those of a car: a bus has a bigger body and bigger wheels, a larger engine and more seats. This chapter will cover the characteristics of different groups of living organisms.

LEARNING OBJECTIVES

- Understand the characteristics shared by living organisms.
- Understand the difference between eukaryotic and prokaryotic organisms.
- Describe the features common to plants and recognise examples of flowering plants such as maize, peas and beans.
- Describe the features common to animals and recognise examples such as mammals and insects.
- Describe the features common to fungi and recognise examples such as *Mucor* and yeast.
- Describe the features common to protoctists and recognise examples such as *Amoeba*, *Chlorella* and *Plasmodium*.
- Describe the features common to bacteria and recognise examples such as *Lactobacillus bulgaricus* and *Pneumococcus*.
- Describe the features common to viruses and recognise examples such as the influenza virus, HIV and the tobacco mosaic virus.
- Understand the term 'pathogen' and know that pathogens may include fungi, bacteria, protoctists or viruses.

THE CHARACTERISTICS OF LIVING ORGANISMS

There are eight 'life processes' which take place in most living things. These processes allow us to recognise whether something is living or dead. They are the characteristics of living organisms. Organisms:

- Need nutrition – plants make their own food, animals eat other organisms
- Respire – release energy from their food
- Excrete – get rid of waste products
- Respond to stimuli – are sensitive to changes in their surroundings
- Move – by the action of muscles in animals and slow growth movements in plants
- Control their internal conditions – maintain a steady state inside the body
- Reproduce – produce offspring
- Grow and develop – increase in size and complexity, using materials from their food.

THE VARIETY OF LIVING ORGANISMS

There are more than 10 million species of organisms alive on the Earth today, and many more once lived on Earth but are now extinct. In order to make sense of this enormous variety, biologists classify organisms, putting them into groups. Members of each group are related – they are descended from a common ancestor by the process of evolution (see **Chapter 10**). That is why the members of a group look similar, for example different species of frogs all look and behave like frogs, because they all evolved from a common frog-like ancestor.

The five main groups of living organisms are plants, animals, fungi, protoctists and bacteria.

PLANTS

You will be familiar with flowering plants, such as those shown in **Figure 1.1**. The plant group also contains simpler non-flowering plants, such as mosses and ferns. All plants are multicellular, which means that they are made up of many cells. A key feature of plants is that many of their cells contain chloroplasts and they carry out photosynthesis. Photosynthesis is the process that uses light energy to convert the simple molecules water and carbon dioxide into complex organic substances (see **Chapter 5**). One of these substances is a carbohydrate called cellulose – all plants have cell walls made of this material.

▲ Figure 1.1 (a) A pea plant. Its leaves contain chloroplasts, giving them their green colour. (b) Maize plants are pollinated by wind. These are the male flowers, which make the pollen. (c) The female maize flowers produce seeds after pollination.

Plants can make many other organic compounds through photosynthesis. One of the first to be made is the storage carbohydrate starch, which is often found inside plant cells. Another is the sugar sucrose, which is transported around the plant and is sometimes stored in fruits and other parts of the plant.

ANIMALS

You will be even more familiar with this group, since it contains the species *Homo sapiens* – humans! The variety of animals is enormous, ranging from organisms such as sponges, molluscs, worms, starfish, insects and crustaceans through to larger animals such as fish, amphibians, reptiles, birds and mammals (**Figure 1.2**). The last five groups are all **vertebrates**, which means they have a backbone (vertebral column). All other animals have no backbone and are called **invertebrates**.

▲ Figure 1.2 (a) A housefly. (b) A mosquito, feeding on human blood. Houseflies and mosquitoes are both insects, which make up the largest sub-group of all the animals. About 60% of all animal species are insects. (c) This high jumper's movement is co-ordinated by a complex nervous system.

Animals are also multicellular organisms. Their cells never contain chloroplasts, so they are unable to carry out photosynthesis. Instead, they gain their nutrition by feeding on other animals or on plants. Animal cells also lack cell walls, which allows their cells to change shape. This is an important feature for organisms that need to move from place to place. Movement in animals is achieved in various ways – for example, running, swimming or crawling, which often involves co-ordination by a nervous system. Another feature common to most animals is that most animals store carbohydrate in their bodies as a substance called **glycogen**.

FUNGI

Fungi include mushrooms and toadstools, as well as moulds. These sub-groups of fungi are multicellular. Another sub-group of fungi is the yeasts, which are **unicellular** (made of single cells). Different species of yeasts live everywhere – on the surface of fruits, in soil, water, and even on dust in the air. The yeast powder used for baking contains millions of yeast cells (**Figure 1.3**). The cells of fungi never contain chloroplasts, so they cannot photosynthesise. Their cells have cell walls, but they are not composed of cellulose. Instead they are made of a substance called **chitin** (**Figure 1.4**).

EXTENSION

Because fungi have cell walls, they were once thought to be plants that had lost their chlorophyll. However, their cell walls are made of chitin, not of cellulose like plants. There are many ways that fungi are very different from plants – the most obvious is that fungi do not carry out photosynthesis. We know now that they are not closely related to plants at all.

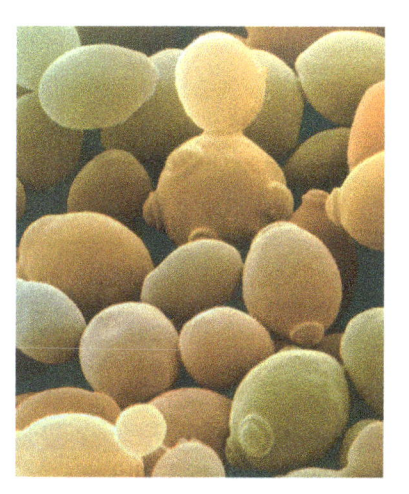

▲ Figure 1.3 Yeast cells, highly magnified

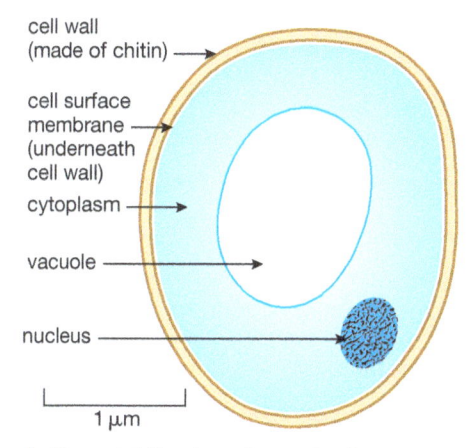

▲ Figure 1.4 Structure of a yeast cell

KEY POINT

The singular of hyphae is hypha.

▲ Figure 1.5 Toadstools growing on a rotting tree trunk

▲ Figure 1.6 The 'pin mould' *Mucor* growing on a piece of bread. The dark spots are structures that produce spores for reproduction.

KEY POINT

Digestive enzymes are chemicals that break down food. They are studied in **Chapter 5**.

The thing we know as a mushroom or toadstool is the reproductive structure of the organism, and this is technically known as a fruiting body (**Figure 1.5**). Under the soil, the mushroom has many fine thread-like filaments called hyphae (pronounced high-fee). A mould consists only of the network of hyphae (**Figure 1.6**) and has no fruiting body. The whole network is called a mycelium (pronounced my-sea-lee-um). Most fungi feed by absorbing nutrients from dead animal or plant material, so they are found wherever this is present, for example in soil, rotting leaves or decaying fruit. Some species of fungi feed on living tissues and cause diseases in other organisms.

If you leave a piece of bread or fruit exposed to the air for a few days, it will soon become mouldy. Mould spores carried in the air have landed on the food and grown into a mycelium of hyphae (**Figure 1.7**).

(a) **Highly magnified tip of a feeding hypha**

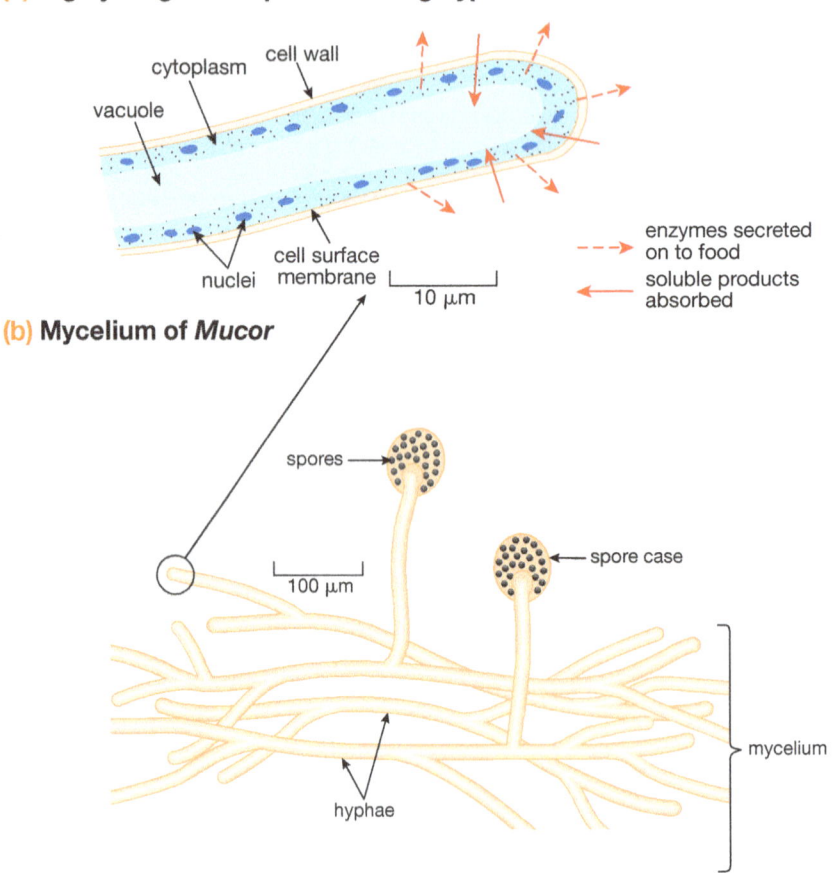

(b) **Mycelium of *Mucor***

▲ Figure 1.7 The structure of a typical mould fungus, the 'pin mould' *Mucor*

The thread-like hyphae of *Mucor* have cell walls surrounding their cytoplasm. The cytoplasm contains many nuclei. In other words the hyphae are not divided up into separate cells.

When a spore from *Mucor* lands on some food, a hypha grows out from it. The hypha grows and branches again and again, until the mycelium covers the surface of the food. The hyphae secrete digestive enzymes on to the food, breaking it down into soluble substances such as sugars, which are then absorbed by the mould. Eventually, the food is used up and the mould must infect another source of food by producing more spores.

When an organism feeds on dead organic material in this way, and digestion takes place outside of the organism, this is called saprotrophic nutrition. Enzymes that are secreted out of cells for this purpose are called *extracellular* enzymes (see **Chapter 5**).

PROTOCTISTS

Protoctists are sometimes called the 'dustbin group', because they are a mixed group of organisms – they are neither plants, animals nor fungi groups. Most protoctists are microscopic single-celled organisms (**Figure 1.8**). Some look like animal cells, such as *Amoeba*, which lives in pond water. These are known as **protozoa**. Other protoctists, called **algae**, have chloroplasts and carry out photosynthesis, so they are more like plants. Most algae are unicellular, but some species such as seaweeds are multicellular and can grow to a great size. Some protoctists cause disease, such as *Plasmodium*, the organism that causes malaria.

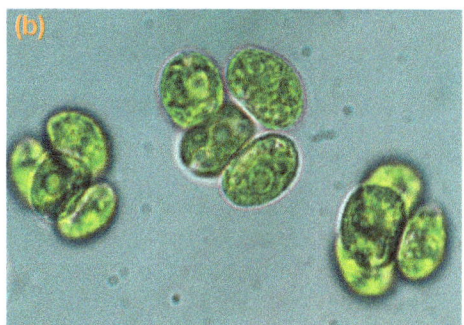

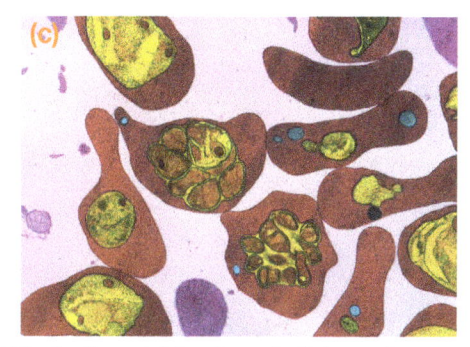

▲ Figure 1.8 (a) *Amoeba*, a protozoan that lives in ponds. (b) *Chlorella*, a unicellular freshwater alga. (c) Blood cells containing the protoctist parasite *Plasmodium*, the organism responsible for causing malaria.

EUKARYOTIC AND PROKARYOTIC ORGANISMS

All the organisms described so far are composed of **eukaryotic** cells and are known as eukaryotic organisms. 'Eukaryotic' means 'having a **nucleus**' – their cells contain a nucleus surrounded by a membrane, along with other membrane-bound **organelles**, such as mitochondria and chloroplasts. The structure of eukaryotic cells is described in **Chapter 2**.

There are also organisms made of simpler cells, which have no nucleus, mitochondria or chloroplasts. These are called **prokaryotic** cells. 'Prokaryotic' means 'before nucleus'. The main forms of prokaryotic organisms are the bacteria.

BACTERIA

Bacteria are small single-celled organisms. Their cells are much smaller than those of eukaryotic organisms and have a much simpler structure. To give you some idea of their size, a typical animal cell might be 10 to 50 μm in diameter (1 μm, or one micrometre, is a millionth of a metre). Compared with this, a typical bacterium is only 1 to 5 μm in length (**Figure 1.9**) and its volume is thousands of times smaller than that of an animal cell.

There are three basic shapes of bacteria – spheres, rods and spirals – but they all have a similar internal structure (**Figure 1.10**).

All bacteria are surrounded by a cell wall, which protects the bacterium and keeps the shape of the cell. Underneath the cell wall is the **cell membrane**, as in other cells. The middle of the cell is made of cytoplasm. Because it is a prokaryotic cell, the bacterium has no nucleus. Instead, its genetic material (DNA) is in a single **chromosome**, loose in the cytoplasm, forming a circular loop.

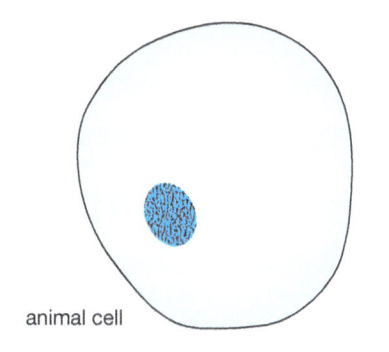

▲ Figure 1.9 A bacterium is much smaller than an animal cell. The relative size of a virus is also shown.

KEY POINT

Bacterial cell walls are not made of cellulose but a complex compound of sugars and proteins called peptidoglycan. Some species have another layer outside this wall, called a capsule or slime layer. Both give the bacterium extra protection.

(a) Some different bacterial shapes

spheres: singles, pairs, chains or groups

rods: singles, chains, with or without flagella

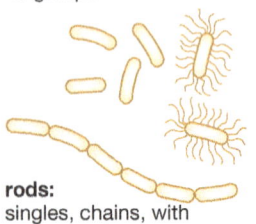

spirals

(b) Internal structure of a bacterium

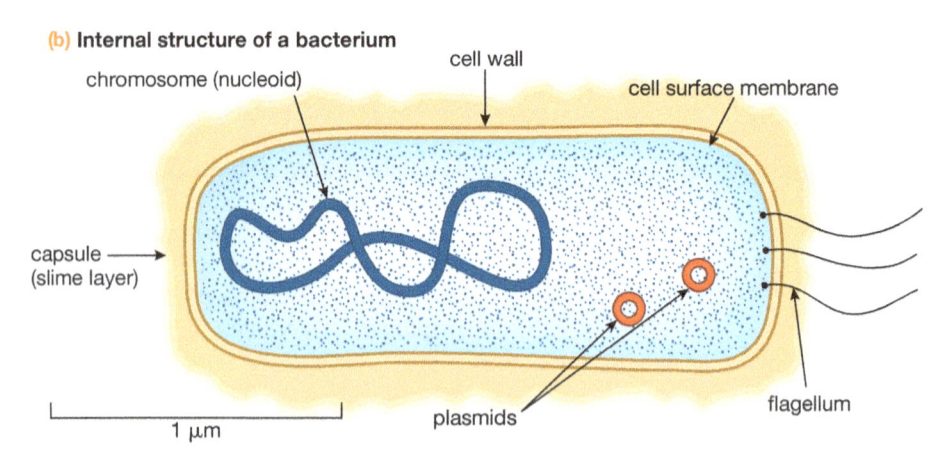

Labels: chromosome (nucleoid), cell wall, cell surface membrane, capsule (slime layer), plasmids, flagellum, 1 μm

◀▲ Figure 1.10 Structure of bacteria

Some bacteria can swim, propelled through water by corkscrew-like movements of structures called flagella (a single one of these is called a **flagellum**). However, most bacteria do not have flagella and cannot move by themselves. Other structures present in the cytoplasm include the **plasmids**. These are small circular rings of **DNA**, carrying some of the bacterium's genes. Not all bacteria contain plasmids, although about three-quarters of all known species do. Plasmids have very important uses in **genetic engineering** (see **Chapter 14**).

Some bacteria contain a form of **chlorophyll** in their cytoplasm, and can carry out photosynthesis. However, most bacteria feed off other living or dead organisms. Along with the fungi, many bacteria are important **decomposers** (see **Chapter 12**), recycling dead organisms and waste products in the soil and elsewhere. Some bacteria are used by humans to make food, such as *Lactobacillus bulgaricus*, a rod-shaped species used in the production of yoghurt from milk (**Figure 1.11**). Other species are **pathogens**, which means that they cause disease (**Figure 1.12**).

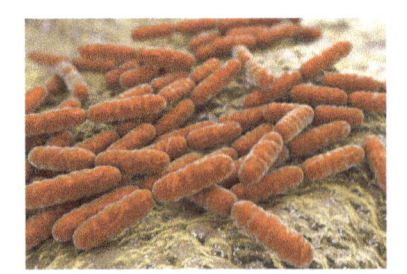

▲ Figure 1.11 The bacterium *Lactobacillus bulgaricus*, used in the production of yoghurt

KEY POINT

Pathogens are organisms that cause disease. Many common animal and plant diseases are caused by bacteria or viruses. Most protoctists are free-living, but a few species are pathogens, such as *Plasmodium* (**Figure 1.8c**). Even some species of fungi can cause disease, for example the skin infection called 'athlete's foot' is caused by a mould.

Despite the relatively simple structure of the bacterial cell, it is a living cell that carries out the normal processes of life, such as respiration, feeding, excretion, growth and reproduction. Some bacteria can move, and they can also respond to a range of stimuli. For example, they may move towards a source of food, or away from a poisonous chemical. You should think about these features when you compare bacteria with the next group, the much simpler viruses.

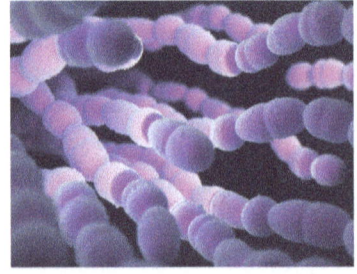

▲ Figure 1.12 Rounded cells of the bacterium *Pneumococcus*, one cause of pneumonia

VIRUSES

All **viruses** are **parasites** and can only reproduce inside living cells. The cell in which the virus lives is called the host. There are many different types of viruses. Some live in the cells of animals or plants, and there are even viruses

1 THE NATURE AND VARIETY OF LIVING ORGANISMS 1 THE CHARACTERISTICS OF LIVING ORGANISMS AND THEIR VARIETY

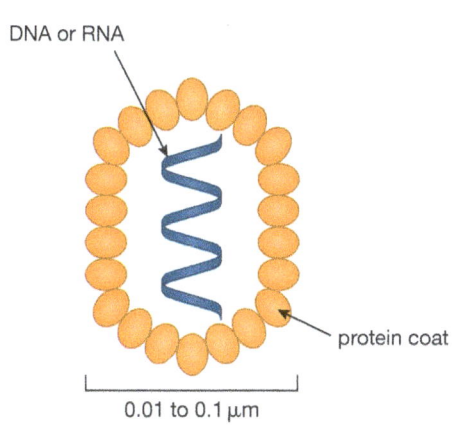

▲ Figure 1.13 The structure of a typical virus, such as the type causing influenza (flu)

that infect bacteria. Viruses are much smaller than bacterial cells: most are between 0.01 and 0.1 μm in diameter (see **Figure 1.9**).

Viruses are not made of cells. A virus particle is very simple. It has no nucleus or cytoplasm, and is composed of a core of genetic material surrounded by a protein coat (**Figure 1.13**). The genetic material can be either **DNA**, or a similar chemical called **ribonucleic acid (RNA)**. In either case, the genetic material makes up just a few genes – all that is needed for the virus to reproduce inside its host cell.

Viruses do not feed, respire, excrete, move, grow or respond to their surroundings. They do not carry out any of the normal characteristics of living things except reproduction, and they can only do this parasitically. This is why biologists do not consider viruses to be living organisms. You can think of viruses as being on the border between an organism and a non-living chemical.

A virus reproduces by entering the host cell and taking over the host's genetic machinery to make more virus particles. After many virus particles have been made, the host cell dies and the particles are released to infect more cells. Many human diseases are caused in this way, such as influenza. Other examples include colds, measles, mumps, polio and rubella. Of course, the reproduction process does not continue forever. Usually, the body's immune system destroys the virus and the person recovers. Sometimes, however, a virus cannot be destroyed by the immune system quickly enough, and it may cause permanent damage or death. With other infections, the virus may attack cells of the immune system itself. This is what happens with HIV (the human immunodeficiency virus), which causes the condition called AIDS (acquired immune deficiency syndrome).

Some viruses, such as the tobacco mosaic virus (**Figure 1.14**), infect plant cells. It interferes with the tobacco plant's ability to make chloroplasts. This causes mottled patches to develop on the leaves (**Figure 1.15**).

EXTENSION

AIDS is not actually a disease but a 'syndrome'. A syndrome is a set of symptoms caused by a medical condition. In the case of HIV, the virus severely damages the person's immune system, so they are more likely to get other diseases, such as tuberculosis. They may also develop some unusual types of cancer. It is this collection of different symptoms that is referred to as AIDS.

▲ Figure 1.15 Discolouration of the leaves of a tobacco plant, caused by infection with tobacco mosaic virus

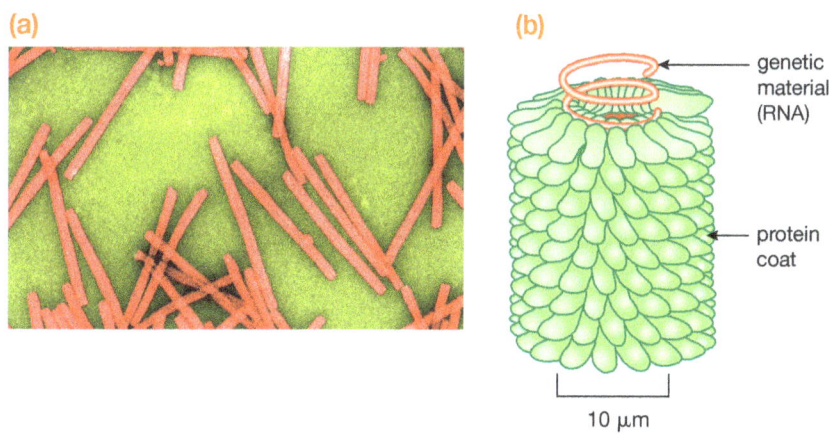

▲ Figure 1.14 (a) Tobacco mosaic virus (TMV), seen through an electron microscope. (b) Structure of part of a TMV particle, magnified 1.25 million times.

CHAPTER QUESTIONS

Exam-style questions on the characteristics of living organisms and their variety can be found at the end of Unit 1 on page 12.

SKILLS CRITICAL THINKING

1 Which of the following is *not* a characteristic of plants?
   A cells contain chloroplasts
   B cell wall made of cellulose
   C they are multicellular
   D they store carbohydrate as glycogen

SKILLS CRITICAL THINKING

2 Fungi carry out *saprotrophic nutrition*. What is the meaning of this term?
   A extracellular digestion of dead organic matter
   B feeding on other living organisms
   C making organic molecules by photosynthesis
   D secreting digestive enzymes

SKILLS CRITICAL THINKING

3 Below are three groups of organisms.
   1. viruses
   2. bacteria
   3. yeasts

   Which of these organisms are prokaryotic?
   A 1 only
   B 2 only
   C 1 and 2
   D 1, 2 and 3

SKILLS CRITICAL THINKING

4 Which of the following is *not* caused by a virus?
   A influenza
   B measles
   C malaria
   D AIDS

5 a The six main groups of living organisms are plants, animals, fungi, protoctists, bacteria and viruses. Name the group to which each of the following organisms belongs.
   i mushroom
   ii *Chlorella*
   iii moss
   iv *Lactobacillus*

SKILLS ANALYSIS, REASONING

b The diagram shows a species of protoctist called *Euglena*. Use the diagram to explain why *Euglena* is classified as a protoctist and not as an animal or plant.

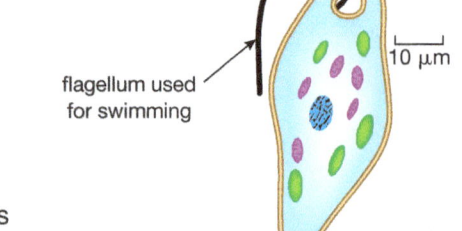

SKILLS INTERPRETATION, CRITICAL THINKING

6 a Draw a diagram to show the structure of a typical virus particle.
  b Is a virus a living organism? Explain your answer.
  c Explain the statement 'viruses are all parasites'.

7 Explain the meanings of the following terms.
  a prokaryotic
  b hyphae
  c saprotrophic

EXAM PRACTICE

SKILLS CRITICAL THINKING

1 Which of the following is a characteristic of *both* bacteria and viruses?

A nutrition

B respiration

C movement

D reproduction

(Total 1 mark)

SKILLS INTERPRETATION

2 The table below shows some features of different groups of organisms. Copy and complete the table, putting a tick in the box if the organism has that feature or a cross if it lacks the feature.

Feature	Type of organism		
	Plant	Fungus	Virus
they are all parasites			
they are made up of a mycelium of hyphae			
they can only reproduce inside living cells			
they feed using extracellular digestion by enzymes			
they store carbohydrate as starch			

(Total 5 marks)

SKILLS CRITICAL THINKING

3 Copy and complete the following account.

Plants have cell walls made of _____ . They store carbohydrate as the insoluble compound called _____ or sometimes as the sugar _____ . Plants make these substances as a result of the process called _____ . Animals, on the other hand, store carbohydrate as the compound _____ . Both animal cells and plant cells have nuclei, but the cells of bacteria lack a true nucleus, having their DNA in a circular chromosome. Bacteria sometimes also contain small rings of DNA called _____ , which are used in genetic engineering. Bacteria and fungi break down organic matter in the soil. They are known as _____ . Some bacteria are pathogens, which means that they _____ .

(Total 8 marks)

1 THE NATURE AND VARIETY OF LIVING ORGANISMS — EXAM PRACTICE

SKILLS INTERPRETATION

4 The diagram shows two types of cell and some features that may or may not be shown by these cells.

Copy the boxes and draw a straight line from each type of cell to any feature that is shown by that cell.

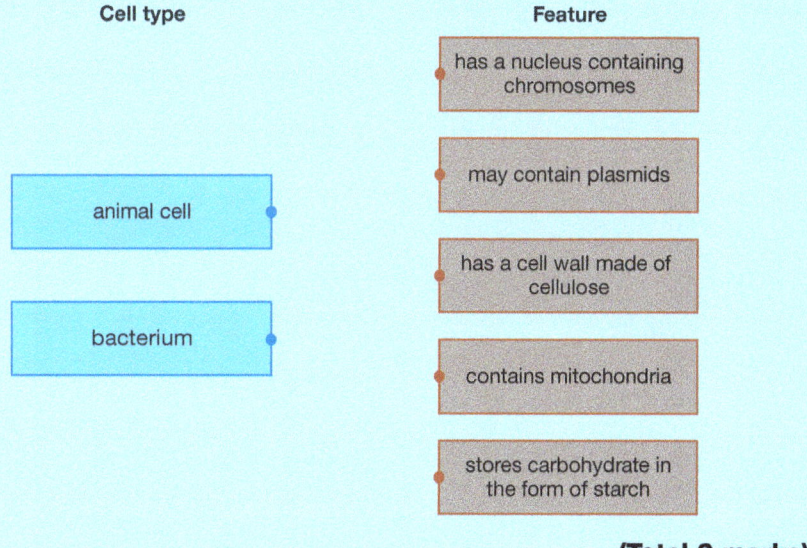

Cell type

- animal cell
- bacterium

Feature

- has a nucleus containing chromosomes
- may contain plasmids
- has a cell wall made of cellulose
- contains mitochondria
- stores carbohydrate in the form of starch

(Total 3 marks)

2 LEVELS OF ORGANISATION AND CELL STRUCTURE 15	3 BIOLOGICAL MOLECULES 20
4 MOVEMENT OF SUBSTANCES INTO AND OUT OF CELLS 28	5 NUTRITION 34	6 RESPIRATION 47
7 GAS EXCHANGE 50	8 TRANSPORT 56

BIOLOGY UNIT 2
STRUCTURE AND FUNCTION IN LIVING ORGANISMS

All living organisms are composed of microscopic units known as cells. These building blocks of life have a number of features in common. This unit starts by looking at the structure and function of cells and how they are put together in the body of an organism. It goes on to consider some of the essential life processes that go on inside cells, and how the structure of the whole organism is adapted to carry out these processes.

2 LEVELS OF ORGANISATION AND CELL STRUCTURE

SPECIFICATION REFERENCES: 2.1–2.4

Note that this chapter only deals with eukaryotic cells. The simpler prokaryotic cells are described in **Chapter 1**. There are some parts of a cell that are present in most cells of living organisms. In this chapter we will look at these features and we will also look at how animal and plant cells are different in structure. We start by seeing how the bodies of organisms are built up from cells.

LEARNING OBJECTIVES

- Describe the levels of organisation in organisms – organelles, cells, organs and systems.
- Describe cell structures, including the nucleus, cytoplasm, cell membrane, cell wall, mitochondria, chloroplasts and vacuole.
- Describe the functions of the nucleus, cytoplasm, cell membrane, cell wall, mitochondria, chloroplasts and vacuole.
- Know the similarities and differences in the structure of plant and animal cells.

LEVELS OF ORGANISATION

All living organisms are composed of units called **cells**. Structures inside a cell, such as the nucleus or a chloroplast, are called **organelles**.

The simplest organisms are made from single cells (**Figure 2.1**) but more complex plants and animals are composed of millions of cells. In many-celled (**multicellular**) organisms, there may be hundreds of different types of cells with different structures. The cells are specialised so that they can carry out particular functions in the animal or plant. Despite all the differences, there are basic features that are the same in all cells.

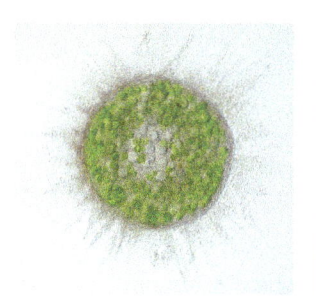

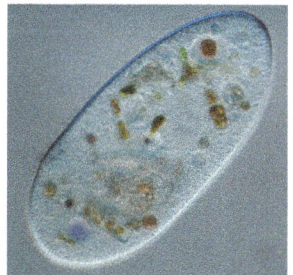

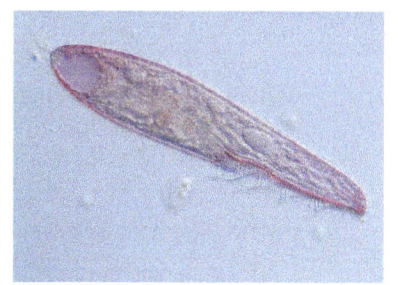

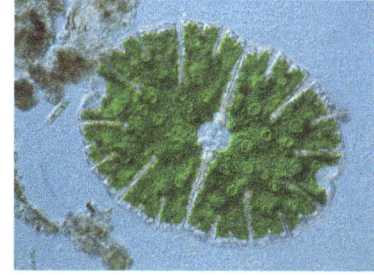

▲ Figure 2.1 Many simple organisms have 'bodies' made from single cells. Here are four examples.

Cells with a similar function are grouped together as **tissues**. For example, the muscles in your arm contains millions of similar muscle cells, all specialised for one function – they contract (shorten) to move the arm bones. This is muscle tissue. However, a muscle also contains other tissues, such as blood and nerves. A collection of several tissues carrying out a particular function is called an **organ**. The main organs of the human body are shown in **Figure 2.2**. Plants also have tissues and organs: leaves, roots, stems and flowers are plant organs.

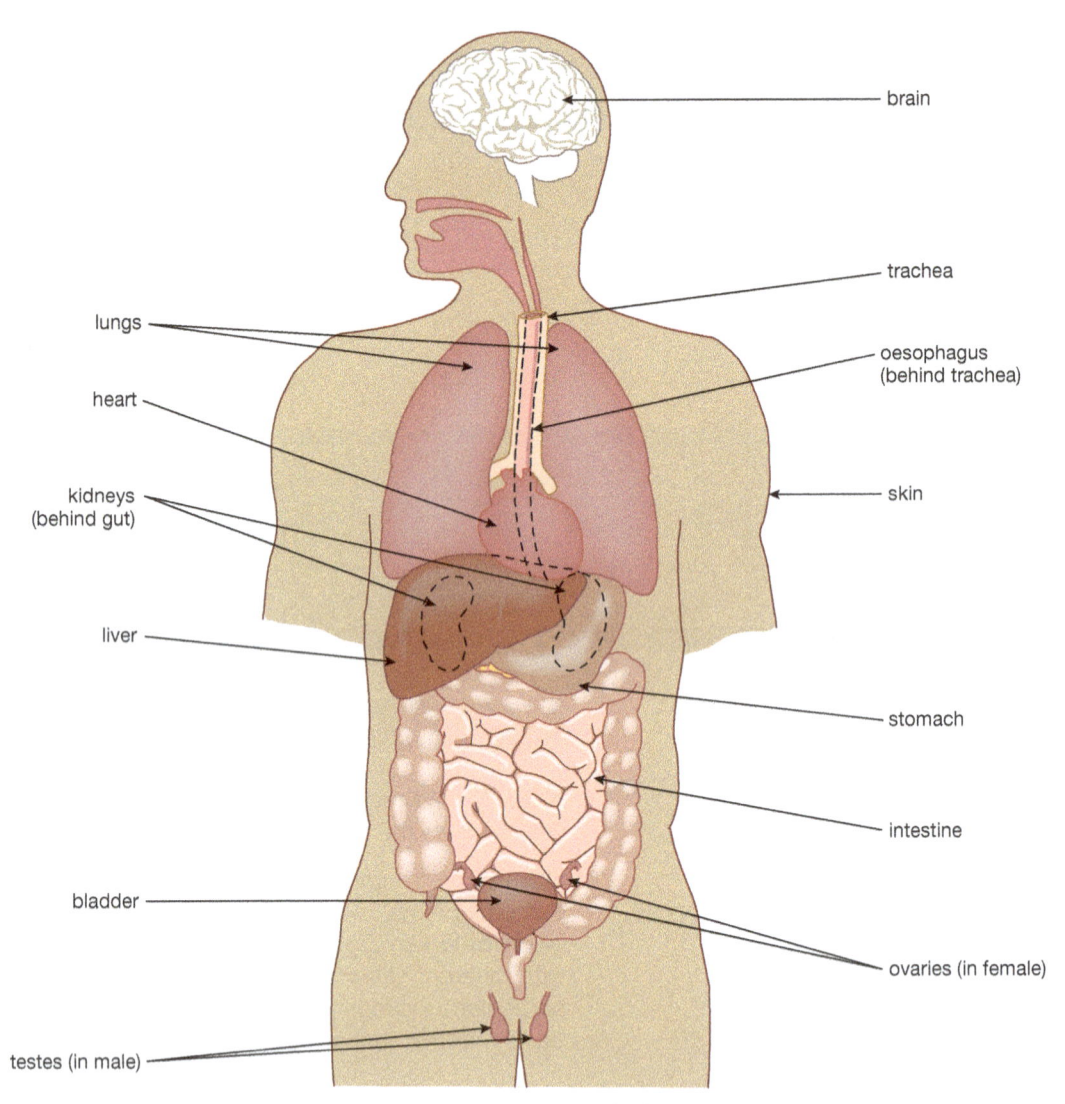

▲ Figure 2.2 Some of the main organs of the human body

In animals, functions are usually carried out by several different organs working together. A group of organs is called an **organ system**. For example, the digestive system consists of the gut, along with organs such as the pancreas and the liver. The function of the whole system is to digest food and absorb the digested products into the blood. There are seven main organ systems in the human body:

- The digestive system.
- The gas exchange system (the airways and lungs), which exchanges oxygen and carbon dioxide between the blood and the air.
- The circulatory system (heart and blood vessels), which transports materials around the body.
- The excretory system (kidneys and bladder), which removes waste materials from the blood.
- The nervous system (brain, spinal cord and nerves), which co-ordinate the body's actions.
- The endocrine system (glands secreting hormones into the blood). The hormones act as chemical messengers.
- The reproductive systems (male and female), producing sperm in males and eggs in females.

CELL STRUCTURE

Most cells contain organelles such as the nucleus, cytoplasm and cell membrane. Note that some cells have certain structures missing, for instance red blood cells are unusual in that they have no nucleus, and cells from a plant root do not contain chloroplasts. **Figure 2.3** shows generalised diagrams of an animal cell and a plant cell.

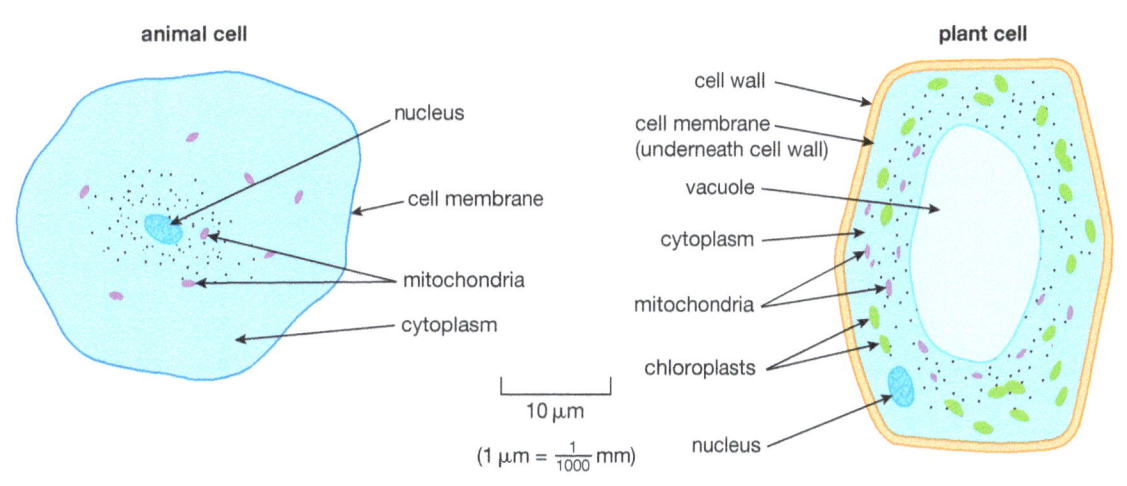

▲ Figure 2.3 The structures of an animal cell and a plant cell

The living material that makes up a cell is called **cytoplasm**. It has a texture rather like runny jelly, so somewhere between a solid and a liquid. Unlike a jelly, it is not made of one substance but is a complex material containing different organelles. You cannot see many of these organelles under an ordinary light microscope. You need to use an electron microscope with a very high magnification to show much detail of the smaller structures (**Figure 2.4**).

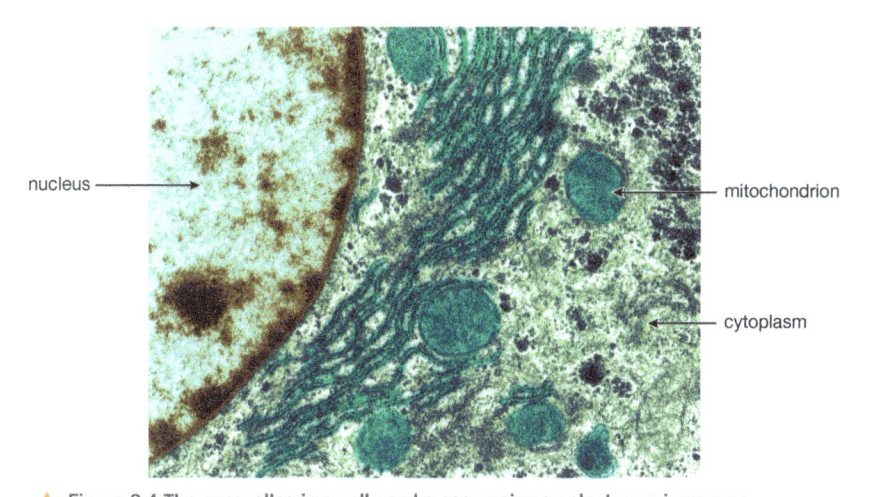

▲ Figure 2.4 The organelles in a cell can be seen using an electron microscope.

The largest organelle in the cell is the **nucleus**. The nucleus contains **chromosomes** (46 in human cells), which carry the genetic material, or **genes**. Genes control the activities going on in the cell.

All cells are surrounded by a **cell membrane**, sometimes called the cell *surface* membrane to distinguish it from other membranes inside the cell.

This is a thin layer like a 'skin' on the surface of the cell. It forms a boundary between the cytoplasm of the cell and the outside. However, it is not a complete barrier. Some chemicals can pass into the cell and others can pass out. We say it is a **partially permeable membrane**. The cell membrane can go further than this and can actually control the movement of some substances – it is *selectively* permeable.

One organelle that is found in the cytoplasm of all living cells is the **mitochondrion** (plural = mitochondria). In cells that need a lot of energy, such as muscle cells or nerve cells, there are many mitochondria. This gives us a clue to their function. Mitochondria carry out some of the reactions of **respiration**, releasing energy that the cell can use (see **Chapter 6**). Most of the energy from respiration is released in the mitochondria.

All of the structures you have seen so far are found in both animal cells and plant cells. However, some structures are only ever found in plant cells. There are three in particular – the cell wall, a permanent vacuole and chloroplasts.

The **cell wall** is a layer of non-living material that is found outside the cell membrane of plant cells. It is made mainly of a carbohydrate called **cellulose**. Cellulose is a tough material that helps the cell keep its shape and is one reason why the 'body' of a plant has a fixed shape. Animal cells do not have a cell wall and tend to be more variable in shape. Plant cells absorb water, producing an internal pressure that pushes against adjacent cells, giving the plant support (see **Chapter 4**). Without a cell wall that is strong enough to resist these pressures, this method of support would be impossible. The cell wall is porous, so it is not a barrier to water or dissolved substances. We call it *freely* permeable.

> **KEY POINT**
>
> Nearly all cells contain cytoplasm, a nucleus, a cell membrane and mitochondria. As well as these structures, plant cells have a cell wall and a permanent vacuole, and plant cells that photosynthesise also contain chloroplasts.

Mature (fully grown) plant cells often have a large central space called a **vacuole**, which is surrounded by a membrane. This vacuole is a permanent feature of the cell. It is filled with a watery liquid called cell sap, which is a store of dissolved sugars, mineral ions and other solutes. Animal cells do contain vacuoles, but they are only small, temporary structures.

Cells of the green parts of plants, especially the leaves, contain another very important organelle, the **chloroplast**. Chloroplasts absorb light energy to make food in the process of photosynthesis (see **Chapter 5**). They contain a green pigment called **chlorophyll**. Cells from the parts of a plant that are not green, such as the flowers, roots and woody stems, have no chloroplasts.

Figure 2.5 shows some animal and plant cells as seen through a light microscope.

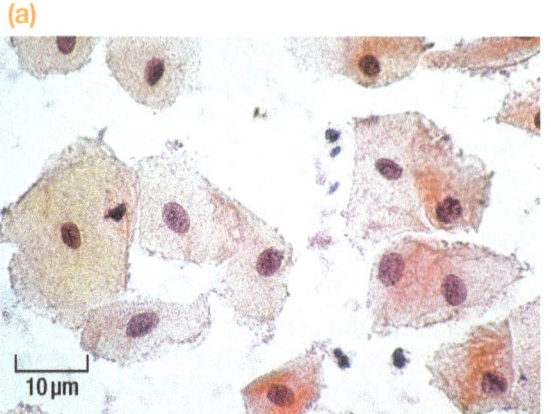

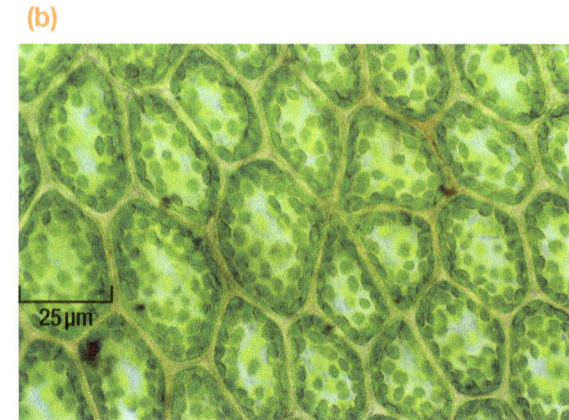

▲ Figure 2.5 (a) Cells from the lining of a human cheek. (b) Cells from the photosynthetic tissue of a leaf.

CHAPTER QUESTIONS

Exam-style questions on levels of organisation and cell structure can be found at the end of Unit 2 on page 67.

SKILLS CRITICAL THINKING

1 Which of the following comparisons of animal and plant cells is *not* true?

	Animal cells	Plant cells
A	do not have chloroplasts	have chloroplasts
B	have mitochondria	do not have mitochondria
C	have temporary vacuoles	have permanent vacuoles
D	do not have cellulose cell walls	have cellulose cell walls

SKILLS CRITICAL THINKING

2 Which of the following descriptions is correct?

A The cell wall is freely permeable and the cell membrane is partially permeable

B The cell wall is partially permeable and the cell membrane is freely permeable

C Both the cell wall and the cell membrane are freely permeable

D Both the cell wall and the cell membrane are partially permeable

SKILLS CRITICAL THINKING, INTERPRETATION

3 a Name the following:
   i the structure made of cellulose that maintains the shape of a plant cell
   ii the organelle that provides a cell with most of its energy
   iii the organelle that contains chlorophyll
   iv the fluid-filled space in the middle of a plant cell, which contains dissolved sugars and ions.

b 'Muscle' is a tissue, whereas 'a muscle' is an organ. Explain this statement.

SKILLS INTERPRETATION

4 a Draw a diagram of a plant cell. Label all of the parts. Alongside each label write the function of that part.

SKILLS CRITICAL THINKING

b Write down three differences between the cell you have drawn and a 'typical' animal cell.

3 BIOLOGICAL MOLECULES

SPECIFICATION REFERENCES: 2.7–2.13

About 60–70% of the human body is water. The rest of your body is mainly made of three groups of substances – carbohydrates, proteins and lipids. Other organisms are composed of the same biological molecules. This chapter deals with the structure of these substances and how we can test for them in samples of food. It also describes an important group of proteins, the enzymes, which control chemical reactions taking place in cells.

LEARNING OBJECTIVES

- Identify the chemical elements present in carbohydrates, proteins and lipids (fats and oils).
- Describe the structure of carbohydrates, proteins and lipids as large molecules made up from smaller basic units – starch and glycogen from simple sugars, protein from amino acids, and lipid from fatty acids and glycerol.
- Investigate food samples for the presence of glucose, starch, protein and fat.
- Understand the role of enzymes as biological catalysts in metabolic reactions.
- Understand how temperature changes can affect enzyme function, including changes to the shape of the active site.
- Investigate how enzyme activity can be affected by changes in temperature.
- Understand how enzyme function can be affected by changes in pH altering the active site.

KEY POINT

A polymer is a large molecule made by joining together lots of small molecules.

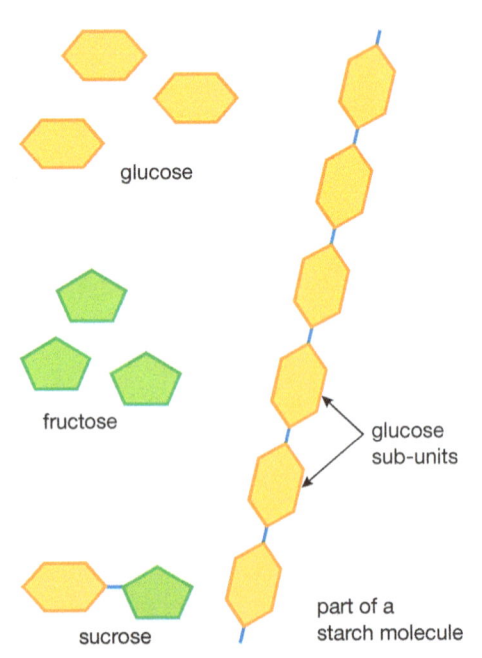

▲ Figure 3.1 Glucose and fructose are 'single sugar' molecules. A molecule of glucose joined to a molecule of fructose forms the 'double sugar' called sucrose. Starch is a polymer of many glucose sub-units.

CARBOHYDRATES

Carbohydrates contain the elements carbon (C), hydrogen (H) and oxygen (O). One example is the simple sugar **glucose**, which has the chemical formula $C_6H_{12}O_6$. The 'carbo' part of the name refers to carbon, and the 'hydrate' part refers to the hydrogen and oxygen atoms being in a 2:1 ratio, as in water (H_2O). There are many other simple sugars, such as **fructose**, a sugar found in fruits. Sometimes simple sugar molecules are joined together in pairs to form a 'double sugar', for example, sucrose. Sucrose is the sugar that some people use to sweeten tea or coffee. Sucrose is stored in some plant cells. Other carbohydrates are made of sugar molecules joined together in long chains. One example is starch, which is a chain or **polymer** of glucose sub-units. Starch is insoluble, which is one reason why plants use it as a storage product. Diagrams of sugars and starch are shown in **Figure 3.1**.

Another polymer of glucose is **cellulose**, the material that makes up plant cell walls. Starch is only found in plant tissues, but animal cells sometimes contain a very similar carbohydrate called **glycogen**. Glycogen is also a polymer of glucose, and is found in tissues such as liver and muscle, where it acts as a store of energy.

EXTENSION

'Single' sugars such as glucose and fructose are called monosaccharides. 'Double' sugars such as sucrose are made of two monosaccharides joined together (sucrose is glucose and fructose), so sucrose is called a disaccharide. Polymers of sugars, such as starch, glycogen and cellulose, are called polysaccharides.

PROTEINS

Proteins are also polymers, but whereas starch is made from a single molecular building block (glucose), proteins are made from 20 different sub-units called **amino acids**. All amino acids contain four chemical elements: carbon, hydrogen and oxygen (as in carbohydrates) along with nitrogen. Two amino acids also contain sulfur. The amino acids are linked together in long chains, which are usually folded up or twisted into spirals, with cross-links holding the chains together (**Figure 3.2**).

EXTENSION

Humans can make about half of the 20 amino acids that they need, but the other 10 have to be taken in as part of the diet. These 10 are called essential amino acids. There are higher amounts of essential amino acids in meat, fish, eggs and dairy products. If you are a vegetarian, you can still get all the essential amino acids you need, as long as you eat a varied diet that includes a range of different plant materials.

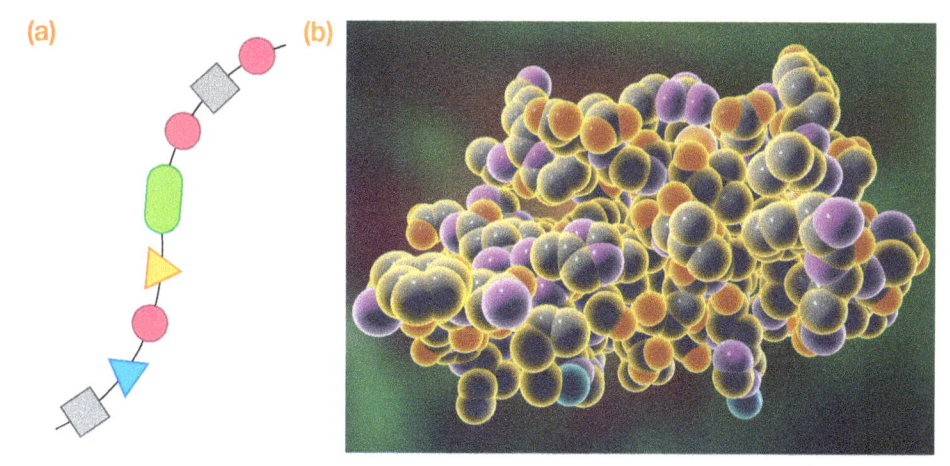

▲ Figure 3.2 (a) A chain of amino acids forming part of a protein molecule. Each shape represents a different amino acid. (b) A computer model of the protein insulin. This substance, like all proteins, is made of a long chain of amino acids arranged in a particular order and folded into a specific shape.

The *shape* of a protein is very important in allowing it to carry out its function, and the *order* of amino acids in the protein decides its shape. Because there are 20 different amino acids, and they can be arranged in any order, the number of different protein structures that can be made is enormous. As a result, there are thousands of different kinds of proteins in organisms. Examples are structural proteins, such as collagen and keratin in skin and nails, and proteins with more specific functions, such as **enzymes** (see below).

LIPIDS (FATS AND OILS)

Lipids contain the same three elements as carbohydrates – carbon, hydrogen and oxygen – but the proportion of oxygen in a lipid is much lower than in a carbohydrate. Meat such as beef or lamb contains a fat called tristearin, which has the formula $C_{51}H_{98}O_6$. This fat, like other animal fats, is a solid at room temperature, but melts if you warm it up. On the other hand, plant lipids are usually liquid at room temperature, and are called oils.

The chemical 'building blocks' of lipids are two types of molecule, called **glycerol** and **fatty acids**. Glycerol is an oily liquid. It is also known as glycerine, and is used in many types of cosmetics. In lipids, one molecule of glycerol is joined to three fatty acid molecules. There are many different fatty acid molecules, which give us the many different kinds of lipid found in food (**Figure 3.3**).

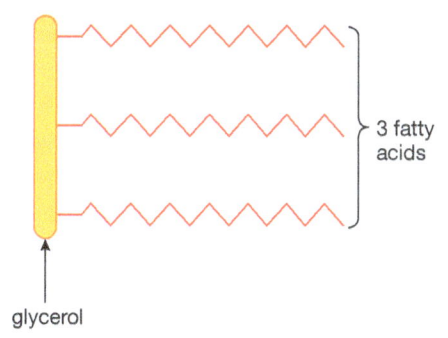

▲ Figure 3.3 Lipids are made up of one molecule of glycerol joined to three fatty acids. The many different fatty acids form the variable part of the molecule.

FOOD TESTS

You can carry out simple chemical tests for starch, glucose, protein or lipid. **Activity 1** uses pure substances for the tests, but it is possible to do them on normal foods too. Unless the food is a liquid, such as milk, it needs to be cut up into small pieces and ground with a pestle and mortar, then shaken with some water in a test tube. This is to extract the components of the food and dissolve any soluble substances, such as sugars.

ACTIVITY 1

▼ PRACTICAL: TESTING FOR SOME BIOLOGICAL MOLECULES

TEST FOR STARCH

A little starch is placed on a spotting tile. A drop of yellow–brown iodine solution is added to the starch. The iodine reacts with the starch, forming a very dark blue, or 'blue–black', colour (**Figure 3.4a**). This test will work on a solid sample of food, such as potato, or a suspension of starch in water.

TEST FOR GLUCOSE

A small spatula measure of glucose is placed in a test tube and a little distilled water is added (about 2 cm deep). The tube is shaken to dissolve the glucose. Several drops of Benedict's solution are added to the tube, enough to colour the mixture blue.

A water bath is prepared by half-filling a beaker with water and heating it on a tripod and gauze. The test tube is placed in the beaker and the water is allowed to boil. After a few seconds, the clear blue solution will gradually change colour, forming a cloudy orange or 'brick red' precipitate (**Figure 3.4b**).

TEST FOR PROTEIN

The test for protein is sometimes called the 'biuret' test, after the coloured compound that is formed.

A little protein, such as powdered egg white (albumen), is placed in a test tube and about 2 cm depth of water is added. The tube is shaken to mix the contents. An equal volume of dilute (5%) potassium hydroxide solution is added and the tube is shaken again. Finally, two drops of 1% copper sulfate solution are added. A pale purple colour will develop (**Figure 3.4c**). (Sometimes these two solutions are supplied already mixed together as 'biuret solution'.)

TEST FOR LIPID

Fats and oils are insoluble in water but will dissolve in ethanol (alcohol). The test for lipid uses this fact.

A pipette is used to place one drop of olive oil in the bottom of a test tube. About 2 cm depth of ethanol is added and the tube is shaken to dissolve the oil. The solution is poured into a test tube that is about three-quarters full with cold water. A white cloudy layer will form on the top of the water (**Figure 3.4d**). The white layer forms as the ethanol dissolves in the water and leaves the lipid behind as a suspension of tiny droplets, called an emulsion.

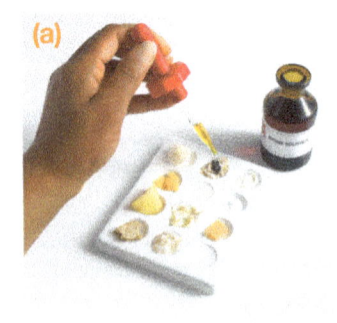

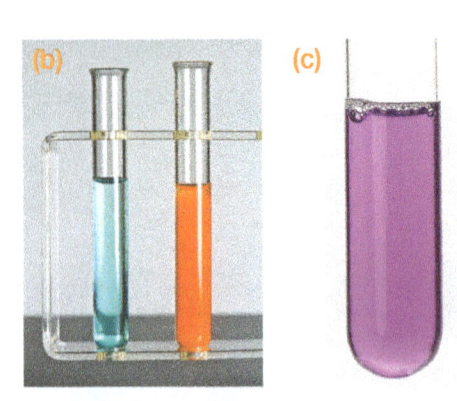

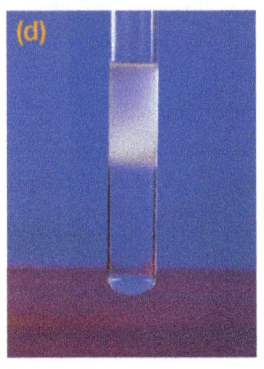

▲ Figure 3.4 (a) Testing for starch using iodine. (b) Testing for glucose using Benedict's solution. (c) Testing for protein using biuret solution. (d) Testing for lipid.

EXTENSION

All other single sugars (e.g. fructose) and some double sugars will give a positive result with Benedict's solution. However, ordinary table sugar (sucrose) will not. If sucrose is boiled with Benedict's solution the mixture will stay a clear blue colour.

ENZYMES: CONTROLLING REACTIONS IN THE CELL

KEY POINT

The chemical reactions taking place in a cell are known as metabolic reactions. The sum of all the metabolic reactions is known as the **metabolism** of the cell. The function of enzymes is to catalyse metabolic reactions.

KEY POINT

In the intestine enzymes are secreted onto the food to break it down. These are called *extracellular* enzymes, which means they function 'outside cells'. However, most enzymes stay inside cells and carry out their function there; they are *intracellular*. You will find out about digestive enzymes in **Chapter 5**.

KEY POINT

Secretion is the release of a fluid or substances from a cell or tissue.

The chemical reactions that take place in a cell are controlled by a group of proteins called enzymes. Enzymes are biological **catalysts**. A catalyst is a chemical which speeds up a reaction without being used up itself. A catalyst takes part in the reaction, but afterwards is unchanged and free to catalyse more reactions. Cells contain hundreds of different enzymes, each catalysing a different reaction. This is how the activities of a cell are controlled – the nucleus contains the genes, which control the production of enzymes, which then catalyse reactions in the cytoplasm:

genes → proteins (enzymes) → catalyse reactions

Everything a cell does depends on which enzymes it can make. In turn, this depends on which genes in its nucleus are 'switched on' (expressed).

Why are enzymes needed at all? They are necessary because the temperatures inside organisms are low (e.g. the human body temperature is about 37 °C) and, without catalysts, most of the reactions that happen in cells would be far too slow to allow life to go on. Just think about the number of reactions in chemistry lessons that you need to heat. The reactions can only take place quickly enough when enzymes speed them up.

There are thousands of different sorts of enzymes because they are proteins, and protein molecules have an enormous range of structures and shapes (see above).

The molecule that an enzyme acts on is called its **substrate**. Each enzyme has a small area on its surface called the **active site**. The substrate attaches to the active site of the enzyme. The formation of this 'enzyme–substrate complex' makes it easier for bonds in the substrate to be broken and new bonds made, to form the products.

The substrate fits into the active site of the enzyme like a key fitting into a lock. Just as a key will only fit one lock, a substrate will only fit into the active site of a particular enzyme. This is known as the **lock and key model** of enzyme action. It is the reason why enzymes are *specific*, that is an enzyme will only catalyse one reaction (**Figure 3.5**).

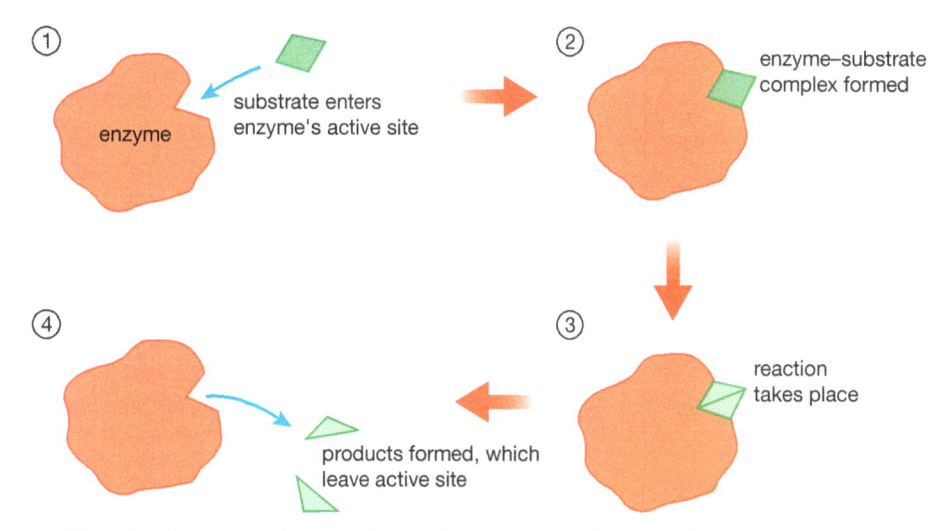

▲ Figure 3.5 Enzymes catalyse reactions at their active site. The active site acts like a 'lock' to the substrate 'key'. The substrate fits into the active site, and products are formed. This happens more easily than without the enzyme – so enzymes act as catalysts.

Enzymes also catalyse reactions where large molecules are built up from smaller ones. In this case, several substrate molecules attach to the active site, the reaction takes place and the larger product molecule is formed.

After an enzyme molecule has catalysed a reaction, the product is released from the active site, and the enzyme is free to act on more substrate molecules.

FACTORS AFFECTING ENZYMES

A number of factors affect the activity of enzymes. Two of these are temperature and pH.

TEMPERATURE

KEY POINT

The 'optimum' temperature means the 'best' temperature, in other words the temperature at which the reaction takes place most rapidly.

The effect of temperature on the action of an enzyme is easiest to see as a graph, where we plot the rate of the reaction against temperature (**Figure 3.6**).

Enzymes in the human body have evolved to work best at body temperature (37 °C). The graph in **Figure 3.6** shows a peak on the curve at this temperature, which is called the *optimum temperature* for the enzyme.

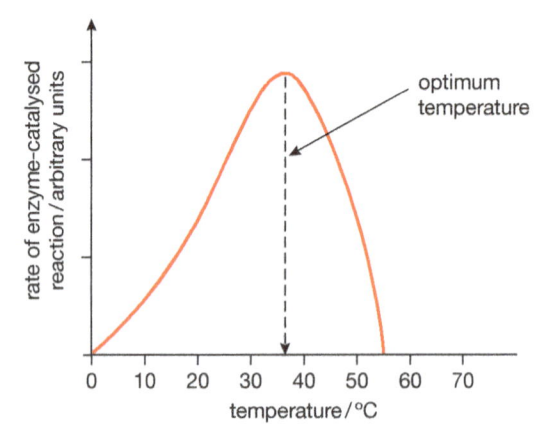

▲ Figure 3.6 Effect of temperature on the action of an enzyme

DID YOU KNOW?

Kinetic energy is the energy an object has because of its movement. The molecules of enzyme and substrate are moving faster, so they have more kinetic energy.

As the enzyme is heated up to the optimum temperature, the rise in temperature increases the rate of reaction. This is because higher temperatures give the molecules of the enzyme and the substrate more kinetic energy, so they collide more often. More collisions means that the reaction will take place more frequently.

Temperature starts to have another effect when it rises above the optimum. Enzymes are made of protein, and proteins are broken down by heat. From 40 °C upwards, heat destroys the enzyme. We say that it is denatured. You can see the effect of **denaturing** when you boil an egg. The egg white is made of protein, and turns from a clear runny liquid into a white solid as the heat denatures the protein. Denaturing changes the shape of the enzyme, including its active site. This means that the substrate (the key) will no longer fit into active site (the lock). Denaturing is permanent – the enzyme molecule cannot go back to its original shape so it can no longer catalyse the reaction.

Not all enzymes have an optimum temperature near 37 °C, only those of animals such as mammals and birds, which all have body temperatures close to this value. Enzymes have evolved to work best at the normal body temperature of the organism. Bacteria that always live at an average temperature of 10 °C will probably have enzymes with an optimum temperature near 10 °C.

pH

The pH around the enzyme is also important. The pH inside cells is neutral (pH 7) and most enzymes have evolved to work best at this pH. At extremes of pH either side of neutral, the enzyme activity decreases, as shown in **Figure 3.7**. The pH at which the enzyme works best is called its *optimum pH*. Either side of the optimum, the pH affects the structure of the enzyme molecule and changes the shape of its active site, so that the substrate will not fit into the active site so well.

KEY POINT

Although most enzymes work best at a neutral pH, a few have an optimum below or above pH 7. The stomach produces hydrochloric acid, which makes its contents very acidic (see **Chapter 5**). Most enzymes stop working at a low pH, but the stomach makes an enzyme called pepsin which has an optimum pH of about 2, so that it is adapted to work well in the unusual acidic surroundings of the stomach.

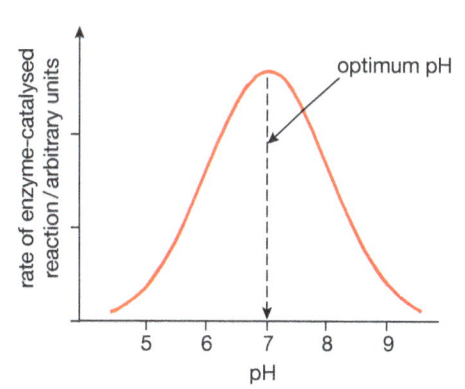

Safety note: Wear eye protection and avoid skin contact with the reactants. Always use a water bath for the glucose test – never use a Bunsen burner to heat the test tube directly.

▲ Figure 3.7 Most enzymes work best at a neutral pH

ACTIVITY 2

▼ PRACTICAL: AN INVESTIGATION INTO THE EFFECT OF TEMPERATURE ON THE ACTIVITY OF AMYLASE

The digestive enzyme amylase breaks down starch into a sugar called maltose. (Maltose is a 'double sugar' made of two glucose molecules joined together.) If the speed at which the starch disappears is recorded, this provides a measure of the activity of the amylase. **Figure 3.8** shows apparatus that can be used to record how quickly the starch is used up.

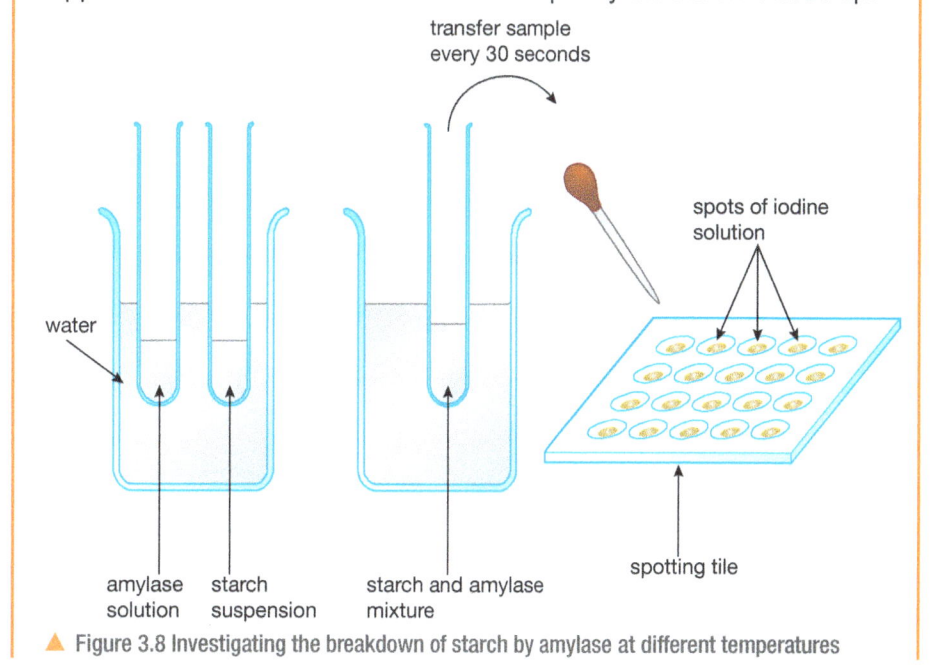

▲ Figure 3.8 Investigating the breakdown of starch by amylase at different temperatures

Spots of iodine solution are placed into the dips on the spotting tile. Using a syringe, 5 cm³ of starch suspension is placed in one boiling tube. 5 cm³ of amylase solution is put in another tube, using a different syringe. The beaker is filled with water at 20 °C. Both boiling tubes are placed in the beaker of water for 5 minutes, and the temperature is recorded.

The amylase solution is then poured into the starch suspension and mixed, leaving the tube containing the mixture in the water bath. Immediately, a small sample of the mixture is removed from the tube with a pipette and added to the first drop of iodine solution on the spotting tile. The colour of the iodine solution is recorded.

A sample of the mixture is then taken every 30 seconds for 10 minutes and tested for starch as above, until the iodine solution remains yellow, showing that all the starch is used up.

The experiment is repeated, maintaining the water bath at different temperatures between 20 °C and 60 °C.

A set of results is shown in the table below.

Time / min	Colour of mixture at different temperatures / (°C)				
	20	30	40	50	60
0.0	blue–black	blue–black	blue–black	blue–black	blue–black
0.5	blue–black	blue–black	brown	blue–black	blue–black
1.0	blue–black	blue–black	yellow	blue–black	blue–black
1.5	blue–black	blue–black	yellow	blue–black	blue–black
2.0	blue–black	blue–black	yellow	brown	blue–black
2.5	blue–black	blue–black	yellow	brown	blue–black
3.0	blue–black	blue–black	yellow	brown	blue–black
3.5	blue–black	blue–black	yellow	yellow	blue–black
4.0	blue–black	blue–black	yellow	yellow	blue–black
5.5	blue–black	blue–black	yellow	yellow	blue–black
6.0	blue–black	brown	yellow	yellow	blue–black
6.5	blue–black	brown	yellow	yellow	blue–black
7.0	blue–black	yellow	yellow	yellow	blue–black
7.5	blue–black	yellow	yellow	yellow	brown
8.0	blue–black	yellow	yellow	yellow	brown
8.5	brown	yellow	yellow	yellow	yellow
9.0	brown	yellow	yellow	yellow	yellow
9.5	yellow	yellow	yellow	yellow	yellow
10.0	yellow	yellow	yellow	yellow	yellow

The rate of reaction can be calculated from the time taken for the starch to be fully broken down, as shown by the colour change from blue–black to yellow.

For example, at 50 °C the starch was fully changed into sugar after 3.5 minutes. The rate is found by dividing the volume of the starch (5 cm³) by the time:

$$\text{Rate} = \frac{5.0 \text{ cm}^3}{3.5 \text{ min}} = 1.4 \text{ cm}^3 \text{ per min}$$

Plot a graph of rate against temperature, using the results in the table. It should produce a curve similar to the one shown in **Figure 3.6**. Better still, you may be able to do this experiment and provide your own results.

If your curve is not quite like the one in **Figure 3.6**, can you suggest why this is? How could you improve the experiment to get more reliable results?

CHAPTER QUESTIONS

Exam-style questions on biological molecules can be found at the end of Unit 2 on page 67.

SKILLS CRITICAL THINKING

1 Which of the following organic molecules contains carbon, hydrogen, oxygen and nitrogen?

　A glycogen　　**B** lipid　　**C** cellulose　　**D** protein

SKILLS CRITICAL THINKING

2 Which of the following substances would give a positive test when boiled with Benedict's solution?

　A glucose　　**B** lipid　　**C** starch　　**D** protein

SKILLS INTERPRETATION

3 Write a short description of the nature and function of enzymes. Include the following in your description:

- a definition of an enzyme
- a description of the 'lock and key' model of enzyme action
- an explanation of the difference between intracellular and extracellular enzymes.

Your description should be about a page in length, including a labelled diagram.

SKILLS ANALYSIS

4 The graph shows the effect of temperature on an enzyme. The enzyme was extracted from a micro-organism that lives in hot mineral springs near a volcano.

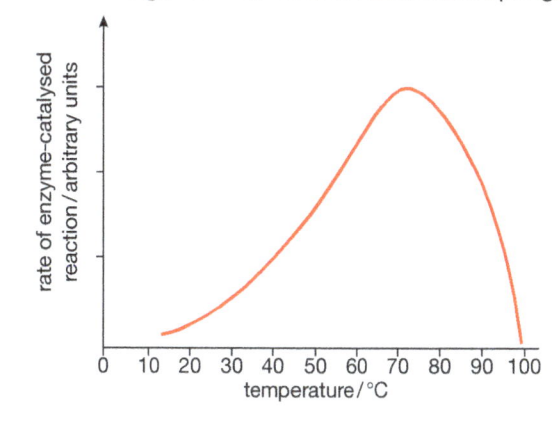

a What is the optimum temperature of this enzyme?

b Explain why the activity of the enzyme is greater at 60 °C than at 30 °C.

c The optimum temperature of enzymes in the human body is about 37 °C. Explain why the enzyme from the micro-organism has a different optimum temperature.

d What happens to the enzyme at 90 °C?

4 MOVEMENT OF SUBSTANCES INTO AND OUT OF CELLS SPECIFICATION REFERENCES: 2.15, 2.16

Cells need to take in some substances, such as oxygen, from their surroundings. They need to get rid of other substances, such as carbon dioxide. The cell membrane acts as a barrier between the inside and the outside of the cell, controlling what can enter and leave. This chapter looks at the ways that molecules and ions pass through the membrane. There are three main ways: diffusion, osmosis and active transport.

LEARNING OBJECTIVES

- Understand the processes of diffusion, osmosis and active transport by which substances move into and out of cells.

- Understand how factors affect the rate of movement of substances into and out of cells, including the effects of surface area to volume ratio, distance, temperature and concentration gradient.

DIFFUSION

Many substances can pass through the cell membrane by **diffusion**. Diffusion happens when a substance is more concentrated in one place than another. For example, if a cell is producing carbon dioxide by respiration (see **Chapter 6**), the concentration of carbon dioxide will be higher inside the cell than outside. This difference in concentration is called *concentration gradient*. The molecules of carbon dioxide are constantly moving about (they have kinetic energy). The cell membrane is permeable to carbon dioxide, so the molecules can move through it in either direction. Over time, more molecules will move out of the cell than into it, because there is a higher concentration of carbon dioxide molecules inside the cell than outside. We say there is a *net* movement of molecules out of the cell (**Figure 4.1**).

KEY TERM

Diffusion is the net movement of particles (molecules or ions) from a region of high concentration to a region of low concentration, i.e. down a concentration gradient.

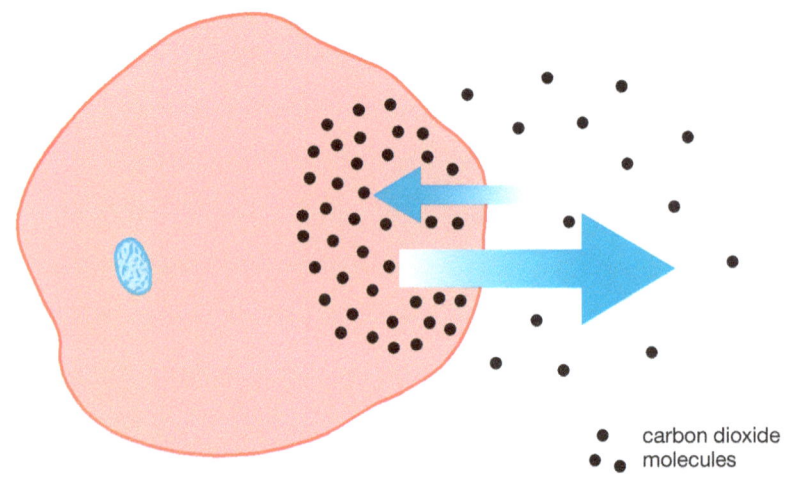

▲ Figure 4.1 Respiration produces carbon dioxide, so the concentration of carbon dioxide inside the cell increases. Although the carbon dioxide molecules diffuse across the cell membrane in both directions, the overall (or net) movement is out of the cell, down the concentration gradient.

The opposite happens with oxygen. Respiration uses up oxygen, so there is a concentration gradient of oxygen from outside the cell to inside. There is therefore a net movement of oxygen into the cell by diffusion.

FACTORS AFFECTING THE RATE OF DIFFUSION

Various factors affect the rate of diffusion.

The surface area to volume ratio: A larger surface area in proportion to the volume will increase the rate of diffusion. Cells that exchange a lot of materials with their surroundings often have a cell surface membrane that is folded to increase its surface area and maximise diffusion.

The distance: The greater the distance that diffusion has to take place over, the slower the rate. For this reason cells in the body that function as an exchange surface are often thin. For example, the lining of the air sacs of the lungs is made of thin, flattened cells so that there is a very short distance for gases to diffuse between the air in the lungs and the blood (see **Chapter 7**).

The temperature: Diffusion is faster at higher temperatures. This is because a high temperature gives particles more kinetic energy. In humans (as well as other mammals and birds) the temperature of the body is constant, so it does not affect the rate of diffusion. However in 'cold blooded' animals, as well as plants, the rate is affected by changes in their body temperature.

The concentration gradient: Diffusion happens more quickly when there is a steep concentration gradient (i.e. a big difference in concentration between two areas). Organisms have evolved ways to maintain a concentration gradient and speed up diffusion. For example, blood vessels surrounding the air sacs of the lungs continuously remove oxygen and take it to the body. This maintains a steep concentration gradient between the air and the blood.

OSMOSIS

Water moves across cell membranes by a special sort of diffusion, called osmosis. Osmosis happens when the total concentration of all the dissolved substances inside and outside the cell are different. Water will move across the membrane from the more dilute solution to the more concentrated one. Notice that this is still obeying the rules of diffusion – the water moves from where there is a higher concentration of water molecules to a lower concentration of water molecules. Osmosis can only happen if the membrane is permeable to water but not to some other solutes. We call such a membrane a partially permeable membrane.

KEY POINT

The cell membrane is both selectively permeable and partially permeable. 'Selectively permeable' means that the membrane can control which molecules it lets through (by active transport, which is explained later). 'Partially permeable' means that small molecules such as water and gases can pass through it, while larger molecules cannot.

An artificial partially permeable membrane called Visking tubing can be used to show osmosis. This membrane is used in kidney dialysis machines to filter the blood of patients with kidney failure. Visking tubing has microscopic holes in it, which let small molecules such as water pass through – it is permeable to water. However, it is not permeable to some larger molecules, such as the sugar sucrose. Like a cell membrane, it is partially permeable. You can show the effects of osmosis by filling a Visking tubing 'sausage' with concentrated sucrose solution, attaching it to a capillary tube and placing the Visking tubing in a beaker of water (**Figure 4.2**).

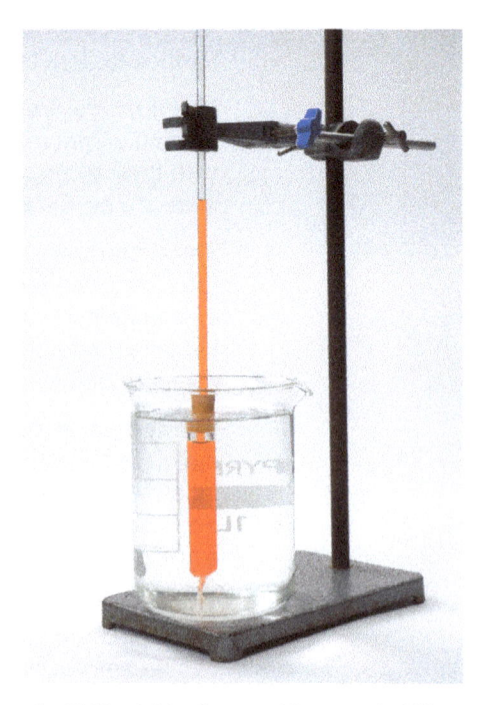

▲ Figure 4.2 Water enters the Visking tubing 'sausage' by osmosis. This causes the level of liquid in the capillary tube to rise. In the photograph the contents of the Visking tubing have had a red dye added to make it easier to see the movement of the liquid.

The level in the capillary tube rises as water moves from the beaker into the Visking tubing. This movement is due to osmosis. You can understand what is happening if you imagine a highly magnified view of the Visking tubing separating the two liquids (**Figure 4.3**).

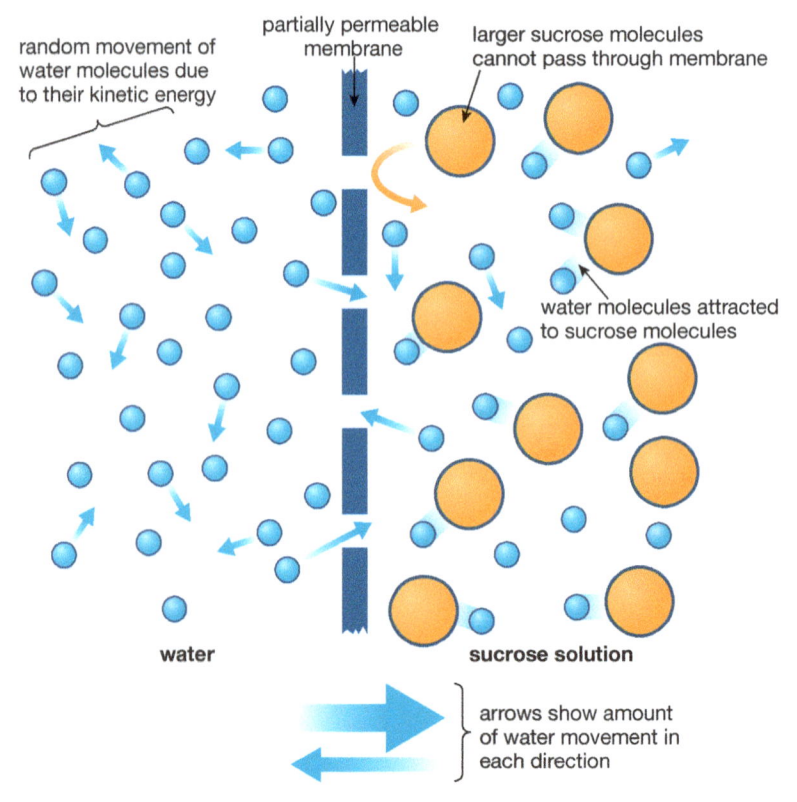

▲ Figure 4.3 In this model of osmosis, more water molecules diffuse from left to right than from right to left

KEY TERM

Osmosis is the net diffusion of water across a partially permeable membrane, from a dilute solution to a more concentrated solution.

The sucrose molecules are too big to pass through the holes in the partially permeable membrane. The water molecules can pass through the membrane in either direction, but those on the right are attracted to the sugar molecules. They cluster around the sugar molecules and are less 'free' to diffuse to other areas. This means that there are more 'free' water molecules on the left-hand side of the membrane than on the right. As a result, more water molecules diffuse from left to right than from right to left. In other words, there is a greater diffusion of water molecules from the more dilute solution (in this case pure water) to the more concentrated solution. The definition of osmosis is given in the key term box.

All cells are surrounded by a partially permeable cell membrane. In the human body, osmosis is important in moving water from cell to cell, and from the blood to the tissues. It is important that the cells of the body are bathed in a solution with the right concentration of solutes; otherwise they could be damaged by osmotic movements of water. For example, if red blood cells are put into water, they will swell up and burst. If the same cells are put into a concentrated salt solution, they lose water by osmosis and shrink, producing cells with crinkly edges (**Figure 4.4**).

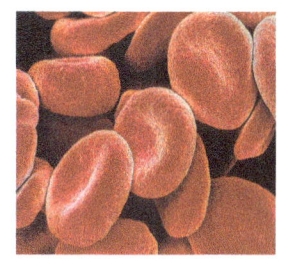

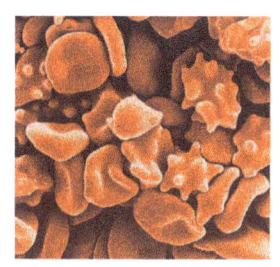

Figure 4.4 The concentration of the liquid part of the blood (plasma) is about the same as a 0.85% salt solution. Compare the normal blood cells on the left, which are in a 0.85% salt solution, with those on the right, in a 3% salt solution.

Osmosis also happens in plant cells. There is a tough cellulose cell wall around plant cells. This gives the cell its shape and it can resist changes in pressure inside the cell. Unlike the cell membrane, the cell wall is freely permeable to water and solutes – it will allow them to pass through. The cell contents, including the sap vacuole, contain many dissolved solutes, such as sugars and ions.

If a plant cell is put into pure water or a dilute solution, there is a higher concentration of solutes inside the cell, so the cell absorbs water by osmosis (**Figure 4.5**). The cell swells up and the cytoplasm pushes against the cell wall. A plant cell that has developed an internal pressure like this is called **turgid**.

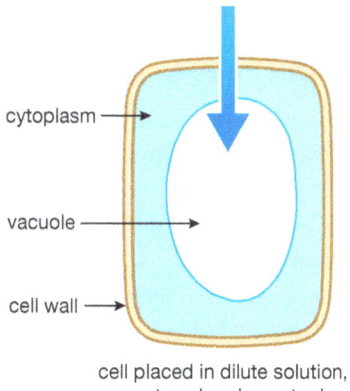

cell placed in dilute solution, or water, absorbs water by osmosis and becomes turgid

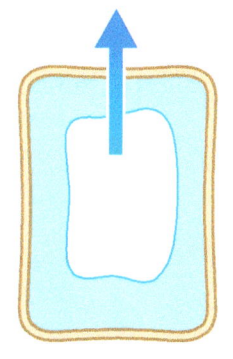

cell placed in concentrated solution loses water by osmosis and becomes flaccid

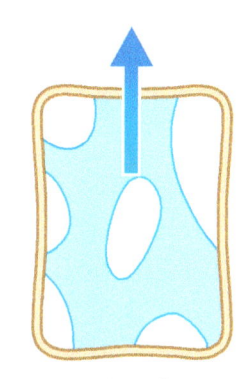

excessive loss of water by osmosis causes the cell to become plasmolysed

▲ Figure 4.5 The effects of osmosis on plant cells

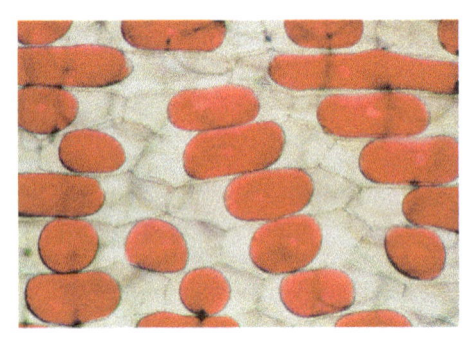

▲ Figure 4.6 Cells of the epidermis of a red onion, showing plasmolysis. The cell membranes and cytoplasm (coloured red) have pulled away from the cell walls.

On the other hand, if the cell is placed in a solution that is more concentrated than the inside of the cell, the cell will *lose* water by osmosis. The cell decreases in volume and the cytoplasm no longer pushes against the cell wall. In this state, the cell is called **flaccid**. Eventually the cell contents shrink so much that the membrane and cytoplasm split away from the cell wall and gaps appear between the wall and the membrane. A cell like this is called **plasmolysed**. You can see plasmolysis happening in the plant cells shown in **Figure 4.6**. The space between the cell wall and the cell surface membrane will now be filled with the sucrose solution.

In a plant water moves from cell to cell by osmosis across the partially permeable cell membranes. The strong cell wall of a plant cell can resist pressure changes in the cell – a plant cell in water will swell up but will not burst. In fact plant cells need to be turgid to give support to the plant.

FACTORS AFFECTING THE RATE OF OSMOSIS

Osmosis is a special sort of diffusion, where water diffuses across a partially permeable membrane from a dilute solution to a more concentrated solution. Since it is just a kind of diffusion, the four factors mentioned above (surface area to volume ratio, distance, temperature and concentration gradient) affect osmosis in the same way as they affect any other diffusion process.

ACTIVE TRANSPORT

Diffusion happens down a concentration gradient as a result of the kinetic energy of the particles. However, sometimes a cell needs to take in a substance when there is very little of that substance outside the cell. In other words, movement needs to go *against* a concentration gradient. This needs another source of energy. It is carried out by a process called **active transport**.

During active transport a cell uses energy from respiration to take up substances, rather like a pump uses energy to move a liquid from one place to another. In fact, biologists speak of the cell 'pumping' ions or molecules in or out. The pumps are protein molecules located in the cell membrane.

An example of a place where active transport takes place is in the human small intestine. Some glucose in the gut is absorbed into the cells lining the intestine by active transport. The roots of plants also take up certain mineral ions in this way. Cells use active transport to control the uptake of many substances.

In **Chapter 6** you will find out about respiration and how it produces a chemical called **ATP**. ATP is used to supply energy for processes in cells. One of these processes is active transport. Most respiration is **aerobic**, which means it needs a supply of oxygen.

Aerobic respiration to make ATP takes place in cell organelles called mitochondria (see **Chapter 2**). Cells that need a lot of energy contain many mitochondria. It follows that a cell that is carrying out active transport usually has many mitochondria and needs a good supply of oxygen for respiration.

A large surface area to volume ratio can increase the rate of active transport in cells. For example, a folded cell membrane may contain more molecular pumps to transport molecules.

KEY POINT

Active transport is the movement of substances against a concentration gradient, using energy from respiration.

EXAM HINT

You should learn the definitions of diffusion, osmosis and active transport.

CHAPTER QUESTIONS

Exam-style questions on movement of substances can be found at the end of Unit 2 on page 67.

SKILLS CRITICAL THINKING

1 A sugar enters a cell by diffusion. Which of the following does *not* affect the rate of diffusion of the sugar?
   A temperature
   B cell surface area to volume ratio
   C concentration of the sugar outside the cell
   D oxygen concentration in the cell

SKILLS CRITICAL THINKING

2 Which of the following is true about active transport?
   A it does not need energy
   B it involves carrier proteins in the cell membrane
   C it produces ATP
   D it moves substances from a high to a low concentration

SKILLS CRITICAL THINKING

3 A plant cell was placed in a concentrated sugar solution. The diagram shows the appearance of the cell after an hour in the solution.

   What is the best description of this cell?
   A turgid
   B flaccid
   C plasmolysed
   D shrunken

SKILLS CRITICAL THINKING, INTERPRETATION

4 The diagram shows a cell from the lining of a human kidney tubule. A major role of this cell is to absorb glucose from the fluid passing along the tubule and pass it into the blood, as shown by the arrows on the diagram.

SKILLS ANALYSIS, INTERPRETATION

   a What is the function of the mitochondria?

   b The tubule cell contains a large number of mitochondria. They are needed for the cell to transport glucose across the cell membrane into the blood at 'A'. Suggest the method that the cell uses to do this and explain your answer.

   c The mitochondria are *not* needed to transport the glucose into the cell from the tubule at 'B'. Name the process by which the glucose molecules move across the membrane at 'B' and explain your answer.

   d The surface membrane of the tubule cell at 'B' is greatly folded. Explain how this adaptation helps the cell to carry out its function.

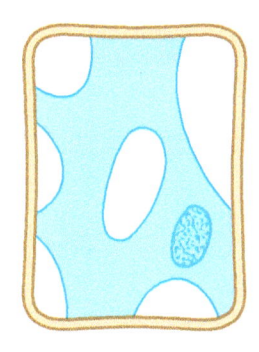

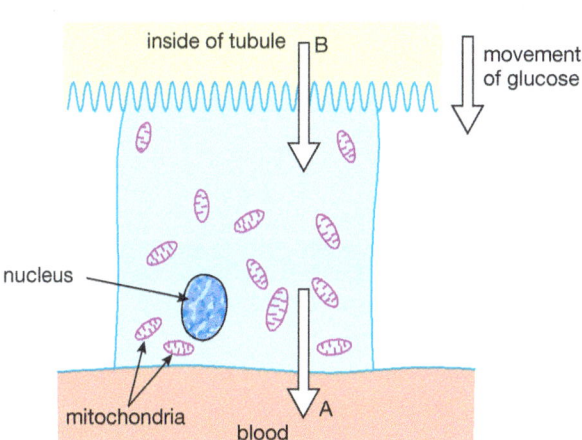

5 NUTRITION

SPECIFICATION REFERENCES: 2.18–2.21, 2.23, 2.27, 2.29

Nutrition is the process by which an organism obtains the nutrients it needs for growth and health. Green plants obtain their nutrients by photosynthesis, which is a chemical reaction where sunlight is used to make organic substances from carbon dioxide and water. Photosynthesis involves the green pigment chlorophyll and generates oxygen gas as a by-product. Animals gain their nutrients by feeding on plants or by eating other animals. This chapter looks at how both groups obtain their nutrition.

LEARNING OBJECTIVES

- Understand the process of photosynthesis and its importance in the conversion of light energy into chemical energy.
- Know the word equation and balanced symbol equation for photosynthesis.
- Understand how carbon dioxide concentration, light intensity and temperature affect the rate of photosynthesis.
- Describe the structure of the leaf and explain how it is adapted for photosynthesis.
- Investigate photosynthesis, showing the evolution of oxygen from a water plant, the production of starch and the need for light, carbon dioxide and chlorophyll.
- Describe the structure and function of the human alimentary canal, including the mouth, oesophagus, stomach, small intestine (duodenum and ileum), large intestine (colon and rectum) and pancreas.
- Understand the role of digestive enzymes, including the digestion of starch to glucose by amylase and maltase, the digestion of proteins to amino acids by proteases and the digestion of lipids to fatty acids and glycerol by lipases.

PHOTOSYNTHESIS

Plants use the simple inorganic molecules carbon dioxide and water, in the presence of chlorophyll and light, to make glucose and oxygen. This process is called **photosynthesis**.

It is summarised by the equation:

$$\text{carbon dioxide} + \text{water} \xrightarrow[\text{chlorophyll}]{\text{light}} \text{glucose} + \text{oxygen}$$

or:

$$6CO_2 + 6H_2O \xrightarrow[\text{chlorophyll}]{\text{light}} C_6H_{12}O_6 + 6O_2$$

EXAM HINT
You will need to know these equations.

DID YOU KNOW?
The 'photo' in photosynthesis comes from the Greek word *photos*, meaning light, and a 'synthesis' reaction is one where small molecules are built up into larger ones.

The function of the chlorophyll is to absorb the light energy needed for the reaction to take place. The products of the reaction (glucose and oxygen) contain more chemical energy than the carbon dioxide and water. In other words, photosynthesis converts light energy into chemical energy.

Starting with glucose, a plant can make many other compounds. These include other sugars, cellulose, proteins and lipids. Leaves also convert glucose into starch for storage. We can use the absence or presence of starch to find out whether or not a plant has been able to carry out photosynthesis. A leaf in the right conditions can make enough starch to give a positive test after a few hours. If no more starch is made, the store may be used up over a 24-hour period. So if we test a leaf for starch and the test is positive, it shows that the plant has been photosynthesising recently.

ACTIVITY 1

▼ PRACTICAL: TESTING LEAVES FOR STARCH

You can test for starch in food by adding a few drops of yellow–brown iodine solution (see **Chapter 3**). If the food contains starch, a blue–black colour is produced.

Leaves that have been in sunlight also contain starch, but you cannot test for it by adding iodine solution to a fresh leaf. The outer waxy surface of the leaf will not absorb the solution, and the green colour of the leaf would hide the colour change. To test for starch in a leaf, the outer waxy layer needs to be removed and the leaf decolourised. This is done by placing the leaf in boiling ethanol (see **Figure 5.1**).

A beaker of water is set up on a tripod and gauze and the water heated until it boils. A leaf is removed from a plant and all chemical reactions in the leaf are stopped by placing the leaf in boiling water for 30 seconds.

The Bunsen burner is turned off (this is important because ethanol is highly flammable), the leaf is placed in a boiling tube containing ethanol, and the tube is placed in the beaker of hot water. The boiling point of ethanol (about 78 °C) is lower than that of water (100 °C) so the ethanol will boil for a few minutes, until the water cools down. This is long enough to remove most of the chlorophyll from the leaf.

When the leaf has turned colourless or pale yellow, it is removed and washed in cold water to soften it, then spread out on a tile and covered with a few drops of iodine solution. After a few minutes, any parts of the leaf that contain starch will turn a dark blue–black colour. This only works if the plant has had plenty of light for some hours before the test.

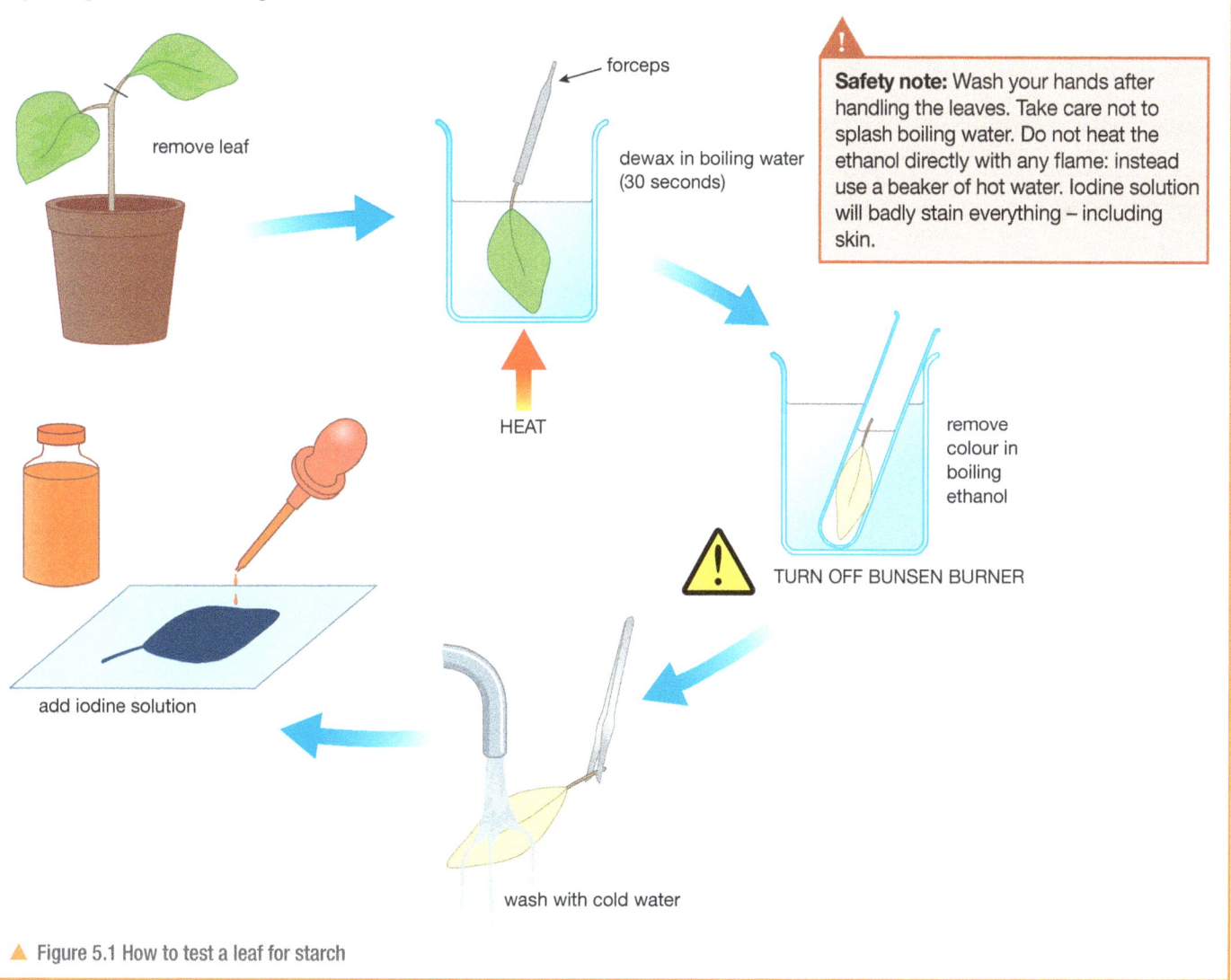

Safety note: Wash your hands after handling the leaves. Take care not to splash boiling water. Do not heat the ethanol directly with any flame: instead use a beaker of hot water. Iodine solution will badly stain everything – including skin.

▲ Figure 5.1 How to test a leaf for starch

KEY POINT

You can 'de-starch' a plant by placing it in the dark for 2 or 3 days. The plant uses up the starch stored in its leaves. De-starched plants are used to find out the conditions needed for the plant to make more starch by photosynthesis.

Figure 5.2 shows the results of a starch test on a leaf. The leaf was taken from a plant that had been under a bright light for 24 hours.

(a)   (b)   (c)

▲ Figure 5.2 Testing a leaf for starch. (a) Leaf before test. (b) Decolourised leaf. (c) Leaf after test, stained blue–black with iodine solution.

Starch is only made in the parts of plants that contain chlorophyll. You can show this by testing a variegated leaf, which has green and white areas. Only the green areas stain blue–black. The white parts of the leaf produce a negative starch test, just staining yellow.

Taking away the source of light is not the only way you can prevent a plant making starch in its leaves. You can also place it in a closed container containing a chemical called soda lime (**Figure 5.3**). This substance absorbs carbon dioxide from the air around the plant. If the plant is kept under a bright light but with no carbon dioxide, it again will not be able to make starch.

You have now found out three important facts about starch production by leaves:

- it uses carbon dioxide from the air
- it needs light
- it needs chlorophyll in the leaves.

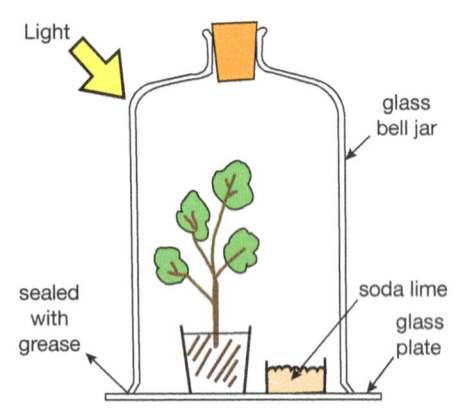

▲ Figure 5.3 Demonstration that carbon dioxide is needed for photosynthesis. The soda lime absorbs carbon dioxide from the air in the bell jar. A **Control** experiment should be set up, using exactly the same apparatus but without the soda lime.

As well as starch, there is another product of this process which is essential to the existence of most living things on the Earth – oxygen. When a plant is in the light, it makes oxygen gas. You can show this using an aquatic plant such as *Elodea* (Canadian pondweed). When a piece of this plant is placed in a test tube of water under a bright light, it produces a stream of small bubbles. If the bubbles are collected and their contents analysed, they are found to contain a high concentration of oxygen (**Figure 5.4**).

▲ Figure 5.4 The bubbles of gas released from this pondweed contain a higher concentration of oxygen than in atmospheric air.

THE STRUCTURE OF LEAVES

Leaves are the parts of a plant that are adapted for photosynthesis. To be able to photosynthesise efficiently, leaves need to have a large surface area to absorb light, many chloroplasts containing the chlorophyll, a supply of water and carbon dioxide, and a system for carrying away the products of photosynthesis to other parts of the plant. They also need to release oxygen (and water vapour) from the leaf cells. Most leaves are thin, flat structures supported by a leaf stalk which can grow to allow the blade of the leaf to be angled to receive the maximum amount of sunlight (**Figure 5.5**).

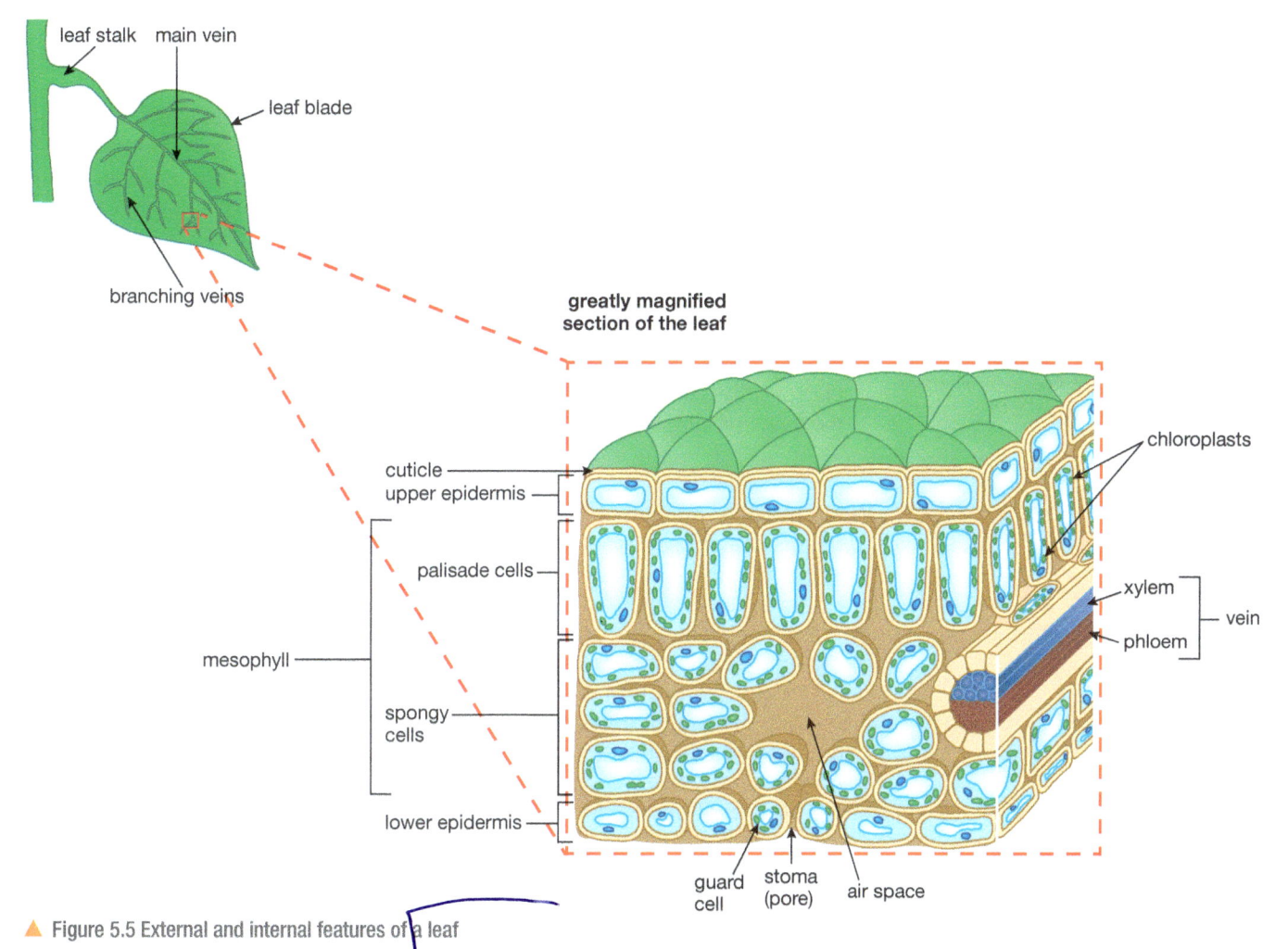

▲ Figure 5.5 External and internal features of a leaf

Inside the leaf are layers of cells with different functions.

- The two outer layers of cells (the upper and lower **epidermis**) have few chloroplasts and are covered by a thin layer of a waxy material called the **cuticle**. This reduces water loss by evaporation, and acts as a barrier to the entry of disease-causing micro-organisms such as bacteria and fungi.
- The lower epidermis has many holes or pores called **stomata** (a single pore is a **stoma**). Usually the upper epidermis contains fewer or no stomata. The stomata allow carbon dioxide to diffuse into the leaf, to reach the photosynthetic tissues. They also allow oxygen and water vapour to diffuse out. Each stoma is formed as a gap between two highly specialised cells called **guard cells**, which can change their shape to open or close the stoma.

- In the middle of the leaf are two layers of photosynthetic cells called the mesophyll ('mesophyll' just means 'middle of the leaf'). Just below the upper epidermis is the palisade mesophyll layer. This is a tissue made of long, narrow cells, each containing hundreds of chloroplasts. It is the main site of photosynthesis. The palisade cells are close to the source of light, and the upper epidermis is relatively transparent, allowing light to pass through to the enormous numbers of chloroplasts which lie below.
- Below the palisade layer is a tissue made of more rounded, loosely packed cells, with air spaces between them, called the spongy mesophyll layer. These cells also photosynthesise, but have fewer chloroplasts than the palisade cells. They form the main gas exchange surface of the leaf, absorbing carbon dioxide and releasing oxygen and water vapour. The air spaces allow these gases to diffuse in and out of the mesophyll.
- Water and mineral ions are supplied to the leaf by vessels in a tissue called the xylem. This consists of non-living, hollow tubes forming a continuous transport system throughout the plant. Water is absorbed by the roots and passes up through the stem and through veins in the leaves. In the leaves, the water leaves the xylem and supplies the mesophyll cells.
- The products of photosynthesis, such as sugars, are carried away from the mesophyll cells by another transport system, the phloem. Phloem contains living cells forming continuous tubes. It supplies all parts of the plant, so that tissues and organs that cannot make their own food can receive products of photosynthesis. The veins in the leaf contain both xylem and phloem tissue; the veins branch again and again to supply all parts of the leaf.

> **KEY POINT**
>
> Starch is insoluble and so cannot be transported around the plant. The phloem carries only soluble substances such as sugars (mainly sucrose) and amino acids. These are converted into other compounds when they reach their destination.

FACTORS AFFECTING THE RATE OF PHOTOSYNTHESIS

When the light intensity rises, the rate of photosynthesis starts to rise too, but eventually it reaches a maximum rate (**Figure 5.6**). The rate 'levels off' (flattens) like this because some other factor needed for photosynthesis is in short supply. Increasing the light intensity further does not affect the rate any more. Normally, the factor which 'holds back' the rate of photosynthesis is the concentration of carbon dioxide in the air. This is only about 0.04%, and the plant can only take up carbon dioxide and use it to make carbohydrate at a certain rate. If the plant is put in a closed container with a higher than normal concentration of carbon dioxide, it will photosynthesise at a faster rate. If there is both a high light intensity and a high level of carbon dioxide, the temperature may limit the rate of photosynthesis, by limiting the rate of the chemical reactions in the leaf. A rise in temperature will then increase the rate. With normal levels of carbon dioxide, very low temperatures (close to 0 °C) slow the reactions, but high temperatures (above about 35 °C) also reduce photosynthesis by denaturing enzymes in the plant cells.

Light intensity, carbon dioxide concentration and temperature can all act as what are called limiting factors in this way (**Figure 5.6**).

> **KEY POINT**
>
> A limiting factor is the component of a reaction that is in 'shortest supply' so that it prevents the rate of the reaction increasing, in other words sets a 'limit' to it.

2 STRUCTURE AND FUNCTION IN LIVING ORGANISMS   5 NUTRITION

KEY POINT

Knowledge of limiting factors is used in some glasshouses (greenhouses) to speed up the growth of crop plants such as tomatoes, strawberries and lettuces (see **Chapter 13**). Extra carbon dioxide is added to the air around the plants, by using gas burners. The higher concentration of carbon dioxide, along with the high temperature in the glasshouse, increases the rate of photosynthesis and boosts the growth of the leaves and fruits.

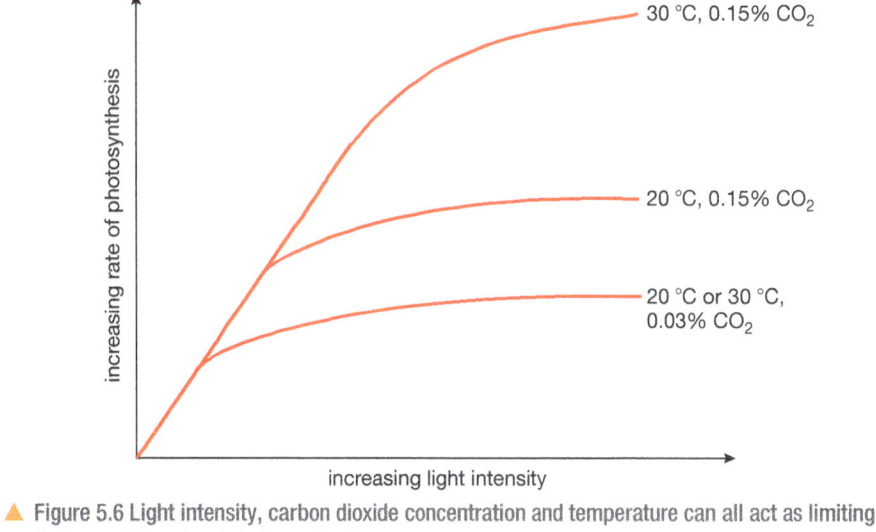

[Graph: increasing rate of photosynthesis vs increasing light intensity, showing three curves:
- 30 °C, 0.15% CO_2
- 20 °C, 0.15% CO_2
- 20 °C or 30 °C, 0.03% CO_2]

▲ Figure 5.6 Light intensity, carbon dioxide concentration and temperature can all act as limiting factors on the rate of photosynthesis.

ACTIVITY 2

▼ PRACTICAL: MEASURING THE RATE OF PHOTOSYNTHESIS USING PONDWEED

You can measure the rate of photosynthesis of a plant by measuring how quickly it produces oxygen. With a land plant this is difficult, because the oxygen is released into the air. However, with an aquatic plant, such as the pondweed *Elodea*, bubbles of oxygen are released into the water around the plant (see **Figure 5.4**).

If the bubbles formed per minute are counted, this is a measure of the rate of photosynthesis of the plant. It is easiest to count the bubbles if the cut piece of weed is placed upside down in a test tube, as shown in **Figure 5.7**. A small paperclip attached to the bottom of the piece of weed makes it sink.

Safety note: Wash hands after collecting and preparing pondweed. Do not handle the lamp, plug or switch with wet hands.

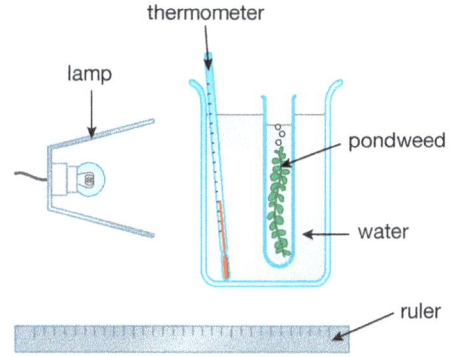

[Diagram: apparatus with lamp, thermometer, pondweed in test tube, water in beaker, and ruler]

▲ Figure 5.7 Measuring the rate of photosynthesis in an aquatic plant

The light intensity is changed by moving the lamp, altering the distance between the lamp and the pondweed. The beaker of water keeps the temperature of the plant constant.

Design an experiment using this apparatus to find out if the rate of photosynthesis is affected by the light intensity. In your plan you should include:

- a hypothesis – state what you think will happen when you change the light intensity, and why
- a systematic way of changing the light intensity
- how the experiment will be controlled so that nothing else is changed apart from the light intensity (e.g. what will you do about the background light in the laboratory?)
- a control that you could use, to show that it is the effect of light on the pondweed that is producing the bubbles
- how you will ensure that your results are reliable.

When you have completed your plan, you may be allowed to use similar apparatus to carry out the experiment. How could you modify your plan to find the effect of changing the *temperature* on the rate of photosynthesis? What factors would you need to keep constant this time? What would be a suitable range of temperatures to use?

DIGESTION IN HUMANS

Food, such as a piece of bread, contains carbohydrates, lipids and proteins, but they are not the same as the carbohydrates, lipids and proteins in our tissues. The components of the bread must first be broken down into their 'building blocks' before they can be absorbed through the wall of the gut. This process is called **digestion**. The digested molecules – sugars, fatty acids, glycerol and amino acids – along with minerals, vitamins and water, can then be carried around the body in the blood. When they reach the tissues they are reassembled into the molecules that make up our cells.

Digestion is speeded up by **enzymes**, which are biological catalysts (see **Chapter 3**). Although most enzymes stay inside cells, the digestive enzymes are made by the tissues and glands in the gut and pass out of cells and into the gut contents where they act on the food. This *chemical* digestion is helped by *mechanical* digestion. Mechanical digestion is the physical breakdown of food. The most obvious place where this happens is in the mouth, where the teeth bite and chew the food, cutting it into smaller pieces that have a larger surface area. This means that enzymes can act on the food more quickly. Other parts of the gut also help with mechanical digestion. For example, muscles in the wall of the stomach contract to churn up the food while it is being chemically digested. Muscles in the gut wall also push the food along the gut so that it can be digested and the products absorbed.

THE DIGESTIVE SYSTEM

Figure 5.8 shows a simplified diagram of the human digestive system, which is also known as the **alimentary canal**.

Figure 5.8 is simplified so that you can see the order of the organs along the gut. The real gut is much longer than this, and coiled up so that it fills the abdomen. Overall, its length in an adult is about 8 m. This gives plenty of time for the food to be broken down and absorbed as it passes through the gut.

EXAM HINT

A good definition of digestion is: 'Digestion is the chemical and mechanical breakdown of food. It converts large insoluble molecules into small soluble molecules, which can be absorbed into the blood.'

DID YOU KNOW?

Alimentary canal means 'the parts of the body that food goes through as it is eaten and digested'.

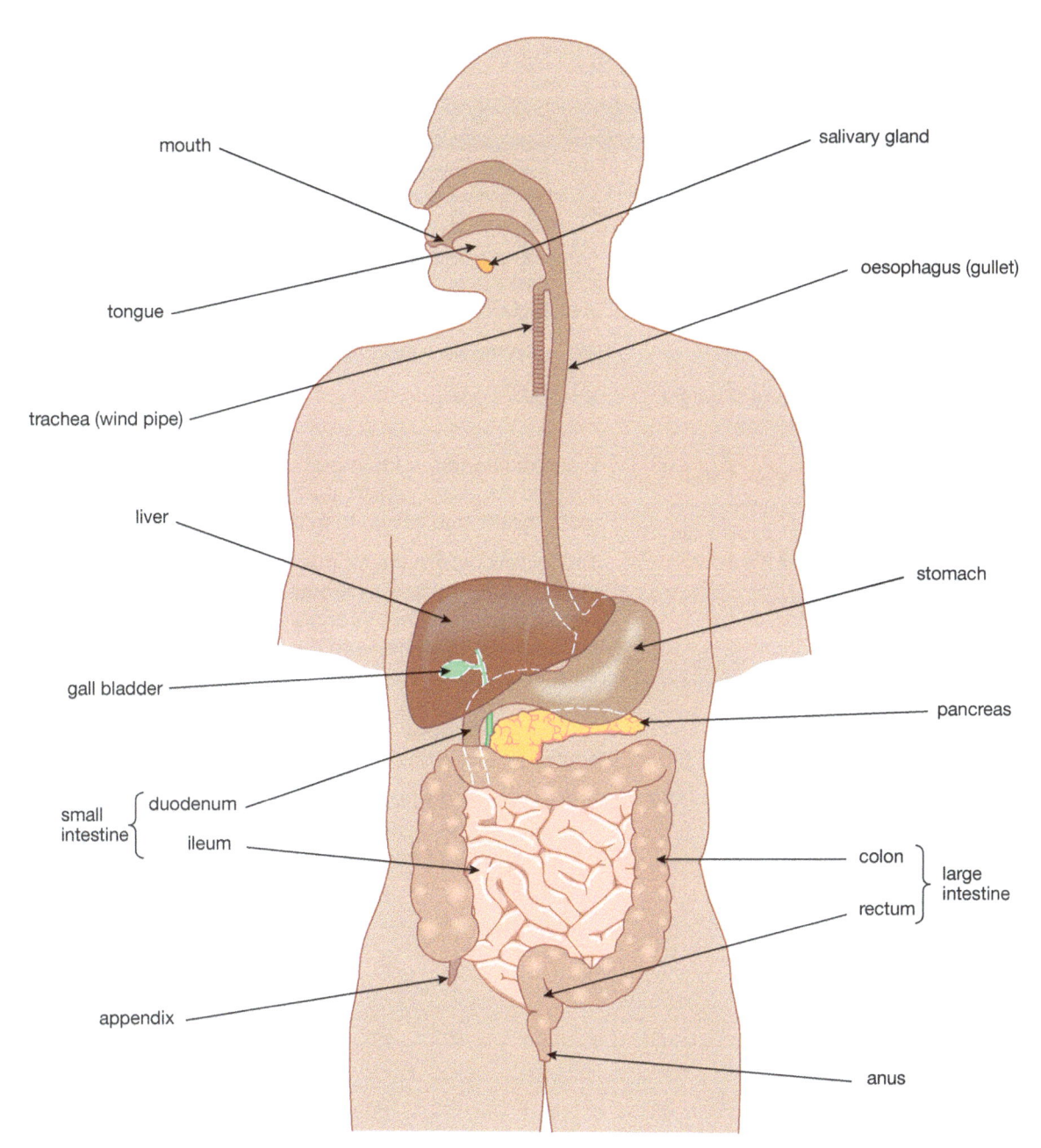

▲ Figure 5.8 The human digestive system

The mouth, stomach and the first part of the small intestine (called the **duodenum**) all break down the food using enzymes. The enzymes are either made in the gut wall itself, or by glands such as the **pancreas**. Digestion continues in the last part of the small intestine (the **ileum**) and it is here that the digested food is absorbed. The last part of the gut, the large intestine, is mainly concerned with absorbing water from what remains, and storing the waste products (**faeces**) before they are removed from the body.

The three main classes of food are broken down by three classes of enzymes. Carbohydrates are digested by enzymes called **carbohydrases**. Proteins are acted upon by **proteases**, and enzymes called **lipases** break down lipids. Some of the places in the gut where these enzymes are made are shown in **Table 5.1**.

Table 5.1 Some of the enzymes that digest food in the human gut. The substances shown in bold are the end products of digestion that can be absorbed from the gut into the blood.

Class of enzyme	Examples	Digestive action	Source of enzyme	Where it acts in the gut
carbohydrases	amylase amylase maltase	starch → maltose[1] starch → maltose maltose → **glucose**	salivary glands pancreas wall of small intestine	mouth small intestine small intestine
proteases	pepsin trypsin peptidases	proteins → peptides[2] proteins → peptides peptides → **amino acids**	stomach wall pancreas wall of small intestine	stomach small intestine small intestine
lipases	lipase	lipids → **glycerol** and **fatty acids**	pancreas	small intestine

[1] Maltose is a 'double sugar' made of two glucose molecules joined together.
[2] Peptides are short chains of amino acids.

> **KEY POINT**
>
> Amylase digests starch into maltose. Amylase is the enzyme, starch is the substrate and maltose is the product.

Digestion begins in the mouth. **Saliva** helps moisten the food and contains the enzyme **amylase**, which starts the breakdown of starch. The chewed lump of food, mixed with saliva, then passes along the **oesophagus** to the stomach.

The food is held in the stomach for several hours, while initial digestion of protein takes place. The stomach wall secretes hydrochloric acid, so the stomach contents are strongly acidic. This has a very important function. It kills bacteria that are taken into the gut along with the food, helping to protect us from food poisoning. The protease enzyme that is made in the stomach, called **pepsin**, has to be able to work in these acidic conditions, and has an optimum pH value of about 2. This is unusually low – most enzymes work best at near neutral pH conditions (see **Chapter 3**).

The semi-digested food is held back in the stomach by a ring of muscle at the outlet of the stomach, called a **sphincter muscle**. When this relaxes, it releases the food into the first part of the small intestine, called the duodenum (**Figure 5.9**).

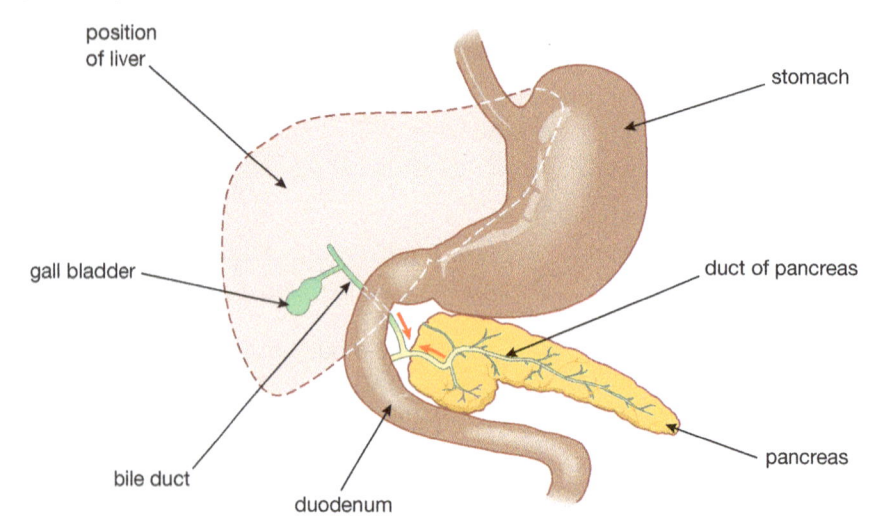

▲ Figure 5.9 The first part of the small intestine, the duodenum, receives digestive juices from the liver and pancreas through tubes called ducts.

Several digestive enzymes are added to the food in the duodenum. These are made by the pancreas, and digest starch, proteins and lipids (see **Table 5.1**).

The mixture of semi-digested food and enzymes coming from the stomach is acidic, and needs to be neutralised by the addition of alkali before it continues on its way through the gut. Pancreatic juice (along with bile from the liver, which is stored in the gall bladder) is alkaline. This neutralises the stomach acid.

2 STRUCTURE AND FUNCTION IN LIVING ORGANISMS 5 NUTRITION

As the food continues along the intestine, more enzymes are added, until the parts of the food that can be digested have been fully broken down into soluble end products, which can be absorbed.

THE ILEUM AND THE LARGE INTESTINE

The products of digestion are absorbed in the ileum. The lining of the ileum has a very large surface area, and is well adapted to absorb the nutrients into the blood. The digested food molecules are distributed around the body by the blood system (see **Chapter 8**). Nutrients pass out from the blood to the tissues, and are used for growth and repair of cells.

By the time that the contents of the gut have reached the end of the small intestine, most of the digested food, as well as most of the water, has been absorbed. The waste material consists mainly of cellulose (fibre) and other indigestible remains, water, dead and living bacteria, and cells lost from the lining of the gut. The function of the first part of the large intestine, called the colon, is to absorb most of the remaining water from the contents, leaving a semi-solid waste material called faeces. This is stored in the rectum, until expelled out of the body through the anus.

CHAPTER QUESTIONS

Exam-style questions on nutrition can be found at the end of Unit 2 on page 67.

SKILLS REASONING

A variegated leaf attached to a plant was placed in a test tube as shown below. The test tube contained soda lime to absorb carbon dioxide.

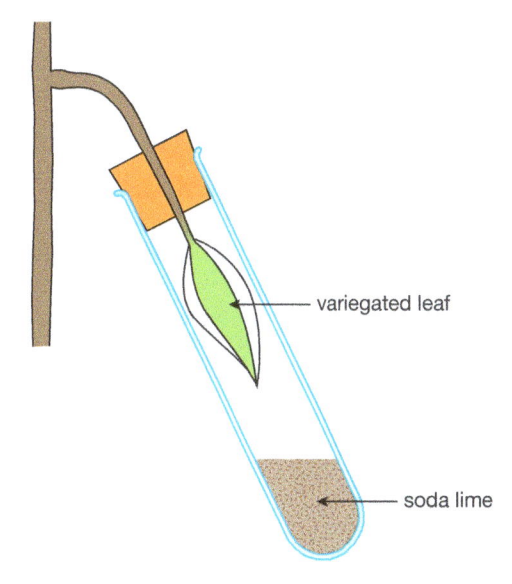

The plant was left in bright light for 24 hours and tested for starch using iodine solution. Which of the following diagrams shows the expected results?

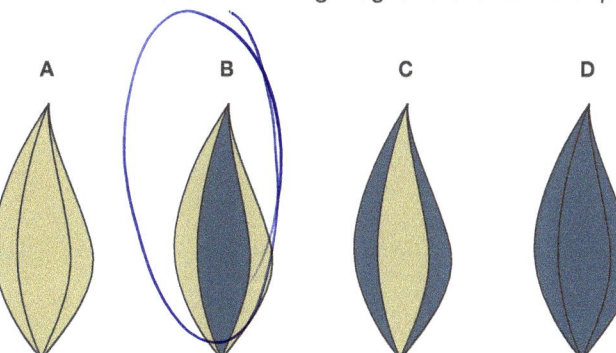

A B C D

44 2 STRUCTURE AND FUNCTION IN LIVING ORGANISMS 5 NUTRITION

SKILLS CRITICAL THINKING

2 Which of the following is *not* normally a factor that limits the rate of photosynthesis?

   A temperature
   B oxygen concentration
   C carbon dioxide concentration
   D light intensity

SKILLS CRITICAL THINKING

3 Which of the following statements about digestion is *not* correct?

   A digestion produces fatty acids and glycerol
   B digestion converts insoluble molecules into soluble molecules
   C digestion changes proteins into amino acids
   D digestion releases energy from food

SKILLS CRITICAL THINKING, ANALYSIS

4 A plant with variegated leaves had a piece of black paper attached to one leaf, as shown in the diagram.

black paper (on both sides of leaf)
edge of leaf lacks chlorophyll

The plant was kept under a bright light for 24 hours. The leaf was then removed, the paper taken off and the leaf was tested for starch.

   a Name the chemical used to test for starch, and describe the colour change if the test is positive.
   b Copy the leaf outline and shade in the areas which would contain starch.
   c Explain how you arrived at your answer to b.
   d What is starch used for in a plant? How do the properties of starch make it suitable for this function?

SKILLS INTERPRETATION

5 Copy and complete the following table to show the functions of different parts of a leaf and how each part is adapted for its function. One row has been done for you.

Part of leaf	Function	How the part is adapted for its function
palisade mesophyll layer	main site of photosynthesis	cells contain many chloroplasts for photosynthesis
spongy mesophyll layer		
stomata		
xylem		
phloem		

SKILLS INTERPRETATION, ANALYSIS

6 A piece of Canadian pondweed was placed upside down in a test tube of water, as shown in the diagram.

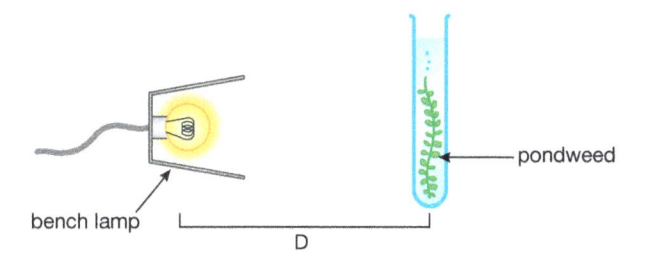

Light from a bench lamp was shone onto the weed, and bubbles of gas appeared at the cut end of the stem. The distance of the lamp from the weed was changed, and the number of bubbles produced per minute was recorded. The results are shown in the table.

Distance of lamp (D) / cm	Number of bubbles per minute
5	126
10	89
15	64
20	42
25	31
30	17
35	14
40	10

a Plot a graph of the number of bubbles per minute against the distance of the weed from the lamp.

b Using your graph, predict the number of bubbles per minute that would be produced if the lamp was placed 17 cm from the weed.

c The student who carried out this experiment arrived at the following conclusion:

'The gas made by the weed is oxygen from photosynthesis, so the faster production of bubbles shows that the rate of photosynthesis is greater at higher light intensities.'

Write down three reasons why the student's conclusion could be criticised. (Hint: is counting the bubbles a reliable method of measuring the rate of photosynthesis?)

SKILLS EXECUTIVE FUNCTION

7 The diagram shows an experiment that was set up as a model to show why food needs to be digested.

The Visking tubing acts as a model of the small intestine because it has tiny holes in it that some molecules can pass through. The tubing was left in the boiling tube for an hour, then the water in the tube was tested for starch and glucose.

a Describe how you would test the water for starch and for glucose. What would the results be for a 'positive' test in each case?

b The tests showed that glucose was present in the water, but starch was not. Explain these results.

c If the tubing takes the place of the intestine, what part of the body does the water in the boiling tube represent?

d What does 'digested' mean?

8 A student carried out an experiment to find out the best conditions for the enzyme pepsin to digest protein. For the protein, she used egg white powder, which forms a cloudy white suspension in water. The table below shows how the four tubes were set up.

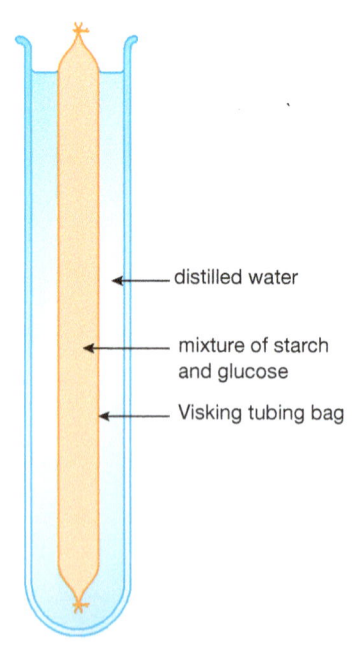

Tube	Contents
A	5 cm³ egg white suspension, 2 cm³ pepsin, 3 drops of dilute acid. Tube kept at 37 °C
B	5 cm³ egg white suspension, 2 cm³ distilled water, 3 drops of dilute acid. Tube kept at 37 °C
C	5 cm³ egg white suspension, 2 cm³ pepsin, 3 drops of dilute acid. Tube kept at 20 °C
D	5 cm³ egg white suspension, 2 cm³ pepsin, 3 drops of dilute alkali. Tube kept at 37 °C

The tubes were left for 2 hours and the results were then observed. Tubes B, C and D were still cloudy. Tube A had gone clear.

a Three tubes were kept at 37 °C. Why was this temperature chosen?

b Explain what had happened to the protein in tube A.

c Why did tube D stay cloudy?

d Tube B is called a Control. Explain what this means.

e Tube C was left for another 3 hours. Gradually it started to clear. Explain why digestion of the protein happened more slowly in this tube.

f The lining of the stomach secretes hydrochloric acid. Explain the function of this.

g When the stomach contents pass into the duodenum, they are still acidic. How are they neutralised?

9 Copy and complete the following table of digestive enzymes.

Enzyme	Food on which it acts	Products
amylase		
trypsin		
		fatty acids and glycerol

6 RESPIRATION

SPECIFICATION REFERENCES: 2.34–2.38

A cell needs a source of energy in order to be able to carry out all the processes needed for life. A cell gets this energy by breaking down food molecules to release the stored chemical energy that they contain. This process is called respiration and is the subject of this chapter.

LEARNING OBJECTIVES

- Understand how the process of respiration produces ATP in living organisms.
- Know that ATP provides energy for cells.
- Describe the differences between aerobic and anaerobic respiration.
- Know the word equation and balanced chemical symbol equation for aerobic respiration.
- Know the word equations for anaerobic respiration.

HOW THE CELL GETS ITS ENERGY

KEY POINT

Respiration is an oxidation reaction, because oxygen is used to break down food molecules.

Respiration takes place in all the cells of the body. Oxygen is used to oxidise food molecules, and carbon dioxide and water are released as waste products. The main food molecule oxidised is the sugar glucose. Glucose contains stored chemical energy that can be converted into other forms of energy that the cell can use. It is rather like burning a fuel to get the energy out of it, except that burning releases most of the energy as heat. Respiration releases some heat energy, but most of the chemical energy from the glucose is used to make a substance called ATP (see below). The energy stored in the ATP molecules can then be used for a variety of purposes, such as:

- contracting muscle cells, producing movement
- active transport of molecules and ions (see **Chapter 4**)
- building large molecules, such as proteins
- cell division
- releasing heat to keep a constant body temperature in mammals and birds.

EXAM HINT

You will need to know these equations.

The overall reaction for respiration is:

glucose + oxygen → carbon dioxide + water (+ energy)

$C_6H_{12}O_6$ + $6O_2$ → $6CO_2$ + $6H_2O$ (+ energy)

This process is called **aerobic respiration**, because it uses oxygen. Aerobic respiration happens in the cells of humans and also in the cells of animals, plants and many other organisms. It is important to realise that the equation above is only a *summary* of the process. It actually takes place gradually, as a sequence of small steps, which release the chemical energy of the glucose in small amounts. Each step in the process is catalysed by a different enzyme. The later steps in the process are the aerobic ones, and these release the most energy. They happen in the mitochondria of the cell.

ATP – THE ENERGY 'CURRENCY' OF THE CELL

Respiration releases energy while other cell processes use it up. Cells have a way of passing the energy from respiration to the other processes that need it. They do this using a chemical called **adenosine triphosphate** or **ATP**. ATP is present in all living cells.

ATP is composed of an organic molecule called adenosine attached to three phosphate groups. In a cell, ATP can be broken down losing one phosphate group and forming adenosine diphosphate or ADP (**Figure 6.1a**).

(a) When energy is needed ATP is broken down into ADP and phosphate (P):

adenosine—P—P—P + H_2O ⟶ adenosine—P—P + P

(b) During respiration ATP is made from ADP and phosphate:

adenosine—P—P + P ⟶ adenosine—P—P—P + H_2O

▲ Figure 6.1 ATP is the energy 'currency' of the cell

When this reaction takes place, chemical energy is released and can be used to drive processes that need it.

During respiration the opposite happens – energy from the oxidation of glucose is used to drive the reverse reaction and a phosphate is added onto ADP (**Figure 6.1b**).

ATP is often described as the energy 'currency' of the cell. It transfers energy between the process that releases it (respiration) and the processes in a cell that use it up. It is called a 'currency' because it is rather like the money that passes from a buyer to a seller.

ANAEROBIC RESPIRATION

There are some situations where cells can respire *without* using oxygen. This is called **anaerobic respiration**. In anaerobic respiration, glucose is not completely broken down, so less energy is released. The advantage of anaerobic respiration is that it can occur in situations where oxygen is in short supply. Two important examples of this are in yeast cells and muscle cells.

Yeasts are single-celled fungi (see **Chapter 1**). They are used in commercial processes such as causing bread to rise before baking it (see **Chapter 13**). When yeast cells are prevented from getting enough oxygen, they stop respiring aerobically and start to respire anaerobically instead. The glucose is partly broken down into ethanol (alcohol) and carbon dioxide:

> **EXAM HINT**
> You will need to know this equation.

glucose → ethanol + carbon dioxide (plus some energy)

The carbon dioxide from this type of respiration is the gas that makes bread dough rise.

Think about the properties of ethanol – it makes a good fuel and will burn to produce a lot of heat, so it still has a lot of chemical energy 'stored' in it.

Muscle cells can also respire anaerobically when they are short of oxygen. If muscles are overworked, the blood cannot reach them fast enough to deliver enough oxygen for aerobic respiration. This happens when a person does a 'burst' of activity, such as a sprint, or quickly lifting a heavy weight. This time the glucose is broken down into a substance called **lactate**:

> **EXAM HINT**
> You will need to know this equation.

glucose → lactate (plus some energy)

2 STRUCTURE AND FUNCTION IN LIVING ORGANISMS — 6 RESPIRATION

> **DID YOU KNOW?**
> Lactate is sometimes called lactic acid.

Anaerobic respiration provides enough energy to keep the overworked muscles going for a short period. During the exercise, the level of lactate in the muscle cells and bloodstream rises.

> **DID YOU KNOW?**
> It was once thought that lactate was toxic and caused muscle fatigue. We now know that this is *not* true. In fact, scientists have shown that lactate actually *delays* muscle fatigue. Fatigue is caused by other changes that happen in the muscles during exercise.

After the exercise the lactate is respired aerobically in the mitochondria. The volume of oxygen needed to completely oxidise the lactate that builds up in the body during anaerobic respiration is called the **oxygen debt**.

CHAPTER QUESTIONS

Exam-style questions on respiration can be found at the end of Unit 2 on page 67.

SKILLS — CRITICAL THINKING

1. Which of the following does *not* use ATP?

   A muscle contraction

   B active transport

   C respiration

   D building proteins

2. What are the products of anaerobic respiration in yeast?

   A ethanol and carbon dioxide

   B lactate and carbon dioxide

   C carbon dioxide and water

   D ethanol and water

SKILLS — INTERPRETATION

3. a Write a balanced chemical symbol equation for aerobic respiration.

   b What is the disadvantage of anaerobic respiration compared with aerobic respiration?

   c Explain why muscles that are exercising vigorously build up an oxygen debt.

7 GAS EXCHANGE

SPECIFICATION REFERENCES: 2.46–2.48

When we breathe, air is moved in and out of our lungs so that gas exchange can take place between the air and the blood. This supplies the tissues with oxygen for respiration and removes carbon dioxide. This chapter looks at the processes of breathing and gas exchange.

LEARNING OBJECTIVES

- Describe the structure of the thorax, including the ribs, intercostal muscles, diaphragm, trachea, bronchi, bronchioles, alveoli and pleural membranes.
- Understand the role of the intercostal muscles and the diaphragm in ventilation.
- Explain how alveoli are adapted for gas exchange by diffusion between air in the lungs and blood in capillaries.

Cells get their energy by oxidising foods such as glucose in the process called respiration. If cells are to respire aerobically, they need a continuous supply of oxygen from the blood. In addition, carbon dioxide from respiration needs to be removed from the body. In humans, these gases are exchanged between the blood and the air in the lungs. Breathing is the mechanism that moves air in and out of the lungs, allowing gas exchange to take place.

THE STRUCTURE OF THE GAS EXCHANGE SYSTEM

The lungs are enclosed in the chest or **thorax** by the ribcage and a muscular sheet of tissue called the **diaphragm** (**Figure 7.1**). The actions of the ribcage and the diaphragm bring about the movements of air into and out of the lungs. Joining each rib to the next are two sets of muscles called **intercostal muscles** ('costals' are rib bones). The diaphragm separates the contents of the thorax from the abdomen. It is not flat, but a shallow dome shape, with a fibrous middle part forming the 'roof' of the dome, and muscular edges forming the walls.

The air passages of the lungs form a highly branching network (**Figure 7.2**). This is why it is sometimes called the **bronchial tree**.

When we breathe in, air enters our nose or mouth and passes down the **trachea** (the windpipe). The trachea splits into two tubes called the **bronchi** (singular = **bronchus**), with one leading to each lung. Each bronchus divides into smaller and smaller tubes called **bronchioles**, eventually ending at microscopic air sacs called **alveoli** (singular = **alveolus**). It is here that gas exchange with the blood takes place.

The walls of trachea and bronchi contain rings of **cartilage**. These support the airways and keep them open when we breathe in. They are rather like the rings in a vacuum cleaner hose – without them the hose would squash flat when the cleaner sucks air in.

The inside of the thorax is separated from the lungs by two thin moist membranes called the **pleural membranes**. They make up a continuous envelope around the lungs, forming an airtight seal. Between the two membranes is a space called the **pleural cavity**, filled with a thin layer of

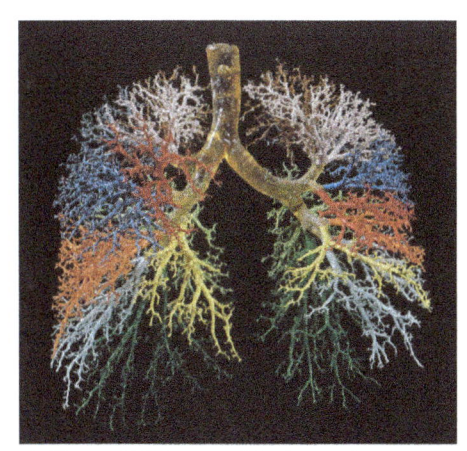

2 STRUCTURE AND FUNCTION IN LIVING ORGANISMS   7 GAS EXCHANGE

▲ Figure 7.2 This cast of the human lungs was made by injecting a pair of lungs with a liquid plastic. The plastic was allowed to set, then the lung tissue was dissolved away with acid.

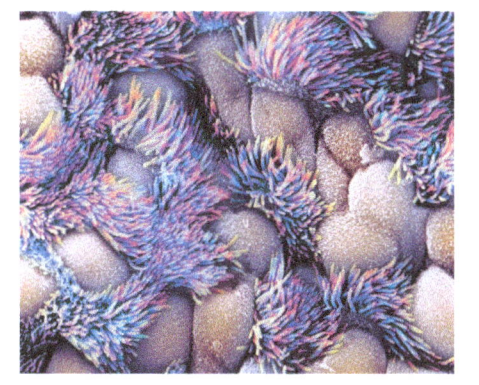

▲ Figure 7.3 This electron microscope picture shows cilia from the lining of the trachea.

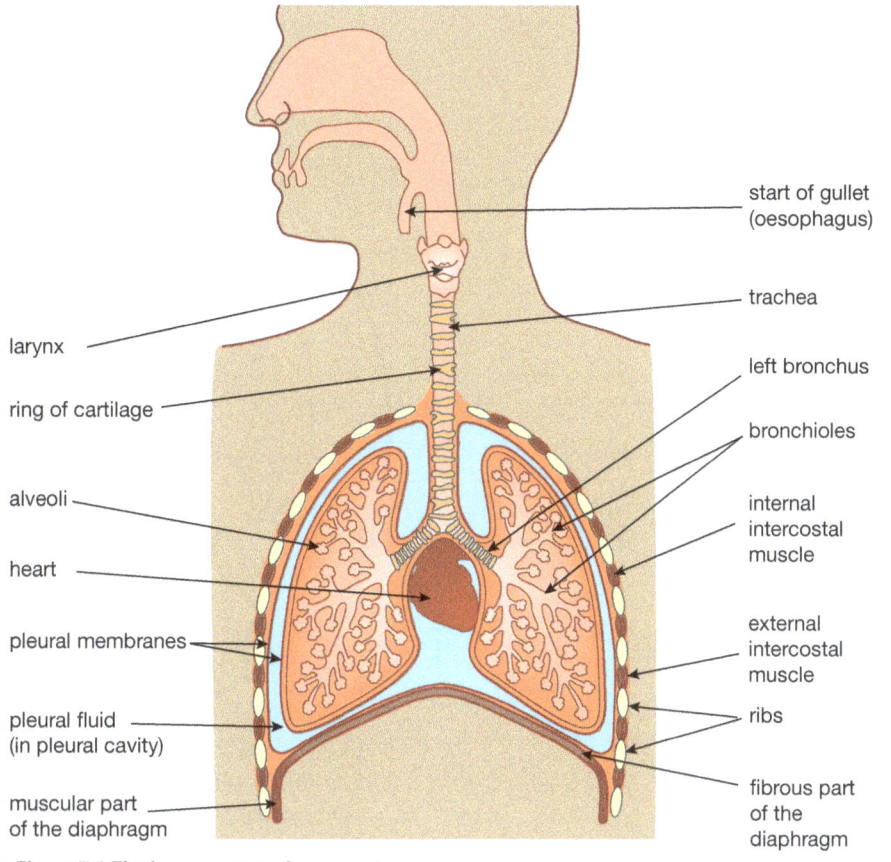

▲ Figure 7.1 The human gas exchange system

liquid called **pleural fluid**. This acts as lubrication, so that the surfaces of the lungs do not stick to the inside of the chest wall when we breathe.

The trachea and larger airways are lined with a layer of cells that have an important role in keeping the airways clean. Some cells in this lining secrete a sticky liquid called **mucus**, which traps particles of dirt or bacteria that are breathed in. Other cells are covered with tiny hair-like structures called **cilia** (**Figure 7.3**). The cilia beat backward and forward, sweeping the mucus and trapped particles out towards the mouth. In this way, dirt and bacteria are prevented from entering the lungs, where they might cause an infection.

VENTILATION OF THE LUNGS

Ventilation means moving air in and out of the lungs. This requires a difference in air pressure – the air moves from a place where the pressure is high to an area where it is low. Ventilation depends on the fact that the thorax is an airtight cavity. When we breathe, we change the volume of our thorax, which alters the pressure inside it. This causes air to move in or out of the lungs.

There are two movements that bring about ventilation: those of the ribs and the diaphragm. If you put your hands on your chest and breathe in deeply, you can feel your ribs move upwards and outwards. They are moved by the intercostal muscles (**Figure 7.4**). The outer (external) intercostals contract, pulling the ribs up. At the same time, the muscles of the diaphragm contract, pulling the diaphragm down into a more flattened shape (**Figure 7.5a**). Both these movements increase the volume of the chest and cause a slight drop in pressure inside the thorax compared with the air outside. Air then enters the lungs (inhalation).

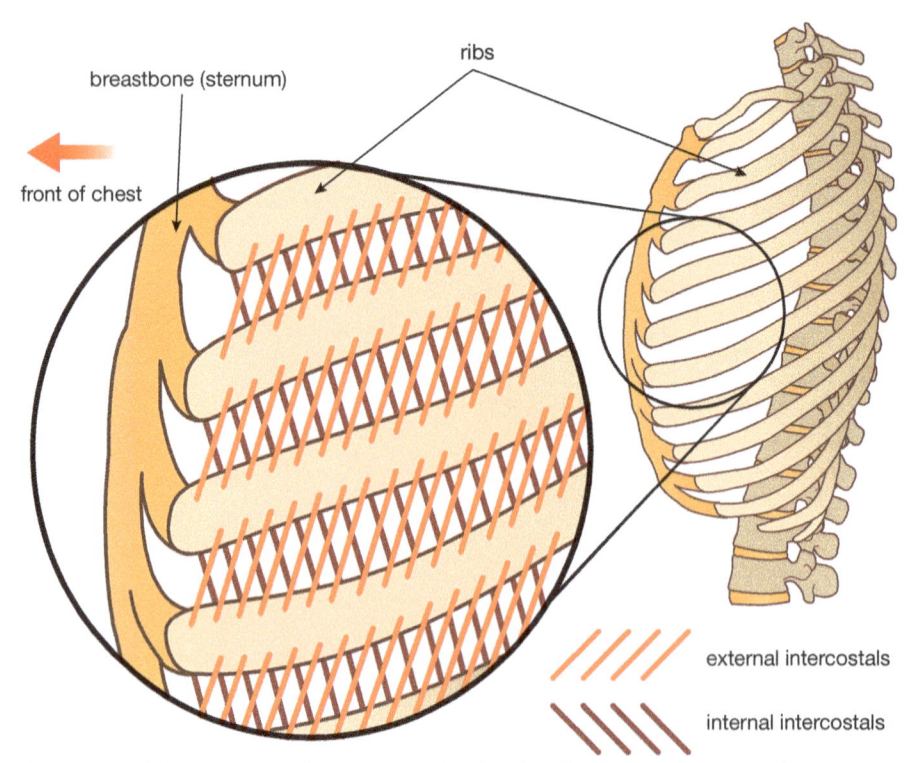

▲ Figure 7.4 Side view of the chest wall, showing the ribs. The diagram shows how the two sets of intercostal muscles run between the ribs. When the external intercostals contract, they move the ribs upwards. When the internal intercostals contract, the ribs are moved downwards.

EXTENSION

During normal (shallow) breathing, the elasticity of the lungs and the weight of the ribs acting downwards is enough to cause exhalation. The internal intercostals are only really used for deep (forced) breathing out, for instance when we are exercising.

The opposite happens when you breathe out deeply. The external intercostals relax, and the internal intercostals contract, pulling the ribs down and in. At the same time, the diaphragm muscles relax and the diaphragm goes back to its normal dome shape. The volume of the thorax decreases, and the pressure in the thorax is raised slightly above atmospheric pressure. This time the difference in pressure forces air out of the lungs (**Figure 7.5b**). Exhalation is helped by the fact that the lungs are elastic, so that they have a tendency to collapse and empty like a balloon.

EXAM HINT

It is important that you remember the changes in volume and pressure during ventilation. If you have trouble understanding these, think of what happens when you use a bicycle pump. If you push the pump handle, the air in the pump is squashed, its pressure rises and it is forced out of the pump. If you pull on the handle, the air pressure inside the pump falls a little, and air is drawn in from outside. This is similar to what happens in the lungs. In exams, students sometimes talk about the lungs forcing the air in and out – they do not!

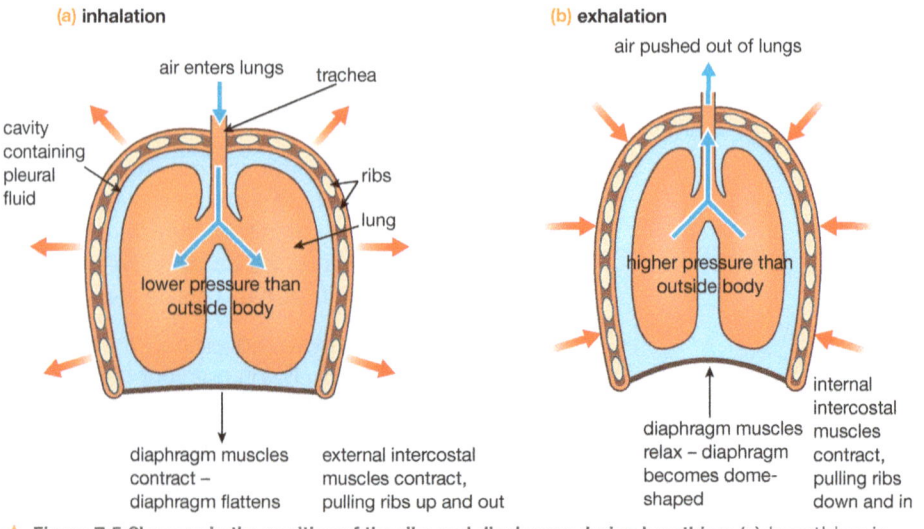

▲ Figure 7.5 Changes in the position of the ribs and diaphragm during breathing: (a) breathing in (inhalation) and (b) breathing out (exhalation).

GAS EXCHANGE IN THE ALVEOLI

You can tell what is happening during gas exchange if you compare the amounts of different gases in atmospheric air with the air breathed out (**Table 7.1**).

Table 7.1 Approximate percentage volume of gases in atmospheric (inhaled) air and exhaled air

Gas	Atmospheric air / %	Exhaled air / %
nitrogen	78	79
oxygen	21	16
carbon dioxide	0.04	4
other gases (mainly argon)	1	1

Exhaled air is also warmer than atmospheric air, and is saturated with water vapour. The amount of water vapour in the atmosphere varies depending on weather conditions.

Clearly, the lungs are absorbing oxygen into the blood and removing carbon dioxide from the blood. This happens in the alveoli. To do this efficiently, the alveoli must have a structure which brings the air and blood very close together, over a very large surface area. There are enormous numbers of alveoli. It has been calculated that the two lungs of a human contain about 700 000 000 of these tiny air sacs, giving a total surface area of 60 m^2. That is bigger than the floor area of an average classroom! Viewed through a high-powered microscope, the alveoli look rather like bunches of grapes, and are covered with tiny blood capillaries (**Figure 7.6**).

> **EXAM HINT**
>
> Be careful when interpreting percentages! The percentage of a gas in a mixture can vary, even if the actual amount of the gas stays the same. This is easiest to understand from an example. Imagine you have a bottle containing a mixture of 20% oxygen and 80% nitrogen. If you used a chemical to absorb all the oxygen in the bottle, the nitrogen left would now be 100% of the gas in the bottle, despite the fact that the amount of nitrogen would still be the same. That is why the percentages of nitrogen in inhaled air and exhaled air are slightly different.

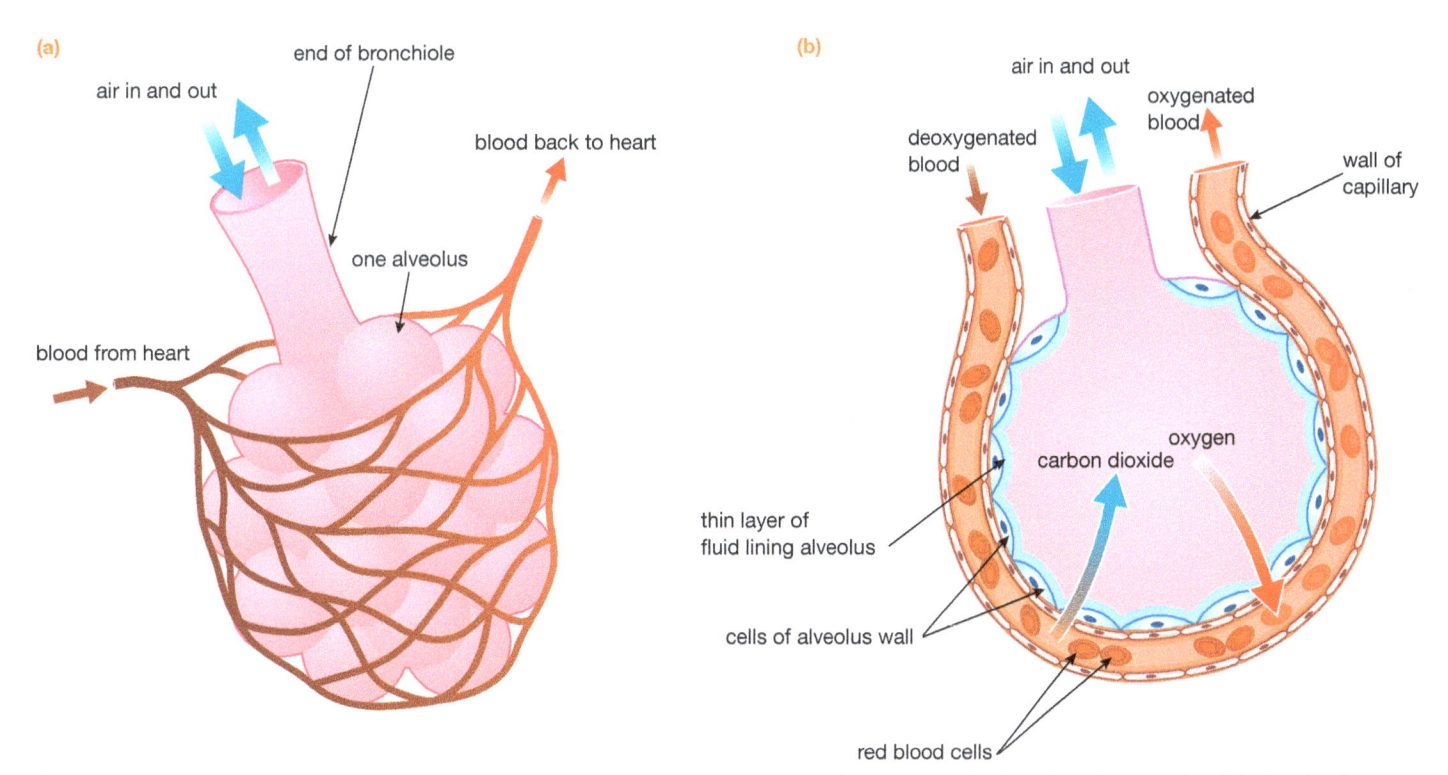

▲ Figure 7.6 (a) Alveoli and the surrounding capillary network. (b) Diffusion of oxygen and carbon dioxide takes place between the air in the alveolus and the blood in the capillaries.

EXAM HINT

Be careful – students sometimes write 'The alveolus has cell walls'. This statement is not correct – a cell wall is part of a plant cell! The correct way to describe the structure is: 'The alveolus has a wall made of cells'.

EXTENSION

The thin layer of fluid lining the inside of the alveoli comes from the blood. The capillaries and cells of the alveolar wall are 'leaky' and the blood pressure pushes fluid out from the blood plasma into the alveolus. Oxygen dissolves in this moist surface before it passes through the alveolar wall into the blood.

Deoxygenated blood is pumped from the heart to the lungs and passes through the capillaries surrounding the alveoli. The blood has come from the respiring tissues of the body, where it has given up some of its oxygen to the cells and gained carbon dioxide. When travelling around the lungs, the blood is separated from the air inside each alveolus by only two layers of cells; the cells making up the wall of the alveolus and the **capillary** wall itself. This is a distance of less than a thousandth of a millimetre.

Because the air in the alveolus has a higher concentration of oxygen than the blood entering the capillary network, oxygen diffuses from the air, across the wall of the alveolus and into the blood. At the same time there is more carbon dioxide in the blood than there is in the air in the lungs. This means that there is a diffusion gradient for carbon dioxide in the other direction, so carbon dioxide diffuses the other way, out of the blood and into the alveolus. The result is that the blood which leaves the capillaries and flows back to the heart has gained oxygen and lost carbon dioxide. The heart then pumps this oxygenated blood around the body again, to supply the respiring cells (see **Chapter 8**).

CHAPTER QUESTIONS

Exam-style questions on gas exchange can be found at the end of Unit 2 on page 67.

SKILLS CRITICAL THINKING

1 The structures below are found in the human bronchial tree
   1. alveoli
   2. trachea
   3. bronchioles
   4. bronchi

   Which of the following shows the route taken by air after it is breathed in through the mouth?
   A 2 → 3 → 4 → 1
   B 1 → 4 → 3 → 2
   C 2 → 4 → 3 → 1
   D 4 → 1 → 2 → 3

SKILLS CRITICAL THINKING

2 Which of the following is *not* a feature of an efficient gas exchange surface?
   A thick walls
   B moist lining
   C close proximity to blood capillaries
   D large surface area

SKILLS CRITICAL THINKING

3 Which row in the table shows the correct percentage of oxygen in atmospheric air and exhaled air?

	Atmospheric air / %	Exhaled air / %
A	78	21
B	21	16
C	16	4
D	4	0.04

SKILLS INTERPRETATION

4 Copy and complete the table, which shows what happens in the thorax during ventilation of the lungs. Two boxes have been completed for you.

	Action during inhalation	Action during exhalation
external intercostal muscles	contract	
internal intercostal muscles		
ribs		move down and in
diaphragm		
volume of thorax		
pressure in thorax		
volume of air in lungs		

SKILLS INTERPRETATION

5 A student wrote the following about the lungs.

When we breathe in, our lungs inflate, sucking air in and pushing the ribs up and out, and forcing the diaphragm down. This is called respiration. In the air sacs of the lungs, the air enters the blood. The blood then takes the air around the body, where it is used by the cells. The blood returns to the lungs to be cleaned. When we breathe out, our lungs deflate, pulling the diaphragm up and the ribs down. The stale air is pushed out of the lungs.

The student does not have a good understanding of the workings of the lungs. Re-write their description, using correct biological words and ideas.

SKILLS REASONING

6 Sometimes, people injured in an accident such as a car crash suffer from a *pneumothorax*. This is an injury where the chest wall is punctured, allowing air to enter the pleural cavity (see **Figure 7.1**). A patient was brought to the emergency department of a hospital, suffering from a pneumothorax on the left side of his chest. His left lung had collapsed, but he was able to breathe normally with his right lung.

a Explain why a pneumothorax caused the left lung to collapse.

b Explain why the right lung was not affected.

c If a patient's lung is injured or infected, a surgeon can sometimes 'reset' it by performing an operation called an *artificial pneumothorax*. What do you think might be involved in this operation?

8 TRANSPORT

SPECIFICATION REFERENCES: 2.51, 2.52, 2.59–2.62, 2.65, 2.68, 2.69

Our blood transports substances to and from the cells of our body. In this chapter you will find out about the structure and functions of the human circulatory system, as well as the composition of blood and its functions.

LEARNING OBJECTIVES

- Understand why simple unicellular organisms can rely on diffusion for movement of substances into and out of the cell.
- Understand the need for a transport system in multicellular animals.
- Describe the composition of the blood: red blood cells, white blood cells, platelets and plasma.
- Understand the role of plasma in the transport of carbon dioxide, digested food, urea, hormones and heat energy.
- Understand how adaptations of red blood cells make them suitable for the transport of oxygen, including shape, the absence of a nucleus and the presence of haemoglobin.
- Understand how the immune system responds to infection using white blood cells, illustrated by phagocytes ingesting pathogens and lymphocytes releasing antibodies specific to the pathogen.
- Describe the structure of the heart and how it functions.
- Understand how the structures of arteries, veins and capillaries relate to their functions.
- Understand the general structure of the circulation system, including the blood vessels to and from the heart and the lungs.

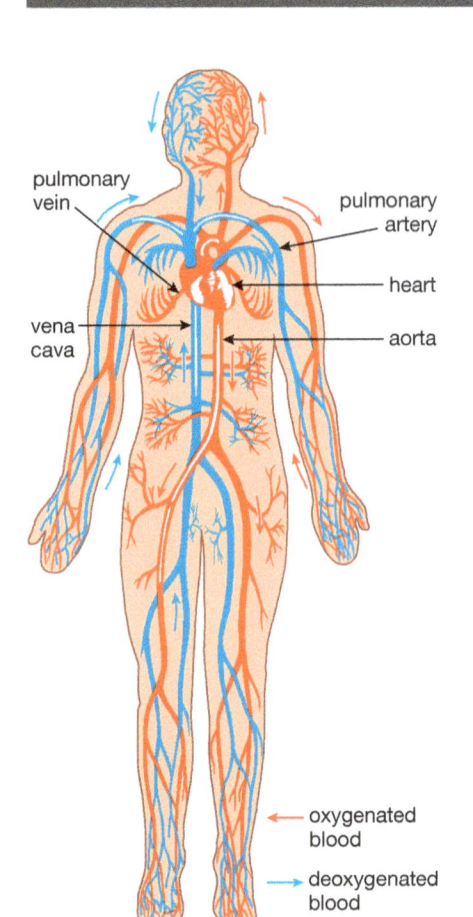

THE NEED FOR CIRCULATORY SYSTEMS

Figure 8.1 shows the human circulatory system.

Blood is pumped around a circuit made up of the heart and blood vessels. As blood travels around the body, it collects materials from some places and unloads them in others. In humans, blood transports:

- oxygen from the lungs to all other parts of the body
- carbon dioxide from all parts of the body to the lungs
- nutrients from the gut to all parts of the body
- **urea** (a waste product) from the liver to the kidneys.

Many other substances, including **hormones** and antibodies, are carried in the blood. It also distributes heat around the body.

Unicellular (single-celled) organisms, like the ones shown in **Figure 8.2**, do not have circulatory systems.

▲ Figure 8.1 The human circulatory system

Amoeba

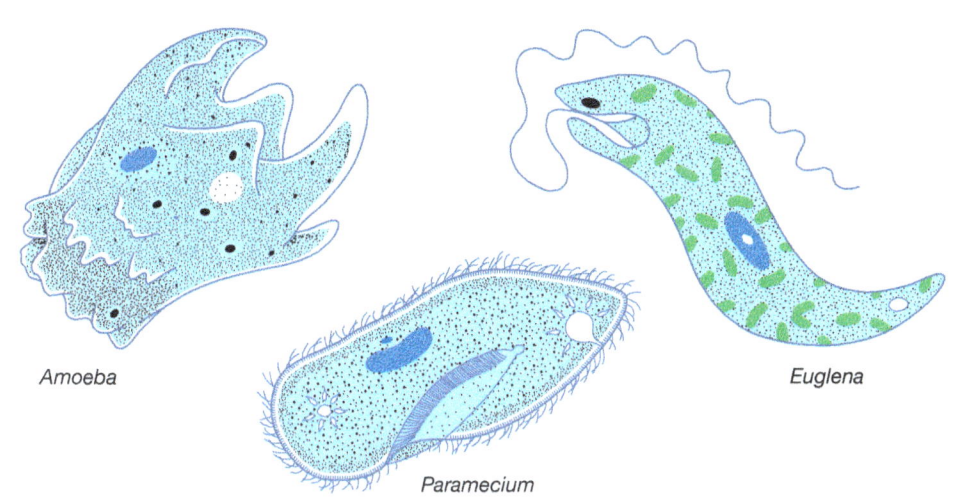

Euglena

Paramecium

▲ Figure 8.2 Unicellular organisms do not have circulatory systems.

There are two reasons why these very small organisms do not need transport systems:

- Their cells are so small that materials can easily move around inside them through movements of the cytoplasm or by diffusion.
- They have a large surface area to volume ratio. This means they can efficiently exchange materials such as oxygen directly across the cell membrane. They do not need special organs like lungs, working with a blood system, to carry the oxygen away.

To help you understand surface area to volume ratio, you can use cubes to model organisms of different sizes (**Table 8.1**).

Table 8.1

Length of side of cube / cm	Surface area of cube / cm² (length × width of one side) × 6	Volume of cube / cm³ (length × width × height)	Ratio of surface area to volume of cube (surface area divided by volume)
2	(2 × 2) × 6 = 24	(2 × 2 × 2) = 8	24/8 = 3
1	(1 × 1) × 6 = 6	(1 × 1 × 1) = 1	6/1 = 6
0.5	(0.5 × 0.5) × 6 = 1.5	(0.5 × 0.5 × 0.5) = 0.125	1.5/0.125 = 12

The surface area to volume ratio is found by dividing the total surface area of the six sides of a cube by its volume (length × width × height). Notice that as the cube gets smaller, its surface area to volume ratio increases. Or to put it another way, a small cube (or a small unicellular organism) has a large surface area in proportion to its volume, so it can rely on diffusion across the cell membrane to supply its needs.

In large animals like humans, materials cannot be obtained and moved around by diffusion alone. Instead we have special gas exchange organs with a large surface area (the lungs) and circulatory systems. The same principle applies to the digestive system – the gut obtains nutrients from food and the circulatory system distributes the nutrients around the body.

THE COMPOSITION OF BLOOD

Blood is a complex tissue composed of several types of cell suspended in a liquid called **plasma**.

Figure 8.3 shows the main types of cells found in blood.

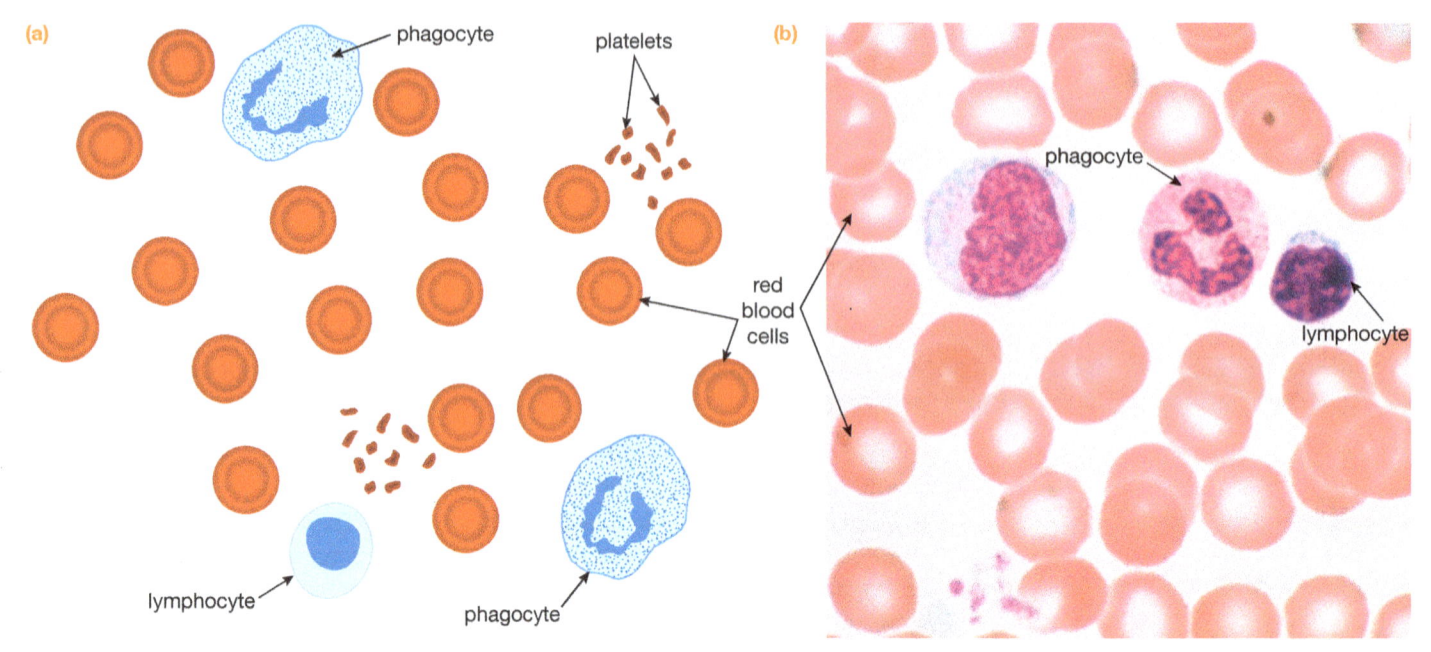

▲ Figure 8.3 The different types of blood cell. (a) Diagram of the different cells. (b) A blood smear seen through a light microscope. The smear contains many red blood cells and three different kinds of white blood cell.

Table 8.2 summarises the functions of the different parts of the blood.

Table 8.2 Functions of the different components of blood

Component of blood	Description of component	Function of component
plasma	liquid part of blood: mainly water	carries the blood cells around the body; carries dissolved nutrients, hormones, carbon dioxide and urea; distributes heat around the body
red blood cells	biconcave, disc-like cells with no nucleus; millions in each mm^3 of blood	transport oxygen – contain mainly haemoglobin, which loads oxygen in the lungs and unloads it in other regions of the body
white blood cells: lymphocytes	about the same size as red blood cells with a large round nucleus	produce antibodies to destroy micro-organisms – some lymphocytes remain in our blood after infection and give us immunity to specific diseases
white blood cells: phagocytes	larger than red blood cells, with a large spherical or lobed nucleus	digest and destroy bacteria and other micro-organisms that have infected our bodies
platelets	fragments of other cells, made in bone marrow	release chemicals to make blood clot when we cut ourselves

DID YOU KNOW?

Hormones are chemical messengers. They are made by organs called glands and travel around the body in the blood until they have an effect on their 'target organ'. For example, the hormone adrenaline is made by the adrenal gland near the kidneys. Adrenaline travels in the blood and affects several organs – for example it speeds up the heart rate.

PLASMA

Plasma is a watery fluid containing many dissolved substances. Carbon dioxide is carried in the plasma, mainly as hydrogencarbonate ions (HCO_3^-). Plasma also contains nutrients from the digestion of food, such as glucose and amino acids. It transports hormones (chemical messengers) and waste products such as urea. Urea is a breakdown product of proteins that is taken to the kidneys for **excretion**. Plasma also carries heat around the body, from 'warm' organs like the muscles and liver to cooler areas such as the skin. This helps to keep the temperature the same in different parts of the body.

RED BLOOD CELLS

Red blood cells are highly specialised cells made in the bone marrow. They have a limited life span of about 100 days; after this, they are destroyed by the body. They have only one function – to transport oxygen. Several features enable them to carry out this function very efficiently.

- Red blood cells contain a protein called **haemoglobin**. When there is a high concentration of oxygen in the surroundings, haemoglobin combines with oxygen to form **oxyhaemoglobin**. We say that the red blood cell is loading oxygen. When the concentration of oxygen is low, oxyhaemoglobin turns back into haemoglobin and the red blood cell unloads its oxygen.

$$\text{haemoglobin + oxygen} \underset{\text{low } O_2 \text{ (tissues)}}{\overset{\text{high } O_2 \text{ (lungs)}}{\rightleftharpoons}} \text{oxyhaemoglobin}$$

As red blood cells pass through the lungs, they load oxygen. As they pass through other tissues, such as the muscles, they unload oxygen. This supplies the tissues with oxygen for respiration.

- Red blood cells do not have a nucleus. It is lost during their development in the bone marrow. This means that more haemoglobin can be packed into each red blood cell so more oxygen can be transported.
- Red blood cells are concave on both sides (biconcave). This shape allows efficient exchange of oxygen into and out of the cell. Each red blood cell has a high surface area to volume ratio, giving a large area for diffusion. The thin shape of the cell means there is a short diffusion distance to the centre of the cell.
- Red blood cells are flexible, so they can squeeze through the narrowest blood vessels (capillaries).

WHITE BLOOD CELLS

There are several types of white blood cell. Their main role is to protect the body against invasion by disease-causing micro-organisms (pathogens) such as bacteria and viruses. They do this in two main ways: **phagocytosis** and the production of **antibodies**.

About 70% of white blood cells are **phagocytes**. Their function is to take up and destroy micro-organisms such as bacteria, in a process called phagocytosis. They do this by changing their shape to produce extensions of their cytoplasm which surround and enclose the micro-organism in a vacuole. Once the micro-organism is inside, the phagocyte secretes enzymes into the vacuole to break the micro-organism down (**Figure 8.4**). Phagocytosis means 'cell eating' – you can see why it is called this.

About 25% of white blood cells are **lymphocytes**. Their function is to make chemicals called antibodies. Antibodies are soluble proteins that pass into the plasma. Their role is to destroy disease-causing organisms such as bacteria and viruses. Antibodies recognise other chemicals, called **antigens**, on the surface of these pathogens. Production of antibodies against particular antigens is known as the **immune response**. Antibodies destroy pathogens in a number of ways, including:

- making bacteria stick together, so that phagocytes can ingest them more easily
- acting as a chemical 'label' on the pathogen, so that it is more easily recognised by phagocytes
- causing bacteria cells to burst open
- neutralising toxins (poisons) produced by pathogens.

EXTENSION

When we are exposed to a particular disease-causing micro-organism for the first time, certain lymphocytes retain a 'memory' of their antigens. This memory may last for many years or even a lifetime. If the same pathogen re-infects us, these *memory cells* can reproduce and make more antibodies. This is called a *secondary* immune response and it is faster and stronger than the first immune response. This gives us *immunity* against the invading organisms as they are killed before they can multiply to a level where they would cause the disease.

THE HUMAN CIRCULATORY SYSTEM

One of the main functions of the circulatory system is to transport oxygen. Blood is pumped to the lungs to load oxygen. It is then pumped to the other parts of the body, where it unloads the oxygen, before returning to the heart. Carbon dioxide is formed in the tissues of the body and travels to the heart before it is carried to the lungs.

Humans and other mammals have a **double circulation** (**Figure 8.5**). There are two parts to a double circulatory system:

- The **pulmonary circulation**: deoxygenated blood leaves the heart through the **pulmonary arteries**. It is circulated through the lungs, where it becomes oxygenated. The oxygenated blood returns to the heart through the **pulmonary veins**.

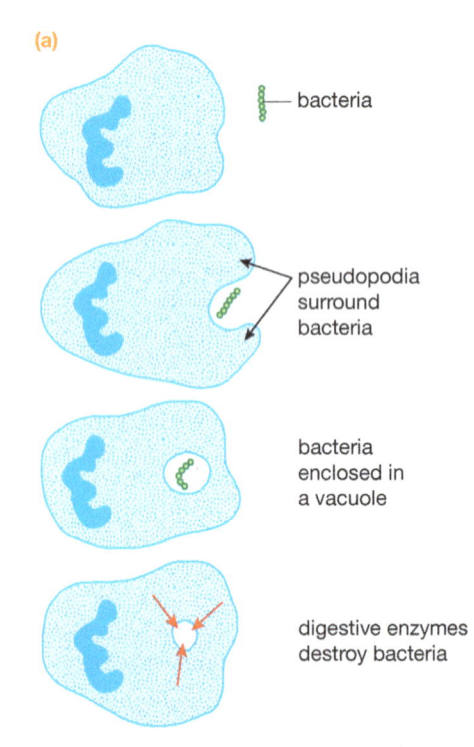

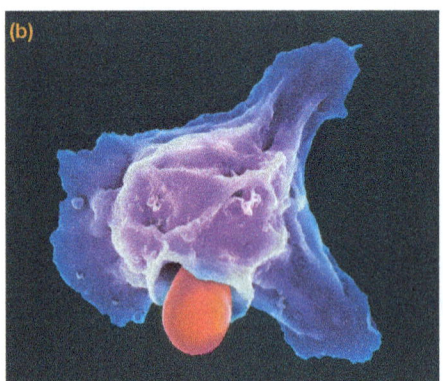

▲ Figure 8.4 (a) Phagocytosis by a white blood cell. (b) A phagocyte ingesting a yeast cell.

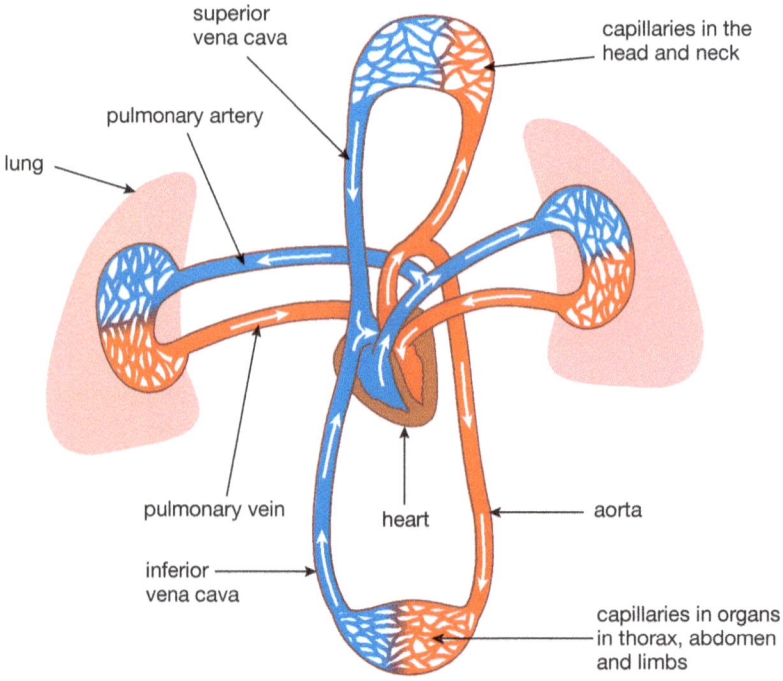

▲ Figure 8.5 The double circulation of blood in the human body. The blood passes through the heart twice during one complete circuit of the body. Red represents oxygenated blood and blue represents deoxygenated blood.

- The **systemic circulation**: oxygenated blood leaves the heart through the aorta and is circulated through all other parts of the body, where it unloads its oxygen. The deoxygenated blood returns to the heart through the **vena cava**.

A double circulatory system allows the blood pressure to be different in the pulmonary and systemic circuits. The pressure in the systemic circulation to the body is higher than the pressure in the pulmonary circulation to the lungs.

The circulatory system is made up of the following parts:

- **The heart:** a muscular pump.
- **Blood vessels:** these carry the blood around the body. **Arteries** carry blood away from the heart and towards other organs. **Veins** carry blood towards the heart and away from other organs. **Capillaries** carry blood through organs, linking the arteries and veins.
- **Blood:** the transport fluid.

Figure 8.6 shows the heart and the main blood vessels in the human circulatory system. The diagram is a 'map' to show the routes taken by blood to and from the heart and to and from the main organs of the body.

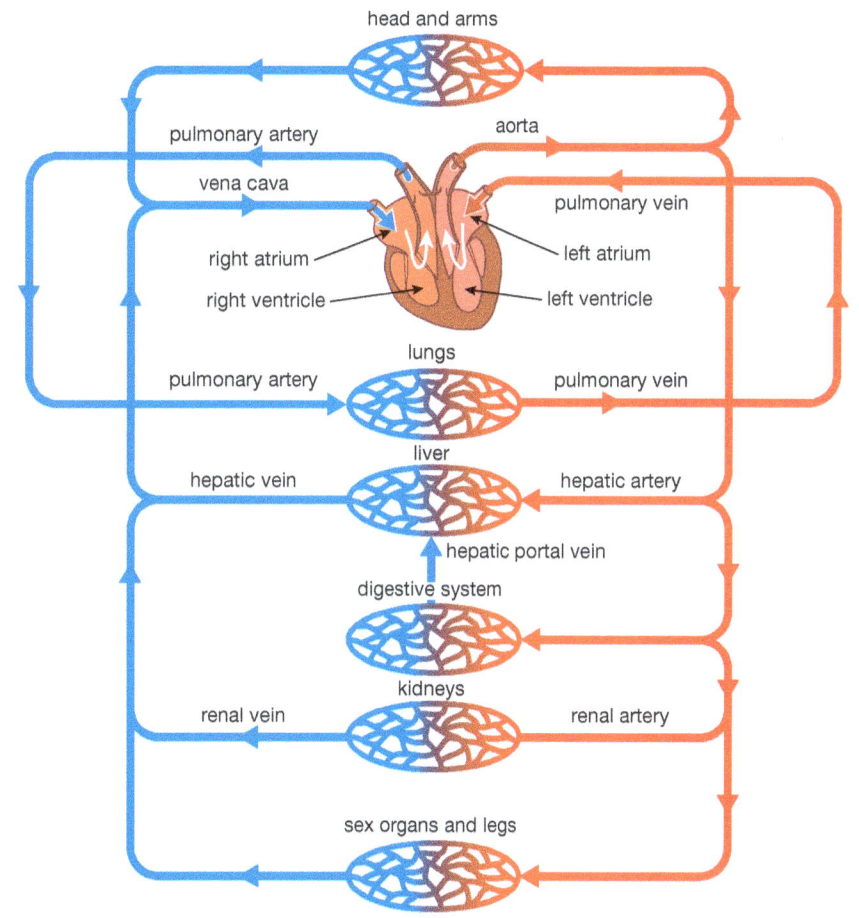

▲ Figure 8.6 A 'map' of the main parts of the human circulatory system. Red represents oxygenated blood and blue represents deoxygenated blood.

THE STRUCTURE AND FUNCTION OF THE HUMAN HEART

The heart is a muscular pump. It pumps blood around the body at different speeds and at different pressures according to the body's needs. In fact, as you have seen, the heart really consists of *two* pumps – the right side of the heart pumps deoxygenated blood to the lungs and the left side pumps oxygenated blood to the rest of the body (see **Figure 8.7**).

62 | **2 STRUCTURE AND FUNCTION IN LIVING ORGANISMS** | **8 TRANSPORT**

(a) Labels: vena cava (superior), aorta, pulmonary artery, pulmonary vein, left atrium, bicuspid (mitral) valve, left ventricle, right ventricle, vena cava (inferior), tricuspid valve, right atrium, semilunar valves.

(b) Labels: aorta, vena cava, pulmonary artery, pulmonary vein, left atrium, coronary arteries, left ventricle, right ventricle, right atrium.

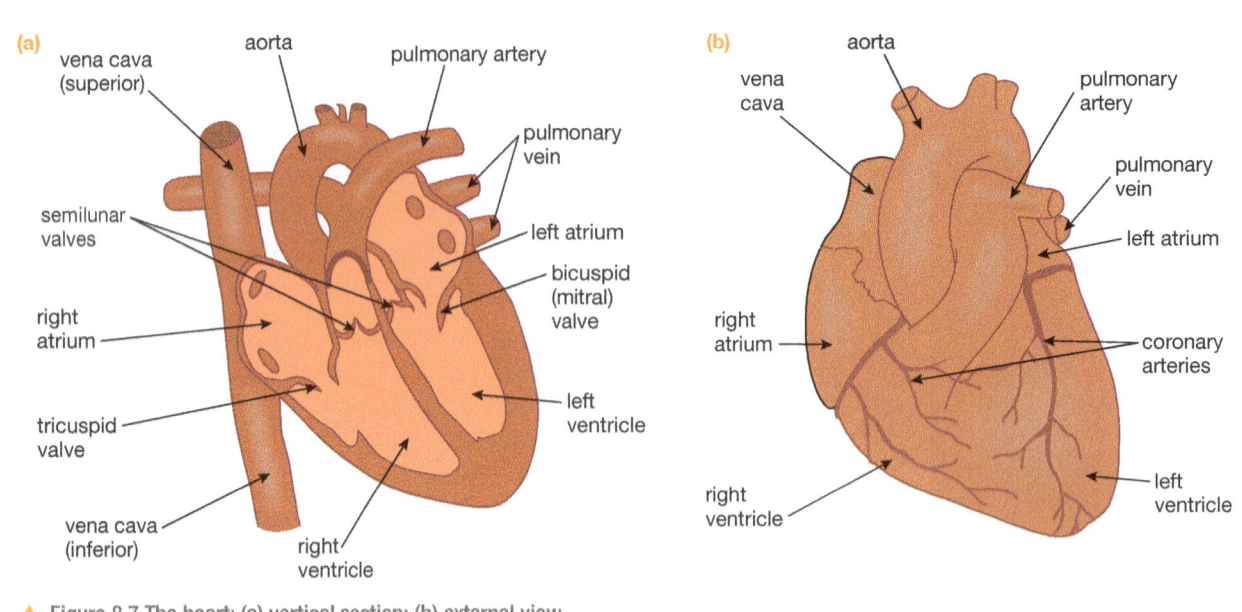

▲ Figure 8.7 The heart: (a) vertical section; (b) external view

THE HEART CYCLE

Blood is moved through the heart by a series of contractions and relaxations of the muscle in the walls of the four chambers. These events are called the heart cycle. The main stages of the heart cycle are shown in **Figure 8.8**.

① Blood enters the atria. It cannot yet pass into the ventricles because the bicuspid (mitral) and tricuspid valves are closed.

② The walls of the atria contract. This raises the pressure of blood in the atria which forces open the bicuspid and tricuspid valves. Blood passes through these valves into the ventricles.

③ When the ventricles are full, they contract. This increases the pressure of blood in the ventricles which closes the bicuspid and tricuspid valves again. Blood cannot return to the atria.

④ The ventricles continue to contract and the pressure continues to increase. This forces open the semi-lunar valves at the base of the aorta and the pulmonary artery. Blood is ejected into these two arteries. The pulmonary artery carries blood to the lungs. The aorta has branches that carry blood to all other parts of the body.

⑤ As the ventricles empty, higher pressure in the aorta and pulmonary artery closes the valves in these blood vessels. The cycle then begins again as the atria start to fill with blood.

Key:
→ oxygenated blood
→ deoxygenated blood

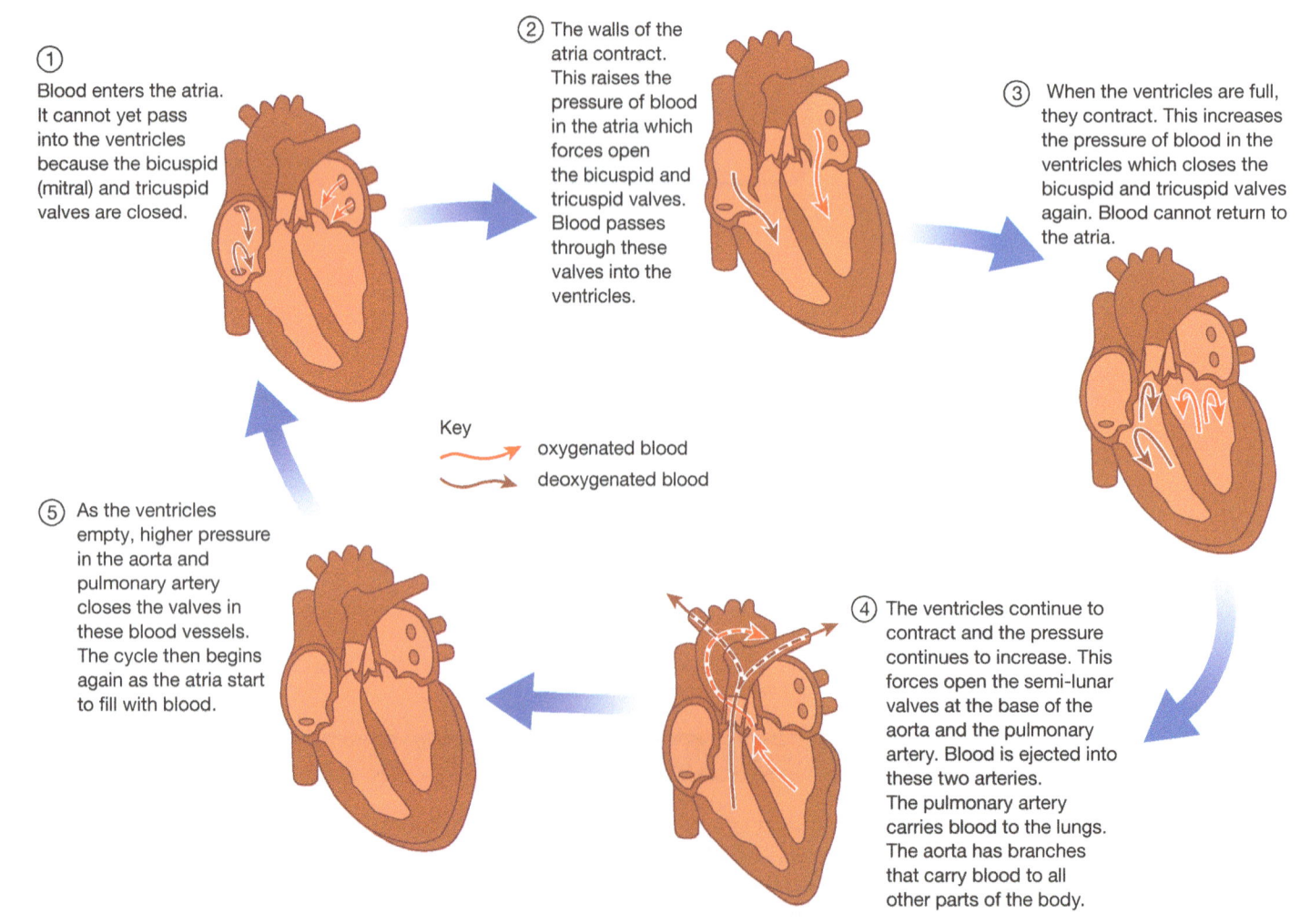

Figure 8.8 The heart cycle

> **EXAM HINT**
>
> Note that during the heart cycle both atria contract at the same time, and then both relax together. After this both ventricles contract at the same time, and then relax together. Students are sometimes confused about this, and think that first one ventricle contracts, followed by the other.

The structure of the heart is adapted for its function in several ways:

- It is divided into a left side and a right side by a wall of muscle. The **right ventricle** pumps blood to the lungs only. The **left ventricle** pumps blood to all other parts of the body, which requires much more pressure. This is why the wall of the left ventricle is much thicker than the wall of the right ventricle.
- Valves ensure that blood can flow only in one direction through the heart.
- The walls of the **atria** are thin. They can be stretched to receive blood as it returns to the heart but can contract with enough force to push blood through the bicuspid and tricuspid valves into the ventricles.
- The walls of the heart are made of a special type of muscle. Heart muscle can contract and relax continuously without becoming fatigued. This is essential – during an average lifetime it will need to contract over two billion times!
- The heart muscle has its own blood supply – the coronary circulation. Blood reaches the muscle through **coronary arteries**. These carry blood to capillaries that supply the heart muscle with oxygen and nutrients. Blood from the heart muscle returns to the right atrium through **coronary veins**.

ARTERIES, VEINS AND CAPILLARIES

> **KEY POINT**
>
> All arteries carry oxygenated blood, except for the pulmonary artery.
> All veins carry deoxygenated blood, except for the pulmonary vein.

Arteries carry blood from the heart to the organs of the body. This arterial blood is pumped out by the ventricles at a high pressure. Elastic tissue in the walls of the arteries allows them to stretch and then recoil, maintaining the high blood pressure. A thick muscular wall helps control the flow of blood by dilating (widening) or constricting (narrowing) the vessels.

Veins carry blood from organs back towards the heart. The pressure of blood in the veins is much lower than that in the arteries. This puts very little pressure on the walls of the veins, so they can be thinner than those of arteries, and contain less elastic tissue and muscle. **Figure 8.9** shows the structure of a typical artery and a typical vein with the same diameter.

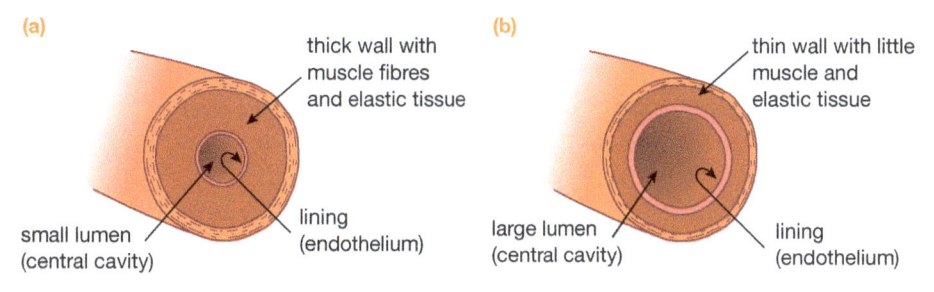

▲ Figure 8.9 The structure of (a) an artery and (b) a vein, as seen in cross-section

Veins also have **semilunar valves** (half-moon shaped), which prevent the backflow of blood. The action of these valves is explained in **Figure 8.10**.

vein in longitudinal section

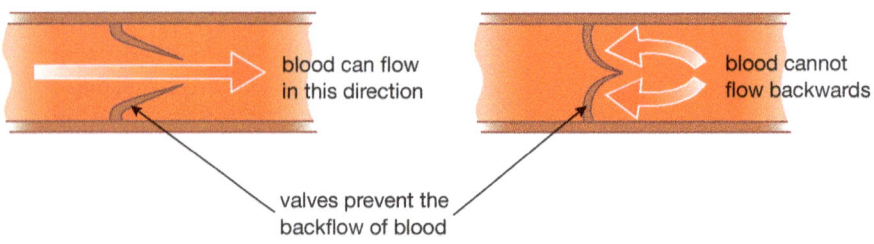

▲ Figure 8.10 The action of semilunar valves in veins

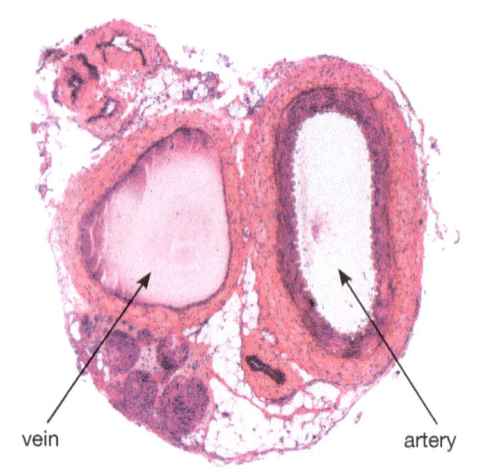

▲ Figure 8.11 The lumen of this artery is the same size as the lumen of the vein – but note the difference in the thickness of the walls of these two vessels.

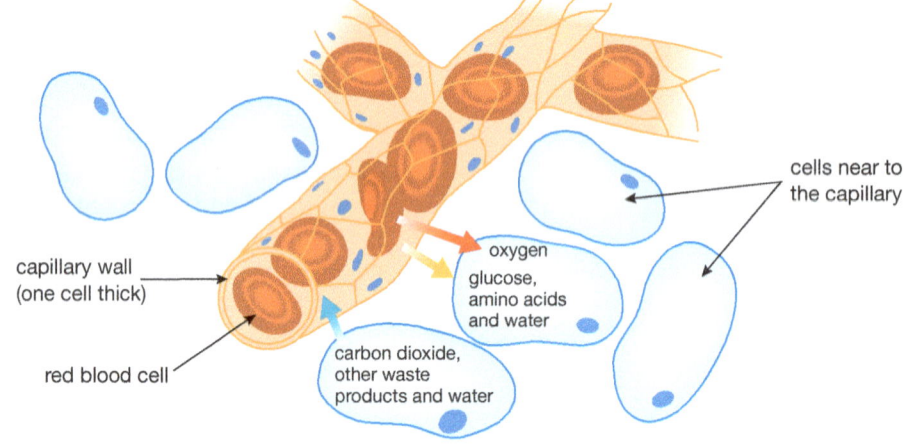

▲ Figure 8.12 How capillaries exchange materials with cells

Figure 8.11 shows a photograph of a cross-section through an artery and a vein.

Capillaries carry blood through organs, bringing the blood close to every cell in the organ. Substances are transferred between the blood in the capillary and the cells. To do this, capillaries must be small enough to fit between cells, and allow materials to pass through their walls easily. **Figure 8.12** shows the structure of a capillary and how exchange of substances takes place between the capillary and nearby cells. The walls of capillaries are one cell thick, providing a short distance for diffusion of substances into and out of the blood. Red blood cells just fit through the capillaries, so they are close to the capillary wall. This means that there is only a short distance for oxygen to diffuse.

CHAPTER QUESTIONS

Exam-style questions on transport can be found at the end of Unit 2 on page 67.

SKILLS CRITICAL THINKING

1 After a period of exercise, which blood vessel will contain the highest concentration of carbon dioxide?

    A aorta

    B vena cava

    C hepatic artery

    D pulmonary vein

2 STRUCTURE AND FUNCTION IN LIVING ORGANISMS   8 TRANSPORT

SKILLS CRITICAL THINKING

2 When the right ventricle contracts, where does the blood flow to next?
   A aorta
   B left atrium
   C pulmonary artery
   D left ventricle

SKILLS CRITICAL THINKING

3 The diagram below shows sections through three blood vessels (not drawn to scale).

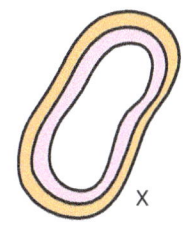

Which row in the table shows the correct names of vessels X, Y and Z?

	X	Y	Z
A	vein	capillary	artery
B	artery	capillary	vein
C	vein	artery	capillary
D	capillary	vein	artery

4 Which component of the blood makes antibodies?
   A red blood cells
   B white blood cells
   C plasma
   D platelets

SKILLS CRITICAL THINKING

5 Blood transports oxygen and carbon dioxide around the body. Oxygen is transported by the red blood cells.
   a Give *three* ways in which a red blood cell is adapted for its function of transporting oxygen.
   b Describe how oxygen:
      i enters a red blood cell from the alveoli in the lungs
      ii passes from a red blood cell to an actively respiring muscle cell.
   c Describe how carbon dioxide is transported around the body.

SKILLS REASONING

6 Blood is carried around the body in arteries, veins and capillaries.
   a Describe *two* ways in which the structure of an artery is adapted for its function.
   b Describe *three* differences between arteries and veins.
   c Describe *two* ways in which the structure of a capillary is adapted for its function.

SKILLS ANALYSIS

7 The diagram shows a section through a human heart.

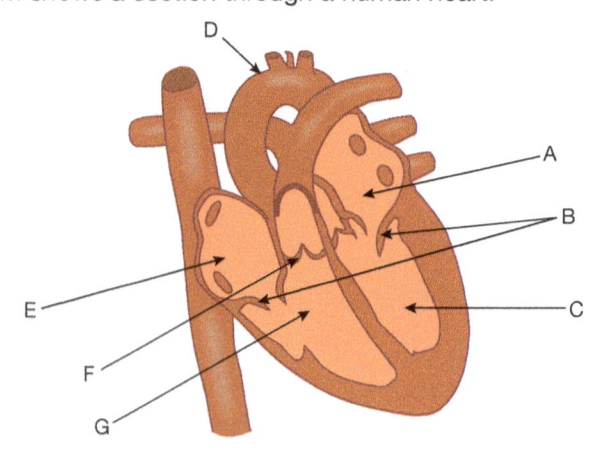

a Name the structures labelled A, B, C, D and E.

SKILLS CRITICAL THINKING

b What is the importance of the structures labelled B and F?

SKILLS ANALYSIS

c Which letters represent the chambers of the heart to which blood returns:
  i from the lungs
  ii from all the other organs of the body?

8 The diagram shows three types of cells found in human blood.

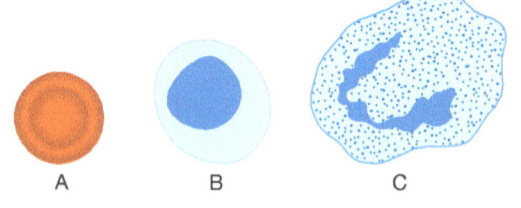

a Giving a reason for each answer, identify the blood cell that:
  i transports oxygen around the body
  ii produces antibodies to destroy bacteria
  iii engulfs and digests bacteria.

SKILLS CRITICAL THINKING

b Name one other component of blood found in the plasma and state its function.

EXAM PRACTICE

SKILLS INTERPRETATION, REASONING

1 In multicellular organisms, cells are organised into tissues, organs and organ systems.

  a The diagram shows a section through an artery and through a capillary.

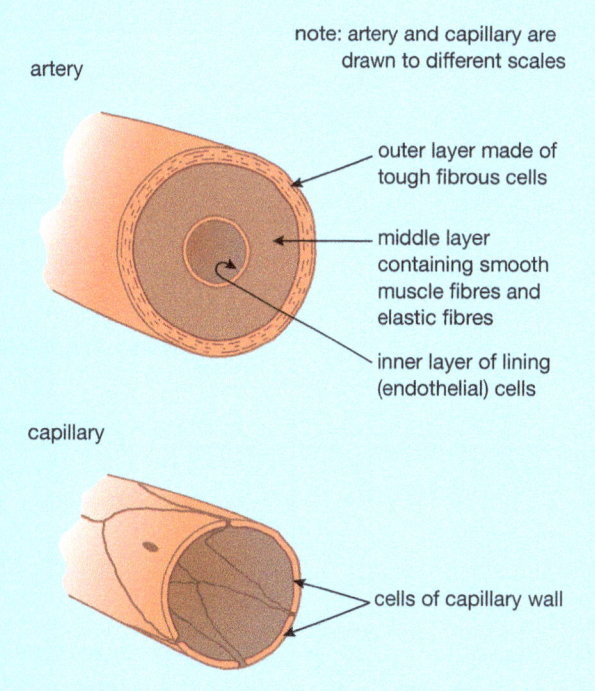

  note: artery and capillary are drawn to different scales

  artery
  - outer layer made of tough fibrous cells
  - middle layer containing smooth muscle fibres and elastic fibres
  - inner layer of lining (endothelial) cells

  capillary
  - cells of capillary wall

  Explain why an artery can be considered to be an organ whereas a capillary cannot. **(2)**

  b Organ systems contain two or more organs whose functions are linked. The digestive system is one human organ system.

SKILLS CRITICAL THINKING

  i Describe the functions of the digestive system. **(2)**

  ii Name *three* organs in the human digestive system. Describe what each organ does as part of the digestive system. **(6)**

  iii Name *two* other human organ systems and, for each system, name *two* organs that are part of the system. **(6)**

  (Total 16 marks)

SKILLS ANALYSIS

2 Catalase is an enzyme found in many plant and animal cells. It catalyses the breakdown of hydrogen peroxide into water and oxygen.

$$\text{hydrogen peroxide} \xrightarrow{\text{catalase}} \text{water} + \text{oxygen}$$

  a In an investigation into the action of catalase in potato, 20 g of potato tissue was put into a small beaker containing hydrogen peroxide. The initial total mass was 80 g. The temperature was maintained at 20 °C throughout the investigation. As soon as the potato was added, the mass of the beaker and its contents was recorded until there was no further change in mass. The results are shown in the graph.

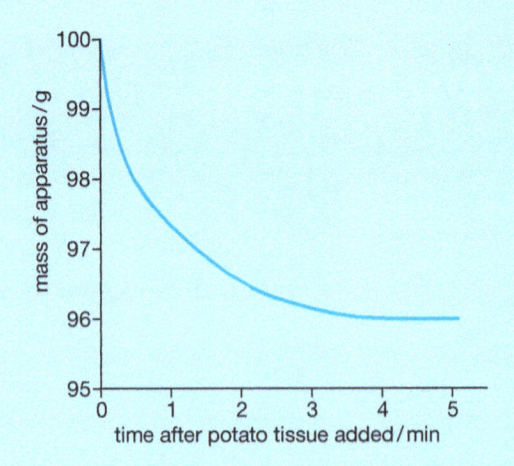

i Determine how much oxygen was formed in this experiment. Explain your answer. (2)
ii Estimate the time by which half this mass of oxygen had been formed. (2)
iii Explain, in terms of collisions between enzyme and substrate molecules, why the rate of reaction changes during the course of the investigation. (2)

b The students repeated the investigation, but carried it out at 30 °C. Predict what difference, if any, would you expect in:
i the mass of oxygen formed.
ii the time taken to form this mass of oxygen.
Explain your answers. (4)

(Total 10 marks)

3 Different particles move across cell membranes using different processes.

a The table below shows some ways in which active transport, osmosis and diffusion are similar and some ways in which they are different.
Copy and complete the table with ticks and crosses, inserting a tick if the statement is correct and a cross if it is wrong. (3)

Feature	Active transport	Osmosis	Diffusion
movement of particles results from their kinetic energy			
movement of particles needs a supply of energy from respiration			
particles move down a concentration gradient			

b The graph shows the results of an investigation into the rate of diffusion of sodium ions across the membranes of potato cells.

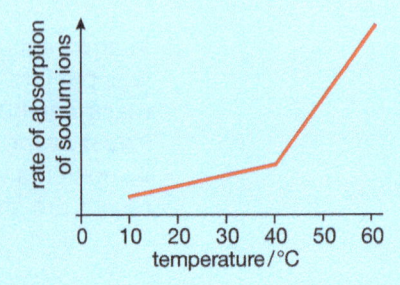

2 STRUCTURE AND FUNCTION IN LIVING ORGANISMS — EXAM PRACTICE

SKILLS ANALYSIS, REASONING

    i Explain the increase in the rate of diffusion up to 40 °C. (2)

    ii Suggest why the rate of increase is much steeper at temperatures above 40 °C. (2)

(Total 7 marks)

SKILLS DECISION MAKING

4 In an investigation of osmosis in potato cells, the following procedure was used.

- Cylinders of tissue were obtained from a potato. Each was the same diameter and cut to a length of 5 cm.
- Each cylinder was gently blotted with filter paper and then weighed.
- Three potato cylinders were placed in each of six different concentrations of sucrose solution and left for 2 hours.
- The cylinders were then removed from the solutions, gently blotted again and reweighed. The percentage change in mass for each piece of potato was calculated, then an average percentage change in mass was found for each solution.

The graph summarises the results.

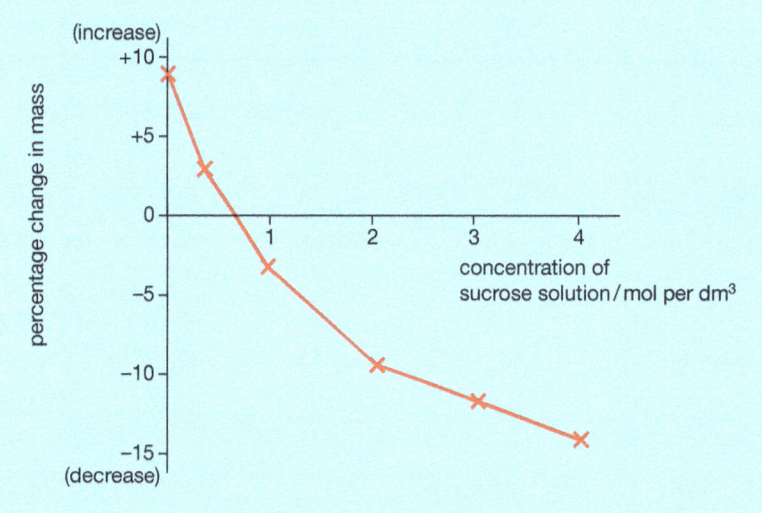

a Suggest why:

    i the cylinders were gently blotted before and after being placed in the sucrose solutions (1)

    ii three cylinders were used for each solution (1)

    iii all the cylinders were the same diameter and were cut to the same length. (1)

b i Using your knowledge of osmosis, explain the result obtained with a 3 mol/dm³ sucrose solution. (3)

    ii Identify the concentration of sucrose solution that is similar in concentration to the contents of the potato cells. Explain how you arrived at your answer. (3)

(Total 9 marks)

SKILLS ANALYSIS

5 Light intensity and the concentration of carbon dioxide in the atmosphere influence the rate of photosynthesis.

a The graph shows the effect of changing light intensity on the rate of photosynthesis at two different carbon dioxide concentrations.

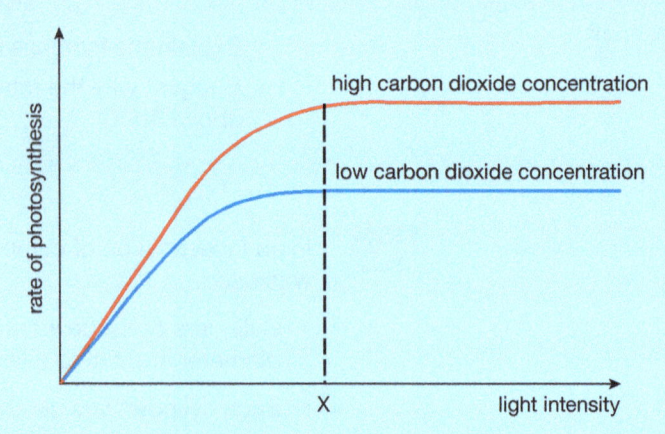

i Describe the effect of light intensity on the rate of photosynthesis at each concentration of carbon dioxide up to light intensity X and beyond light intensity X. (4)

ii State the factor which limits the rate of photosynthesis up to light intensity X and the factor that limits the rate beyond light intensity X. (2)

Explain your answers in each case. (3)

b i Name *two* other factors which influence the rate of photosynthesis. (2)

ii Explain why each factor you chose in part **b i** is a limiting factor. (4)

c 'Photosynthesis is a means of converting light energy into chemical energy.'
Explain the meaning of this statement. (2)

(Total 17 marks)

SKILLS ANALYSIS

6 Digestion is brought about by enzymes converting large insoluble molecules into smaller soluble molecules that can be more easily absorbed.

a The activity of enzymes is affected by pH and temperature. The graph shows the activity of two human enzymes from different regions of the gut that are at different pH values.

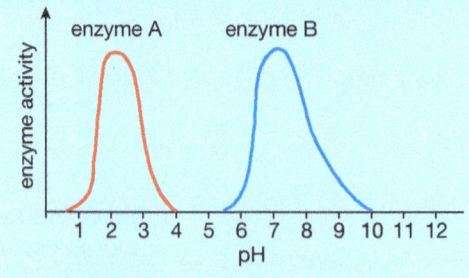

i Suggest which regions of the gut the two enzymes come from. Explain your answer. (4)

ii Name the nutrient digested by enzyme A. (1)

b Describe how enzyme function is affected by changes in pH. (3)

(Total 8 marks)

SKILLS CREATIVITY

7 A piece of meat is a tissue composed of muscle fibres. Muscle fibres use ATP when they contract. Describe an experiment you could carry out to find out if a solution of ATP will cause the contraction of muscle fibres. Your answer should include experimental details and be written in full sentences.

(Total 6 marks)

2 STRUCTURE AND FUNCTION IN LIVING ORGANISMS — EXAM PRACTICE

SKILLS CRITICAL THINKING

8 The table shows the percentage of gases in inhaled and exhaled air.

Gas	Inhaled air / %	Exhaled air / %
nitrogen	78	79
oxygen		
carbon dioxide		
other gases (mainly argon)	1	1

a Copy and complete the table by choosing from the following numbers:
21   4   0.04   16 (2)

b Explain why the percentage of carbon dioxide is different in inhaled and exhaled air. (2)

c The following features can be seen in the lungs:
  i thin membranes between the alveoli and the blood supply
  ii a good blood supply
  iii a large surface area.
Explain how each feature helps gas exchange to happen quickly. (6)

(Total 10 marks)

SKILLS INTERPRETATION

SKILLS CRITICAL THINKING

9 The immune system responds to infections using white blood cells. A phagocyte is one type of white blood cell.

a Draw and label a phagocyte. (3)

b State one way that the structure of a phagocyte differs from that of a red blood cell. (1)

c Phagocytes carry out phagocytosis. Describe the process of phagocytosis. (2)

d Describe how other white blood cells are involved in the immune response. (3)

(Total 9 marks)

SKILLS CREATIVITY

10 Protein supplements are foods that some body-builders use to increase the bulk of their muscles. Describe an investigation to find out if adding a protein supplement to the diet of rats will increase their growth.

Your answer should include experimental details and be written in full sentences.

(Total 6 marks)

| 9 REPRODUCTION 73 | 10 INHERITANCE 81 |

BIOLOGY UNIT 3
REPRODUCTION AND INHERITANCE

One feature that is unique to living organisms is their ability to reproduce and form new individuals. Chapter 9 looks at the process of reproduction in flowering plants and in humans. Chapter 10 deals with the topic of inheritance. This is the science of genetics and how genes are passed on from one generation to the next.

9 REPRODUCTION

SPECIFICATION REFERENCES: 3.1–3.4, 3.8, 3.13

One of the characteristics of living organisms that makes them different from non-living things is their ability to produce offspring, that is, to reproduce. Reproduction is all about an organism passing on its genes to the next generation. Reproduction can be sexual, when it takes place through the formation of special sex cells called gametes, and it can also be asexual, without the production of gametes. This chapter looks at the differences between sexual and asexual reproduction, and sexual reproduction in flowering plants and humans.

LEARNING OBJECTIVES

- Understand the differences between sexual and asexual reproduction.
- Understand that fertilisation involves the fusion of a male and female gamete to produce a zygote that undergoes cell division and develops into an embryo.
- Describe the structures of an insect-pollinated and wind-pollinated flower and explain how each is adapted for pollination.
- Understand that the growth of the pollen tube followed by fertilisation leads to seed formation.
- Understand how the structure of the male and female reproductive systems are adapted for their functions.
- Understand the roles of oestrogen and testosterone in the development of secondary sexual characteristics.

SEXUAL AND ASEXUAL REPRODUCTION COMPARED

There are two types of reproduction: **sexual reproduction** and **asexual reproduction**.

In sexual reproduction, specialised sex cells called **gametes** are produced.

- In animals there are two types, a mobile male gamete called a **sperm** and a stationary female gamete called an egg cell or **ovum** (plural = ova).
- Flowering plants also produce two types of gamete. The female gamete is an egg cell, contained within an **ovule**, and the male gamete is a cell contained within a **pollen grain**.

Sexual reproduction brings together genes from two parents. This means that the offspring will be genetically different from each other and the parent organisms. Sexual reproduction produces **genetic variation**.

The male gamete must fuse with the female gamete to start the process of sexual reproduction.

This is called **fertilisation** (**Figure 9.1**). The single cell formed by fertilisation is called a **zygote**. This cell divides many times to form an **embryo**, which develops into the new organism.

In asexual reproduction there are no specialised gametes and there is no fertilisation. Instead, cells in one part of the body divide to form a structure that breaks away from the parent body and grows into a new organism. There is only one parent organism involved – sexual reproduction normally involves two. In addition, the offspring from asexual reproduction are genetically the same – asexual reproduction does not produce genetic variation.

▲ Figure 9.1 A sperm fertilising an egg

SOME EXAMPLES OF ASEXUAL REPRODUCTION

> **DID YOU KNOW?**
> Individuals that are produced asexually from the same adult organism are genetically identical and are called **clones**.

A few animal species can reproduce asexually. **Figure 9.2** shows *Hydra*. This is a small animal similar to a jellyfish that lives in ponds. It reproduces by a process called budding. Cells in the body wall of the *Hydra* divide to form a small version of the adult. This eventually breaks off and becomes a free-living *Hydra*. One animal may produce several 'buds' in a short space of time.

All the offspring produced from *Hydra* buds are genetically identical – they have exactly the same genes. This is because all the cells of the new individual are produced from just one cell in the body of the adult. When the cell from the adult divides the new cells that are produced are exact copies of the original cell.

Asexual reproduction is rarely used in animals and tends to be restricted to simple animals like *Hydra*.

▲ Figure 9.2 *Hydra* reproducing asexually by budding

However, asexual reproduction is much more common in plants. There are many different methods of asexual reproduction in plants. Most involve some part of the plant growing, and then breaking away from the parent plant before developing into a new plant. Many plants will grow from pieces of root, stem or leaf, and gardeners often use this fact when they grow new plants from cuttings (**Figure 9.3**).

> **KEY POINT**
> A **gene** is a section of DNA that determines a particular characteristic or feature. Genes are found in the nucleus of a cell, on the chromosomes (see **Chapter 10**).

▲ Figure 9.3 These geranium cuttings have started to grow roots

SEXUAL REPRODUCTION IN PLANTS

Plants produce gametes in their flowers. The male gametes are contained within the pollen grains. The female gametes are egg cells that are found within a structure called the ovule. Like animals, the male gametes must be transferred to the female gametes. This takes place through **pollination**, which is normally carried out either by wind or insects. Following pollination, fertilisation takes place and the zygote formed develops into a **seed**.

Pollen grains are produced in the **anthers** of the **stamens**. The ova are produced in ovules in the **ovaries**.

During pollination, pollen grains are transferred from the anthers of a flower to the **stigma**. If this occurs within the same flower it is called **self-pollination**. If the pollen grains are transferred to a different flower, it is called **cross-pollination**.

Plants that are wind-pollinated produce flowers with a structure that is different from those of insect-pollinated flowers. **Figure 9.4** shows the structure of a typical insect-pollinated flower and **Figure 9.5** shows the structure of a typical wind-pollinated flower. **Table 9.1** summarises the main differences between insect-pollinated flowers and wind-pollinated flowers.

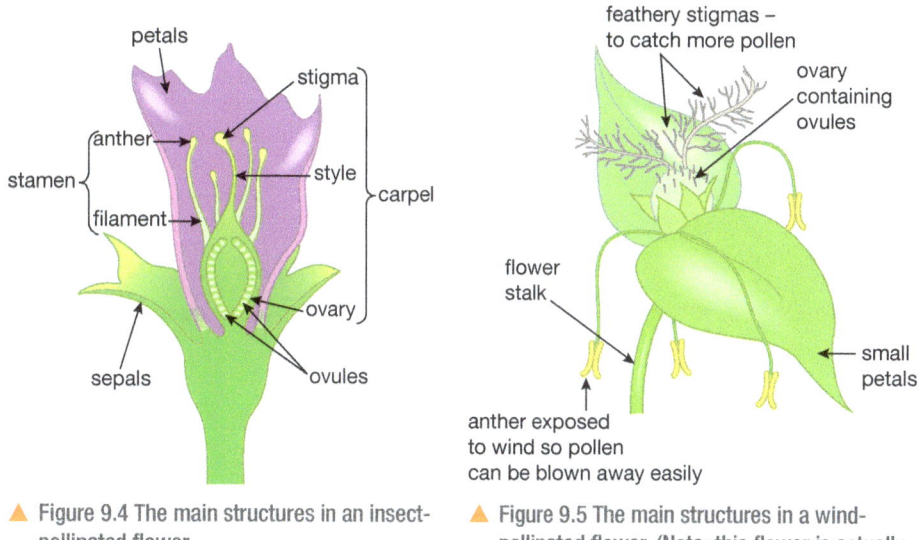

▲ Figure 9.4 The main structures in an insect-pollinated flower

▲ Figure 9.5 The main structures in a wind-pollinated flower. (Note: this flower is actually much smaller than the insect-pollinated flower but it is drawn here to a larger scale.)

Table 9.1 Differences between insect-pollinated and wind-pollinated flowers

Feature of flower	Type of flower	
	Insect-pollinated	Wind-pollinated
position of stamens	enclosed within flower so that insect must make contact	exposed so that wind can easily blow pollen away
position of stigmas	enclosed within flower so that insect must make contact	exposed to catch pollen blowing in the wind
type of stigma	sticky so pollen grains attach from insects	feathery, to catch pollen grains blowing in the wind
size of petals	large to attract insects	small
colour of petals	brightly coloured to attract insects	not brightly coloured, usually green
nectaries	present – they produce nectar, a sweet liquid containing sugars as a 'reward' for insects	absent
pollen grains	large, sticky grains or grains with hooks, to stick to insects' bodies	small, smooth, inflated grains to carry in the wind

Pollination transfers the pollen grain to the stigma. However, for fertilisation to take place, the nucleus of the pollen grain (the male gamete) must fuse with the nucleus of the egg cell, which is inside an ovule in the ovary. To transfer the nucleus to the ovum, the pollen grain forms a **pollen tube**, which grows down through the tissue of the **style** and into the ovary. Here it curves around to enter the opening in an ovule. The tip of the tube dissolves and allows the pollen grain nucleus to move out of the tube and into the ovule. Here it fertilises the ovum nucleus. These events are summarised in **Figure 9.6**.

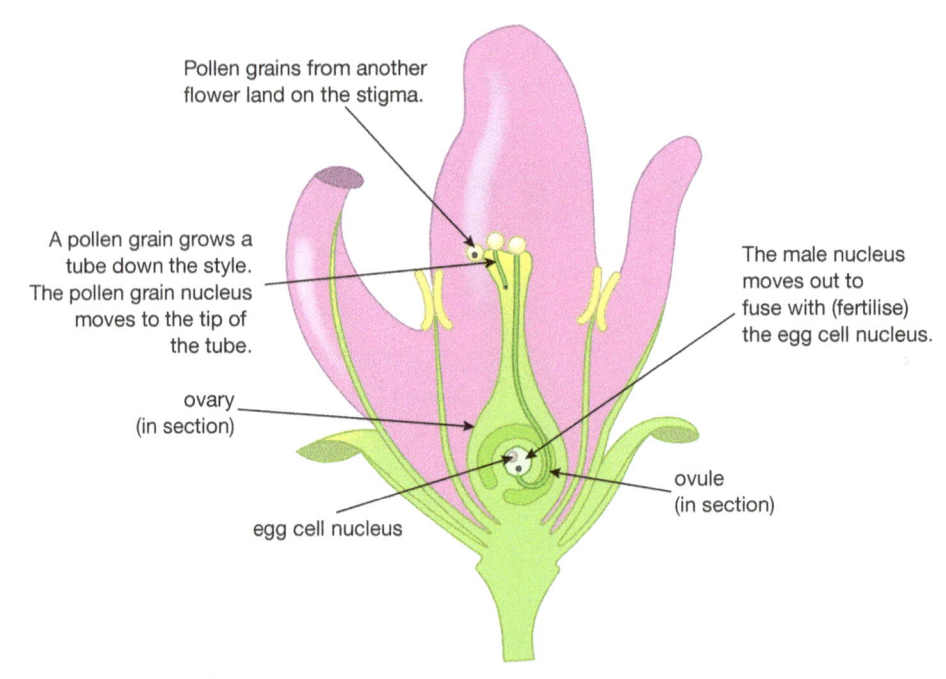

▲ Figure 9.6 Pollination and fertilisation

Fertilisation produces a zygote, which develops into an embryo plant within a seed. Eventually seeds will be dispersed away from the parent plant and grow into new plants.

THE HUMAN REPRODUCTIVE SYSTEMS

Figures 9.7 and **9.8** show the structure of the human female and male reproductive systems.

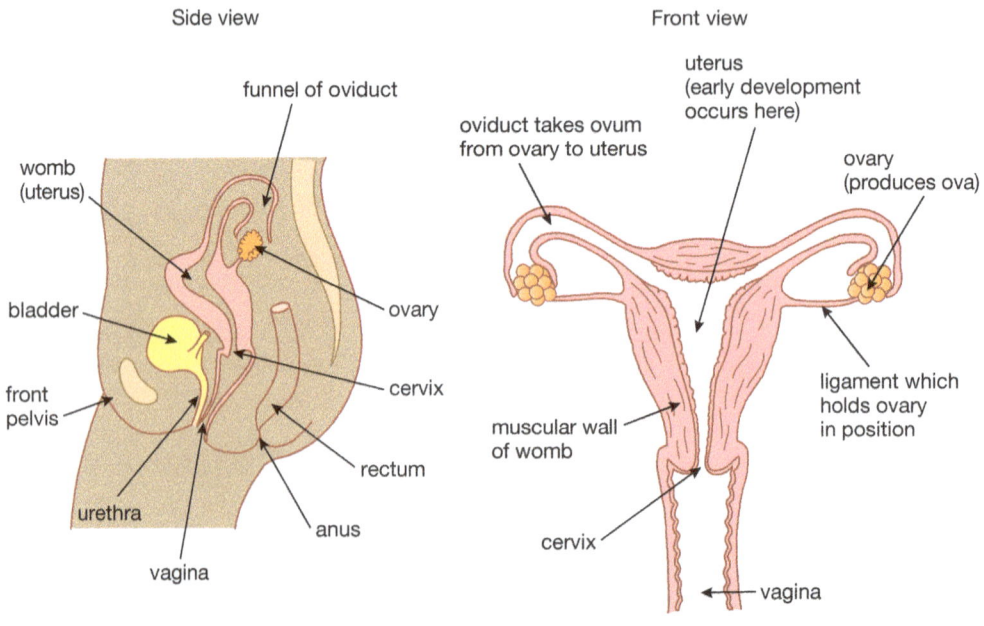

▲ Figure 9.7 The human female reproductive system

Eggs are produced inside the woman's *ovaries*. Eggs are formed by a special sort of cell division that halves the number of chromosomes in the nucleus of each egg cell. (The number of chromosomes is restored to normal at fertilisation, when a sperm fuses with the egg.) Sperm are produced in the

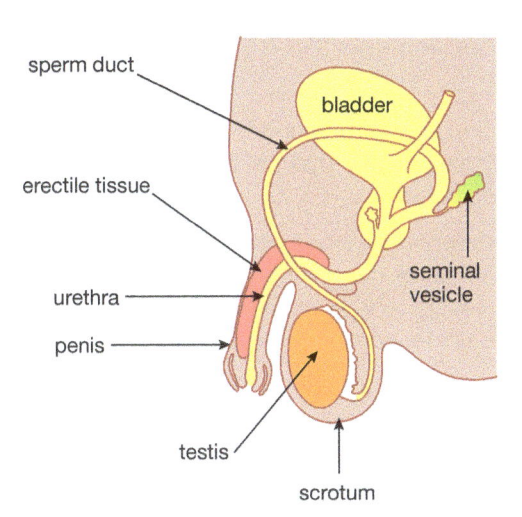

Figure 9.8 The human male reproductive system

man's **testes** (singular = testis). They are formed by the same sort of cell division that produces the eggs. The testes are found inside a structure called the **scrotum**, located outside the rest of the body. The location of the testes in the scrotum means that their temperature is a few degrees lower than the core body temperature (37 °C). This lower temperature is ideal for sperm production.

During **sexual intercourse** increased amounts of blood flows through erectile tissue in the man's penis. The penis becomes erect (bigger and harder) and is moved repeatedly in and out of the woman's vagina. Sperm pass along the sperm duct and urethra and are released into the vagina in a special fluid from the seminal vesicles. This fluid, together with the sperm, is called **semen**. Release of semen is called **ejaculation**. Semen provides nutrients for the sperm, and allows them to swim towards the oviducts to meet the egg.

Each month, an egg is released into an **oviduct** from one of the ovaries. This is called **ovulation**. If an egg is present in the oviduct, it may be fertilised by sperm introduced during intercourse. The zygote formed begins to develop into an embryo, which moves down the oviduct and sinks into ('implants' in) the lining of the uterus. Here, the embryo develops an organ called the **placenta**, which allows it to exchange nutrients with the mother's blood. As the embryo develops it becomes more and more complex. When it becomes recognisably human, we no longer call it an embryo but a fetus. **Figure 9.9** shows the position of a human fetus in the uterus just before birth.

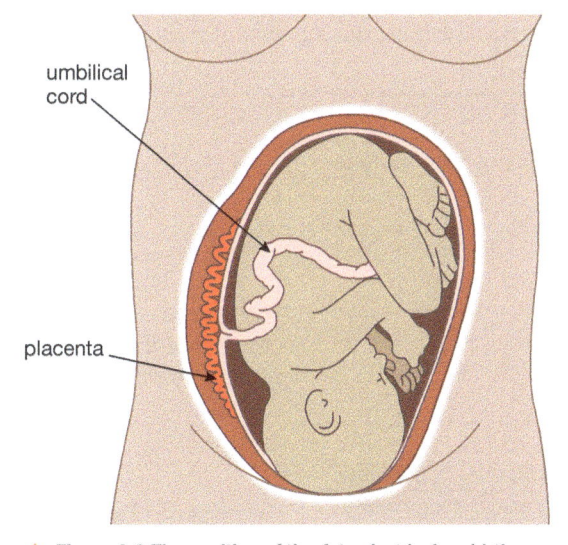

Figure 9.9 The position of the fetus just before birth

THE SECONDARY SEXUAL CHARACTERISTICS

When a baby is born, it can be recognisable as a boy or girl by its sex organs. The male or female sex organs are known as the primary sexual characteristics. However, like most animals, humans are unable to reproduce when they are young. During their teens, changes happen to boys and girls that lead to sexual maturity; this means that they are able to have babies. These changes are controlled by hormones, and the time when these changes happen is called **puberty**.

Puberty involves two developments. The first is that the gametes (eggs and sperm) start to mature and be released. The second is that the bodies of both sexes adapt to allow reproduction to take place.

In boys, the testes secrete the male sex hormone, **testosterone**. Testosterone controls the development of the male **secondary sexual characteristics**. These include growth of the penis and testes, growth of facial and body hair, muscle development and 'breaking' of the voice, when the voice gets lower in tone (**Table 9.2**).

In girls, the ovaries release a female sex hormone called **oestrogen**. Oestrogen produces the female secondary sexual characteristics, such as breast development and the beginning of menstruation ('periods').

Table 9.2 Changes at puberty

In boys	In girls
sperm production starts	the menstrual cycle begins, and eggs are released by the ovaries every month
growth and development of male sexual organs	growth and development of female sexual organs
growth of armpit and pubic hair, and chest and facial hair (beard)	growth of armpit and pubic hair
increase in body mass; growth of muscles, e.g. chest muscles	increase in body mass; development of 'rounded' shape to hips
voice breaks	voice deepens without sudden 'breaking'
sexual 'drive' develops	sexual 'drive' develops
	breasts develop

The age when puberty takes place can vary a good deal, but it is usually between about 11 and 14 years in girls and 13 and 16 years in boys. It takes several years for puberty to be completed.

CHAPTER QUESTIONS

Exam-style questions on reproduction can be found at the end of Unit 3 on page 97.

SKILLS CRITICAL THINKING

1 Consider the following statements about reproduction in plants:

 1. Large numbers of offspring are produced quickly.

 2. There is little genetic variation in the offspring.

 3. A mechanism such as wind or insects is not needed for pollination.

 Which of the above are features of *asexual* reproduction in plants?

 A 1 and 2

 B 1 and 3

 C 2 and 3

 D 1, 2 and 3

SKILLS CRITICAL THINKING

2 Which of the following features are shown by wind-pollinated flowers?

  A large petals, a scent and sticky pollen grains

  B small petals, no scent and light pollen grains

  C large petals, no scent and light pollen grains

  D small petals, a scent and sticky pollen grains

SKILLS CRITICAL THINKING

3 During pollination, between which of the following structures are pollen grains transferred?

  A from anther to stigma

  B from anther to ovary

  C from stigma to style

  D from stigma to ovary

SKILLS ANALYSIS

4 The diagram below shows a section through an insect-pollinated flower. Pollination happens when pollen grains land on part X.

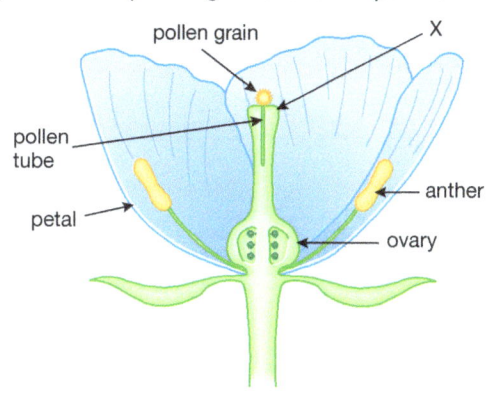

  a Name part X.

SKILLS REASONING

  b Give *two* ways that insects are attracted to a flower like this.

SKILLS INTERPRETATION

  c Copy the diagram and extend the pollen tube to show where it would go when fully grown.

SKILLS REASONING

5 The drawing shows a strawberry plant reproducing in two ways.

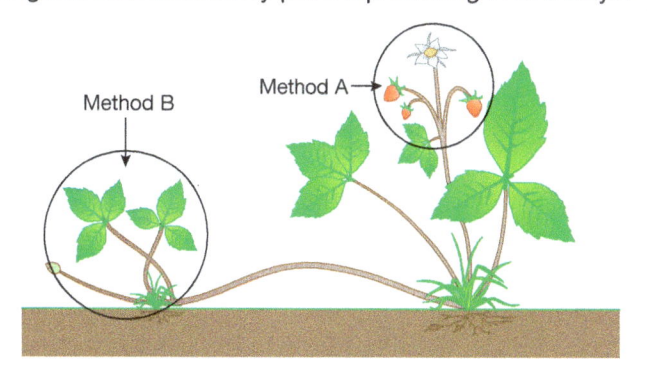

  a Which of the two methods of reproduction shown will result in offspring that show genetic variation? Explain your answer.

  b Is the strawberry flower likely to be wind-pollinated or insect-pollinated? Give reasons for your answer.

SKILLS ANALYSIS

6 The diagram shows the human female reproductive system.

Which letter represents:

a the site of production of oestrogen

b the place where fertilisation usually occurs

c the place where the embryo develops

d the structure that releases eggs?

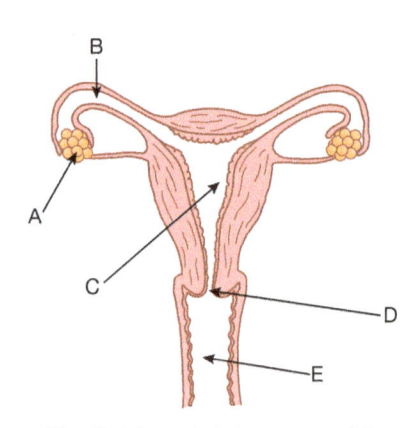

SKILLS INTERPERSONAL SKILLS

7 The number of sperm cells per cm^3 of semen (the fluid containing sperm) is called the 'sperm count'. Some scientists believe that over the last 50 years, the sperm counts of adult male humans have decreased. They think that this is caused by a number of factors, including drinking water becoming polluted with oestrogens and other chemicals. Carry out an internet search to find out the evidence for this. Summarise your findings in about two sides of A4 paper.

10 INHERITANCE

SPECIFICATION REFERENCES: 3.15, 3.19, 3.20, 3.23, 3.25–3.27, 3.31, 3.33, 3.38

The science of inheritance is called genetics. It looks at how the characteristics of an organism are passed from generation to generation. Genetic crosses follow simple mathematical rules and can be explained using diagrams. This chapter deals with how to interpret genetic crosses and make predictions about the outcomes of a cross. The chapter ends with a look at Darwin's theory of evolution by natural selection.

LEARNING OBJECTIVES

- Understand that the nucleus of a cell contains chromosomes on which genes are located.
- Understand how genes exist in alternative forms called alleles, which give rise to differences in inherited characteristics.
- Understand the meaning of the terms dominant, recessive, homozygous, heterozygous, phenotype and genotype.
- Describe patterns of monohybrid inheritance using a genetic diagram.
- Predict probabilities of outcomes from monohybrid crosses.
- Understand how the sex of a person is controlled by one pair of chromosomes, XX in a female and XY in a male.
- Describe the determination of the sex of offspring at fertilisation using a genetic diagram.
- Understand how random fertilisation produces genetic variation in offspring.
- Understand that variation in a species can be genetic, environmental, or a combination of both.
- Explain Darwin's theory of evolution by natural selection.

CHROMOSOMES AND GENES

The characteristics of an organism are determined by instructions carried in the nucleus of each cell. The chemical that is the basis of inheritance is **DNA**. DNA is found in structures called **chromosomes**. A section of DNA that controls a particular feature is called a **gene** (Figure 10.1).

DID YOU KNOW?
DNA stands for deoxyribonucleic acid. This is the famous 'double helix'. The nucleus contains chromosomes, chromosomes contain genes, genes are made of DNA.

DID YOU KNOW?
Most cells in the human body contain 46 chromosomes.

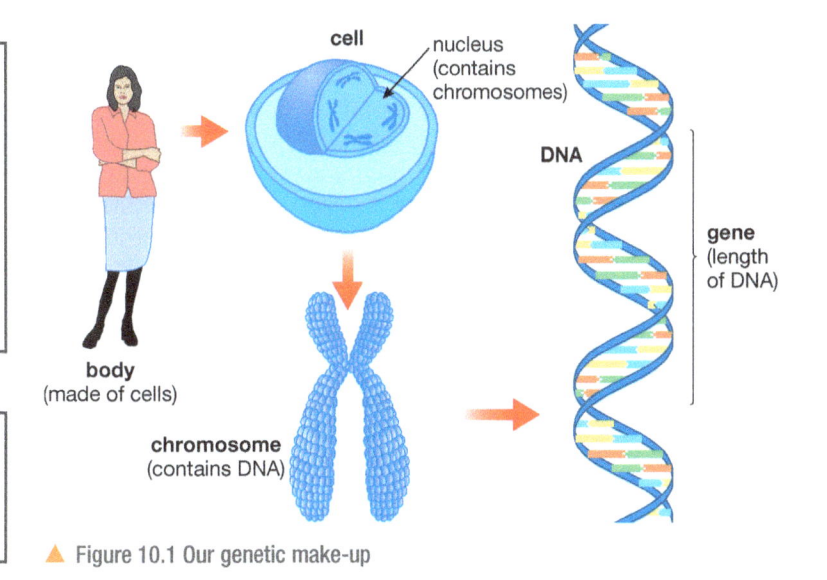

▲ Figure 10.1 Our genetic make-up

GENES AND ALLELES

The features controlled by genes are called 'characteristics'. Sometimes the characteristic is visible, such as the colour of a plant's flowers or a person's height. Sometimes the characteristic is not visible, such as the production of a digestive enzyme, or a person's blood group.

Most genes have more than one form. Let us look at a simple example of this. In garden pea plants the gene controlling flower colour has two forms, one of which produces purple flowers and the other white flowers (**Figure 10.2**).

▲ Figure 10.2 Purple and white flowers in garden pea plants. These colours are produced by two different forms of one gene.

These alternative forms of the gene are called **alleles**. The chromosomes in the cells of a pea plant are in pairs. A plant develops from a zygote (see **Chapter 9**). At fertilisation, the zygote gained one chromosome from the male gamete in the pollen, and one from the female gamete in the ovule.

Both chromosomes of each pair carry genes for the same characteristics. However, the alleles of each gene may be the same or different.

> **EXTENSION**
>
> Most animals and plants have their chromosomes in pairs, although the number varies from species to species. For example, pea plants have 7 pairs of chromosomes, humans 23 pairs, mice 10 pairs and dogs 78 pairs. In each case an individual inherits one chromosome from each parent.

Suppose that, for the gene controlling pea flower colour, a plant has one allele for purple flowers and one for white flowers. What happens? Are some flowers purple and some white, or are they all pale purple? In fact, neither of these happens. In this example, all flowers will be purple. The allele for purple flowers is called **dominant**. This means that it will show its effect, whether or not the allele for white flowers is present. The allele for white flowers is called **recessive**. The recessive allele will only show its effect if there is no dominant allele present. The scientific way to say that a gene 'shows its effect' is to say that the gene is 'expressed'.

> **EXTENSION**
>
> In this chapter, all the examples of genetic crosses involve only one gene with two alleles. In fact, most characteristics are controlled by *many* genes. For example, coat colour in mice is affected by at least five different genes, each with different alleles. Starting with 'single gene' crosses will help you to understand the principles involved, which apply to all genes.

3 REPRODUCTION AND INHERITANCE **10 INHERITANCE**

▲ Figure 10.3 The coats of guinea pigs can be many different colours, with long or short hair and the presence or absence of circular whorls called rosettes.

GENETIC CROSSES

We usually show the dominant allele of a gene with a capital letter (e.g. A) and the recessive allele with the corresponding small letter (a). Consider the coats of guinea pigs (**Figure 10.3**). Several features of their coats are controlled by single genes with dominant and recessive alleles. For example, short hair is dominant to long hair, straight hair is dominant to curls and the presence of rosettes is dominant to smooth hair.

Let us look at the genetics of rosettes. The allele for rosettes (R) is dominant over the allele for smooth hair (r). There are three possible combinations of alleles (**Table 10.1**).

Table 10.1 The genotypes controlling the presence or absence of rosettes in guinea pigs.

Genotype	Description of genotype	Appearance of guinea pig (phenotype)
RR	homozygous dominant	rosettes
rr	homozygous recessive	smooth
Rr	heterozygous	rosettes

There are some new terms here that need to be explained:
- the **genotype** is the genetic make-up of an organism (RR, rr or Rr in this example)
- the **phenotype** is the appearance of an organism (rosettes or smooth hair)
- **homozygous** means that the two alleles of the gene are the same (RR or rr)
- **heterozygous** means that the two alleles of the gene are different (Rr).

Remember that the dominant allele always shows its effect (is expressed) if it is present. This means that the heterozygote and dominant homozygote have the same phenotype – both RR and Rr guinea pigs have rosettes. The recessive allele is only expressed in the recessive homozygote (rr).

KEY POINT

The noun from the word homozygous is 'homozygote'. You can say that an animal is homozygous or is 'a homozygote'. Similarly, an animal can be heterozygous or 'a heterozygote'.

CONSTRUCTING GENETIC DIAGRAMS

We can use the symbols for alleles to explain how they are passed on to the offspring of a cross between two animals. If we are only dealing with one gene, this is called a **monohybrid cross**.

First, consider a cross between two guinea pigs, one that is homozygous dominant and one that is homozygous recessive (**Figure 10.4**).

Phenotype of parents	rosettes	smooth	Explanation
genotypes of parents	RR	rr	Each parent has two copies of only one allele
gametes (eggs and sperm)	R	r	Cell division produces gametes with one allele
genotype of first (F_1) generation		Rr	F_1 are all heterozygous
phenotype of F_1 generation	all have rosettes		The R allele is expressed – all offspring have rosettes

▲ Figure 10.4 A cross between a guinea pig that is homozygous dominant for rosettes and one that is homozygous recessive for smooth hair (RR × rr). Note that the sex of the parents does not matter – the male guinea pig could be either RR or rr and vice versa. The cross would produce the same results either way.

KEY POINT

Gametes are formed by a special sort of cell division, where the members of each pair of chromosomes are separated. For example, in body cells of guinea pigs there are 64 chromosomes, which is reduced to 32 in eggs and sperm. So a gamete only receives one copy of each allele from each parent. The alleles are brought back together again at fertilisation.

> **KEY TERM**
>
> The first generation produced by crossing the parents is called the **F₁ generation**. This stands for 'first filial' generation, from the Latin for 'son of'. The next generation, produced by crossing the animals from the F₁ generation, is called the **F₂ generation**.

Now look at what happens when two of the heterozygous animals from the F₁ generation are crossed (**Figure 10.5**).

Phenotype of parents	rosettes	rosettes	Explanation
genotypes of parents (F₁)	Rr	Rr	Each parent has a copy of both alleles
gametes (eggs and sperm)	R or r	R or r	Half of the gametes from each parent carry the R allele and half the r allele
genotype of second (F₂) generation	RR Rr Rr rr 1 RR : 2 Rr : 1 rr		The ratio of the genotypes in the F₂ is the result of random fertilisation of eggs by sperm
phenotypes of F₂ generation	3 rosettes : 1 smooth		The *probability* is that the offspring will be in this ratio

▲ Figure 10.5 A cross between two heterozygous guinea pigs (Rr × Rr).

If you construct a genetic diagram like that in **Figure 10.5**, using arrows, it is easy to make mistakes. A better way is to use a diagram called a **Punnett square** (**Figure 10.6**).

Gametes	R	r
R	RR rosettes	Rr rosettes
r	Rr rosettes	rr smooth

▲ Figure 10.6 The cross between two heterozygous guinea pigs drawn as a Punnett square.

The Punnett square produces the same expected ratio in the F₂ generation: three animals with rosettes to one animal with smooth fur. This is a 3 : 1 ratio.

There is an important point here. These are only the *expected* ratios, based on the laws of probability. What this means is that if the cross produced a *large number* of offspring, the probability is that their genotypes would be in the ratio 1 RR : 2 Rr : 1 rr or their phenotypes would be in the ratio 3 with rosettes : 1 smooth.

If you carried out the same cross lots of times with many pairs of heterozygous guinea pigs, you could produce 400 baby guinea pigs. With a large number like this, the most likely outcome would be that you would get 300 animals with rosettes and 100 with smooth coats. However, the laws of probability mean it is quite likely that the numbers would be 307 : 93, or 295 : 105 – close to the expected ratio, but not exactly the same.

With a small number of offspring, the ratios are likely to be quite different from the expected values. Just by chance, a pair of heterozygous guinea pigs could produce four babies with rosettes, or even four smooth ones. Fertilisation of an egg by a sperm is a random event, so it is impossible to be certain about the outcome.

So far the examples have involved animals. The same rules apply to crossing plants, where the gametes are contained within the ovule and pollen grain (see **Chapter 9**).

For example, there are two alternative varieties of garden pea plants. One grows long stems and is called 'tall'. The other variety has very short stems and is called 'dwarf'. Crossing a pure-breeding tall plant with a dwarf plant produces all tall plants in the F₁ generation. Crossing two F₁ plants together produces a ratio of 3 tall : 1 dwarf in the F₂ generation (**Figure 10.7**).

> **KEY POINT**
>
> Ratios and probabilities can be written as a percentage or as a decimal fraction of 1. For example, a 3 : 1 ratio can be written as 75% : 25% or 0.75 : 0.25. A 50% probability can be written as 0.5.

3 REPRODUCTION AND INHERITANCE   10 INHERITANCE

KEY TERM

'Pure-breeding' means that the parent tall plants were homozygous for stem length. This can be proven by crossing them for several generations to check that no dwarf plants are produced. (Dwarf plants can only be homozygous – see explanation below.)

Parents

tall parent   dwarf parent

F₁

all tall plants

F₂

tall plant   tall plant   tall plant   dwarf plant

3 tall : 1 dwarf

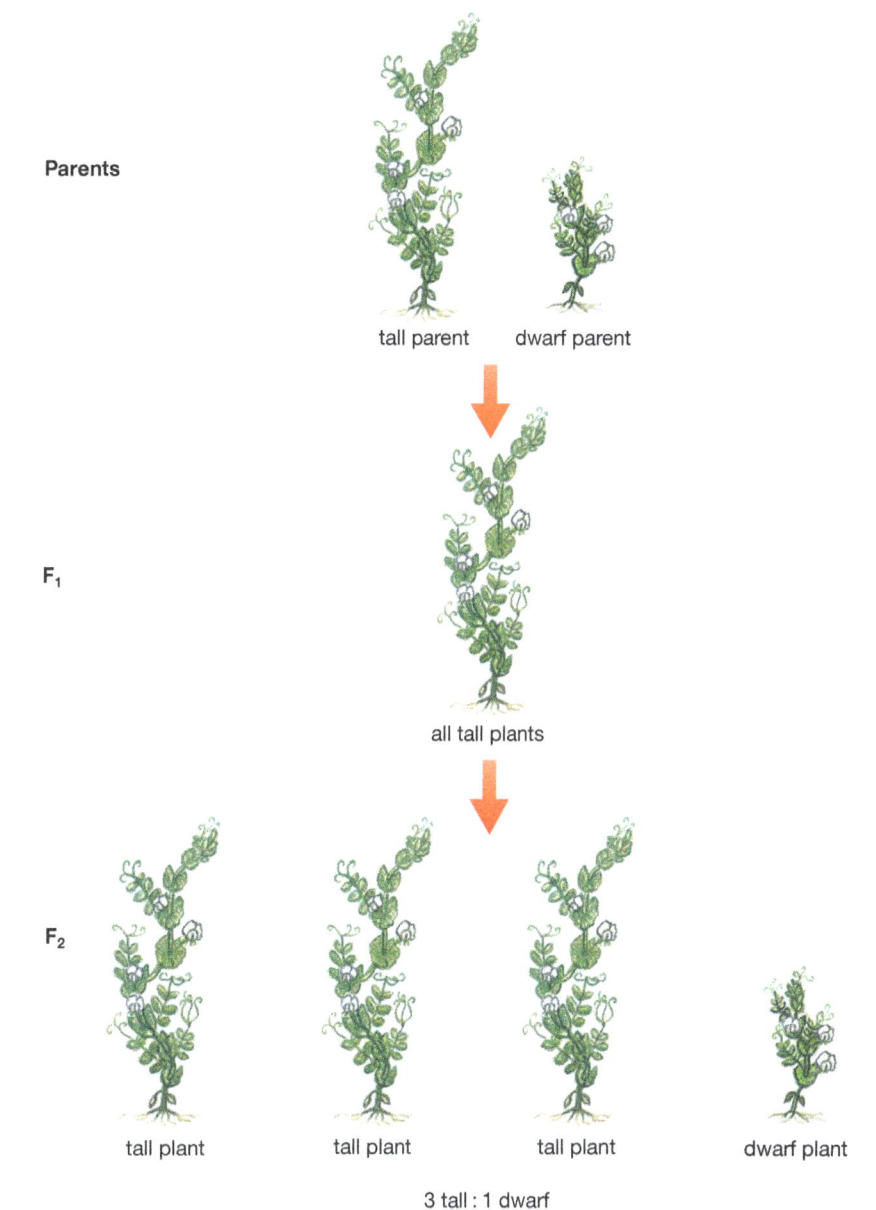

▲ Figure 10.7 Results from a cross between tall and dwarf pea plants.

To draw a genetic diagram to explain these crosses, we use the symbol T for the allele for tall and t for the allele for dwarf. The parent plants must have the genotypes TT (tall) and tt (dwarf). **Figure 10.8** explains the crosses that give the F₁ plants (all genotype Tt) and the 3:1 ratio of tall to dwarf plants in the F₂.

phenotype of parents   tall   dwarf

genotype of parents   TT   tt

gametes   (T)   (t)

genotype of F₁   Tt

phenotype of F₁   all tall

gametes from the   male gametes   female gametes
F₁ plants   (T) or (t)   (T) or (t)

genotypes of F₂   female gametes
                            T   t
            male gametes T TT   Tt
                         t Tt   tt

                        1 TT : 2 Tt : 1 tt

phenotypes of F₂   3 tall : 1 dwarf

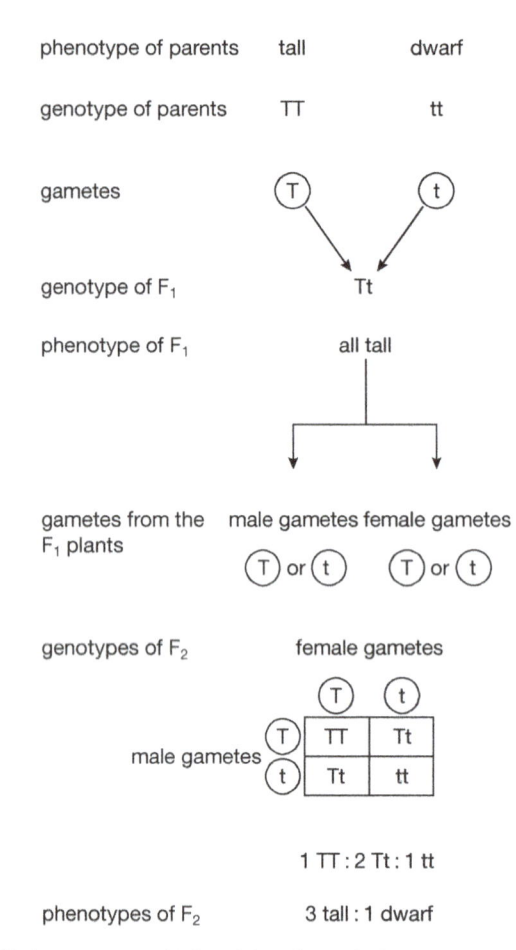

▲ Figure 10.8 Results from crosses of tall and dwarf pea plants.

FAMILY TREES

We can often tell the genotypes of individuals from their family tree.

Take the example of polydactyly. This is an inherited condition in which a person develops extra digits (fingers or toes) on their hands or feet. It is controlled by a dominant allele. The recessive allele causes the normal number of digits to develop.

If we use the symbol D for the polydactyly allele and d for the normal-number allele, the possible genotypes and phenotypes are:

- DD – person has polydactyly
- Dd – person has polydactyly (remember, only one dominant allele is needed for the gene to be expressed)
- dd – person has the normal number of digits.

The *family tree* for polydactyly is shown in **Figure 10.9**.

You can tell which allele is dominant from the family tree. In **Figure 10.9** the parents 1 and 2 both show polydactyly, but their children 4 and 6 do not. That means that 1 and 2 must each carry a 'hidden' (recessive) allele for the normal number of digits (d). They must both be heterozygous (Dd) and their children – numbers 4 and 6 – must be homozygous recessive (dd).

> **EXAM HINT**
>
> You might wonder why we do not use P and p to represent the alleles. This is because the capital P and small p look very similar and could easily be confused in a genetic diagram. It is better to use letters that look different, such as D and d.

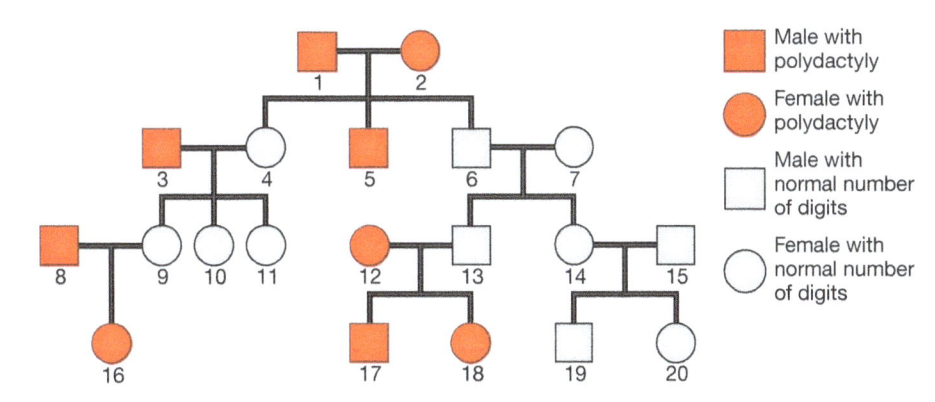

▲ Figure 10.9 A family tree showing the inheritance of polydactyly

From here, you can begin to work out some of the other genotypes, knowing that:

- all the people with the normal number of digits *must* have the genotype dd, because if they had even one D allele, they would show polydactyly
- all the people with polydactyly must be either DD or Dd
- any person with polydactyly who has children with the normal number of digits must be heterozygous (Dd)
- any person with polydactyly who has one parent with the normal number of digits must also be heterozygous (the 'normal-number' parent only has 'normal-number' alleles to pass on).

From these rules we can tell that individuals 1, 2, 3, 16, 17 and 18 must be heterozygous (Dd) and individuals 4, 6, 7, 9, 10, 11, 13, 14, 15, 19 and 20 must be homozygous recessive (dd). This is shown in **Figure 10.10**.

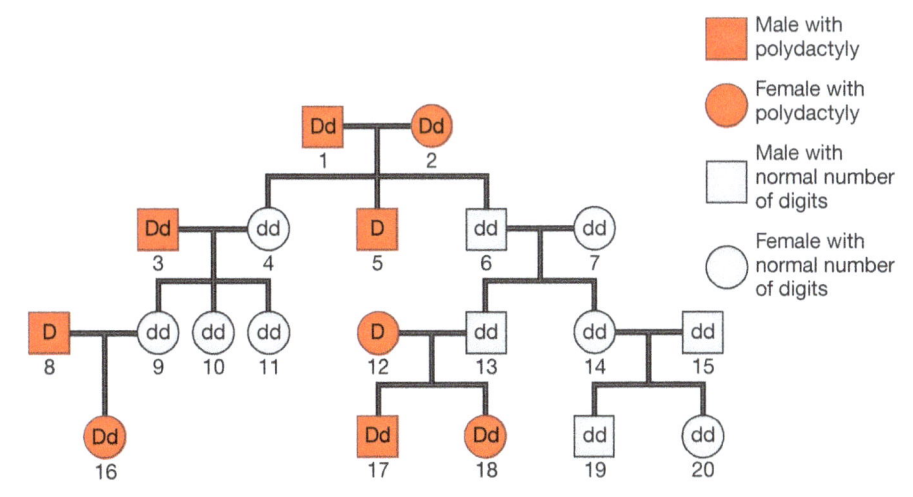

▲ Figure 10.10 The family tree from Figure 10.9, with known genotypes added

We cannot be sure about the genotypes of individuals 5, 8 and 12. They could be homozygous dominant (DD) or heterozygous (Dd). All we can tell is that they must each have at least one dominant allele.

SEX DETERMINATION

Our sex – whether we are male or female – is not under the control of a single gene. It is determined by the X and Y chromosomes, which are therefore known as the **sex chromosomes**. Human body cells contain 46 chromosomes. These are made up of 44 'non-sex' chromosomes and two sex chromosomes.

In females there are two X chromosomes in all cells (apart from the egg cells), and in males one X chromosome and one Y chromosome in all cells (except the sperm). Our sex is effectively determined by the presence or absence of the Y chromosome – Y present gives male, Y absent gives female. The full set of chromosomes of a man is shown in **Figure 10.11**.

> **REMINDER**
>
> We should really say *nearly* all body cells have 46 chromosomes. Some cells have no nucleus and no chromosomes, e.g. red blood cells.

▲ Figure 10.11 A man's chromosomes. One of each of the 22 pairs of 'non-sex' chromosomes are shown, along with the X and Y sex chromosomes. A woman's chromosomes are the same, except that she has two X chromosomes.

The inheritance of sex follows the pattern shown in **Figure 10.12**. The sex chromosomes ensure that the probability of having a female child or a male child is 50%. However, predicted genetic ratios are usually only met when large numbers are involved. Even in a large family it is not unusual to have, for example, five girls and one boy. Overall, the ratio of male to female births throughout the world is 1:1.

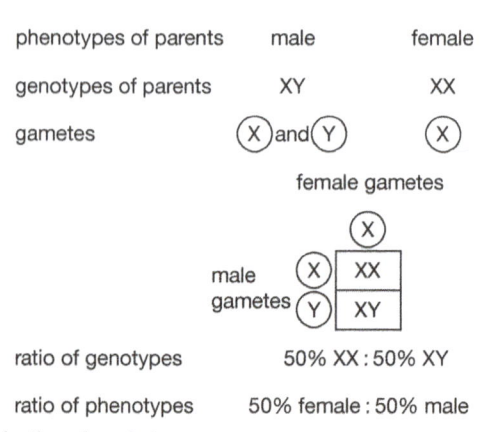

phenotypes of parents	male	female
genotypes of parents	XY	XX
gametes	X and Y	X

female gametes

	X
male gametes X	XX
Y	XY

ratio of genotypes   50% XX : 50% XY

ratio of phenotypes   50% female : 50% male

▲ Figure 10.12 Determination of sex in humans

> **DID YOU KNOW?**
> Not quite every individual is genetically unique. Identical twins are formed from the *same zygote*. When the zygote starts to divide, the two cells formed do not stay together. For some reason they separate and each cell behaves as though it were an individual zygote, dividing and developing into an embryo. Because they have developed from genetically identical cells, the embryos (and, later, the children and the adults they become) will be genetically identical too.

GENETIC VARIATION

Sexual reproduction in any multicellular organism involves the fusion of two gametes to form a zygote. The offspring from sexual reproduction differ in their genetic make-up. We say that they show **genetic variation**. One reason for this is because of the huge variation in the gametes.

At the start of this chapter it was mentioned that gametes are produced by a special sort of cell division. You do not need to know the details of this process, but it results in new combinations of alleles of different genes being passed to each gamete.

Another source of genetic variation is the random way in which fertilisation takes place. In humans, any one of the billions of sperm formed by a male during his life could, potentially, fertilise any one of the thousands of eggs formed by a female.

Taken together, these two sources of variation mean that every individual is likely to be genetically unique.

GENES AND ENVIRONMENT BOTH PRODUCE VARIATION

The appearance of an organism is not just a product of its genes. The organism's surroundings (environment) also plays a part in deciding its characteristics.

You have seen that there are two varieties of pea plants that are either tall or dwarf. This difference in height is due to the genes they inherit. There are no 'intermediate height' pea plants. However, all the tall pea plants are not *exactly* the same height and neither are all the dwarf pea plants *exactly* the same height. **Figure 10.13** shows the variation in height of pea plants.

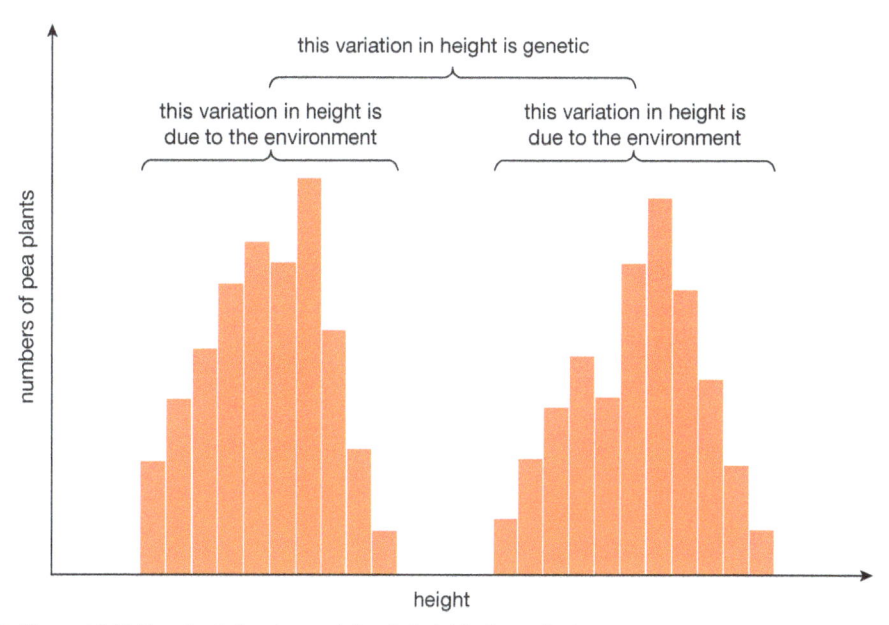

▲ Figure 10.13 Bar chart showing variation in height of pea plants

Several environmental factors can affect the height of the plants. For example:

- they may not all receive the same amount of light and so some will not photosynthesise as well as others
- they may not all receive the same amount of water and mineral ions from the soil – this could affect the manufacture of a range of substances in the plant
- they may not all receive the same amount of carbon dioxide; again, some plants will not photosynthesise as well as others.

Similar effects can be observed in animals. For example, body height in humans is partly due to the effects of genes controlling bone and muscle growth but it is also affected by how much food is available and what type of food a person consumes.

Identical twins have the same genes, and often grow up to look very alike (although not quite identical). Identical twins will sometimes develop similar talents. However, identical twins never look *exactly* the same. This is especially true if, for some reason, they grow up apart. The different environments affect their physical, social and intellectual development in different ways.

DARWIN'S THEORY OF EVOLUTION BY NATURAL SELECTION

The meaning of 'evolution' is that species of animals and plants are not fixed in their form, but change over time. It is not a new idea. For thousands of years philosophers have discussed this theory. By the beginning of the 19th century there was overwhelming evidence for evolution, and many scientists had accepted that it had taken place. What was missing was an understanding of the *mechanism* by which evolution could have occurred.

The person who proposed the mechanism for evolution that is accepted today was the English biologist Charles Darwin (**Figure 10.14**). He called the mechanism natural selection.

At the age of 22, Charles Darwin became the unpaid biologist aboard the survey ship HMS *Beagle*, which left England for a five-year voyage in 1831 (**Figure 10.15**).

▲ Figure 10.14 Charles Darwin (1809–1882)

DID YOU KNOW?

Charles Darwin was the son of a country doctor. He did not do very well at school or university and was unable to decide on a profession. His father is supposed to have said: 'you're good for nothing but shooting guns and rat-catching … you'll be a disgrace to yourself and all of your family'. He was wrong – Darwin went on to become one of the most famous scientists of all time!

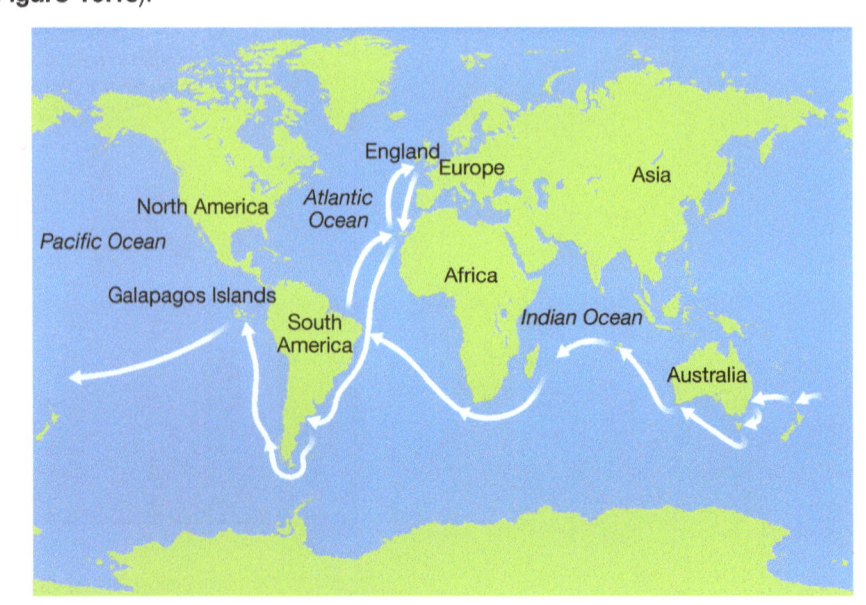

▲ Figure 10.15 The five-year journey of HMS *Beagle*

DID YOU KNOW?

A fossil is the remains of an animal or plant that lived thousands or millions of years ago, preserved in sedimentary rocks. Fossils are formed when minerals replace the materials in bone and tissue, creating a replica of the original organism in the rock.

During the voyage, Darwin collected hundreds of specimens and made many observations about the variety of organisms and the ways in which they were adapted to their environments. He gained much information, in particular, from the variety of life forms in South America and the Galapagos Islands. Darwin was influenced by the work of Charles Lyell who was, at the time, laying the foundations of modern geology. Lyell was using the evidence of rock layers to suggest that the surface of the Earth was constantly changing. The layers of sediments in rocks represented different time periods. Darwin noticed that the fossils often changed slightly through the layers. He suggested that life forms were continually changing – evolving.

On his return to England, Darwin began to evaluate his data and wrote several essays, introducing the ideas of natural selection. He arrived at his theory of natural selection from observations made during his voyage on HMS *Beagle* and from deductions made from those observations. Darwin made three key observations.

- Organisms generally produce more offspring than are needed to replace them. For example, a single female salmon can release 5 million eggs per year; a giant puffball fungus produces 40 million spores.

- Despite this over-reproduction, stable, established populations of organisms generally remain the same size. The seas are not overflowing with salmon, and we are not surrounded by lots of giant puffball fungi!

- Members of the same species are not identical – they show variation.

He made two important deductions from these observations.

- From the first two observations he deduced that there is a 'struggle for existence'. Many offspring are produced, yet the population stays the same size. There must be competition for resources and many individuals must die.

KEY POINT

The phrase 'survival of the fittest' does not mean *physical* fitness, but *biological* fitness. This depends on how well adapted an organism is to its environment so that it is successful in *reproducing*. A good way of putting it is; 'survival of the individuals that will leave most offspring in later generations'.

- From the third observation he deduced that, if some offspring survive while others die, those organisms best suited to their environment would survive to reproduce. Those less suited will die. This gave rise to the phrase 'survival of the fittest'.

Notice a key phrase in the second deduction – the best-suited organisms survive *to reproduce*. This means that the characteristics that give the organism a better chance of surviving will be passed on to the next generation. Fewer of the individuals that are less suited to the environment survive to reproduce. The next generation will have more of the type that is better adapted and fewer of the less well-adapted type. This will be repeated in each generation.

Another naturalist, Alfred Russel Wallace, had also studied life forms in South America and Indonesia and had reached the same conclusions as Darwin. Darwin and Wallace jointly published a scientific paper on natural selection, although it was Darwin who went on to develop the ideas further. In 1859, he published his now famous book *On the Origin of Species by Means of Natural Selection* (usually shortened to *On The Origin of Species*).

This book changed forever the way in which biologists think about how species originate. Darwin went on to suggest that humans could have evolved from ape-like ancestors. For this he was ridiculed, largely by people who had misunderstood his ideas (**Figure 10.16**). He also carried out considerable research in other areas of biology.

▲ Figure 10.16 Darwin's ideas were unpopular and many newspapers of the time made fun of them.

The theory of natural selection proposes that some factor in the environment 'selects' which forms of a species will survive to reproduce. Forms that are not well adapted will not survive.

The following is a summary of how we think natural selection works:

1. There is variation within the species.
2. Changing conditions in the environment favour one particular form of the species.
3. The frequency of the favoured form increases under these conditions (survival of the fittest).
4. The frequency of the less well-adapted form decreases under these conditions.

SOME EXAMPLES OF HOW NATURAL SELECTION MIGHT HAVE WORKED

> **KEY POINT**
>
> When Darwin proposed his theory of natural selection, genes had not been identified. Darwin realised that characteristics must be inherited in some way, but he had no knowledge of how genes control characteristics or how they are passed from one generation to the next. In the first edition of his book *On the Origin of Species* he said, 'The Laws governing inheritance are quite unknown'.

THE HOVERFLY

Figure 10.17 shows two species of insect: a wasp and a hoverfly. Wasps can defend themselves against predators using a sting. They also have a body with yellow and black stripes. This is called a 'warning colouration'. Predators such as birds soon learn that these colours mean that wasps have a sting, and they avoid attacking them.

Hoverflies do not have a sting. However, they have an appearance that is very like a wasp, with similar yellow and black stripes – they are 'mimics' of wasps. Predators treat hoverflies as if they do have a sting.

Clearly, mimicking a wasp is an advantage to the hoverfly. How could they have evolved this appearance? We can explain how it could have happened by natural selection.

The *selection pressure* was predation by birds and other animals. Among the ancestors of present-day hoverflies there would have been variation in colours. In addition, some hoverflies gained new alleles (mutations) that produced stripes on their bodies. These insects were less likely to be eaten by predators than hoverflies without the stripes – they had a *selective advantage*.

> **DID YOU KNOW?**
>
> Random changes in the DNA give rise to new alleles. They are called **mutations**, and are the source of new variation.

▲ Figure 10.17 Two insects showing 'warning colouration': (a) a wasp, which has a sting, and (b) a harmless hoverfly

> **KEY POINT**
>
> Note that perfect stripes did not have to appear straight away. Even a slightly stripy appearance could give a small selective advantage over hoverflies without stripes. This would be enough to result in an increase in stripy hoverflies in the next generation.

Since the hoverflies with stripes were more likely to survive being eaten, they were more likely to reproduce, and would pass on the genes for stripes to their offspring. This process continued over many generations. Gradually selection for 'better' stripes took place, until the hoverflies evolved the excellent warning colouration that they have today.

3 REPRODUCTION AND INHERITANCE   10 INHERITANCE

THE POLAR BEAR

▲ Figure 10.18 A polar bear hunting on the Arctic sea ice

DID YOU KNOW?
Polar bear fur appears to be white, but the individual hairs are actually transparent. The white colour results from the light being refracted through the clear hair strands.

The polar bear lives in the Arctic, inhabiting landmasses and sea ice covering the waters within the Arctic Circle (**Figure 10.18**). It is a large predatory carnivore, mainly hunting seals. One way the bear hunts is to wait near holes in the ice where seals come up to breathe. It also silently approaches and attacks seals that are resting on the ice.

Polar bears have many *adaptations* that suit them to their habitat. These include:

- A thick layer of white fur, which reduces heat loss and acts as camouflage in the snow.
- Wide, large paws. These help with walking in the snow, and are used for swimming.
- Strong, muscular legs – a bear can swim continuously in the cold Arctic waters for days.
- Nostrils that close when the bear is swimming under water.
- A large body mass. Polar bears are the largest bears on Earth. An adult male averages 350 to 550 kilograms, and the record is over 1000 kilograms. This large size results in the animal having a small surface area to volume ratio, which reduces heat loss.
- A 10-centimetre thick layer of insulating fat under the skin.
- A well-developed sense of smell – used to detect the bear's prey.
- Bumps on the pads of the paws to provide grip on the ice.
- Short, powerful claws, which also provide grip, and are needed for holding the heavy prey.

The polar bear is thought to have evolved from a smaller species, the brown bear, about 150 000 years ago. How did it evolve its adaptations for life in the Arctic? Let's consider just one of the adaptations: the thick white fur.

There are two main *selection pressures* in favour of thick white fur. The first is the need for insulation to reduce heat loss. The polar bear often has to survive temperatures of −30 °C, and temperatures in the Arctic can fall as low as −70 °C. The second is camouflage; white fur camouflages the animal against the snow so that it can approach its prey unseen and then attack it.

Among the brown bears that were the ancestors of the polar bear there would have been variations in fur length and colour. When some of these bears came to live in colder, more northerly habitats, those individuals with longer and paler fur would have had a *selective advantage* over others with shorter, darker fur. Any new alleles (mutations) that produced long, pale fur increased this advantage. Bears with these genes were less likely to die from the cold or from lack of food. As a result, well-adapted bears were more likely to reproduce and pass on their genes. Over many thousands of years more mutations and selection for long, white fur produced the adaptation we see in the polar bear today. The same process of natural selection is thought to have happened to bring about the other adaptations shown by the polar bear.

CHAPTER QUESTIONS

Exam-style questions on inheritance can be found at the end of Unit 3 on page 97.

SKILLS CRITICAL THINKING

1 Which of the following is true of dominant alleles?

   A they are only expressed if present as a pair

   B they determine the most favourable of a pair of alternative features

   C they are inherited in preference to recessive alleles

   D a dominant allele is expressed if present with a recessive allele

SKILLS PROBLEM SOLVING

2 In pea plants, the allele for purple petals is dominant to the allele for white petals. A pea plant heterozygous for petal colour was crossed with a plant with white petals. What would be the ratio of genotypes in the offspring?

   A 1 : 1   B 2 : 1

   C 1 : 0   D 3 : 1

SKILLS PROBLEM SOLVING

3 The allele for yellow coat colour in mice (Y) is dominant to the allele for non-yellow coat colour (y).

   - Mice with the genotype yy have non-yellow coats.
   - Mice with the genotype Yy have yellow coats.
   - Mice with the genotype YY die as embryos.

   Two heterozygous mice were crossed. What is the probability that a surviving mouse in the F_1 generation will be yellow?

   A 0.00   B 0.25

   C 0.50   D 0.67

SKILLS CRITICAL THINKING

4 How many chromosomes are there in the body cells of a man?

   A 23 pairs + XX

   B 23 pairs + XY

   C 22 pairs + XX

   D 22 pairs + XY

SKILLS CRITICAL THINKING

5 Which of the following best describes the meaning of biological 'fitness'?

   A a measure of an organism's ability to survive in different habitats

   B a measure of the reproductive success of an organism

   C a measure of the relative health of an organism

   D a measure of the strength of an organism

SKILLS REASONING

6 In guinea pigs, the allele for short hair is dominant to that for long hair.

   a Two short-haired guinea pigs were bred and their offspring included some long-haired guinea pigs. Explain these results.

   b One of the short-haired guinea pigs that was used for breeding in part a was crossed with a long-haired guinea pig. What hair type(s) would you expect the offspring to have? Explain your answer.

SKILLS REASONING

7 Predict the *ratios* of the phenotypes of the offspring from the following crosses between tall and dwarf pea plants.

   a TT × TT

   b TT × Tt

   c TT × tt

   d Tt × Tt

   e Tt × tt

   f tt × tt

SKILLS INTERPRETATION

8 In nasturtiums, a single pair of alleles controls flower colour.

The allele for red flower colour is dominant to the allele for yellow flower colour. The diagram represents the results of a cross between a pure-breeding red-flowered nasturtium and a pure-breeding yellow-flowered nasturtium.

R = dominant allele for red flower colour

r = recessive allele for yellow flower colour

phenotypes of parents	red	yellow	
genotypes of parents	RR	rr	
gametes	(R)	( )	

genotypes of F₁ — male gametes / female gametes

genotypes of F₁ parents   ?   ?

gametes   ( ) and ( )   ( ) and ( )

genotypes of F₂ — male gametes / female gametes, with squares A, B, C, D

   a Copy and complete the genetic diagram.

   b What are the colours of the flowers of A, B, C and D?

SKILLS CRITICAL THINKING, REASONING

9 Variation in organisms can be caused by the environment as well as by the genes they inherit. For each of the following examples, state whether the variation described is likely to be genetic, environmental or both. In each case, give a reason for your answer.

   a Humans have brown, blue or green eyes.

   b Half the human population is male, half is female.

   c Cuttings of hydrangea plants grown in soils with different pH values develop flowers with slightly different colours.

d Some pea plants are tall; others are dwarf. However, the tall plants are not all exactly the same height and neither are all the dwarf plants the same height.

e People in some families are more at risk of heart disease than people in other families. However, not every member of the 'high risk' families has a heart attack and some members of the 'low risk' families do.

10 Warfarin is a pesticide that was developed to kill rats. When it was first used in 1950, it was very effective. Some rats, however, gained a new allele of a gene that made them resistant to warfarin. Nowadays the pesticide is much less effective.

a Use the ideas of natural selection to explain why warfarin is much less effective than it used to be.

b Suggest what might happen to the number of rats carrying the allele for warfarin resistance if warfarin were no longer used. Explain your answer.

11 Read the description below and answer the questions that follow.

Natural selection happens when a selection pressure favours individuals with particular characteristics, so that they have a selective advantage.

Some plants growing in areas contaminated by waste from mines have developed a tolerance to toxic metals such as lead and copper. They are able to grow on polluted soil, while non-tolerant plants are killed by the metals in the soil.

a How did the new tolerant varieties of plants arise?

b With reference to this example, explain the terms
  i selection pressure
  ii selective advantage
  iii natural selection.

c When metal-tolerant plants are grown on uncontaminated soil, they are out-competed by non-tolerant plants. Suggest a reason for this.

EXAM PRACTICE

SKILLS CRITICAL THINKING

1 The diagram shows *Hydra* (a small water animal) reproducing in two ways.

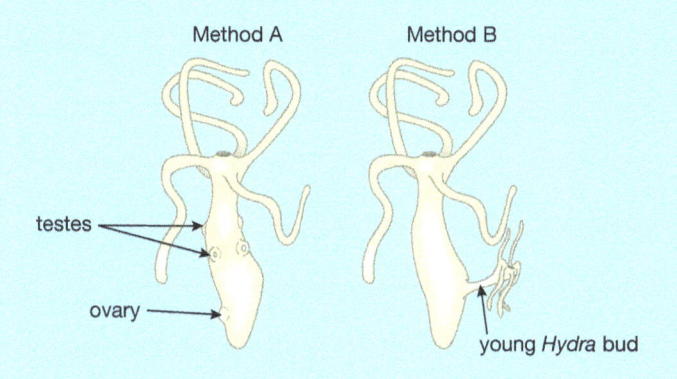

Method A — testes, ovary
Method B — young *Hydra* bud

a State which of the two methods shows asexual reproduction. Give a reason for your answer. (2)

b Explain why organisms produced asexually are genetically identical to each other and to the organism that produced them. (2)

c Explain why sexual reproduction increases genetic variation. (2)

d When the surroundings do not change for long periods, *Hydra* reproduces mainly asexually. When the conditions change, *Hydra* begins to reproduce sexually. Suggest how this pattern of asexual and sexual reproduction helps *Hydra* to survive. (2)

(Total 8 marks)

SKILLS CRITICAL THINKING

2 The drawing shows a wind-pollinated flower.

a Name the structures labelled A, B, C and D. (4)

b Give *three* pieces of evidence *visible in the diagram* that show that this flower is wind-pollinated. (3)

c Describe how fertilisation takes place once a flower has been pollinated. (3)

d Describe *four* ways in which you would expect an insect-pollinated flower to be different from the flower shown above. (4)

(Total 14 marks)

SKILLS CRITICAL THINKING

3 In cattle, a pair of alleles controls coat colour. The allele for black coat colour is dominant to the allele for red coat colour. The genetic diagram represents a cross between a pure-breeding black bull and a pure-breeding red cow.

B = dominant allele for black coat colour

b = recessive allele for red coat colour

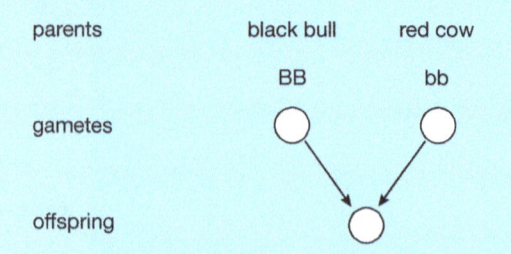

parents: black bull BB × red cow bb

gametes

offspring

a i Name the term that describes the genotypes of the pure-breeding parents. (1)
  ii Explain the terms dominant and recessive. (2)

SKILLS CRITICAL THINKING

b i State the genotypes of the gametes of each parent. (2)
  ii State the genotype of the offspring. (1)

c Cows and bulls both having the same genotype as the offspring were crossed with each other.
  i State the genetic term for this genotype. (1)

SKILLS INTERPRETATION, PROBLEM SOLVING

  ii Draw a genetic diagram to show this cross, and work out the ratios of:
     the genotypes of the offspring (2)
     the phenotypes of the offspring. (2)

(Total 11 marks)

SKILLS REASONING

4 For natural selection to operate, some factor has to exert a 'selection pressure'. In each of the following situations, identify both the selection pressure and the likely result of this selection pressure.

a Near old copper mines, the soil becomes polluted with copper ions that are toxic to most plants. (2)

b In the Serengeti (northern Tanzania), wildebeest are hunted by lions. (2)

c A farmer uses a pesticide to try to eliminate pests of a potato crop. (2)

(Total 6 marks)

SKILLS CRITICAL THINKING

5 In humans, which of the following produces egg cells?

A ovule

B ovary

C ovum

D oviduct

(Total 1 mark)

3 REPRODUCTION AND INHERITANCE — EXAM PRACTICE

SKILLS ANALYSIS

6 In the Galapagos Islands, Charles Darwin identified a number of species of birds, now known as Darwin's finches. He found evidence to suggest that they had all evolved from one ancestral type, which had colonised the islands having travelled from South America. The main differences between the finches were their beaks. The diagram shows some of the beak types for Darwin's finches and the beak type of the likely ancestral finch.

SKILLS FOOD SOURCE

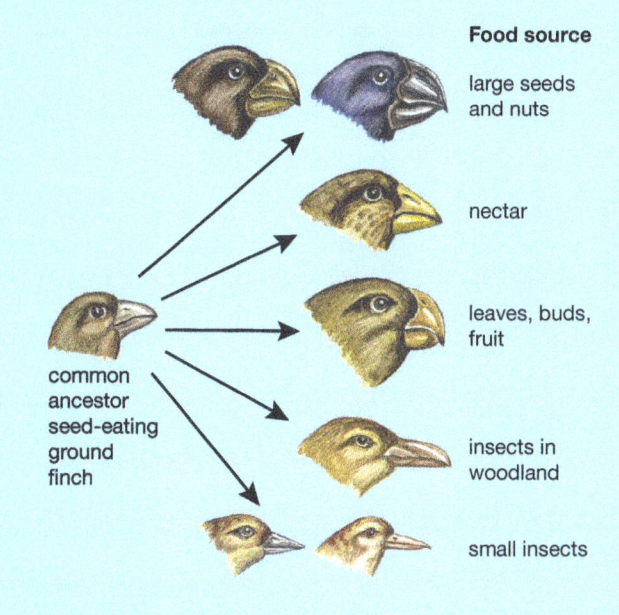

Food source
- large seeds and nuts
- nectar
- leaves, buds, fruit
- insects in woodland
- small insects

common ancestor seed-eating ground finch

a Describe how the finches that eat large seeds and nuts are adapted to their environment. (2)

b Describe how the finches that eat insects and live in woodland are adapted to their environment. (2)

SKILLS REASONING

c Using the information in the diagram, explain how the common ancestor could have evolved into the different type of finches. (4)

(Total 8 marks)

11 THE ORGANISM IN THE ENVIRONMENT 101 | 12 FEEDING RELATIONSHIPS AND CYCLES WITHIN ECOSYSTEMS 107

BIOLOGY UNIT 4
ECOLOGY AND THE ENVIRONMENT

Ecology is the scientific study of the interactions between organisms and their surroundings. It deals with both the interactions that living things have with each other and the interactions they have with their non-living, physical environment. Chapter 11 looks at the components of ecosystems and some of these interactions. Chapter 12 deals with feeding relationships and one example of a nutrient cycle in nature – the carbon cycle.

4 ECOLOGY AND THE ENVIRONMENT
11 THE ORGANISM IN THE ENVIRONMENT

11 THE ORGANISM IN THE ENVIRONMENT
SPECIFICATION REFERENCES: 4.1, 4.2, 4.5

This chapter looks at the make-up of ecosystems and some of the factors affecting organisms in an ecosystem.

LEARNING OBJECTIVES

- Understand the terms population, community, habitat and ecosystem.
- Investigate the population size of an organism in two different areas using quadrats.
- Understand how biotic and abiotic factors affect the population size and distribution of organisms.

THE COMPONENTS OF ECOSYSTEMS

An **ecosystem** consists of a distinct, self-supporting group of organisms *and* the physical surroundings that they live in. An ecosystem can be small, such as a pond (**Figure 11.1**), or large, such as a tropical rainforest or a mangrove swamp (**Figure 11.2**).

▲ Figure 11.1 A pond is a small ecosystem.

▲ Figure 11.2 A mangrove swamp is a larger ecosystem.

Whatever their size, ecosystems usually have the same components:

- **producers** – plants which photosynthesise to produce food
- **consumers** – animals that eat plants or other animals

- **decomposers** – organisms that break down dead material and help to recycle nutrients
- the physical environment – all the non-biological components of the ecosystem; for example, the water and soil in a pond or the soil and air in a forest.

The living components of an ecosystem are called the *biotic* components. (They are described in more detail in **Chapter 12**.) The non-living (physical) components are the *abiotic* components (compare these terms with **biotic factors** and **abiotic factors**, below).

An ecosystem contains a variety of habitats. A **habitat** is the place where an organism lives. For example, habitats in a pond ecosystem include the open water, the mud at the bottom of the pond and the surface water.

All the organisms of a particular species found in an ecosystem at a certain time form the **population** of that species. All the immature frogs (tadpoles) swimming in a pond are a population of tadpoles; all the water lily plants growing in the pond make up a population of water lilies.

The populations of *all* species (animals, plants and other organisms) found in an ecosystem at a particular time form the **community**. **Figure 11.3** illustrates the main components of a pond ecosystem.

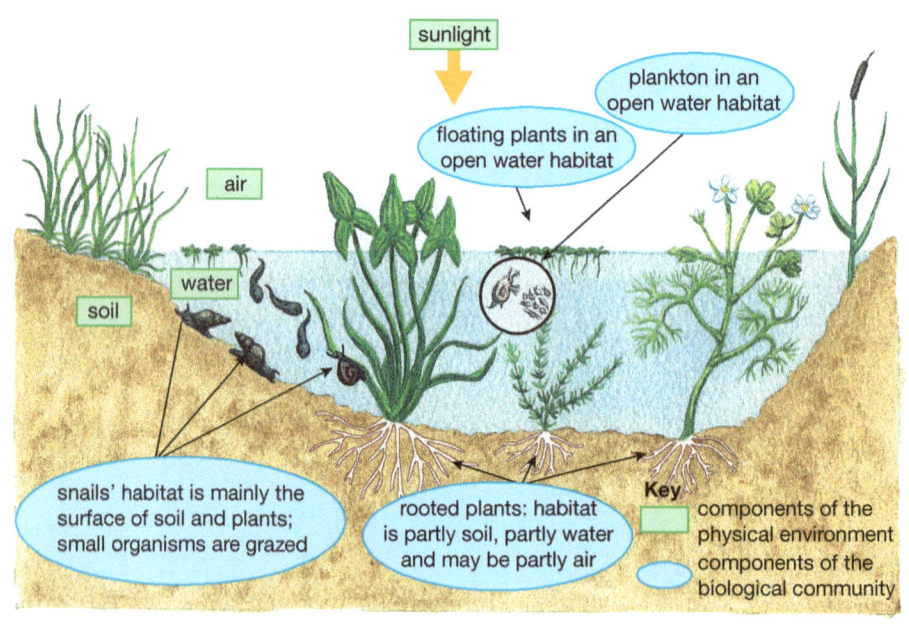

▲ Figure 11.3 A pond ecosystem

When an ecologist wants to know how many organisms there are in a particular habitat, it would not be possible to count them all. Instead, it is necessary to count a smaller representative part of the population, called a *sample*. Sampling of plants, or animals that do not move much (such as snails), can be done using a sampling square called a **quadrat**. A quadrat is usually made from metal, wood or plastic. The size of quadrat used depends on the size of the organisms being sampled. For example, to count plants growing on a school field, you could use a quadrat with sides 0.5 or 1 metre in length (**Figure 11.4**).

> **EXAM HINT**
>
> People often mistakenly call quadrats 'quadrants', with an unwanted 'n'. A *quadrant* is quite different – it is a quarter of a circle.

4 ECOLOGY AND THE ENVIRONMENT   11 THE ORGANISM IN THE ENVIRONMENT   103

KEY POINT

Some books (and even some teachers!) talk about 'throwing' quadrats. The idea is that you stand in the middle of a field and throw the quadrat over your shoulder. This is supposed to be random, but it certainly is not! The place where the quadrat falls will depend on where you choose to stand, how hard you throw it, etc. It is wrong to use this method.

Safety note: Wash hands after handling the quadrat, plants and soil.

▲ Figure 11.4 A student sampling with a quadrat

It is important that sampling in an area is carried out *at random*, to avoid bias. For example, if you were sampling from a school field, but for convenience only placed your quadrats next to a path, this probably would not give you a sample that was representative of the whole field. It would be a *biased* sample.

ACTIVITY 1

▼ PRACTICAL: USING QUADRATS TO COMPARE THE SIZE OF A PLANT POPULATION IN TWO AREAS OF A FIELD

One way that you can sample randomly is to place quadrats at co-ordinates on a numbered grid.

Imagine that there are two areas of a school field (A and B) that seem to contain different numbers of dandelion plants. Area A is more trampled than area B and looks like it contains fewer dandelions. This might lead you to propose the hypothesis: 'The dandelion population in area A is smaller than the dandelion population in area B'.

In area A, two 10-metre tape measures are arranged to form the sides of a square (**Figure 11.5**).

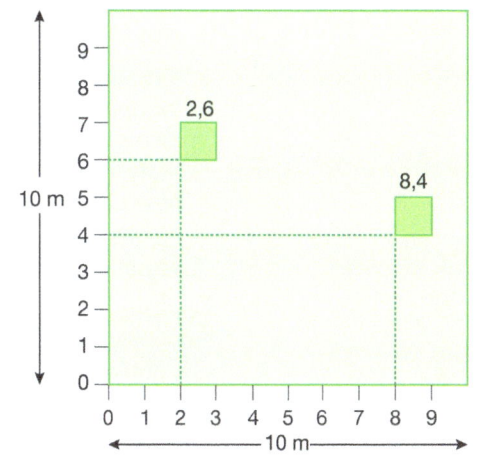

▲ Figure 11.5 A 10 m × 10 m grid with 1 m^2 quadrats positioned at co-ordinates 2,6 and 8,4.

A pair of random numbers is generated, using the random number function on a calculator. These numbers are used as co-ordinates to position the quadrat in the large square.

The numbers of dandelions in the quadrat are counted. The process is then repeated for nine more quadrats. The tape measures are then moved to area B and the process repeated to sample from ten more quadrats in that part of the field.

Table 11.1 shows a set of results for a study like this.

Table 11.1

Quadrat number	Number of dandelions in each quadrat in area A	Number of dandelions in each quadrat in area B
1	4	10
2	7	7
3	1	9
4	0	14
5	3	12
6	8	7
7	3	16
8	12	9
9	1	11
10	6	15

Calculate the mean number of dandelions per m² in each area. Do the results support the hypothesis that the population numbers are different? How could you improve the **reliability** of the results?

INTERACTIONS IN ECOSYSTEMS

The organisms in an ecosystem are continually interacting with each other and with their physical environment. Interactions include the following.

- Feeding among the organisms – the plants, animals and decomposers are continually recycling the same nutrients through the ecosystem.
- Competition among the organisms – animals compete for food, shelter, mates, nesting sites; plants compete for carbon dioxide, mineral ions, light and water.
- Interactions between organisms and the environment – plants absorb mineral ions, carbon dioxide and water from the environment; plants also give off water vapour and oxygen into the environment; animals use materials from the environment to build shelters; the temperature of the environment can affect processes occurring in the organisms; processes occurring in organisms can affect the temperature of the environment (all organisms produce some heat).

REMINDER

Do not forget that plants take in carbon dioxide and give out oxygen only when there is enough light for photosynthesis to occur efficiently. When there is little light, plants take in oxygen and give out carbon dioxide. You should be able to explain the reasons for this (see **Chapters 5** and **6**).

BIOTIC AND ABIOTIC FACTORS

There are many factors that influence the numbers and distribution of organisms in an ecosystem. There are two types of factor – *biotic* and *abiotic*.

Biotic factors are biological. Many (but not all) involve feeding relationships. They include:

- availability of food and competition for food resources
- predation
- parasitism
- disease
- presence of pollinating insects
- availability of nest sites.

Abiotic factors are physical or chemical factors. They include:

- climate, such as light intensity, temperature and water availability
- hours of daylight
- soil conditions, such as clay content, nitrate level, particle size, water content and pH
- other factors specific to a particular habitat, such as salinity (salt content) in an estuary, flow rate in a river or oxygen concentration in a lake
- pollution.

Clearly *which* factors affect population sizes and distribution of organisms will depend on the *type* of ecosystem. If you take the example of a river, some of the main abiotic factors could be:

- depth of water
- flow rate
- type of material at the bottom of the river (stones, sand, mud, etc.)
- concentration of minerals in the water
- pH
- oxygen concentration
- cloudiness of the water
- presence of any pollution.

The main biotic factors affecting animals in the river will be food supply, either from plants or other animals. But other factors are important too – for example, very large fish could not live in a shallow stream!

It is impossible to generalise about which factors are the most important. In a heavily polluted river all the organisms could be killed by the pollution, while in a clean river the depth and flow rate might have a greater effect on the animals that could live there. The different factors may also affect one another. For example, a faster flow rate could mix the water with air, increasing the amount of dissolved oxygen.

The main factor affecting large ecosystems is climate, particularly temperature and rainfall. Climate is the reason why **tropical rainforests** are restricted to a strip near the equator of the Earth, while pine forests grow in the higher latitudes of the Northern Hemisphere.

> **KEY POINT**
>
> A **predator** is an animal that kills and eats another animal. A **parasite** is an organism (animal or plant) that lives in or on another organism (called its host) and gets its nutrition from the host. For example, mosquitoes are parasites of humans (and other animals), and the human is the host of the mosquito.

> **EXTENSION**
>
> Large areas of the Earth that are dominated by a specific type of vegetation are called *biomes*. Temperate grassland and tropical rainforest are two examples of biomes. You could carry out some research to find out about these and other biomes.

CHAPTER QUESTIONS

Exam-style questions on the organism in the environment can be found at the end of Unit 4 on page 115.

SKILLS CRITICAL THINKING

1 Which of the following terms is defined as 'all the organisms living in a particular place and their interactions with each other and with their environment'?

   A habitat

   B population

   C community

   D ecosystem

SKILLS CRITICAL THINKING

2 Which of the following is a biotic factor?

   A light intensity

   B food supply

   C pollution

   D temperature

SKILLS CRITICAL THINKING

3 Which of the following is an abiotic factor?

   A predation

   B pollination

   C parasites

   D pollution

SKILLS CRITICAL THINKING

4 a Explain what is meant by each of the terms habitat, community, environment and population.

   b What are the roles of plants, animals and decomposers in an ecosystem?

SKILLS CRITICAL THINKING, CREATIVITY

5 a What is a quadrat?

   b What is meant by random sampling?

   c A student thought that more moss grew on the shady side of a wall than on the sunny side. Describe how you could use a quadrat to test her hypothesis.

12 FEEDING RELATIONSHIPS AND CYCLES WITHIN ECOSYSTEMS

SPECIFICATION REFERENCES: 4.6–4.10

The main biotic factors in any ecosystem are feeding relationships. This chapter looks at how substances and energy are passed between organisms in an ecosystem.

LEARNING OBJECTIVES

- Understand the names given to different trophic levels, including producers, primary, secondary and tertiary consumers, and decomposers.
- Understand the concept of food chains, food webs, pyramids of number, pyramids of biomass and pyramids of energy transfer.
- Understand the transfer of substances and energy along a food chain.
- Understand why only about 10% of energy is transferred from one trophic level to the next.
- Describe the stages in the carbon cycle, including respiration, photosynthesis, decomposition and combustion.

FEEDING RELATIONSHIPS

The simplest way of showing feeding relationships within an ecosystem is a **food chain** (**Figure 12.1**).

In any food chain, the arrow (→) means 'is eaten by'. In the food chain illustrated, the grass is the **producer**. It is a plant so it can photosynthesise and *produce* food materials. The grasshopper is the **primary consumer**. It is an animal which eats the producer and so is also known as a **herbivore** (something that eats plants). The lizard is the **secondary consumer**. It eats the primary consumer and is also known as a **carnivore** (something that eats animals). The different stages in a food chain (producer, primary consumer and secondary consumer) are called **trophic levels**.

Many food chains have more than three links in them. Here are two examples of longer food chains:

filamentous algae → mayfly nymph → caddis fly larvae → salmon

In this freshwater food chain, the extra link in the chain makes the salmon a **tertiary consumer**.

plankton → crustacean → fish → ringed seal → polar bear

This is a marine (sea) food chain. The polar bear is one step up from a tertiary consumer (sometimes called a quaternary consumer). Because nothing eats the polar bear, it is also called the *top carnivore*.

Food chains are a convenient way of showing the feeding relationships between a few organisms in an ecosystem, but they oversimplify the situation. The marine food chain above implies that only crustaceans feed on plankton, which is not true. Some whales and other mammals also feed on plankton. For a fuller understanding, you need to consider how the different food chains in an ecosystem relate to each other. **Figure 12.2** gives a clearer picture of the

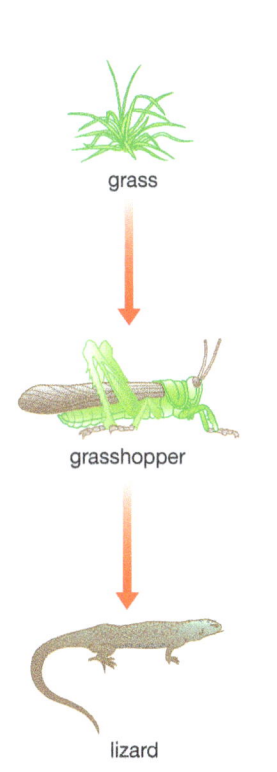

▲ Figure 12.1 A simple food chain

feeding relationships involved in a freshwater ecosystem in which salmon are the top carnivores. This is the **food web** of the salmon.

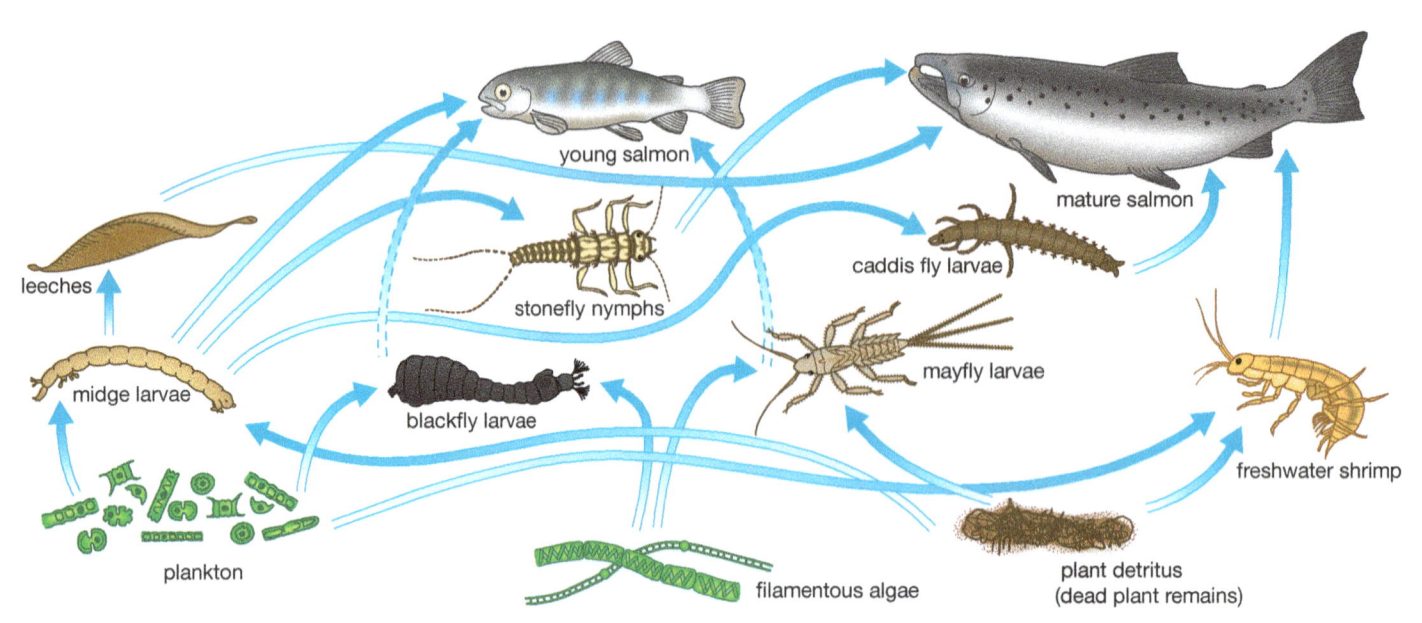

▲ Figure 12.2 The food web of the salmon. As you can see, young salmon have a slightly different diet from mature salmon.

Even **Figure 12.2** is a simplified version of the true situation, as some feeding relationships are still not shown. It does, however, give some idea of the interrelationships between food chains in an ecosystem. With a little thought, you can predict how changes in the numbers of one organism in a food chain in the web might affect the numbers of organisms in another food chain in the web. For example, if the leech population in **Figure 12.2** declined through disease, there could be several possible consequences:

- the stonefly nymph population could increase, as there would be more midge larvae to feed on
- the stonefly nymph population could decrease, as the mature salmon might eat more of them as there would be fewer leeches for the mature salmon to eat
- the numbers could remain the same due to a combination of the above.

Although food webs give us more information than food chains, they do not tell us how many organisms are involved, or what the mass of the organisms is. Nor do they show the role of the **decomposers**.

THE ROLE OF DECOMPOSERS

The food web shown in **Figure 12.2** is incomplete. It does not show what happens to substances in the bodies of organisms when they die and decay. Plants die and shed leaves, flowers and other parts. Animals die and also produce waste products. All of these materials are recycled by certain groups of organisms. Larger animals such as worms feed upon them, starting the process of breakdown. Dead material and waste products are also used as a food source by decomposers. Decomposers are saprotrophic bacteria and fungi (see **Chapter 1**). These micro-organisms make up the final stage in any food chain. **Decomposition** releases nutrients so that they can be used again. For example, organic molecules are respired by decomposers, producing carbon dioxide. The carbon dioxide is then available to plants for photosynthesis (see the carbon cycle, below). Eventually decomposers themselves die and are broken down by other decomposers. And so the cycle continues…

ECOLOGICAL PYRAMIDS

Ecological pyramids are diagrams that represent the relative amounts of organisms at each trophic level in a food chain. There are two main types:

- **pyramids of numbers**, which represent the numbers of organisms in each trophic level in a food chain, irrespective of their mass
- **pyramids of biomass**, which show the total mass of the organisms in each trophic level, irrespective of their numbers.

Consider these two food chains:

a grass → grasshopper → frog → bird
b oak tree → aphid → ladybird → bird

Figures 12.3 and **12.4** show the pyramids of numbers and biomass for these two food chains.

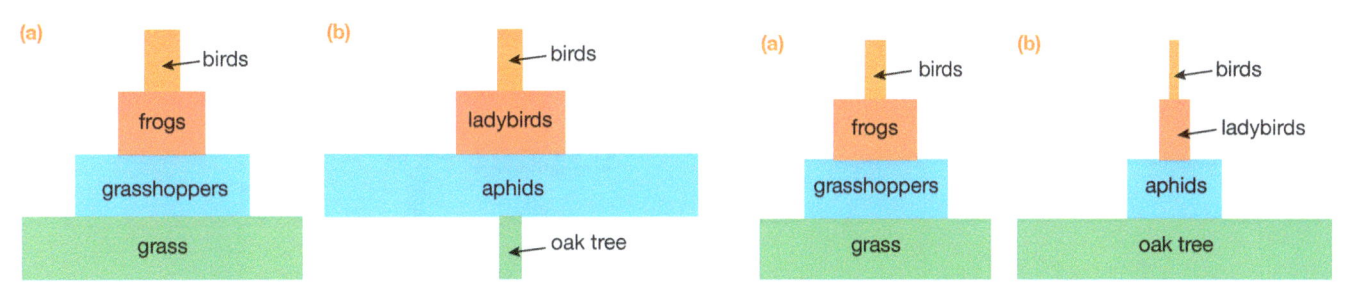

▲ Figure 12.3 Pyramids of numbers for two food chains

▲ Figure 12.4 Pyramids of biomass for the same two food chains

KEY POINT

Biomass is the total mass of organisms. If it refers to living organisms, this is called the *fresh biomass*. More commonly the *dry biomass* is used. This is the mass of plant or animal material after water has been removed, by drying in an oven. Dry biomass is a more reliable measure, since the water content of organisms (especially plants) varies with environmental conditions.

KEY POINT

Another way of describing a food chain is that it shows how energy is moved from one organism to another as a result of feeding. The arrows show the direction of energy flow.

The two pyramids for the 'grass' food chain look the same – the numbers at each trophic level decrease. The *total* biomass also decreases along the food chain – the mass of *all* the grass plants in a large field would be more than the mass of *all* the grasshoppers, which would be more than the mass of *all* the frogs, and so on.

The two pyramids for the 'oak tree' food chain look different because of the size of an oak tree. Each oak tree can support many thousands of aphids, so the numbers *increase* from the first trophic level to second. But each ladybird will need to eat many aphids and each bird will need to eat many ladybirds, so the numbers *decrease* at the third and fourth trophic levels. However, the total biomass *decreases* at each trophic level – the biomass of one oak tree is much greater than that of the thousands of aphids it supports. The total biomass of all these aphids is greater than that of the ladybirds, which is greater than that of the birds.

Suppose the birds in the second food chain have nematode worms as parasites (small worms living in the bird's gut). The food chain now becomes:

oak tree → aphid → ladybird → bird → nematode worm

The pyramid of numbers now takes on a very strange appearance, because of the large numbers of parasites in each bird (**Figure 12.5a**). The pyramid of biomass, however, has a true pyramid shape because the total biomass of the nematode worms must be less than that of the birds in which they are parasites (**Figure 12.5b**).

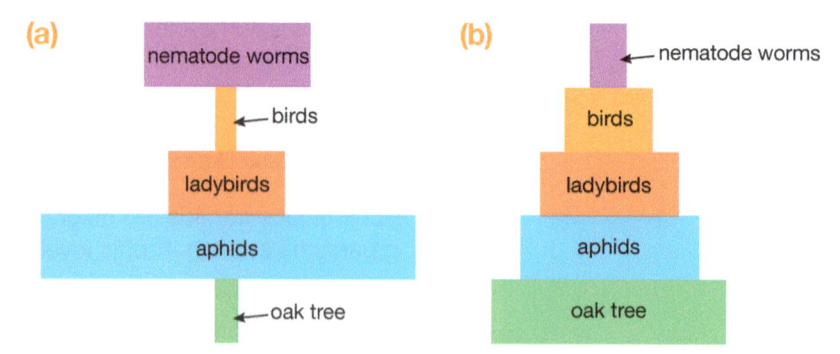

▲ Figure 12.5 (a) A pyramid of numbers and (b) a pyramid of biomass for a food chain involving parasites

WHY ARE DIAGRAMS OF FEEDING RELATIONSHIPS PYRAMID SHAPED?

The explanation for the pyramid-shaped diagrams is relatively straightforward (**Figure 12.6**). When a rabbit eats grass, not all of the materials in the grass plant end up as rabbit. There are losses:

- some parts of the grass are not eaten (the roots for example)
- some parts are not digested and so are not absorbed
- some of the materials absorbed become excretory products
- many of the materials are respired to release energy, with the loss of carbon dioxide and water.

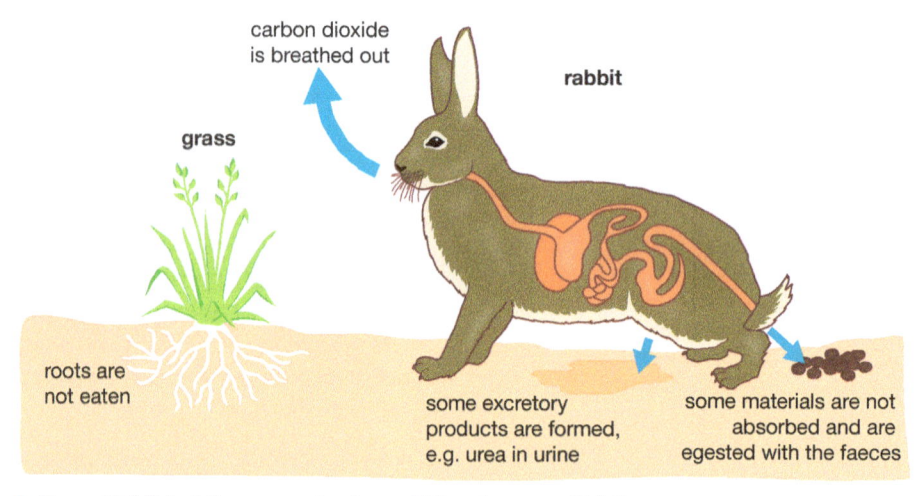

▲ Figure 12.6 Not all the grass eaten by a rabbit ends up as rabbit tissue

In fact, only a small fraction of the materials in the grass ends up in new cells in the rabbit. Similar losses are repeated at each stage in the food chain, so smaller and smaller amounts of biomass are available for growth at successive trophic levels. The shape of pyramids of biomass reflects this.

Feeding is a way of transferring energy between organisms. Another way of modelling ecosystems looks at the energy flow between the various trophic levels.

THE FLOW OF ENERGY THROUGH ECOSYSTEMS

Energy flow diagrams show the transfer of energy between trophic levels in the whole ecosystem. There are a number of key ideas involved:

- photosynthesis fixes light energy into chemical energy in organic compounds such as glucose and starch

- respiration releases energy from compounds such as glucose
- other biological processes (e.g. muscle contraction, growth, active transport) use the energy released from respiration.
- if the energy from respiration is used to drive chemical reactions to produce new cells, then the energy remains 'fixed' in molecules in that organism and it can be passed on to the next trophic level through feeding.
- if the energy from respiration is used for other processes then it will eventually be lost from organisms as heat; energy is therefore lost from food chains and webs at each trophic level.

Figure 12.7 is an energy flow diagram. It shows the main ways in which energy is transferred in an ecosystem. It also gives the amounts of energy transferred between the trophic levels of this particular (grassland) ecosystem.

As you can see, only about 10% of the energy entering a trophic level is passed on to the next trophic level. This explains why not many food chains have more than five trophic levels. Think of the food chain:

$$A \rightarrow B \rightarrow C \rightarrow D \rightarrow E$$

If we assume that only about 10% of the energy entering a trophic level is passed on to the next level, then, of the original 100% at A (a producer), 10% passes to B, 1% (10% of 10%) passes to C, 0.1% passes to D and only 0.001% passes to E. There is just not enough energy left for another trophic level. Some marine food chains have six trophic levels because of the huge amount of light energy reaching the surface waters, but most food chains have fewer stages than this.

THE CARBON CYCLE

The atoms that make up our bodies have always existed on the Earth. When we die, they are recycled by decomposers and passed through food chains, becoming part of the bodies of other plants and animals. This constant recycling of substances is all part of the cycle of life, death and decay.

Micro-organisms play a key role in this recycling. Bacteria and fungi in the soil and elsewhere are decomposers. They break down complex organic molecules in the bodies of dead plants and animals into simpler substances, which are released into the environment.

Carbon is an element present in most biological molecules (see **Chapter 3**). Carbohydrates, proteins, lipids, DNA and many other molecules contain carbon. It is recycled by a number of different processes linked together to form the carbon cycle.

The following processes are important in cycling carbon through ecosystems:
- photosynthesis turns carbon atoms from carbon dioxide into organic compounds
- feeding, digestion and building new organic molecules pass carbon atoms already in organic compounds along food chains
- respiration produces inorganic carbon dioxide from organic compounds (mainly carbohydrates) as they are broken down to release energy
- formation of fossil fuels traps carbon in coal, oil and gas (note: the process of fossilisation takes millions of years)
- combustion (burning) of fossil fuels or wood releases carbon dioxide into the atmosphere when fuels are burned.

▲ Figure 12.7 The main ways in which energy is transferred in an ecosystem. The amounts of energy transferred through 1 m² of a grassland ecosystem per year are shown in brackets.

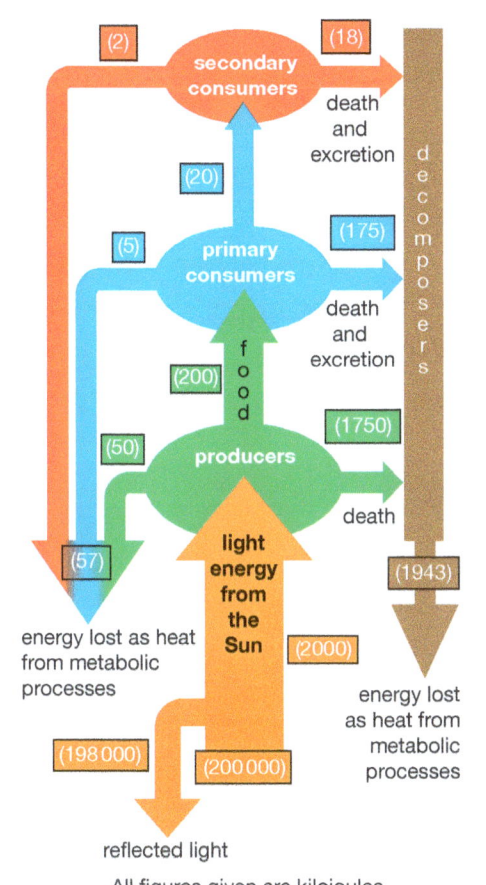

All figures given are kilojoules (×10⁵) per m² per year.

DID YOU KNOW?
Could you explain what an organic compound is? There is no precise definition! All organic compounds contain carbon and *most* contain hydrogen. Starch and glucose are organic molecules, but carbon dioxide (CO_2) is not; it is inorganic.

Figures 12.8 and **12.9** show the role of these processes in the carbon cycle in two different ways.

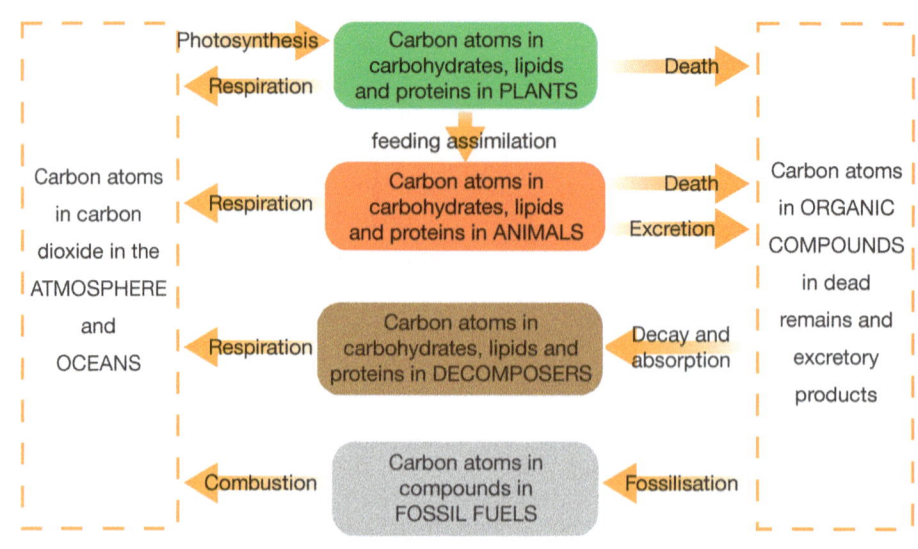

▲ Figure 12.8 The main processes in the carbon cycle

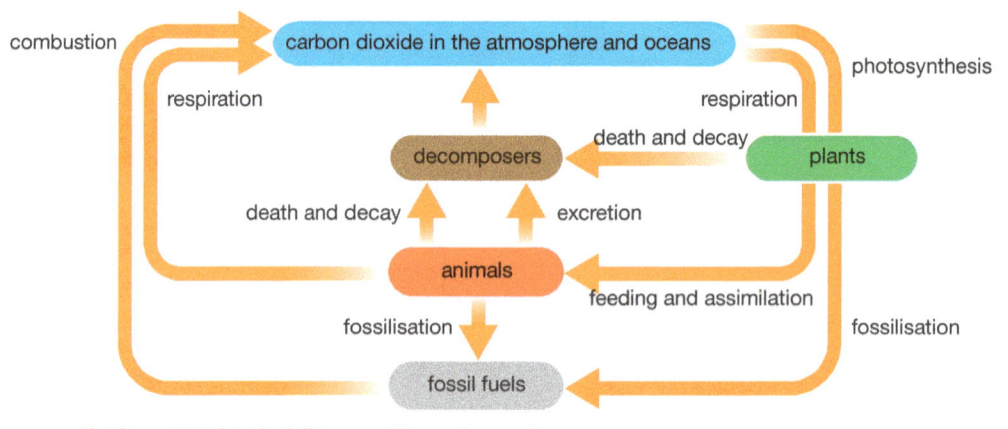

▲ Figure 12.9 A typical diagram of the carbon cycle

CHAPTER QUESTIONS

Exam-style questions on feeding relationships and cycles within ecosystems can be found at the end of Unit 4 on page 115.

SKILLS CRITICAL THINKING

1 The diagram below shows a food web containing four food chains.

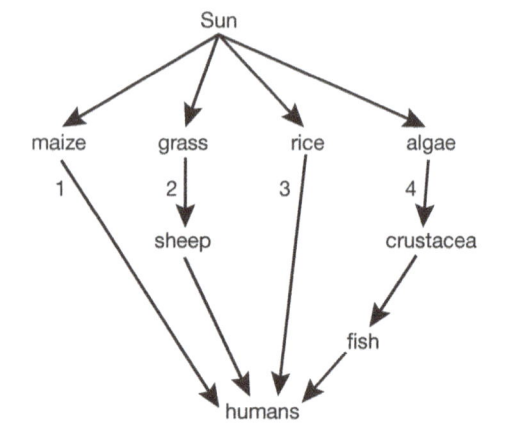

4 ECOLOGY AND THE ENVIRONMENT   12 FEEDING RELATIONSHIPS AND CYCLES WITHIN ECOSYSTEMS   113

Which food chains are most efficient at using energy from the Sun?

A 1 and 3

B 2 and 4

C 2 and 3

D 3 and 4

SKILLS CRITICAL THINKING

2 Which of the following processes does *not* affect the carbon cycle today?

A fossilisation

B respiration

C combustion

D photosynthesis

SKILLS CRITICAL THINKING

3 A marine food chain is shown below.

plankton → small crustacean → krill → seal → killer whale

a Which organism is:

  i the producer

  ii the secondary consumer?

b What term best describes the killer whale?

SKILLS REASONING

c Suggest why five trophic levels are possible in this case, when many food chains only have three or four.

SKILLS INTERPRETATION

4 Part (a) of the diagram below shows a woodland food web. Part (b) shows a pyramid of numbers and a pyramid of biomass for a small part of this wood.

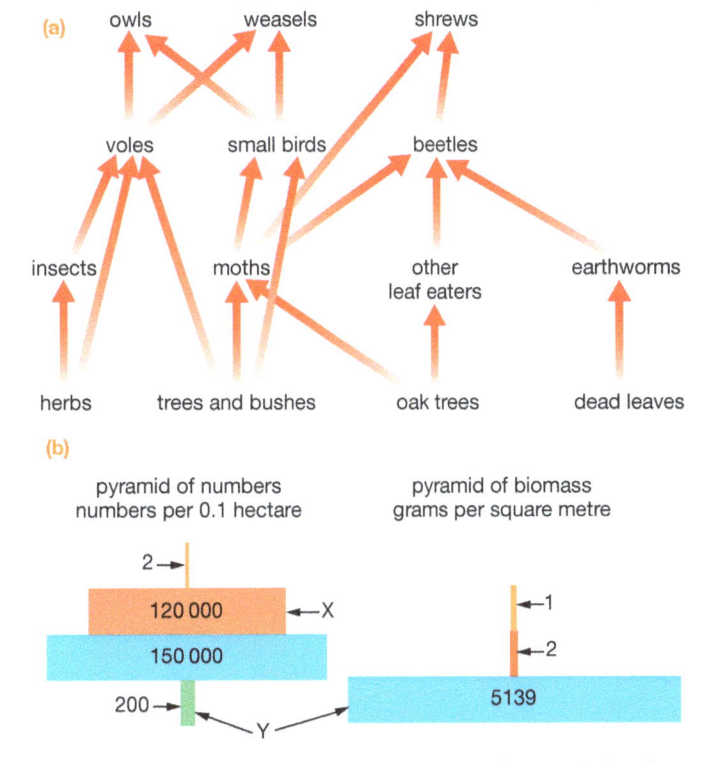

(a) owls, weasels, shrews, voles, small birds, beetles, insects, moths, other leaf eaters, earthworms, herbs, trees and bushes, oak trees, dead leaves

(b) pyramid of numbers — numbers per 0.1 hectare: 2, 120 000 ←X, 150 000, 200→ ...Y

pyramid of biomass — grams per square metre: 1, 2, 5139

a Write out *two* food chains (from the food web) containing four organisms, both involving moths.

b Name *one* organism in the food web which is both a primary consumer and a secondary consumer.

c Suggest how a reduction in the quantity of dead leaves may lead to a reduction in the numbers of shrews.

d In part (b) of the diagram, explain why level Y is such a different width in the two pyramids.

SKILLS INTERPRETATION

5 A tree contains a population of 200 herbivorous beetles. The beetles are preyed upon by a pair of insect-eating birds. Several parasitic mites live in the birds' feathers, feeding on the birds' blood.

a Sketch a pyramid of numbers and a pyramid of biomass for this ecosystem.

b Explain why the two pyramids are a different shape.

c State *three* ways that energy is lost by the birds.

EXAM PRACTICE

SKILLS CRITICAL THINKING

1 What is the approximate amount of energy that passes from one trophic level to the next higher level?

A 0.1%

B 1%

C 10%

D 100%

(Total 1 mark)

SKILLS INTERPRETATION

2 The diagram shows a simplified food web of a fish, the herring.

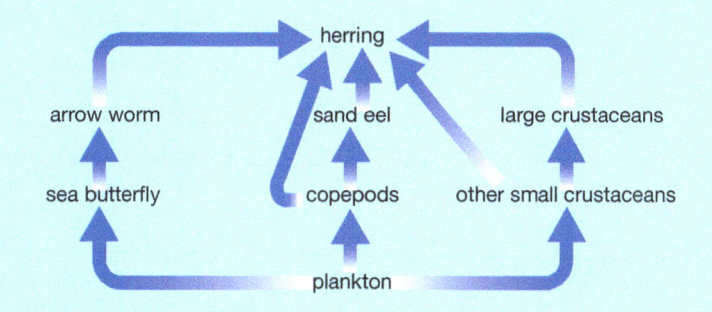

SKILLS ANALYSIS

a i From the food web, draw a food chain containing four organisms. (1)

ii From your food chain, name the primary consumer and secondary consumer. (2)

iii Name one organism in the web that is both a secondary consumer and a tertiary consumer. Explain your answer. (2)

b The amount of energy in each trophic level is shown in the following food chain. The units are kJ per m^2 per year.

plankton (8869) → copepod (892) → herring (91)

SKILLS INTERPRETATION

SKILLS PROBLEM SOLVING

i Sketch a pyramid of energy for this food chain. (1)

ii Calculate the percentage of energy entering the plankton that passes to the copepod. (2)

iii Calculate the percentage of energy entering the copepod that passes to the herring. (2)

SKILLS REASONING

iv Describe *two* ways in which energy is lost in the transfer from the copepod to the herring. (2)

(Total 12 marks)

3 The carbon cycle shows how carbon is passed through ecosystems by the actions of plants, animals and decomposers. Humans influence the carbon cycle more than other animals.

   a Explain the importance of plants in the carbon cycle. (2)

   b State what human activity significantly affects the world carbon cycle. (1)

   c The graph shows the activity of decomposers acting on the bodies of dead animals under different conditions.

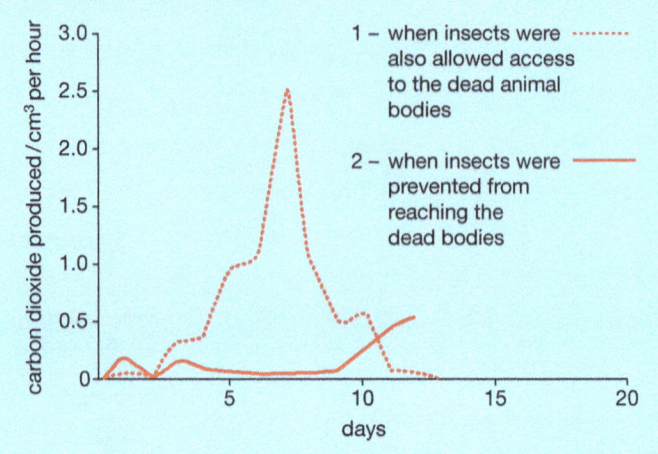

   i Explain why carbon dioxide production was used as a measure of the activity of the decomposers. (2)

   ii Describe and suggest a reason for the changes in decomposer activity when insects were also allowed access to the dead bodies (curve 1). (3)

   iii Describe *two* differences between curves 1 and 2. Suggest an explanation for the differences you describe. (4)

   (Total 12 marks)

4 Copy and complete the following description of the carbon cycle:

Plants take up _____ from the air during photosynthesis, using the carbon to form organic substances such as glucose. Plants are eaten by _____ consumers and the carbon is passed along a food chain.

Dead organic material and _____ products provide the energy source for decomposers, which are bacteria and _____ .

Most organisms pass carbon dioxide to the air by the process of _____ . Burning fossil fuels such as _____ , natural gas and oil adds to the level of carbon dioxide in the air.

(Total 6 marks)

4 ECOLOGY AND THE ENVIRONMENT — EXAM PRACTICE

SKILLS PROBLEM SOLVING

5 In a year, 1 m² of grass produces 21 500 kJ of energy. The diagram below shows the fate of the energy transferred to a cow feeding on the grass.

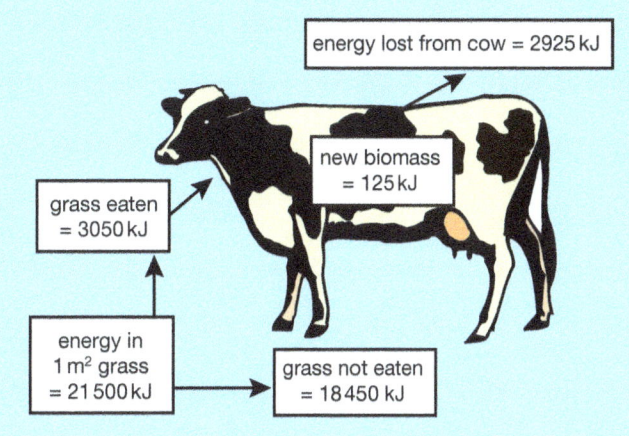

- energy lost from cow = 2925 kJ
- new biomass = 125 kJ
- grass eaten = 3050 kJ
- energy in 1 m² grass = 21 500 kJ
- grass not eaten = 18 450 kJ

a Calculate the energy efficiency of the cow from the following equation. (2)

$$\text{energy efficiency} = \frac{\text{energy that ends up as part of cow}}{\text{energy available}} \times 100$$

SKILLS CRITICAL THINKING

SKILLS REASONING

b State *two* ways that energy is lost from the cow. (2)

c Suggest what may happen to the 18 450 kJ of energy in the grass that was not eaten by the cow. (3)

(Total 7 marks)

| 13 FOOD PRODUCTION 119 | 14 GENETIC MODIFICATION (GENETIC ENGINEERING) 125 |

BIOLOGY UNIT 5
USE OF BIOLOGICAL RESOURCES

This unit covers some aspects of the use of biological resources. Chapter 13 looks at two ways we have used our understanding of biology in food production. There are a few species of micro-organisms that are grown by humans to make useful products. One of these is yeast, a fungus used to make traditional biotechnology products such as bread. In modern biotechnology, micro-organisms can be genetically engineered to make new products. This is described in Chapter 14.

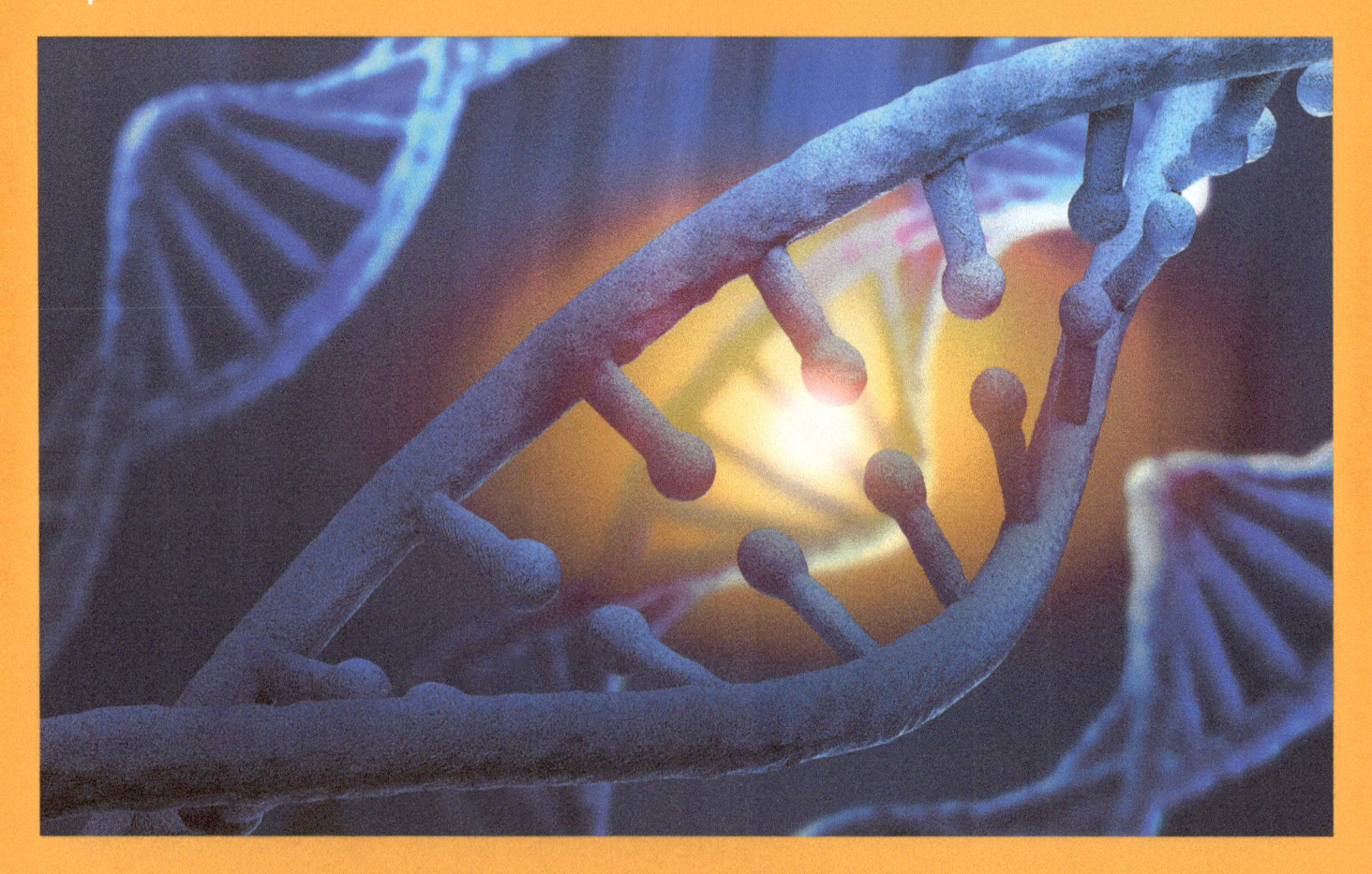

13 FOOD PRODUCTION

SPECIFICATION REFERENCES: 5.1, 5.2, 5.5, 5.6

This chapter looks at two ways that our understanding of biology is useful in food production – the use of glasshouses to increase the growth of crops and the use of yeast in the production of bread.

LEARNING OBJECTIVES

- Describe how glasshouses and polythene tunnels can be used to increase the yield of certain crops.
- Understand the effects on crop yield of increased carbon dioxide and increased temperature in glasshouses.
- Understand the role of yeast in the production of food, including bread.
- Investigate the rate of anaerobic respiration by yeast in different conditions.

DID YOU KNOW?
The *yield* of a crop is the total amount of crop produced for sale.

GLASSHOUSES AND POLYTHENE TUNNELS

Glasshouses (**Figure 13.1**) and polythene tunnels (**Figure 13.2**) are both used to increase the rate of growth of certain crop plants and so increase their yield.

▲ Figure 13.1 A glasshouse maintains a favourable environment for plants. These plants are being grown in a soil-free culture solution (hydroponics).

▲ Figure 13.2 Many crops are grown in large tunnels made of transparent polythene.

Glasshouses (also known as 'greenhouses') and polythene tunnels ('polytunnels') can provide very controlled conditions for plants to grow. There are a number of reasons for this.

- The transparent walls of a glasshouse allow enough natural light for photosynthesis during the summer months. During the winter additional artificial lighting can be used to increase light intensity and extend the 'length of daylight'.
- The temperature inside a glasshouse is raised by the 'greenhouse effect'. Infrared radiation from the Sun entering the glasshouse is absorbed by the soil and re-radiated at a longer wavelength. This radiation cannot escape through the glass, so the inside of the glasshouse heats up. The glasshouse also reduces convection currents in the air, which would otherwise cause cooling.

- The glasshouse can be heated to raise the temperature inside if the outside temperature falls too low.
- If heaters are used that burn fossil fuels such as natural gas, this produces carbon dioxide and water vapour. Carbon dioxide is a raw material for photosynthesis. Water vapour maintains a moist atmosphere and reduces water loss from the plants.
- Carbon dioxide can be directly added to the air in the glasshouse, from tanks of the gas or other sources.
- In some glasshouses, the plants are grown with their roots in a soil-free culture solution (see **Figure 13.1**). This is called hydroponics. The solution provides exactly the right balance of minerals that the plant needs. It is also easier to keep the plants free from soil pathogens that could cause disease and reduce yield.

> **DID YOU KNOW?**
> One simple and cheap way of adding extra carbon dioxide is to use 'exhale bags', which are filled with a mycelium of fungi that give off steady amounts of the gas from their respiration.

THE EFFECTS OF INCREASED CARBON DIOXIDE AND INCREASED TEMPERATURE ON CROP YIELD IN GLASSHOUSES

Around the world, the most commonly grown commercial glasshouse crops are:
- fruits, such as tomatoes, strawberries, melons, peppers and cucumbers
- leaves such as lettuce, Chinese cabbage and some herbs.

All parts of a plant are made by photosynthesis, so the yield of any of these crops is directly related to the rate of photosynthesis.

How can we predict how carbon dioxide and temperature will affect crop yield in a glasshouse or polythene tunnel? To do this, we can use our knowledge of photosynthesis. You saw in **Chapter 5** that the rate of photosynthesis mainly depends on three limiting factors – light intensity, carbon dioxide concentration in the air and temperature (**Figure 13.3**).

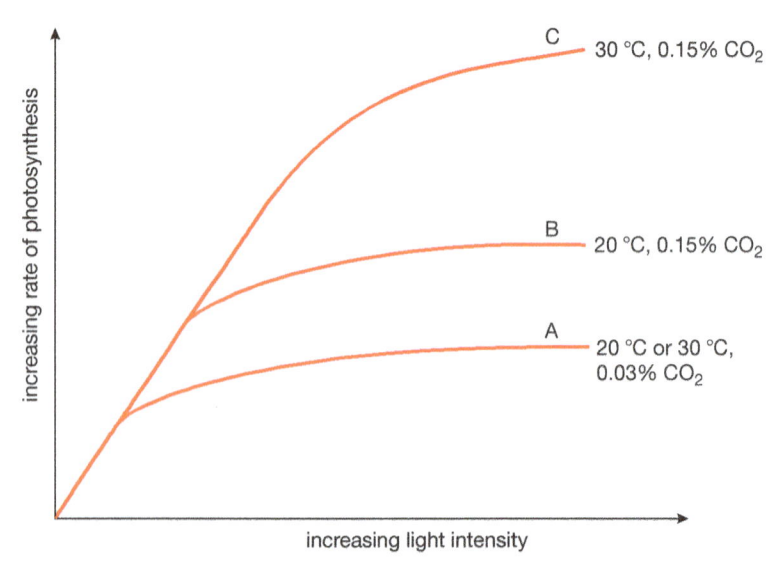

▲ Figure 13.3 Light intensity, carbon dioxide concentration and temperature can all affect the rate of photosynthesis

Curve C: 30 °C, 0.15% CO_2
Curve B: 20 °C, 0.15% CO_2
Curve A: 20 °C or 30 °C, 0.03% CO_2

If the light intensity in the glasshouse is high, the limiting factor for photosynthesis is the concentration of carbon dioxide in the air (point A on the lowest curve in **Figure 13.3**). Raising the carbon dioxide levels increases the rate of photosynthesis (point B on the middle curve). At this point temperature is the limiting factor, so increasing temperature increases the rate again (point C on the upper curve).

The glasshouse owner may decide to raise the concentration of carbon dioxide and increase the temperature, in order to maximise photosynthesis and the yield of the crop.

You might expect the owner to try to maintain conditions at point C on the graph. There are two reasons why this may not be a good idea:

- Different plant species vary in their responses to changing levels of carbon dioxide and temperature. A particular crop species may not fit on the curves shown in **Figure 13.3**.
- The farmer has to balance the income gained from the crop against the costs involved in lighting and heating the glasshouse and in burning the fuel to make carbon dioxide. If the farmer's costs are greater than the profits, there is no point in getting the extra yield, because overall there will be a financial loss.

Each crop needs some scientific research to find out the optimum levels of light, carbon dioxide and temperature to achieve the best growth and yield. However, altering these factors can have a big effect on the yield. For example, raising the amount of carbon dioxide from the normal level in the air (0.04%) to 0.1% can increase the yield of some types of tomatoes by 50%.

USING YEAST TO MAKE BREAD

You saw in **Chapter 6** that when yeast cells are deprived of oxygen, they respire anaerobically, breaking sugar down into ethanol and carbon dioxide:

glucose → ethanol + carbon dioxide

This process has been used for thousands of years to make bread, using a species of yeast called *Saccharomyces cerevisiae*.

Yeast is used to make bread. Wheat flour and water are mixed together and yeast added, forming the bread dough. Enzymes from the original cereal grains break down starch to sugars, and the sugars are respired by the yeast. Extra sugar may be added at this stage. In bread-making, the yeast begins by respiring aerobically, producing water and carbon dioxide. The carbon dioxide makes the dough rise. When the air runs out, conditions become anaerobic, so the yeast begins to respire anaerobically making ethanol and more carbon dioxide.

Later, when the dough is baked in the oven, the gas bubbles expand. This gives the bread a light, cellular texture (**Figure 13.4**). Baking also kills the yeast cells and evaporates any ethanol.

(a)

(b)

▲ Figure 13.4 (a) The 'holes' in this bread were produced by bubbles of carbon dioxide released from the respiration of the yeast. (b) Bread that is made without yeast is called unleavened bread. What is the difference in texture and appearance between leavened and unleavened bread?

Safety note: Wear eye protection and avoid skin contact with the indicator.

ACTIVITY 1

▼ **PRACTICAL: INVESTIGATING THE RATE OF ANAEROBIC RESPIRATION IN YEAST**

Some simple apparatus and materials can be used to investigate the rate of anaerobic respiration in yeast.

A small amount of water is gently boiled in a boiling tube to remove any air that is dissolved in the water. The water is allowed to cool, and a small amount of sugar (glucose or sucrose) is dissolved in the water. Finally, a little yeast is added and the mixture is stirred.

The apparatus is set up as shown in **Figure 13.5**.

liquid paraffin

limewater or hydrogen-carbonate indicator solution

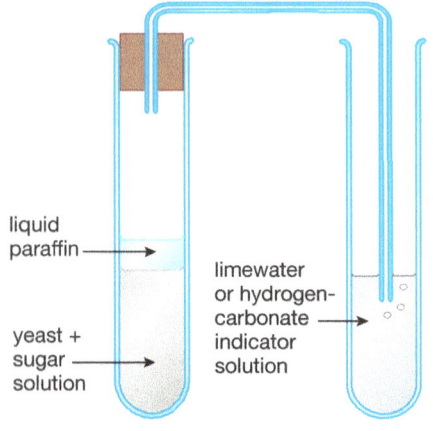

yeast + sugar solution

▲ Figure 13.5 Apparatus to test for carbon dioxide produced by anaerobic respiration in yeast

5 USE OF BIOLOGICAL RESOURCES 13 FOOD PRODUCTION

A thin layer of liquid paraffin is added to the surface of the mixture, using a pipette. Boiling the water ensures that there is no oxygen in the mixture at the start of the experiment, and the layer of paraffin stops any oxygen diffusing in from the air. A control apparatus is set up. This is exactly the same as that shown in **Figure 13.5**, except that boiled (killed) yeast is used instead of living yeast.

Both sets of apparatus are left in a warm place for an hour or two. The mixture with living yeast will be seen to produce gas bubbles. The gas passes through the delivery tube and into the indicator in the second boiling tube.

If this second tube contains limewater, it will turn cloudy (milky). If it contains hydrogencarbonate indicator, the indicator will change from orange to yellow. Both tests show that the gas is carbon dioxide. The time taken for the indicator to change colour is recorded and compared with the control (which will not change).

(If the bung is taken out of the first boiling tube and the liquid paraffin removed using a pipette, the tube will smell of alcohol.)

This method can be used to test predictions, such as how:

- the type of sugar (glucose, sucrose, maltose, etc.) affects the rate of respiration of the yeast
- the concentration of sugar affects the rate of respiration of the yeast
- the temperature affects the rate of respiration of the yeast.

The rate can be found by timing how quickly the indicator changes colour, or from the rate of production of bubbles of carbon dioxide. You could plan experiments to test these hypotheses.

CHAPTER QUESTIONS

Exam-style questions on food production can be found at the end of Unit 5 on page 132.

SKILLS CRITICAL THINKING

1 What is the main factor that can increase crop yield in an unheated polytunnel?

 A temperature

 B carbon dioxide concentration

 C light intensity

 D day length

SKILLS CRITICAL THINKING

2 The apparatus below was used to measure the rate of anaerobic respiration of yeast by counting bubbles of gas passing through the water in the second test tube. What is the purpose of the layer of liquid paraffin?

 A to prevent oxygen leaving the tube

 B to prevent oxygen entering the tube

 C to prevent carbon dioxide leaving the tube

 D to prevent carbon dioxide entering the tube

[Diagram: test tube containing yeast + sugar solution with liquid paraffin layer, connected via delivery tube to another test tube containing water]

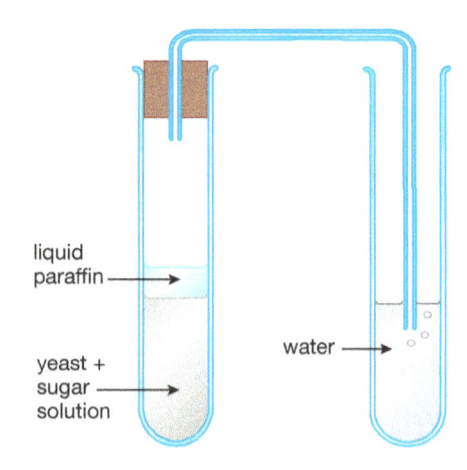

SKILLS INTERPRETATION

3 a Glasshouses allow crops to be grown under very controlled conditions. Explain how glasshouses can be used to control the following:
   i light intensity
   ii temperature
   iii carbon dioxide level.

b A farmer grows tomatoes in a glasshouse. On a bright sunny day, the temperature in the glasshouse is 28 °C and the atmosphere inside the greenhouse contains 0.04% carbon dioxide. Which factor is likely to be limiting the rate of photosynthesis of the tomato plants?

SKILLS INTERPRETATION

4 a Explain the role of yeast in making bread.

b What happens to the bread if a baker forgets to add yeast to the dough mix?

14 GENETIC MODIFICATION (GENETIC ENGINEERING) SPECIFICATION REFERENCES: 5.12–5.16

In this chapter we will look at ways in which it is possible to manipulate genes and produce genetically modified (GM) organisms. This is the science of 'genetic engineering'.

LEARNING OBJECTIVES

- Understand how restriction enzymes are used to cut DNA at specific sites and ligase enzymes are used to join pieces of DNA together.
- Understand how plasmids and viruses can act as vectors, which take up pieces of DNA, and then insert this recombinant DNA into other cells.
- Understand how large amounts of human insulin can be manufactured from genetically modified bacteria.
- Understand how genetically modified plants can be used to improve food production.
- Understand that the term *transgenic* means the transfer of genetic material from one species to a different species.

KEY POINT

A transgenic organism is one that contains a gene that has been introduced from another species. The transgenic organism is commonly a micro-organism such as a bacterium or yeast, but there are also transgenic plants and animals that have been engineered with genes from other species.

RECOMBINANT DNA

The production of **recombinant DNA** is the basis of genetic engineering. A section of DNA – a gene – is cut out of the DNA of one species and inserted into the DNA of another. This new DNA is called recombinant because the DNA from two different organisms has been 'recombined'. The organism that receives the gene from a different species is a **transgenic** organism.

The organism receiving the new gene will be able to express that gene. For example, if a bacterium is given the human gene that codes for the production of the hormone insulin, the bacterium will then be able to make human insulin. Countless billions of these transgenic bacteria can be grown in a special vessel called a bioreactor. They then become a 'factory' for making human insulin.

PLASMIDS, RESTRICTION ENZYMES AND LIGASES

The breakthrough in being able to transfer DNA from cell to cell came when it was found that bacteria have two sorts of DNA – the DNA found in their bacterial chromosome and much smaller circular pieces of DNA called **plasmids** (see **Chapter 1**, **Figure 1.10**).

Bacteria naturally 'swap' plasmids, and biologists found ways of transferring plasmids from one bacterium to another. The next stage was to find molecular 'scissors' and a molecular 'glue' that could cut out genes from one molecule of DNA and stick them back into another. Research led to the discovery of two key types of enzymes:

EXTENSION

There is a lot more to producing recombinant DNA and transgenic bacteria than is described here. You could carry out some research to find out more about this topic.

- **Restriction enzymes** are enzymes that cut DNA molecules at specific points. Different restriction enzymes cut DNA at different places. They can be used to cut out specific genes from a molecule of DNA.
- **Ligases** (or DNA ligases) are enzymes that join the cut ends of DNA molecules.

5 USE OF BIOLOGICAL RESOURCES   **14 GENETIC MODIFICATION (GENETIC ENGINEERING)**

> **DID YOU KNOW?**
> The word 'vector' has several different meanings. In biology, it is used to describe an organism that transmits an infection (e.g. mosquitoes transmit the malaria parasite). In genetic engineering, it is used to describe something that can transfer a gene (most commonly a plasmid). Note that the meaning is completely different in maths and physics!

Biologists now had a method of transferring a gene from any cell into a bacterium. They could insert the gene into a plasmid and then transfer the plasmid into a bacterium. The plasmid is called a **vector** because it is the means of transferring the gene.

PRODUCING A TRANSGENIC BACTERIUM

The main processes involved in producing a transgenic bacterium are shown in **Figure 14.1**. Some restriction enzymes make a staggered cut in the DNA, producing 'sticky ends' (as in **Figure 14.1**). They are called 'sticky ends' because they are easily joined with the DNA in the recombinant plasmids. (Other restriction enzymes make straight cuts across the DNA, called 'blunt ends'.)

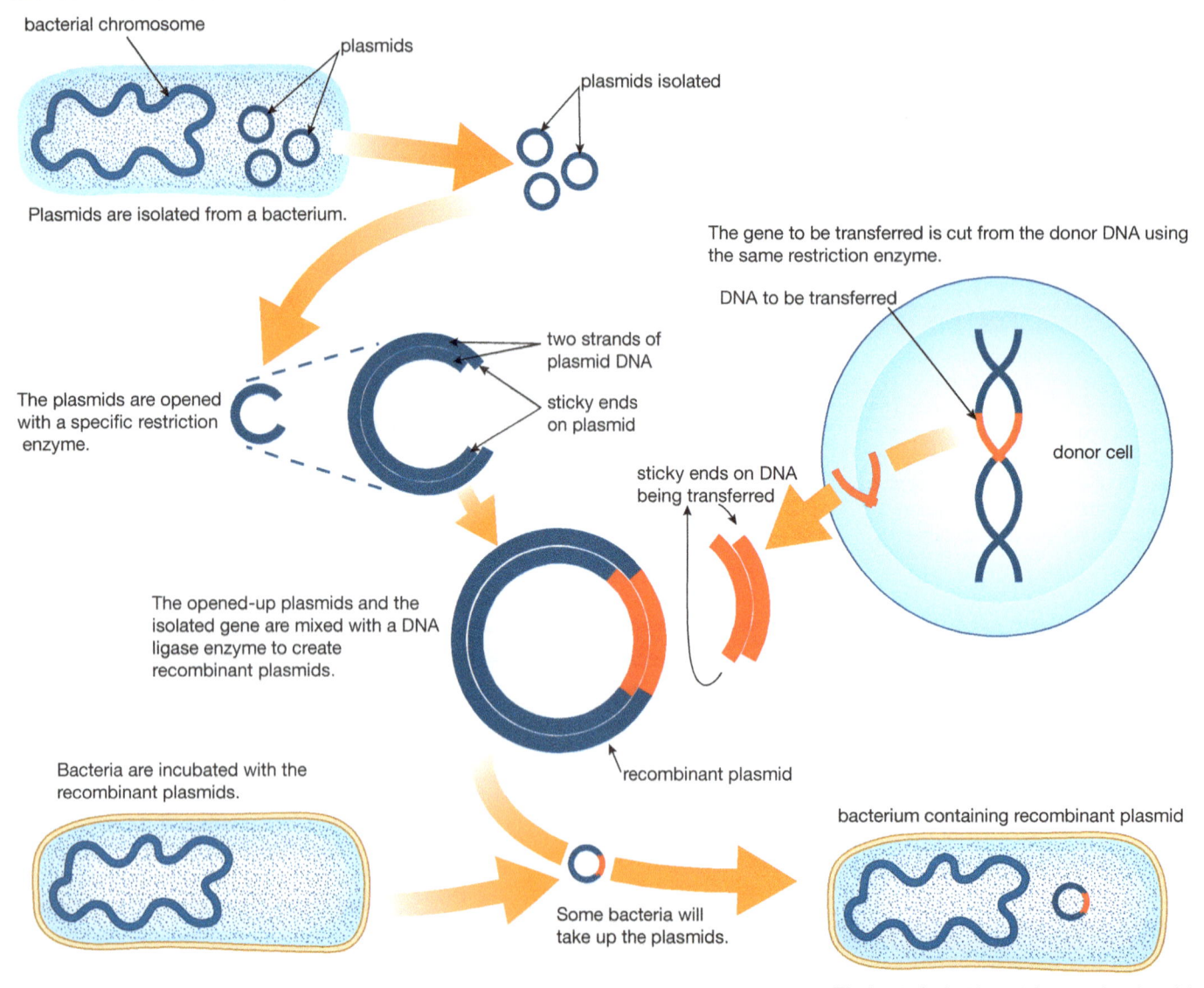

▲ Figure 14.1 Stages in producing a transgenic bacterium

MAKING HUMAN INSULIN

Insulin is a hormone made by the pancreas that acts to decrease glucose levels in the blood. People with the disease diabetes often have to inject insulin to control their blood glucose levels. Before the use of genetic engineering, the only insulin available was made from the pancreases of animals. Insulin from these animals does not have quite the same structure as human insulin and does not give the same level of control of blood glucose levels. We can now make human insulin by genetic modification of bacteria. The bacteria are grown in large vessels called bioreactors or fermenters (**Figure 14.2**). This means that we can 'harvest' large amounts of human insulin and reduce the need to extract the hormone from animal tissues.

▲ Figure 14.2 An industrial bioreactor or fermenter holds thousands of dm³ of a liquid culture of bacteria. It can produce large amounts of products such as human insulin.

Many other products of genetic engineering are made in this way. Some are made in bacteria, others in genetically modified yeast. They include:

- enzymes for the food industry
- enzymes used in biological washing powders
- human growth hormone
- proteins to develop vaccines against some disease-causing viruses
- blood-clotting factors
- proteins that help to destroy cancers.

EXTENSION

Do some research to find out more about the range of products that are made by genetic modification of micro-organisms.

USING VIRUSES AS VECTORS

Viruses can also be used as vectors to transfer genes. One type of virus that is used is the **bacteriophage**. A bacteriophage is a virus that attacks a bacterium. It does this by attaching to the cell wall of the bacterium and injecting its own DNA into the bacterial cell (**Figure 14.3**). This DNA becomes incorporated into the DNA of the host cell, and eventually causes the production of many virus particles.

If a foreign gene can be inserted into the DNA of the virus, the virus will inject it into the bacterium along with its own genes.

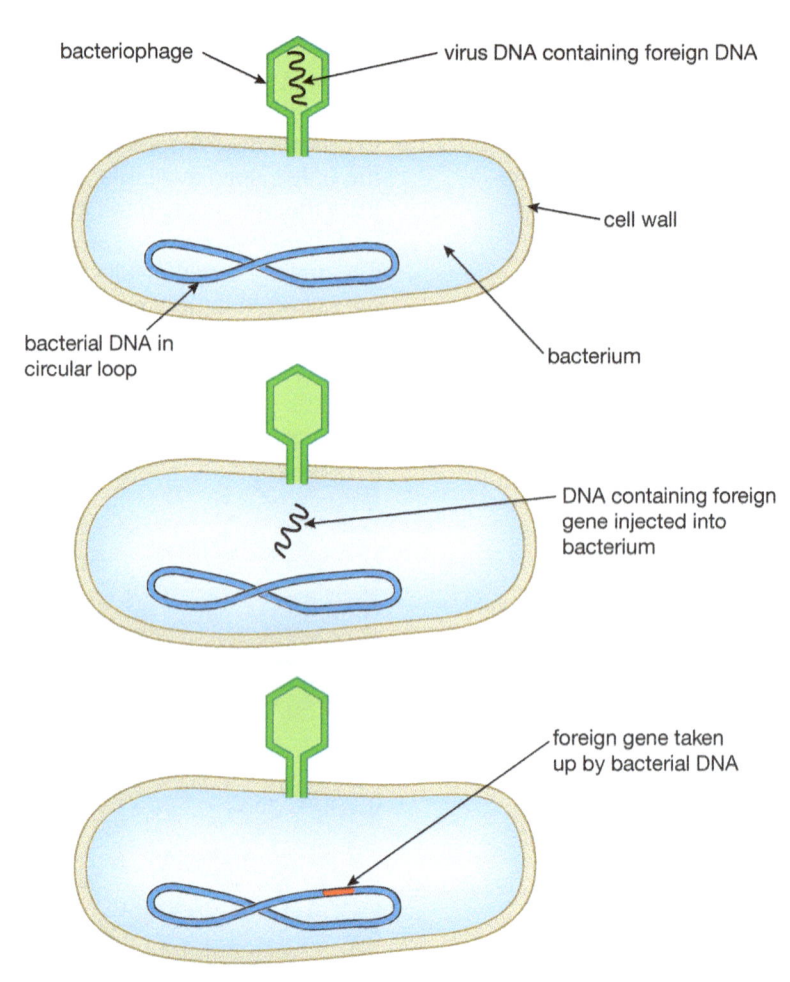

▲ Figure 14.3 A bacteriophage attacking a bacterial cell

Most gene transfer in bacteria is carried out using plasmids. However, in recent years there has been an increasing use of bacteriophages and other viruses as vectors, and they have been used to transfer genes to a number of different animal, plant and human cells.

PRODUCING GENETICALLY MODIFIED PLANTS

The gene technology described so far can transfer DNA from one cell to another cell. In the case of bacteria, this is fine – a bacterium only has one cell. But plants have billions of cells. In order to genetically modify a plant, each cell must receive the new gene. So, any procedure for genetically modifying plants has two main stages:

- introducing the new gene or genes into plant cells
- producing whole plants from just a few cells.

At first, biologists had problems inserting genes into plant cells. Then they discovered a soil bacterium called *Agrobacterium*, which regularly inserts its plasmids into plant cells. Now that a vector had been found, gene transfer to plants became possible. **Figure 14.4** shows a process that uses plasmids from *Agrobacterium* as a vector.

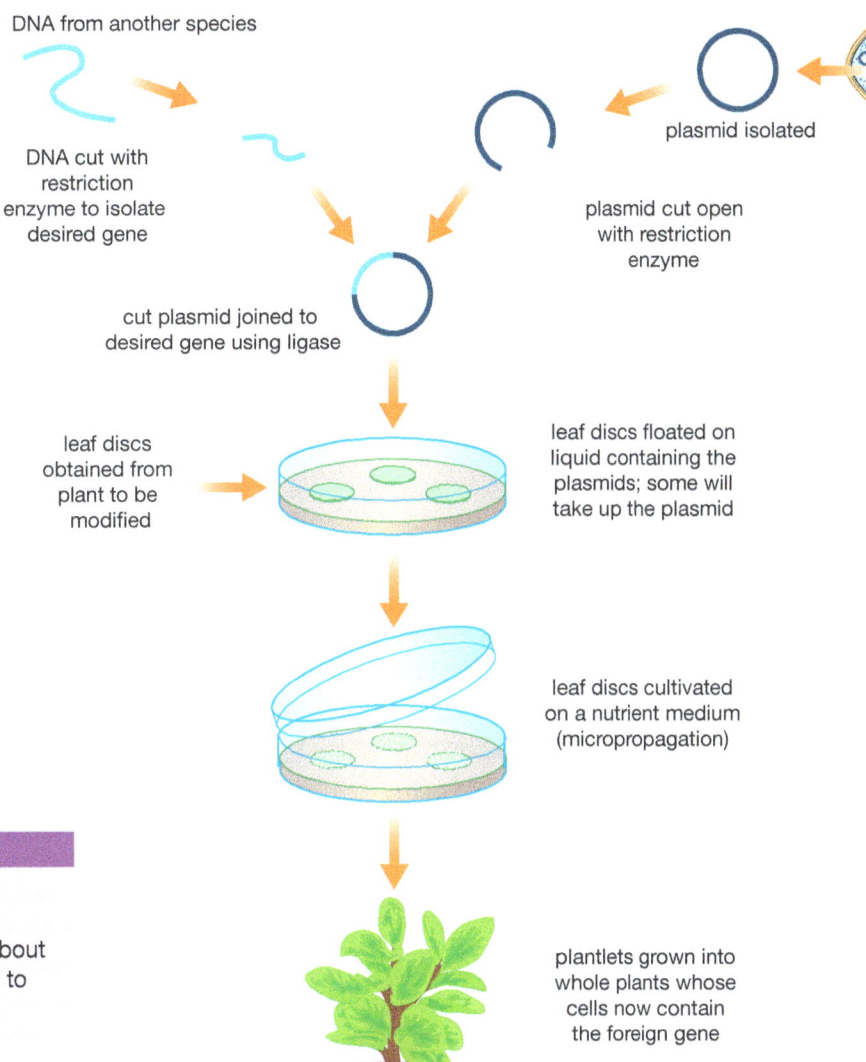

5 USE OF BIOLOGICAL RESOURCES — 14 GENETIC MODIFICATION (GENETIC ENGINEERING)

▲ Figure 14.4 Genetically modifying plants using *Agrobacterium*

Diagram labels:
- DNA from another species
- DNA cut with restriction enzyme to isolate desired gene
- plasmid isolated
- *Agrobacterium tumefaciens*
- plasmid cut open with restriction enzyme
- cut plasmid joined to desired gene using ligase
- leaf discs obtained from plant to be modified
- leaf discs floated on liquid containing the plasmids; some will take up the plasmid
- leaf discs cultivated on a nutrient medium (micropropagation)
- plantlets grown into whole plants whose cells now contain the foreign gene

EXTENSION

There is much debate about the rights and wrongs of growing GM crops. Carry out some research about this. What do you think? Is it right to genetically modify plants?

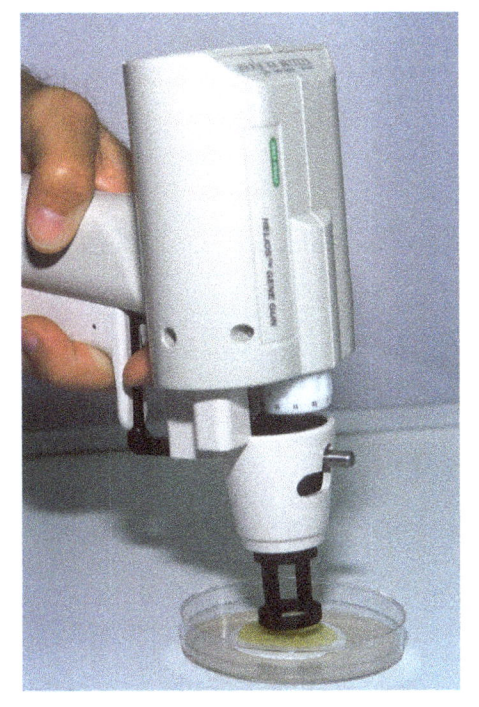

▲ Figure 14.5 A gene gun

This technique cannot be used on all plants. *Agrobacterium* will not infect cereals so another technique was needed for these. The 'gene gun' was invented. This is, quite literally, a gun that fires a golden bullet (**Figure 14.5**). Tiny pellets of gold are coated with DNA that contains the gene to be transferred. These are then 'fired' directly into plant tissue. Research has shown that if young, delicate tissue is used, there is a good uptake of the DNA. The genetically modified tissue can then be grown into new plants using the same techniques used in the *Agrobacterium* procedure. The gene gun has made it possible to genetically modify many cereal plants, as well as tobacco, carrot, soybean, apple, oilseed rape, cotton and many others.

Some fruit and vegetables have been engineered to have extended 'shelf lives' – they last longer before they start to go bad. Other crop plants have been modified to be resistant to herbicides (weedkillers). This allows farmers to spray herbicides to kill weeds, without affecting the crop plant. There are concerns that this will encourage farmers to be less careful in their use of herbicides. In another example, genes from Arctic fish that code for an 'antifreeze' in their blood have been transferred to some plants to make them frost resistant.

▲ Figure 14.6 Golden rice

EXTENSION

Golden rice sounds like a good idea, but there have been several problems with it. Some people believe that there are ethical and environmental reasons why golden rice should not be grown and that it is better to provide other, natural crops containing enough beta-carotene. You could carry out some research into the advantages and disadvantages of golden rice.

The gene gun allowed biologists to produce genetically modified rice called 'golden rice' (**Figure 14.6**). This rice has three genes added to its normal DNA content. Two of these come from daffodils and one from a bacterium. Together, these genes allow the rice to make beta-carotene – the chemical that gives carrots their colour. It also colours the rice, hence the name 'golden rice'. More importantly, the beta-carotene is converted to vitamin A when eaten. This could save the eyesight of millions of children in less economically developed countries, who go blind because they do not have enough vitamin A in their diet.

Further research into genetic modification is being carried out, in the hope of developing better crop plants with features such as:

- increased resistance to pests and pathogens
- increased tolerance of hot, dry climates
- increased salt tolerance
- a better balance of proteins, carbohydrates, lipids, vitamins and minerals.

DID YOU KNOW?

Genetically modified plants are also helping the fight against disease. Biologists have succeeded in modifying tobacco plants and soybean plants to produce antibodies against a range of infectious diseases. If these plants can be produced on a large scale, the antibodies could be given to people who do not produce enough of their own antibodies.

CHAPTER QUESTIONS

Exam-style questions on genetic modification can be found at the end of Unit 5 on page 132.

SKILLS CRITICAL THINKING

1 Why is it relatively easy to genetically modify bacteria?

   A they reproduce slowly and accurately

   B they are able to take up plasmids

   C they only contain a single chromosome

   D they make restriction enzymes

SKILLS CRITICAL THINKING

2 The statements below show some stages in the production of human insulin from genetically modified bacteria.

   1. DNA for insulin inserted into plasmids
   2. bacteria grown in a bioreactor
   3. plasmids inserted into bacteria
   4. DNA for insulin cut out using restriction enzyme

   Which of the following shows the correct sequence of steps in the process?

   A 2 → 1 → 4 → 3

   B 4 → 2 → 3 → 1

   C 4 → 1 → 3 → 2

   D 2 → 3 → 4 → 1

SKILLS CRITICAL THINKING

3 Which of the following enzymes is used to join together pieces of DNA?

  A ligase

  B lipase

  C amylase

  D restriction enzyme

SKILLS ANALYSIS

4 The diagram shows the main stages in transferring the human insulin gene to a bacterium.

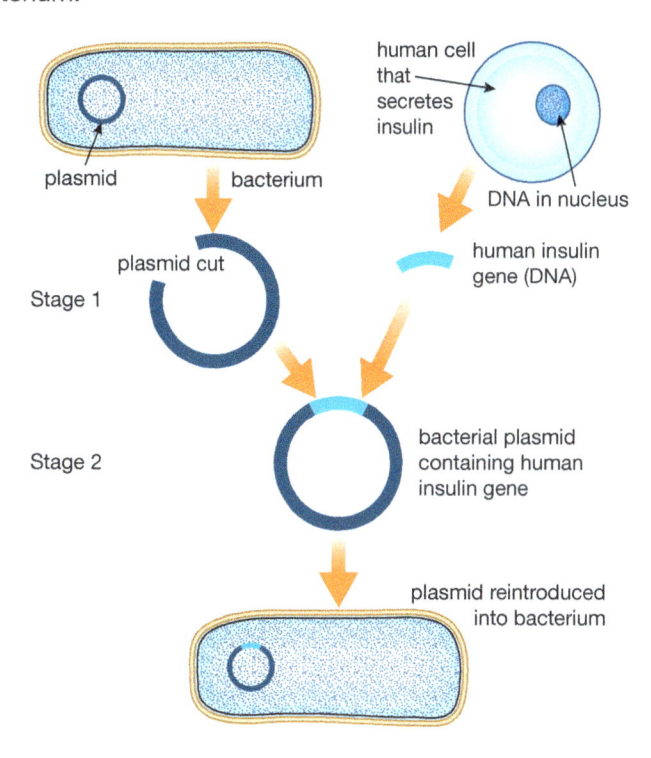

a Name the enzymes used at stages 1 and 2.

SKILLS CRITICAL THINKING

b What is the role of the plasmid in this procedure?

c How would the insulin-producing bacteria be used to produce significant amounts of insulin?

SKILLS REASONING

d Why is the insulin produced this way preferred to insulin extracted from other animals?

SKILLS CRITICAL THINKING

5 Producing genetically modified plants and animals is more complex than producing genetically modified bacteria.

  a Describe *two* ways in which genes can be introduced into plant cells.

  b How are these genetically modified cells used to produce whole organisms?

EXAM PRACTICE

1 The apparatus in the diagram was used to investigate anaerobic respiration in yeast.

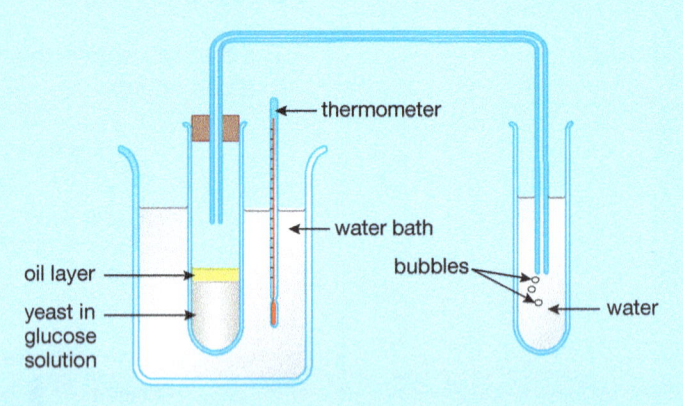

SKILLS INTERPRETATION

a Describe the role of the layer of oil above the yeast in glucose solution. (2)

b Before the yeast was added to the glucose solution, the solution was boiled and cooled. Explain the purpose of this. (2)

SKILLS ANALYSIS, REASONING

c The rate of respiration of the yeast was measured by counting the number of bubbles of gas produced per minute. The effect of temperature on the rate was investigated by changing the temperature of the water bath. The results are shown in the table below.

| Temperature / °C | Number of bubbles per minute ||||
	1st trial	2nd trial	3rd trial	Mean of the three trials
20	11	12	12	12
28	30	27	22	26
36	35	37	33	
42	33	32	36	34
49	21	18	20	20
62	2	5	2	3

i Calculate the mean of the three trials at 36 °C. Give your answer correct to the nearest whole number. (1)

ii Using graph paper, plot a line graph of bubble rate against temperature. (4)

iii Describe the shape of the curve in the graph. (3)

iv Explain the change in the rate of respiration of the yeast as the temperature increases from 42 °C to 62 °C. (3)

(Total 15 marks)

5 USE OF BIOLOGICAL RESOURCES   EXAM PRACTICE   133

SKILLS PROBLEM SOLVING, CREATIVITY

2 Using the apparatus shown in question **1**, design an experiment to test the hypothesis that yeast respires faster when supplied with sucrose instead of glucose for respiration. Your answer should be written in full sentences.

(Total 6 marks)

SKILLS CRITICAL THINKING, INTERPRETATION

3 An organism called *Saccharomyces cerevisiae* is used in making bread. The diagram shows a cell of *Saccharomyces cerevisiae*.

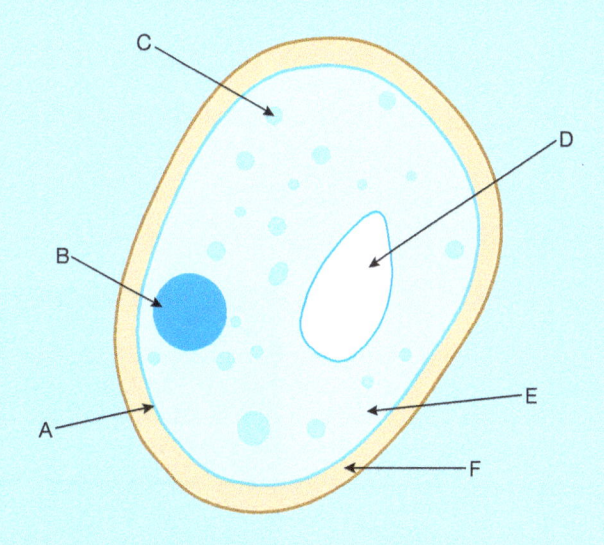

a Name the group of organisms that *Saccharomyces cerevisiae* belongs to. (1)

b State the letter of the structure in the cell that is made of:
   i chitin
   ii glycogen. (2)

c 'The anaerobic respiration of *Saccharomyces cerevisiae* is essential to the production of bread'. Explain this statement. Include a chemical word equation in your answer. (3)

(Total 6 marks)

SKILLS INTERPRETATION

4 a Describe plasmids and their role in genetic engineering. (3)

b i Describe what a bacteriophage is. (2)
   ii Describe how bacteriophages reproduce. (2)
   iii Describe how bacteriophages are used in genetic engineering. (3)

c Explain the importance of the following enzymes in genetic engineering:
   i restriction enzymes
   ii ligase enzymes. (6)

(Total 16 marks)

1 STATES OF MATTER 135   2 ELEMENTS, COMPOUNDS AND MIXTURES 142   3 ATOMIC STRUCTURE 151
4 THE PERIODIC TABLE 158   5 CHEMICAL FORMULAE AND EQUATIONS 162
6 IONIC BONDING 170   7 COVALENT BONDING 178

CHEMISTRY UNIT 1
PRINCIPLES OF CHEMISTRY

The universe is made of three things!

Up to the present day scientists have discovered 118 elements. Most of these have been made naturally in stars but some are made artificially. As far as we know these are the only elements in the universe, so we basically have a model kit containing 118 different atoms. Chemistry can be described as the study of how these different atoms are joined together in various ways to make everything around us, from a tree, to a person, to the tallest skyscraper. Many of these elements are not very common so most of the things we see around us are made up of different combinations of only about a quarter of these elements. What makes this even more amazing is that each atom is made up of just three subatomic particles, which are called protons, neutrons and electrons. So, the world around us is made of only three things arranged in different ways.

1 PRINCIPLES OF CHEMISTRY
1 STATES OF MATTER

SPECIFICATION REFERENCES: 1.1–1.3

Everything around us is made of particles that we cannot see because they are so small. This chapter looks at the arrangement of particles in solids, liquids and gases, and the ways in which the particles can move around.

▲ Figure 1.1 Everything you look at is a solid, a liquid or a gas . . .

▲ Figure 1.2 . . . metals, concrete, water, air, clouds – everything!

LEARNING OBJECTIVES

- Understand the three states of matter in terms of the arrangement, movement and energy of the particles.
- Understand the interconversions between the three states of matter in terms of:
  - the names of the interconversions
  - how they are achieved
- the changes in arrangement, movement and energy of the particles.
- Understand how the results of experiments involving the dilution of coloured solutions and diffusion of gases can be explained.

STATES OF MATTER

Solids, liquids and gases are known as the three states of matter.

THE ARRANGEMENT OF THE PARTICLES

Think about these facts:

- You cannot walk through a brick wall, but you can move (with some resistance – it pushes against you) through water. Moving through air is easy.
- When you melt most solids their volume increases slightly. Most liquids are less dense than the solid they come from.
- If you boil about 5 cm^3 of water, the steam will fill an average bucket.

1 PRINCIPLES OF CHEMISTRY   1 STATES OF MATTER

EXAM HINT

When you draw a diagram of the particles in a solid, the particles should be touching the ones next to them and arranged regularly. When you draw a liquid, it is important to remember that the particles should also be mostly touching the particles next to them. The arrangement of the particles in a liquid is irregular/random.

KEY POINTS

- You cannot walk through a brick wall because of the strong forces of attraction between the particles – the particles cannot move out of your way.
- You can swim through water because you can push the particles out of the way.
- It is easy to move through a gas because there are no forces between the particles.

The arrangement of the **particles** in solids, liquids and gases explains these facts (see **Figure 1.3**).

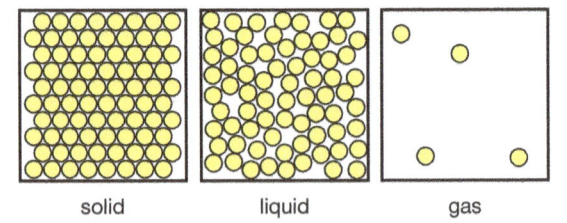

▲ Figure 1.3 The arrangement of particles in different states of matter

In a solid, the particles are usually arranged regularly and packed closely together. The particles are only able to vibrate about fixed positions; they cannot move around. The particles have strong forces of attraction between them, which keep them together.

In a liquid, the particles are still mostly touching, but some gaps have appeared. This is why liquids are usually less dense than solids. The forces between the particles are less effective, and the particles can move around each other. The particles in a liquid are arranged randomly.

The particles in a gas are moving randomly at high speed in all directions. In a gas, the particles are much further apart and there are (almost) no forces of attraction between them.

The particles in a solid have less energy than the particles in a liquid, which have less energy than the particles in a gas.

INTERCONVERSIONS BETWEEN THE THREE STATES OF MATTER

CHANGING STATE BETWEEN SOLID AND LIQUID

If you heat a solid, the energy provided by the heat source makes the particles in the solid vibrate faster and faster. Eventually, they vibrate so fast that the forces of attraction between the particles are no longer strong enough to hold them together; the particles are then able to move around each other – the solid melts to form a liquid (see **Figure 1.4**). The temperature at which the solid **melts** is called its **melting point**. The particles in the liquid have more energy than the particles in the solid so energy has to be supplied to convert a solid to a liquid.

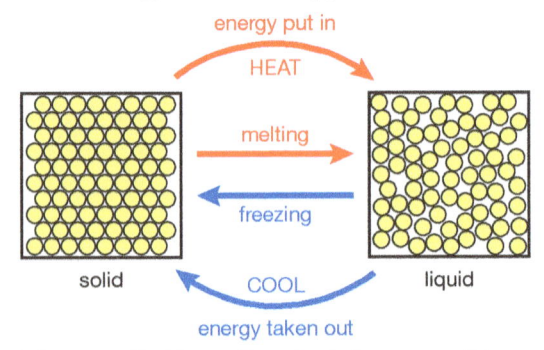

▲ Figure 1.4 Melting to become a liquid – and **freezing** to become a solid

If the liquid is cooled again, the liquid particles will move around more and more slowly. Eventually, they are moving so slowly that the forces of attraction between them will hold them in a fixed position and the particles pack more closely together into a solid. The liquid freezes, forming a solid. The temperature at which this occurs is called the **freezing point**.

Although they are called different things depending which way you are going, the temperature of the melting point and that of the freezing point of a substance are exactly the same.

CHANGING STATE BETWEEN LIQUID AND GAS

> **KEY POINT**
>
> Another way of thinking about this is that energy has to be supplied to boil a liquid in order to overcome the forces of attraction between the particles in the liquid.

> **KEY POINT**
>
> Evaporation occurs at any temperature, but boiling only occurs at one temperature – the boiling point of the liquid. Puddles of water disappear quite quickly despite the outside temperature often being below 5 °C in the winter in the UK. The water in the puddles certainly does not boil at this temperature; the water evaporates. So water will evaporate at, for example, 5 °C but only boil at 100 °C.

There are two different ways this can happen, called **boiling** and **evaporation**.

BOILING

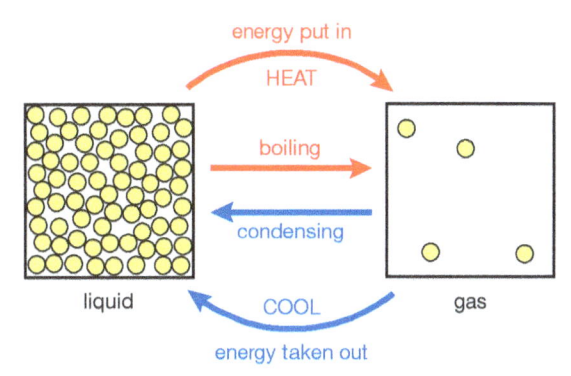

▲ Figure 1.5 Boiling to become a gas – and condensing to become a liquid

Boiling occurs when a liquid is heated so strongly that the particles are moving fast enough to overcome all the forces of attraction between them (see **Figure 1.5**). The stronger the forces of attraction between particles, the higher the boiling point of the liquid. This is because more energy is needed to overcome these forces of attraction.

If a gas is cooled, the particles eventually move slowly enough that forces of attraction between them start to form and hold them together as a liquid. The gas condenses.

EVAPORATION

Evaporation is different. In any liquid or gas, the average speed of the particles varies with the temperature. But at each temperature, some particles will be moving faster than the average and others more slowly.

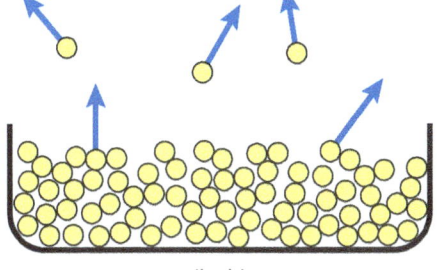

Some very fast particles at the surface of the liquid will have enough energy to overcome the forces of attraction between the particles – they will break away to form a gas (see **Figure 1.6**). This is evaporation. You do not see any **bubbling**; the liquid just slowly disappears if it is open to the air. If the liquid is in a closed container, particles in the gas will also be colliding with particles at the surface of the liquid. If they are moving slowly enough they will be held by the attractive forces and become part of the liquid. In a closed container evaporation and **condensation** will both be occurring at the same time.

▲ Figure 1.6 Evaporation

CHANGING STATE BETWEEN SOLID AND GAS: SUBLIMATION

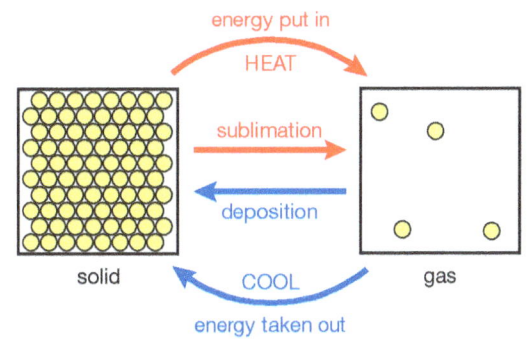

> **KEY POINT**
>
> The process of a gas changing into a solid is given various names. Some people call it 'de-sublimation' or 'deposition' and others just use the word 'sublimation' again.

▲ Figure 1.7 This change of state goes directly from a solid to a gas and from a gas to a solid.

A small number of substances can change directly from a solid to a gas, or from a gas to a solid, at normal **pressure** without involving any liquid in the process. The conversion of a solid into a gas is known as **sublimation** and the reverse process is usually called **deposition** (see **Figure 1.7**).

An example of a substance that sublimes is carbon dioxide. At ordinary pressures, there is no such thing as liquid carbon dioxide – it turns directly from a solid to a gas at −78.5 °C. Solid carbon dioxide is known as **dry ice** (see **Figure 1.8**).

▲ Figure 1.8 Dry ice subliming. Notice the white solid carbon dioxide in the beaker. The white cloud is because the carbon dioxide gas produced is so cold that it causes water vapour in the air to condense. Carbon dioxide gas itself is invisible.

WORKING OUT THE PHYSICAL STATE OF A SUBSTANCE AT A PARTICULAR TEMPERATURE

A substance:

- is a solid at temperatures below its melting point,
- is liquid between its melting point and its boiling point
- is a gas above its boiling point.

We can deduce whether a substance is a solid, a liquid or a gas at room temperature by looking at where its melting and boiling points are in relation to room temperature.

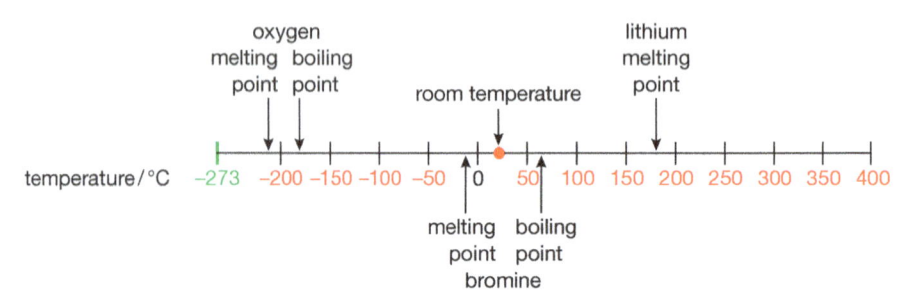

▲ Figure 1.9 A temperature line can be used to work out whether substances are solids, liquids or gases.

If we look at the temperature line in **Figure 1.9** we can see that room temperature is above the boiling point of oxygen; this means that oxygen is a gas at room temperature.

Let us look at what happens when we heat bromine from −100 °C to 100 °C. As −100 °C is below bromine's melting point, bromine is a solid at −100 °C. As it is heated to −7 °C (its melting point) it becomes a liquid and it remains as a liquid until its temperature reaches the boiling point at 59 °C. Room temperature is between the melting point and the boiling point, which means that bromine is a liquid at room temperature. Above 59 °C bromine is a gas.

Lithium's melting point is above room temperature and so it is a solid at room temperature.

KEY POINT

Room temperature is different in different places but in science it is usually taken to mean a temperature between 20 and 25 °C. Because there is not just one fixed value, for changes of state that occur near room temperature we must be careful when making comparisons and make clear what value is being used as room temperature.

DIFFUSION

DIFFUSION IN GASES

▲ Figure 1.10 An ammonia particle bouncing off air particles

Suppose someone accidentally releases some smelly gas in the lab, ammonia for example. Within a minute or so, everybody in the lab will be able to smell it. That is not surprising – particles in the gas are free to move around. What does need explaining, though, is why it takes so long.

At room temperature, ammonia particles travel at speeds of about 600 metres per second so they should be able to travel from one end of a lab to the other in less than 1/100 s (0.01 s). This would be the case if they travelled in a straight line without bumping into anything else. However, each particle is bouncing off air particles on its way (see **Figure 1.10**). In the time that it takes for the smell to reach all corners of the lab, each ammonia particle may have travelled 30 or more kilometres!

1 PRINCIPLES OF CHEMISTRY
1 STATES OF MATTER

The spreading out of particles in a gas or liquid is known as **diffusion**. We say that ammonia particles *diffuse* through the air. A formal definition of diffusion is:

Diffusion is the spreading out of particles from where they are at a high concentration (there are lots of them in a certain volume) to where they are at a low concentration (there are fewer of them in a certain volume).

How the distribution of particles changes during diffusion is shown in **Figure 1.11**.

higher concentration of particles in a certain region

diffusion

particles spread out until there is equal concentration throughout the container

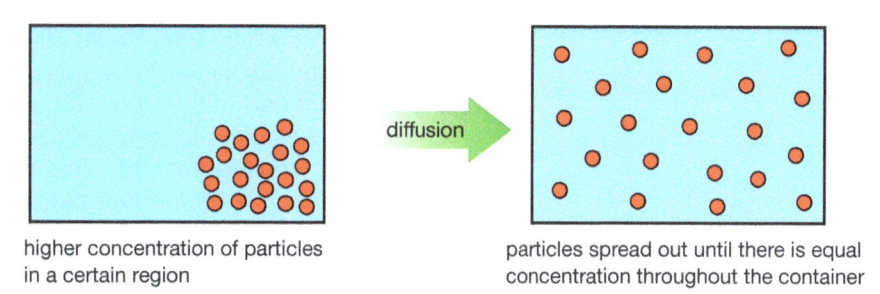

▲ Figure 1.11 Diffusion involves the spreading out of particles.

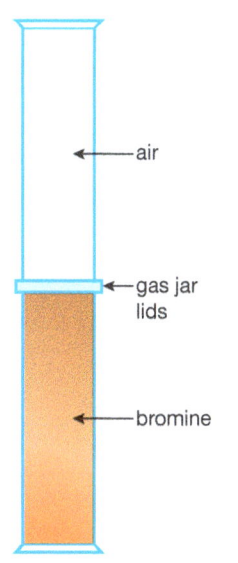

▲ Figure 1.12 Demonstrating diffusion in gases

Safety note: The teacher demonstration must be prepared in a working fume cupboard wearing eye protection and chemical-resistant gloves. Inhalation of bromine by anyone with breathing difficulties may produce a reaction, possibly delayed, requiring urgent medical attention.

You can show diffusion in gases very easily by using the apparatus in **Figure 1.12**. The lower gas jar contains bromine gas; the top one contains air. If the lids are removed, the brown colour of the bromine diffuses upwards until both gas jars are uniformly brown (the air particles also diffuse downwards). The bromine particles and air particles move around at random to give an even mixture – both gas jars contain air and bromine particles.

You can carry out the same experiment with hydrogen and air, but in this example you have to put a lighted splint in at the end to find out where the gases have gone. People often expect that the much less dense hydrogen will all go to the top gas jar. In fact, you will get identical explosions from both jars.

SHOWING THAT PARTICLES OF DIFFERENT GASES TRAVEL AT DIFFERENT SPEEDS

This experiment relies on the reaction between ammonia (NH_3) and hydrogen chloride (HCl) gases to give white solid ammonium chloride (NH_4Cl):

$$NH_3(g) + HCl(g) \rightarrow NH_4Cl(s)$$

HINT
Do not worry if you do not know how to write symbol equations. This one is included here so that you can refer to it again in later revision.

cotton wool soaked in concentrated ammonia solution

cotton wool soaked in concentrated hydrochloric acid

white ring forms closer to the hydrochloric acid end

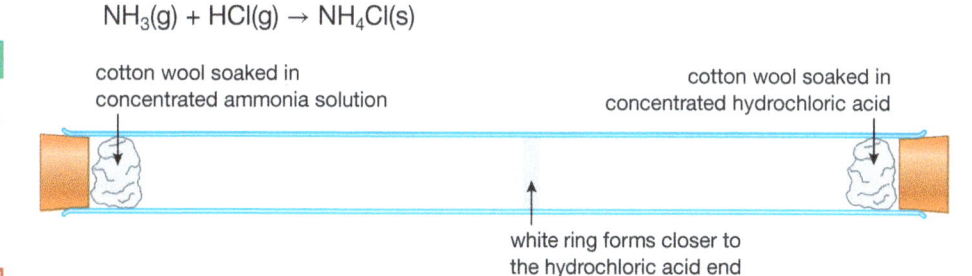

▲ Figure 1.13 Demonstrating that particles in ammonia and hydrogen chloride travel at different speeds

Safety note: The teacher demonstration requires eye protection and the avoidance of skin contact and inhalation of any **fumes**. The apparatus must be cleaned up in a working fume cupboard.

Pieces of cotton wool are **soaked** in concentrated ammonia solution (as a source of ammonia gas) and concentrated hydrochloric acid (as a source of hydrogen chloride gas). These are placed in the ends of a long glass tube with rubber bungs to stop the poisonous gases escaping (see **Figure 1.13**).

KEY POINT
You will learn about relative molecular mass in **Chapter 5**. The relative molecular mass of ammonia is 17 and that of hydrogen chloride is 36.5.

Ammonia particles and hydrogen chloride particles diffuse along the tube. A white ring of solid ammonium chloride forms where they meet. The white ring of ammonium chloride takes time to form (as it takes some time for the particles of ammonia and hydrogen chloride to diffuse along the tube), and appears *closer to the hydrochloric acid end*. Ammonia particles are lighter than hydrogen chloride particles and therefore move faster. The ammonia particles travel further in the same amount of time, which means that the ring forms further away from the ammonia end.

DIFFUSION IN LIQUIDS

KEY POINT

If the gas jar is left long enough, the purple colour should become uniform throughout the solution: it has the same intensity of colour everywhere.

Diffusion through a liquid is very slow if the liquid is completely still. For example, if a small jar of strongly coloured solution (such as potassium manganate(VII) solution) is placed in a gas jar of water the colour will be initially most intense around the small jar, and the water in the parts furthest away from the jar will be colourless. After a few minutes the colour will have spread around the bottom part of the jar but it can take days for the colour to diffuse throughout all the water (see **Figure 1.14**). This is because *the particles in a liquid move more slowly than the particles in a gas*. The particles in a liquid are also much closer together than those in a gas and so there is less space for particles to move into without colliding with another one.

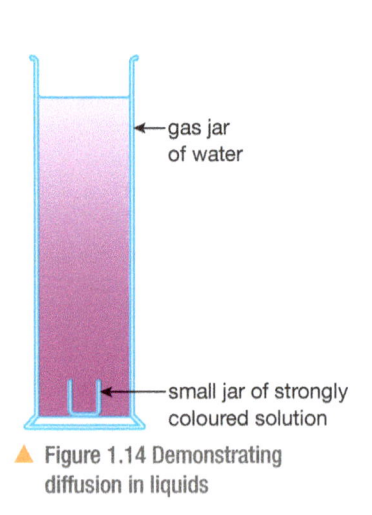

▲ Figure 1.14 Demonstrating diffusion in liquids

THE DILUTION OF COLOURED SOLUTIONS

KEY POINT

The colour of the solution becomes paler because there are fewer 'particles' of potassium manganate(VII) per cm^3 of solution.

REMINDER

Why the inverted commas around 'particle'? Potassium manganate(VII) is an *ionic compound* and contains more than one sort of particle (these separate when it is dissolved in water). You will find out more about ionic compounds in **Chapter 6**.

Imagine you dissolve 0.01 g of potassium manganate(VII) in 1 cm^3 of water to make a deep purple solution. If we take the volume of 1 drop as 0.05 cm^3 we can work out that there are 20 drops in 1 cm^3 and each drop will contain 0.0005 g of potassium manganate(VII).

If you dilute this solution by adding water until the total volume is 10 000 cm^3, the colour will be much paler but you should still just be able to see the purple colour.

There are now 200 000 drops in the solution. In order to see the colour each drop must contain at least one 'particle' of potassium manganate(VII), so there must be at least 200 000 'particles' in 0.01 g of potassium manganate(VII). This means that each 'particle' cannot weigh more than 50 billionths of a gram (0.00000005 g).

This answer is not even close to the real answer. A potassium manganate(VII) 'particle' actually weighs about 0.000000000000000000000026 g and there are about 38 000 000 000 000 000 000 particles in 0.01 g! In reality, you need very large numbers of particles in each drop in order to see the colour.

CHAPTER QUESTIONS

Exam-style questions on states of matter can be found at the end of Unit 1 on page 184.

SKILLS CRITICAL THINKING

SKILLS INTERPRETATION

1 What name is given to each of the following changes of state?
   a solid to liquid   b liquid to solid   c solid to gas

2 a Draw diagrams to show the arrangement of the particles in a solid, a liquid and a gas.

   b Describe the difference between the movement of particles in a solid and a liquid.

   c The change of state from a liquid to a gas can be either evaporation or boiling. Explain the difference between evaporation and boiling.

3 The questions refer to the substances in the table.

	Melting point / °C	Boiling point / °C
A	−259	−253
B	0	100
C	3700 (sublimes)	
D	−116	34.5
E	801	1413

SKILLS ANALYSIS

a Write down the physical states of each compound at
   i   30 °C
   ii −100 °C
   iii 80 °C

SKILLS PROBLEM SOLVING

b Which substance has the greatest distance between its particles at 25 °C? Explain your answer.

SKILLS REASONING

c Why is no boiling point given for substance **C**?

d Which liquid substance would evaporate most quickly in the open air at 25 °C? Explain your answer.

4 Refer to **Figure 1.13** on page 139 showing the diffusion experiment.

a Explain why the ring takes a few minutes to form.

SKILLS INTERPRETATION

b i   If you heat a gas, what effect will this have on the movement of the particles?

SKILLS CRITICAL THINKING

   ii In the light of your answer to **i**, what difference would you find if you did this experiment outside on a day when the temperature was 2 °C instead of in a warm lab at 25 °C? Explain your answer.

SKILLS INTERPRETATION

c Explain why the ring was formed nearer the hydrochloric acid end of the tube.

d Suppose you replaced the concentrated hydrochloric acid with concentrated hydrobromic acid. This releases the gas hydrogen bromide (HBr). Hydrogen bromide also reacts with ammonia to form a white ring.

SKILLS CRITICAL THINKING

   i   Suggest a name for the white ring in this case.
   ii Hydrogen bromide particles are about twice as heavy as hydrogen chloride particles. Explain two effects this will have on the experiment.

SKILLS REASONING

5 A crystal of dark purple potassium manganate(VII) is placed into a small beaker of water. The diagram shows the appearance of the beaker after a few minutes.

a Describe how the appearance of the beaker changes over the next few hours and state the name of the two processes occurring in the beaker.

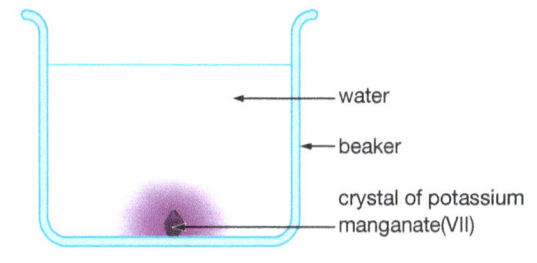

b The student stirs the beaker then leaves it in a warm laboratory for two days. Describe how the appearance of the beaker will have changed after two days. State the name of the process that has occurred.

1 PRINCIPLES OF CHEMISTRY
2 ELEMENTS, COMPOUNDS AND MIXTURES

SPECIFICATION REFERENCES: 1.8–1.13

Most of the substances that we are familiar with from everyday life are mixtures. For example, the air that we breathe is a mixture containing elements such as nitrogen and oxygen, and compounds such as carbon dioxide and nitrogen oxides. The food that we eat and the drinks that we drink are mixtures. This chapter looks at the properties of elements, compounds and mixtures, and also how to separate the components of a mixture. Separation of mixtures is very important in the analysis of substances, such as in forensics.

▲ Figure 2.1 Gold is an element, but a gold ring made from 18-carat gold only contains 75% gold. The metal is a mixture of gold and, usually, copper.

▲ Figure 2.2 Pure water is a compound, but the water we drink is a mixture of water and other dissolved substances.

LEARNING OBJECTIVES

- Understand how to classify a substance as an element, compound or mixture.
- Understand that a pure substance has a fixed melting and boiling point, but that a mixture may melt or boil over a range of temperatures.
- Describe these experimental techniques for the separation of mixtures:
  - simple distillation
  - filtration
  - paper chromatography
  - fractional distillation
  - crystallisation.
- Understand how a chromatogram provides information about the composition of a mixture.
- Understand how to use the calculation of R_f values to identify the components of a mixture.
- Practical: Investigate paper chromatography using inks/food colourings.

REMINDER
You might want to look at **Chapter 3** if you do not already know the term *atom*.

KEY POINT
It is not completely true to say that elements consist of only one type of atom. A better way of saying it would be that *all the atoms in an element have the same atomic number*. Most elements consist of mixtures of isotopes, which have the same atomic number, but different mass numbers (due to different numbers of neutrons). When we draw diagrams or make models, we are not usually interested in the differences between the isotopes. Isotopes will be discussed in **Chapter 3**.

ELEMENTS

Elements are *substances that cannot be split into anything simpler by* **chemical means**. An element contains only one type of atom (but see the key point in the margin). In models or diagrams they are shown as atoms of a single colour or size (**Figure 2.3**).

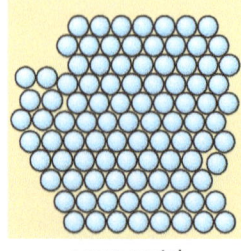

a pure metal such as magnesium

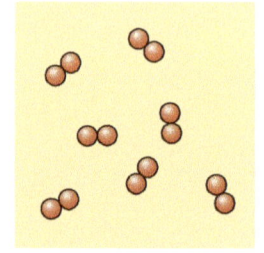

oxygen gas

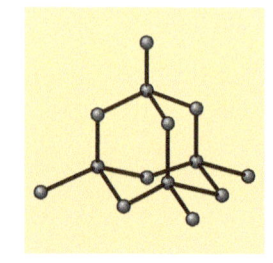

diamond (a form of carbon)

▲ Figure 2.3 Elements contain only one type of atom.

There are 118 elements and these are shown in the **Periodic Table**. Most of the elements occur naturally, such as hydrogen, helium and sulfur. Some others have to be made artificially, such as einsteinium.

COMPOUNDS

Compounds are formed when *two or more elements chemically combine*. The elements always combine in fixed proportions. For example, hydrogen and fluorine always combine to form hydrogen fluoride, with **formula** HF, whereas magnesium and fluorine always combine to form magnesium fluoride, with formula MgF_2 – the elements must combine in these ratios. Examples of other compounds are carbon dioxide (CO_2) and methane (CH_4). Diagrams of compounds show more than one type of atom bonded together (see **Figure 2.4**).

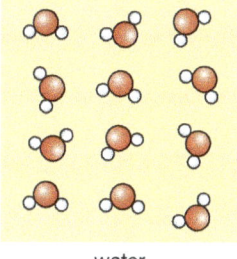

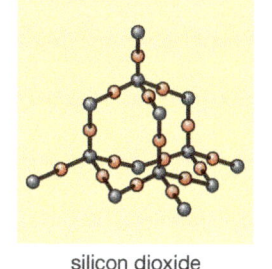

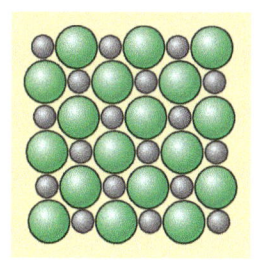

water   silicon dioxide   sodium chloride

▲ Figure 2.4 Some compounds

MIXTURES

In a **mixture**, the various substances are mixed together and no chemical reaction occurs. Mixtures can be made from elements and/or compounds (see **Figure 2.5**). The various components can be in any proportion, for example you can put any amount of sugar into your cup of tea or coffee (until it becomes saturated).

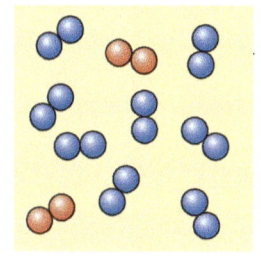

mixture of elements – nitrogen and oxygen

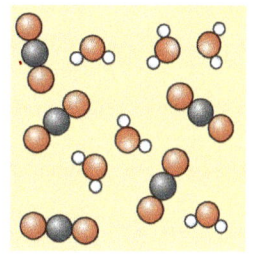

mixture of compounds – carbon dioxide and water (vapour)

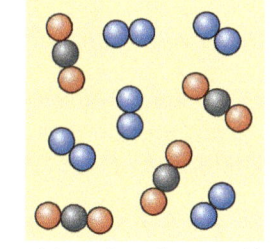

mixture of an element with a compound – carbon dioxide and nitrogen

▲ Figure 2.5 Some mixtures

SIMPLE DIFFERENCES BETWEEN MIXTURES AND COMPOUNDS

PROPORTIONS

In water (a compound), every single water molecule has two hydrogen atoms combined with one oxygen atom. It never varies. In a mixture of hydrogen and oxygen gases, the two could be mixed together in any proportion.

If you had some iron metal and some sulfur, you could mix them in any proportion you wanted to. In iron sulfide (FeS), a compound, the proportion of iron to sulfur is always exactly the same.

PROPERTIES

REMINDER
You can find out about the reactions of metals with dilute acids on pages 209–210. The reaction between iron sulfide and acids is not needed for exam purposes at International GCSE.

In a mixture of elements, each element keeps its own properties, but the properties of the compound are quite different. For example, in a mixture of iron and sulfur, the iron is grey and the sulfur is yellow. The iron reacts with dilute acids such as hydrochloric acid to produce hydrogen; the sulfur does not react with the acid. However, the compound iron sulfide (FeS) reacts quite differently with acids to produce poisonous hydrogen sulfide gas, which smells of bad eggs.

A mixture of hydrogen and oxygen is a colourless gas which explodes when you put a flame to it. The compound, water, is a colourless liquid which puts out a flame.

EASE OF SEPARATION

Mixtures can be separated by **physical means**. Physical means are things like changing the temperature or dissolving part of the mixture in a solvent such as water; in other words, methods that do not involve any chemical reactions.

For example, a mixture of iron and sulfur is quite easy to separate into the two elements using a magnet. The iron sticks to the magnet and the sulfur does not. The elements in a compound cannot be separated by physical means. To convert iron sulfide into separate samples of iron and sulfur requires chemical reactions.

You can cool a mixture of hydrogen and oxygen gases to separate it by a physical process. Oxygen condenses into a liquid at a much higher temperature than hydrogen (–183 °C as opposed to –253 °C). This would leave you with liquid oxygen and hydrogen gas, which are easy to separate. But to separate water into hydrogen and oxygen, you have to change it chemically using **electrolysis**.

MELTING POINT AND BOILING POINT

Pure substances, such as elements and pure compounds, melt and boil at fixed temperatures. For example, the melting point of water is 0 °C and the boiling point 100 °C. However, mixtures usually melt or boil over a **range** of temperatures.

KEY POINT
A mixture is not a pure substance. If a sample contains only a small amount of an unwanted substance, the unwanted substance might be called an *impurity*.

The presence of impurities lowers the melting point of a substance and raises the boiling point. For instance, dissolving 10 g of common (table) salt (sodium chloride) in 1 **litre** of water lowers the melting point of the water to about –0.6 °C and raises the boiling point to about 100.2 °C.

The melting point can be very useful in determining whether or not a substance is pure. If you continue to study chemistry you might carry out a practical experiment to make some aspirin. In order to determine whether your sample is pure or not you can measure the melting point. You would record the temperature at which your sample starts to melt, and then you would record the temperature at which it has fully melted to completely form a liquid. Aspirin is a white powder that melts at 138 °C. If the melting point of the sample you made is 128–134 °C you can see that it is quite impure because it melts over a wide range of temperature (below the melting point of pure aspirin).

EXTENSION
Enrichment of uranium is the process of increasing the proportion of the uranium-235 isotope compared with the uranium-238 isotope in a sample. One of the techniques used involves converting the uranium to UF_6 and then relying on the fact that gaseous $^{235}UF_6$ diffuses slightly faster than $^{238}UF_6$.

SEPARATION OF MIXTURES

Separating mixtures is extremely important in chemistry. For example, we can see this in the processing of crude oil, in producing fresh water from salt water and in the enrichment of uranium. In forensic science, the components of a mixture usually have to be separated before they can be analysed.

1 PRINCIPLES OF CHEMISTRY   2 ELEMENTS, COMPOUNDS AND MIXTURES

FILTRATION

Filtration can be used to separate a solid from a liquid.

For example, sand can be separated from water by filtration. The apparatus for filtration is shown in **Figure 2.6**.

The substance left in the filter paper is called the residue and the liquid that comes through is called the filtrate.

Filtration can also be used to separate two solids from each other if only one of them is soluble in water (see below – rock salt).

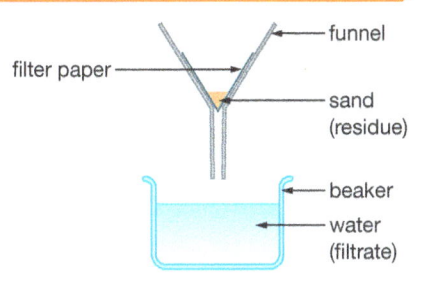

▲ Figure 2.6 Filtration can be used to separate a mixture of sand and water.

CRYSTALLISATION

Crystallisation can be used to separate a solute from a solution. For example, it could be used to separate sodium chloride from a sodium chloride solution. The solution is heated in an evaporating basin to boil off some of the water until the solution is more concentrated. The Bunsen burner is then turned off and the crystals allowed to form as more water evaporates and the solution cools. The crystals can now be removed from the mixture by filtration.

The apparatus for crystallisation is shown in **Figure 2.7**.

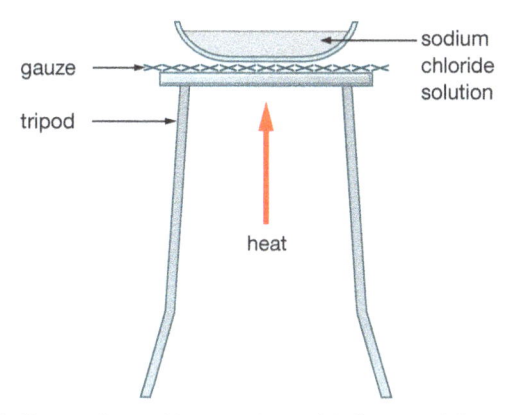

REMINDER

When a solid dissolves in a liquid:
- the substance that dissolves is called the solute
- the liquid it dissolves in is called the solvent
- the liquid formed is a solution.

KEY POINT

If the solution is heated until all the water has been boiled off, the solid can spit out of the evaporating basin and the crystals formed will be very small. If large crystals are required it is better to allow the crystals to form slowly.

▲ Figure 2.7 Crystallisation can be used to separate a solute from a solution.

MAKING PURE SALT FROM ROCK SALT

We can use filtration and crystallisation to obtain pure salt from rock salt.

Rock salt (see **Figure 2.8**) consists of salt contaminated by various earthy or rocky impurities. These impurities are not soluble in water.

If you crush the rock salt and mix it with hot water, the salt dissolves, but the impurities do not. The impurities can be filtered off, and remain on the filter paper. The filtrate is then a salt solution. The solid salt can be obtained from the solution by crystallisation.

This is typical of the way you can separate any mixture of two solids, one of which is soluble in water and one of which is not.

▲ Figure 2.8 Rock salt

SIMPLE DISTILLATION

Simple distillation can be used to separate the components of a solution. Although we can use crystallisation to separate sodium chloride from a sodium chloride solution, we can also collect the water if we use simple distillation. The apparatus for simple distillation is shown in **Figure 2.9**.

The water boils and is condensed back to a liquid by the condenser. The salt remains in the flask.

KEY POINT

Notice that water is always fed into the condenser at the lower end. That way it fills the condenser jacket better and if the flow of water stops for any reason the condenser jacket remains full of water.

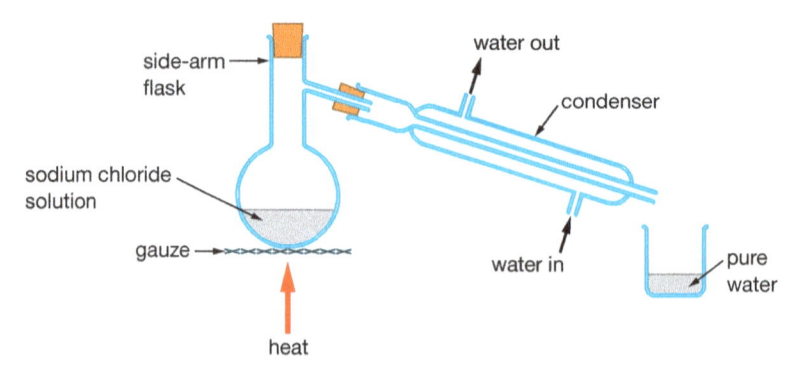

▲ Figure 2.9 Distilling pure water from sodium chloride solution

You could, of course, collect the salt from the solution as well as collecting pure water. The sodium chloride solution eventually becomes so concentrated that the salt will crystallise out.

FRACTIONAL DISTILLATION

EXTENSION

The fractionating column is often packed with glass beads or something similar, although the separation of ethanol and water in the lab works perfectly well just with an empty column. For reasons that are beyond International GCSE, a high surface area in the column helps separation of the two vapours. The ethanol produced by this experiment is about 96% pure. For complicated reasons, again beyond International GCSE, it is impossible to remove the last 4% of water by distillation.

Fractional distillation is used to separate a mixture of liquids such as ethanol (alcohol) and water. You can separate them by taking advantage of their different boiling points: water boils at 100 °C, ethanol at 78 °C. The experimental set-up for using fractional distillation to separate a mixture of ethanol and water is shown in **Figure 2.10**.

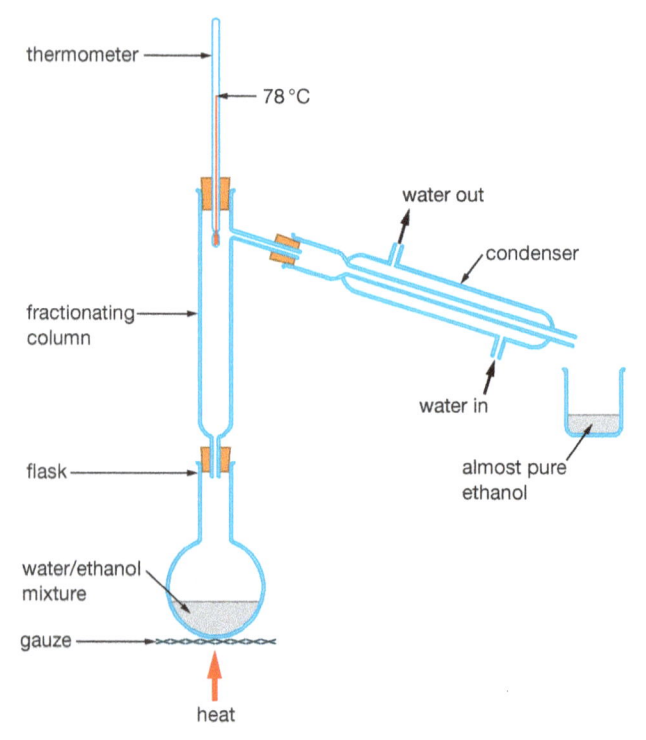

▲ Figure 2.10 Fractional distillation

Both liquids boil, but by careful heating you can control the temperature of the column so that all the water condenses in the column and **trickles** back into the flask. Only the ethanol remains as a vapour all the way to the top of the **fractionating column** and out into the condenser.

PAPER CHROMATOGRAPHY

EXTENSION

Paper chromatography can also be used to separate a mixture of colourless substances such as amino acids or sugars, but then some method must be used to make the spots visible on the paper. Amino acids show up as purple spots when they are sprayed with a chemical called ninhydrin.

Safety note: Avoid skin contact with the solvents and dyes, especially if you have sensitive skin.

KEY POINT

If the dye does not move from the pencil line during an experiment, then the dye is not at all soluble in the solvent you are using. In this case, you need to find a different solvent. If the dye moves up the paper with the solvent front, the dye is too soluble in that solvent and, again, you have to try a different solvent.

Paper chromatography can be used to separate a variety of mixtures. However, at International GCSE level we will usually use it to separate mixtures of coloured inks or food colourings. Most inks and food colourings are not just made up of one colour but contain a mixture of dyes.

ACTIVITY 1

▼ **PRACTICAL: INVESTIGATING THE COMPOSITION OF A MIXTURE WITH PAPER CHROMATOGRAPHY**

We can investigate the composition of a mixture of coloured dyes using paper chromatography. To do this we carry out the following steps.
- Draw a line with a pencil across a piece of chromatography paper; this line should be about 1 cm from the bottom of the paper. Do not use a pen as the colours in the ink may move up the chromatography paper with the solvent.
- Put a spot (use a teat pipette or a capillary tube) of the mixture of dyes on the pencil line and allow it to dry.
- Suspend the chromatography paper in a beaker that contains a small amount of solvent so that the bottom of the paper goes into the solvent. It is important that the solvent is below the pencil line so that the dyes do not just dissolve in the solvent.
- Put a lid (such as a watch glass) on the beaker so that the atmosphere becomes saturated with the solvent. This is to stop evaporation of the solvent from the surface of the paper.
- When the solvent has moved up the paper to about 1 cm from the top, remove the paper from the beaker and draw a pencil line to show where the solvent got to. The highest level of the solvent on the paper at any time is called the *solvent front*.
- Leave the paper to dry so that all the solvent evaporates.

For the solvent you can use water or a non-aqueous solvent (a solvent other than water). Which solvent you use depends on what substances are present in the mixture. A suitable solvent is usually found by experimenting with different ones.

The dyes that make up the mixture will be different in two important ways:
- the affinity they have for the paper (how well they 'stick' to the paper)
- how soluble they are in the solvent which moves up the paper.

In **Figure 2.11** spot C has hardly moved. Either it was not very soluble in the solvent or it has a very high affinity for the paper (or both). On the other hand, spot A has moved almost as far as the solvent. It must be very soluble in the solvent and not have much affinity for the paper.

◀ Figure 2.11 Paper chromatography

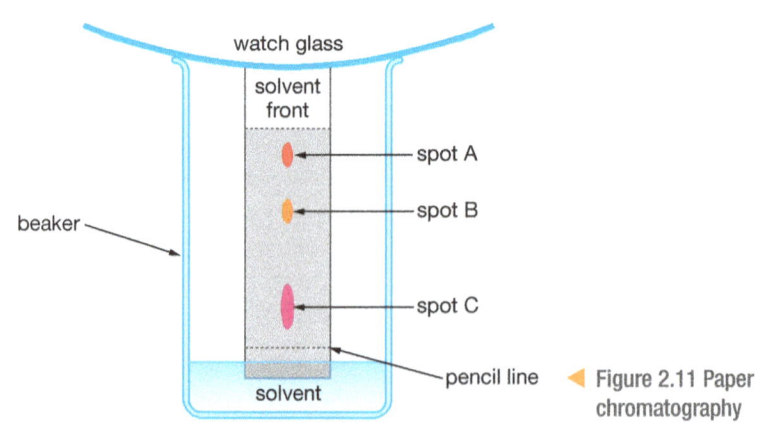

The pattern of spots you get is called a **chromatogram**. In this example, the mixture must have contained a minimum of three different dyes. We say a *minimum* of three dyes because there could be more – it is possible that one of the spots is made up of two coloured dyes that by coincidence moved the same distance. You could only confirm this by doing the experiment again with a different solvent. The chromatogram from a different experiment is shown in **Figure 2.12** and the separation of the dyes in several different inks can be clearly seen.

▲ Figure 2.12 A paper chromatography experiment

USING PAPER CHROMATOGRAPHY IN ANALYSIS

You can use paper chromatography to identify the particular dyes in a mixture. If you think that your mixture (m) could contain dyes d1, d2, d3 and d4, you can carry out an experiment to determine this.

A pencil line is drawn on a larger sheet of paper and pencil marks are drawn along the line to show the original positions of the various dyes placed on the line (see **Figure 2.13**). One spot is your unknown mixture; the others are single, known dyes. The chromatogram is then allowed to develop as before.

The mixture (m) has spots corresponding to dyes d1, d3 and d4. They have the same colour as spots in the mixture, and have travelled the same distance on the paper. Although dye d2 is the same colour as one of the spots in the mixture, it has travelled a different distance and so must be a different compound.

Instead of just saying the spots move different distances we can use the **R_f value** to describe how far the spots move. R_f stands for **retardation factor**. Each time we do a chromatography experiment the solvent (and therefore the spots) will move different distances along the paper. This means we cannot just report the distance moved by a particular spot so we have to work out a ratio instead.

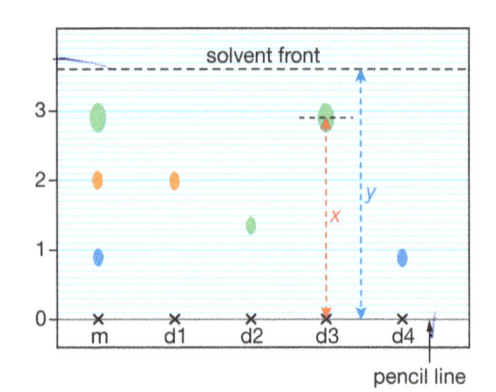

▲ Figure 2.13 Paper chromatography can be used to analyse a mixture. Lines will not be present on your paper, but they have been added here to help you measure the distances.

1 PRINCIPLES OF CHEMISTRY 2 ELEMENTS, COMPOUNDS AND MIXTURES

$$R_f = \frac{\text{distance moved by a spot (from the pencil line)}}{\text{distance moved by the solvent front (from the pencil line)}}$$

In **Figure 2.13** $R_f = \frac{x}{y}$.

So in **Figure 2.13** the R_f value for dye d3 is:

$$R_f = \frac{2.9}{3.6} = 0.81$$

EXAM HINT
Measure to the centre of the spot.

The R_f values of the dyes in mixture m are:

blue spot: $R_f = \frac{0.9}{3.6} = 0.25$

orange spot: $R_f = \frac{2.0}{3.6} = 0.56$

green spot: $R_f = \frac{2.9}{3.6} = 0.81$

The R_f values of dyes d1 to d4 are:

d1: $R_f = 0.56$
d2: $R_f = 0.36$
d3: $R_f = 0.81$
d4: $R_f = 0.25$

EXAM HINT
An R_f value must be between 0 and 1. If you get a number bigger than 1 you have probably divided the numbers the wrong way round. An R_f value has no units.

Because the spots in mixture m have the same R_f values as d1, d3 and d4, we can conclude that the mixture contains these dyes.

You have to be careful when using R_f values as they depend on the solvent used and on the type of paper. There was no problem in the experiment described above because the mixture and the individual dyes were all put on the same piece of paper. However, if the mixture was put on one piece of chromatography paper and the individual dyes on a separate piece, you can still compare R_f values as long as you use the same type of paper and the same solvent.

CHAPTER QUESTIONS

Exam-style questions on elements, compounds and mixtures can be found at the end of Unit 1 on page 184.

SKILLS CRITICAL THINKING

1 Classify each of the following substances as an element, compound or mixture:

seawater   hydrogen   honey
magnesium oxide copper(II) sulfate blood
calcium   mud   potassium iodide solution

SKILLS ANALYSIS

2 Look at the diagrams below and classify each one as an element, compound or mixture.

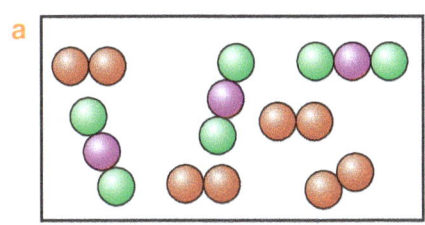

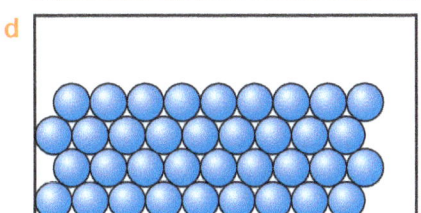

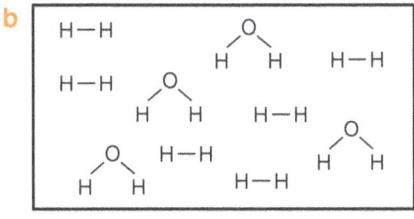

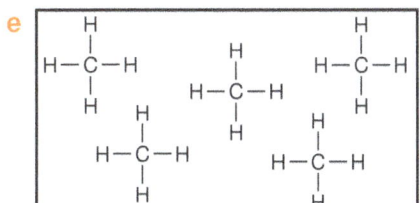

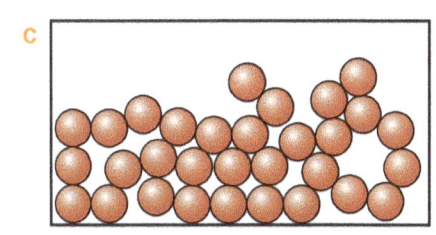

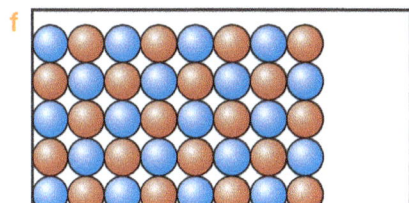

SKILLS REASONING, PROBLEM SOLVING

3 A teacher has found two white powders on a desk in the chemistry laboratory. She wants to test to see if they are pure substances, so she measures the melting points. Substance X melts at 122 °C and substance Y melts between 87 °C and 93 °C. Explain which one is the pure substance.

SKILLS DECISION MAKING

4 State which separation method you would use to carry out the following separations.

   a Potassium iodide from a potassium iodide solution.

   b Water from a potassium iodide solution.

   c Ethanol from a mixture of ethanol and water.

   d Red dye from a mixture of red and blue dyes.

   e Calcium carbonate (insoluble in water) from a mixture of calcium carbonate and water.

SKILLS CREATIVITY, DECISION MAKING

5 Suppose you had a valuable collection of small diamonds, which you kept safe from thieves by mixing them with white sugar crystals. You store the mixture in a jar labelled 'sugar'. Now you want to sell the diamonds. Describe how you would separate all the diamonds from the sugar.

SKILLS ANALYSIS

6 In order to identify the writer of an anonymous letter, a sample of ink from the letter was dissolved in a solvent and then placed on some chromatography paper. Spots of ink from the pens of five possible writers, **G**, **M**, **P**, **R** and **T**, were placed next to the sample on the chromatography paper. The final chromatogram looked like this:

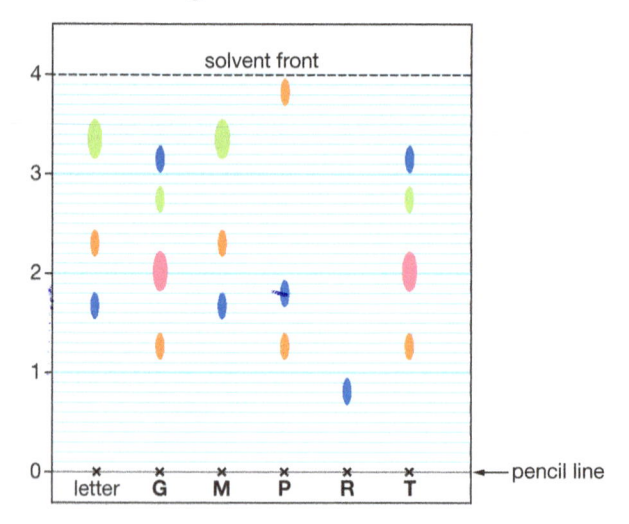

   a Which of the five writers is using ink that matches the sample from the letter?

   b Which of the writers is using a pen that contains ink made from a single dye?

SKILLS PROBLEM SOLVING

   c What is the R_f value of the blue dye in suspect **P**'s pen?

SKILLS ANALYSIS

   d Which two of the five writers are using pens containing the same ink?

   e Whose pen contained the dye that was most soluble in the solvent?

1 PRINCIPLES OF CHEMISTRY **3 ATOMIC STRUCTURE**

3 ATOMIC STRUCTURE

SPECIFICATION REFERENCES: 1.14–1.17

This chapter explores the nature of atoms and how they differ from element to element. The 118 elements are the building blocks from which everything is made, from a simple substance, such as water, to a complex molecule, such as DNA.

▲ Figure 3.1 New atoms are produced in stars . . .

▲ Figure 3.2 . . . or in nuclear processes such as nuclear bombs, nuclear reactors or radioactive decay.

LEARNING OBJECTIVES

- Know what is meant by the terms atom and molecule.
- Know the structure of an atom in terms of the positions, relative masses and relative charges of sub-atomic particles.
- Know what is meant by the terms atomic number, mass number, isotopes and relative atomic mass (A_r).
- Be able to calculate the relative atomic mass of an element (A_r) from isotopic abundances.

Copper is an element. If you tried to cut it up into smaller and smaller pieces, the final result would be the smallest possible piece of copper. At that stage, you would have an individual copper atom. You can, of course, split that atom into smaller pieces (**protons**, **neutrons** and **electrons**), but you would no longer have copper. Therefore, an **atom** is the smallest piece of an element that can still be recognised as that element.

ATOMS AND MOLECULES

REMINDER

Covalent bonds will be discussed in **Chapter 7**.

Atoms can be joined together to make molecules. A **molecule** consists of two or more atoms chemically bonded (by covalent bonds). The atoms that make up a molecule can be of the same element or different elements. A hydrogen (H_2) molecule (**Figure 3.3a**) consists of 2 hydrogen atoms chemically bonded together. A water (H_2O) molecule (**Figure 3.3b**) consists of 2 hydrogen atoms and an oxygen atom chemically bonded.

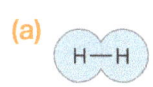

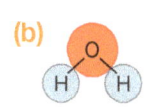

(a) H—H (b) H–O–H

▲ Figure 3.3 (a) A H_2 molecule and (b) a H_2O molecule. The lines between the atoms represent chemical (covalent) bonds.

3 ATOMIC STRUCTURE

THE STRUCTURE OF THE ATOM

Atoms are made of protons, neutrons and electrons. These particles are sometimes called *subatomic particles* because they are smaller than an atom.

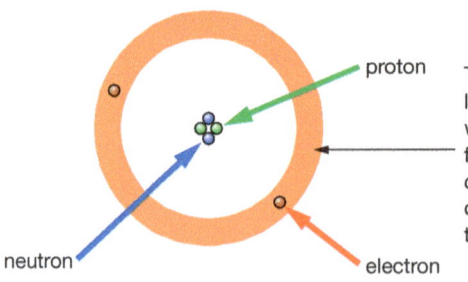

The **electrons** are found at large distances (compared with the size of the nucleus) from the nucleus. In this case, they are found most of the time somewhere in the shaded pink area.

▲ Figure 3.4 The structure of a helium atom

The **nucleus** of the atom contains protons and neutrons, and is shown highly magnified in **Figure 3.4**. In reality, if you **scale up** a helium atom to the size of a sports hall the nucleus would be no more than the size of a grain of sand.

The electrons in an atom are constantly moving around the nucleus. We usually describe the electrons as occupying *shells* and orbiting the nucleus.

The relative masses and charges of protons, neutrons and electrons are shown in **Table 3.1**.

Table 3.1 The properties of protons, neutrons and electrons

Particle	Relative mass	Relative charge
proton	1	+1
neutron	1	0
electron	$\frac{1}{1836}$	−1

Virtually all the mass of the atom is concentrated in the nucleus because electrons have a much smaller mass than protons and neutrons.

The masses and charges are measured relative to each other because the actual values are incredibly small. For example, it would take about 600 000 000 000 000 000 000 000 (6×10^{23}) protons to weigh 1 g.

ATOMIC NUMBER AND MASS NUMBER

The number of protons in an atom's nucleus is called its **atomic number** or **proton number**. Each of the 118 different elements has a different number of protons. For example, if an atom has 8 protons it must be an oxygen atom:

   atomic number = number of protons

The **mass number** (sometimes known as the **nucleon number**) shows the total number of protons and neutrons in the nucleus of the atom:

   mass number = number of protons + number of neutrons

HINT

$\frac{1}{1836}$ is approximately 0.0005.

KEY POINT

The mass of an electron is negligible (virtually nothing) compared with the mass of protons and neutrons.

If the mass of a proton were the same as the mass of a basketball, an electron would have a mass approximately the same as 10 grains of rice.

KEY POINT

The atomic number defines an element and is unique to that element. We can identify an element by its atomic number instead of its name. We could talk about a wristwatch made from the element with atomic number 79 instead of talking about 'a gold wristwatch', or say that the element with atomic number 17 is poisonous instead of saying 'chlorine is poisonous'. However, these are more complicated ways of describing things!

For any particular atom, this information can be shown as, for example:

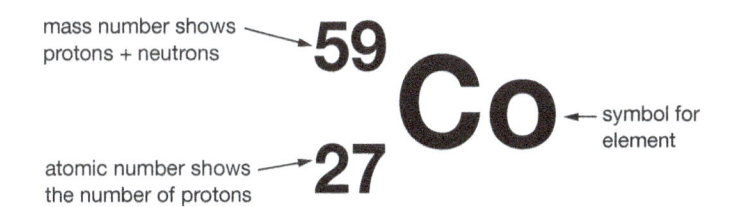

mass number shows protons + neutrons → 59
atomic number shows the number of protons → 27
Co ← symbol for element

This particular atom of cobalt contains 27 protons. To make the total number of protons and neutrons up to 59, there must also be 32 neutrons.

You can see from this that:

number of neutrons = mass number – atomic number

> **HINT**
> **Be careful!** When you are writing symbols with two letters, the first is a capital letter and the second must be lower case. If you write CO you are talking about carbon monoxide, not cobalt.

ISOTOPES

The number of neutrons in an atom can vary slightly. For example, there are three kinds of carbon atom, called carbon-12, carbon-13 and carbon-14 (see **Figure 3.5**). They all have the same number of protons (because all carbon atoms have 6 protons, its atomic number), but the number of neutrons varies. These different atoms of carbon are called **isotopes**.

Isotopes are atoms (of the same element) which have the same atomic number but different mass numbers. They have the same number of protons but different numbers of neutrons.

The fact that they have varying numbers of neutrons makes no difference to their chemical reactions. The chemical properties (how something reacts) are controlled by the number and arrangement of the electrons, and that is identical for all three isotopes.

$^{12}_{6}C$ — 6 protons, 6 neutrons
$^{13}_{6}C$ — 6 protons, 7 neutrons
$^{14}_{6}C$ — 6 protons, 8 neutrons

○ proton ○ neutron

▲ Figure 3.5 The nuclei of the three isotopes of carbon

RELATIVE ATOMIC MASS

You might have seen the following in a Periodic Table:

35.5
Cl
chlorine
17

Chlorine appears to have a mass number of 35.5. If you calculate the number of neutrons for chlorine you obtain:

number of neutrons = 35.5 – 17 = 18.5

It is not possible to have half a neutron and so there must be something wrong with this. The number 35.5 is not actually the mass number for chlorine but rather the **relative atomic mass** (A_r). Chlorine consists of two isotopes, ^{35}Cl and ^{37}Cl, and a naturally occurring sample contains a mixture of these.

> **KEY POINT**
> The number above each symbol in the Periodic Table used in International GCSE papers is a relative atomic mass and not a mass number. However, in most cases the relative atomic mass stated is the same as the mass number of the most common isotope. The only exceptions to this are chlorine (35.5) and copper (63.5).

> **KEY POINT**
>
> This type of average is called a **weighted average** or weighted mean.

Relative atomic mass is the average mass of an atom, taking into account the amount of each isotope present in a naturally occurring sample of an element. It is explained in more detail in **Chapter 5**.

You can probably see that a naturally occurring sample of chlorine must contain more of the ^{35}Cl isotope than the ^{37}Cl isotope. This is because the relative atomic mass is closer to 35 than to 37.

We can calculate the relative atomic mass of an element by knowing how much of each isotope is present in a sample (the isotopic abundances) of that element, and then working out the average mass of an atom. This is done in exactly the same way as you would calculate a weighted average in maths. It can be understood more easily by looking at a worked example.

> **EXAMPLE 1**
>
> A naturally occurring sample of the element boron contains 20% ^{10}B and 80% ^{11}B. Calculate the relative atomic mass.
>
> If we imagine there are 100 atoms we can work out that 20% of them, that is 20, will have mass 10 and 80 will have mass 11.
>
> The total mass of the 20 atoms with mass 10 is 20 × 10
>
> The total mass of the 80 atoms with mass 11 is 80 × 11
>
> The total mass of all the atoms in the sample is 20 × 10 + 80 × 11
>
> There are 100 atoms so we can work out the average by dividing the total mass by the total number of atoms (100):
>
> $$\text{relative atomic mass} = \frac{20 \times 10 + 80 \times 11}{100} = 10.8$$
>
> Therefore, the relative atomic mass of boron is 10.8.
>
> Even if there are three or four different isotopes, you still do the calculation in the same way: calculate the total mass of 100 atoms, then divide the answer by 100.

THE ELECTRONS

> **COUNTING THE NUMBER OF ELECTRONS IN AN ATOM**

Atoms are electrically neutral (they have no overall charge). The charge on a proton (+1) is equal but opposite to the charge on an electron (−1), and therefore in an atom:

number of electrons = number of protons

> **HINT**
>
> Remember that the number of protons is the same as the atomic number of the element.

So, if an oxygen atom (atomic number = 8) has 8 protons, it must also have 8 electrons; if a chlorine atom (atomic number = 17) has 17 protons, it must also have 17 electrons.

You will see that the key feature in this is knowing the atomic number. You can find the atomic number from the Periodic Table.

The number of protons in an atom is equal to the number of electrons. However, the atomic number is defined in terms of the number of protons because the number of electrons can change in chemical reactions, for example when atoms form **ions** (see **Chapter 6**).

1 PRINCIPLES OF CHEMISTRY 3 ATOMIC STRUCTURE

DIAGRAMS OF ATOMS

REMINDER

You do not need to be able to work out or understand why there are different numbers of electrons in each shell.

You will often see diagrams of atoms drawn as in **Figure 3.6**. The nucleus is shown at the centre and the electrons are in shells around the nucleus.

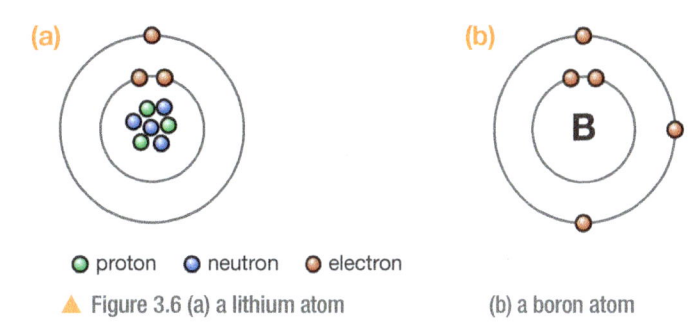

○ proton ● neutron ● electron

▲ Figure 3.6 (a) a lithium atom   (b) a boron atom

In **Figure 3.6a**, we can tell that the diagram represents a lithium atom because there are 3 protons in the nucleus. We can also tell that it is the ^{7}Li isotope because there are 4 neutrons as well as the 3 protons.

In **Figure 3.6b**, the B in the middle tells us that the element is boron, so we know there must be 5 protons in the nucleus. We do not, however, know how many neutrons there are so we cannot identify which isotope it is (there are 2 common isotopes of boron, ^{10}B and ^{11}B).

THE PERIODIC TABLE

Chapter 4 deals in detail with what you need to know about the Periodic Table for International GCSE purposes.

Atoms are arranged in the Periodic Table in order of increasing atomic number. You will find a full version of the Periodic Table in Appendix A on page 452. Most Periodic Tables have two numbers against each symbol; be careful to choose the right one. The atomic number will always be the smaller number. The other number will either be the mass number of the most common isotope of the element or the relative atomic mass of the element. The Periodic Table will clarify this.

CHAPTER QUESTIONS

Exam-style questions on atomic structure can be found at the end of Unit 1 on page 184.

You will need to use the Periodic Table in Appendix A on page 452.

SKILLS CRITICAL THINKING

1 Atoms contain three types of particle: proton, neutron and electron.
   a State where the protons and neutrons are in an atom.
   b State which type of particle in the atom orbits the nucleus.
   c State which one of the particles has a positive charge.
   d State which two particles have approximately the same mass.

SKILLS CRITICAL THINKING

2 Fluorine atoms have a mass number of 19.
   a Use the Periodic Table to find the atomic number of fluorine.
   b Explain what *mass number* means.
   c State the number of protons, neutrons and electrons in a fluorine atom.

SKILLS REASONING

   d Explain why the number of protons in an atom must always equal the number of electrons.

3 The symbol for an osmium atom is $^{190}_{76}$Os. From this it can be deduced that

A there are 190 protons in an osmium atom

B there are 266 neutrons in an osmium atom

C the number of protons + electrons in an osmium atom is 190

D the number of neutrons is an osmium atom is 114

4 Work out the numbers of protons, neutrons and electrons in each of the following atoms:

a $^{56}_{26}$Fe   **b** $^{93}_{41}$Nb   **c** $^{235}_{92}$U

5 Chlorine has two isotopes, chlorine-35 and chlorine-37.

a Explain what *isotopes* are.

b State the numbers of protons, neutrons and electrons in the two isotopes.

6 The table shows the number of protons, neutrons and electrons in four atoms. The symbols are not the actual chemical symbols of the elements.

	Protons	Neutrons	Electrons
Q	12	12	12
Z	18	19	18
D	12	14	12
A	17	19	17

a Explain why all the atoms are neutral.

b State the letters of two atoms that are isotopes.

c What is the atomic number of A?

d What is the mass number of Z?

e Write the full symbol for Q showing its atomic number and mass number.

f An atom of D loses 2 electrons in a chemical reaction. Explain how this affects the charge on the atom and the mass of the atom.

7 Which of the following produces the greatest number?

A the number of neutrons in an atom of ^{55}Mn – the number of electrons in an atom of ^{37}Cl

B the number of neutrons in an atom of ^{65}Cu – the number of protons in an atom of ^{66}Zn

C the number of electrons in an atom of ^{23}Na + the number of protons in an atom of ^{18}O

D the total number of protons, neutrons and electrons in an atom of ^{14}C

8 Nitrogen has two naturally occurring stable isotopes, ^{14}N and ^{15}N. The relative atomic mass of nitrogen is 14.01. Which of the following is correct?

A the nucleus of a ^{15}N atom contains 1 more proton than the nucleus of a ^{14}N atom

B a naturally occurring sample of nitrogen contains more ^{14}N than ^{15}N

C the nuclei of ^{14}N and ^{15}N contain the same number of electrons

D the number of neutrons in an atom of ^{15}N is equal to the number of electrons in an atom of ^{14}N

1 PRINCIPLES OF CHEMISTRY   **3 ATOMIC STRUCTURE**

SKILLS   PROBLEM SOLVING

9. Lithium has two naturally occurring isotopes, ^{6}Li (abundance 7%) and ^{7}Li (abundance 93%). Calculate the relative atomic mass of lithium, giving your answer to 2 decimal places.

10. Magnesium has three naturally occurring stable isotopes, ^{24}Mg (abundance 78.99%), ^{25}Mg (abundance 10.00%) and ^{26}Mg (abundance 11.01%). Calculate the relative atomic mass of magnesium, giving your answer to 2 decimal places.

11. Lead has four naturally occurring stable isotopes. Calculate the relative atomic mass of lead given the data in the table.

Mass number	Natural abundance / %
204	1.4
206	24.1
207	22.1
208	52.4

12. Iridium has two naturally occurring isotopes, ^{191}Ir and ^{193}Ir.
    a. State the number of protons, neutrons and electrons in an ^{191}Ir atom.
    b. Explain the difference between the two isotopes.
    c. The relative atomic mass of iridium is 192.22. Explain whether a naturally occurring sample of iridium contains more ^{191}Ir or ^{193}Ir.

SKILLS   REASONING

4 THE PERIODIC TABLE

SPECIFICATION REFERENCES: 1.18, 1.21

The Periodic Table shows all the elements in the universe and is one of the most important tools that a chemist has. The arrangement of the elements allows us to understand trends in properties and make predictions. The modern Periodic Table was first presented in 1869 by a famous Russian chemist, Dmitri Mendeleev (left). This chapter explores some of the features of the Periodic Table.

LEARNING OBJECTIVES

- Understand how elements are arranged in the Periodic Table:
  - in order of atomic number
  - in groups and periods.
- Identify an element as a metal or a non-metal according to its position in the Periodic Table.

THE PERIODIC TABLE

The search for patterns in chemistry during the 19th century resulted in the modern Periodic Table (**Figure 4.1**). *The elements are arranged in order of atomic number* – the number of protons in the nuclei of the atoms.

▲ Figure 4.1 The Periodic Table

The vertical columns in the Periodic Table are called **groups**. The first seven groups are numbered from 1 to 7 and the final group is numbered 0. Elements are placed in a particular group because of the way they react – their chemical properties. For example, all the elements in Group 1 react in the same way with water to form hydrogen gas and a hydroxide with formula MOH (e.g. LiOH, NaOH, KOH) and all the elements in Group 0 are very unreactive.

DID YOU KNOW?

You will sometimes see Group 0 labelled as Group 8. In more advanced Periodic Tables the groups are numbered from 1 to 18, including the transition metals.

1 PRINCIPLES OF CHEMISTRY   4 THE PERIODIC TABLE

The elements in orange in **Figure 4.1** are called the transition metals or transition elements. At this level, they are not usually included in the numbering of the groups. Some of the groups have names, e.g. Group 1 is the **alkali metals**, Group 7 is the **halogens** and Group 0 is the **noble gases**.

The horizontal rows in the Periodic Table are called **periods**. It is important to remember that hydrogen and helium make up Period 1.

The lanthanoids and actinoids are usually dropped out of their proper places and written separately at the bottom of the Periodic Table. There is a good reason for this. If you put them where they should be (as in **Figure 4.2**), everything has to be drawn slightly smaller to fit on the page. That makes it more difficult to read.

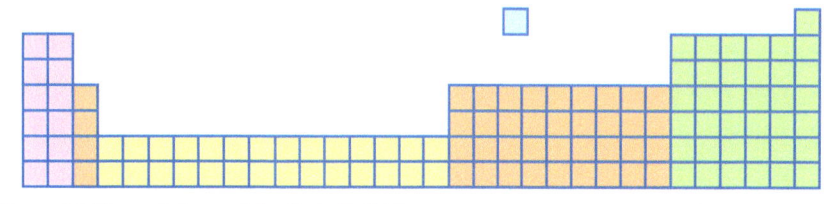

▲ Figure 4.2 The real shape of the Periodic Table

THE PERIODIC TABLE AND THE NUMBER OF PROTONS, NEUTRONS AND ELECTRONS

Most Periodic Tables have two numbers against each symbol. The atomic number will always be the smaller number. The other number will either be the mass number of the most common isotope of the element or the relative atomic mass of the element. The Periodic Table will tell you which.

You can use a Periodic Table to work out the number of protons, neutrons and electrons there are in atoms. Remember:

- the number of protons in an atom is equal to the atomic number
- the number of electrons in an atom is equal to the number of protons
- the number of neutrons in an atom = mass number − atomic number.

> **REMINDER**
> For a larger version of the Periodic Table, including atomic numbers and other information, see **Appendix A**.

> **DID YOU KNOW?**
> The most up-to-date Periodic Table contains the elements up to atomic number 118. At International GCSE level the lanthanoids and actinoids are usually omitted from Periodic Tables because the emphasis is placed on a general understanding, which can easily be achieved without them. Although sometimes called the rare earth metals, the lanthanoids are actually not that rare and are quite important in modern technology. Most of the actinoids are unstable and **undergo** radioactive decay.

238
U
Uranium
92

▲ Figure 4.3

EXAMPLE 1

Figure 4.3 shows the symbol for uranium as given in a Periodic Table. Calculate the number of protons, neutrons and electrons in an atom of uranium.

The atomic number is the smaller number, so the atomic number of uranium is 92. The atomic number tells us the number of protons, therefore a uranium atom contains 92 protons.

The number of protons is equal to the number of electrons, therefore a uranium atom contains 92 electrons.

The number of neutrons = mass number − atomic number.

The number of neutrons = 238 − 92 = 146.

1 PRINCIPLES OF CHEMISTRY 4 THE PERIODIC TABLE

> **REMINDER**
> You do not need to know the physical properties for the exam (although you will probably remember them from earlier study).

> **DID YOU KNOW?**
> Not all metals have high melting and boiling points: sodium has a melting point of 98 °C and mercury is a liquid at room temperature. We still classify sodium and mercury as metals however, due to their other properties.

> **DID YOU KNOW?**
> Not all non-metals show all of these properties: diamond and graphite (both forms of carbon) sublime at around 4000 °C, which is higher than the melting point of any metallic element. Diamond is also the best conductor of heat of any element and graphite conducts electricity.

> **EXTENSION**
> Hydrogen does not really fit in the Periodic Table properly. With an atomic number of 1 and 1 electron it its outer shell, there is a case for putting it in Group 1, but it does not have similar properties to the other elements in Group 1: it is not a metal and does not have similar chemical properties to the alkali metals. If you are interested, you could try an internet search for 'metallic hydrogen'.

METALS AND NON-METALS

We can divide elements into two categories – metals and non-metals – based on their properties.

Metals:

- tend to be solids with high melting and boiling points
- are **malleable** and **ductile**
- are good conductors of electricity and heat.

Non-metals:

- tend to have low melting and boiling points
- do not usually conduct electricity
- are usually poor conductors of heat.

The metals are on the left-hand side of the Periodic Table and the non-metals are on the right-hand side. Although the division into metals and non-metals is shown clearly in **Figure 4.4**, in practice there is a lot of uncertainty on the dividing line. For example, arsenic (As) has properties of both metals and non-metals.

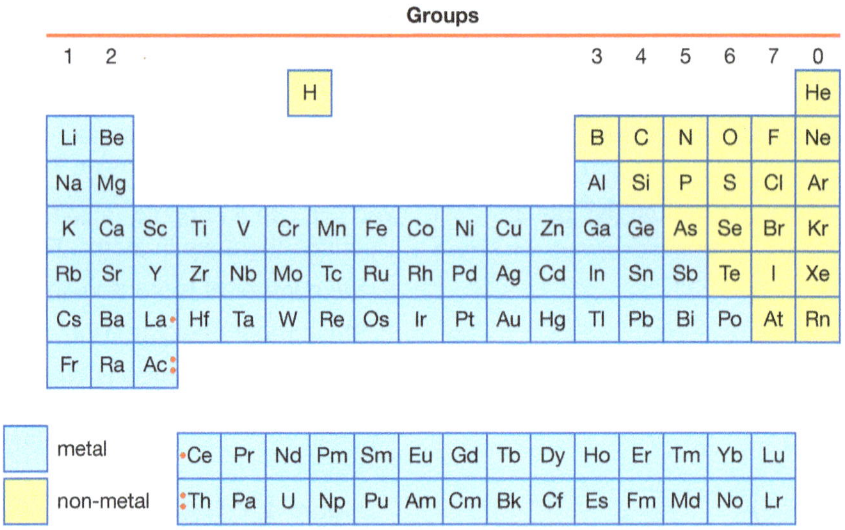

▲ Figure 4.4 Metals and non-metals

CHAPTER QUESTIONS

Exam-style questions on the Periodic Table can be found at the end of Unit 1 on page 184.

You will need to use the Periodic Table in Appendix A on page 452.

SKILLS CRITICAL THINKING

1 Answer the questions that follow using only the elements in this list:

caesium, chlorine, molybdenum, neon, nickel, nitrogen, strontium, tin.

   a State the name of an element which is:

   i in Group 2

   ii in the same period as silicon

iii in the same group as phosphorus
iv in Period 6
v a noble gas.

b Divide the list of elements at the beginning of the question into two groups, metals and non-metals.

2 a Give the symbol of the element in Period 5 and Group 1.

b Give the symbol of the element in Group 3 and Period 4.

3 The diagram shows a blank Periodic Table in which the symbols of certain elements are represented by letters – these letters are not the actual symbols for the elements.

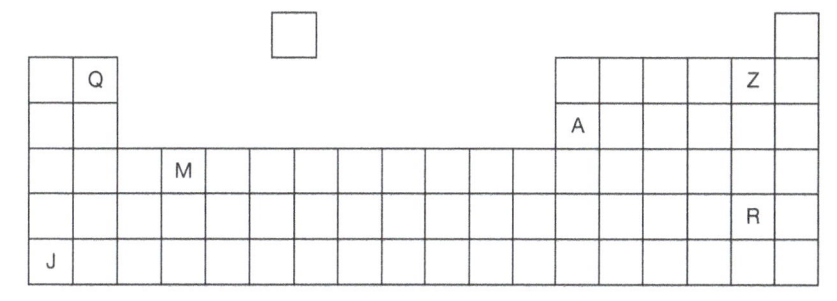

Answer the following questions using the letters in the Periodic Table above, not the actual symbols of the elements.

a State the letters of two elements in the same group.

b State the letters of two elements in the same period.

c How many elements shown are metals?

d Explain whether M has a higher or lower atomic number than A.

e Which of the following *must* be true about R and J?

A	An atom of J contains 2 more protons than an atom of R
B	An atom of J contains 2 more neutrons than an atom of R
C	R and J have similar chemical properties
D	R and J are isotopes

4 Find each of the following elements in the Periodic Table and state the number of protons in the nucleus.

a arsenic, As

b bromine, Br

c tin, Sn

d xenon, Xe

5 The elements in the Periodic Table are arranged in order of atomic number. If they were arranged in order of mass number, give the names of two elements that would be in different positions. Explain why this would cause a problem.

6 Use the Periodic Table to explain whether the following statement is true or false.

Considering only the most common isotope of each element, there is only one element that has more protons than neutrons.

5 CHEMICAL FORMULAE AND EQUATIONS

SPECIFICATION REFERENCES: 1.25, 1.26

Chemistry has its own language and chemists can communicate important information using formulae and equations. In this chapter we will learn how to write chemical equations.

▲ Figure 5.1 Water (H_2O) and hydrogen peroxide (H_2O_2) have very similar formulae but there is a big difference between them. You can drink a glass of H_2O, however, if you drink H_2O_2 you will get very ill.

LEARNING OBJECTIVES

- Write word equations and balanced chemical equations (including state symbols):
  - for reactions studied in this specification
  - for unfamiliar reactions where suitable information is provided.
- Calculate relative formula masses (including relative molecular masses) (M_r) from relative atomic masses (A_r).

Table 5.1 Some names and formulae of chemicals

Water	H_2O
Hydrogen peroxide	H_2O_2
Sodium	Na
Sodium chloride	NaCl
Potassium permanganate	$KMnO_4$
Oxygen	O_2
Ozone	O_3
Ammonia	NH_3
Hydrazine	N_2H_4

FORMULAE

The words *chemicals* or *chemical substances* are used to describe the elements and compounds that make up the world around us. All chemical substances can be described using chemical formulae. Each chemical has a fixed formula and if two chemicals have different formulae they are different substances. Examples of some chemical formulae are given in **Table 5.1**.

All chemical formulae are made up of letters representing the elements present, for example NH_3 contains atoms of two different elements (N and H) but $KMnO_4$ has atoms of three different elements (K, Mn, O).

Formulae may also contain numbers representing how many of each atom are present. The numbers in a chemical formula are always **subscripts** (small numbers below the line) and they are fixed – if the number is different then it is not the same chemical. For example, you can safely drink H_2O but you would be very ill if you drank H_2O_2!

1 PRINCIPLES OF CHEMISTRY 5 CHEMICAL FORMULAE AND EQUATIONS

COUNTING ATOMS IN A FORMULA

In order to be able to balance equations (see below) we need to count the number of atoms in a formula. If there is a subscript number *after* the symbol for an atom it indicates how many of *that* atom are present in the formula. If there is no number then there is just one atom present. In the formula H_2O, the 2 after the H indicates that there are 2 H atoms present in a molecule; there is no number after the O, so there is only 1 O atom present. In H_2O_2 there are 2 H atoms and 2 O atoms in each molecule.

Some other examples are given in **Table 5.2**.

Table 5.2 The numbers and types of atoms in some chemicals

CO_2	1 C atom and 2 O atoms
NH_3	1 N atom and 3 H atoms
HNO_3	1 H atom, 1 N atom and 3 O atoms
C_4H_{10}	4 C atoms and 10 H atoms

If there are brackets in a formula then the subscript after the brackets refers to everything in the brackets. For example, $Ca(OH)_2$ contains 1 Ca atom, 2 O atoms and 2 H atoms whereas $Mg(NO_3)_2$ contains 1 Mg atom, 2 N atoms and $3 \times 2 = 6$ O atoms.

Occasionally big numbers appear in formulae – an example of this is $CuSO_4 \cdot 5H_2O$ – like other big numbers (see below) the 5 multiplies everything after it; therefore there are 5 H_2O molecules per formula unit, so a total of 10 H atoms and 14 O atoms in $CuSO_4 \cdot 5H_2O$.

REMINDER
$CuSO_4 \cdot 5H_2O$ contains water of crystallisation and will be discussed again on page 167.

EXAM HINT
Unless the exam question states explicitly that you should write a word equation, when asked to write an equation, *always* write a balanced symbol equation.

WRITING EQUATIONS

There are two types of chemical equation that you could be asked to write: **word equations** and symbol equations. Symbol equations are usually called *chemical equations*, or just, *equations*. All chemical equations must be balanced.

COUNTING ATOMS IN A CHEMICAL EQUATION

An example of a balanced chemical equation is:

$$CaCO_3 + 2HCl \rightarrow CaCl_2 + CO_2 + H_2O$$

When you write equations, it is important to be able to count how many of each type of atom you have. In particular, you must understand the difference between big numbers written in front of formulae (sometimes called **coefficients**), such as the **2** in **2**HCl, and the smaller, subscript numbers in the formulae, such as the **3** in $CaCO_3$. The big number (coefficient) multiplies everything after it, so 2HCl means that there are 2HCl molecules and a total of 2H atoms and 2Cl atoms. Remember: a subscript only multiplies the atom immediately before it (unless there are brackets), so $CaCO_3$ contains 1Ca, 1C and 3O atoms.

Another balanced chemical equation is $H_2S_2O_7 + H_2O \rightarrow 2H_2SO_4$

Look at the way the numbers work in $2H_2SO_4$. The big number in front tells you that you have 2 sulfuric acid (H_2SO_4) molecules. The subscript 4 tells you that you have 4 oxygen atoms in each molecule. If you count the atoms in $2H_2SO_4$ (see **Figure 5.2**) you will find 4 hydrogens, 2 sulfurs and 8 oxygens.

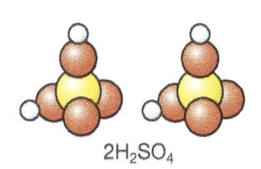

▲ Figure 5.2 $2H_2SO_4$. The sulfur atoms are shown in yellow, the oxygens in red and the hydrogens in white.

> **HINT**
> A thermal **decomposition reaction** is one in which heat is used to break down a substance into simpler substances.

The balanced equation for the **thermal decomposition** of calcium nitrate is

$2Ca(NO_3)_2 \rightarrow 2CaO + 4NO_2 + O_2$

In $2Ca(NO_3)_2$ the large 2 multiplies everything after it and the small 2 multiplies everything in the brackets, so there are $2 \times 3 \times 2 = 12$ O atoms.

BALANCING EQUATIONS

Chemical reactions involve taking elements or compounds and moving their atoms around into new combinations. It follows that you must always end up with the same number of atoms that you started with.

Imagine you had to write an equation for the reaction between methane, CH_4, and oxygen, O_2. Methane burns in oxygen to form carbon dioxide and water. Think of this in terms of rearranging the atoms in some models (see **Figure 5.3**).

methane   oxygen   carbon dioxide   water

▲ Figure 5.3 Rearranging the atoms in methane and oxygen

If you count the atoms you had at the beginning (on the left-hand side of the arrow) and the atoms you have at the end (on the right-hand side of the arrow), you can see that this cannot be right! During the rearrangement, we seem to have gained an oxygen atom and lost two hydrogens. The reaction must be more complicated than this. Since the substances are all correct, the proportions must be wrong.

Try again:

> **EXAM HINT**
> You should learn the formulae of carbon dioxide (CO_2) and water (H_2O).

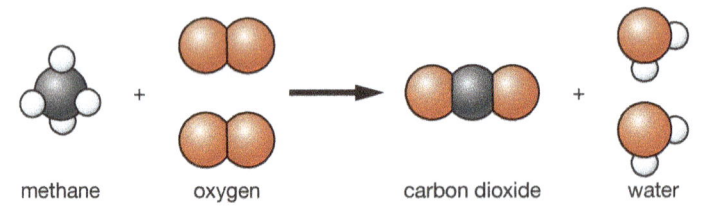

methane   oxygen   carbon dioxide   water

▲ Figure 5.4 A balanced equation for the reaction between methane and oxygen.

There are now the same number of each type of atom before and after (see **Figure 5.4**). This process is called **balancing the equation**.

In symbols, this equation would be:

$CH_4 + 2O_2 \rightarrow CO_2 + 2H_2O$

Think of each symbol (C or H or O) as representing one atom of that element. Count them up in the equation, and check that there is the same number of atoms on both sides.

HOW TO BALANCE EQUATIONS

In order to balance equations you should adopt a systematic approach.

- Work across the equation from left to right, checking one element after another, except if an element appears in several places in the equation. In that case, leave the element until the end and you will often find that it has sorted itself out.

1 PRINCIPLES OF CHEMISTRY
5 CHEMICAL FORMULAE AND EQUATIONS

- If you have a group of atoms (like a sulfate group (SO_4), for example), which is unchanged from one side of the equation to the other, count that up as a whole group, rather than counting individual sulfurs and oxygens – saves time.
- Check everything at the end to make sure you have not changed something that you have already counted.

> **HINT**
> This is really important! You must never, never change a formula when balancing an equation. All you are allowed to do is to write big numbers in front of the formula.

> **HINT**
> The symbol for a metal is always just the element symbol – there is never a subscript. For example, magnesium is Mg, zinc is Zn and sodium is Na. If you write Mg_2, Zn_2 or Na_2, this is wrong.

> **HINT**
> Most elements that are gases have a 2 in their formula:
> Hydrogen is H_2 Oxygen is O_2
> The only gaseous elements that do not have this 2 are the noble gases: He, Ne, Ar, Kr and Xe.

> **EXAM HINT**
> In more advanced work scientists often balance equations with fractions, but in the International GCSE examination it is probably best to avoid leaving halves in equations. To get rid of the halves you just need to double all the large numbers in the equation (do not forget about the 1s – although we do not show them they are still there!).

> **EXTENSION**
> The problem of having fractions in an equation is resolved if you consider the equations as representing *moles* of substances rather than *molecules*. Moles are not covered in this course but there is a full treatment in the Triple Award Chemistry book.

EXAMPLE 1

Balance the equation for the reaction between zinc and hydrochloric acid:

$$Zn + HCl \rightarrow ZnCl_2 + H_2$$

Work from left to right. Count the zinc atoms: 1 on each side; no problem!

Count the hydrogen atoms: 1 on the left, 2 on the right. If you have 2 at the end, you must have started with 2. The only way of achieving this is to have 2HCl. (You must not change the formula to H_2Cl because this substance does not exist.)

$$Zn + 2HCl \rightarrow ZnCl_2 + H_2$$

Now count the chlorines: there are 2 on each side. Good! Finally check everything again to make sure, and you have finished.

	Zn + 2HCl	→	$ZnCl_2 + H_2$
numbers of atoms	Zn 1		Zn 1
	H 2		H 2
	Cl 2		Cl 2

EXAMPLE 2

Balance the equation for the **combustion** of ethane:

$$C_2H_6 + O_2 \rightarrow CO_2 + H_2O$$

Starting from the left, balance the carbons:

$$C_2H_6 + O_2 \rightarrow 2CO_2 + H_2O$$

Now the hydrogens:

$$C_2H_6 + O_2 \rightarrow 2CO_2 + 3H_2O$$

Finally the oxygens: there are 7 oxygens ((2×2) + 3) on the right-hand side, but only 2 on the left (**Figure 5.5**). The problem is that the oxygens have to go around in pairs. So how can you obtain an odd number (7) of oxygens on the left-hand side?

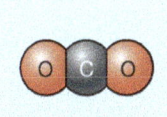

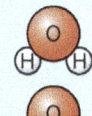

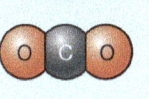

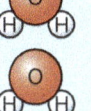

▲ Figure 5.5 There are 7 O atoms in $2CO_2 + 3H_2O$

The trick with this is to allow yourself to have halves in your equation. 7 oxygen atoms, O, is the same as $3\frac{1}{2}$ oxygen molecules, O_2.

$$C_2H_6 + 3\tfrac{1}{2}O_2 \rightarrow 2CO_2 + 3H_2O$$

Now double all the large numbers to get rid of the half:

$$2C_2H_6 + 7O_2 \rightarrow 4CO_2 + 6H_2O$$

> **HINT**
> Do not worry if this chemistry is new to you, or if at this stage you do not know what the state symbols should be. That is not important at the moment.

> **EXAM HINT**
> Remember that water is a liquid (l), not an aqueous solution (aq). An aqueous solution is formed when something is *dissolved in water*.

> **REMINDER**
> Remember that isotopes are atoms of the same element, but with different masses. Isotopes are explained in **Chapter 3** (page 153).

> **EXTENSION**
> This is a slight approximation. To be accurate, each of these hydrogen atoms has a mass of 1.008 on the carbon-12 scale. For International GCSE purposes, we take it as being exactly 1.

> **KEY POINT**
> Remember, to work out a weighted average we have to know how much of each isotope is present in a sample.

STATE SYMBOLS

State symbols are often, but not always, written after the formulae of the various substances in an equation to show what physical state everything is in. You need to know four different state symbols:

(s) solid   (l) liquid   (g) gas   (aq) in **aqueous** solution (dissolved in water)

So an equation might look like this:

$$2K(s) + 2H_2O(l) \rightarrow 2KOH(aq) + H_2(g)$$

This shows that *solid* potassium reacts with *liquid* water to make a *solution* of potassium hydroxide in water and hydrogen *gas*.

RELATIVE ATOMIC MASS (A_r)

We have already looked at how to calculate relative atomic masses from the isotopic abundances in **Chapter 3**. Here we will look a little more closely at what exactly the relative atomic mass is.

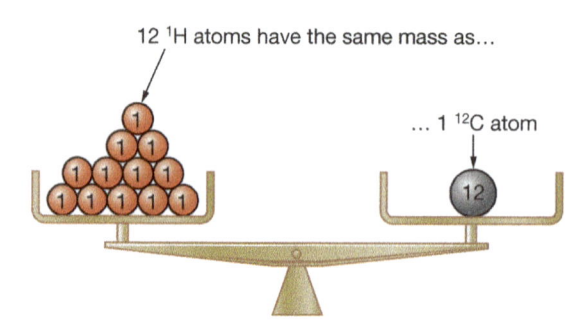

Atoms are amazingly small. The mass of a hydrogen atom is about 1.67×10^{-24} g (0.00000000000000000000000167 g). It is really difficult to use numbers such as this and so we use a scale of *relative* masses instead. The masses of atoms (and molecules) are compared with the mass of an atom of the carbon-12 isotope. We call this the carbon-12 scale. On this scale, one atom of the carbon-12 isotope weighs *exactly* 12 units and the mass of the most common hydrogen isotope is 1 (see **Figure 5.6**).

▲ Figure 5.6 The most common hydrogen atom weighs one-twelfth as much as a ^{12}C atom.

From this you can see that $\frac{1}{12}$ of a ^{12}C atom has a relative mass of 1 and we compare everything to this. A fluorine-19 atom has a relative mass of 19 because its atoms have a mass 19 times that of $\frac{1}{12}$ of a ^{12}C atom. An atom of the most common isotope of magnesium weighs 24 times as much as $\frac{1}{12}$ of a ^{12}C atom, and is therefore said to have a relative mass of 24.

The masses we are talking about here are the masses of individual *isotopes*, but samples of an actual element contain different isotopes and so we need a measure of the average mass of an *atom* taking into account the different isotopes. This is the relative atomic mass.

The relative atomic mass of an element is given the symbol A_r and it is defined like this:

The relative atomic mass of an element is the weighted average mass of the isotopes of the element. It is measured on a scale on which a carbon-12 (^{12}C) atom has a mass of exactly 12.

Because we are talking here about *relative* masses they have no units.

On this scale, the relative atomic mass of chlorine is 35.45, that of lithium is 6.94 and that of sodium is 22.99 because we are taking into account the different isotopes, and are quoting an average mass for an atom. Although all elements consist of a mixture of isotopes, at International GCSE we only use relative atomic masses including decimal places for Cl (35.5) and Cu (63.5), therefore we will take the relative atomic mass of lithium as 7 and that of sodium as 23.

RELATIVE FORMULA MASS (M_r)

You can measure the masses of compounds on the same carbon-12 scale. For example, a water molecule, H_2O, has a mass of 18 on the carbon-12 scale. This means that a water molecule has 18 times the mass of $\frac{1}{12}$ of a ^{12}C atom.

If you are talking about compounds, you use the term **relative formula mass**. Relative formula mass is sometimes called relative molecular mass.

Relative formula mass is given the symbol M_r.

> **HINT**
> Avoid the term relative *molecular* mass because it can only properly be applied to substances which are actually molecules, that is, to covalent substances. You should not use it for things like magnesium oxide or sodium chloride, which are ionic. Relative *formula* mass covers everything.

CALCULATING SOME RELATIVE FORMULA MASSES

> **EXAM HINT**
> Relative atomic masses will always be given to you in an exam, either in the question or on the Periodic Table. If you use the Periodic Table, be sure to *use the right number!* It will always be the larger of the two numbers given.

To find the relative formula mass (M_r) of magnesium carbonate, $MgCO_3$

Relative atomic masses: C = 12, O = 16, Mg = 24.

Add up the relative atomic masses to give the relative formula mass of the whole compound. In this case, you need to add up the masses of 1 × Mg, 1 × C and 3 × O.

$$M_r = 24 + 12 + (3 \times 16) = 84$$
$$\text{Mg} \quad \text{C} \quad (3 \times \text{O})$$

To find the relative formula mass of calcium hydroxide, $Ca(OH)_2$

Relative atomic masses: H = 1, O = 16, Ca = 40.

$$M_r = 40 + (16 + 1) \times 2 = 74$$
$$\text{Ca} \quad \text{O} \quad \text{H}$$

To find the M_r of copper(II) sulfate crystals, $CuSO_4 \cdot 5H_2O$

We met this formula above. When some substances crystallise from solution, water becomes chemically bound up with the salt. This is called **water of crystallisation**. The $5H_2O$ in $CuSO_4 \cdot 5H_2O$ is water of crystallisation. The water is necessary to form crystals of copper(II) sulfate (and some other substances). There are always 5 water molecules associated with 1 $CuSO_4$ unit and they are part of the formula (see **Figure 5.7**).

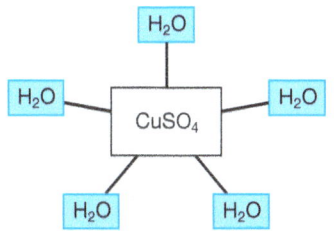

▲ Figure 5.7 A schematic diagram showing the formula of copper(II) sulfate crystals: there are five water molecules bonded to each copper(II) sulfate unit.

Relative atomic masses: H = 1, O = 16, S = 32, Cu = 63.5.

It is easiest to work out the relative formula mass of water first:

$$H_2O: \quad M_r = 2 \times 1 + 16 = 18$$

> **HINT**
> It is dangerous to calculate the number of hydrogens and oxygens separately. The common mistake is to work out 10 hydrogens (quite correctly!), but then only count 1 oxygen rather than 5.

> **KEY POINT**
> Salts containing water of crystallisation are said to be **hydrated**. Other examples include $Na_2CO_3 \cdot 10H_2O$ and $MgCl_2 \cdot 6H_2O$.

Now add the correct number of waters on to the rest of the formula:

$$CuSO_4 \cdot 5H_2O: \quad M_r = 63.5 + 32 + (4 \times 16) + (5 \times 18) = 249.5$$
$$\text{Cu} \quad \text{S} \quad (4 \times \text{O}) \quad (5 \times H_2O)$$

CHAPTER QUESTIONS

Exam-style questions on chemical formulae and equations can be found at the end of Unit 1 on page 184.

SKILLS CRITICAL THINKING

1 For each of the following compounds state how many different elements are present.

   a sulfur dioxide, SO_2
   b carbon disulfide, CS_2
   c phosphorus trichloride, PCl_3
   d silver nitrate, $AgNO_3$
   e potassium dichromate, $K_2Cr_2O_7$
   f nitrobenzene, $C_6H_5NO_2$

SKILLS CRITICAL THINKING

2 Sometimes we use prefixes to indicate the number of a particular atom in a formula. You will have seen names such as carbon dioxide (CO_2) and carbon monoxide (CO). The most common prefixes are:

prefix	number
mono-	1
di-	2
tri-	3
tetra-	4
penta-	5
hexa-	6

   a Phosphorus trichloride has the formula PCl_3. Work out the formulae of phosphorus pentachloride and phosphorus tribromide.
   b Xenon is a noble gas and so is very unreactive but it does, however, form a few compounds with fluorine and oxygen. Suggest the names of XeF_2, XeF_4 and XeF_6.

SKILLS CRITICAL THINKING

3 Work out the formulae of the molecules shown in the table.

A	B	C
$Cl-P(=O)-Cl$ with Cl	$O=Cl(=O)-O-Cl(=O)=O$	$H_3C-CH_2-CH_2-C(=O)-O-H$ displayed

HINT

Technically, the diagrams shown here are also types of formulae and are called displayed formulae. The formulae you are being asked to work out are, more correctly, called molecular formulae. The different types of formulae will be discussed in **Chapter 16**.

SKILLS CRITICAL THINKING

4 For each of the following compounds, work out how many oxygen atoms are present in one formula unit.

   a $KMnO_4$
   b $Al(OH)_3$
   c $FeSO_4 \cdot 7H_2O$

SKILLS PROBLEM SOLVING

5 Balance the following equations.

   a $Fe + HCl \rightarrow FeCl_2 + H_2$
   b $Zn + H_2SO_4 \rightarrow ZnSO_4 + H_2$
   c $Ca + H_2O \rightarrow Ca(OH)_2 + H_2$
   d $Al + Cr_2O_3 \rightarrow Al_2O_3 + Cr$
   e $Fe_2O_3 + CO \rightarrow Fe + CO_2$
   f $NaHCO_3 + H_2SO_4 \rightarrow Na_2SO_4 + CO_2 + H_2O$
   g $C_8H_{18} + O_2 \rightarrow CO_2 + H_2O$
   h $Fe_3O_4 + H_2 \rightarrow Fe + H_2O$
   i $Pb + AgNO_3 \rightarrow Pb(NO_3)_2 + Ag$
   j $AgNO_3 + MgCl_2 \rightarrow Mg(NO_3)_2 + AgCl$
   k $C_3H_8 + O_2 \rightarrow CO_2 + H_2O$

1 PRINCIPLES OF CHEMISTRY — 5 CHEMICAL FORMULAE AND EQUATIONS

SKILLS PROBLEM SOLVING

6 Which of the following equations is *not* balanced?

  A $Pb(NO_3)_2 + 2NaCl \rightarrow PbCl_2 + 2NaNO_3$

  B $4FeS_2 + 11O_2 \rightarrow 2Fe_2O_3 + 8SO_2$

  C $2NH_3 + 5O_2 \rightarrow 2NO + 3H_2O$

  D $3Cu + 8HNO_3 \rightarrow 3Cu(NO_3)_2 + 4H_2O + 2NO$

SKILLS REASONING

7 a Write the formulae of the following, including state symbols.

  i water

  ii ice

  iii carbon dioxide gas

  iv dry ice – solid carbon dioxide

SKILLS PROBLEM SOLVING

  b Write equations including state symbols for the following processes.

  i the melting of ice

  ii the sublimation of carbon dioxide

SKILLS PROBLEM SOLVING

8 Write balanced chemical equations, including state symbols, from each of the following descriptions.

  a Solid copper(II) carbonate ($CuCO_3$) decomposes when heated to form solid copper(II) oxide (CuO) and carbon dioxide gas.

  b Solid zinc metal reacts with copper(II) sulfate ($CuSO_4$) solution to form solid copper metal and zinc sulfate ($ZnSO_4$) solution.

  c Ethanol (C_2H_5OH) is a liquid at room temperature and burns in oxygen (O_2) gas to form carbon dioxide and water.

  d Solid calcium carbonate ($CaCO_3$) reacts with hydrochloric acid (a solution of HCl in water) to form a solution of calcium chloride ($CaCl_2$), carbon dioxide and water.

SKILLS PROBLEM SOLVING

9 Calculate the relative formula masses of the following compounds.

  a NaOH

  b CO_2

  c NH_3

  d $CaCl_2$

  e CH_3CO_2H

  f Na_2SO_4

  g $(NH_4)_2SO_4$

  h $Cr_2(SO_4)_3$

  i $Na_2CO_3 \cdot 10H_2O$

  j $Fe(NO_3)_3 \cdot 9H_2O$

(A_r: H = 1, C = 12, N = 14, O = 16, Na = 23, S = 32, Cl = 35.5, Ca = 40, Cr = 52, Fe = 56)

6 IONIC BONDING

SPECIFICATION REFERENCES: 1.37–1.39, 1.41, 1.42

We have already looked at the definition of a compound. A compound is formed when two or more elements chemically combine. In this chapter we are going to look at one way in which elements can chemically combine: by the transfer of electrons to form ionic compounds.

chlorine + sodium → sodium chloride

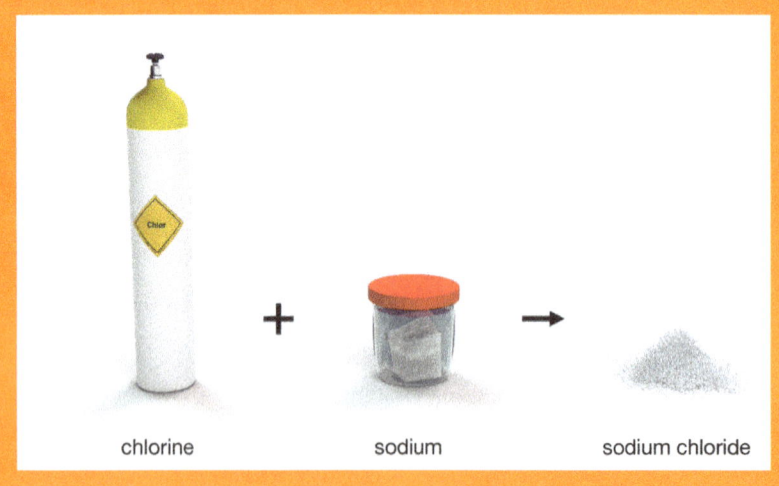

▲ Figure 6.1 The properties of a compound are very different from those of the elements. Sodium (an element) is a dangerously reactive metal. It is stored under oil to prevent it reacting with air or water. Chlorine (an element) is a very poisonous, reactive gas. But salt, sodium chloride (an ionic compound), is safe to eat in small quantities.

LEARNING OBJECTIVES

- Understand how ions are formed by electron loss or gain.
- Know the charges of these ions:
  - metals in Groups 1, 2 and 3
  - non-metals in Groups 5, 6 and 7
  - hydrogen (H^+), hydroxide (OH^-), ammonium (NH_4^+), carbonate (CO_3^{2-}), nitrate (NO_3^-), sulfate (SO_4^{2-}).
- Write formulae for compounds formed between the ions listed above.
- Understand ionic bonding in terms of electrostatic attractions.
- Understand why compounds with giant ionic lattices have high melting and boiling points.

IONIC BONDING

Sodium chloride (common salt) is probably the best-known example of an ionic compound. Ionic compounds contain **ions**, for example, a crystal of sodium chloride contains Na^+ and Cl^- ions.

Ions are charged particles formed when atoms (or groups of atoms) lose or gain electrons. Ions can have either a positive or a negative charge.

- A positive ion is called a **cation**, for example Na^+
- A negative ion is called an **anion**, for example Cl^-

1 PRINCIPLES OF CHEMISTRY 6 IONIC BONDING

FORMATION OF IONS

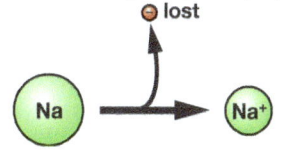

▲ Figure 6.2 A sodium atom loses 1 electron to form a sodium ion.

EXAM HINT

For the International GCSE exam, you do not need to understand how many electrons are in each shell in diagrams like this. You do need to understand how many electrons are lost/gained when ions are formed. If you are asked to complete a diagram like this, remember that electrons are only lost from the outermost shell.

KEY POINT

The name changes when an atom gains an electron to form a negative ion. For example, chlorine (Cl) forms a chloride ion (Cl⁻) and oxygen forms an oxide ion (O^{2-}). The names of positive ions do not change.

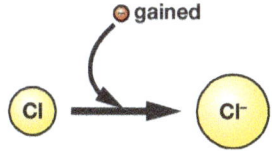

▲ Figure 6.4 Chlorine gains an electron to form a negative ion.

Positive ions are formed when atoms lose (an) electron(s).

Because an electron has a negative charge, when an atom loses an electron it becomes positively charged. **Figure 6.2** shows a sodium atom losing an electron to form a positively charged sodium ion (Na⁺).

You can check that sodium does have a positive charge. If you look at the Periodic Table you will see that sodium has an atomic number of 11, so it has 11 protons in its nucleus. Protons have a positive charge so the charge on the nucleus is 11+. In the sodium *atom* there are 11 electrons, each with a negative charge. These cancel out the 11+ on the nucleus and there is no overall charge.

However, in the sodium *ion* there are only 10 electrons, so with 11+ and 10– there is an overall charge of 1+.

When magnesium forms an ion it loses 2 electrons to form Mg^{2+}. **Figure 6.3** shows how the number of electrons changes as a magnesium atom forms a magnesium ion.

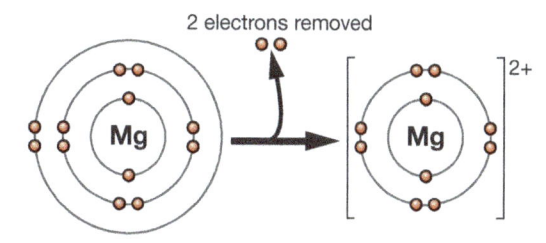

▲ Figure 6.3 A 2+ ion is formed when a magnesium atom loses 2 electrons.

Metal atoms always *lose* electrons to form positive ions. Metal atoms can lose up to 3 electrons. How many electrons a metal atom loses depends on its position in the Periodic Table. We will look at this below.

Negative ions are formed when atoms gain (an) electron(s).

Because an electron has a negative charge, when an atom gains an electron it becomes negatively charged. **Figure 6.4** shows a chlorine atom gaining an electron to form a negatively charged chloride ion (Cl⁻).

An oxygen atom gains 2 electrons to form an oxide ion (O^{2-}). This is shown in **Figure 6.5**.

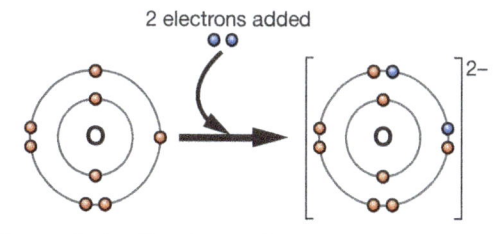

▲ Figure 6.5 Oxygen forms a 2– ion. The electrons here are identical but are shown in different colours for clarity.

Non-metal atoms *gain* electrons to form negative ions. Atoms can gain up to 3 electrons. The number of electrons an atom gains depends on its position in the Periodic Table.

When an ionic compound such as sodium chloride is formed, the sodium atom loses an electron (metals lose electrons) to form a positive ion. The electron lost by the sodium atom is gained by a chlorine atom (non-metals gain electrons) to form a negatively charged chloride ion. The overall effect of this is an electron is transferred from a sodium atom to a chlorine atom. This is shown in **Figure 6.6**.

172 1 PRINCIPLES OF CHEMISTRY 6 IONIC BONDING

> **EXAM HINT**
> The symbols for electrons in diagrams like this are often shown as dots for one atom, and crosses for the other atom. Therefore this is called a dot-and-cross diagram. You do not have to draw dot-and-cross diagrams for the International GCSE exam.

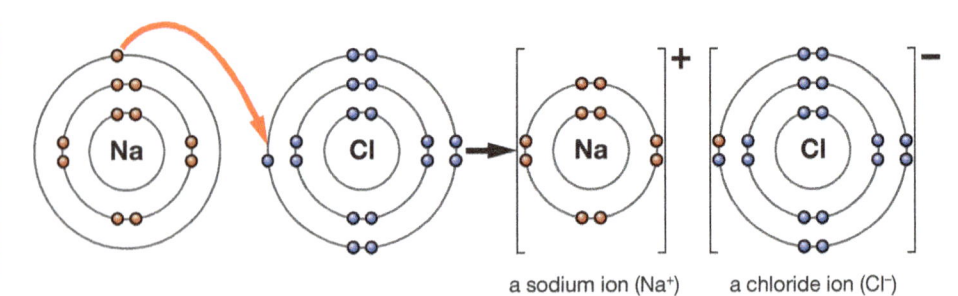

a sodium ion (Na$^+$)   a chloride ion (Cl$^-$)

▲ Figure 6.6 **ionic bonding** in sodium chloride. Ionic bonding involves the transfer of electrons.

FORMULAE OF IONIC COMPOUNDS

RECOGNISING THE FORMULAE OF IONIC COMPOUNDS

You can recognise ionic compounds because they (usually) contain a metal.

Examples of ionic compounds are magnesium oxide (MgO), calcium fluoride (CaF$_2$) and zinc bromide (ZnBr$_2$). All these compounds contain a metal combined with a non-metal.

> **HINT**
> There are one or two exceptions to this: there are ionic compounds that do not contain a metal, for example those containing the ammonium ion (such as NH$_4$Cl or (NH$_4$)$_2$SO$_4$).

FORMULAE AND CHARGES ON IONS

You can work out the charges on some ions from the position of an element in the Periodic Table. The connection between the group an element is in and the charge on the ion formed is shown in **Table 6.1**.

Table 6.1 The charges on an ion in Groups 1–7.

Group in Periodic Table	Charge on ion	Example
1	1+	Na$^+$
2	2+	Mg^{2+}
3	3+	Al^{3+}
5	3–	N^{3-}
6	2–	O^{2-}
7	1–	Br$^-$

> **EXAM HINT**
> You will have a copy of the Periodic Table in the exam. That means that you can always find out which group an element is in.

> **EXAM HINT**
> Elements in Group 4 only form a few ionic compounds and the situation is a bit more complicated. You will be told in the question what the charge on the ion of a Group 4 element is if you need it.

You cannot work out the charges for certain ions, you have to learn them. Ions that need to be learned are shown in **Table 6.2** – be sure to learn both the formula and the charge for each ion.

Table 6.2 Ions that you should learn.

Charge	Substance	Ion
positive	hydrogen	H$^+$
	ammonium	NH$_4^+$

Charge	Substance	Ion
negative	nitrate	NO$_3^-$
	hydroxide	OH$^-$
	carbonate	CO$_3^{2-}$
	sulfate	SO$_4^{2-}$

You may encounter compounds such as lead(II) oxide, iron(III) chloride or copper(II) sulfate during the course. For these compounds the number in Roman numerals tell you directly about the charge on the metal ion.

- lead(II) oxide contains a Pb^{2+} ion
- iron(III) chloride contains an Fe^{3+} ion
- copper(II) sulfate contains a Cu^{2+} ion

CONFUSING ENDINGS!

When naming ionic compounds, the name of the metal (cation) in a formula always stays the same but the name of the non-metal (anion) changes. Look carefully at the ending of the non-metal to see whether it is *ide* or *ate* as this will tell you if there is oxygen (and possibly other elements) also present.

The *ide* ending in magnesium sulf**ide** tells you that the only elements present are magnesium and sulfur; this compound is made of Mg^{2+} and S^{2-} ions (see **Figure 6.7**).

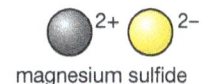

▲ Figure 6.7 Magnesium sulfide is MgS.

Similarly, sodium chlor**ide** contains only the elements sodium and chlorine. The ions present in sodium chloride are Na^+ and Cl^-.

The *ate* ending in magnesium sulf**ate** indicates that oxygen is also present in the compound. Magnesium sulf**ate** contains Mg^{2+} and SO_4^{2-} ions (see **Figure 6.8**).

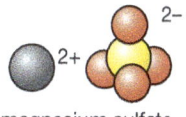

▲ Figure 6.8 Magnesium sulfate is $MgSO_4$

Lithium nitr**ide** (Li_3N) contains only lithium and nitrogen but lithium nitr**ate** ($LiNO_3$) contains oxygen as well.

> **HINT**
> One of the most common mistakes that students make when they start to write formulae is not looking carefully at word endings. Be careful!

DEDUCING THE FORMULA FOR AN IONIC COMPOUND

Ionic compounds are formed when a metal atom transfers electrons to a non-metal atom (or group of atoms). The electrons cannot just disappear so this means that the number of electrons lost when positive ions are formed will be exactly the same as the number of electrons gained when negative ions are formed. Another way of saying this is that, although ions have charges, the overall ionic compound is electrically neutral: it does not have an overall charge.

We can use this idea to work out the formula of an ionic compound. The total charges on the ions must always balance out, that is, there must be equal numbers of positive and negative charges.

KEY POINT

Why are ion charges not shown in formulae? Actually, they can be shown. For example, the formula for sodium chloride is NaCl. It is sometimes written Na^+Cl^- if you are trying to make a particular point, but for most purposes the charges are left out. In an ionic compound, the charges are there, whether you write them or not.

EXAMPLE 1

To find the formula for sodium oxide

Sodium is in Group 1, so the ion is Na^+

Oxygen is in Group 6, so the ion is O^{2-}

To have equal numbers of positive and negative charges, you would need two sodium ions to provide the two positive charges to cancel the two negative charges on one oxide ion. In other words, you need:

$Na^+ \quad Na^+ \quad O^{2-}$

The formula is therefore **Na_2O**.

EXAMPLE 2

To find the formula for barium nitrate

Barium is in Group 2, so the ion is Ba^{2+}

Nitrate ions are NO_3^-. You will have to remember this.

To have equal numbers of positive and negative charges, you would need two nitrate ions for each barium ion.

The formula is **$Ba(NO_3)_2$**

Notice the brackets around the nitrate group. *Brackets must be written if you have more than one of these complex ions* (ions containing more than one atom). In any other situation, they are completely unnecessary.

KEY POINT

If you do not write the brackets, the formula would look like this: $BaNO_{32}$. That would read as 1 barium, 1 nitrogen and 32 oxygens!

EXAMPLE 3

To find the formula for aluminium sulfate

Aluminium is in Group 3 in the Periodic Table, so the ion is Al^{3+}

Sulfate ions are SO_4^{2-}

To have equal numbers of positive and negative charges, you would need two aluminium ions for every three sulfate ions, giving 6+ and 6− in total.

The formula is **$Al_2(SO_4)_3$**

A shortcut to working out complicated formulae such as these is to just swap over the numbers in the charges. This is shown in **Figure 6.9**.

$$Al^{3+} \quad SO_4^{2-} \Rightarrow Al_2(SO_4)_3$$

▲ Figure 6.9 If you cross over the numbers in the charges you will get the formula.

CALCIUM CHLORIDE PROVIDES ANOTHER EXAMPLE

$$Ca^{2+} \quad Cl^- \rightarrow CaCl_2$$

▲ Figure 6.10 To work out the formula of calcium chloride we cross over the numbers in the charges. There is no extra number in front of the charge in Cl^- because we do not tend to write in a 1.

THE FORMULA OF CALCIUM OXIDE

You have to be careful using this method because you can get the wrong answer when the charges on the ions are the same. For example, the formula of calcium oxide is CaO and not Ca$_2$O$_2$ (see **Figure 6.11**). When the charges on the positive and negative ions are the same you can deduce that there will be 1 of each ion in the formula, so there is no need to swap anything over.

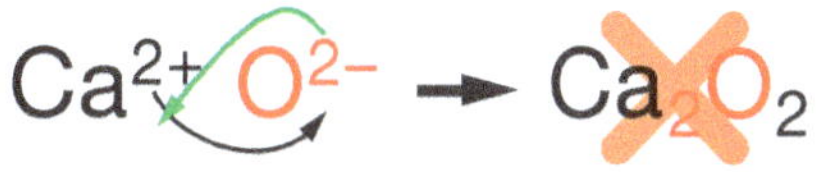

$$Ca^{2+} \, O^{2-} \rightarrow Ca_2O_2$$

▲ Figure 6.11 The formula of calcium oxide is CaO and not Ca$_2$O$_2$.

GIANT IONIC STRUCTURES

All ionic compounds form crystals (**Figure 6.12**) that consist of positive and negative ions packed together in a regular way. A simplified 2-D diagram of part of a sodium chloride crystal is shown in **Figure 6.13**. In this structure each positive ion is surrounded by negative ions and each negative ion is surrounded by positive ions. The ions are held together by *the strong electrostatic attraction between positive and negative ions – this is called ionic bonding.*

KEY POINT

Electrostatic attraction simply means that positively charged particles attract negatively charged particles.

▲ Figure 6.12 Sodium chloride crystals

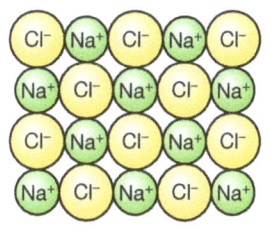

▲ Figure 6.13 Part of the structure of a sodium chloride crystal. The structure is held together by the attraction between positive and negative ions.

THE STRUCTURE OF SODIUM CHLORIDE

Figure 6.14 shows how the ions in a crystal of sodium chloride are arranged in three dimensions.

In diagrams, the ions are usually drawn in an 'exploded' view (**Figure 6.15**). Each sodium ion is surrounded by 6 chloride ions. In turn, each chloride ion is surrounded by 6 sodium ions. You have to remember that this pattern repeats itself throughout the structure over vast numbers of ions.

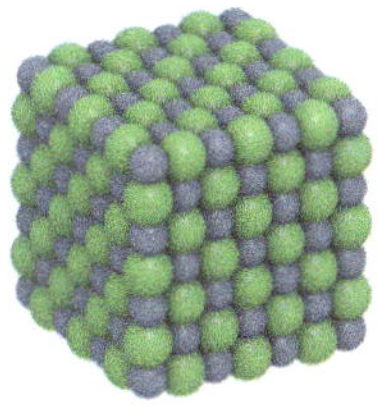

▲ Figure 6.14 A model of a small part of a sodium chloride crystal

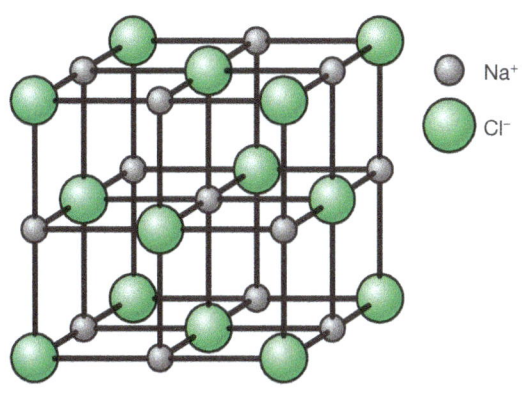

▲ Figure 6.15 An 'exploded' view of sodium chloride. The lines in this diagram are not bonds, they are just there to help show the arrangement of the ions. Those ions joined by lines are touching each other.

EXAM HINT

This is really important: you must not talk about *molecules* of an ionic compound. This will be marked wrong in the exam and you could lose all the marks for a question!

The structure of sodium chloride is described as a **giant ionic lattice**. A **lattice** is a regular **array** of particles and the word '**giant**' is used here not in the sense of big but rather to describe a structure where there are no individual molecules. All the sodium ions in the structure attract all the chloride ions; we cannot pick out individual sodium chloride molecules. The bonding in a giant ionic lattice extends throughout the structure in all directions. There is no limit to the number of particles present, all we know is that there must be the same number of sodium and chloride ions.

▲ Figure 6.16 A lattice fence. A lattice is a regular, repeating structure.

ICONIC COMPOUNDS: MELTING AND BOILING POINTS

Ionic compounds have high melting points and boiling points because a lot of energy has to be supplied to break the strong electrostatic forces of attraction between oppositely charged ions in the giant lattice structure. The key word here is *strong*: a lot of energy must be supplied to overcome the forces in the lattice because they are so strong.

EXAM HINT

You must not use the term *intermolecular forces* (see **Chapter 7**) when when writing answers about ionic compounds.

CHAPTER QUESTIONS

Exam-style questions on ionic bonding can be found at the end of Unit 1 on page 184.

SKILLS INTERPRETATION

1 Explain what is meant by
   a an ion
   b ionic bonding.

SKILLS PROBLEM SOLVING

2 In each of the following cases state the charge on the ion formed.
   a an atom of A loses two electrons
   b an atom of Q gains three electrons

SKILLS CRITICAL THINKING

3 a State the formula of the ion formed by:
   i   magnesium   vii chlorine
   ii strontium   viii iodine
   iii potassium   ix   aluminium
   iv oxygen   x   calcium
   v   sulfur   xi   nitrogen
   vi caesium

   b State the name of each negative ion in **a**.

4 The diagrams show the arrangement of electrons in an atom and an ion of element X (not its actual symbol).

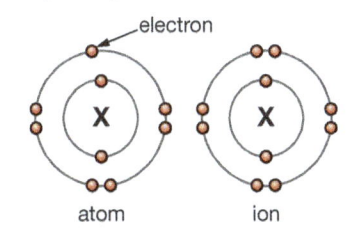

atom   ion

a Deduce the charge on the X ion.

b Explain whether X is a metal or a non-metal.

c Deduce which group of the Periodic Table element X is in.

5 Work out the formulae of the following compounds:

a magnesium sulfate
b potassium carbonate
c calcium nitrate
d aluminium sulfate
e cobalt(II) chloride
f ammonium nitrate
g sodium sulfate
h sodium bromide
i ammonium sulfide
j calcium hydroxide
k calcium oxide
l rubidium iodide

6 Name the following compounds of lithium.

a LiCl
b Li_3N
c Li_2SO_4
d Li_2S
e $LiNO_3$
f Li_2O
g LiOH

7 Which of the following formulae is *not* correct?
A $NaNO_3$
B $MgCO_3$
C Na_2S
D Mg_2Cl

8 Imagine that scientists have just discovered a new element that they have called excelium and given it the symbol Ex. They know that excelium forms a 3+ ion.

a Explain whether excelium is a metal or a non-metal.

b Write the formulae of excelium chloride and excelium sulfate.

9 Describe the structure of sodium chloride and explain why it has a high melting point.

7 COVALENT BONDING

SPECIFICATION REFERENCES: 1.44, 1.47, 1.49

We met ionic compounds in **Chapter 6** and in this chapter we will understand what covalent bonding is. There are a lot more covalent compounds than ionic compounds so it is important that you understand how the bonding works.

▲ Figure 7.1 Water is a covalent compound but the salt dissolved in seawater is an ionic compound.

LEARNING OBJECTIVES

- Know that a covalent bond is formed between atoms by the sharing of a pair of electrons.
- Explain why substances with a simple molecular structure are gases or liquids, or solids with low melting and boiling points.
- Understand that the term intermolecular forces of attraction can be used to represent all forces between molecules.
- Explain why substances with giant covalent structures are solids with high melting and boiling points.

KEY POINT

Ammonium chloride (NH_4Cl) is an example of an ionic compound that does not contain a metal. There is ionic bonding between the NH_4^+ and Cl^- ions. There is, however, also covalent bonding in this compound: the NH_4^+ ion is held together by covalent bonding.

EXAM HINT

If the compound contains a metal it almost certainly has ionic bonding.

RECOGNISING WHETHER A COMPOUND CONTAINS IONIC OR COVALENT BONDING

Ionic compounds are formed between metals and non-metals. The formulae of some ionic compounds are MgO, $CaCl_2$, Li_3N.

Covalent compounds are formed between two or more non-metals. The formulae of some covalent compounds are H_2O, CH_4, PCl_3.

COVALENT BONDING

In covalent substances, the atoms are held together by **covalent bonds**. A covalent bond is formed when two atoms *share a pair of electrons*. The sharing of a pair of electrons in a hydrogen molecule, H_2, is shown in **Figure 7.2**.

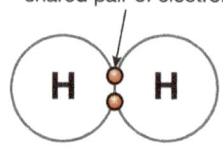

▲ Figure 7.2 The covalent bond in an H_2 molecule

1 PRINCIPLES OF CHEMISTRY   7 COVALENT BONDING   179

EXAM HINT

When describing covalent bonding in the exam it is important to state that 'the atoms share a *pair* of electrons' and not just 'share electrons'.

The atoms are held together because the negatively charged electron pair is attracted to the nuclei of both atoms simultaneously. This is shown in **Figure 7.3**.

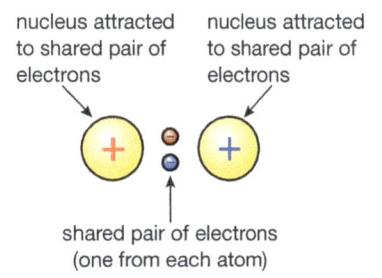

▲ Figure 7.3 How the atoms are held together in a covalent bond

DIAGRAMS OF COVALENT MOLECULES

There are various ways that we can show the covalent bonding within a molecule. **Figure 7.4** shows the bonding in hydrogen chloride, HCl. Although these diagrams look very different, the key point to notice in each one is the shared pair of electrons.

HINT

Remember that, although the electrons are shown in different colours, there is absolutely no difference between them in reality; the different colours simply show that the electrons have come from two different atoms.

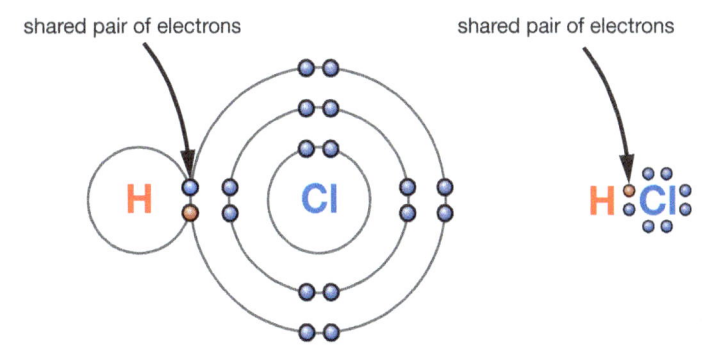

▲ Figure 7.4 The covalent bonding in a hydrogen chloride molecule

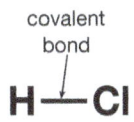

▲ Figure 7.5 The line between the atoms represents a covalent bond

The simplest way to show the bonding in a covalent molecule is by using a line to represent a covalent bond – **Figure 7.5**.

THE COVALENT BONDING IN CH_4

The covalent bonding in a methane, CH_4, molecule is shown in three different ways in **Figure 7.6**.

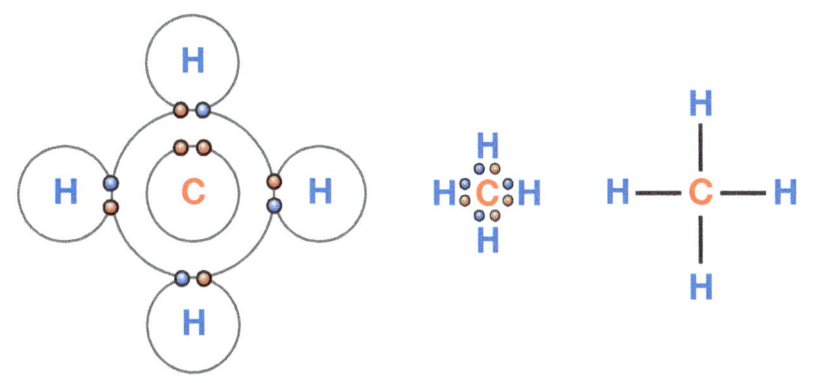

▲ Figure 7.6 The covalent bonding in methane

THE COVALENT BONDING IN H₂O

Water contains two covalent bonds – **Figure 7.7**.

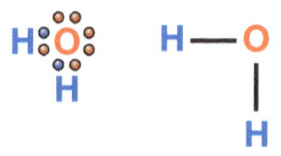

▲ Figure 7.7 Two different representations of the covalent bonding in water

DOUBLE COVALENT BONDS

Sometimes two atoms share more than one pair of electrons. A double covalent bond (usually just called a **double bond**) between oxygen atoms in O_2 is shown in **Figure 7.8**.

KEY POINT

It is important to remember that each line in O=O represents a shared pair of electrons.

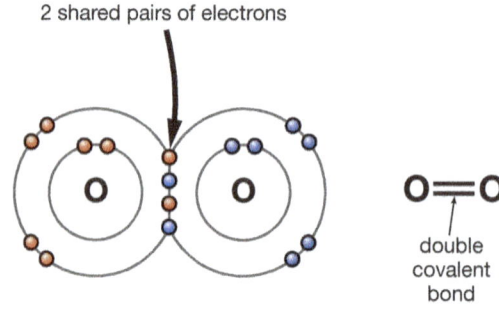

▲ Figure 7.8 There is a double bond between the atoms in an O_2 molecule.

TRIPLE COVALENT BONDS

In a nitrogen, N_2, molecule there is a **triple bond** between the nitrogen atoms – **Figure 7.9**.

HINT

The diagram on the right is called a dot-and-cross diagram. We often show the electrons in a covalent bond with different symbols (dots and crosses) to make it clear that one is coming from each atom and that the two atoms are sharing the electrons, but remember that all electrons are actually identical.

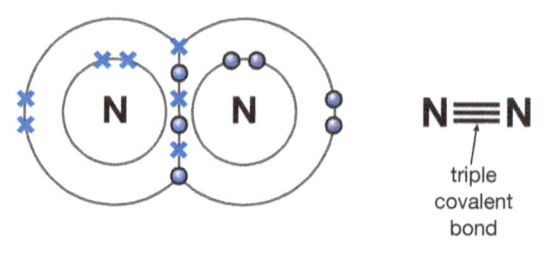

▲ Figure 7.9 N_2 has a triple bond.

SIMPLE MOLECULAR STRUCTURES

Most covalent substances are made up of molecules. Molecules contain fixed numbers of atoms joined by strong covalent bonds. If we look closely at liquid water (**Figure 7.10**), there are individual water molecules, where the H and O atoms are joined together with strong covalent bonds. But there must also be some forces between water molecules which keep them in the liquid state. These forces are **intermolecular forces**.

KEY POINT

We often use the term *covalent molecular compound* to mean a covalent compound with a simple molecular structure.

DID YOU KNOW?

Intermolecular literally means *between molecules*.

strong covalent bonds join hydrogen and oxygen atoms…

… but the intermolecular attractions between the water molecules are weaker

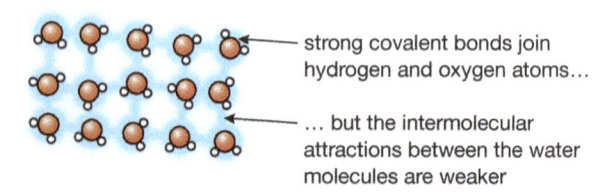

▲ Figure 7.10 Water is a simple molecular compound.

1 PRINCIPLES OF CHEMISTRY   7 COVALENT BONDING

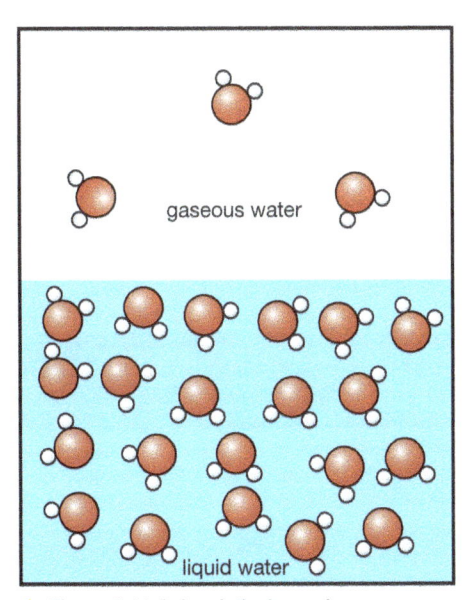

▲ Figure 7.11 Only relatively weak intermolecular forces of attraction are broken when water evaporates/boils.

Intermolecular (between molecules) forces are much weaker than covalent bonds. When we boil water it is only these weak intermolecular forces of attraction that are broken; covalent bonds are not broken. Looking at **Figure 7.11** you can see that there are H_2O molecules in liquid water and in gaseous water. The covalent bonds between the H and O atoms in the molecules have not changed in any way. All that has changed in gaseous water is that there are no intermolecular forces, they have been broken.

When a substance consists of molecules with intermolecular forces of attraction between them, we say that it has a *simple molecular structure*. Examples of things that have simple molecular structures are H_2O, CO_2, CH_4, NH_3 and C_2H_4. Almost all the compounds you will encounter that have covalent bonding will have simple molecular structures.

Substances with simple molecular structures tend to be gases or liquids or solids with low melting points and boiling points. The reason for this is that not much energy is required to break the *weak* intermolecular forces of attraction between molecules. Remember, no covalent bonds are broken, covalent bonds are strong.

EXAM HINT

Use the phrase *intermolecular forces of attraction* when explaining why substances with a simple molecular structure have low melting and boiling points and remember, these forces are *weak*.

EXTENSION

If you continue with chemistry you will learn that there are different types of intermolecular forces. You will come across terms like van der Waals' forces, London dispersion forces and hydrogen bonds. There is a special type of intermolecular force between water molecules called **hydrogen bonds**. Hydrogen bonding gives water some of its very special properties, for example the solid form (ice) is less dense than the liquid form.

GIANT COVALENT STRUCTURES

There are some covalent substances that do not consist of individual molecules but have a *giant* structure. One such substance is diamond, a form of carbon.

Each carbon atom in a diamond forms four covalent bonds. In **Figure 7.12** we can see just a small part of the structure which shows some of the covalent bonds. It is important to remember that this structure carries on in three dimensions and all the atoms shown actually form 4 bonds.

This is a giant covalent structure; it is *not* a molecule because the number of atoms joined up in a real diamond (**Figure 7.13**) is completely variable and depends on the size of the crystal. Molecules always contain *fixed numbers* of atoms joined by covalent bonds.

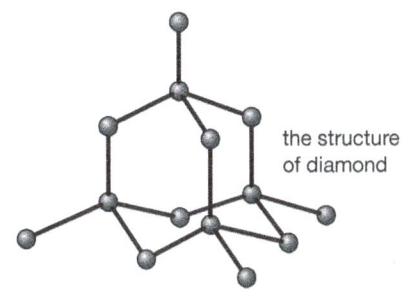

▲ Figure 7.12 Part of the structure of diamond

KEY POINT

In **Figure 7.12** some carbon atoms seem to be forming only two bonds (or even one bond), but that is not really the case. We are only showing a small part of the whole structure. The structure continues in three dimensions, and each of the atoms drawn here is attached to four others. Each of the lines in this diagram represents a covalent bond.

1 PRINCIPLES OF CHEMISTRY

7 COVALENT BONDING

The properties of substances with giant covalent structures are very different from those with simple molecular structures. In general, *all substances with giant covalent structures are solids with high melting and boiling points* because a lot of energy has to be supplied to break all the *strong* covalent bonds throughout the giant structure.

Other examples of covalent substances with giant structures are graphite, another form of carbon, and silicon dioxide, SiO_2 (**Figure 7.14**). Both graphite and silicon dioxide have high melting and boiling points.

▲ Figure 7.13 Diamond has a very high melting point because it has a giant structure.

▲ Figure 7.14 SiO_2 has a giant structure. The grey spheres represent Si atoms and the red spheres are O atoms. Only some of the covalent bonds are shown and the structure continues in three dimensions.

COMPARISON OF COVALENT SUBSTANCES WITH SIMPLE MOLECULAR AND GIANT STRUCTURES

Table 7.1 A comparison of the properties of covalent substances with simple molecular and giant structures.

Simple molecular	Giant structures
individual molecules	no individual molecules
strong covalent bonding within molecules	strong covalent bonding throughout the structure
weak intermolecular forces of attraction between molecules	no intermolecular forces
gases or liquids or solids with low melting and boiling points	solids with high melting and boiling points
only weak intermolecular forces of attraction broken when substance melts/boils	strong covalent bonds broken when substance melts/boils

CHAPTER QUESTIONS

Exam-style questions on covalent bonding can be found at the end of Unit 1 on page 184.

You will need to use the Periodic Table in Appendix A on page 452.

SKILLS CRITICAL THINKING

1 State whether each of the following compounds is ionic or covalent.
   a MgO
   b CH_3Br
   c H_2O_2
   d $FeCl_2$
   e NaF
   f HCN

SKILLS REASONING

2 The structure of an ammonia molecule is shown below.

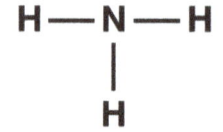

H—N—H
   |
   H

Explain what each of the lines between the atoms represents.

SKILLS REASONING

3 Carbon and silicon are two elements in the same group in the Periodic Table. Carbon dioxide has a simple molecular structure whereas silicon dioxide has a giant structure. Explain why carbon dioxide sublimes at −78.5 °C but silicon dioxide melts at over 1700 °C.

SKILLS REASONING

4 Hexane has the formula C_6H_{14}. It is a liquid at room temperature. Explain whether hexane has a simple molecular or giant structure.

SKILLS REASONING

5 Explain why the following statements are *false*.

  a Oxygen has a higher boiling point (−183 °C) than hydrogen (−253 °C) because there is a double covalent bond between the oxygen atoms (O=O) but only a single covalent bond between the hydrogen atoms (H–H) and a double covalent bond is stronger than a single covalent bond.

  b Sodium chloride has a higher melting point (801 °C) than carbon tetrachloride (CCl_4, −23 °C) because ionic bonds are stronger than covalent bonds.

SKILLS REASONING

6 The boiling points of the halogens are shown in the table.

Halogen	Boiling point / °C
Fluorine, F_2	−188
Chlorine, Cl_2	−34
Bromine, Br_2	59
Iodine, I_2	184

Explain whether the following statement is true or false.

The boiling point increases down the group therefore it can be deduced that the strength of the covalent bond between two F atoms is weaker than that between two I atoms.

SKILLS PROBLEM SOLVING

7 Which of the following will have the highest melting point?

  A NaCl

  B SCl_2

  C PCl_3

  D CCl_4

EXAM PRACTICE

You may need to refer to the Periodic Table on page 452.

SKILLS CRITICAL THINKING

1 Hydrogen is the most common element in the Universe.

a The melting point and boiling point of hydrogen are shown in the table:

Melting point / °C	Boiling point / °C
−259	−253

Identify a temperature at which hydrogen is a liquid. (1)

A −265 °C   B −260 °C   C −255 °C   D −250 °C

SKILLS INTERPRETATION

b The circle in the diagram represents 1 molecule of hydrogen. Copy and complete the diagram to show the arrangement of particles in liquid hydrogen. You should add at least 10 more circles to the diagram. (2)

SKILLS PROBLEM SOLVING

c Hydrogen has three isotopes, the least common of which is tritium, ^{3}H. Determine, using the Periodic Table, the number of protons, neutrons and electrons in an atom of tritium. (3)

d Under certain conditions, hydrogen gas reacts with nitrogen gas to form ammonia gas (NH_3).
Write a chemical equation for this reaction, including state symbols. (3)

e Ammonia forms salts that contain the ammonium ion. Which of the following formulae for ammonium compounds is *incorrect*? (1)

A NH_4SO_4 B NH_4NO_3 C NH_4Cl D $(NH_4)_2CO_3$

SKILLS CRITICAL THINKING

f Two more compounds that contain hydrogen are water and ethanol. Which method can be used to separate a mixture of ethanol and water? (1)

A crystallisation
B filtration
C simple distillation
D fractional distillation

(Total 11 marks)

SKILLS REASONING

2 a Copy and complete the following passage by using the words below. You may use the words once, more than once, or not at all. (3)

mass number   atomic number   groups   periods
physical properties   electrons   chemical properties   nucleus

The elements in the Periodic Table are arranged in order of _____.

The vertical columns are called _____ and contain elements which have similar _____.

b Which elements are non-metals? (2)

A H   B V   C Pb   D Ar   E W

(Total 5 marks)

3 The diagrams show the structures of some atoms and ions. The structures are represented by letters which are not the symbols of the elements.

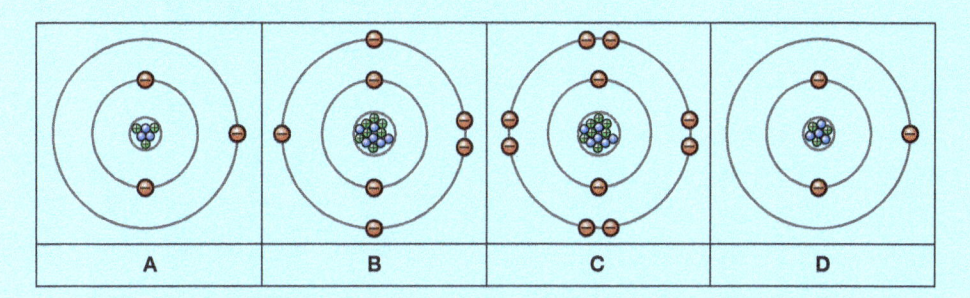

| A | B | C | D |

Use letters A, B, C, D from the diagrams above to answer the following questions.

a Which two atoms are isotopes? (1)

b i   Which diagram shows an ion? (1)
   ii State the charge on the ion identified in **b i**. (1)

c Deduce the atomic number and mass number of B. (2)

d Identify element C. (1)

(Total 6 marks)

4 Strontium is an element in Group 2 of the Periodic Table and bromine is an element in Group 7.

a Strontium bromide is an ionic compound.
   i   State the charge on the ion formed by strontium. (1)
   ii   Explain how a strontium atom forms a strontium ion. (2)
   iii Deduce the formula of strontium bromide. (1)
   iv   Explain in terms of structure and bonding whether you would expect strontium bromide to have a high or a low melting point. (3)

b Explain what you understand by the term *relative atomic mass* of an element. (2)

c The natural abundances of the two isotopes of bromine are:

^{79}Br   50.69%
^{81}Br   49.31%

Calculate the relative atomic mass of bromine. Give your answer to 2 decimal places. (2)

(Total 11 marks)

186　1 PRINCIPLES OF CHEMISTRY　　EXAM PRACTICE

5 Carbon exists in several different forms. The diagrams show the structures of two forms of carbon. C_{60} fullerene has a simple molecular structure and diamond has a giant structure.

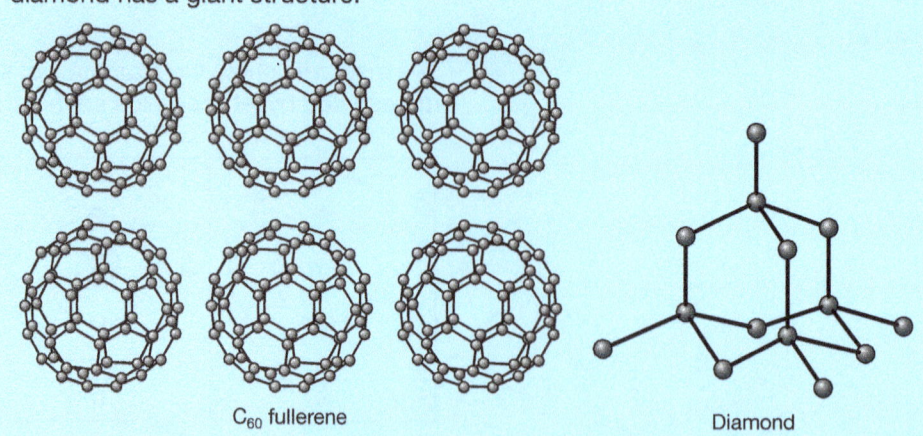

C_{60} fullerene　　　　　　Diamond

SKILLS PROBLEM SOLVING
a Calculate the relative formula mass (M_r) of C_{60} fullerene. (1)

SKILLS INTERPRETATION
b Describe the type of bonding between the carbon atoms in both structures. (2)

SKILLS REASONING
c Both C_{60} fullerene and diamond are solids at room temperature. Explain whether C_{60} fullerene or diamond will have the higher melting point. (4)

SKILLS PROBLEM SOLVING
d When a heated diamond is placed in liquid oxygen it will react to form carbon dioxide gas. Complete the equation, including state symbols, for this reaction. (2)

$C(s) + O_2(.....) \rightarrow$

SKILLS PROBLEM SOLVING
e Carbon dioxide can be used to put out fires but it would not work on a fire involving burning magnesium because the magnesium reacts with carbon dioxide. If a piece of burning magnesium is put into a gas jar containing carbon dioxide, magnesium oxide and carbon are formed.

　i Deduce the formula of magnesium oxide. (1)

　ii Deduce a chemical equation for the reaction between magnesium and carbon dioxide. (3)

(Total 13 marks)

6 A student placed a large crystal of blue hydrated copper(II) sulfate, $CuSO_4 \cdot 5H_2O$, in a beaker containing 100 cm³ of cold water. They kept the beaker still and observed how the appearance changed over 30 minutes.

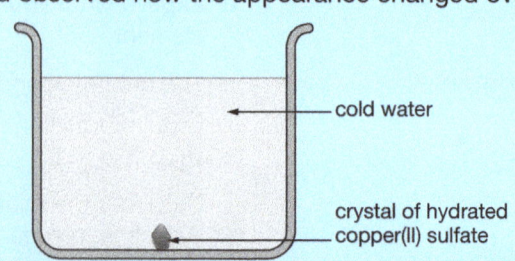

— cold water

— crystal of hydrated copper(II) sulfate

SKILLS CRITICAL THINKING
a Which *two* processes occur in the beaker? (2)

　A sublimation
　B dissolving
　C diffusion
　D melting

1 PRINCIPLES OF CHEMISTRY   EXAM PRACTICE   187

SKILLS REASONING

b Describe how the appearance of the crystal will have changed after 30 minutes. (1)

SKILLS REASONING

c After 30 minutes, the student stirred the water until there was no further change. Describe the appearance of the contents of the beaker. (1)

SKILLS REASONING

d The student added 50 cm³ of water to the beaker and stirred the liquid.

 i Name a piece of apparatus that can be used to measure out 50 cm³ of water accurately. (1)

 ii Describe how the appearance of the liquid in the beaker now differs from that in **c**. (1)

SKILLS REASONING

e Describe the process by which the student could obtain large crystals of copper(II) sulfate from the contents of the beaker. (3)

SKILLS PROBLEM SOLVING

f The formula of hydrated copper(II) sulfate is CuSO₄·5H₂O. How many different elements are present in a crystal of hydrated copper(II) sulfate? (1)

  A 2   **B** 3   **C** 4   **D** 5

SKILLS INTERPRETATION

g When a crystal of hydrated copper(II) sulfate is heated strongly a white solid, anhydrous copper(II) sulfate, and water vapour are formed. Copy and complete the equation for this process by inserting state symbols. (1)

CuSO₄·5H₂O (....) → CuSO₄ (....) + 5H₂O (.....)

(Total 11 marks)

SKILLS CRITICAL THINKING, REASONING

7 A student is given a bottle containing a purple liquid and told that it contains a mixture of dyes. Describe, giving essential practical details, an experiment to determine how many different dyes are present in the mixture.

(Total 6 marks)

SKILLS CRITICAL THINKING, REASONING

8 A student researched the properties of some elements and their nitrides and collected the following data.

Element	Metal or non-metal	Name of nitride	Formula of nitride	Melting point of nitride / °C
lithium	metal	lithium nitride	Li₃N	~800
boron	non-metal	boron nitride	BN	~3000
sulfur	non-metal	tetrasulfur tetranitride	S₄N₄	~180

From these data the student came to the following conclusion:

lithium nitride and boron nitride have high melting points so have ionic bonding but tetrasulfur tetranitride has covalent bonding because it has a low melting point.

Discuss the student's conclusion with regard to the data in the table and to structure and bonding.

(Total 8 marks)

8 GROUP 1 (ALKALI METALS) 189   9 GROUP 7 (HALOGENS) 196   10 GASES IN THE ATMOSPHERE 199
11 REACTIVITY SERIES 206   12 ACIDS AND ALKALIS 214   13 CHEMICAL TESTS 219

CHEMISTRY UNIT 2
INORGANIC CHEMISTRY

Inorganic chemistry is the study of all the elements in the Periodic Table and the compounds they form, except organic compounds formed by carbon. The elements all have very different properties and they form a huge variety of compounds. Inorganic chemists use the Periodic Table as the unifying principle for understanding the behaviour of the elements and their compounds. Most of the elements in the Periodic Table are metals and these are some of the most important materials that we use in everyday life. However, scientists are always searching for new materials with exciting properties. Inorganic chemists are involved in the development of these new materials, for instance high-temperature superconductors that can be used in trains that levitate above the tracks.

8 GROUP 1 (ALKALI METALS): LITHIUM, SODIUM AND POTASSIUM

SPECIFICATION REFERENCES: 2.1–2.3

We have already looked at the Periodic Table in Chapter 4. Here we will look at the properties of the elements in Group 1 of the Periodic Table: the alkali metals.

▶ Figure 8.1 Potassium reacting with water. The alkali metals are all reactive metals that react vigorously with water.

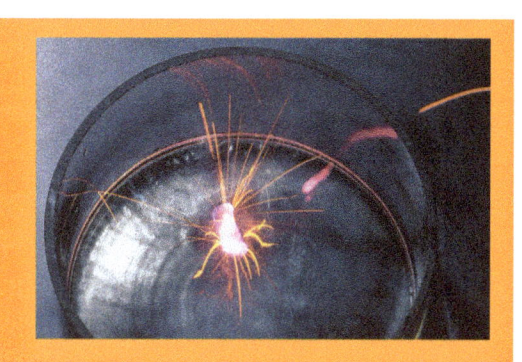

LEARNING OBJECTIVES

- Understand how the similarities in the reactions of these elements with water provide evidence for their recognition as a family of elements.

- Understand how the differences between the reactions of these elements with air and water provide evidence for the trend in reactivity in Group 1.

- Use knowledge of trends in Group 1 to predict the properties of other alkali metals.

The elements in Group 1 of the Periodic Table are called the alkali metals. The group contains all the elements shown in **Figure 8.2**, but we will concentrate specifically on the properties of lithium, sodium and potassium in this chapter.

Li lithium
Na sodium
K potassium
Rb rubidium
Cs caesium
Fr francium

▲ Figure 8.2 The alkali metals

PHYSICAL PROPERTIES

	Melting point / °C	Boiling point / °C	Density / g/cm^3
Li	181	1342	0.53
Na	98	883	0.97
K	63	760	0.86
Rb	39	686	1.53
Cs	29	669	1.88

Table 8.1 Some physical properties of the alkali metals

The melting and boiling points of the elements are very low for metals, and get lower as you move down the group.

Their densities tend to increase down the group, although not regularly. Lithium, sodium and potassium are all less dense than water, and so will float on it.

The metals are also very soft and are easily cut with a knife, becoming softer as you move down the group. They are shiny and silver when freshly cut, but tarnish very quickly on exposure to air.

A FAMILY OF ELEMENTS

Lithium, sodium and potassium are put in the same group in the Periodic Table because they have very similar chemical properties — they react in very similar ways and form compounds with the same formula (only the metal is different).

- They all react with water (this will be discussed below) in the same way to form a hydroxide with the formula MOH (e.g. LiOH, NaOH) and hydrogen.
- They react with oxygen to form an oxide with the formula M_2O (e.g. Na_2O, K_2O).
- They react with halogens to form compounds with the formula MX (e.g. LiCl, KBr).
- They form ionic compounds which contain an M^+ ion (e.g. Na^+, K^+).

> **KEY POINT**
>
> 'M' simply represents any one of the alkali metals. 'X' represents any one of the halogens.

> **EXTENSION**
>
> The chemical properties depend on the number of electrons in the outer shell of an atom. The Group 1 elements react in very similar ways because they all have the same number of electrons in the outer shell (one).

REACTIONS WITH WATER

All the alkali metals react in the same way with water to produce a metal hydroxide and hydrogen:

alkali metal + water → alkali metal hydroxide + hydrogen
2M + $2H_2O$ → 2MOH + H_2

> **REMINDER**
>
> You might need to remind yourself why the formula is MOH by looking at **Chapter 6**. The charge on the hydroxide ion is 1–.

The main difference between the reactions is how quickly they happen.

As you go down the group, the metals become more reactive and the reactions occur more rapidly.

The reaction between sodium and water is typical.

SODIUM

$2Na(s) + 2H_2O(l) \rightarrow 2NaOH(aq) + H_2(g)$

> **HINT**
>
> Strictly speaking, most of the time the sodium is reacting it is present as molten sodium, not solid sodium. Writing (l) for the state symbol has the potential to confuse an examiner and is probably best avoided!

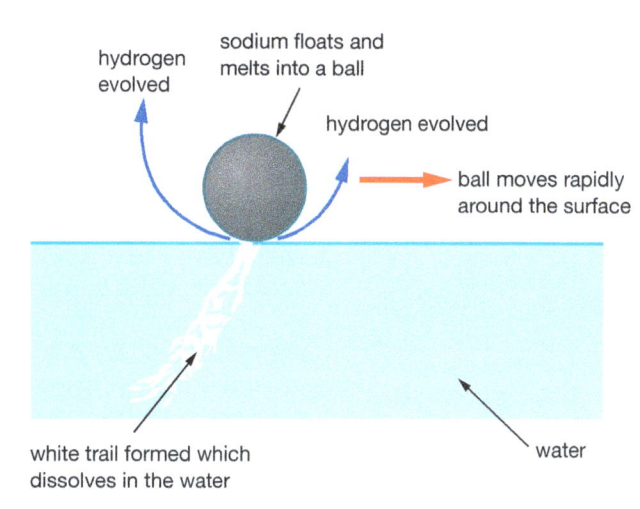

▲ Figure 8.3 Sodium reacting with water. The white trail is the sodium hydroxide, which dissolves in water to form a strongly alkaline solution.

A piece of sodium reacting with water is shown in **Figure 8.3**. The main *observations* you can make when this reaction occurs are:

- *The sodium floats* because it is less dense than water.
- *The sodium melts into a ball* because its melting point is low and a lot of heat is produced by the reaction.
- There is *fizzing* because hydrogen gas is produced.
- *The sodium moves around on the surface of the water*. Because the hydrogen is not given off symmetrically around the ball, the sodium is pushed around the surface of the water.
- *The piece of sodium gets smaller and eventually disappears*. The sodium is used up in the reaction.
- If you test the solution that is formed with universal indicator solution, you will see that the universal indicator goes blue, indicating an alkaline solution has been formed. The metal hydroxide solution is alkaline (the solution contains the OH⁻ ion).

LITHIUM

$$2Li(s) + 2H_2O(l) \rightarrow 2LiOH(aq) + H_2(g)$$

The reaction is very similar to sodium's reaction, except that it is slower. Lithium's melting point is higher and the heat is not produced so quickly, so the lithium does not melt.

POTASSIUM

$$2K(s) + 2H_2O(l) \rightarrow 2KOH(aq) + H_2(g)$$

Potassium's reaction is faster than sodium's. Enough heat is produced to ignite the hydrogen, which burns with a lilac flame. The reaction often ends with the potassium *spitting* around and exploding.

RUBIDIUM AND CAESIUM

These react even more violently than potassium, and the reaction can be explosive. Rubidium hydroxide and caesium hydroxide are formed.

EXAM HINT

When asked to write *observations* in the exam it is better to write 'fizzing/bubbling/effervescing' rather than 'a gas is given off' because the fizzing/bubbling/effervescing, is what you actually *see*.

EXAM HINT

When you are asked about this in the exam, you are often asked to compare the reactions of sodium and lithium so you should explain how you can see that the reaction of lithium is slower. So, for example, you can say that it fizzes *more slowly*, or the lithium moves around *more slowly*, or *takes longer* to disappear.

EXAM HINT

Again, if you are asked to compare potassium with sodium use phrases such as:
'fizzes *more* vigorously'
'moves around *more* quickly'
'disappears *more* quickly'
The key difference though is that with potassium the hydrogen bursts into flames but with sodium it usually does not.

▲ Figure 8.4 Lithium, sodium and potassium have to be kept in oil to stop them reacting with oxygen and water vapour in the air.

Safety note: The reactions of rubidium and caesium would be too hazardous to attempt in school as they would explode.

REMINDER

Remember the charge on the oxide ion is O^{2-} and the charge on an alkali metal ion is M^+.

▲ Figure 8.5 A piece of sodium. The left-hand edge has been freshly cut, so it is shiny.

REACTIONS WITH AIR

Lithium, sodium and potassium are all stored in oil (see **Figure 8.4**) because they react with the air. If we look at a piece of sodium which has been taken out of the oil, it usually has a crust on the outside. It is not shiny unless it has been freshly cut.

When the piece of sodium is cut, the fresh surface is shiny (**Figure 8.5**) but it tarnishes rapidly as the freshly exposed sodium reacts with oxygen in the air. If we do the same with a piece of lithium it tarnishes more slowly because lithium reacts more slowly than sodium. A freshly cut piece of potassium tarnishes extremely rapidly, more quickly than sodium. In this way we can see again that potassium is more reactive than sodium, which is more reactive than lithium. In each case the metal reacts with oxygen in the air to form an oxide with the formula M_2O.

If we heat each of the metals in the air using a Bunsen burner, we get a much more vigorous reaction and it is more difficult to see which metal is most reactive because all the reactions are so rapid.

Lithium burns with a red flame to form lithium oxide.

Sodium burns with a yellow flame to form sodium oxide.

Potassium burns with a lilac flame to form potassium oxide.

The equation for all these reactions is:

$$4M(s) + O_2(g) \rightarrow 2M_2O(s)$$

In each case the product formed is a white powder – the alkali metal oxide.

COMPOUNDS OF THE ALKALI METALS

All Group 1 metal ions are colourless. That means that their compounds will be colourless or white unless they are combined with a coloured negative ion. Potassium dichromate(VI) is orange, for example, because the dichromate(VI) ion is orange, and potassium manganate(VII) is purple because the manganate(VII) ion is purple. Group 1 compounds are typical ionic solids and are mostly soluble in water.

GROUP 1 ELEMENTS: A SUMMARY

The main features of the Group 1 elements are:
- they are metals
- they are soft with melting points and densities which are very low for metals
- they have to be stored out of contact with air or water
- they react rapidly with air to form coatings of the metal oxide
- they react with water to produce an alkaline solution of the metal hydroxide and hydrogen gas
- they increase in reactivity as you go down the group
- they form compounds in which the metal is present as a 1+ ion
- they have mainly white/colourless compounds which dissolve in water to produce colourless solutions.

PREDICTING THE PROPERTIES OF FRANCIUM

All elements in a group in the Periodic Table have similar chemical properties. However, as we move down a group in the Periodic Table the physical properties of the elements change gradually. So, if we know the chemical and physical properties of most of the elements in a group, we should be able to predict the properties of elements we do not know. Francium (pronounced frans-ee-um) is extremely **radioactive** and at any time, anywhere in the world, there is only a tiny amount present; nobody has actually seen a piece of francium. We can, however, predict the properties of francium using the properties of the other alkali metals.

We can predict that francium:

- is very soft
- will have a melting point around room temperature
- has density which is probably just over 2 g/cm^3
- will be a silvery metal, but will tarnish almost instantly in air
- will react violently with water to give francium hydroxide and hydrogen
- will be more reactive than caesium
- will have a hydroxide, francium hydroxide, with the formula FrOH, which will be soluble in water and form a strongly alkaline solution
- will form compounds that are white/colourless and dissolve in water to give colourless solutions.

We could use a graphical method to predict the melting point of francium (**Figure 8.6**). If we **plot** the melting point of the alkali metals against atomic number then draw a line of best fit we get:

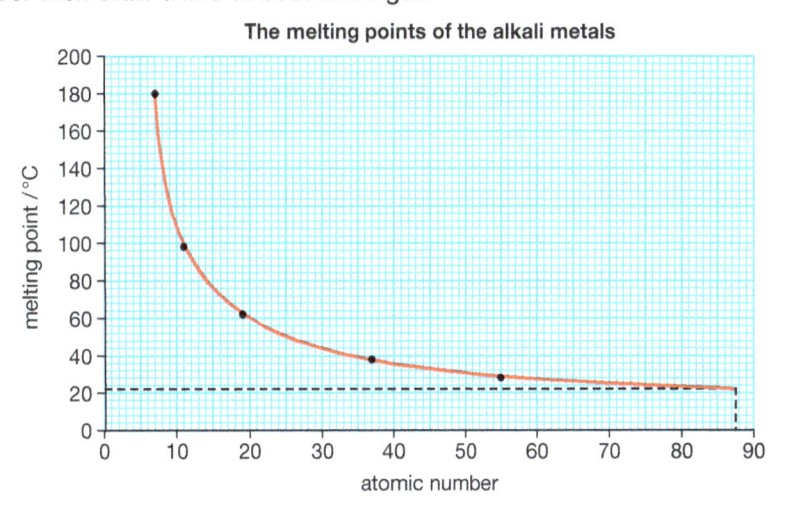

▲ Figure 8.6 This graph allows us to predict the melting point of francium.

If we carry on the line to atomic number 87 we can predict a melting point of about 22 °C.

> **REMINDER**
> The chemical properties of an element indicate how the element reacts, and give clues about the formulae of compounds formed.

> **REMINDER**
> See **Table 8.1** for melting points and densities.

> **REMINDER**
> Remember, you cannot actually observe any of these properties.

> **KEY POINT**
> Various other predictions give a melting point for francium between 21 °C and 27 °C.

CHAPTER QUESTIONS

Exam-style questions on Group 1 (alkali metals): lithium, sodium and potassium can be found at the end of Unit 2 on page 224.

SKILLS REASONING

1. Explain why lithium, sodium and potassium are put in the same group in the Periodic Table.

SKILLS CRITICAL THINKING

2. a State the formula of the ion formed by sodium.
   b Write the formulae of the following compounds.
      i lithium hydroxide
      ii sodium hydroxide
      iii rubidium hydroxide
      iv sodium oxide
      v potassium oxide
      vi caesium oxide.

SKILLS REASONING

3. Which of the following is correct?
   A potassium has a higher melting point than sodium but a lower melting point than lithium
   B rubidium has a higher melting point than potassium and lithium
   C lithium is the alkali metal with the highest melting point
   D sodium has a melting point lower than that of lithium and potassium

SKILLS REASONING

4. a State *three* observations you could make when a small piece of sodium is put into a trough of water.
   b Explain one observation that would be different if lithium is used instead of sodium.

SKILLS PROBLEM SOLVING

   c Write a word equation for the reaction that occurs in **a**.
   d Write a chemical equation, including state symbols, for the reaction in **b**.

SKILLS CRITICAL THINKING

5. This question concerns the chemistry of the elements Li, Na, and K.
   In **a** and **b**, *you should name the substances represented by letters. These letters are not the chemical symbols of the elements.*
   a **A** is the least dense of the metals.
   b When metal **B** is dropped onto water it melts into a ball and moves rapidly around the surface. A gas, **C**, is given off and this burns with a lilac flame. A solution of **D** is formed.
   c Write an equation for the reaction of **B** with water. *Use the actual symbol of element* **B**.

SKILLS REASONING

   d What do you expect to see if solution **D** is tested with universal indicator paper?
   e Explain why **B** melts into a ball when it is dropped onto water.

SKILLS CRITICAL THINKING

   f **E** burns in air with a yellow flame to form compound **F**. Write a word equation and balanced symbol equation for the reaction that occurs.

SKILLS REASONING

6. Which of the following is correct?
   A a freshly cut piece of lithium tarnishes more rapidly in air than a freshly cut piece of sodium
   B lithium, sodium and potassium are stored under oil to prevent them from reacting with nitrogen in the air
   C potassium reacts violently with air because hydrogen gas is produced, which ignites
   D a freshly cut piece of potassium tarnishes rapidly in air because it reacts to form an oxide

7 Explain whether each of the following statements is true or false.
   a Sodium forms mostly covalent compounds.
   b All the alkali metals react with air to form oxides.
   c Lithium reacts with chlorine to form lithium chloride, which has the formula Li₂Cl.

8 Imagine that a new alkali metal has recently been discovered and that it fits into the Periodic Table below francium. We will call this new element edexcelium.
   a Explain whether you would expect edexcelium to have a higher or lower melting point than francium.
   b State the names of the products that will be formed when edexcelium reacts with water.
   c Explain whether edexcelium will be more or less reactive than francium.
   d If the symbol for edexcelium is Ed, write a balanced chemical equation for the reaction of edexcelium with water.
   e When edexcelium reacts with water, will the solution formed be acidic, alkaline or neutral?
   f Write the formula for the compound formed when edexcelium reacts with air.

9 GROUP 7 (HALOGENS): CHLORINE, BROMINE AND IODINE

SPECIFICATION REFERENCES: 2.5, 2.6

The elements in Group 7 of the Periodic Table are called the halogens. In this chapter we will look at some of the properties of these elements. When we first look at them, it is hard to see that they form a family of elements because they look so different, but they react in very similar ways.

▶ Figure 9.1 Chlorine, bromine and iodine are three of the halogens.

LEARNING OBJECTIVES

- Know the colours, physical states (at room temperature) and trends in physical properties of the halogens.
- Use knowledge of trends in Group 7 to predict the properties of other halogens.

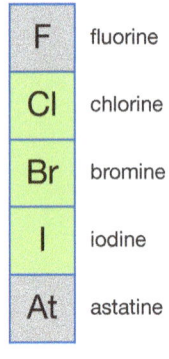

▲ Figure 9.2 The halogens

KEY POINT

Diatomic means that there are 2 atoms per molecule.

▲ Figure 9.3 Iodine is a grey solid but has a purple vapour.

THE HALOGENS

Fluorine, chlorine, bromine, iodine and astatine are the elements in Group 7 of the Periodic Table (**Figure 9.2**). The elements are all placed in the same group because they have similar chemical properties. In this chapter we will concentrate on the properties of chlorine, bromine and iodine (see **Table 9.1**, **Figure 9.3**).

The halogens are non-metallic elements with diatomic molecules: F_2, Cl_2, etc.

The name 'halogen' means 'salt-producing'. When they react with metals, these elements produce a wide range of salts, for example, calcium fluoride, sodium chloride, silver bromide and potassium iodide. All the salts contain the X^- ion (where X stands for any halogen).

Table 9.1 The melting and boiling points of the halogens increase and the colour becomes darker down the group.

	Physical state at room temperature	Colour
Cl_2	gas	green
Br_2	liquid	red–brown liquid, orange–brown vapour
I_2	solid	grey solid, purple vapour

2 INORGANIC CHEMISTRY
9 GROUP 7 (HALOGENS): CHLORINE, BROMINE AND IODINE

REMINDER

Remember that intermolecular forces are the forces of attraction between molecules.

The halogens are all covalent substances with simple molecular structures and so when they boil, only the intermolecular forces of attraction are broken – no covalent bonds are broken. The fact that the melting and boiling points of the halogens increase down the group from chlorine to bromine to iodine must mean that the intermolecular forces of attraction become stronger down the group, therefore more energy must be supplied to overcome these stronger forces of attraction.

REACTIONS OF THE HALOGENS

The halogens react with hydrogen to form **hydrogen halides**: hydrogen chloride, hydrogen bromide and hydrogen iodide. For example:

$$H_2(g) + Br_2(g) \rightarrow 2HBr(g)$$

The hydrogen halides are all acidic, poisonous gases. In common with all the compounds formed between the halogens and non-metals, the gases are covalently bonded. They are very soluble in water, reacting with it to produce solutions of **acids**. For example, hydrochloric acid is a solution of hydrogen chloride in water:

$$HCl(g) \xrightarrow{\text{dissolve in water}} HCl(aq)$$

hydrogen chloride   hydrochloric acid

KEY POINT

Make sure you understand these distinctions:
- Hydrogen chloride is a gas and when it dissolves in water it becomes hydrochloric acid.
- Hydrogen chloride gas consists of HCl molecules.
- Hydrochloric acid is a solution containing H$^+$ and Cl$^-$ ions.

The acids formed by other hydrogen halides are:
HBr(aq)   hydrobromic acid
HI(aq)   hydroiodic acid

The halogens react with alkali metals to form salts, which contain the X$^-$ ion (Cl$^-$, Br$^-$ or I$^-$). For instance, sodium burns in chlorine with its typical yellow flame to produce white, solid sodium chloride:

$$2Na(s) + Cl_2(g) \rightarrow 2NaCl(s)$$

SUMMARISING THE MAIN FEATURES OF THE GROUP 7 ELEMENTS

Group 7 elements:
- have diatomic molecules, X$_2$ (e.g. Cl$_2$, Br$_2$, I$_2$)
- go from gases to liquid to solid as you move down the group: the melting points and boiling points increase down the group
- become darker in colour down the group
- form compounds with the formula HX (e.g. HCl, HBr, HI) when reacted with hydrogen and these dissolve in water to form acids
- form ionic salts with metals and covalent compounds with non-metals
- form X$^-$ (e.g. Cl$^-$, Br$^-$, I$^-$) ions in ionic compounds.

EXAM HINT

If asked in the exam about safety precautions when carrying out experiments involving the halogens, it is important to realise that they have extremely poisonous **vapours** and have to be handled in a **fume cupboard**.

We can use these properties and trends to predict the properties of astatine, the element below iodine in Group 7. Astatine is an extremely rare radioactive element and no one has ever seen a sample of it, but we can predict that it:
- will be diatomic and contain At$_2$ molecules
- will be a solid at room temperature and have a higher melting point than iodine
- will be a darker colour than iodine, very dark grey or black
- will react with hydrogen to form HAt, which will dissolve in water to form an acid
- will form the salt NaAt with sodium or KAt with potassium
- will contain the astatide ion (At$^-$) in its ionic salts.

CHAPTER QUESTIONS

Exam-style questions on Group 7 (halogens): chlorine, bromine and iodine can be found at the end of Unit 2 on page 224.

SKILLS REASONING

1 Explain why chlorine, bromine and iodine are placed in the same group in the Periodic Table.

SKILLS INTERPRETATION

2 The colour of liquid bromine is:
 A blue–purple
 B yellow–green
 C red–brown
 D grey–black

3 The table shows the boiling points of fluorine, chlorine and bromine.

	Boiling point / °C
fluorine, F_2	−188
chlorine, Cl_2	−34
bromine, Br_2	59

SKILLS ANALYSIS
SKILLS PROBLEM SOLVING

a Predict the boiling point of iodine.

b The melting point of chlorine is −101 °C and that of bromine is −7 °C. Explain whether there is a temperature at which both chlorine and bromine are liquids.

SKILLS INTERPRETATION

4 a State the colour of
  i solid iodine
  ii iodine vapour.
 b State the formula, with state symbol, of iodine vapour.

SKILLS PROBLEM SOLVING

 c Iodine sublimes. Write an equation with state symbols to show this process.
 d State the formula of the ion formed by iodine.
 e State the formula of potassium iodide.

SKILLS REASONING, PROBLEM SOLVING

5 In 2010, scientists discovered a new element which they called tennessine. They placed this element in Group 7 below astatine. The symbol for tennessine is Ts. Scientists have never seen samples of astatine or tennessine.
 a What would be the formula of tennessine gas?
 b Explain whether you would expect tennessine to be a solid, liquid or gas at room temperature.
 c Predict whether tennessine would have a higher or lower melting point than astatine.
 d Use your knowledge of the colours of other halogens to suggest whether tennessine would be darker or lighter in colour than astatine.
 e i Chlorine gas reacts with hydrogen gas to form hydrogen chloride (HCl) gas. Write an equation for this reaction including state symbols.
  ii Write an equation for the reaction of tennessine with hydrogen gas. *You do not need to include state symbols.*
 f Bromine reacts with potassium to form potassium bromide.
  i Deduce the formula of potassium bromide.
  ii Predict the name and formula of the compound formed when tennessine reacts with potassium.

10 GASES IN THE ATMOSPHERE

SPECIFICATION REFERENCES: 2.9–2.11, 2.13, 2.14

This chapter looks at the most common gases in the atmosphere, concentrating on oxygen. We will also look at carbon dioxide, which is a greenhouse gas and is a cause of climate change.

▶ Figure 10.1 Despite the gases added by industry, the air around us is mostly nitrogen and oxygen.

LEARNING OBJECTIVES

- Know the approximate percentages by volume of the four most abundant gases in dry air.
- Understand how to determine the percentage by volume of oxygen in air using experiments involving the reactions of metals (e.g. iron) and non-metals (e.g. phosphorus) with air.
- Describe the combustion of elements in oxygen, including magnesium, hydrogen and sulfur.
- Know that carbon dioxide is a greenhouse gas and that increasing amounts in the atmosphere contributes to climate change.
- Practical: Determine the approximate percentage by volume of oxygen in air using a metal or a non-metal.

THE COMPOSITION OF THE AIR

The approximate percentages (by volume) of the four most abundant gases present in *unpolluted, dry* air are shown in **Table 10.1**.

Table 10.1 Approximate percentages (by volume) of the main gases in unpolluted, dry air

Gas	Amount in air / %	Amount in air / fraction
nitrogen	78.1	about 4/5
oxygen	21.0	about 1/5
argon	0.9	
carbon dioxide	0.04	

KEY POINT

It is important to realise that these figures apply only to dry, unpolluted air. Air can have anywhere between 0 and 4% water vapour. The percentage of carbon dioxide in the air, although very small, is rising steadily because of human activity.

There are also very small amounts of the other noble gases in the air.

SHOWING THAT AIR CONTAINS ABOUT ONE-FIFTH OXYGEN

We will look at two different methods for measuring the percentage of oxygen in the air. Both methods rely on the same basic principle: we react something with the oxygen in the air and look at how much the volume decreases as the oxygen is removed.

KEY POINT

Iron needs oxygen and water to rust. The rusting of iron is discussed in **Chapter 11**.

> **Safety note:** Iron filings can irritate the skin and are a particular hazard if they get in the eyes.

ACTIVITY 1

▼ PRACTICAL: USING THE RUSTING OF IRON

Iron rusts in **damp** air, using up oxygen as it does so. We can use this reaction to determine how much oxygen there is in the air.

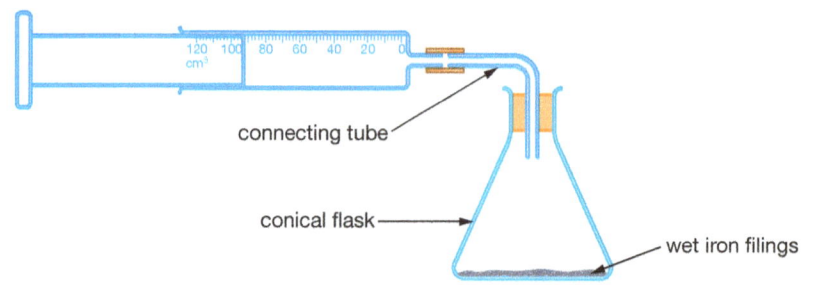

▲ Figure 10.2 This apparatus can be used to find the percentage of oxygen in the air.

We will use the apparatus in **Figure 10.2**, but before we start we need to know the volume of air present in the apparatus. We can find this by filling up the conical flask and connecting tube with water and then transferring the water to a measuring cylinder. On the conical flask we mark the position of the bung and only fill with water to that point. We will assume that the small volume occupied by the **iron filings** is negligible (very small compared with the overall volume).

The procedure for the experiment is as follows:

- Set up the apparatus as shown in **Figure 10.2**.
- Put wet iron filings into the conical flask.
- Record the initial reading on the gas syringe.
- Leave the apparatus in place for about a week, until the reading on the gas syringe stops changing.
- Record the final reading on the gas syringe.

Volume of air in conical flask / cm^3	130
Volume of air in connecting tube / cm^3	12
Initial reading on gas syringe / cm^3	92
Final reading on gas syringe / cm^3	43

We can see that the total volume of air inside the apparatus at the beginning of the experiment is 130 + 12 + 92 = 234 cm^3.

The total volume of 'air' in the apparatus at the end = 130 + 12 + 43 = 185 cm^3

Volume of oxygen used up = 234 − 185 = 49 cm^3

The percentage of oxygen in the air is 49/234 × 100 = 21%.

Sometimes when you do this experiment, the answer comes out as less than 21%. Possible reasons for this could be:

- The experiment was not left set up for long enough. The iron has not had enough chance to react with all the oxygen in the apparatus.
- Not enough iron was added at the beginning. The iron must be in excess, that is, there must be enough iron to react with all the oxygen present.

KEY POINT

Oxygen is needed for things to burn. There are inverted commas (' ... ') around 'air' because oxygen has been removed. The 'air' is therefore mostly nitrogen. Nitrogen is very unreactive, so if you put a lighted splint into this 'air', it will be extinguished.

2 INORGANIC CHEMISTRY   10 GASES IN THE ATMOSPHERE

KEY POINT

Phosphorus does not react with water.

> **Safety note:** The teacher demonstrating this experiment needs to wear eye protection or a face shield. The room must be well ventilated. After igniting the phosphorus, the bell-jar needs to be held down, because the pressure will rise at the beginning of the experiment. After all the fumes have dissolved the evaporating basin needs to be sunk using a glass rod to prevent any unreacted phosphorus re-igniting.

ACTIVITY 2

▼ PRACTICAL: USING PHOSPHORUS

Phosphorus is a very reactive element that reacts with the oxygen in the air to form a phosphorus oxide. This oxide is very soluble in water.

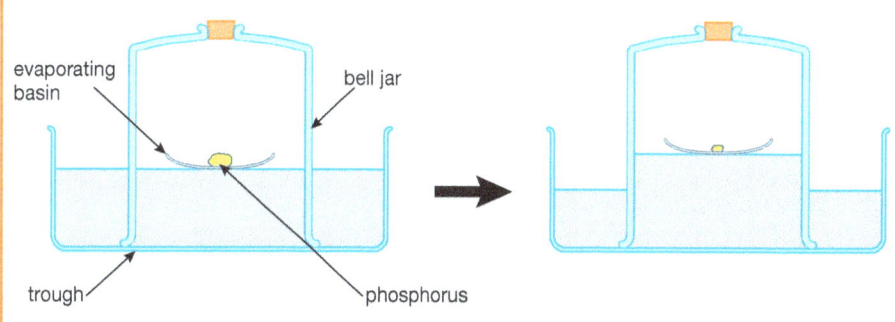

▲ Figure 10.3 Finding the percentage of oxygen in air using phosphorus

- The apparatus shown in **Figure 10.3** is set up with the piece of phosphorus on an evaporating basin, which is floating in the water.
- The initial level of water is marked on the side of the bell jar with a waterproof pen or a sticker.
- The bung is removed from the bell jar and the phosphorus is touched with a hot metal wire in order to ignite it.
- The bung is quickly put back into the bell jar.
- The phosphorus burns, the bell jar becomes filled with a white smoke (phosphorus oxide) and the level of water rises inside the bell jar. The smoke eventually clears as the phosphorus oxide dissolves in the water.
- When the level of water inside the bell jar stops rising, the final level is marked.
- To find how much the water level has changed, the bell jar is turned upside down, filled with water to each mark in turn and the water is poured into a large measuring cylinder.

It is important that there is still some phosphorus left in the evaporating basin at the end of the experiment. We use an excess of phosphorus so that there is more than enough to react with all the oxygen. If there was no phosphorus left, then we would probably get a lower value for the percentage of oxygen in the air because not all the oxygen would have been used up.

THE COMBUSTION OF ELEMENTS IN OXYGEN

Some elements burn in oxygen, these reactions are called *combustion reactions*. Elements burn more brightly and rapidly in pure oxygen than in air because air only contains 21% oxygen.

BURNING MAGNESIUM

Magnesium burns in oxygen with an extremely bright white flame (**Figure 10.4**) to give a white, powdery ash of magnesium oxide:

$$2Mg(s) + O_2(g) \rightarrow 2MgO(s)$$

The white powder formed is not very soluble in water but a very small amount does dissolve to form an alkaline solution:

$$MgO(s) + H_2O(l) \rightarrow Mg(OH)_2(aq)$$

▲ Figure 10.4 Magnesium ribbon burning in air

BURNING SULFUR

KEY POINT

Sulfur dioxide is also called sulfur(IV) oxide.

Sulfur burns in oxygen with a blue flame (**Figure 10.5**). Poisonous, colourless sulfur dioxide gas is produced.

$$S(s) + O_2(g) \rightarrow SO_2(g)$$

▲ Figure 10.5 Sulfur burning in oxygen

KEY POINT

Sulfurous acid (H_2SO_3), not sulfuric acid (H_2SO_4), is formed.

The sulfur dioxide dissolves in water to form an acidic solution of *sulfurous acid*:

$$SO_2(g) + H_2O(l) \rightarrow H_2SO_3(aq)$$

BURNING HYDROGEN

Hydrogen burns in oxygen with a pale blue flame. The product is water:

$$2H_2(g) + O_2(g) \rightarrow 2H_2O(l)$$

If you ignite a mixture of hydrogen and oxygen it will explode. This is the basis of the 'squeaky pop' test for hydrogen (see **Chapter 13**).

CARBON DIOXIDE AND GLOBAL WARMING: THE GREENHOUSE EFFECT

Carbon dioxide is produced when fossil fuels (coal, oil and gas) burn. For instance, when coal, which is mostly carbon, burns in excess oxygen:

$$C(s) + O_2(g) \rightarrow CO_2(g)$$

REMINDER

A hydrocarbon is a molecule containing carbon and hydrogen only. These are discussed more fully in **Unit 4**.

Petrol (the fuel in most cars) is a mixture containing many different hydrocarbons. An example of a reaction that occurs when petrol burns is:

$$2C_8H_{18}(l) + 25O_2(g) \rightarrow 16CO_2(g) + 18H_2O(l)$$

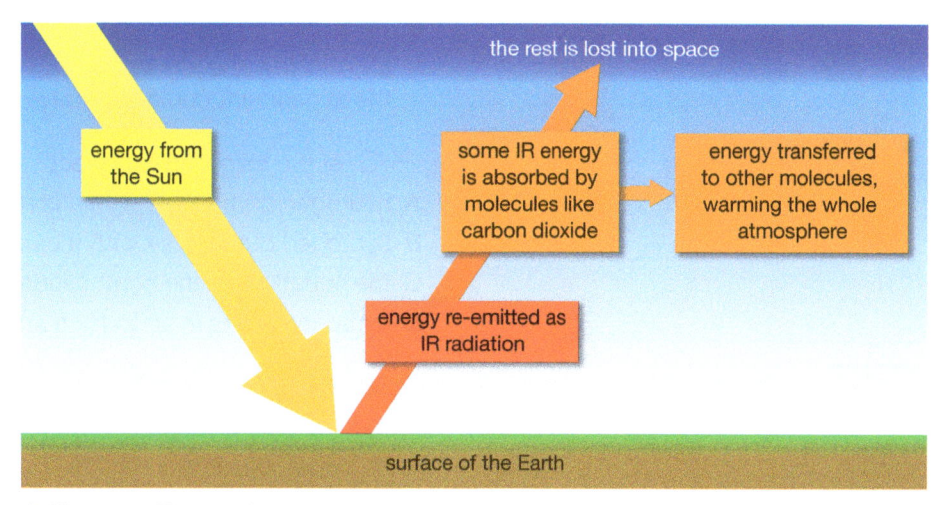

2 INORGANIC CHEMISTRY
10 GASES IN THE ATMOSPHERE

▲ Figure 10.6 The greenhouse effect

Carbon dioxide is a **greenhouse gas**. The greenhouse effect occurs when high-energy **UV** and visible light from the sun pass through the atmosphere and warm up the surface of the Earth (see **Figure 10.6**). The surface of the Earth (like any other warm surface) radiates infrared (IR) radiation. This IR radiation is absorbed by molecules such as CO_2 in the atmosphere. These then give out this energy again in all directions, heating the atmosphere.

For approximately the last 200 years the level of CO_2 in the atmosphere has been increasing. This has occurred since the industrial revolution and is mainly due to the burning of fossil fuels and deforestation (cutting down trees to create more land, mostly for agriculture). Scientists have shown that increasing levels of carbon dioxide in the atmosphere resulting from human activities are driving an increase in global temperatures and climate change. Some of the evidence of climate change that we are seeing is:

- polar ice caps melting
- sea levels rising
- more extreme weather (such as floods, droughts and heat waves).

CHAPTER QUESTIONS

Exam-style questions on gases in the atmosphere can be found at the end of Unit 2 on page 224.

SKILLS CRITICAL THINKING

1 State the approximate percentage of each of the following gases in dry air:
   a nitrogen   b oxygen   c carbon dioxide   d argon

SKILLS PROBLEM SOLVING

2 A student carried out an experiment to measure the percentage oxygen in the air by using the rusting of iron. The experimental **set-up** is shown below. The initial reading on the measuring cylinder was 95 cm³. They left the apparatus for 2 days and the new reading on the measuring cylinder was 80 cm³.

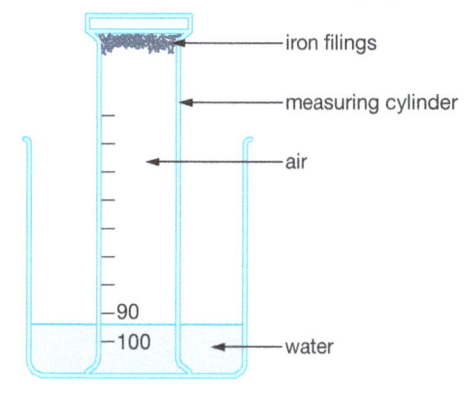

a Calculate the percentage oxygen in the air using these data.
b Explain why the answer is not the same as you had expected and how the experiment could be improved.

3 Which of the following is correct?
   A hydrogen burns in air with a green flame and forms ammonia
   B hydrogen burns in air with a blue flame and forms water
   C the equation for the combustion of hydrogen is 2H + O → H$_2$O
   D hydrogen burns in air to form an acidic gas

4 a State the formulae of the following:
     i magnesium oxide
     ii carbon dioxide
     iii sulfur dioxide.
   b Write balanced chemical equations for the reactions of
     i magnesium with oxygen gas
     ii sulfur with oxygen gas
     iii sulfur dioxide with water.
   c Name the product of the reaction in b iii.

5 Copper reacts with oxygen, when heated, to form copper(II) oxide:

   2Cu(s) + O$_2$(g) → 2CuO(s)
   copper + oxygen → copper(II) oxide

   A student used the apparatus shown below to measure the percentage oxygen in the air. Before heating they took the readings on the gas syringes. They then passed the air back and forth over the heated copper filings until there was no further change. They let the apparatus cool down and then took the final readings on the gas syringes.

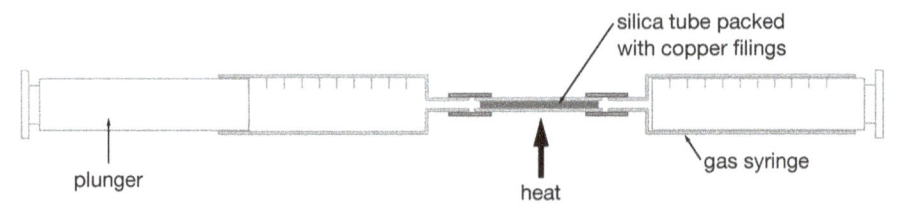

   The gas syringes are shown below.
   At start of experiment:

   At end of experiment:

   The total volume of the connecting tubes was 10 cm^3.

SKILLS ANALYSIS

a Copy and complete the table with the readings on the gas syringes at the beginning and end of the experiment.

	Left-hand syringe volume of gas / cm³	Right-hand syringe volume of gas / cm³
start of experiment		
end of experiment		

SKILLS PROBLEM SOLVING

b Calculate the total volume of gas in the apparatus at the start and end of the experiment.

c Calculate the percentage oxygen in the air from these experimental data.

SKILLS EXECUTIVE FUNCTION

d Several other students in the class also carried out this experiment. For each of the following suggested flaws in the experiment state whether the flaw would cause the result obtained by the students for the percentage oxygen in air to be lower or higher than 21.0%. Write either an L (lower) or an H (higher) for each statement.

  i The copper was not in excess - there was no unreacted copper left at the end.

  ii Some gas escaped from the apparatus as the student moved the plungers of the gas syringes in and out.

  iii The student did not allow the apparatus to cool down before taking the final readings on the gas syringe.

  iv The student did not wait until there was no further change in the total volume of gas.

  v Some magnesium powder was mixed with the copper. *(Heated magnesium reacts with oxygen and nitrogen.)*

SKILLS CRITICAL THINKING

6 Carbon dioxide is described as a *greenhouse gas*. Explain what this means.

SKILLS INTERPRETATION

7 Which of the following is correct?

  A carbon dioxide is only produced when trees burn in forest fires

  B carbon dioxide levels in the atmosphere have been falling for the last 100 years

  C increasing levels of carbon dioxide in the atmosphere could cause climate change

  D in the next 100 years carbon dioxide will become the most common gas in the atmosphere

11 REACTIVITY SERIES

SPECIFICATION REFERENCES: 2.15, 2.17–2.19

The reactivity series lists elements (mainly metals) in order of decreasing reactivity. It is likely that you will have come across some of this chemistry already in earlier years. This chapter looks at some of the reactions of metals and one of the most important reactions in the world – the rusting of iron and steel.

▲ Figure 11.1 Iron and steel react with air and water to form rust. Rusting costs the world billions of dollars each year.

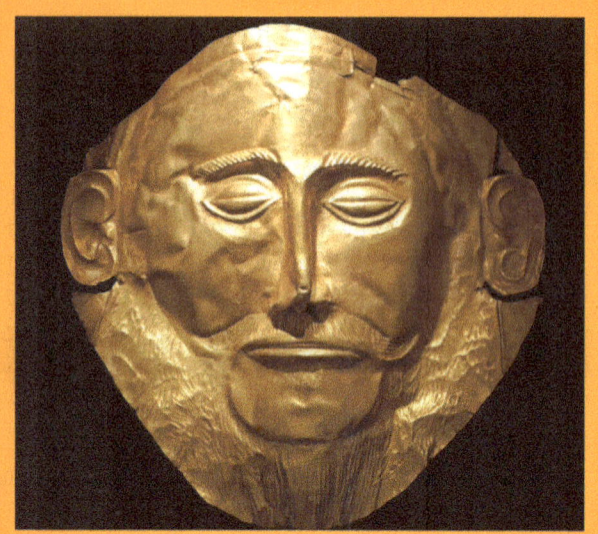

▲ Figure 11.2 Gold is so unreactive that it will remain chemically unchanged in contact with air or water basically forever.

LEARNING OBJECTIVES

- Understand how metals can be arranged in a reactivity series based on their reactions with:
  - water
  - dilute hydrochloric or sulfuric acid.
- Know the order of reactivity of these metals: potassium, sodium, lithium, calcium, magnesium, aluminium, zinc, iron, copper, silver, gold.
- Know the conditions under which iron rusts.
- Understand how the rusting of iron may be prevented by:
  - barrier methods
  - galvanising.

KEY POINT

You need to be careful when using this series of reactions to deduce a reactivity series because how vigorously a metal reacts with a dilute acid depends not only on its position in the series, but also on its surface area, and whether the surface is free from dirt or an oxide coating.

Metals can be placed in a **reactivity series** according to how vigorously they react with water and dilute acids.

ARRANGING METALS IN A REACTIVITY SERIES

Imagine you have been given pieces of calcium, zinc, iron and copper and want to arrange them in order of reactivity. To do this you could carry out the following sequence of reactions:

Add a small piece of the metal to a small volume of cold water in a test tube and observe if there is any fizzing. Calcium reacts with cold water but the others do not. We therefore know that calcium is the most reactive of the four metals.

potassium
sodium
lithium
calcium
magnesium
aluminium
(carbon)
zinc
iron
(hydrogen)
copper
silver
gold

decreasing reactivity ↓

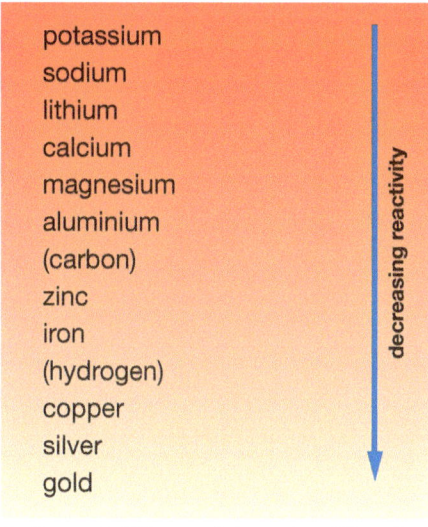

▲ Figure 11.3 The reactivity series. Although carbon and hydrogen are not metals, they are usually included in the series.

A GENERAL SUMMARY

You could then try reacting the other three metals with steam. Zinc and iron react with steam but copper does not, so you know that copper is the least reactive of the four metals.

To distinguish between zinc and iron you can add a small piece of each to a small amount of either dilute hydrochloric acid or dilute sulfuric acid in a test tube. Both metals will fizz in the acid but the zinc fizzes more vigorously so you can conclude that zinc is more reactive than iron.

> **KEY POINT**
>
> The experiments must always be done in this order – cold water, then steam, then acid – because if you had been given a very reactive metal and started off by reacting it with acid the reaction could be very violent and dangerous. Metals will always react less violently with cold water than with acids.

Metals are arranged in a reactivity series from the most reactive at the top to the least reactive at the bottom (**Figure 11.3**).

REACTIONS OF METALS WITH WATER

METALS ABOVE HYDROGEN IN THE REACTIVITY SERIES

Metals above hydrogen in the reactivity series react with water (or steam) to produce hydrogen.

If the metal reacts with cold water, the metal *hydroxide* and hydrogen are formed.

metal + water → metal hydroxide + hydrogen

If the metal reacts with steam, the metal *oxide* and hydrogen are formed.

metal + steam → metal oxide + hydrogen

As you move down the reactivity series, the reactions become less vigorous.

METALS BELOW HYDROGEN IN THE REACTIVITY SERIES

Metals below hydrogen in the reactivity series (such as copper) do not react with water or steam. This is why copper can be used for both hot and cold water pipes.

REACTIONS WITH COLD WATER

POTASSIUM, SODIUM, LITHIUM

These reactions are described in detail on pages 190–191. They are very vigorous reactions, but become less violent in the following order: potassium > sodium > lithium. The equations all look like this:

$$2M(s) + 2H_2O(l) \rightarrow 2MOH(aq) + H_2(g)$$

Replace M with K, Na or Li, depending on which metal you want.

CALCIUM

Calcium reacts gently with cold water. When grey calcium granules are put into a boiling tube or beaker of cold water, the granules sink, but are carried back to the surface again as bubbles of hydrogen are formed around them (**Figure 11.4**). The mixture becomes warm as heat is produced.

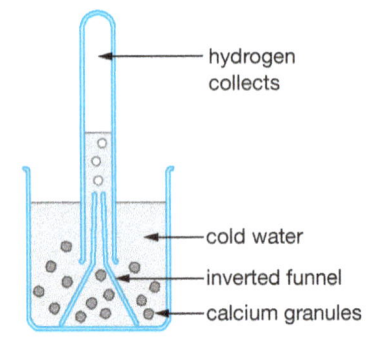

▲ Figure 11.4 Calcium reacting with cold water

Calcium hydroxide is formed. This is not very soluble in water. Some of it dissolves to give a colourless solution, but most of it is left as a white, insoluble solid.

$$Ca(s) + 2H_2O(l) \rightarrow Ca(OH)_2(aq \text{ or } s) + H_2(g)$$

MAGNESIUM

There is almost no reaction. If the magnesium is very clean, a few bubbles of hydrogen form on it, but the reaction soon stops again. This is because the magnesium becomes coated with insoluble magnesium hydroxide, which prevents any more water coming into contact with the magnesium.

REACTIONS WITH STEAM

MAGNESIUM

Magnesium ribbon can be heated in steam using the apparatus shown in **Figure 11.5**.

> **KEY POINT**
>
> You might wonder why there is no description for aluminium and steam. The reactivity of aluminium is supposed to be between that of magnesium and that of zinc. However, aluminium has only a very slow reaction with steam because it is covered in a very thin, but very strong, layer of aluminium oxide. It only really shows its true reactivity if that layer can be penetrated in some way. Water or steam do not do that very well. We will talk about this again when we look at reactions between metals and acids.

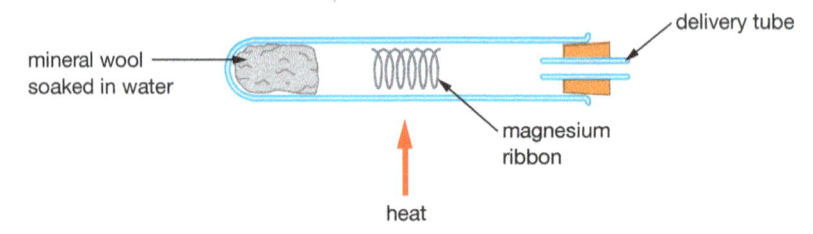

▲ Figure 11.5 Magnesium reacting with steam

The mineral wool is not heated directly. Enough heat moves back along the test tube to turn the water to steam.

The magnesium burns with a bright white flame in the steam, producing hydrogen, which can be ignited at the end of the delivery tube. White magnesium oxide is formed:

$$Mg(s) + H_2O(g) \rightarrow MgO(s) + H_2(g)$$

With both zinc and iron, the hydrogen comes off slowly enough to be collected. Neither metal burns.

ZINC

Zinc oxide is formed. This is yellow when it is hot, but white on cooling.

$$Zn(s) + H_2O(g) \rightarrow ZnO(s) + H_2(g)$$

IRON

The iron becomes slightly darker grey. A complicated oxide is formed, called triiron tetraoxide, Fe_3O_4:

$$3Fe(s) + 4H_2O(g) \rightarrow Fe_3O_4(s) + 4H_2(g)$$

> **KEY POINT**
>
> Notice that in these equations, water now has a state symbol (g) because we are talking about it as steam.

> **REMINDER**
>
> Remember that *metals below hydrogen* in the reactivity series, such as copper, *do not react* with water or steam.

REACTIONS OF METALS WITH DILUTE ACIDS

The pattern for the reaction of metals with acids is the same as for the reaction between the metals and water, but in each case the reaction is much more vigorous.

METALS ABOVE HYDROGEN IN THE REACTIVITY SERIES

Metals above hydrogen react with acids to form a salt (e.g. magnesium sulfate or zinc chloride) and hydrogen. The higher the metal in the series, the more violent the reaction.

metal + acid → salt + hydrogen

metal + dilute sulfuric acid → metal sulfate + hydrogen

metal + dilute hydrochloric acid → metal chloride + hydrogen

METALS BELOW HYDROGEN IN THE REACTIVITY SERIES

Metals such as copper, silver and gold do not react with simple dilute acids such as sulfuric or hydrochloric acid.

POTASSIUM, SODIUM, LITHIUM AND CALCIUM WITH DILUTE ACIDS

These are too reactive to add safely to acids – the reaction is too violent. Calcium can be used if the acid is very dilute.

METALS FROM MAGNESIUM TO IRON IN THE REACTIVITY SERIES

Magnesium reacts vigorously with cold dilute acids, and the mixture becomes hot. A colourless solution of magnesium sulfate or chloride is formed. With dilute sulfuric acid:

$$Mg(s) + H_2SO_4(aq) \rightarrow MgSO_4(aq) + H_2(g)$$

Aluminium is slow to start reacting, but after warming it reacts very vigorously. There is a very thin, but very strong, layer of aluminium oxide on the surface of the aluminium, which stops the acid from getting to it. On heating, the acid removes this layer, and the aluminium can show its true reactivity. With dilute hydrochloric acid:

$$2Al(s) + 6HCl(aq) \rightarrow 2AlCl_3(aq) + 3H_2(g)$$

Zinc and ***iron*** react slowly in the cold (**Figure 11.6**), but more rapidly on heating. The vigour of the reactions is less than that of aluminium. The zinc forms zinc sulfate or zinc chloride and hydrogen. The iron forms iron(II) sulfate or iron(II) chloride and hydrogen. For example:

$$Zn(s) + H_2SO_4(aq) \rightarrow ZnSO_4(aq) + H_2(g)$$
$$Fe(s) + 2HCl(aq) \rightarrow FeCl_2(aq) + H_2(g)$$

> **KEY POINT**
> The general trends on this page apply to simple acids such as dilute sulfuric acid or dilute hydrochloric acid. Nitric acid and concentrated sulfuric acid behave completely differently with most metals. These are problems beyond International GCSE.

> **HINT**
> You can remember the general equation using the mnemonic MASH.

> **Safety note:** Wear eye protection and avoid splashing the acid when stirring.

▲ Figure 11.6 Iron reacting with dilute hydrochloric acid

ACTIVITY 1

▼ PRACTICAL: INVESTIGATING THE REACTIONS BETWEEN METALS AND DILUTE ACIDS

The reactions between metals and dilute acids can be investigated in the laboratory using the following procedure.

- Set up four test tubes and put about 2 cm^3 of dilute hydrochloric acid into each one.
- Put a small piece of magnesium, zinc, iron or copper into each test tube and observe any reaction that occurs.
- If there is fizzing, collect or trap the gas and test with a lighted splint – a squeaky pop indicates the presence of hydrogen gas.
- Repeat the experiments with dilute sulfuric acid.

The results that we could obtain from the experiments with dilute hydrochloric acid are shown in **Figure 11.7** and **Table 11.1**.

Safety note: Wear eye protection. Keep hands and face away from the mouths of the tubes as some acid aerosol (tiny droplets) may be carried out by the gas.

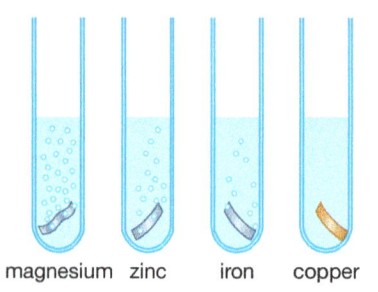

▲ Figure 11.7 The reactions between metals and hydrochloric acid

Table 11.1 The results of experiments on the reaction between hydrochloric acid and some metals

Metal	Reaction with dilute hydrochloric acid
magnesium	Reacts vigorously with lots of fizzing. The gas produced gave a squeaky pop with a lighted splint. A colourless solution is formed. The test tube gets hot.
zinc	Steady reaction. Fizzing. Enough gas eventually collected to produce a squeaky pop with a lighted splint. A colourless solution formed. The test tube gets warmer.
iron	Slow fizzing. Very little gas was collected in the time available. A very pale green solution formed. The test tube got slightly warmer.
copper	No change.

These reactions are all **exothermic** (they give out heat). See **Chapter 14** for more about exothermic reactions.

RUSTING OF IRON

Iron **rusts** in the presence of *oxygen* and *water*. Rusting occurs with iron and the most common **alloy** of iron, steel (**Figure 11.8**).

The formula of rust is $Fe_2O_3 \cdot xH_2O$, where x is a variable number. It can be called 'hydrated iron(III) oxide'.

> **HINT**
>
> **Warning!** Many metals corrode, but *rusting* refers only to the **corrosion** of iron.

> **KEY POINT**
>
> Both water *and* oxygen are needed for rusting to occur.

> **KEY POINT**
>
> Steel is mostly iron and reacts in the same way as iron. Cars, bridges etc are made from steel rather than pure iron as steel has superior properties, e.g. it is stronger.

▲ Figure 11.8 Salty water accelerates rusting.

PREVENTING RUSTING BY USING BARRIERS

The most obvious way of preventing rusting is to keep the iron/steel from coming into contact with air and water. You can do this by painting it, coating it in oil or grease, or covering it in plastic. The paint, oil or grease act as a barrier between the iron/steel and the air and water. These methods of preventing rusting are therefore called **barrier methods**. Coating the iron with a metal *below* it in the reactivity series (e.g. coating steel with tin for tin cans) is also a barrier method.

Barrier methods are usually quite cheap ways of preventing rusting. A problem with barrier methods is that once the coating is broken, the iron underneath is exposed to oxygen and water and will rust (even the bits that are not directly exposed to the air/water).

PREVENTING RUSTING BY GALVANISING

> **REMINDER**
>
> Zinc is higher than iron in the reactivity series.

Galvanised iron is iron that is coated with a layer of zinc (**Figure 11.9**). As long as the zinc layer is unscratched, it serves as a barrier to air and water. However, the iron still does not rust even when some of the zinc on the surface is scratched away to expose the iron. This is because the zinc is more reactive than iron, and so reacts with oxygen/water more readily than the iron does. Therefore the zinc corrodes instead of the iron.

▲ Figure 11.9 Galvanised iron does not rust even when the outer coating is scratched.

CHAPTER QUESTIONS

Exam-style questions on reactivity series can be found at the end of Unit 2 on page 224.

SKILLS CRITICAL THINKING

1 This question is about the reactivity of magnesium, copper, iron and sodium.
   a List the metals in order of decreasing reactivity.
   b Two of the metals react with cold water. Write an equation for the reaction of the most reactive metal with water.
   c One of the metals only reacts slowly with cold water but reacts vigorously when heated in steam. Write an equation, including state symbols, for the reaction of this metal with steam.
   d Three of the metals react with dilute hydrochloric acid. State the name of the gas produced in these reactions.
   e Write a word equation for the reaction between magnesium and dilute hydrochloric acid.
   f Iron reacts with dilute sulfuric to form a solution of iron(II) sulfate ($FeSO_4$). Write an equation including state symbols for this reaction.

2 A student designs an experiment to put four metals in a reactivity series by reacting them with dilute sulfuric acid. The metals are D, X, Q, Z (these are not the actual chemical symbols of the metals). The student took 0.1 g of each metal and added it to 5 cm³ of dilute sulfuric acid. They observed the metals for 1 minute. Their observations are shown in the table.

Metal	Observation
D	no bubbles
X	fizzing
Q	fizzing
Z	fizzing

SKILLS EXECUTIVE FUNCTION

   a The student told their teacher that they can at least tell that D is the least reactive metal. The teacher, however, told the student that they cannot even make that conclusion from their results.
   Discuss whether the student or the teacher is correct.
   b Explain what additional information the student needs to record so that they can put X, Q and Z in order of reactivity.

SKILLS PROBLEM SOLVING

   c The formula of the salt formed when X reacts with sulfuric acid is XSO_4. XSO_4 is soluble in water. Write an equation, including state symbols, for the reaction of metal X with dilute sulfuric acid.

SKILLS CRITICAL THINKING

3 If you add some powdered aluminium to a small amount of cold dilute hydrochloric acid in a boiling tube, very little happens. If you warm this it starts to fizz very rapidly.
   a State the name of the gas given off to produce the fizzing.
   b If you used an excess of hydrochloric acid, the result would be a colourless solution. State the name of the solution.

SKILLS PROBLEM SOLVING

   c Write the full balanced equation for the reaction.

SKILLS REASONING

    d Explain why the aluminium hardly reacts at all with the dilute acid in the cold, but reacts vigorously when it is heated.

SKILLS EXECUTIVE FUNCTION

4 If you have some small pieces of the metal titanium and any simple apparatus that you might need, describe how you would find out the approximate position of titanium in the reactivity series, using only water and dilute hydrochloric acid. You only need to find out that the reactivity is 'similar to iron' or 'similar to magnesium', for example. Your experiments should be done in an order that guarantees maximum safety.

SKILLS CRITICAL THINKING

5 In the past, cars were made from steel, which was then painted. In more modern cars, the steel is galvanised before it is painted.
    a State the conditions under which iron/steel rusts.
    b Explain how painting prevents iron/steel from rusting.
    c What is meant by *galvanised steel*?
    d i An old car in which the steel is painted but not galvanised is scratched. Explain whether the steel rusts.
       ii A modern car in which the steel is galvanised before it is painted is scratched. Explain whether the steel rusts.

SKILLS INTERPRETATION

6 Which of the following is *not* a barrier method for rust prevention?
    A coating a bicycle chain with oil or grease
    B painting a car door
    C coating the wires of a garden fence with plastic
    D putting silica gel (absorbs water) in a tin containing steel nails

12 ACIDS AND ALKALIS

SPECIFICATION REFERENCES: 2.28–2.32

This chapter explores what indicators, acids and alkalis are.

▲ Figure 12.1 Acids range from the extremely dangerous, needing protective clothing to clean up spills . . .

▲ Figure 12.2 . . . to a natural part of our diet: oranges contain citric acid.

LEARNING OBJECTIVES

- Describe the use of litmus to distinguish between acidic and alkaline solutions.
- Understand how the pH scale, from 0–14, can be used to classify solutions as strongly acidic (0–3), weakly acidic (4–6), neutral (7), weakly alkaline (8–10) and strongly alkaline (11–14).
- Describe the use of universal indicator to measure the approximate pH value of an aqueous solution.
- Know that acids in aqueous solution are a source of hydrogen ions, and alkalis in an aqueous solution are a source of hydroxide ions.
- Know that alkalis can neutralise acids.

pH AND INDICATORS

THE pH SCALE

The **pH scale** ranges from about 0 to about 14, and tells you how acidic or how alkaline a solution is.

KEY POINT

We talk about an 'alkali' or an 'alkaline solution'. The word 'alkali' is a noun and 'alkaline' is an adjective.

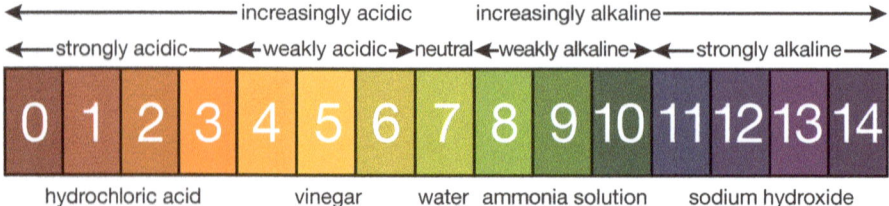

increasingly acidic — increasingly alkaline
strongly acidic — weakly acidic — neutral — weakly alkaline — strongly alkaline

0 1 2 3 4 5 6 7 8 9 10 11 12 13 14

hydrochloric acid — vinegar — sodium chloride solution — water — ammonia solution — sodium hydroxide solution

▲ Figure 12.3 The pH scale. **Vinegar** is a solution of ethanoic *acid*.

2 INORGANIC CHEMISTRY 12 ACIDS AND ALKALIS

> **KEY POINT**
> Remember, when writing pH, use a small p and a big H (the symbol for hydrogen).

> **EXTENSION**
> These are actually only approximate ranges and depend on the concentration of the acid/alkali solution. A 0.10 mol/dm³ solution of ethanoic acid actually has a pH of 2.88.

We can classify substances as strongly acidic/alkaline or weakly acidic/alkaline based on their pH (**Table 12.1**).

Table 12.1 We can classify solutions according to their pH

	pH	Solution
strongly acidic	0–3	hydrochloric acid
weakly acidic	4–6	ethanoic acid (vinegar)
neutral	7	sodium chloride
weakly alkaline	8–10	ammonia
strongly alkaline	11–14	sodium hydroxide

ACID–ALKALI INDICATORS

Litmus is an **indicator** and we can use it to distinguish between acidic and alkaline solutions. Litmus is red in acidic solutions and blue in alkaline ones. In neutral solutions, the colour is purple, which is an equal mixture of the red and blue forms.

Litmus can be used as a solution or as litmus paper. If we want to test for an acid we use blue litmus paper – this goes red if the solution is acidic. If we want to test for an alkali we use red litmus paper – this goes blue if the solution is alkaline.

Litmus can only be used to determine whether a solution is acidic or alkaline, it cannot be used to measure the pH; for that we use universal indicator. Litmus only has two colours but universal indicator has a whole range.

MEASURING pH

> **HINT**
> You can measure pH much more accurately using a pH meter.

> **KEY POINT**
> Universal indicator is red in strongly acidic solutions, green in neutral solutions and blue/purple in strongly alkaline solutions.

Universal indicator can be used to measure the approximate pH of a solution. Universal indicator is made from a mixture of indicators, which change colour in a gradual way over a range of pH values. It can be used as a solution or as paper. The most common form is known as *full-range* universal indicator. It changes through a variety of colours from pH 1 right up to pH 14, but it is not very accurate. The colours for universal indicator paper are shown in **Figure 12.3**.

▲ Figure 12.4 Using universal indicator solution to measure the pH of various solutions. The colours are checked against a pH colour chart.

In order to find the approximate pH of a solution using universal indicator solution, add a few drops of the indicator to the solution you want to test (**Figure 12.4**) and check the colour against the pH colour chart. If using universal indicator paper, place a drop of your test solution on a piece of the indicator paper and compare with the pH colour chart.

ACIDS

The formulae of some acids are given in **Table 12.2**.

All acids contain hydrogen and when acids react the hydrogen shown in red in **Table 12.2** is replaced by something else; all acids have replaceable H. For example, when hydrochloric acid reacts with sodium hydroxide we obtain:

$$HCl(aq) + NaOH(aq) \rightarrow NaCl(aq) + H_2O(l)$$

The H of the HCl has been replaced by an Na.

Not all of the hydrogens in acids are replaceable, for example in ethanoic acid only the H attached to the O is replaceable, not the ones joined to the C.

When acids are in water they dissociate (break apart) to form hydrogen ions (H^+), for example:

$$HCl(aq) \rightarrow H^+(aq) + Cl^-(aq)$$
$$HNO_3(aq) \rightarrow H^+(aq) + NO_3^-(aq)$$
$$H_2SO_4(aq) \rightarrow 2H^+(aq) + SO_4^{2-}(aq)$$

We can define acids as *substances that act as a source of hydrogen ions (H^+) in solution*.

When we are measuring pH we are actually measuring the concentration of these H^+ ions in the solution. This is why the H in pH is written with a capital letter.

Table 12.2 Some acids showing the replaceable hydrogen

Acid	Formula
hydrochloric acid	HCl
nitric acid	HNO$_3$
sulfuric acid	H$_2$SO$_4$
ethanoic acid	CH$_3$COOH
phosphoric acid	H$_3$PO$_4$

ALKALIS

Examples of alkalis are solutions of sodium hydroxide and potassium hydroxide (and solutions of all the other Group 1 hydroxides). Alkalis are solutions – if a metal hydroxide is insoluble in water it cannot form an alkali.

Alkalis are a source of hydroxide (OH^-) ions in solution.

When sodium hydroxide is in water it breaks apart to form sodium and hydroxide ions:

$$NaOH(aq) \rightarrow Na^+(aq) + OH^-(aq)$$

The other common alkali you will meet is a solution of ammonia (NH_3) (**Figure 12.5**). The ammonia reacts with the water to form ammonium ions and hydroxide ions:

$$NH_3(aq) + H_2O(l) \rightarrow NH_4^+(aq) + OH^-(aq)$$

Only some of the ammonia molecules react with water to form hydroxide ions, so ammonia solution is only weakly alkaline. All alkalis have a pH greater than 7.

> **KEY POINT**
>
> Most metal hydroxides are insoluble in water and so do not form alkalis. Other hydroxides that you might come across that are alkalis are calcium hydroxide solution (limewater) and barium hydroxide solution.

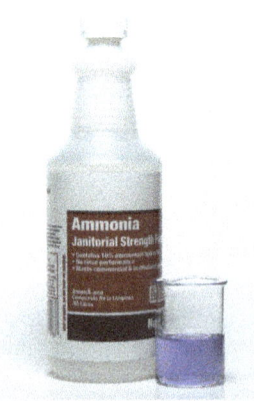

▲ Figure 12.5 Ammonia solution is sometimes called ammonium hydroxide. It is an alkali and is used in some cleaning products. Some universal indicator solution has been added to it in the beaker.

OTHER ALKALINE SOLUTIONS

There are some other substances, such as soluble metal carbonates, that react with water to form hydroxide ions:

$$Na_2CO_3(aq) + H_2O(l) \rightarrow Na^+(aq) + OH^-(aq) + Na^+(aq) + HCO_3^-(aq)$$

There are not many soluble carbonates, but sodium carbonate and potassium carbonate are both alkalis with a pH greater than 7. This is due to the OH^- ions in the solution. Only some of the carbonate ions react with water, so these solutions are only weakly alkaline.

2 INORGANIC CHEMISTRY   12 ACIDS AND ALKALIS

NEUTRALISATION REACTIONS

Acids react with alkalis in a neutralisation reaction.

The word equation for the reaction is

acid + alkali → salt + water

A **salt** is obtained when a metal (or ammonium) ion takes the place of the replaceable hydrogen of an acid.

The salts formed from:

- hydrochloric acid (HCl) are chlorides, e.g. sodium chloride (NaCl)
- sulfuric acid (H_2SO_4) are sulfates, e.g. potassium sulfate (K_2SO_4)
- nitric acid (HNO_3) are nitrates, e.g. ammonium nitrate (NH_4NO_3).

Sodium hydroxide solution (an alkali) reacts with dilute hydrochloric acid to form sodium chloride and water:

NaOH(aq) + HCl(aq) → NaCl(aq) + H_2O(l)

This is a neutralisation reaction.

In the neutralisation reaction between an acid and an alkali the H^+ from the acid reacts with the OH^- from the alkali to form water. This can be written as:

OH^-(aq) + H^+(aq) → H_2O(l)

This is an ionic equation. All neutralisation reactions for an acid reacting with an alkali will have the same ionic equation. This is because they all involve the OH^- ions from the alkali reacting with the H^+ ions from the acid to form water.

KEY POINT

The reaction of ammonia solution with acids is usually written slightly differently and we do not include the water, e.g.

NH_3 + HCl → NH_4Cl

or

$2NH_3$ + H_2SO_4 → $(NH_4)_2SO_4$

The reactions, however, can be seen to be the same if we write ammonia as ammonium hydroxide, e.g.

NH_4OH + HCl → NH_4Cl + H_2O

HINT

Refer back to **Chapter 6** if you cannot remember the charges on ions.

CHAPTER QUESTIONS

Exam-style questions on acids and alkalis can be found at the end of Unit 2 on page 224.

SKILLS CRITICAL THINKING

1 State the colour of litmus in each of the following solutions.

   a sodium hydroxide solution

   b hydrochloric acid solution

SKILLS ANALYSIS

2 **Table 12.3** gives the pH of some solutions. Classify each as strongly acidic, strongly alkaline, weakly acidic, weakly alkaline or neutral by copying the table and putting ticks in the appropriate boxes.

Table 12.3

Solution	pH	Strongly acidic	Weakly acidic	Neutral	Weakly alkaline	Strongly alkaline
potassium iodide	7					
propanoic acid	4.2					
sodium carbonate	9.5					
potassium hydroxide	13					
iron(III) chloride	2.4					
nitric acid	1.3					

SKILLS ▸ PROBLEM SOLVING

3 When acids react with alkalis, salts are formed. State the name of the salt formed in each of the following reactions.
   a sodium hydroxide + hydrochloric acid
   b potassium hydroxide + nitric acid
   c ammonia solution + sulfuric acid

SKILLS ▸ CRITICAL THINKING

4 Deduce the formulae of the following salts (you may need to refer back to **Chapter 6**).
   a potassium bromide
   b rubidium nitrate
   c calcium sulfate
   d ammonium nitrate

SKILLS ▸ INTERPRETATION

5 State the formula of the ion that makes a solution of HCl acidic.

SKILLS ▸ REASONING

6 Explain, using an equation, why ammonia solution is an alkali.

SKILLS ▸ PROBLEM SOLVING

7 a Write equations for the following reactions.
      i potassium hydroxide + sulfuric acid
      ii sodium hydroxide + nitric acid
      iii ammonia solution + hydrochloric acid
   b State the name of the type of reaction occurring in part a.

SKILLS ▸ REASONING

SKILLS ▸ CRITICAL THINKING

8 Suggest the names of acids and alkalis that could be reacted together to make the following salts.
   a potassium nitrate
   b barium sulfate
   c calcium chloride

SKILLS ▸ REASONING

9 The reaction that occurs when sodium carbonate reacts with water can be shown using an ionic equation.

An ionic equation only shows the ions that react.

$$CO_3^{2-}(aq) + H_2O(l) \rightarrow OH^-(aq) + HCO_3^-(aq)$$

Explain what happens when a piece of red litmus paper is put into the solution.

SKILLS ▸ REASONING

10 A few drops of litmus solution are added to each of the following. In which one would litmus solution go blue?
   A $HNO_3(aq)$
   B $Ba(OH)_2(aq)$
   C $NaCl(aq)$
   D $H_2SO_4(aq)$

13 CHEMICAL TESTS

SPECIFICATION REFERENCES: 2.44–2.46, 2.48, 2.49

In this chapter we will look at how to identify substances using chemical tests.

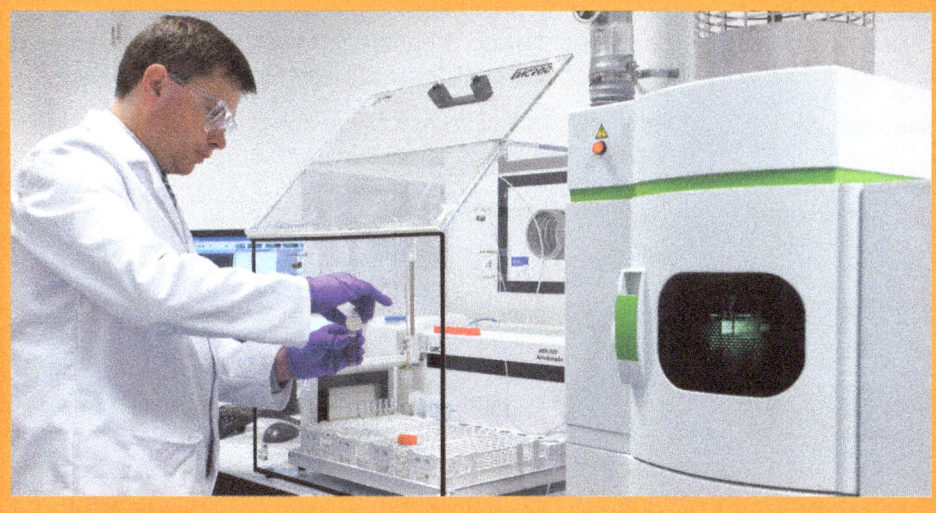

▲ Figure 13.1 Although the reactions we learn here are useful for identifying substances in the lab and we are also introduced to some interesting chemistry, analysis of substances is now routinely carried out using sophisticated machines.

LEARNING OBJECTIVES

- Describe tests for these gases:
  - hydrogen
  - oxygen
  - carbon dioxide
  - ammonia
  - chlorine.
- Describe how to carry out a flame test.
- Know the colours formed in flame tests for these cations:
  - Li$^+$ (red)
  - Na$^+$ (yellow)
  - K$^+$ (lilac)
  - Ca^{2+} (orange–red)
  - Cu^{2+} (blue–green).
- Describe a test for CO$_3^{2-}$ using hydrochloric acid and identifying the gas evolved.
- Describe a test for the presence of water using anhydrous copper(II) sulfate.

TESTING FOR GASES

HYDROGEN, H$_2$

THE TEST FOR HYDROGEN GAS

A lighted splint is held to the mouth of the tube. The hydrogen explodes with a squeaky pop.

The hydrogen combines explosively with oxygen in the air to make water.

$$2H_2(g) + O_2(g) \rightarrow 2H_2O(l)$$

OXYGEN, O₂

THE TEST FOR OXYGEN GAS

A glowing splint is put into the tube containing the gas. Oxygen relights a glowing splint.

CARBON DIOXIDE, CO₂

KEY POINT

If you keep bubbling the carbon dioxide through the limewater, the white precipitate will eventually disappear again. This is because the CO₂ reacts with the calcium carbonate to form calcium hydrogencarbonate, which is soluble in water:

$$CaCO_3(s) + H_2O(l) + CO_2(g) \rightarrow Ca(HCO_3)_2(aq)$$

THE TEST FOR CARBON DIOXIDE GAS

The carbon dioxide is bubbled through limewater. Carbon dioxide turns limewater milky/chalky/cloudy (see **Figure 13.9**, below).

Limewater is calcium hydroxide solution. Carbon dioxide reacts with it to form a white **precipitate** of calcium carbonate.

$$Ca(OH)_2(aq) + CO_2(g) \rightarrow CaCO_3(s) + H_2O(l)$$

CHLORINE, Cl₂

THE TEST FOR CHLORINE GAS

A piece of damp litmus paper or universal indicator paper is put into the test tube or held over its mouth. Chlorine is a green gas that bleaches (turns white) the damp litmus paper or universal indicator paper (**Figure 13.2**).

If blue litmus paper or universal indicator paper are used for this test, they go red first (the chlorine dissolves in the water to form an acidic solution) and then white.

Safety note: Wear eye protection. Avoid inhaling or 'sniffing' chlorine or ammonia, especially if you have a breathing problem such as asthma.

EXAM HINT

If you are asked for the *final* colour of the litmus or universal indicator paper, the answer is *white*.

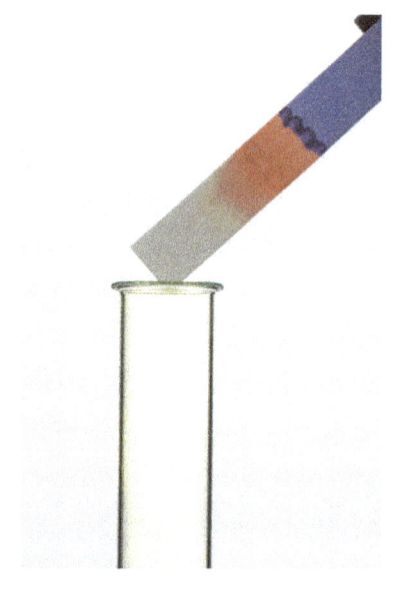

▲ Figure 13.2 Chlorine bleaches damp litmus paper.

AMMONIA, NH₃

KEY POINT

The piece of universal indicator paper or litmus paper must be damp. The ammonia dissolves in the water to form an alkali.

THE TEST FOR AMMONIA GAS

Hold a piece of damp universal indicator paper or red litmus paper at the mouth of the test tube. Ammonia turns the universal indicator paper/litmus paper blue.

Ammonia is the only alkaline gas that you will meet at International GCSE.

2 INORGANIC CHEMISTRY   13 CHEMICAL TESTS

TESTING FOR WATER

USING ANHYDROUS COPPER(II) SULFATE

Water turns white **anhydrous** copper(II) sulfate blue (**Figure 13.3**).

Anhydrous copper(II) sulfate lacks water of crystallisation and is white. Dropping water onto it replaces the water of crystallisation and turns it blue.

anhydrous copper(II) sulfate + water → hydrated copper(II) sulfate

$$CuSO_4(s) + 5H_2O(l) \rightarrow CuSO_4 \cdot 5H_2O(s)$$
white   blue

This test works for anything that contains water, so would work with sodium chloride solution or sulfuric acid. It does not show that the water is *pure*.

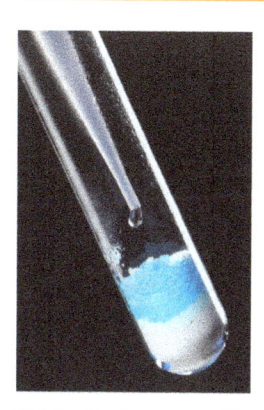

> **REMINDER**
>
> When many salts form their crystals, water from the solution becomes chemically bound up with the salt. This is called *water of crystallisation*. A salt which contains water of crystallisation is said to be *hydrated*.

▲ Figure 13.3 Testing for water with anhydrous copper(II) sulfate

Safety note: Avoid skin contact with the copper salts.

TESTING FOR IONS

All salts contain at least one cation (positive ion) and anion (negative ion). In this section we will learn how to test for these anions and cations. We do the tests for anions and cations separately.

FLAME TESTS

A flame test is used to show the presence of certain metal ions (cations) in a compound. A clean platinum or nichrome wire is dipped into concentrated hydrochloric acid and then into the salt you want to test, so that some salt sticks on the end. The wire and the salt are then held just within a non-luminous (roaring) Bunsen burner flame and the colour observed (**Figures 13.4–13.8**).

> **KEY POINT**
>
> If a new piece of wire is not being used, it is usually cleaned by **dipping** it into concentrated hydrochloric acid and then holding it in a non-luminous Bunsen flame. This is repeated until the wire does not give any colour to the flame.

> **HINT**
>
> The colour for sodium is described as yellow in the specification, but you will also see it described as orange. Both are usually acceptable.

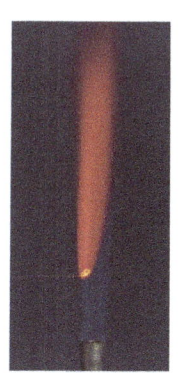

▲ Figure 13.4 Red shows lithium ions

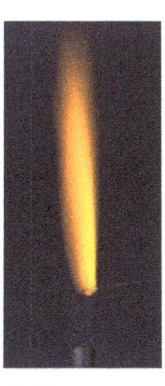

▲ Figure 13.5 Yellow shows the presence of sodium ions

▲ Figure 13.6 Lilac shows potassium ions

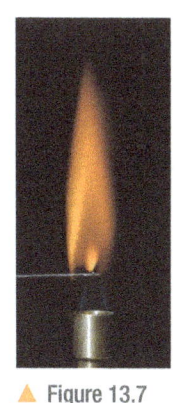

▲ Figure 13.7 Orange–red shows calcium ions

▲ Figure 13.8 Blue–green shows the presence of copper(II) ions

Safety note: Wear eye protection and take great care with the concentrated acid. Do not get it on your skin and watch out for 'spitting' when heating it on the wire.

> **KEY POINT**
>
> Lithium is not the only ion to give a red flame colour. Strontium gives a very similar colour. The only way to be sure is to compare the flame colour next to the flame colour of a known compound of lithium or strontium.

TESTING FOR CARBONATES (CO_3^{2-})

EXTENSION

The ionic equation shows any carbonate reacting with any acid.

$CO_3^{2-}(s) + 2H^+(aq) \rightarrow CO_2(g) + H_2O(l)$

HINT

You can use any acid to do this test, but you have to be careful, especially with sulfuric acid, as some acid–carbonate combinations can produce an insoluble salt that coats the solid carbonate and stops the reaction. The test works well with dilute hydrochloric acid or dilute nitric acid.

Safety note: Wear eye protection for all these tests and avoid skin contact with the reactants and products.

The general equation for a carbonate reacting with an acid is:

carbonate + acid → salt + carbon dioxide + water

For example, using zinc carbonate and dilute hydrochloric acid:

$ZnCO_3(s) + 2HCl(aq) \rightarrow ZnCl_2(aq) + CO_2(g) + H_2O(l)$

To test whether a substance contains carbonate ions, add a little dilute hydrochloric acid to your sample and look for fizzing/bubbles of gas. Fizzing indicates that a gas is given off. You can test the gas by bubbling it through limewater to show that it is carbon dioxide (**Figure 13.9**).

Most carbonates are insoluble in water and so you will usually be doing this test on a sample of a solid. Soluble carbonates are sodium carbonate, potassium carbonate and ammonium carbonate, and the test also works on solutions of these.

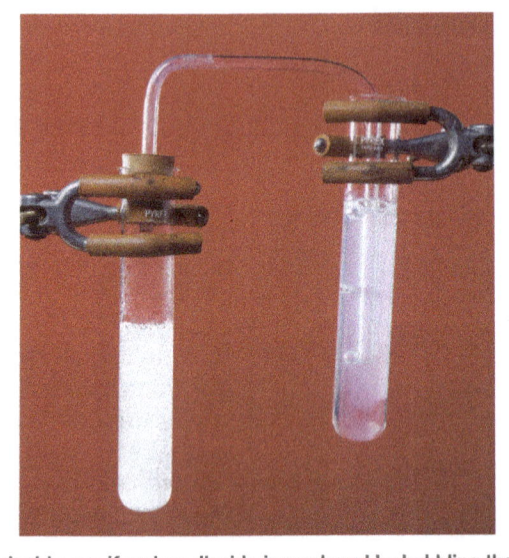

▲ Figure 13.9 We can test to see if carbon dioxide is produced by bubbling the gas through limewater (in the tube on the right) and looking to see whether the limewater goes cloudy/milky (white precipitate of calcium carbonate formed).

CHAPTER QUESTIONS

Exam-style questions on chemical tests can be found at the end of Unit 2 on page 224.

SKILLS CRITICAL THINKING

1 Name the gas being described in each of the following cases.
   a A green gas that bleaches damp litmus paper.
   b A gas that dissolves readily in water to produce a solution with a pH of about 11.
   c A gas that produces a white precipitate with limewater.
   d A gas that pops when a lighted splint is placed in it.
   e A gas that relights a glowing splint.

SKILLS EXECUTIVE FUNCTION

2 You have found a white powder in the laboratory which is insoluble in water. You suspect that the powder is calcium carbonate. Describe in detail how you would carry out the following tests to prove that the powder is calcium carbonate. In each case describe what you would expect to see happen.
   a A flame test to show it contains calcium ions.
   b A test to show the presence of carbonate ions.

SKILLS REASONING

3 A student carried out a series of flame tests on different salts. In each case identify the ion responsible for the flame colour.
   a lilac flame
   b red flame
   c blue–green flame
   d orange–red flame
   e yellow flame

SKILLS PROBLEM SOLVING

4 **G** is a colourless crystalline solid which reacts with dilute hydrochloric acid to give a colourless solution, **H**, and a colourless, odourless gas, **I**, which turns limewater milky. **G** has a lilac flame colour.

SKILLS CRITICAL THINKING
SKILLS PROBLEM SOLVING

   a State the names of **G**, **H** and **I**.
   b Write an equation for the reaction between **G** and dilute hydrochloric acid.

SKILLS EXECUTVE FUNCTION

5 A student has found that her sample of potassium nitrate is contaminated with small amounts of a green solid. She picks out a small piece of the green solid and finds that it is insoluble in water.

SKILLS CRITICAL THINKING

   a Potassium nitrate is soluble in water. Describe how you would make a pure sample of potassium nitrate from the impure mixture.
   b The student believes that the green solid could be copper(II) carbonate. Describe a series of tests that the student could use to confirm this.

6 A student finds a bottle containing a colourless liquid in the laboratory.
   a Describe a test to show that the bottle contains water.
   b Write a word equation for the reaction that occurs in the test you have described in a.

SKILLS PROBLEM SOLVING, CRITICAL THINKING

   c Write a symbol equation, including state symbols, for the reaction that occurs in the test in a.
   d The student is told that the bottle contains either dilute hydrochloric acid or a solution of sodium carbonate.

   Describe chemical tests that would enable the student to distinguish between these two solutions.

   Your answer should include a positive test for each and the results that both solutions would give with each test.

EXAM PRACTICE

You may need to refer to the Periodic Table on page 452.

SKILLS REASONING

1 Some solid potassium chlorate is heated in a test tube. A student collected the gas produced and tested it with a glowing splint. The gas relighted the glowing splint. The gas produced when potassium chlorate is heated is

   A ammonia   **C** carbon dioxide

   B hydrogen   **D** oxygen   **(Total 1 mark)**

SKILLS REASONING

2 A student adds some sodium hydroxide solution to a white solid in a test tube. When they warm the test tube a gas is produced which turns moist universal indicator paper blue. The formula of the gas is

   A NH_3 **C** N_2

   B NH_4 **D** NH_4OH **(Total 1 mark)**

SKILLS INTERPRETATION

3 Metals can be placed in a reactivity series. Which of the following is correct?

   A calcium is more reactive than lithium but less reactive than sodium

   B zinc is more reactive than iron but less reactive than magnesium

   C aluminium is lower in the reactivity series than iron

   D copper is the least reactive metal   **(Total 1 mark)**

SKILLS REASONING

4 Lithium, sodium and potassium are three elements in Group 1 of the Periodic Table. All these elements are stored under oil so that they cannot react with air and water.

SKILLS CRITICAL THINKING

   a State the name of the product obtained when potassium reacts with air. **(1)**

   b Which *two* statements about the reaction of lithium with water given below are correct? **(2)**

      A The water turns blue

      B The piece of lithium floats

      C The lithium burns with a lilac flame

      D Hydrogen gas is formed

      E The lithium explodes

      F Lithium reacts more violently than sodium

   c The solution formed when sodium reacts with water is alkaline.

SKILLS INTERPRETATION

      i State the name and formula of the ion that makes the solution alkaline. **(2)**

SKILLS EXECUTIVE FUNCTION

      ii Describe how universal indicator paper could be used to determine the approximate pH of the solution formed. **(2)**

2 INORGANIC CHEMISTRY — EXAM PRACTICE

SKILLS INTERPRETATION

SKILLS PROBLEM SOLVING

SKILLS INTERPRETATION

iii Predict the approximate pH of the solution. (1)

iv Write a balanced equation, including state symbols, for the reaction of sodium with water. (3)

v The teacher adds some dilute nitric acid to the solution formed. State what type of reaction occurs. (1)

d Some data about the physical properties of lithium, sodium and potassium are shown in the table.

	Melting point in °C	Boiling point in °C	Density in g/cm³
Li	181	1342	0.53
Na	98	883	0.97
K	63	760	0.86

Caesium is another element in Group 1 of the Periodic Table.

i Which two are likely to be properties of caesium? (2)

    A It forms a 1+ ion in compounds

    B It has a melting point of 60 °C

    C It is a non-metal

    D It reacts with water and air

    E It is an alkali

SKILLS REASONING

SKILLS EXECUTIVE FUNCTION, REASONING

ii Explain why the data in the table cannot be used to predict whether caesium has a higher or lower density than potassium. (2)

e Flame tests can be used to distinguish between the compounds of lithium, sodium and potassium.

i Describe how you would carry out a flame test on a sample of lithium chloride. (3)

ii Explain how the results of flame tests would allow you to distinguish between samples of lithium chloride and sodium chloride. (2)

(Total 21 marks)

5 A student tested four unknown metals (the names and reactions are all imaginary) with cold water and dilute hydrochloric acid to determine the order of reactivity. This is the procedure the student followed:

- Set up four test tubes and put about 2 cm³ of water into each one.
- Put a small piece of mollium, pearsonium, rosium or amelium into each test tube and observe any reaction that occurs.
- If there is fizzing, collect or trap the gas and test with a lighted splint.
- Repeat the experiments with dilute hydrochloric acid.

The student's results are shown in the table.

	Reaction with cold water	Reaction with dilute hydrochloric acid
mollium (Ml)	no reaction	Some fizzing, the test tube gets slightly warmer – approximately half a test tube of gas was produced after 5 minutes. The gas produced gave a squeaky pop with a lighted splint. A green solution was formed.
pearsonium (Pe)	no reaction	no reaction
rosium (Ro)	Violent reaction – lots of fizzing. The gas produced gave a squeaky pop with a lighted splint.	not attempted
amelium (Ae)	Fizzes slowly – not enough gas was produced after 5 minutes to test.	Reacts vigorously with lots of fizzing. The gas produced gave a squeaky pop with a lighted splint. A pink solution is formed. The test tube gets hot.

SKILLS EXECUTIVE FUNCTION

a State the most important safety precaution the student must take when carrying out these experiments. (1)

b Explain why the student did not attempt the reaction between rosium and dilute hydrochloric acid. (2)

SKILLS PROBLEM SOLVING

c Deduce the reactivity series for these four metals. (1)

d Identify the gas produced in some of these reactions. (1)

e The formula of mollium chloride is $MlCl_2$. Write an equation for the reaction between mollium and dilute hydrochloric acid. (2)

(Total 7 marks)

6 Fluorine and chlorine are elements in Group 7 of the Periodic Table.

SKILLS INTERPRETATION

a State the name given to the elements in Group 7 of the Periodic Table. (1)

SKILLS INTERPRETATION

b Chlorine, the element below fluorine in the Periodic Table is a green gas with a boiling point of –34°C.

 i Predict whether fluorine will be lighter or darker in colour than chlorine. (1)

 ii Predict whether fluorine will have a higher or lower boiling point than chlorine. (1)

SKILLS REASONING

c Chlorine can be prepared in the laboratory by the reaction between concentrated hydrochloric acid and potassium manganate(VII). The equation for the reaction is:

$2KMnO_4 + 16HCl \rightarrow 2KCl + 2MnCl_2 + 8H_2O + ...Cl_2$

 i The equation is not balanced. Give the number that should be put in front of Cl_2 in order to balance it. (1)

 ii Describe a test for chlorine gas. Include the positive result. (2)

2 INORGANIC CHEMISTRY — EXAM PRACTICE — 227

SKILLS — PROBLEM SOLVING, REASONING

d When chlorine reacts with hydrogen a gas called hydrogen chloride is formed. Hydrogen chloride has the formula HCl.

  i Predict the name and formula of the product formed when fluorine reacts with hydrogen. (2)

  ii When hydrogen chloride is dissolved in water hydrochloric acid is formed. State the formula of the particle which makes the solution acidic. (1)

  iii Explain the colour change that occurs when a few drops of dilute hydrochloric acid are added to some anhydrous copper(II) sulfate. (3)

(Total 12 marks)

SKILLS — CRITICAL THINKING

7 a State the name of the most common gas in the air. (1)

b A student carried out an experiment to measure the percentage of oxygen in the air. He used the following apparatus:

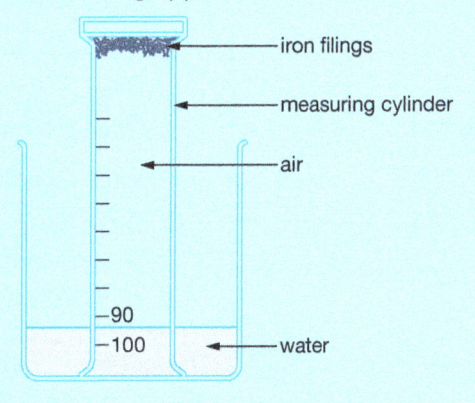

He carried out the following procedure:

- Put some damp iron filings at the bottom of a 100 cm³ measuring cylinder.
- Invert the measuring cylinder in a beaker of water.
- Take the initial reading of the level of water in the measuring cylinder.
- Take a reading of the level of water in the measuring cylinder every day for 1 week.

The student's results were:

Initial reading on measuring cylinder / cm³	94
Reading on measuring cylinder after 1 day / cm³	85
Reading on measuring cylinder after 2 days / cm³	80
Reading on measuring cylinder after 3 days / cm³	77
Reading on measuring cylinder after 4 days / cm³	76
Reading on measuring cylinder after 5 days / cm³	75
Reading on measuring cylinder after 6 days / cm³	75
Reading on measuring cylinder after 7 days / cm³	75

SKILLS REASONING
    i Explain why the water level in the measuring cylinder rises. (2)

    ii Explain why the reading on the measuring cylinder eventually remains constant. (1)

SKILLS CRITICAL THINKING
    iii Give the name of the iron compound that is formed in this experiment. (1)

SKILLS REASONING
    iv The student trapped the gas in the measuring cylinder and put a lighted splint into it. Explain why the splint goes out. (2)

SKILLS PROBLEM SOLVING
    v Use the results in the table to calculate the percentage oxygen present in the air in the measuring cylinder after 1 day. (4)

SKILLS CRITICAL THINKING
    vi The student decided that 1 week is too long to wait for results so suggested using a more reactive metal such as calcium or lithium in this experiment. Explain one reason, other than that it might be too dangerous, why the experiment will not work with these metals. (2)

SKILLS EXECUTIVE FUNCTION
    vii Suggest one change that the student could make to the experiment so he does not have to wait so long for the results. (1)

c Sulfur reacts with oxygen. A teacher burns a piece of sulfur in a gas jar of oxygen.

SKILLS CRITICAL THINKING
    i State the colour of the flame. (1)

SKILLS PROBLEM SOLVING
    ii Write a balanced equation for the reaction that occurs. (1)

SKILLS REASONING
    iii State the colour observed when a few drops of litmus solution are added to the gas jar. (1)

(Total 17 marks)

8 This question is about limestone. Limestone is an impure form of calcium carbonate that is used in the production of cement and concrete. In the process to produce cement, the limestone is heated and decomposes to form calcium oxide and carbon dioxide. This industrial process accounts for about 5% of the global production of carbon dioxide.

SKILLS CRITICAL THINKING
a A student is given a sample of powdered limestone. Describe how they could show that it contains calcium carbonate. (5)

SKILLS PROBLEM SOLVING
b i Give the formula of calcium carbonate. (1)

    ii State the formulae of the ions present in calcium oxide. (2)

    iii Write an equation for the decomposition of calcium carbonate. (1)

SKILLS CRITICAL THINKING
c When calcium oxide is added to water, a solution of calcium hydroxide is formed. This solution is often called *limewater*. Explain what will be observed when a few drops of litmus solution are added to limewater. (3)

SKILLS INTERPRETATION
d Explain one environmental problem associated with heating limestone to make cement. (2)

(Total 14 marks)

SKILLS CRITICAL THINKING

9 A student is given unlabelled solid samples of the following substances:

sodium hydroxide   citric acid   potassium chloride   potassium hydroxide

All the substances are white solids that are soluble in water. Describe how the student could distinguish between the four substances using chemical tests.

(Total 7 marks)

14 ENERGETICS 231 15 RATES OF REACTION 244

CHEMISTRY UNIT 3
PHYSICAL CHEMISTRY

In a world where the population has more than trebled in the last 100 years, fighting against hunger is an extremely important challenge. At the beginning of the 20th century scientists developed industrial processes to make artificial fertilisers that can be used to increase crop yields. In order to develop these processes, chemists and chemical engineers from around the world have had to understand the principles of energy changes and rates of reaction. The world's resources are limited and it is vital that these processes are as efficient and environmentally friendly as possible.

14 ENERGETICS

SPECIFICATION REFERENCES: 3.1–3.3, 3.8

Some chemical reactions produce heat. Others need to be heated constantly to make them occur at all. This chapter explores some examples of both kinds of reaction and examines how energy changes during reactions can be measured by experiments.

LEARNING OBJECTIVES

- Know that chemical reactions in which heat energy is given out are described as exothermic, and those in which heat energy is taken in are described as endothermic.
- Describe simple calorimetry experiments for reactions such as combustion, displacement, dissolving and neutralisation.
- Calculate the heat energy change from a measured temperature change using the expression $Q = mc\Delta T$.

- Practical: Investigate the temperature changes accompanying some of the following types of change:
  - salts dissolving in water
  - neutralisation reactions
  - displacement reactions
  - combustion reactions.

DID YOU KNOW?

Calcium oxide is known as **quicklime**. Adding water to it is described as *slaking* it. The calcium hydroxide produced is known as **slaked lime**.

Safety note: It is less hazardous to use a **lump** of calcium oxide, rather than powered calcium oxide.

EXOTHERMIC REACTIONS

Some chemical reactions give out energy in the form of heat. A reaction that *gives out heat to the surroundings* is said to be **exothermic**. If you are holding a test tube in which an exothermic reaction is occurring, you will notice that the test tube *gets warmer*.

An example of an exothermic reaction is adding water to calcium oxide (see **Figure 14.1**). If you add water to solid calcium oxide, the heat produced is enough to boil the water and produce steam. Calcium hydroxide is produced.

$$CaO(s) + H_2O(l) \rightarrow Ca(OH)_2(s)$$

In an *exothermic* reaction, *the products of the reaction have less (chemical) energy than the reactants*. In the reaction, *chemical energy* (stored in the bonds of chemicals) *is converted to heat energy*, which is released to the surroundings (see **Figure 14.2**). The temperature of the reaction mixture and its surroundings *goes up*.

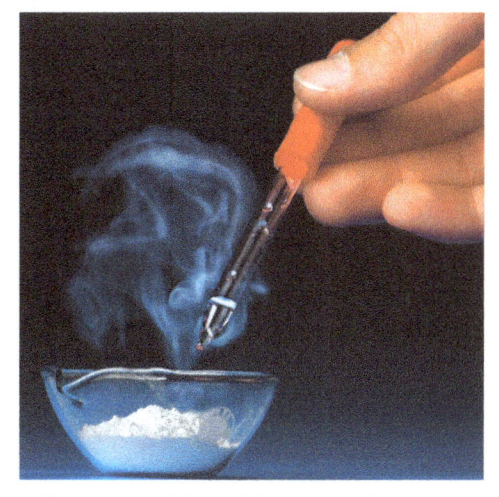

▲ Figure 14.1 Calcium oxide reacting with water

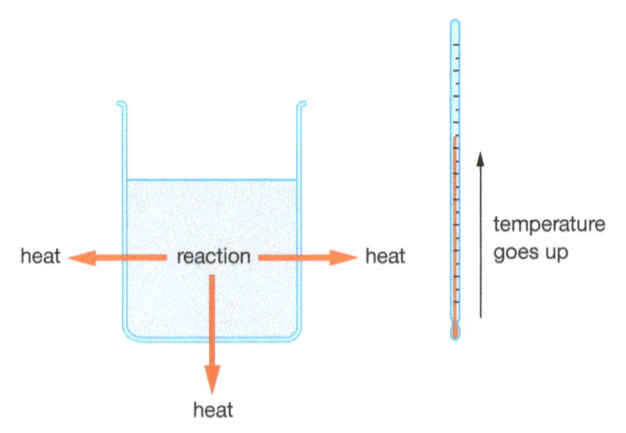

▲ Figure 14.2 In an exothermic reaction, chemical energy is converted to heat energy. Heat is released so the temperature goes up.

You will come across lots of exothermic reactions in this course. Some examples are given below.

COMBUSTION REACTIONS

Any reaction that produces a flame is exothermic. Burning things produces heat energy.

For instance, hydrogen burns in oxygen, producing water and lots of heat (see **Figure 14.3**):

$$2H_2(g) + O_2(g) \rightarrow 2H_2O(l)$$

Apart from burning, other exothermic changes include:

- the reactions of metals with acids
- neutralisation reactions.

▲ Figure 14.3 The burning of hydrogen is used in oxy-hydrogen cutting equipment underwater.

THE REACTIONS OF METALS WITH ACIDS

When magnesium reacts with dilute sulfuric acid, for example, the mixture gets very warm:

$$Mg(s) + H_2SO_4(aq) \rightarrow MgSO_4(aq) + H_2(g)$$

REMINDER

This reaction is described in detail in Chapter 11 (page 209).

NEUTRALISATION REACTIONS

About the only interesting thing that you can observe happening when sodium hydroxide solution reacts with dilute hydrochloric acid is that the temperature rises:

$$NaOH(aq) + HCl(aq) \rightarrow NaCl(aq) + H_2O(l)$$

REMINDER

You can read about this reaction in Chapter 12 (page 217). We will investigate how much heat energy is released in a typical neutralisation reaction later in this chapter (pages 240–241).

ENDOTHERMIC REACTIONS

A reaction that absorbs heat from the surroundings is said to be **endothermic** (see **Figure 14.4**). If you hold a test tube in which an endothermic reaction is occurring you will notice that it *gets colder*.

In an endothermic reaction, *the products have more (chemical) energy than the reactants*. In order to supply the extra energy that is needed to convert the reactants (lower energy) into the products (higher energy), heat energy needs to be absorbed from the surroundings (see **Figure 14.5**). This *heat energy is converted to chemical energy* (energy stored in the bonds of chemicals). The temperature of the reaction mixture and the surroundings *goes down* because heat energy has been converted into a different form of energy.

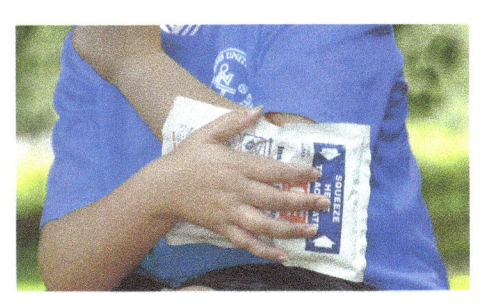

▲ Figure 14.4 A boy using a cold pack to relieve pain in his elbow. Endothermic processes occur in the chemical cold pack to **absorb** heat from the surroundings and reduce the temperature of his arm.

> **EXAM HINT**
>
> For a chemical reaction, the term *system* means the reactants and the products. Everything else around the system including the apparatus and the air in the laboratory is called the *surroundings*.

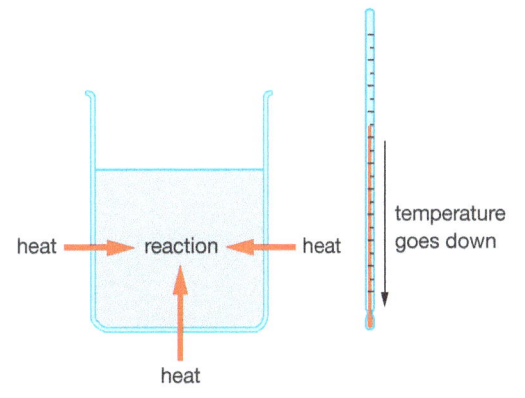

▲ Figure 14.5 In an endothermic reaction, heat energy is converted to chemical energy. Heat is absorbed so the temperature goes down.

The *thermal decomposition* of metal carbonates is an example of an endothermic reaction. You have to heat a carbonate constantly to make it decompose.

For example, copper(II) carbonate (green) decomposes on heating to produce copper(II) oxide (black).

$$CuCO_3(s) \rightarrow CuO(s) + CO_2(g)$$

Similarly, zinc carbonate decomposes to form zinc oxide when heated.

$$ZnCO_3(s) \rightarrow ZnO(s) + CO_2(g)$$

MEASURING HEAT ENERGY CHANGES OF REACTIONS

Here we discuss how we can measure how much heat is taken in or given out by a chemical reaction.

SPECIFIC HEAT CAPACITY

> **KEY POINT**
>
> The unit for specific heat capacity is J/g/°C or J g^{-1}°C^{-1}.

> **KEY POINT**
>
> The delta (Δ) symbol is used to indicate a change. ΔT means a temperature change.
>
> The concept of specific heat capacity also applies to the cooling of a substance. For example, to cool 1 g of water by 1 °C we need to take out 4.18 J of energy.

When we heat something up, it gets hotter. The **specific heat capacity** tells us about *how much* energy has to be put in to increase the temperature of something. The specific heat capacity of a substance is defined as *the amount of heat needed to raise the temperature of 1 gram of a substance by 1 °C*.

For water, the value is 4.18 J/g/°C (joules per gram per degree Celsius). This means that 4.18 J of heat energy is needed if we want to increase the temperature of 1 g of water by 1 °C. If you want the temperature of 1 g of water to go up by 2 °C, then 4.18 × 2 = 8.36 J of heat energy must be supplied. If now you have 2 g of water, then 2 × 8.36 J of energy would be needed to raise the temperature by 2 °C.

The amount of heat energy required is *directly proportional* to the mass (*m*) and the temperature change (Δ*T*) of the substance. The following equation can be used to calculate how much heat energy needs to be supplied to raise the temperature of mass *m* by Δ*T* °C:

heat energy change = mass × specific heat capacity × temperature change

$$Q = m \times c \times \Delta T$$

CALORIMETRY EXPERIMENTS FOR DETERMINING THE HEAT ENERGY CHANGES OF REACTIONS

It is fairly uncomplicated to measure the amount of heat absorbed or given out in several kinds of chemical reactions and physical changes. The technique used to do this is called **calorimetry** and it is based on the idea that if we use the heat from a reaction to heat another substance, such as water, we can then use the equation introduced above (*Q* = *mc*Δ*T*) to calculate the amount of heat released. Here the mass, the specific heat capacity and the temperature change are all referring to *the substance heated*.

The following activity illustrates how we can use calorimetry to determine the heat energy change of combustion of an alcohol, that is, how much heat energy is released when a certain amount of alcohol burns.

ACTIVITY 1

▼ PRACTICAL: MEASURING HEAT ENERGY CHANGES IN COMBUSTION REACTIONS

> **Safety note:** Wear eye protection. Do not carry a lit spirit burner and do not fill or re-fill a spirit burner when there is a naked flame nearby.

One of the most common calorimetry experiments at International GCSE is to measure the amount of heat given off when a number of small alcohols are burned. You could use methanol, ethanol, propan-1-ol and butan-1-ol.

The alcohols are burned in a small spirit burner, and the heat produced is used to heat some water in a copper can (the calorimeter).

The following procedure could be used:

- Measure 100 cm³ of cold water using a measuring cylinder and transfer the water to a copper can.
- Take the initial temperature of the water.

> **KEY POINT**
>
> A *calorimeter* is simply something that we do a calorimetry experiment in; here it is a copper can, in other experiments it can be a polystyrene cup.

3 PHYSICAL CHEMISTRY   14 ENERGETICS

- Weigh a spirit-burner containing ethanol with its lid *on*. The lid should be kept on when the **wick** is not lit to prevent the alcohol from evaporating.
- Arrange the apparatus as shown in **Figure 14.6** so that the spirit-burner can be used to heat the water in the copper can. The apparatus is shielded as far as possible to prevent draughts.
- Light the wick to heat the water. Stop heating when you have a reasonable temperature rise of water (say, about 40.0 °C). The flame can be extinguished by putting the lid back on the wick.
- Stir the water thoroughly and measure the maximum temperature of the water.
- Weigh the spirit-burner again with its lid *on*.
- The experiment can be repeated with the same alcohol to check for reliability, and then carried out again with whatever other alcohols are available.

KEY POINT

You may see other versions of this experiment recommending a different temperature rise or suggesting that you heat the water for a fixed number of minutes. There is no ideal answer to this. The higher the temperature the water reaches, the greater the heat losses during the experiment. On the other hand, if you just increase the temperature of the water by a small amount, errors in reading the thermometer or in finding the mass change of the alcohol become too significant.

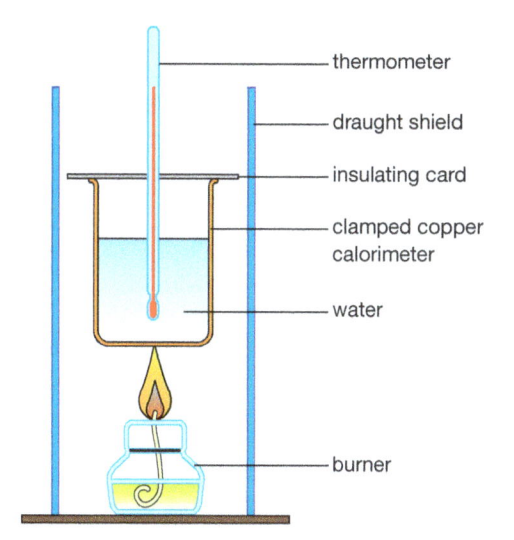

▲ Figure 14.6 A calorimetry experiment to measure the heat energy change of combustion of alcohols.

SAMPLE DATA

Volume of water / cm³	100
Mass of burner + ethanol before experiment / g	137.36
Mass of burner + ethanol after experiment / g	136.58
Original temperature of water / °C	21.5
Final temperature of water / °C	62.8

Combustion is an exothermic reaction so the temperature of the water goes up. As ethanol is burned, the total mass of the burner and ethanol goes down.

Using the above data we can determine how much heat energy is released during the combustion of ethanol.

CALCULATIONS FOR ACTIVITY 1

We are going to use the equation $Q = mc\Delta T$ so we need to find out what each quantity is.

Temperature change of water = ΔT = 62.8 − 21.5 = 41.3 °C.

Mass of water being heated = m = 100 g, the density of water is approximately 1 g/cm^3 at room temperature, so 100 cm^3 of water has a mass of 100 g.

c is the specific heat capacity of the water (it is the water that is being heated): c = 4.18 J/g/°C

Heat gained by water = $Q = mc\Delta T$ = 100 × 4.18 × 41.3 = 17 260 J.

Divide Q by 1000 to give energy in kJ = 17.26 kJ.

> **EXAM HINT**
> Energy can have the units J or kJ. To convert J to kJ, you need to divide the number by 1000. To convert kJ to J, you need to times the number by 1000.

> **EXAM HINT**
> We have quoted the final answer to *3 significant figures*. In the exam, it is usually best to quote answers to 3 significant figures. When we are doing experiments we should actually base our answers on *the piece of data with the fewest significant figures*. When you are doing calculations carry more significant figures through on your calculator and then round the value at the end.

This means 17.26 kJ of heat energy is released by the combustion of the ethanol in this experiment. In order to compare the heat energy produced from different types of alcohols or fuels, you might want to work out the amount of heat produced when 1 gram of ethanol, burns. For this, you need to find out how many grams of ethanol are burned in your experiment.

Heat energy change per gram of fuel = $\dfrac{Q}{\text{mass of ethanol}} = \dfrac{17.26}{0.78} = 22.1$ kJ/g

The amount of heat released in the **complete combustion** of 1 gram of ethanol is therefore:

$$C_2H_6O + 3O_2 \rightarrow 2CO_2 + 3H_2O \qquad \text{Heat released = 22.1 kJ/g}$$

EVALUATION OF THE EXPERIMENTAL RESULTS

How accurate is the figure of 22.1 kJ/g for the heat energy change of the combustion of ethanol? The accepted value found in data booklets for ethanol is 29.7 kJ/g, which means that 29.7 kJ of heat should be given out when 1 gram of ethanol burns. You can see that the value we obtained is less exothermic than expected; our reaction seemed to give out less heat than expected.

There are many sources of error in this experiment, in particular *large amounts of heat loss* to the surroundings.

The warm water gives out heat to the air, heat is lost from the flame, which goes straight into the air rather than into the water, and heat is used to raise the temperature of the copper can and the thermometer.

Another major source of error is the **incomplete combustion** of alcohol. We will talk about incomplete combustion in more detail in **Chapter 17**. Incomplete combustion of an alcohol occurs when there is not enough oxygen present. Incomplete combustion releases less heat than complete combustion. We can see that the combustion in **Activity 1** is incomplete because the flame of the wick is often yellow orange rather than blue, and **soot** (carbon) is produced at the bottom of the copper can. If the combustion is complete, the flame should be blue and carbon dioxide should be produced instead of carbon.

That does not mean you cannot use this experiment to make useful comparisons. If you repeat it with other alcohols, under conditions that are as similar as possible, you can find how the heat evolved (given out) changes as the alcohol gets bigger.

In **Figure 14.7** we can see that the combustion reaction gets more exothermic as the alcohol chain becomes longer. In other words, longer alcohols give out more heat energy per gram when they burn than shorter ones.

> **KEY POINT**
>
> You may sometimes see these plotted as smooth graphs, but that is technically wrong. A smooth curve should only be used for a continuous **independent variable**, one which can take any value. There is no such thing as an alcohol with 0.5 or 1.64 carbon atoms! The number of carbon atoms is a **non-continuous variable** because it can only take whole number values.

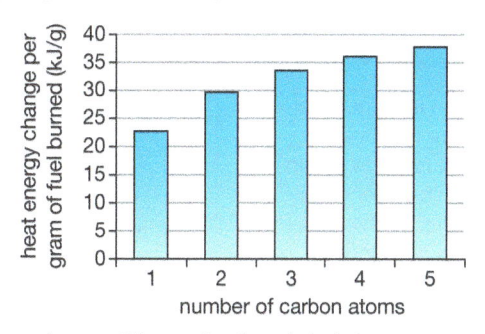

▲ Figure 14.7 Heat energy change of the combustion of alcohols

WORKING OUT HEAT ENERGY CHANGES FOR REACTIONS INVOLVING SOLUTIONS USING CALORIMETRY EXPERIMENTS

You can use very similar methods for measuring heat energy changes in **displacement reactions** (e.g. zinc and copper(II) sulfate solution), dissolving (e.g. dissolving ammonium chloride in water to form a solution) and neutralisation reactions (e.g. between potassium hydroxide solution and dilute hydrochloric acid). These experiments also involve heating water, but this time the water is part of the solutions we are using. We will look at how to do this in the next few practicals.

3 PHYSICAL CHEMISTRY 14 ENERGETICS

Safety note: Avoid skin contact with the chemicals.

HINT
A displacement reaction is a chemical reaction in which a more reactive element replaces a less reactive one in its compound. In this experiment, the more reactive zinc displaces the less reactive copper from its compound, copper(II) sulfate, to form zinc(II) sulfate solution and copper metal.

ACTIVITY 2

▼ PRACTICAL: MEASURING HEAT ENERGY CHANGES FOR DISPLACEMENT REACTIONS

In order to determine the heat energy change of the reaction of zinc and copper(II) sulfate, the following procedure could be used:
- Place a polystyrene cup in a 250 cm³ glass beaker (**Figure 14.8**).
- Transfer 50 cm³ of aqueous copper(II) sulfate solution into the polystyrene cup using a measuring cylinder.
- Weigh 1.20 g of zinc using a weighing boat on a balance.
- Record the initial temperature of the copper(II) sulfate solution.
- Add the zinc.
- Stir the solution as quickly as possible.
- Record the maximum temperature reached.

▲ Figure 14.8 A calorimetry experiment to measure the heat energy change of a displacement reaction.

SAMPLE DATA

Initial temperature of copper(II) sulfate solution / °C	17.0
Maximum temperature of the reaction mixture / °C	27.3

We can use this data to calculate the heat energy change for this displacement reaction, when copper(II) sulfate reacts with zinc.

CALCULATIONS FOR ACTIVITY 2

Heat given out in this reaction: $Q = mc\Delta T = 50 \times 4.18 \times (27.3 - 17.0)$
$$= 2152.7 \, \text{J}$$
$$= 2.1527 \, \text{kJ}$$

Here we assume the following:

EXAM HINT
The m in the formula for calculating Q is the mass of the solution heated, rather than the mass of the zinc metal added in the reaction.

1. The density of the copper sulfate solution is the same as that of water, so 1 cm³ of solution has a mass of 1 g.
2. The specific heat capacity of the mixture is the same as that of water. This is a fairly reasonable assumption because the reaction mixture is mostly water.

You could repeat this experiment with metals of different reactivities, still using copper(II) sulfate solution. The more reactive a metal is in comparison to copper, the more heat should be released in the displacement reaction. To ensure a fair comparison, you need to keep everything else the same: the mass of the metals, the size of the solid particles, and the volume and concentration of the copper(II) sulfate solution. Do not use metals that are more reactive than magnesium, otherwise you are measuring the heat released when the metal reacts with water instead!

> **Safety note:** Wear eye protection and avoid skin contact with the salts and their solutions.

ACTIVITY 3

▼ PRACTICAL: MEASURING HEAT ENERGY CHANGES WHEN SALTS DISSOLVE IN WATER

We can also use calorimetry experiments to work out the amount of heat given out/taken in when salts dissolve in water. The following procedure could be used:

- Place a polystyrene cup in a 250 cm³ glass beaker.
- Transfer 100 cm³ of water into the polystyrene cup using a measuring cylinder.
- Record the initial temperature of the water.
- Weigh 5.20 g of ammonium chloride using a weighing boat on a balance.
- Add the ammonium chloride to water and stir the solution vigorously until all the ammonium chloride has dissolved.
- Record the minimum temperature.

The set-up is very similar to the one used in **Activity 2**; see **Figure 14.8**.

SAMPLE DATA

Initial temperature of water / °C	18.3
Minimum temperature of salt solution / °C	15.1

Note: the temperature of the water decreases, so the process is endothermic and heat is absorbed from the surroundings for the dissolving to occur.

We can use this data to calculate the heat energy change for dissolving ammonium chloride.

CALCULATIONS FOR ACTIVITY 3

Heat absorbed: $Q = mc\Delta T = 100 \times 4.18 \times (18.3 - 15.1) = 1337.6\,J = 1.3376\,kJ$

Here we assume the following:

1. The specific heat capacity of the diluted solution of ammonium chloride is the same as that of water. This is quite a reasonable assumption because the mixture is mostly water.
2. The mass of the solution is 100 g. The mass of the ammonium chloride is relatively small and it is ignored in the calculation. There are other major sources of error in the experiment, for example heat absorbed from the surrounding air, which makes much more difference to the results.

KEY POINT

Dissolving is a physical process rather than a chemical reaction. When some salts dissolve in water heat is given out (exothermic), but when others dissolve the process is endothermic.

Safety note: Wear eye protection and avoid skin contact with the acid and alkali.

If you want to compare how much heat energy is given out or absorbed when dissolving different solutes into water, you can calculate the heat energy change per gram.

In this experiment, the amount of heat absorbed per gram of ammonium chloride is:

$$\frac{Q}{\text{mass of ammonium chloride}} = \frac{1.3376}{5.20} = 0.257 \text{ kJ/g}$$

ACTIVITY 4

▼ PRACTICAL: MEASURING HEAT ENERGY CHANGES OF NEUTRALISATION BETWEEN AN ALKALI AND AN ACID

Let us look at the reaction between potassium hydroxide (an alkali) and hydrochloric acid.

$$KOH(aq) + HCl(aq) \rightarrow KCl(aq) + H_2O(l)$$

If you want to find out how much of the acid is required to neutralise a certain amount of the alkali, the following method could be used to find out the exact volume of the acid required for complete neutralisation and how much heat is released during the reaction.

- Place a polystyrene cup in a 250 cm³ glass beaker.
- Transfer 25 cm³ of aqueous potassium hydroxide into the polystyrene cup using a measuring cylinder.
- Record the initial temperature.
- Fill a burette with 50.00 cm³ of dilute hydrochloric acid.
- Use the burette to add 5.00 cm³ of dilute hydrochloric acid to the potassium hydroxide.
- Stir vigorously and record the maximum temperature reached.
- Continue adding further 5.00 cm³ portions of dilute hydrochloric acid to the cup, stirring and recording the maximum temperature each time, until a total volume of 50.00 cm³ has been added.

We can plot a graph of the temperature of the mixture versus the volume of acid added.

SAMPLE DATA

In this reaction the temperature increases at first but then decreases (see **Figure 14.9**). The reaction between the acid and the alkali is exothermic. At the beginning the temperature goes up because the acid reacts with the alkali, giving out heat. But when all the alkali has been used up, we are just adding cold acid to our warm solution (there is no reaction because there is nothing for the acid to react with) and the temperature goes down.

Two lines of best fit can be drawn on our graph. The point where the lines cross represents complete neutralisation. From the graph, we can identify the maximum temperature reached during the experiment as 31.5 °C. At this point, 28.00 cm³ of acid has been used.

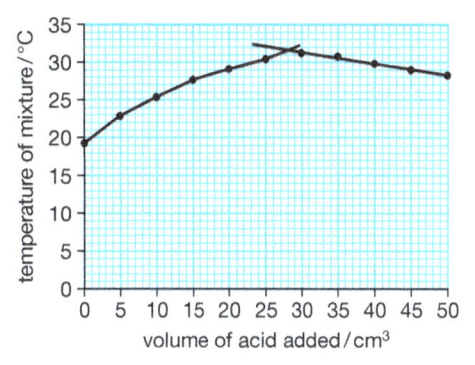

▲ Figure 14.9 Temperature change in the neutralisation reaction between KOH and HCl

CALCULATIONS FOR ACTIVITY 4

To work out how much heat is released in the neutralisation reaction, we can use the same calculation as before.

The total volume of the solution at the neutralisation point is 25 + 28 = 53 cm³.

Heat given out is shown by $Q = mc\Delta T$ = 53 × 4.18 × (31.5 − 19.3) = 2702.8 J.

If we divide by 1000 we get 2.7028 kJ.

Here we assume the following:

1. The density of the reaction mixture is the same as that of water, so 1 cm³ of solution has a mass of 1 g.
2. The specific heat capacity of the mixture is the same as that of water. This is a fairly reasonable assumption because the neutralised solution is mostly water.

EXAM HINT

The m in the formula for calculating Q in this reaction is the mass of the neutral solution, so you need to add the volume of the alkali to the volume of the acid required at the neutralisation point.

CHAPTER QUESTIONS

Exam-style questions on energetics can be found at the end of Unit 3 on page 256.

1. When potassium hydroxide (KOH) reacts with nitric acid (HNO₃), the temperature of the reaction mixture increases. The reaction can be described as

   A neutralisation and endothermic

   B combustion and endothermic

   C neutralisation and exothermic

   D combustion and exothermic

2. When 2 g of a liquid fuel is burned, the temperature of 50 cm³ of water heated with the fuel increases from 23.0 °C to 52.0 °C. How much heat is absorbed by the water?

   A 2 × 4.18 × 23.0

   B 50 × 4.18 × 29.0

   C 50 × 4.18 × 52.0

   D 2 × 4.18 × 29.0

SKILLS INTERPRETATION

3 Copy and complete the following sentences.

   a In an exothermic reaction, _____ energy is converted to _____ energy. The products have _____ energy than the reactants. The temperature of the reaction mixtures and the surroundings _____

   b In an endothermic reaction, _____ energy is converted to _____ energy. The products have _____ energy than the reactants. The temperature of the reaction mixtures and the surroundings _____

   c Combustion reactions are always _____

   d The specific heat capacity is the amount of heat needed to raise the _____ of one gram of a substance by _____ _____ _____

SKILLS PROBLEM SOLVING

4 Calculate the heat energy released/absorbed in kJ in each of the following experiments, using the data provided.

   Assume the specific heat capacity of all the solutions is the same as that of water = 4.2 J/g/°C and the density of the solutions = 1 g/cm³.

   a Neutralisation of 50 cm³ of hydrochloric acid with 120 cm³ of potassium hydroxide solution. The temperature of the reaction mixture went from 21.3 °C at the start to 29.6 °C at the highest.

   b 0.45 g of butanol in an alcohol burner was burned to heat up 100 cm³ of water in a copper can. The temperature of the water increased from 17.0 °C to 40.5 °C.

   c 6 g of sodium chloride solid was dissolved in 25 cm³ of distilled water in a polystyrene cup with fast stirring. The temperature of the salt solution decreased by 2.8 °C.

SKILLS CRITICAL THINKING, PROBLEM SOLVING

5 Write balanced chemical equations for two exothermic changes.

SKILLS CRITICAL THINKING

6 Identify each of the following changes as exothermic or endothermic. In some cases you will have to rely on your previous knowledge of chemistry. Several reactions are likely to be completely new to you.

   a The reaction between sodium and water.

   b Burning methane (major constituent of natural gas).

   c The reaction between sodium carbonate and ethanoic acid. A thermometer placed in the reaction mixture shows a temperature drop.

   d $S(s) + O_2(g) \rightarrow SO_2(g)$

   e If you dissolve solid sodium hydroxide in water, the solution becomes very hot.

3 PHYSICAL CHEMISTRY 14 ENERGETICS

SKILLS INTRAPERSONAL

7 Self-heating cans are used to provide warm food in situations where it is inconvenient to use a more conventional form of heat. By doing an internet (or other) search, find out how self-heating cans work. Write a short explanation of your findings (not exceeding 200 words). You should include equation(s) for any reaction(s) involved, and a diagram or picture if it is useful.

SKILLS EXECUTIVE FUNCTION

8 A student investigated the amount of heat given out when hexane, C_6H_{14}, burns using the apparatus in **Figure 14.6**. Hexane is a highly flammable liquid which is one of the components of petrol (gasoline).

In each case, the student calculated the amount of heat evolved per gram of hexane. Her first two experiments produced answers of 37.1 and 45.2 kJ/g of heat evolved. She then decided to do a third experiment. Her results were as follows:

Volume of water in copper calorimeter / cm^3	100
Mass of burner + hexane before experiment / g	35.62
Mass of burner + hexane after experiment / g	35.23
Original temperature of water / °C	19.0
Final temperature of water / °C	55.0

a Suggest a reason why the student decided to do a third experiment.

b Apart from wearing eye protection, suggest two other safety precautions the student should take during the experiment.

SKILLS PROBLEM SOLVING

c Use the results table to calculate the amount of heat in **kJ** evolved by the burning hexane during the experiment.

(Specific heat capacity of water = 4.18 J/g/°C; density of water = 1 g/cm^3.)

d Calculate the amount of heat energy released per gram of hexane.

SKILLS REASONING

e To calculate the average value of the heat evolved per gram when hexane burns, the student took an average of her results. She decided not to use the figure of 45.2 in calculating the average because it was so different from the other two. Suggest two reasons why this reaction might have been more exothermic than the others.

f A data book gave a figure of 48.7 kJ of heat evolved when 1 gram of hexane burns. Suggest two reasons why all the results in the student's experiment were lower than this.

SKILLS PROBLEM SOLVING

9 When 5.15 g of lithium chloride (LiCl) is dissolved in 50 cm^3 of water the temperature of the solution goes from 17.0 °C to 33.5 °C.

a Calculate the heat energy released in this experiment. (Specific heat capacity of water = 4.18 J/g/°C; mass of 1 cm^3 of solution = 1 g.)

b Using your answers from **a** calculate the heat energy change when 1 gram of lithium chloride dissolves in water in kJ/g.

SKILLS REASONING

c A data book gives a figure of 0.874 kJ/mol for heat released when 1 gram of lithium chloride is dissolved in water. Suggest two reasons why the value you calculated in **b** might be different from the value given in the data book.

15 RATES OF REACTION

SPECIFICATION REFERENCES: 3.9, 3.10, 3.12, 3.15

Reactions can vary in speed between those that happen within fractions of a second – explosions, for example – and those that never happen at all. Gold can be exposed to the air for thousands of years and not react in any way.

This chapter looks at the factors controlling the speeds of chemical reactions.

▲ Figure 15.1 Some reactions are very fast, for example, explosions of fireworks.

▲ Figure 15.2 Some reactions happen over several minutes, for example, when antacid tablets react with hydrochloric acid.

▲ Figure 15.3 Rusting takes days or weeks.

▲ Figure 15.4 The weathering of limestone and the formation of stalagmites and stalactites takes a very long time.

LEARNING OBJECTIVES

- Describe experiments to investigate the effects of changes in the surface area of a solid, the concentration of a solution, the temperature and the use of a catalyst on the rate of a reaction.

- Describe the effects of changes in the surface area of a solid, the concentration of a solution, the pressure of a gas, the temperature and the use of a catalyst on the rate of a reaction.

- Know that a catalyst is a substance that increases the rate of a reaction, but is chemically unchanged at the end of the reaction.

- Practical: Investigate the effect of changing the surface area of marble chips and of changing the concentration of hydrochloric acid on the rate of reaction between marble chips and dilute hydrochloric acid.

EXPERIMENTS TO MEASURE THE RATE OF REACTION

The **rate of a reaction** is the speed at which the amount of reactants decreases or the amount of products increases. It is measured as *a change in the concentration (or amount) of reactants or products per unit time* (per second, per minute etc.).

$$\text{rate of reaction} = \frac{\text{change in concentration, volume or mass}}{\text{time}}$$

ACTIVITY 1

▼ **PRACTICAL: AN INVESTIGATION OF THE RATE OF REACTION BETWEEN MARBLE CHIPS AND DILUTE HYDROCHLORIC ACID**

Marble chips are made of calcium carbonate and react with hydrochloric acid to produce carbon dioxide gas. Calcium chloride solution is also formed.

$$CaCO_3(s) + 2HCl(aq) \rightarrow CaCl_2(aq) + H_2O(l) + CO_2(g)$$

Safety note: Wear eye protection and avoid skin contact with the acid.

Figure 15.5 shows some apparatus that can be used to measure how the mass of carbon dioxide produced changes with time. Part (a) is drawn as the apparatus would look before the reaction starts.

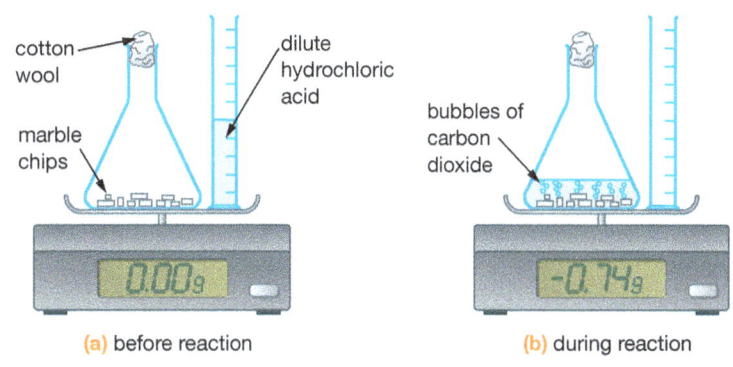

(a) before reaction   (b) during reaction

▲ Figure 15.5 Investigating the reaction between calcium carbonate and hydrochloric acid

The following procedure could be used:

- Use a measuring cylinder to measure 25 cm³ of dilute hydrochloric acid.
- Add 5.00 g of large marble chips to a conical flask and place a piece of cotton wool at the opening of the flask. The marble is in *excess* – some of it will be left over when the acid is all used up.
- Place everything on a balance and reset it to zero.
- Add the acid to the marble chips and record the reading on the balance every 30 seconds.

Part (b) shows what happens during the reaction. The acid has been **poured** into the flask and everything has been replaced on the balance. Once the reaction starts, the balance shows a negative mass. The mass goes down because the carbon dioxide escapes through the cotton wool.

When we plot a graph of mass of carbon dioxide lost against time, we obtain something similar to the one in **Figure 15.6**.

The steeper the slope (gradient) of the line, the faster the reaction. We can see from **Figure 15.6** that about 0.47 g of carbon dioxide is produced in the first minute. Only about 0.20 g of extra carbon dioxide is produced in the second minute, the reaction is slowing down.

> **EXAM HINT**
> The cotton wool is there to allow the carbon dioxide to escape during the reaction, but to stop any acid spitting out.

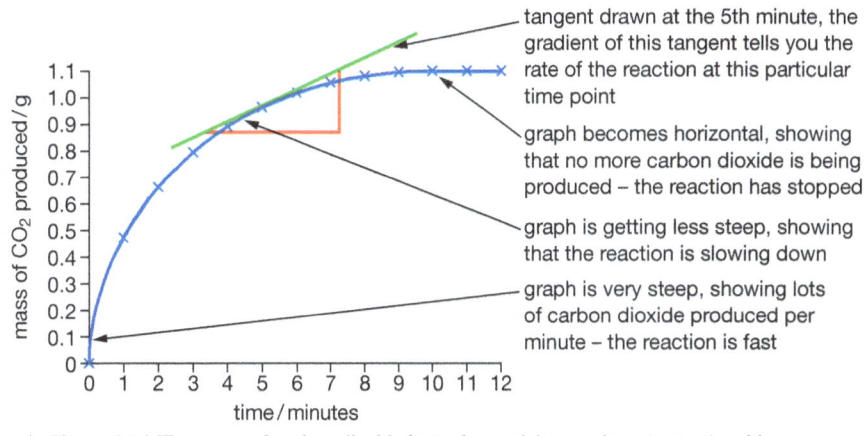

▲ Figure 15.6 The mass of carbon dioxide lost when calcium carbonate reacts with hydrochloric acid.

We can calculate the *average rate* of the reaction during any time interval by using

$$\text{rate} = \frac{\text{mass of CO}_2 \text{ lost}}{\text{time}}$$

For example, the average rate of the reaction in the *first* minute

$$= \frac{0.47}{1} = 0.47\,\text{g/min}$$

The average rate of the reaction in the *second* minute

$$= \frac{0.20}{1} = 0.20\,\text{g/min}$$

The average rate of the reaction over the *first two* minutes

$$= \frac{0.67}{2} = 0.34\,\text{g/min}$$

We can see the reaction is fastest at the beginning. It then slows down as the concentration of the hydrochloric acid decreases. Eventually the reaction stops because *all the hydrochloric acid has been used up*.

We can measure how fast the reaction is going *at any time point* by finding the slope (gradient) of the line at that point. This is the rate of the reaction *at that point* (rather than the average). This is done by drawing a **tangent** to the line at the time you are interested in and finding its slope (gradient). For example, at 5 minutes the carbon dioxide is being lost at the rate of about 0.05 g per minute (see **Figure 15.6**).

We can also follow the rate of this reaction by measuring the *volume* of carbon dioxide given off. The apparatus shown in **Figure 15.7** can be used.

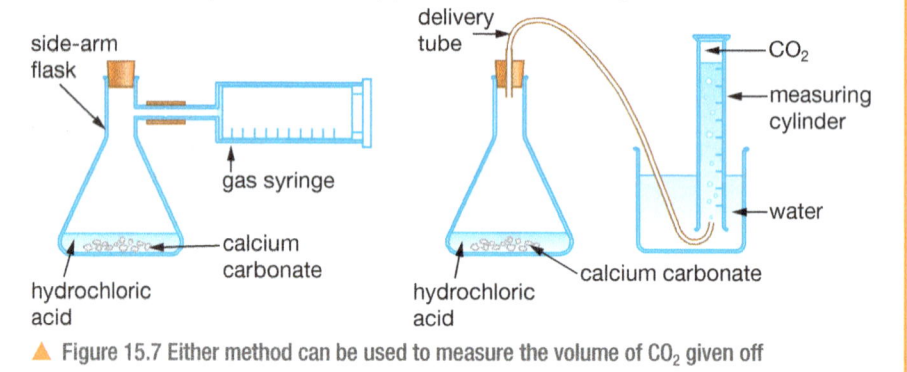

▲ Figure 15.7 Either method can be used to measure the volume of CO_2 given off

REMINDER

Remember, the marble chips were in excess (there was more than enough to react with all the hydrochloric acid). There will still be unreacted marble chips in the flask at the end.

A DIFFERENT FORM OF GRAPH

At International GCSE you normally plot graphs showing the mass or volume of product *formed* during a reaction. It is possible, however, that you will see graphs showing the fall in the concentration of one of the *reactants* – in this case, the concentration of the dilute hydrochloric acid (see **Figure 15.8**).

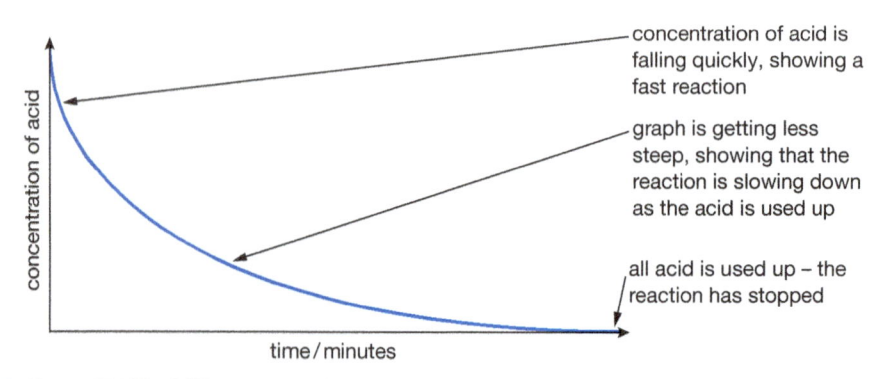

▲ Figure 15.8 The fall in concentration of hydrochloric acid over time

Where the graph is falling most quickly (is steepest), it shows that the reaction is fastest.

Eventually, the graph becomes horizontal because the reaction has stopped when all the acid has been consumed.

CHANGING THE SURFACE AREA OF THE REACTANTS

ACTIVITY 2

Safety note: Wear eye protection and avoid skin contact with the acid.

▼ PRACTICAL: INVESTIGATING THE EFFECT OF CHANGING THE SURFACE AREA OF MARBLE CHIPS ON THE RATE OF REACTION BETWEEN MARBLE CHIPS AND DILUTE HYDROCHLORIC ACID

HINT

If we are going to investigate the effect of changing the size of the marble chips, it is important that everything else stays exactly the same to make this a valid (fair) test.

We can repeat the experiment in **Activity 1** using exactly the same quantities of everything, but using much smaller marble chips. The reaction with the smaller chips happens faster.

We can plot both sets of results (Activities 1 and 2) on the same graph (see **Figure 15.9**). Notice that the same mass of carbon dioxide is produced because we are using the same quantities of everything in both experiments. However, the reaction with the smaller chips starts off much faster and finishes sooner.

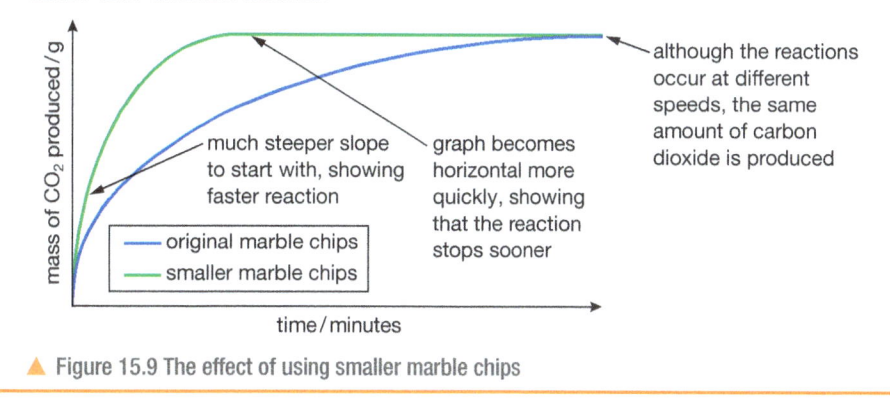

EXAM HINT

If you are asked to design an experiment to measure the rate of a reaction, check the physical properties of the reactants and the products (for example, physical states and colour) to decide which method is the most suitable. You could be measuring, for example, the volume of a gas given off, a change in mass, a colour change or the formation of a precipitate.

▲ Figure 15.9 The effect of using smaller marble chips

Reactions between solids and liquids are faster if the solids are present as a lot of small pieces rather than a few big ones. The more finely divided the solid, the faster the reaction. This is because the *surface area* in contact with the liquid is *much greater* and there are more particles of the solid exposed on the surface (see **Figure 15.10**). Only the particles on the surface are available for reactions.

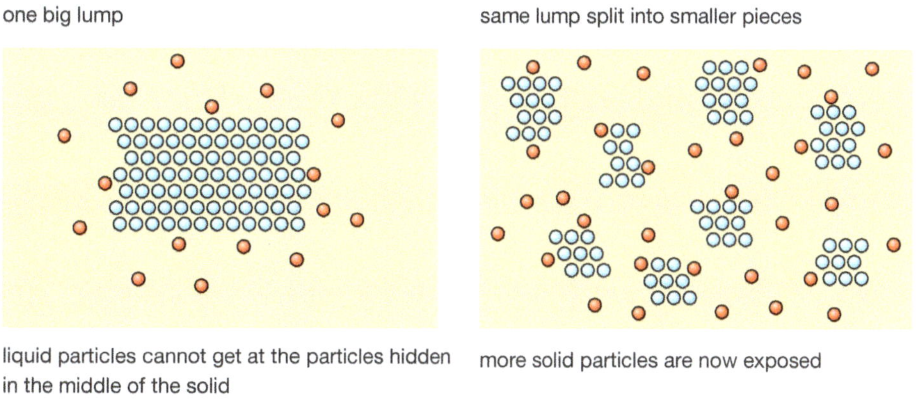

one big lump

same lump split into smaller pieces

liquid particles cannot get at the particles hidden in the middle of the solid

more solid particles are now exposed

▲ Figure 15.10 The more divided the solid, the faster the reaction

▲ Figure 15.11 A catalytic converter has a honeycomb structure to give a very large surface area for the exhaust gases to flow through.

Large surface areas are frequently used to speed up reactions outside the lab. For example, a **catalytic converter** for a car uses expensive metals such as platinum, palladium and rhodium coated onto a honeycomb structure in a very thin layer to give the maximum possible surface area (see **Figure 15.11**).

In the presence of these metals, harmful substances such as carbon monoxide and nitrogen oxides are converted into relatively harmless carbon dioxide and nitrogen. The large surface area means the reaction is very rapid. This is important because the gases in the exhaust system are in contact with the catalytic converter for only a very short time.

CHANGING THE CONCENTRATION OF THE REACTANTS

THE EFFECT OF CHANGING THE CONCENTRATION

We can repeat our original experiment with large marble chips and hydrochloric acid. Everything is kept the same except we use hydrochloric acid of half the concentration.

We find that reducing the concentration of the acid makes the reaction slower. We can see this on our graph (see **Figure 15.12**) because the graph (red line) is less steep than for our original experiment (blue line).

HINT

You can make an acid solution of half the concentration of the original by mixing 12.5 cm³ of the original acid with 12.5 cm³ of distilled water. Make sure you mix the solution thoroughly before adding it into the conical flask.

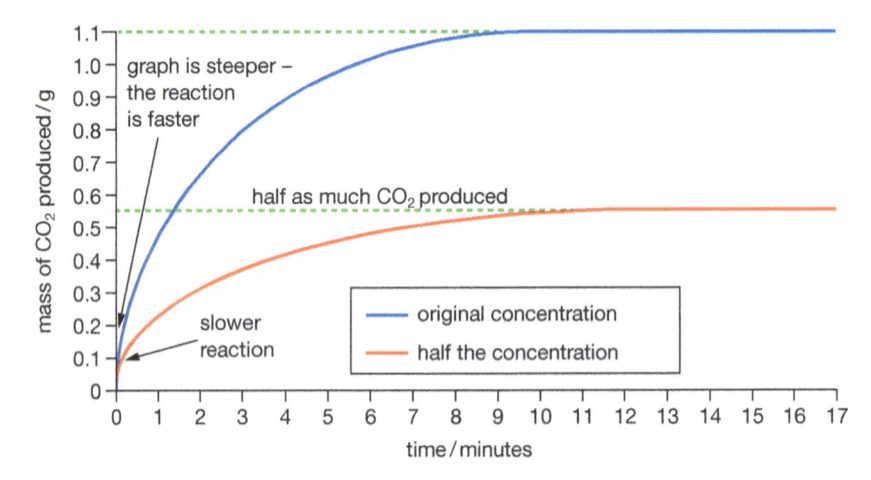

▲ Figure 15.12 The effect of changing the concentration of the acid

In our original experiment we used 25 cm³ of the hydrochloric acid stock solution. In this experiment we used 25 cm³ of hydrochloric acid of half of the concentration. Since we have started with half the amount of hydrochloric acid, we will produce half as much carbon dioxide.

In general, if you increase the concentration of the reactants, the reaction becomes faster. *Increasing the concentration increases the number of acid particles within a fixed volume* (see **Figure 15.13**), therefore they are more likely to react with the marble chips in a certain amount of time.

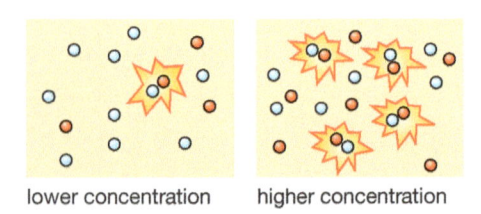

▲ Figure 15.13 At a higher concentration, more reactions occur per unit time.

3 PHYSICAL CHEMISTRY   **15 RATES OF REACTION**   249

Safety note: Wear eye protection and avoid skin contact with the acid.

ACTIVITY 3

▼ PRACTICAL: INVESTIGATING THE EFFECT OF CHANGING THE CONCENTRATION OF THE ACID ON THE RATE OF REACTION BETWEEN MARBLE CHIPS AND DILUTE HYDROCHLORIC ACID

We can repeat our previous experiment in **Activity 1** using the original large marble chips, but using hydrochloric acid of different concentrations. Everything else would be the same, that is, the mass of the marble chips (5.00 g) and the total volume of the acid (25 cm^3). We can dilute the acid by adding distilled water to the original acid solution but making sure the total volume of water and acid remains at 25 cm^3.

For example, if 12.5 cm^3 of the original HCl is mixed with 12.5 cm^3 of distilled water, we get an acid solution of half of the original concentration. If only 5 cm^3 of the original HCl is mixed with 20 cm^3 of distilled water, the acid solution is now 20% (5 out of 25) of the original concentration.

In this experiment we are going to calculate the average rate during the first 30 seconds, so we record the mass of carbon dioxide lost in 30 seconds.

We can calculate the average rate of reaction within the first 30 seconds by dividing the mass loss by 30. For example, if we obtain a loss of 0.32 g:

$$\text{average rate} = \frac{0.32}{30} = 0.011 \text{ g/s}$$

To identify the effect of changing concentration on rate, we can plot the results for the different concentrations on a piece of graph paper with rate on the y-axis and concentration of acid on the x-axis (see **Figure 15.14**). The line of best fit should go through the origin (0, 0). If there is no acid, there should be no rate. A straight line going through the origin shows that the rate of the reaction is *directly proportional* to the concentration of the hydrochloric acid. If the concentration doubles, the rate should double. If the concentration triples, the rate should triple.

DID YOU KNOW?
The words *proportional* and *directly proportional* mean the same thing. If the graph we plotted was a straight line that did not go through the origin, this is not a proportional relationship. In that case we would describe the relationship as *linear*.

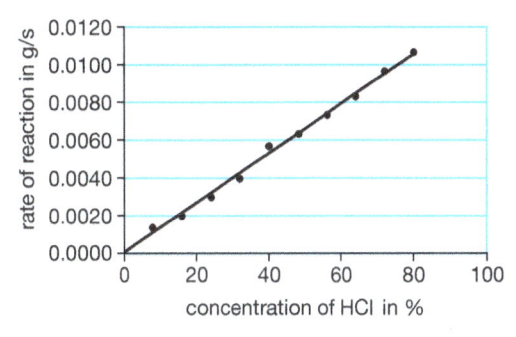

▲ Figure 15.14 The more concentrated the acid, the faster the reaction

CHANGING THE TEMPERATURE OF THE REACTION

We can do the original experiment again, but this time at a higher temperature. We keep everything else exactly the same as before.

Reactions get faster as the temperature is increased; the graph is *steeper* and *finishes sooner* (see **Figure 15.15**). The same mass of gas is given off because we have used the same quantities of everything in the mixture.

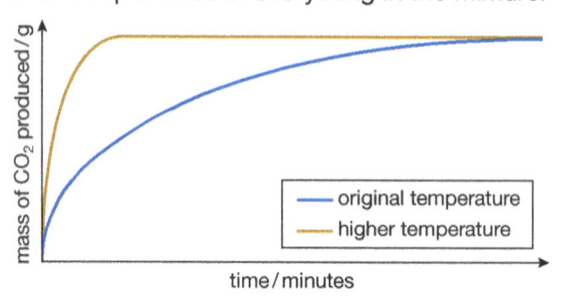

▲ Figure 15.15 The effect of changing the temperature of the reaction

HINT

As an approximation, a 10 °C increase in temperature approximately doubles the rate of a reaction. This works for quite a lot of reactions that we meet in the lab.

Increasing the temperature means that the particles in the reaction mixture have more **kinetic energy** so more reactions occur per unit time (see **Figure 15.16**). This increases the rate of a reaction.

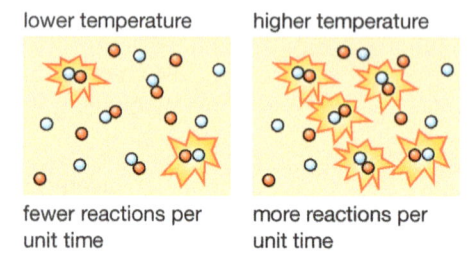

▲ Figure 15.16 A small increase in temperature produces a large increase in the rate of a reaction.

CHANGING THE PRESSURE ON THE REACTION

Changing the **pressure** of a reaction in which the reactants are only solids or liquids makes almost no difference to the rate of reaction. But increasing the pressure of a reaction where the reactants are *gases* does speed up the reaction.

If we have a fixed mass of a gas, we increase the pressure by squeezing it into a smaller volume.

This forces the particles *closer together*, so they react faster (see **Figure 15.17**). This is exactly the same as increasing the concentration of the gas.

KEY POINT

In solids and liquids, particles are packed closely together and there is hardly any space in between. Increasing the pressure would not change the volumes of the solids or liquids much, therefore there would hardly be any change in the number of particles in a certain volume.

3 PHYSICAL CHEMISTRY   **15 RATES OF REACTION**   251

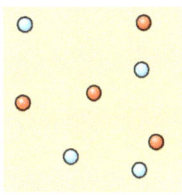

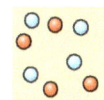

▲ Figure 15.17 Increased pressure means gas particles react faster.

CATALYSTS

WHAT ARE CATALYSTS?

Catalysts are *substances that speed up chemical reactions*, but are not used up in the process. They are still there, *chemically unchanged, at the end of the reaction*. Because they are not consumed, small amounts of catalyst can be used to process lots and lots of reactant particles. Different reactions need different catalysts.

THE CATALYTIC DECOMPOSITION OF HYDROGEN PEROXIDE

Bombardier beetles defend themselves by spraying a hot, unpleasant liquid at their attackers. Part of the reaction involves splitting hydrogen peroxide into water and oxygen, using the enzyme catalase (see **Figure 15.18**). **Enzymes** are *biological catalysts*. This reaction happens almost explosively, and produces a lot of heat. The same enzyme can be found in potatoes, or even liver tissues.

There are a lot of other things that also catalyse the decomposition of hydrogen peroxide. Some examples are manganese(IV) oxide (also called manganese dioxide), MnO_2, and lead(IV) oxide, PbO_2. Manganese(IV) oxide is what is normally used in the lab to speed up the decomposition of hydrogen peroxide.

▲ Figure 15.18 Bombardier beetles use hydrogen peroxide as part of their defence mechanism.

The reaction happening with the hydrogen peroxide is:

$$\text{hydrogen peroxide} \rightarrow \text{water} + \text{oxygen}$$

$$2H_2O_2(aq) \rightarrow 2H_2O(l) + O_2(g)$$

Notice that we do not write catalysts into the equation because they are chemically unchanged at the end of the reaction. If you like, you can write their name or formula over the top of the arrow.

SHOWING THAT A SUBSTANCE IS A CATALYST

It is not difficult to show that manganese(IV) oxide speeds up the decomposition of hydrogen peroxide to produce oxygen. **Figure 15.19** shows two beakers, both of which contain hydrogen peroxide solution. Without the catalyst, there is only a **trace** of bubbles in the solution. With it, oxygen is given off quickly.

How can you show that the manganese(IV) oxide is chemically unchanged by the reaction? It still looks the same, but has any been used up? You can only find out by weighing it before you add it to the hydrogen peroxide solution and then reweighing it at the end.

▲ Figure 15.19 The beakers both contain hydrogen peroxide solution, the right-hand one has MnO_2 added to speed up oxygen production.

You can separate the manganese(IV) oxide from the liquid by filtering it through a weighed filter paper, allowing the paper and residue to dry, and then reweighing to calculate the mass of the remaining manganese(IV) oxide. You should find that the mass has not changed.

Safety note: Wear eye protection and avoid skin contact with the solution.

HINT

The experiment in **Figure 15.20** is very simple and easy to set up. However, using this set-up has the disadvantage that some oxygen will escape at the beginning of the reaction when MnO_2 is added to H_2O_2 before the bung can be put back on the conical flask. Using a weighing bottle like the one in **Figure 15.21** is a simple way of mixing the chemicals together without losing any oxygen before you can get the bung in. When you are ready to start the reaction, shake the flask so that the weighing bottle falls over and the manganese(IV) oxide comes into contact with the hydrogen peroxide. You need to keep shaking so that an even mixture is formed.

DID YOU KNOW?

'*vol*', meaning volume, is a measurement for concentration for hydrogen peroxide. 1 cm^3 of 2 *vol* hydrogen peroxide solution decomposes completely to give 2 cm^3 of oxygen.

ACTIVITY 4

▼ PRACTICAL: INVESTIGATE THE USE OF A CATALYST ON THE DECOMPOSITION OF HYDROGEN PEROXIDE SOLUTION

Figure 15.20 shows apparatus that can be used to measure how the volume of oxygen produced changes with time in the decomposition of hydrogen peroxide solution.

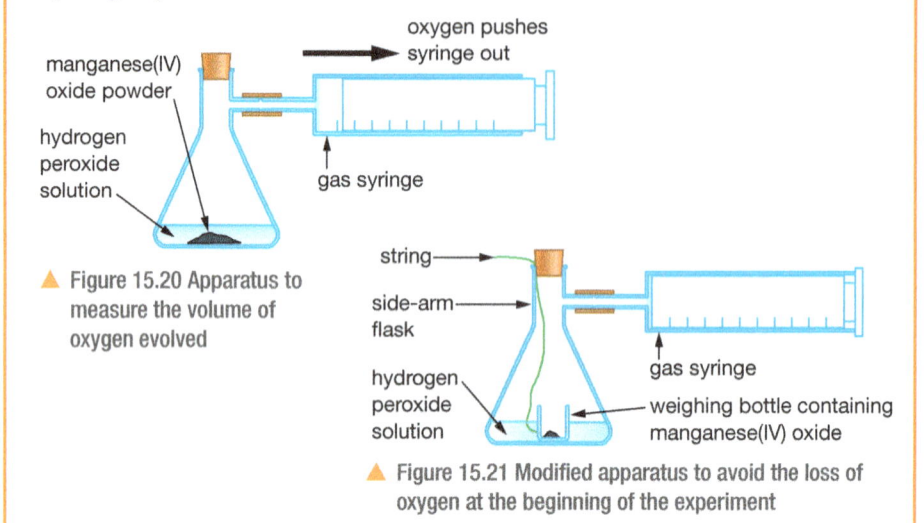

▲ Figure 15.20 Apparatus to measure the volume of oxygen evolved

▲ Figure 15.21 Modified apparatus to avoid the loss of oxygen at the beginning of the experiment

The following procedure could be used:

- Measure 100 cm^3 of 2 *vol* hydrogen peroxide and transfer to a 250 cm^3 conical flask with the gas syringe already attached.
- Weigh out 0.20 g of manganese(IV) oxide on a balance.
- Add the manganese(IV) oxide to the hydrogen peroxide and quickly replace the bung. Swirl the reaction mixture at a constant speed.
- Record the amount of oxygen produced every 20 seconds for 3 minutes and plot a graph of volume of oxygen versus time.

The sample data below show manganese(IV) oxide is a very effective catalyst for the decomposition of hydrogen peroxide (see **Figure 15.22**). Without the catalyst, there is no oxygen released during the experiment.

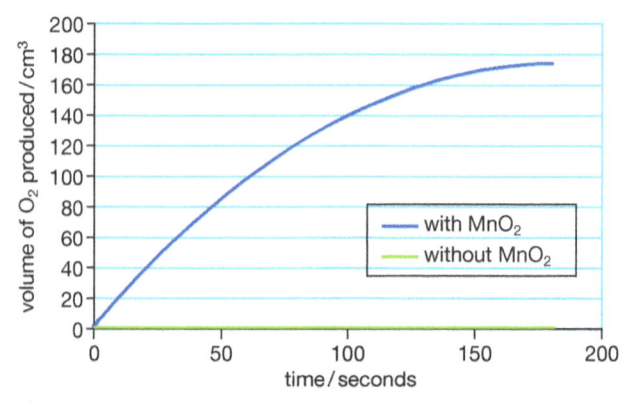

▲ Figure 15.22 The catalytic effect of MnO_2 on the decomposition of H_2O_2.

CATALYSTS IN INDUSTRY

Catalysts are especially important in industrial reactions because they help substances to react quickly at lower temperatures and pressures than would otherwise be needed. This saves money.

15 RATES OF REACTION

CHAPTER QUESTIONS

Exam-style questions on rates of reaction can be found at the end of Unit 3 on page 256.

SKILLS — PROBLEM SOLVING

1. Calculate the average rates of the following reactions; include the units in your answers.
   a. 64 cm³ of hydrogen gas was produced in the reaction between zinc powder with dilute hydrochloric acid in 30 seconds.
   b. In the reaction between sodium hydrogen carbonate ($NaHCO_3$) and dilute hydrochloric acid (HCl), there was a decrease in mass of 0.35 g in 2 minutes.
   c. In the reaction between dilute hydrochloric acid (HCl) and sodium thiosulfate ($Na_2S_2O_3$), 1.54 g of sulfur precipitate was produced over a period of 2 minutes and 30 seconds.

SKILLS — INTERPRETATION

2. Copy and complete the following sentences.
   a. The rate of a reaction can be measured as a change in the _____ of _____ or _____ per unit time.
   b. The rate of a reaction can be affected by the surface area of a solid reactant, the concentration of a solution, the temperature of a reaction mixture and the presence of a catalyst:
      i. When a solid reactant is broken down into smaller particles, this _____ the surface area of the reactant and the rate of the reaction _____.
      ii. When the concentration of a reactant increases, the rate of the reaction _____ Sometimes when the concentration of a reactant doubles the rate also doubles. The rate is said to be _____ _____ to the concertation of the reactant.
      iii. When the temperature of a reaction mixture increases, the particles gain more _____ energy. This _____ the rate of a reaction.
      iv. Catalysts _____ the rate of a reaction but are chemically _____ at the end of the reaction.

3. To investigate the rate of a reaction between sodium thiosulfate ($Na_2S_2O_3$) and hydrochloric acid (HCl), a student used the following method.
   - Measure 50 cm³ of the sodium thiosulfate stock solution using a 50 cm³ measuring cylinder and transfer it into a 250 cm³ conical flask.
   - Place the conical flask onto a white tile marked with a black cross (X) (see figure below).
   - Measure 50 cm³ of the dilute hydrochloric acid solution using a 50 cm³ measuring cylinder.
   - Add the acid into the conical flask with sodium thiosulfate and immediately start the timer.
   - Observe the conical flask from above and time how long it takes before you can no longer see the cross through the solution.

The equation for this reaction is:

$Na_2S_2O_3(aq) + 2HCl(aq) \rightarrow 2NaCl(aq) + H_2O(l) + SO_2(aq) + S(s)$

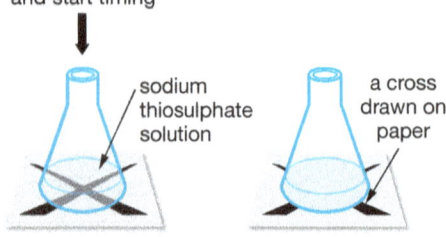

a Explain why the cross gets blocked as this reaction proceeds.

b The experiment was repeated using different concentrations of the acid. The table below shows the results.

Experiment number	Concentration of HCl (as percentage of the stock solution)	Volume of sodium thiosulfate stock solution / cm³	Volume of hydrochloric acid stock solution / cm³	Volume of distilled water / cm³	Time taken for the cross to disappear / sec
1	100%	50	50	0	25
2	80%	50	40		31
3	60%	50	30	20	42
4	40%	50	20		115
5	20%	50	10	40	126

i Explain why is it important to add distilled water into the reaction mixtures when carrying out experiments 2–5.

ii Calculate the volumes of distilled water to be added in experiments 2 and 4.

iii Plot the student's result on a piece of graph paper, with concentration of HCl on the x-axis and time taken for the cross to disappear on the y-axis. Draw a line a best fit.

iv One of the results is anomalous. Identify this result on your graph from iii by circling around the point.

v What could be the reason for the anomalous point?

A too little distilled water was added into the reaction mixture

B the student started the timer too late

C too little sodium thiosulfate was added into the reaction mixture

D the student stopped the timer too early

vi The rate of the reaction can be calculated as rate = 1/time taken for the cross to disappear. Calculate the rate of the reaction when the acid concentration was 20%, to 3 significant figures **with units**.

4 A student carried out an experiment to investigate the rate of a reaction between an excess of dolomite (magnesium carbonate) and 50 cm³ of dilute hydrochloric acid. The dolomite was in small pieces. The reaction is:

$MgCO_3(s) + 2HCl(aq) \rightarrow MgCl_2(aq) + H_2O(l) + CO_2(g)$

He measured the volume of carbon dioxide given off at regular intervals, with the results shown in the table below.

Time / s	0	30	60	90	120	150	180	210	240	270	300	330	360
Volume / cm³	0	27	45	59	70	78	85	90	94	97	99	100	100

SKILLS CREATIVITY

SKILLS INTERPRETATION

SKILLS ANALYSIS, REASONING

SKILLS PROBLEM SOLVING

SKILLS CRITICAL THINKING

a Draw a diagram of the apparatus you would use for this experiment and label it.

b Plot these results on a piece of graph paper, with time on the *x*-axis and volume of gas on the *y*-axis.

c At what time is the gas being given off most quickly? Explain why the reaction is fastest at that time.

d Use your graph to find out how long it took to produce 50 cm³ of gas.

e Use your graph to calculate the average rate of this reaction in the first 80 seconds.

f In each of the following questions, state what would happen to the initial rate of the reaction and to the total volume of gas given off if various changes were made to the experiment.

   i The mass of dolomite and the volume and concentration of acid were kept constant, but the dolomite was in one big lump instead of small pieces.

   ii The mass of dolomite was unchanged and it was still in small pieces. 50 cm³ of hydrochloric acid was used, which had half the original concentration.

   iii The dolomite was unchanged again. This time 25 cm³ of the original acid was used instead of 50 cm³.

   iv The acid was heated to 40 °C before the dolomite was added to it.

5 Catalysts speed up reactions, but can be recovered chemically unchanged at the end of the reaction.

Design an experiment to compare which one of the two following solids, iron(III) chloride ($FeCl_3$) and manganese(IV) oxide (MnO_2), act as a better catalyst for the decomposition of H_2O_2. The rate of the reaction will be calculated from the time taken for 50 cm³ of oxygen gas to be collected.

SKILLS ANALYSIS

SKILLS EXECUTIVE FUNCTION

SKILLS DECISION MAKING

a Suggest the independent variable (what you are varying) and the dependent variable (what you are measuring) in this experiment.

b Suggest *four* controlled variables (that should be kept the same) for this experiment, so that you are carrying out a fair test to compare the effect of the two different solid catalysts.

c The experiment was carried out using the following steps:

   A Time how long it takes to collect 50 cm³ of oxygen.

   B Weigh out 0.50 g of iron(III) chloride on a balance.

   C Add the iron(III) chloride powder into the hydrogen peroxide solution in a conical flask.

   D Start the timer and stir the reaction mixture constantly.

   E Measure 50 cm³ of a dilute H_2O_2 solution using a measuring cylinder and transfer to a 250 cm³ conical flask.

   F Repeat with 0.50 g of manganese(IV) oxide.

   Deduce the correct order of the steps.

SKILLS ANALYSIS

d The following table shows the results of the experiments. Identify the better catalyst for the decomposition of hydrogen peroxide.

Solid catalyst	Time to collect 50 cm³ of oxygen gas / s
iron(III) chloride	55
manganese(IV) oxide	12

EXAM PRACTICE

1 Which of the following changes does *not* increase the rate of the reaction between magnesium metal and dilute hydrochloric acid?

A increasing the temperature

B increasing the concentration of the acid

C decreasing the particle size of the magnesium

D increasing the particle size of the magnesium

(Total 1 mark)

SKILLS CRITICAL THINKING

2 State whether the following changes are exothermic or endothermic.

a Water boiling (1)

b Mg ribbon reacts with dilute HCl (1)

c Thermal decomposition of $CuCO_3$ to form CuO and CO_2 (1)

d $MgCl_2$ dissolves in water, temperature increases from 25 °C to 42 °C (1)

e Combustion of petrol (1)

f Baking soda reacting with vinegar, temperature decreases from 23.1 °C to 18.6 °C (1)

g CaO reacting with water — a reaction used to heat up coffee in self-heating cans (1)

(Total 7 marks)

3 A group of students wanted to investigate the energy changes when salts dissolve in water. The teacher suggested that they should measure the temperature changes that occur when the salts were dissolved.

This is the method they followed:

- Add 100 cm³ of water to a beaker.
- Record the temperature of the water.
- Weigh 5.00 g of salt and add it to the water in the beaker.
- Stir the mixture with a glass rod vigorously until all the solid has dissolved.
- Record the maximum (or minimum) temperature of the solution.

a The diagram below shows the readings on the thermometer before and after the student dissolved a salt, potassium chloride, in water.

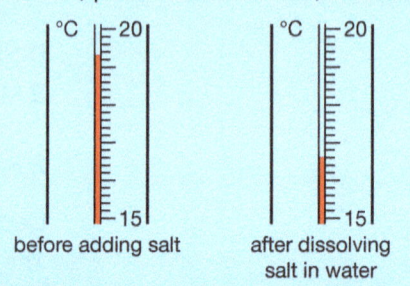

SKILLS ANALYSIS, PROBLEM SOLVING

i Copy and complete the thermometer readings below and calculate the temperature change. (3)

Temperature before   .... °C
Temperature after   .... °C
Temperature change   .... °C

3 PHYSICAL CHEMISTRY — EXAM PRACTICE

SKILLS CRITICAL THINKING

   ii Which one of the following statements is true about the dissolving of potassium chloride in water? (1)

   A The process is endothermic and ΔT is positive.
   B The process is exothermic and ΔT is positive.
   C The process is endothermic and ΔT is negative.
   D The process is exothermic and ΔT is negative.

SKILLS PROBLEM SOLVING

b Another student repeated the experiment with a different salt, calcium chloride, using the same method and recorded these results.

Volume of water = 100 cm³

Starting temperature of water = 15.9 °C

Maximum temperature of solution = 23.2 °C

Mass of salt = 5.00 g

   i Calculate the heat energy released in this experiment. The specific heat capacity of the solution c = 4.2 J/g/°C and the mass of 1 cm³ of mixture = 1 g. (2)

   ii Calculate the heat energy change per gram, in kJ/g, for dissolving calcium chloride in water. (2)

SKILLS REASONING

c Another student dissolved magnesium chloride in water. She compared her result with a data book value.

Student's value = 1.10 kJ/g

Data book value = 1.48 kJ/g

There are no errors in the calculation of her result.

Suggest *two* reasons why the student's value is lower than the data book value. (2)

(Total 10 marks)

4 In an experiment to investigate the rate of decomposition of hydrogen peroxide solution in the presence of manganese(IV) oxide, a student mixed 10 cm³ of hydrogen peroxide solution with 30 cm³ of water and added 0.20 g of manganese(IV) oxide. She measured the volume of oxygen evolved at 60 s intervals. The results of her experiment are recorded in the table below.

Time / s	0	60	120	180	240	300
Volume / cm³	0	30	48	57	60	60

SKILLS PROBLEM SOLVING

a Write a balanced equation for the decomposition of hydrogen peroxide H_2O_2 to form water and oxygen. (2)

SKILLS REASONING

b Explain why the manganese(IV) oxide was added in a weighing bottle rather than directly into the hydrogen peroxide solution. (1)

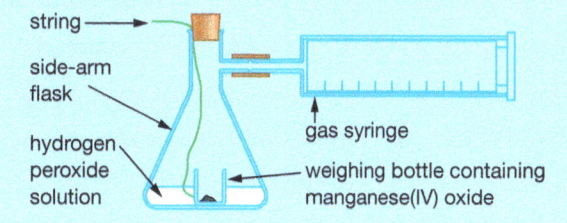

SKILLS INTERPRETATION

c Plot a graph of her results and draw a line of best fit. Make sure that you label the axes. (4)

d Use your graph to determine the following:
  i The time it took to produce 50 cm³ of oxygen. (1)
  ii The volume of gas produced after 100 seconds. (1)
  iii The average rate (with unit) in the first 150 seconds. (2)
  iv By drawing tangents, calculate the rate of reaction at 90 seconds. (3)

e Explain why the graph becomes horizontal after 240 seconds. (2)

f Describe a method you could use to show that the manganese(IV) oxide is acting as a catalyst in this reaction. (4)

g Suppose the experiment had been repeated using the same quantities of everything, but with the reaction flask immersed in ice.
Sketch the graph you would expect to get. Use the same grid as in **c**. Label the new graph **G**. (2)

h On the same grid as in **c** and **g** sketch the graph you would expect to get if you repeated the experiment at the original temperature using 5 cm³ of hydrogen peroxide solution, 35 cm³ of water and 0.20 g of manganese(IV) oxide. Label this graph **H**. (2)

(Total 24 marks)

5 A student investigates the heat energy change of displacement reaction between zinc powder and copper(II) sulfate solution. This method was followed:

- Use a 50 cm³ measuring cylinder to measure out 50 cm³ of the copper(II) sulfate solution, transfer it into a polystyrene cup.
- Use a weighing boat to measure out 3.40 g of zinc powder on a balance.
- Add the zinc powder into the copper(II) sulfate solution and put the lid onto the polystyrene cup.
- Measure and record the maximum temperature of the reaction mixture.

a Identify two steps that were missing in the student's method. (2)

b Draw and label the apparatus used for carrying out this experiment. (2)

c The temperature of the reaction mixture changed from 18.2 °C to 49.6 °C. A student performed the following calculation to work out the heat energy released in this reaction, assuming the specific heat capacity of the solution c = 4.2 J/g/°C and mass of 1 cm³ of the reaction mixture = 1 g. Identify three mistakes the student made in his calculation and calculate the correct value for the heat energy released in this reaction in kJ.

$Q = mc\Delta T = 3.40 \times 4.2 \times 49.6 = 708.288$ kJ $= 708288$ J (4)

d The theoretical value for the heat energy released in this experiment is 10.9 kJ. Evaluate your answer from **c**, with suggestions on the difference between your answer and the theoretical value. (4)

e In the experiment above, the zinc powder was in excess. Another experiment was done when the student used the same mass of zinc powder, but 25 cm³ of the copper(II) sulfate solution with double the concentration. Determine the expected temperature rise in the second experiment. (1)

(Total 13 marks)

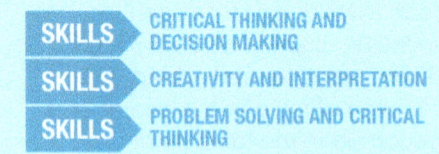

3 PHYSICAL CHEMISTRY — EXAM PRACTICE

6 A group of students investigated the effect of changing the concentration of dilute hydrochloric acid on the rate of its reaction with marble chips (calcium carbonate).

The equation for this reaction is

$$CaCO_3(s) + 2HCl(aq) \rightarrow CaCl_2(aq) + H_2O(l) + CO_2(g)$$

They used the following method:

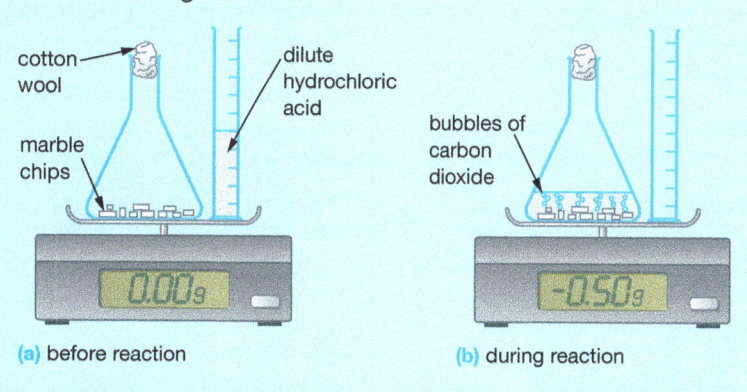

(a) before reaction (b) during reaction

The students recorded the time taken for the mass of the flask and contents to decrease by 0.50 g.

The experiment was then repeated using different concentrations of hydrochloric acid.

a To ensure it was a valid (fair) test, the students kept the number of marble chips constant in each experiment. Suggest *two* other properties of the marble chips that should be kept the same in each experiment. (2)

b Give a reason why cotton wool was used in the experiment. (1)

c The teacher gave the students some hydrochloric acid that was labelled 100%. The table below shows the results.

Student	Mass of $CaCO_3$ / g	Volume of aqueous HCl / cm^3	Volume of water / cm^3	Concentration of HCl / %	Time to lose 0.50 g / s
1	5.00	25	0	100	105
2	5.00	20	5	80	150
3	5.00	15		60	175
4	5.00	10	15	40	272
5	5.00	5	20	20	520

  i The results of Student 3 are incomplete.
  Calculate the volume of water the student should have used for the result to be comparable with the other four (choose one answer). (1)
  A 5   B 10   C 15   D 20

  ii Plot a graph of the results on a separate piece of graph paper, with concentration of acid on the *x*-axis and time on the *y*-axis. Draw a line of best fit. (4)

  iii Use your graph in **ii** to identify the time taken for the loss of 0.50 g of mass from the flask when the concentration of acid is 70%. (1)

iv One of the points on the graph is anomalous. Give a reason for this (choose one answer). (1)

    A The student started the stopwatch too late.
    B The student stopped the stopwatch before mass loss reached 0.50 g.
    C The student added too much water at the beginning of the experiment.
    D The student spilt some water before adding it into the reaction mixture.

d Another group of students repeated the experiment, but this time they measured the mass loss after 1 minute.

The table below shows the results obtained by the students.

Mass of carbon dioxide given off / g	0.36	0.72	0.88	1.28	1.44	1.65
% Concentration of acid	20	40	50	70	80	90

Describe the relationship between the mass of carbon dioxide given off in 1 minute and the concentration of the acid. (2)

e A third student repeated the experiments with hydrochloric acid and an excess of marble chips using the same apparatus as shown above. The graph shows the results of two experiments, L and M.

Which change could have caused the change from L to M? (1)

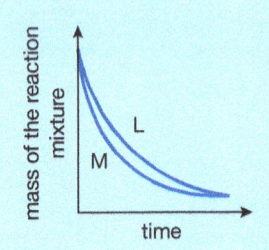

    A increasing the concentration of the acid in M
    B increasing the size of the marble chips in M
    C decreasing the temperature of the reaction mixture in M
    D increasing the volume of the acid in M

(Total 13 marks)

7 Curve **i** in the following graph shows the volume of hydrogen gas given off when magnesium powder reacts with excess dilute hydrochloric acid. The other product formed in the reaction is a soluble salt of magnesium chloride.

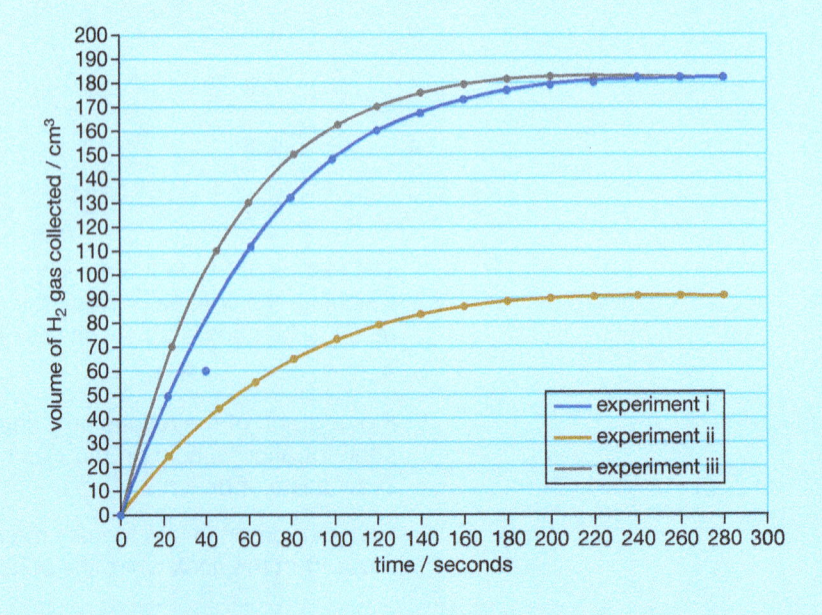

3 PHYSICAL CHEMISTRY — EXAM PRACTICE

SKILLS CRITICAL THINKING AND PROBLEM SOLVING

a Copy and complete the chemical equation for this reaction. Balance the equation and add in the state symbols. (3)

.... Mg ( ) + ... HCl ( ) → .... MgCl$_2$( ) + ...H$_2$( )

SKILLS ANALYSIS

b Using the graph, calculate the volume of hydrogen gas produced in the second minute of the reaction for experiment **i**. (1)

SKILLS PROBLEM SOLVING

c Determine the average rate of reaction for experiment **i**, with units, in the first 20 seconds. (2)

SKILLS PROBLEM SOLVING

d By drawing tangents, calculate the initial rate of the experiment **i**. (3)

SKILLS INTERPRETATION

e Describe and explain what happens to the rate of the reaction as the reaction continues. (2)

SKILLS REASONING

f The point at $t = 40$ seconds in experiment **i** is an anomaly. Suggest a reason for this anomalous result. (1)

SKILLS CRITICAL THINKING

g Another method to find out how much gas is produced in a reaction is by weighing the reaction mixture on a balance and let the gas escape into the air. Give a reason why the loss of mass may not be a good idea for measuring the rate of this reaction. (1)

SKILLS CRITICAL THINKING

h Describe what changes could have caused: (2)

curve **ii**

curve **iii**.

(Total 15 marks)

SKILLS CRITICAL THINKING, DECISION MAKING, CREATIVITY

8 Antacids are medicines which can neutralise stomach acid containing hydrochloric acid (HCl), to relieve indigestion or heartburn. Antacids usually contain calcium carbonate or magnesium carbonate or sodium hydrogen carbonate or a combination of them. Using the following chemicals and apparatus provided, design an experiment to investigate the effect of surface area on the rate of a reaction between an antacid containing calcium carbonate and an aqueous solution of dilute hydrochloric acid. You should describe your method clearly and draw a diagram to show how you would set up the apparatus.

Chemicals:

Antacid tablets containing 500 mg of CaCO$_3$ each

Excess dilute hydrochloric acid

Apparatus:

- 250 cm^3 conical flasks with side arm to connect onto a gas syringe
- pestle and mortar
- 50 cm^3 measuring cylinders
- gas syringes
- bungs
- stopwatch
- weighing boats
- clamps, bosses, stands

(Total 7 marks)

16 INTRODUCTION TO ORGANIC CHEMISTRY 263 | 17 CRUDE OIL 267 | 18 ALKANES 274 | 19 ALKENES 280
20 SYNTHETIC POLYMERS 284

CHEMISTRY UNIT 4
ORGANIC CHEMISTRY

Organic chemistry is the study of the compounds of carbon (there are some inorganic carbon compounds as well). There are more organic compounds than all the other compounds put together. These compounds include naturally occurring ones that are found in our bodies, for example proteins, DNA and fats. There are also artificially made compounds such as plastics, dyes and drugs. The artificial compounds are derived from chemicals obtained from crude oil. When all the crude oil has been used we will have to find new sources for more than just fuel for cars and making electricity. Organic chemists are involved in the synthesis of a huge variety of new compounds, including drugs and medicines used to treat diseases such as cancer, AIDS, influenza and asthma. The synthesis of these drugs can involve a large number of steps and requires the knowledge and understanding of a great number of organic chemistry reactions. It can take many years and millions of dollars to develop a new drug.

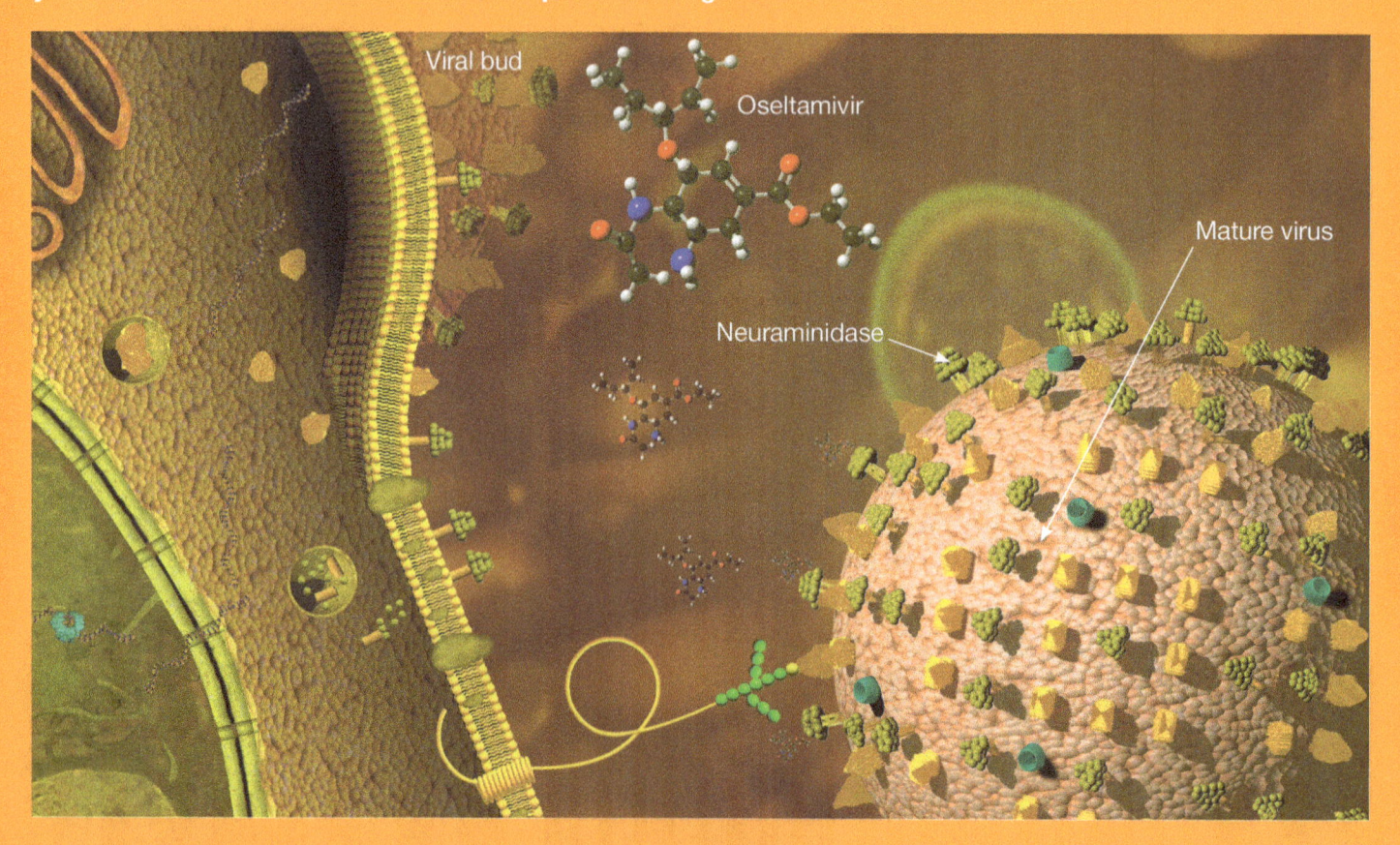

16 INTRODUCTION TO ORGANIC CHEMISTRY

SPECIFICATION REFERENCES: 4.1, 4.2

There are millions of different organic compounds. They all contain carbon and hydrogen, and often other elements such as oxygen, nitrogen and chlorine. Carbon atoms can join together to form chains and rings, which is why there are so many carbon compounds. This chapter introduces you to some of the important ideas that you need to know before you can start to understand organic chemistry.

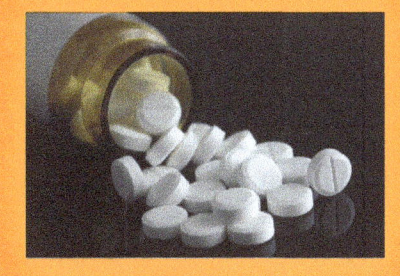

▲ Figure 16.1 What do caffeine, aspirin and dyes have in common? They are all organic compounds.

LEARNING OBJECTIVES

- Know that a hydrocarbon is a compound made up of hydrogen and carbon only.
- Understand how to represent organic molecules using, molecular formulae, general formulae, structural formulae and displayed formulae.

In the next few chapters we will be looking at organic compounds. The term 'organic' was originally used because it was believed that organic compounds could only come from living things. Now it is used for any carbon compound except for the very simplest (carbon dioxide, carbon monoxide, the carbonates and the hydrogencarbonates).

Organic compounds can exist as chains, branched chains or rings of carbon atoms with hydrogens attached.

When you start doing **organic chemistry**, you are suddenly faced with a whole lot of new compounds with strange names and unfamiliar ways of drawing them (see **Figure 16.2**). It can be quite scary!

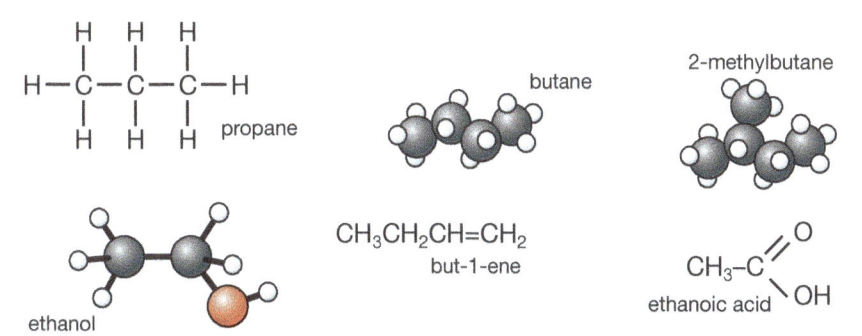

▲ Figure 16.2 Organic chemistry involves a lot of new compounds.

The secret at the beginning is to spend a lot of time exploring the subject – understanding names, drawing structures and making models.

HINT

Your school may have models you can use. Otherwise, you can make your own out of modelling clay and matchsticks or small nails to use as bonds.

HYDROCARBONS

The simplest organic compounds are **hydrocarbons** (see **Figure 16.3**). *These are molecules that contain carbon and hydrogen only.*

> **EXAM HINT**
>
> The word *only* is important here for the definition. Almost all organic compounds contain carbon and hydrogen but hydrocarbons contain *only* carbon and hydrogen.

The carbon atoms are joined together with single, double or triple bonds. Carbon atoms are joined to hydrogen atoms by single bonds.

> **KEY POINT**
>
> Organic compounds can be described as **saturated** (containing only single C–C bonds) or **unsaturated** (containing double C=C or triple C≡C bonds). This is discussed in **Chapters 18 and 19**.

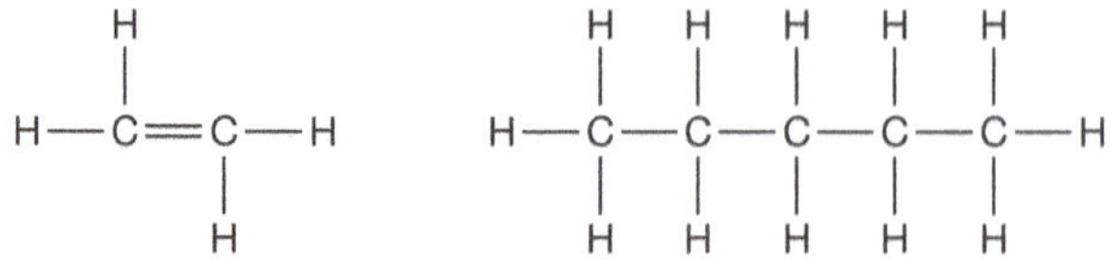

ethene   pentane

▲ Figure 16.3 Examples of hydrocarbons

TYPES OF FORMULA FOR ORGANIC MOLECULES

MOLECULAR FORMULAE

A **molecular formula** *counts the actual number of each type of atom present in a molecule.* For example, the molecular formula of butane is C_4H_{10} and the molecular formula of ethene is C_2H_4.

The molecular formula tells you nothing about the way the atoms are joined together. Both the compounds in **Figure 16.4** have the same molecular formula, C_4H_{10}.

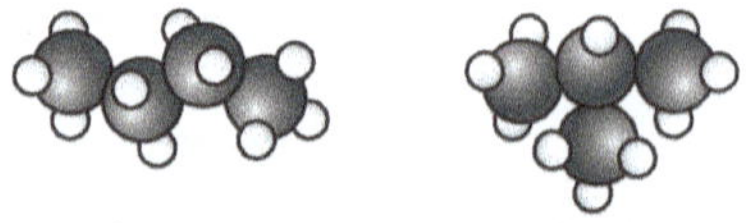

▲ Figure 16.4 These two compounds have the same molecular formula but different structures.

Molecular formulae are used very rarely in organic chemistry because they do not give any useful information about the bonding in the molecule. You might use them in equations for the combustion of simple hydrocarbons, where the structure of the molecule does not matter. For example:

$$2C_4H_{10}(g) + 13O_2(g) \rightarrow 8CO_2(g) + 10H_2O(l)$$

In almost all other cases, you use a structural or a displayed formula (see page 265).

GENERAL FORMULAE

Table 16.1 The first few members of the alkane and alkene families

Alkanes	Alkenes
CH_4	
C_2H_6	C_2H_4
C_3H_8	C_3H_6
C_4H_{10}	C_4H_8

There are many different families of organic compounds, for example, **alkanes** and **alkenes**.

Members of a family of organic compounds with similar chemical properties can be represented using a **general formula**. The first few members of the alkane family are shown in **Table 16.1**.

In the case of alkanes, if there are n carbons in a molecule, there are always $2n + 2$ hydrogens. The general formula of alkanes is C_nH_{2n+2}. For methane, CH_4, there is 1 carbon atom in the molecule and $2 \times 1 + 2 = 4$ hydrogen atoms. For propane C_3H_8, there are 3 carbon atoms in the molecule and $2 \times 3 + 2 = 8$ hydrogen atoms. We can therefore work out that dodecane, which has 12 carbon atoms, will have 26 hydrogen atoms and the molecular formula $C_{12}H_{26}$.

Different families of organic compounds usually have different general formulae. For example, the general formula for alkenes is C_nH_{2n}.

STRUCTURAL FORMULAE

A **structural formula** shows *how the atoms in a molecule are joined together*. There are two ways of representing structural formulae: they can be drawn as a **displayed formula** (full structural formula), or they can be written out in condensed form (*condensed structural formula*) by omitting all the carbon–carbon single bonds and carbon–hydrogen single bonds, for example CH₃CH₂CH₃. You need to be confident about using either way.

DISPLAYED FORMULAE

A displayed formula (sometimes called a full structural formula) shows *all* the atoms in the molecule and all the bonds as individual lines. You need to remember that each line represents *a pair of shared electrons in a covalent bond*.

Figure 16.5 shows a model of butane, together with its displayed formula. Notice that the way the displayed formula is drawn is different from the shape of the actual molecule. Displayed formulae are always drawn with the molecule straightened out and flattened. They do, however, show exactly how all the atoms are joined together.

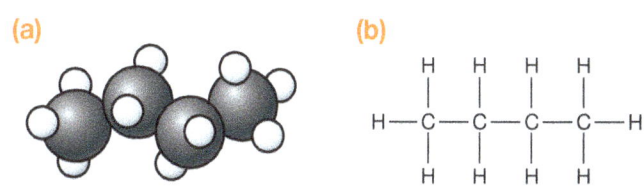

▲ Figure 16.5 Butane. The angles between neighbouring C–H bonds in butane are shown as 90° in the two-dimensional displayed formula (b). In reality they are about 109.5° in a tetrahedral arrangement in three dimensions (a).

HOW TO DRAW A STRUCTURAL FORMULA

For anything other than the smallest molecules, drawing a fully displayed formula is very time-consuming. You can simplify the formula by writing, for example, CH₃ or CH₂ instead of showing all the carbon–hydrogen bonds.

The structural formula for butane can be shown as

CH₃CH₂CH₂CH₃ or CH₃—CH₂—CH₂—CH₃

These both show exactly how the atoms in the molecule are joined together. The corresponding molecular formula, C₄H₁₀, does not give you the same sort of useful information about the molecule.

All the structures in **Figure 16.6** represent butane: even though they look different they are exactly the same molecule.

▲ Figure 16.6 All three structures represent butane. The convention is to write the structure with all the carbon atoms in a straight line.

Each structure shows four carbon atoms joined together in a chain, but the chain has simply twisted. This happens in real molecules as well: the atoms can rotate around single carbon–carbon bonds, as shown in **Figure 16.7**.

> **REMINDER**
>
> It is important to remember when you draw structures that C always forms four bonds and H always forms one bond. If you are not sure about why these atoms form this number of bonds, you need to look back at **Chapter 7**.

> **EXAM HINT**
>
> If you are asked to draw the structure for a molecule in an International GCSE exam, always draw it as a displayed formula. You cannot lose any marks by doing this, whereas you might if you use the simplified form. If, on the other hand, you are simply writing a structure in an equation, for example, you can use whichever version you prefer.

> **HINT**
>
> The best way to understand that these are all the same is to make some models. If you do not have access to molecular models, use blobs of modelling clay joined together with pieces of matchstick or small nails to represent the bonds. You will find that you can change the shape of the model by rotating around the bonds. That is what happens in real molecules.

266 4 ORGANIC CHEMISTRY   16 INTRODUCTION TO ORGANIC CHEMISTRY

KEY POINT
Structural formulae may be drawn in various ways. Sometimes no bonds are shown and other times some bonds are shown. The easiest way to think about it is like this: if all the bonds are shown, then it is a displayed formula. If not all of them are shown (but you can still see what the structure is), then it is a structural formula.

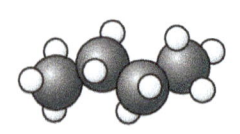

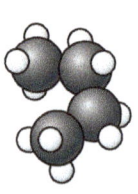

▲ Figure 16.7 These diagrams show the shape of a butane molecule better, but you would not draw these in an exam.

A molecule like propene, C_3H_6, has a carbon–carbon double bond. This is shown by drawing two lines between the carbon atoms to show *the two pairs of shared electrons* (**Figure 16.8**). You would normally write this in a simplified structural formula as $CH_3CH=CH_2$.

KEY POINT
In more advanced work the structural formula of propene would just be written as CH_3CHCH_2 but at International GCSE the C=C will normally be shown.

▲ Figure 16.8 The displayed formula for propene

CHAPTER QUESTIONS

SKILLS CRITICAL THINKING

1 Copy and complete the following table.

Molecular formula	Displayed formula	Structural formula	General formula
C_3H_8			
		$CH_3CH=CHCH_3$	
	(displayed formula of pentane)		
		CH_3CH_2OH	$C_nH_{2n+2}O$
C_2H_4			

2 The table below shows the formulae of some organic compounds.

Compound	Formula
A	C_2H_6
B	$CH_3CH=CH_2$
C	$CH_3CH_2CH_2OH$
D	$CH_3CH_2CH_2CH_2CH_3$

SKILLS CRITICAL THINKING

a Select one compound from the table which is not a hydrocarbon. Explain your choice.

b Draw the full displayed formula of compound **B**. Include all bonds in your drawing.

SKILLS CRITICAL THINKING

c Compounds **A** and **D** are from the same family of organic compounds. State the general formula for this family.

17 CRUDE OIL

SPECIFICATION REFERENCES: 4.7, 4.9–4.16

The oil industry is at the very heart of modern life. It provides fuels, plastics and the organic chemicals which go to make things as different as solvents, drugs, dyes and explosives. This chapter explores how an unappealing, sticky, black liquid is converted into useful things.

▲ Figure 17.1 The oil industry is big business!

LEARNING OBJECTIVES

- Know that crude oil is a mixture of hydrocarbons.
- Know the names and uses of the main fractions obtained from crude oil: refinery gases, gasoline, kerosene, diesel, fuel oil and bitumen.
- Know the trend in colour, boiling point and viscosity of the main fractions.
- Know that a fuel is a substance that, when burned, releases heat energy.
- Know the possible products of complete and incomplete combustion of hydrocarbons with oxygen in the air.
- Understand why carbon monoxide is poisonous, in terms of its effect on the capacity of blood to transport oxygen.
- Know that in car engines the temperature reached is high enough to allow nitrogen and oxygen from air to react, forming oxides of nitrogen.
- Explain how the combustion of some impurities in hydrocarbon fuels results in the formation of sulfur dioxide.
- Understand how sulfur dioxide and oxides of nitrogen contribute to acid rain.

WHAT IS CRUDE OIL?

THE ORIGIN OF CRUDE OIL

Millions of years ago, plants and animals living in the sea died and fell to the bottom. Layers of sediment formed on top of them. Their shells and skeletons formed limestone. The soft tissue was gradually changed by heat and high pressure into **crude oil** (see **Figure 17.2**). Crude oil is a *finite, non-renewable resource*. Once all the existing supplies have been used, they will not be replaced, or at least not for many millions of years.

▲ Figure 17.2 This sticky black liquid is essential to modern life.

CRUDE OIL CONTAINS HYDROCARBONS

Crude oil is a mixture of hydrocarbons, *compounds containing carbon and hydrogen only*. There are lots of different hydrocarbons of various sizes in crude oil, ranging from molecules with just a few carbon and hydrogen atoms to molecules containing over 100 atoms.

HOW THE PHYSICAL PROPERTIES OF HYDROCARBONS CHANGE WITH MOLECULE SIZE

As the number of carbon atoms in hydrocarbon molecules increases, the physical properties of the compounds change. Most of these changes are the result of increasing attractions between neighbouring molecules. *As the molecules become bigger, the intermolecular forces of attraction become stronger* and it becomes more difficult to separate one molecule from its neighbours.

REMINDER
Intermolecular forces are explained in **Chapter 7** (page 180).

As the molecules become bigger, the following changes occur.

- *Boiling point increases*: the larger the molecule, the higher the boiling point. This is because large molecules are attracted to each other more strongly than smaller ones. More energy is needed to break these stronger intermolecular forces of attraction to produce the widely separated molecules in the gas.

- *The liquids become less* volatile: the bigger the hydrocarbon, the more slowly it evaporates at room temperature. This is again because the bigger molecules are more strongly attracted to their neighbours and so do not turn into a gas so easily.

HINT
We usually count a substance as being volatile if it turns to a vapour easily at room temperature. That means it will evaporate quickly at that temperature.

- *The liquids become more* viscous *and flow less easily*: liquids containing small hydrocarbon molecules are runny. Those containing large molecules flow less easily because of the stronger forces of attraction between their molecules.

- The liquids become darker in colour.

- Bigger hydrocarbons do not burn as easily as smaller ones. This limits the use of the bigger ones as fuels.

SEPARATING CRUDE OIL

Crude oil itself has no uses and it has to be separated into *fractions* before it can be used. These fractions are all mixtures, but each one contains a narrow range of sizes of hydrocarbons with similar boiling points. We use **fractional distillation** to separate crude oil into fractions. This is carried out in an oil refinery.

4 ORGANIC CHEMISTRY
17 CRUDE OIL

FRACTIONAL DISTILLATION

> **HINT**
> You do not need to be able to describe how fractional distillation works in separating the fractions in the crude oil.

Crude oil is heated until it boils and the vapours pass into a **fractionating column**, which is cooler at the top and hotter at the bottom (see **Figure 17.3**). The vapours rise up the column. How far up the column a particular hydrocarbon moves depends on its boiling point.

> **KEY POINT**
> The boiling point is the same as the temperature at which a gas condenses to form a liquid; it could also be called the *condensation point*.

Suppose a hydrocarbon boils at 120 °C. At the bottom of the column, the temperature is much higher than 120 °C and so the hydrocarbon remains as a gas. As it travels up the column, the temperature of the column becomes lower. When the temperature falls to 120 °C, that hydrocarbon will turn into a liquid, it *condenses* and can be removed.

Smaller molecules have lower boiling points and get further up the column before they condense. Longer chain hydrocarbons have higher boiling points and condense lower down in the column. This way, the crude oil is split into various *fractions*.

ACTIVITY 1

▼ PRACTICAL

The fractional distillation of crude oil can be approximated in a school laboratory using the apparatus shown in **Figure 17.4**.

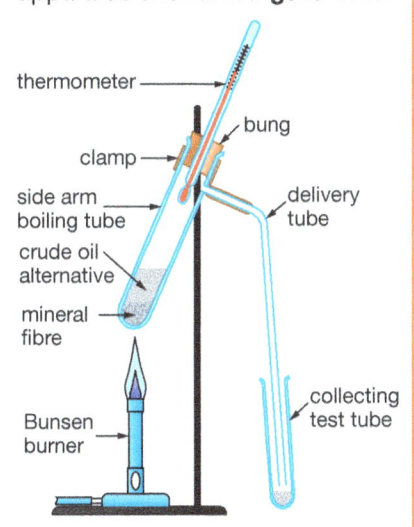

▲ Figure 17.4 Separating the fractions of crude oil in a laboratory.

Different fractions can be collected at different boiling points. You can test the ease of ignition of the fractions by pouring them from the test tubes onto watch glasses and setting light to them. The viscosity of the fractions can be assessed on how easily they can be poured onto the watch glasses.

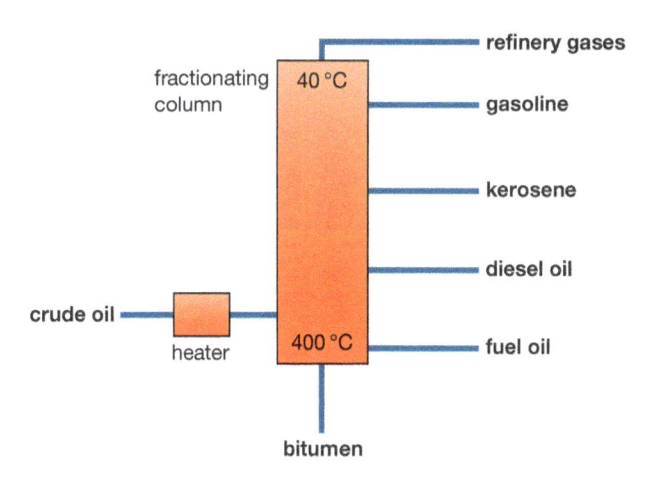

▲ Figure 17.3 Fractional distillation of crude oil

> **EXAM HINT**
> You will find a lot of disagreement, from various sources, about exactly what fractions are produced in fractional distillation. **Figure 17.3** matches the requirements of the Edexcel International GCSE specification, but this is a major simplification of what really goes on.

USES OF THE FRACTIONS

AS FUELS

All hydrocarbons burn in air (oxygen) to form *carbon dioxide and water*, and release a lot of heat in the process. The various fractions can therefore be used as **fuels**.

A fuel is a substance which, when burned, releases heat energy.

EXAM HINT

Do not try to learn these equations as there are too many possible hydrocarbons you could be asked about. Provided you know (or are told) the formula of the fuel and remember the products of the combustion reaction, you can balance the equation yourself.

For example, burning methane (the major constituent of natural gas):

$$CH_4(g) + 2O_2(g) \rightarrow CO_2(g) + 2H_2O(l)$$

or burning octane (one of the hydrocarbons present in gasoline (petrol)):

$$2C_8H_{18}(l) + 25O_2(g) \rightarrow 16CO_2(g) + 18H_2O(l)$$

If there is not enough air (or oxygen), you get **incomplete combustion**. This leads to the formation of *carbon (soot)* or *carbon monoxide* instead of carbon dioxide.

For example, if methane burns in a badly maintained gas appliance, there may not be enough oxygen available to produce carbon dioxide, and so you get toxic carbon monoxide instead:

$$2CH_4(g) + 3O_2(g) \rightarrow 2CO(g) + 4H_2O(l)$$

The formation of carbon monoxide from the incomplete combustion of hydrocarbons is very dangerous (see **Figure 17.5**). Carbon monoxide is colourless and odourless, and is very poisonous. *Carbon monoxide is poisonous because it reduces the ability of the blood to carry oxygen around the body.* This will make you ill, or you may even die, because not enough oxygen gets to the cells in your body for respiration to provide energy.

▲ Figure 17.5 As well as all the other poisonous or cancer-causing compounds, cigarette smoke contains carbon monoxide due to incomplete combustion.

DID YOU KNOW?

Carbon monoxide combines with *haemoglobin* (the molecule that carries oxygen in the red blood cells), preventing it from carrying the oxygen. It binds more strongly to the haemoglobin than oxygen does.

REFINERY GASES

Refinery gases are *a mixture of methane, ethane, propane and butane*, which can be separated into individual gases if required. These gases are commonly used as liquefied petroleum gas (LPG) for domestic heating and cooking.

GASOLINE (PETROL)

As with all the other fractions, gasoline (petrol) is a mixture of hydrocarbons with similar boiling points. It is used as a fuel in cars.

KEROSENE

Kerosene is used as a fuel for jet aircraft (see **Figure 17.6**), as domestic heating oil and as 'paraffin' for small heaters and lamps.

▲ Figure 17.6 Kerosene is used as aviation fuel.

4 ORGANIC CHEMISTRY   17 CRUDE OIL   271

DIESEL

Diesel is used as a fuel for buses, lorries, some cars, and some railway engines (**Figure 17.7**). Some is also converted to other more useful organic chemicals, including gasoline (petrol), in a process called cracking.

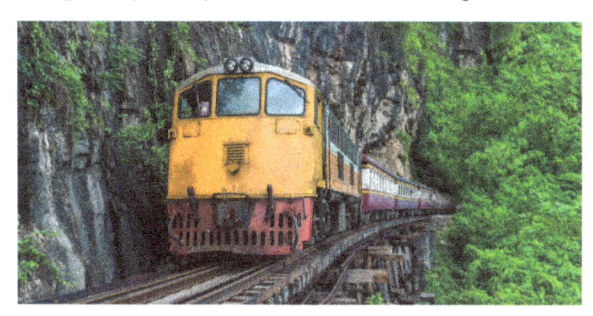

▲ Figure 17.7 A train powered by diesel

FUEL OIL

Fuel oil is used as a fuel for ships (**Figure 17.8**) and for industrial heating.

▲ Figure 17.8 Ships' boilers burn fuel oil.

BITUMEN

Bitumen is a thick, black material, which is melted and mixed with small pieces of rock to make the top surface of roads (**Figure 17.9**).

▲ Figure 17.9 Bitumen is used in road construction.

ENVIRONMENTAL PROBLEMS ASSOCIATED WITH THE BURNING OF FOSSIL FUELS FROM CRUDE OIL

There are major environmental problems associated with the burning of fossil fuels derived from crude oil. First of all, the carbon dioxide produced when hydrocarbons are burned is a greenhouse gas. Greenhouse gases *trap the heat radiated from the Earth's surface (originally from the Sun)* and scientists have shown that this is contributing to climate change. For more discussion on the greenhouse effect, see **Chapter 10**.

> **KEY POINT**
>
> **Fossil fuels** include coal, gas and fuels derived from crude oil. These all come from things that were once alive.

ACID RAIN: SULFUR DIOXIDE AND OXIDES OF NITROGEN

KEY POINT

Several oxides of nitrogen are involved, including NO and NO_2. They are often given the general formula NO_x.

EXAM HINT

Carbon dioxide may contribute to climate change, but it does not cause acid rain.

▲ Figure 17.10 Use of very low-sulfur fuels limits the production of sulfur dioxide, but the spark in a petrol engine causes oxygen and nitrogen from the air to combine to make oxides of nitrogen, NO_x.

▲ Figure 17.11 Trees dying from the effects of acid rain.

Rain is naturally slightly acidic (pH = ~5.6) because of dissolved carbon dioxide. Acid rain is rain with a pH lower than this (pH < 5.6) because of the presence of various pollutants. The pH of acid rain is often about 4.

Acid rain is formed when water and oxygen in the atmosphere react with sulfur dioxide to produce sulfuric acid (H_2SO_4), or with various oxides of nitrogen, NO_x, to give nitric acid (HNO_3). SO_2 and NO_x come mainly from power stations and factories burning fossil fuels, or from motor vehicles (**Figure 17.10**).

Fossil fuels contain a small amount of sulfur. When the fuel is burned, the sulfur reacts with oxygen, producing sulfur dioxide:

$$S(s) + O_2(g) \rightarrow SO_2(g)$$

Reactions in the atmosphere with oxygen and water can convert this to *sulfuric acid (H_2SO_4)*, a strong acid and an important component of acid rain:

$$2SO_2(g) + 2H_2O(l) + O_2(g) \rightarrow 2H_2SO_4(aq)$$

Note: when sulfur dioxide reacts with water, a weaker acid called *sulfurous acid (H_2SO_3)* is formed:

$$SO_2(g) + H_2O(l) \rightarrow H_2SO_3(aq)$$

In petrol engines, **sparks** are used to ignite the petrol–air mixture to power the car. The temperature reached in the engine is high enough to allow nitrogen and oxygen in the air to combine to produce oxides of nitrogen. For example:

$$N_2(g) + O_2(g) \rightarrow 2NO(g)$$

These nitrogen oxides can be converted to *nitric acid (HNO_3)* in the atmosphere and therefore contribute to acid rain.

Acid rain is a major problem, mainly because of its devastating effect on trees (see **Figure 17.11**) and on life in lakes. Acid rain kills trees and fish in lakes. In some lakes the water is so acidic that it will not support life at all. Limestone buildings and marble statues (both made of *calcium carbonate*) and some metals such as iron are also attacked by acid rain.

Reaction between limestone and sulfuric acid:

$$CaCO_3(s) + H_2SO_4(aq) \rightarrow CaSO_4(s) + H_2O(l) + CO_2(g)$$

The solution to acid rain involves removing sulfur from fuels (this is usually done for petrol used in cars), '**scrubbing**' the gases from power stations and factories to remove SO_2 and NO_x, and using catalytic converters in cars.

CHAPTER QUESTIONS

Exam-style questions on crude oil can be found at the end of Unit 4 on page 290.

1 Which method can be used to separate gasoline from diesel?
   A crystallisation
   B filtration
   C distillation
   D diffusion

2 Which use is *not* correct for the named fraction?
   A bitumen for building roads
   B gasoline for ship fuel
   C refinery gas for cooking
   D kerosene for aircraft fuel

3 Copy and complete the following sentences.
   a Hydrocarbons are compounds containing _____ and _____ only.

SKILLS CRITICAL THINKING

b Crude oil is a type of _____ _____ It is a _____ of hydrocarbons. The different _____ of crude oil are separated by _____ distillation due to their different _____ _____ The names of the main fractions obtained from crude oil are _____ _____, _____, _____, _____, _____, _____, _____, and _____ As you go down the fractionating column, the colour of the fractions becomes _____, the boiling point of the fractions _____ and the viscosity of the fractions _____

c Fuel is a substance that, when burned, releases _____ _____

d Sulfur dioxide in the air can react with _____ and _____ to form a strong acid called _____ acid, which contributes to the environmental problem of _____ _____

e Incomplete combustion of hydrocarbons produces _____ _____ which is toxic, because it reduces the capacity of blood to transport _____

SKILLS CRITICAL THINKING

4 Crude oil is a mixture of hydrocarbons.
   a State which two elements are present in the compounds in crude oil.
   b Crude oil is separated into fractions by fractional distillation. Why does distillation separate different types of liquids?
   c Two of the fractions are gasoline and diesel. State one use of each.
   d Name two fractions formed in the fractional distillation of crude oil, other than gasoline and diesel.
   e Describe the differences between gasoline and diesel. In your answer you should refer to the average size of the molecules in the two liquids, the colour of the two liquids and the viscosities of the two liquids.
   f One of the hydrocarbons found in the diesel fraction is $C_{18}H_{38}$. Suggest the formula of a hydrocarbon that could be found in the gasoline fraction.

SKILLS PROBLEM SOLVING

   g i Write a balanced chemical equation for the complete combustion of butane, C_4H_{10}.

SKILLS REASONING

      ii Incomplete combustion of hydrocarbons produces carbon monoxide. Explain why carbon monoxide is harmful to humans.

SKILLS REASONING

5 Explain why:
   a burning a fuel containing sulfur as an impurity causes acid rain
   b petrol engines produce oxides of nitrogen
   c the presence of too much sulfur dioxide, SO_2, in the atmosphere has a damaging effect on many buildings made of marble, a form of calcium carbonate, $CaCO_3$.

SKILLS REASONING AND ANALYSIS

6 a State the difference in the following properties for two different hydrocarbons: pentane C_5H_{12} and dodecane $C_{12}H_{26}$
      i colour
      ii viscosity
      iii boiling point
   b Name a process that could be used to separate pentane and dodecane.

18 ALKANES

SPECIFICATION REFERENCES: 4.19–4.21

The hydrocarbons separated from the fractional distillation of crude oil are mainly alkanes. This is the simplest family of hydrocarbons, containing only carbon–carbon and carbon–hydrogen single bonds. Here we look into the structures and chemical reactions of these compounds in more detail. It is assumed that you have already read **Chapter 16** (Introduction to Organic Chemistry).

LEARNING OBJECTIVES

- Know the general formula for alkanes.
- Explain why alkanes are classified as saturated hydrocarbons.
- Understand how to draw the structural and displayed formulae for alkanes with up to five carbon atoms in the molecule and to name the unbranched-chain isomers.

The alkanes are the simplest family of hydrocarbons. Hydrocarbons are compounds that contain carbon and hydrogen only.

Many of the alkanes are used as fuels (**Figure 18.1**). Methane is the major component of natural gas. Ethane and propane are also present in small quantities in natural gas. Propane and butane are important constituents of liquefied petroleum gases (LPG) from crude oil distillation (discussed in **Chapter 17**).

The first five members of the alkanes family are shown in **Table 18.1**.

▲ Figure 18.1 The small alkanes are gases and are burned as fuels.

Table 18.1 The first five unbranched alkanes.

Name	Molecular formula	Structural formula	Displayed formula
methane	CH_4	CH_4	
ethane	C_2H_6	CH_3CH_3	
propane	C_3H_8	$CH_3CH_2CH_3$	
butane	C_4H_{10}	$CH_3CH_2CH_2CH_3$	
pentane	C_5H_{12}	$CH_3CH_2CH_2CH_2CH_3$	

EXAM HINT

The alkanes are described as *saturated* hydrocarbons because they contain only C–C single bonds and have no double (C=C) or triple (C≡C) bonds. A way of thinking about this is that the alkanes are saturated with hydrogen, in other words they have the maximum number of hydrogen atoms possible for that number of carbon atoms. But do not write this down as a definition in the exam!

4 ORGANIC CHEMISTRY 18 ALKANES

NAMING ORGANIC COMPOUNDS

Names for organic compounds can appear quite complicated, but they are simply a code that describes the molecule. Each part of a name tells you something specific about the molecule. One part of a name tells you how many carbon atoms there are in the longest chain, another part tells you whether there are any carbon–carbon double bonds, and so on.

CODING FOR THE CHAIN LENGTH

Look for the code letters in the name – these are given in **Table 18.2**.

Table 18.2 Coding for the chain length

Code letters	Number of carbons in chain
meth	1
eth	2
prop	3
but	4
pent	5

EXAM HINT

You have to learn these! The first four are the difficult ones because there is no pattern. However, a mnemonic can help, something like **M**onkeys **E**at **P**ink **B**ananas. Or you could think of one of your own that you can remember!
'**Pent**' means five as in **pent**agon.

CODING FOR THE TYPE OF COMPOUND

Alkanes are *saturated hydrocarbons and their names* are coded with the ending '**ane**'. For example, eth*ane* is a two-carbon chain (because of 'eth') with a carbon–carbon single bond, CH_3-CH_3. Other types of organic compounds will have different endings in their names.

STRUCTURAL VARIATIONS OF ORGANIC MOLECULES

Sometimes it is possible to have molecules with the same molecular formula, but different structural or displayed formulae.

Examples will make this clear.

DIFFERENT MOLECULES OF C_5H_{12}

If you had some molecular models and picked out 5 carbon atoms and 12 hydrogen atoms, you would find it was possible to join them together in more than one way (see **Figure 18.2**). The different molecules formed are known as isomers. All have the molecular formula C_5H_{12}, but different structures.

HINT

You do not need to worry about how to name any molecules which have a branched carbon chain.

$CH_3-CH_2-CH_2-CH_2-CH_3$ pentane

$CH_3-CH(CH_3)-CH_2-CH_3$ 2-methylbutane

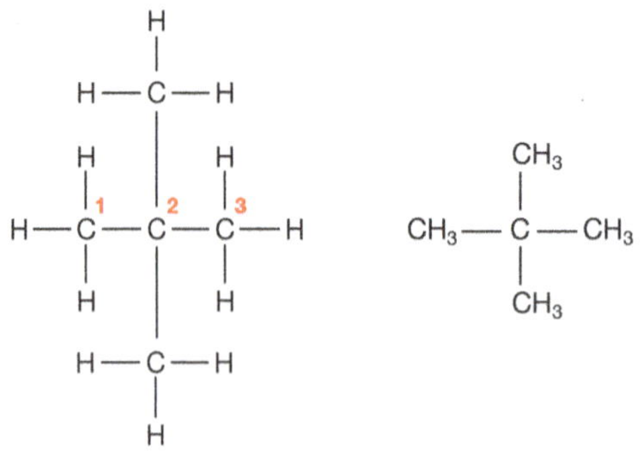

▲ Figure 18.2 There are three different molecules with the molecular formula C_5H_{12}. These can be shown as either displayed formulae or structural formulae.

If you look carefully at the structures in **Figure 18.2** you can see that you could not change one into the other simply by bending or twisting the molecule. You would have to break some bonds and reconnect the atoms.

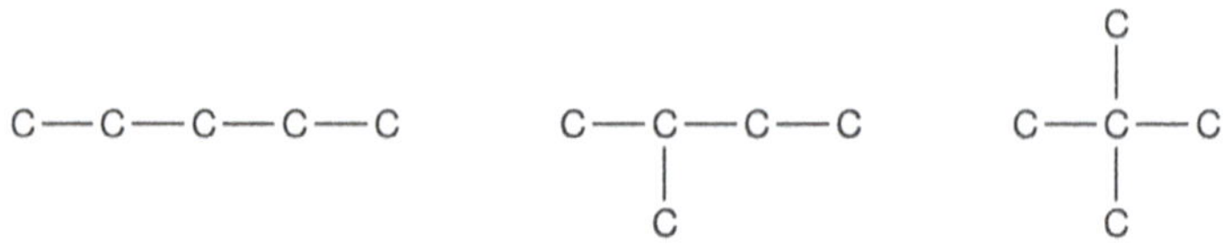

The **straight chain** molecule is called pentane. The *branched chain* molecule in the middle has a four-carbon chain ('butane') and a CH_3 group on the second carbon. The final *branched chain* molecule, which has a three-carbon chain ('propane') and two CH_3 groups on the second carbon, is yet another form.

Students frequently think they can find another molecule as well. If you look closely at this 'fourth' one (see **Figure 18.3**) you will see that it is just the second molecule rotated in space.

To avoid this sort of problem, always draw your structural or displayed formula so that *the longest carbon chain is drawn horizontally* (or draw them out again without the H atoms to check).

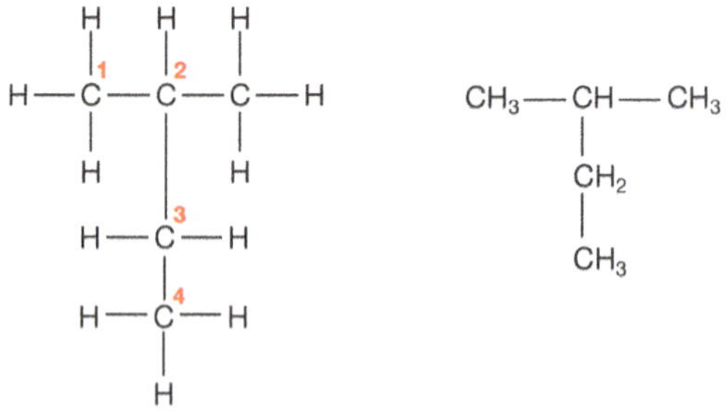

▲ Figure 18.3 There is no fourth isomer for C_5H_{12}.

> **EXAM HINT**
>
> It is sometimes easier to see that the molecules are different by drawing only the C atoms joined together, without the hydrogens.
>
> But you must show the hydrogen atoms in the exam!

> **REMINDER**
>
> A straight chain is an unbranched chain.

MEMBERS OF THE ALKANE FAMILY

The members of the alkane family
- can be described by the same general formula
- differ from the next by a $-CH_2-$ unit
- show a trend (gradation) in physical properties
- have similar chemical properties.

The alkanes form the simplest organic compounds and they are all saturated. The alkanes contain only single C–C and C–H bonds, which are the basis of all other organic compounds.

MEMBERS OF THE ALKANE FAMILY HAVE THE SAME GENERAL FORMULA

In the case of the alkanes, if there are n carbons, there are $2n + 2$ hydrogens.

The general formula for the alkanes is **C_nH_{2n+2}**.

So, for example, if there are three carbons, there are $(2 \times 3) + 2 = 8$ hydrogens. The formula for propane is C_3H_8.

If you want the formula for an alkane with 15 carbons, you could work out that it is $C_{15}H_{32}$ and so on.

The reason that the alkanes can be described by a general formula is that each member differs from the next by a –CH$_2$– unit (see **Figure 18.4**).

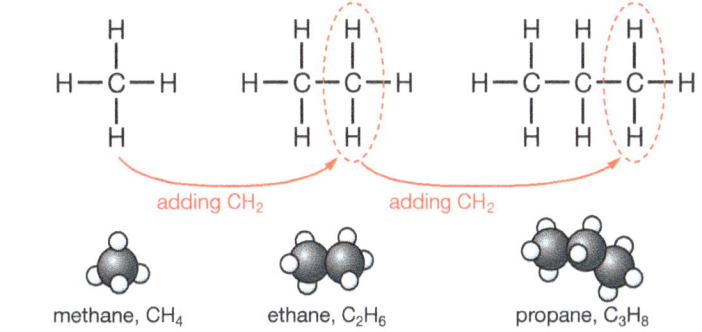

▲ Figure 18.4 The three smallest alkanes. Each member differs from the next by a –CH$_2$– unit.

MEMBERS OF THE ALKANE FAMILY SHOW A TREND (GRADATION) IN PHYSICAL PROPERTIES

Figure 18.5 shows the boiling points of the first eight alkanes.

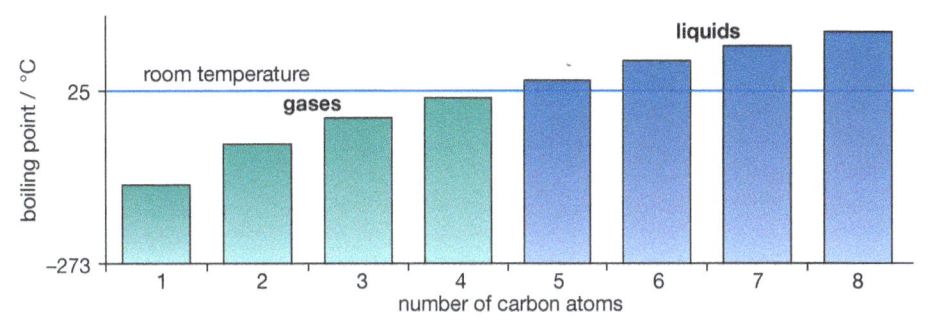

▲ Figure 18.5 Boiling points of the first eight alkanes

The first four alkanes are gases at room temperature (~25 °C). All the other alkanes you are likely to see at International GCSE are liquids. Solids start to appear at about $C_{18}H_{38}$.

The molecules of the alkane family increase in size in a regular way and you can see that the *boiling points* also *increase* in a regular way.

As the molecules become bigger, the strength of the *intermolecular forces of attraction* between them *increases*. This means that *more energy* has to be put in to *break* the attractions between one molecule and its neighbours.

MEMBERS OF THE ALKANE FAMILY HAVE SIMILAR CHEMICAL PROPERTIES

Chemical properties are dependent on the bonding within the molecules. Because alkanes only contain carbon–carbon single bonds and carbon–hydrogen bonds, they are all going to behave in the same way. These are strong bonds, therefore alkanes are fairly unreactive organic compounds and are often thought of as being quite **inert**.

KEY POINT

The alkanes are not inert in the sense that they do not react with anything, like neon for example, but they are not very reactive for organic compounds.

COMBUSTION OF THE ALKANES

COMBUSTION

HINT

Do not try to learn these equations! Practise working them out for a wide range of different hydrocarbons. You will find guidance on how to work out the ethane equation in **Chapter 5**, page 165.

All alkanes burn in air or oxygen. If there is enough oxygen, they burn *completely* to give *carbon dioxide* and *water*, for example:

$$2C_2H_6(g) + 7O_2(g) \rightarrow 4CO_2(g) + 6H_2O(l)$$

Propane is frequently used in camping stoves outdoors (see **Figure 18.6**).

Propane burning:

$$C_3H_8(g) + 5O_2(g) \rightarrow 3CO_2(g) + 4H_2O(l)$$

▶ Figure 18.6 The burning of a camping stove

EXAM HINT

Remember, in combustion reactions it is highly unlikely that hydrogen, H_2, will be formed as a product because hydrogen is very flammable. You always obtain water, H_2O, even if there is insufficient oxygen.

If there is not enough oxygen, the hydrocarbons undergo incomplete combustion. You obtain *carbon monoxide* or *carbon (soot)* instead of carbon dioxide, for example:

$$2C_2H_6(g) + 5O_2(g) \rightarrow 4CO(g) + 6H_2O(l)$$

or

$$2C_2H_6(g) + 3O_2(g) \rightarrow 4C(s) + 6H_2O(l)$$

CHAPTER QUESTIONS

Exam-style questions on alkanes can be found at the end of Unit 4 on page 290.

1 Which compound is *not* an alkane?

   A C_2H_4 **B** C_3H_8 **C** C_2H_6 **D** C_4H_{10}

SKILLS CRITICAL THINKING

2 a Alkanes are *saturated* hydrocarbons. Explain the term *saturated*.

   b Undecane is an alkane with 11 carbon atoms.

     i Write down the molecular formula for undecane.

SKILLS REASONING

     ii What physical state (solid, liquid or gas) would you expect undecane to be in at room temperature (25 °C)?

SKILLS PROBLEM SOLVING

     iii Write a balanced chemical equation for the complete combustion of undecane.

     iv Write a balanced chemical equation for the incomplete combustion of undecane to produce carbon monoxide and explain why this reaction is harmful to humans.

4 ORGANIC CHEMISTRY — 18 ALKANES

SKILLS CRITICAL THINKING

3 a Write down the names of the following hydrocarbons.
   i CH_4
   ii $CH_3CH_2CH_3$
   iii $CH_3CH_2CH_2CH_2CH_3$

SKILLS INTERPRETATION

b Draw displayed and structural formulae for.
   i ethane
   ii pentane

SKILLS ANALYSIS

4 a Write the molecular formulae of the following compounds.

   i, ii, iii (displayed structural formulae shown)

b Name compound **ii** in **a**.

SKILLS INTERPRETATION

5 Draw two molecules which have the same molecular formula but different displayed formulae to the following compound.

   (displayed formula of a 5-carbon straight-chain alkane shown)

6 Below is a table of the first four members of the alkane family and their boiling points:

Alkane	Boiling point (°C)
methane	−162
ethane	−89
propane	−42
butane	−1

SKILLS INTERPRETATION

a Plot the data on a bar chart (plot boiling points on the y-axis against the number of carbon atoms in the alkanes on the x-axis).

SKILLS ANALYSIS AND PROBLEM SOLVING

b Use your graph to predict the boiling point of pentane.

SKILLS REASONING

c Explain the trend in the boiling point in the alkane family.

19 ALKENES

SPECIFICATION REFERENCES: 4.23–4.26, 4.28

The alkenes are another family of hydrocarbons. They all contain a carbon–carbon double bond. Alkenes can be produced from alkanes and they are much more reactive than the alkanes.

▶ Figure 19.1 Sunflower oil is unsaturated and contains lots of C=C groups.

LEARNING OBJECTIVES

- Know that alkenes contain the functional group >C=C<.
- Know the general formula for alkenes.
- Explain why alkenes are classified as unsaturated hydrocarbons.
- Understand how to draw the structural and displayed formulae for alkenes with up to four carbon atoms in the molecule, and name the unbranched-chain isomers.
- Describe how bromine water can be used to distinguish between an alkane and an alkene.

HINT

A way of thinking about this is: the functional group is what makes the behaviour of a particular compound different from that of an alkane.

KEY POINT

It is not possible to have an alkene with one carbon atom because alkenes must contain a C=C group so you need a minimum of two carbon atoms.

The alkenes are a family of hydrocarbons which contain a carbon–carbon double bond. The **C=C** bond is the functional group of the alkenes.

A **functional group** is *an atom or a group of atoms that determine the chemical properties of a compound*. All compounds in the same family have the same functional group.

The first three members of the alkene series are shown in **Table 19.1**.

Table 19.1 The first three alkenes

Name	Molecular formula	Structural formula	Displayed formula
ethene	C_2H_4	$CH_2=CH_2$	
propene	C_3H_6	$CH_2=CHCH_3$	
but-1-ene	C_4H_8	$CH_2=CHCH_2CH_3$	

The presence of the C=C double bond in the alkenes family is shown in their name by the ending '**ene**'. For example, eth*ene* is a two-carbon chain containing a C=C double bond, $CH_2=CH_2$. With longer chains, the position of the double bond could vary in the chain. This is shown by numbering the chain and noting which carbon atom the double bond *starts* from (**Table 19.2**).

Table 19.2 Indicating the position of the double bond in the name of alkenes

Formula	Name	Description
CH$_2$=CHCH$_2$CH$_3$	but-1-ene	a four-carbon chain with a double bond starting on the first carbon
CH$_3$CH=CHCH$_3$	but-2-ene	a four-carbon chain with a double bond starting on the second carbon

How do you know which end of the chain to number from? The rule is that *you number from the end which produces the smaller numbers in the name*.

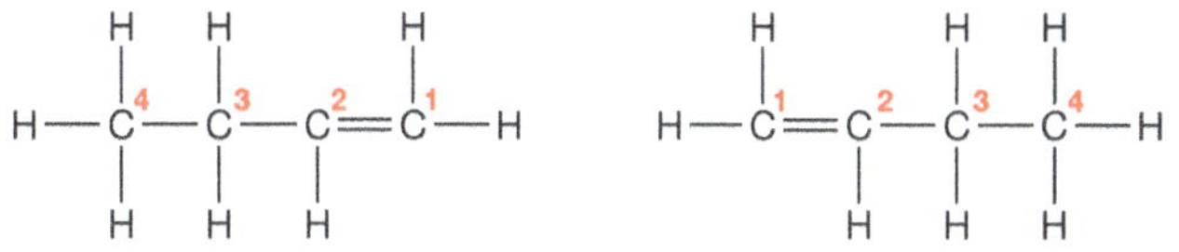

▲ Figure 19.2 Both structures represent but-1-ene.

> **HINT**
>
> Both parts of **Figure 19.2** show the same molecule, but in one case it has been turned over so that what was originally on the left is now on the right, and vice versa. It would be silly to change the name every time the molecule moved! Both of the forms in **Figure 19.2** are called but-1-ene.

STRUCTURAL VARIATIONS IN THE ALKENES

ETHENE AND PROPENE

It is not possible to draw an alternative alkene molecule with the same molecular formula but different structural formula to ethene CH$_2$=CH$_2$ or propene CH$_3$CH=CH$_2$.

> **EXTENSION**
>
> There is a form of C$_3$H$_6$ that does not have a C=C double bond. It has three carbon atoms joined in a ring. It is called cyclopropane, which indicates 'a ring of three carbons with only single bonds between them'.

STRUCTURAL VARIATIONS OF C$_4$H$_8$

There are three structural forms with the molecular formula C$_4$H$_8$ and containing a C=C double bond (see **Figure 19.3**).

Notice the way that you can vary the position of the double bond as well as branching the chain.

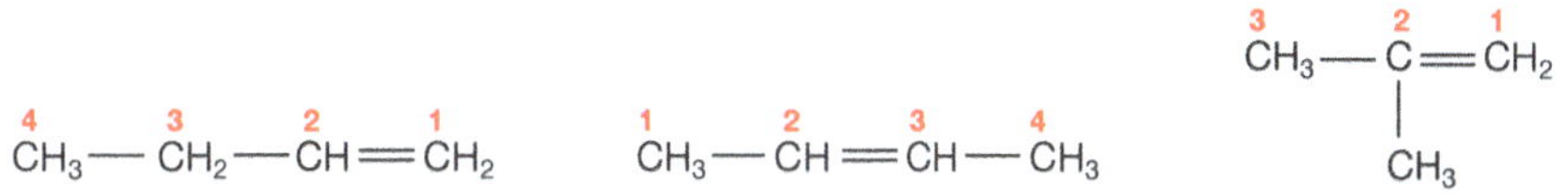

> **HINT**
>
> A way of thinking about this is that the alkenes are not saturated with H atoms, they do not have the maximum number of H atoms for that number of C atoms.

▲ Figure 19.3 Structural variations with the molecular formula of C$_4$H$_8$

UNSATURATED HYDROCARBONS

Alkenes are **unsaturated compounds** because they contain a C=C bond. *A saturated compound contains single C–C bonds only whereas an unsaturated compound contains one or more double C=C or triple C≡C bonds.*

THE GENERAL FORMULA

Alkenes have the general formula **C$_n$H$_{2n}$**. The number of hydrogen atoms is twice the number of carbon atoms.

The alkene with 11 carbon atoms will have 22 hydrogen atoms and the molecular formula C$_{11}$H$_{22}$.

PHYSICAL PROPERTIES

These are very similar to those of the alkanes. Remember that the small alkanes with up to four carbon atoms are gases at room temperature. The same is true for the alkenes. They are gases up to C_4H_8, and the next dozen or so are liquids. Again, the members of the same family of organic compounds *show a trend in physical properties*.

CHEMICAL REACTIONS OF THE ALKENES

COMBUSTION

In common with all hydrocarbons, alkenes burn in air or oxygen to give carbon dioxide and water, for example:

$$C_2H_4(g) + 3O_2(g) \rightarrow 2CO_2(g) + 2H_2O(l)$$

This is not a reaction anybody would ever choose to do. Alkenes are much too useful to waste by burning them.

THE ADDITION OF BROMINE

Bromine can react with alkenes at room temperature. The reaction is often carried out using bromine water (aqueous bromine solution).

You know a reaction has happened because bromine water is *orange* but the product of the reaction is a *colourless* liquid.

THE TEST FOR UNSATURATED COMPOUNDS

Any compound with a C=C double bond will react with bromine in a similar way. If you shake an unknown organic compound with bromine water and the orange bromine water is *decolourised* (the colour changes from orange to colourless), the compound contains a C=C double bond. If your unknown compound is a gas, you can simply bubble it through bromine water with the same effect.

> **EXAM HINT**
>
> You must be careful with the words you use here: the final mixture is *colourless* and not clear. Do not use the word clear. Clear means not cloudy, you can see through it. The bromine water is clear as well as the product of the reaction.

The left-hand tube in **Figure 19.4** shows the effect of shaking a liquid alkene with bromine water. The organic layer (containing the alkene) is on top. You can see that the bromine water has been completely decolourised, showing the presence of the C=C double bond.

The right-hand tube in **Figure 19.4** shows what happens if you use a liquid alkane, which does not have a C=C double bond. The colour of the bromine is still there. Alkanes do not decolourise bromine water because they do not contain a C=C double bond.

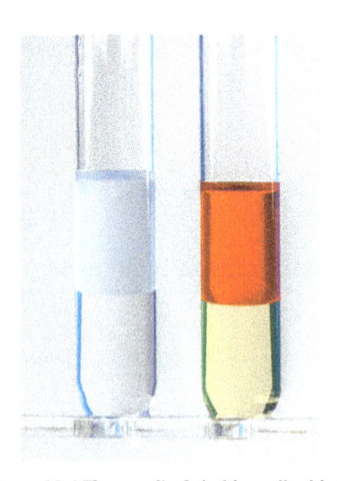

▲ Figure 19.4 The result of shaking a liquid alkene (left) or alkane (right) with bromine water.

CHAPTER QUESTIONS

Exam-style questions on alkenes can be found at the end of Unit 4 on page 290.

1 Which of the following describes the correct colour change of bromine water when propene is bubbled into it?

    A clear to orange   C orange to colourless
    B colourless to orange   D brown to clear

4 ORGANIC CHEMISTRY
19 ALKENES

SKILLS CRITICAL THINKING

2 a Write down the names of the following hydrocarbons.
       i $CH_3CH=CH_2$ ii $CH_2=CH_2$ iii $CH_2=CHCH_2CH_3$

SKILLS INTERPRETATION

  b Draw the displayed and structural formulae for but-2-ene.

3 The alkenes all belong to the same family of organic compounds.

SKILLS CRITICAL THINKING

  a i State two characteristics of the members of this family.
       ii Explain the term *unsaturated*.

  b Ethene is the simplest member of the alkenes. Bromine water can be used to distinguish alkenes from alkanes.

SKILLS PROBLEM SOLVING, INTERPRETATION

    i Bromine water is added to ethene. State the starting colour of the bromine water and the finishing colour of the reaction mixture.
       ii The same experiment is repeated with ethane instead of ethene. State the finishing colour of the mixture.

SKILLS INTERPRETATION

  c Sometimes compounds can have the same molecular formula but different displayed formulae. Draw the displayed formulae of three alkene molecules that have the molecular formula C_4H_8.

  d Draw any other structural variations of C_4H_8 which are *not* alkenes.

4 A gaseous hydrocarbon, **P**, with three carbon atoms, decolourises bromine water.

SKILLS CRITICAL THINKING

  a Explain what the decolorisation of the bromine water tests for.

  b Draw the displayed formula for the hydrocarbon.

5 The table shows the structures of some organic compounds.

Compound	Formula
A	(cyclopropane: three carbons in a ring, each with 2 H)
B	$CH_3CH_2CH_2CH_2CH_3$
C	H–C(H)(H)–C(H)=C–C(H)(H)–C(H)(H)–H (pent-2-ene displayed)
D	H–C(H)(H)–C(H)(H)–C(H)(H)–O–H
E	C_4H_{10}

SKILLS CRITICAL THINKING

  a Which of these compounds are hydrocarbons?

SKILLS CRITICAL THINKING

  b Which of these compounds are unsaturated?

  c One of the possible molecules with the molecular formula in **E** is butane.

SKILLS INTERPRETATION

    i Draw the structural formula of butane.

SKILLS REASONING

    ii Explain why butane is an alkane, not an alkene.

20 SYNTHETIC POLYMERS

SPECIFICATION REFERENCES: 4.44–4.47

Polymers are everywhere, ranging from naturally occurring polymers, for example proteins (polypeptides) and sugar (polysaccharides), which you probably have met before, to synthetic polymers used for plastic bags and clothing. Polymers are large molecules consisting of many repeat units. This chapter looks at one way that polymers can be made: addition polymerisation for polymers such as poly(ethene).

▲ Figure 20.1 Synthetic polymers are extremely useful for making a variety of products, from the coating for electrical wires to plastic bottles and intelligent label chips.

LEARNING OBJECTIVES

- Know that an addition polymer is formed by joining up many small molecules called monomers.
- Understand how to draw the repeat unit of the addition polymer poly(ethene).
- Understand how to deduce the structure of a monomer from the repeat unit of an addition polymer and vice versa.
- Explain problems in the disposal of addition polymers, including:
  - their inertness and inability to biodegrade
  - the production of toxic gases when they are burned.

ADDITION POLYMERISATION

THE POLYMERISATION OF ETHENE

Ethene is the smallest hydrocarbon containing a C=C double bond. **Figure 20.2** shows different ways of representing an ethene molecule.

C_2H_4 $CH_2{=}CH_2$

▲ Figure 20.2 Ethene

Under the right conditions, molecules containing C=C double bonds can join together to produce very long chains (see **Figure 20.3**). Part of the double bond is broken to become a single bond, and the electrons in it are used to join to neighbouring molecules.

Polymerisation is the joining up of lots of small molecules (**monomers**) to make one big molecule (**polymer**). In the case of ethene, lots of ethene molecules join together to make *poly(ethene)*, which is more usually called *polythene. Molecules simply add onto each other without anything else being formed*. This is called **addition polymerisation**.

4 ORGANIC CHEMISTRY   20 SYNTHETIC POLYMERS   285

KEY POINT

An *initiator* is used to start the process. You must not call it a catalyst because it is consumed in the reaction.

EXTENSION

People occasionally wonder what happens at the ends of the chains. They do not end tidily! Bits of the initiator are bonded on at either end. You do not need to worry about that for International GCSE.

KEY POINT

In this structure for poly(ethene) *n* represents a large but variable number. It simply means that the structure in the brackets (called the *repeat unit*) repeats itself many times in the molecule. When representing a polymer, the bonds on the two sides of the repeat unit should extend outside the square brackets to show that the carbon atoms are joined to the next ones in a chain, as shown in **Figure 20.4**.

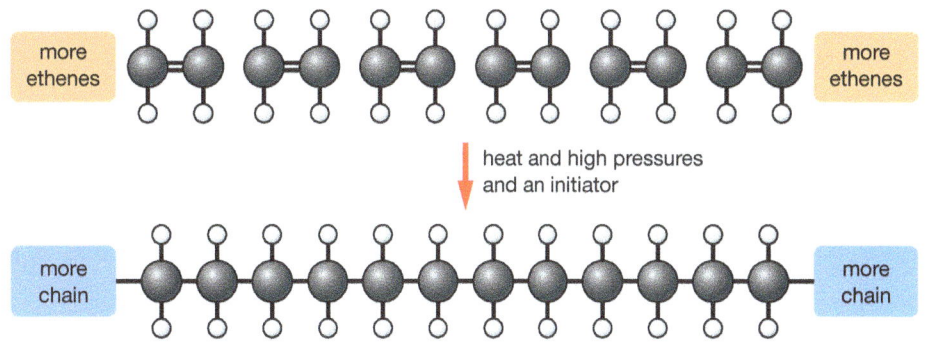

▲ Figure 20.3 The polymerisation of ethene

The chain length can vary from about 4000 to 40 000 carbon atoms.

For normal purposes, the polymerisation reaction is written using displayed formulae (see **Figure 20.4**).

▲ Figure 20.4 Formation of poly(ethene)

EXAM HINT

Make sure you can distinguish between the different terms monomer, polymer and **repeat unit**. In the equation in **Figure 20.4**, the monomer is $CH_2=CH_2$, the polymer is $-[CH_2-CH_2]_n-$ and the repeat unit is $-CH_2-CH_2-$.

USES FOR POLY(ETHENE)

KEY POINT

Although the polymer is called *poly(ethene)* it is actually an *alkane*. The polymer is saturated and will not decolourise bromine water.

Poly(ethene) comes in two types: low-density poly(ethene) (LDPE) and high-density poly(ethene) (HDPE). Low-density poly(ethene) is mainly used as a thin film to make polythene bags (**Figure 20.5**). It is very flexible and not very strong.

▲ Figure 20.5 Plastic bags made from poly(ethene)

High-density poly(ethene) is used where greater strength and rigidity are needed, for example to make plastic bottles such as milk bottles. If you can find a recycling symbol with the letters HDPE next to it, then the bottle is made of high-density poly(ethene).

HOW TO DEDUCE THE POLYMERISATION REACTION FOR ANY ALKENE

Figure 20.6 shows how to work out a polymerisation reaction starting from any alkene. The key thing is to always draw the alkene as shown with just the C=C in the middle.

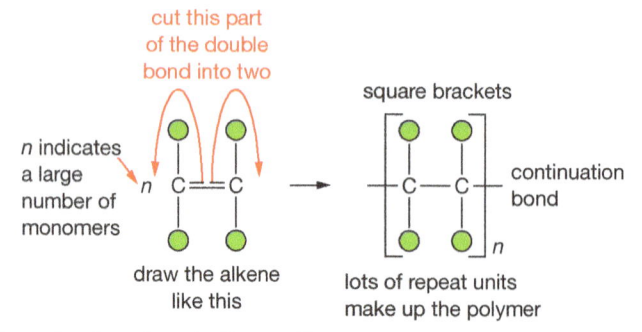

▲ Figure 20.6 How to work out a polymerisation reaction

OTHER TYPES OF ADDITION POLYMERS

THE POLYMERISATION OF PROPENE

Propene is another alkene, this time with three carbon atoms in each molecule. Its formula is normally written as $CH_3CH=CH_2$. Think of it as a modified ethene molecule, with a CH_3 group attached in place of one of the hydrogen atoms (**Figure 20.7**).

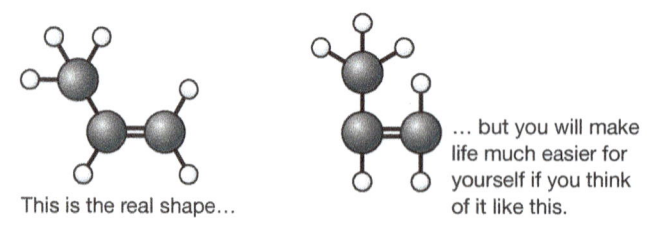

▲ Figure 20.7 Propene

When propene is polymerised you obtain *poly(propene)* (see **Figures 20.8** and **20.9**). This used to be called *polypropylene*.

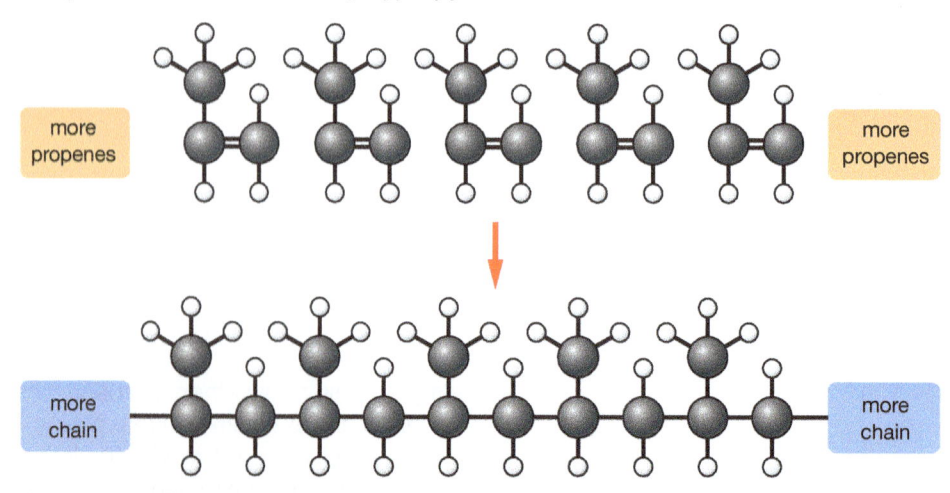

▲ Figure 20.8 The polymerisation of propene

4 ORGANIC CHEMISTRY
20 SYNTHETIC POLYMERS

EXAM HINT

When you draw an addition polymerisation reaction never change anything except opening out the double bond and drawing the continuation bonds on each side.

Write this as:

$$n \begin{array}{c} CH_3 \; H \\ C=C \\ H \; \; H \end{array} \longrightarrow \left[\begin{array}{c} CH_3 \; H \\ -C-C- \\ H \; \; H \end{array} \right]_n$$

▲ Figure 20.9 Formation of poly(propene)

THE POLYMERISATION OF CHLOROETHENE

Chloroethene is a molecule in which one of the hydrogen atoms in ethene is replaced by a chlorine. Its formula is $CH_2=CHCl$. In the past, it was called vinyl chloride. Polymerising chloroethene gives you *poly(chloroethene)* (see **Figures 20.10** and **20.11**). This is usually known by its old name, polyvinylchloride or PVC.

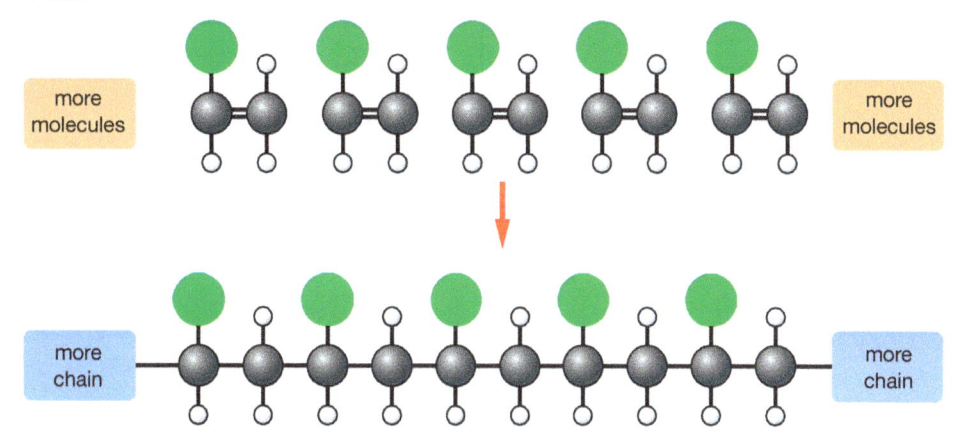

▲ Figure 20.10 The polymerisation of chloroethene

Write this as:

$$n \begin{array}{c} Cl \; \; H \\ C=C \\ H \; \; H \end{array} \longrightarrow \left[\begin{array}{c} Cl \; \; H \\ -C-C- \\ H \; \; H \end{array} \right]_n$$

▲ Figure 20.11 Formation of poly(chloroethene)

HINT

When you draw this, it is not important whether you put the chlorine atom on the left-hand carbon atom or the right-hand one.

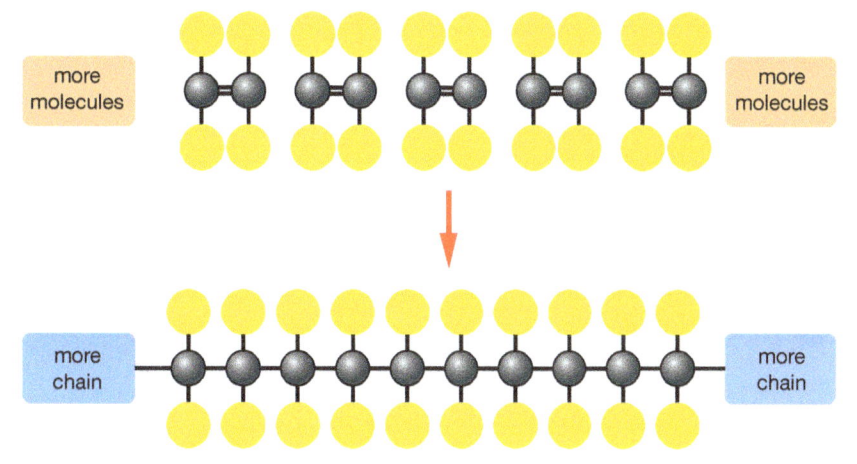

THE POLYMERISATION OF TETRAFLUOROETHENE

Tetrafluoroethene is another molecule derived from ethene in which all four hydrogen atoms are replaced by fluorine. Its formula is $CF_2=CF_2$. Polymerising tetrafluoroethene gives you poly(tetrafluoroethene) or PTFE, more commonly known as Teflon® (see **Figures 20.12** and **20.13**).

▲ Figure 20.12 The polymerisation of tetrafluoroethene

KEY POINT

If you look at this reaction, you can see it is exactly the same as the polymerisation of ethene except that each H has been replaced by an F.

▲ Figure 20.13 Formation of poly(tetrafluoroethene)

WORKING OUT THE MONOMER FOR A GIVEN ADDITION POLYMER

In an exam you may find that you are given the structure of a polymer and asked to deduce what the repeat unit is or what monomer it was made from. **Figure 20.14** shows you how to do this.

▲ Figure 20.14 How to work out the repeat unit and monomer for poly(styrene)

The C_6H_5 group is complicated, but we do not need to worry about that when we write the structure of the monomer; work from the structure you are given. First find the repeat unit, which can be done simply by taking any two adjacent carbon atoms in the main polymer chain. To derive the monomer, a double bond needs to be put back between the two middle carbon atoms of the repeat unit.

DISPOSAL OF ADDITION POLYMERS

Recycling of plastics is important, not just to save raw materials, but because it takes a very long time for addition polymers like poly(ethene) and poly(chloroethene) to break down in the environment. They contain strong covalent bonds, making them essentially *inert* at ordinary temperatures. They are **non-biodegradable**, meaning *they cannot be broken down by bacteria in the environment*.

One solution to the problem of their disposal is to *bury them in landfill sites* (**Figure 20.15**), which are basically just big holes in the ground. However the plastic will remain unchanged for thousands of years.

Some countries, including Denmark and Japan, *incinerate (burn) plastics* in order to tackle the problem of disposal. This releases a lot of heat energy, which can be used to generate electricity. However, there are problems associated with this. For example, carbon dioxide is produced, which contributes to **global warming**. Toxic gases are also released, including carbon monoxide and hydrogen chloride.

▲ Figure 20.15 Plastics (and other rubbish) can be disposed of in landfill sites.

There are advantages and disadvantages for using either method to dispose of plastics.

Disposal method	Advantages	Disadvantages
landfill	No greenhouse gases or toxic gases produced from plastics Cheap	Ugly, smelly and noisy; no one wants to live next to a landfill site Uses large areas of land The waste will be there for thousands of years
incineration	Requires little space Can produce heat for local homes/offices and/or produce electricity	It is expensive to build and maintain the plant Produces greenhouse gases Releases toxic gases The ash produced must still be disposed of in landfill sites

CHAPTER QUESTIONS

Exam-style questions on synthetic polymers can be found at the end of Unit 4 on page 290.

1 Ethene, C_2H_4, is an important molecule used in industry. It is an *unsaturated hydrocarbon*.

   a Explain the terms *unsaturated* and *hydrocarbon*.

   b Ethene burns easily and releases a large amount of heat during combustion. Write a balanced chemical equation for the complete combustion of ethene.

   c Explain why in industry ethene is considered too valuable to be used as a fuel.

2 Propene, $\text{CH}_2=\text{CHCH}_3$, can be polymerised to make poly(propene).

   a Explain the term *polymerisation*.

   b Draw a diagram to represent the structure of a poly(propene) chain showing three repeat units.

   c The formation of poly(propene) is an example of *addition* polymerisation. Explain what is meant by the word *addition*.

   d Styrene has the formula $\text{C}_6\text{H}_5\text{CH}=\text{CH}_2$.

   Write a balanced chemical equation to show what happens when styrene is polymerised to make polystyrene. Your equation should clearly show the structure of the polystyrene (Show the C_6H_5 group as a whole).

   e A small part of a Perspex molecule, another addition polymer used as an alternative to glass, looks like this:

   [structure showing repeating units with H, CH₃, and C=O with OCH₃ side groups]

   Draw the structure of the monomer from which Perspex is made.

EXAM PRACTICE

1 Crude oil is a complex mixture of hydrocarbons. The diagram shows the separation of crude oil into simpler mixtures called fractions.

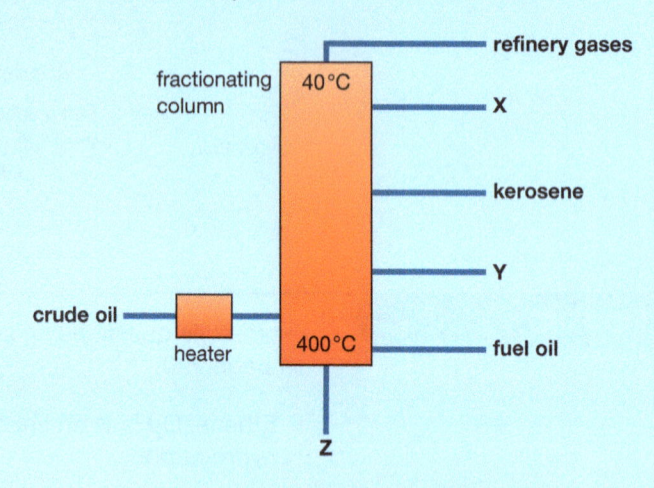

SKILLS ANALYSIS

a What could X, Y and Z represent (choose one answer)? (1)

	X	Y	Z
A	gasoline	bitumen	diesel
B	diesel	gasoline	bitumen
C	bitumen	gasoline	diesel
D	gasoline	diesel	bitumen

SKILLS CRITICAL THINKING

b State a use for the refinery gas fraction. (1)

c Name the liquid that leaves the fractionating column at the lowest temperature. (1)

d Different fractions in the crude oil are separated in the fractionating column due to their different boiling points. Describe and explain the relationship between the number of carbon atoms in a hydrocarbon and its boiling point. (3)

SKILLS PROBLEM SOLVING

e One of the hydrocarbons, $C_{15}H_{32}$, called pentadecane, is present in the kerosene fraction. It could be used as a fuel in jet engines. Write an equation for the incomplete combustion of pentadecane to produce carbon monoxide. (2)

f Give a reason why the incomplete combustion of kerosene can be poisonous to humans. (1)

(Total 9 marks)

2 The table shows the formulae of some organic compounds.

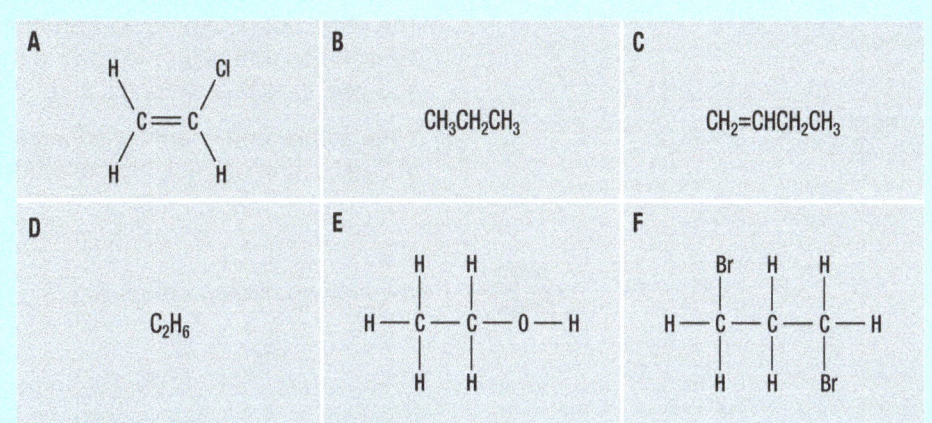

A	B	C
H₂C=CHCl (H,H on left C; H,Cl on right C)	CH₃CH₂CH₃	CH₂=CHCH₂CH₃

D	E	F
C₂H₆	H-C(H,H)-C(H,H)-O-H	H-C(Br,H)-C(H,H)-C(H,Br)-H

a Give a reason why compound **E** is *not* a hydrocarbon. (1)

b State the name of compound **B**. (1)

c Give the letters of compounds which are unsaturated. (1)

d Two of the compounds shown belong to the alkanes family.
  i Give the letters of these two compounds. (1)
  ii State the general formula of this family of compounds. (1)
  iii State *two* other characteristics of the compounds in this family apart from having the same general formula. (2)

e Compound **A** is a monomer which can undergo addition polymerisation.
  i Explain what is meant by the term monomer. (1)
  ii Draw the repeat unit of the addition polymer of compound **A**. (1)
  iii Many addition polymers, for example those used for making plastic bags, are not biodegradable. Used plastic bags can be either buried underground in landfill sites or incinerated. Evaluate both methods of disposal and describe which method you think is better, giving two advantages and two disadvantages of your choice. (4)

(Total 13 marks)

3 The set-up below is used to confirm the combustion products of a candle, which consists of a mixture of solid hydrocarbons.

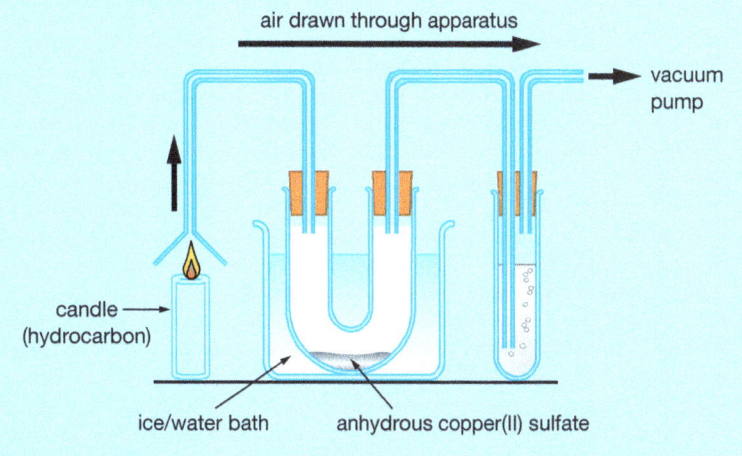

a One of the combustion products is water. State the starting and finishing colours of the anhydrous copper(II) sulfate in the U-tube. (2)

b State the purpose of the ice water bath. (1)

c The other possible product from the combustion is carbon dioxide. Name the solution that could be used in the boiling tube to test for carbon dioxide and give the observations if carbon dioxide is present. (3)

d Write a balanced chemical equation for the complete combustion of $C_{21}H_{44}$, one possible hydrocarbon present in wax. (3)

(Total 9 marks)

4 Below are two hydrocarbons with the molecular formula C_3H_6.

compound 1   compound 2

a Describe a chemical test for distinguishing between the two hydrocarbons and give the results for this test. (3)

b Compound 3 is in the same family of organic compounds as compound 1. Draw the displayed formulae for two other molecules which have the same molecular formula as compound 3, but different structures.

compound 3 (2)

(Total 5 marks)

5 This question is about addition polymers.

a Poly(propene) is an addition polymer made from propene, $CH_2=CHCH_3$. Draw a length of the poly(propene) chain showing two repeat units. (2)

b Another addition polymer, polyacrylamide, is used to make hydrogel in contact lenses, nappies and drug delivery systems. The structure of the polymer is shown in the diagram. Draw the structural formula of the monomer used to make polyacrylamide. (1)

(Total 3 marks)

6 The figure below shows a short length of a polymer.

```
    H   H   H   H   H   H
    |   |   |   |   |   |
  — C — C — C — C — C — C —
    |   |   |   |   |   |
    H  CH₂  H  CH₂  H  CH₂
        |       |       |
       CH₃     CH₃     CH₃
```

a What is the structure of the monomer used to make this polymer? (1)

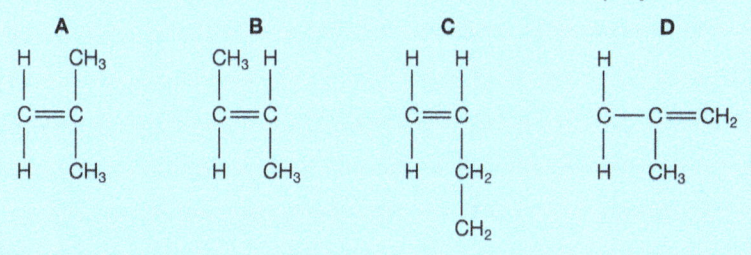

```
      A              B              C              D
   H   CH₃        CH₃  H         H   H          H
   |   |          |    |         |   |          |
   C = C          C =  C         C = C          C — C = CH₂
   |   |          |    |         |   |          |   |
   H   CH₃        H    CH₃       H   CH₂        H   CH₃
                                     |
                                     CH₂
```

b Draw the repeat unit for this polymer. (1)

c State the colour change when bromine water is added into this polymer and explain your reasoning. (2)

d Name the monomer used to make poly(chloroethene). (1)

(Total 5 marks)

1 MOVEMENT AND POSITION 295 | 2 FORCES AND SHAPE 308 | 3 FORCES AND MOVEMENT 314

PHYSICS UNIT 1
FORCES AND MOTION

Forces make things move, like this Atlas V rocket carrying the Cygnus spacecraft up to the International Space Station. Forces hold the particles of matter together and keep us on the Earth. Forces can make things slow down. This is useful when we apply the brakes when driving a car! Forces can change the shape of things, sometimes temporarily and sometimes permanently. Forces make things rotate and change direction.

1 MOVEMENT AND POSITION

SPECIFICATION REFERENCES: 1.1, 1.3–1.9

It is very useful to be able to make predictions about the way moving objects behave. In this chapter you will learn about some equations of motion that can be used to calculate the speed and acceleration of objects, and the distances they travel in a certain time.

▲ Figure 1.1 The world is full of speeding objects.

LEARNING OBJECTIVES

- Plot and explain distance–time graphs.
- Know and use the relationship between average speed, distance moved and time taken:

  $$\text{average speed} = \frac{\text{distance moved}}{\text{time taken}}$$

- Practical: Investigate the motion of everyday objects such as toy cars or tennis balls.
- Know and use the relationship between acceleration, change in velocity and time taken:

  $$\text{acceleration} = \frac{\text{change in velocity}}{\text{time taken}} \qquad a = \frac{(v-u)}{t}$$

- Plot and explain velocity–time graphs.
- Determine acceleration from the gradient of a velocity–time graph.
- Determine the distance travelled from the area between a velocity–time graph and the time axis.

KEY POINT

Sometimes the symbol v is used to represent average speed. Later you will see that we use v to represent the final velocity of an object and u to represent the starting velocity of an object.

UNITS

In this section you will need to use kilogram (kg) as the unit of mass, metre (m) as the unit of length, and second (s) as the unit of time, You will find measurements of mass made in subdivisions of the kilogram, like grams (g) and milligrams (mg), measurements of length in multiples of the metre, like the kilometre (km), and subdivisions like the centimetre (cm) and millimetre (mm). You will also be familiar with other units for time: minutes, hours, days and years etc. You will need to take care to convert units in calculations to the base units of kg, m and s when you meet these subdivisions and multiples.

Other units come from these base units. In the first chapter you will meet the units for:
- speed and velocity: metre per second (m/s)
- acceleration: metre per second squared (m/s^2).

In later chapters you will meet the units for:
- **force:** newton (N)
- gravitational field strength: newton per kilogram (N/kg).

Speed is a term that is often used in everyday life. Action films often feature high-speed chases. Speed is a cause of fatal accidents on the road. Sprinters aim for greater speed in competition with other athletes. Rockets must reach a high enough speed to put communications satellites in **orbit** around the Earth. This chapter will explain how speed is defined and measured and how distance–time graphs are used to show the movement of an object as time passes. We shall then look at changing speed – **acceleration** and **deceleration**. We shall use velocity–time graphs to find the acceleration of an object. We shall also find how far an object has travelled using its velocity–time graph.

AVERAGE SPEED

A car travels 100 kilometres in 2 hours so the average speed of the car is 50 km/h. You can work this out by doing a simple calculation using the following definition of speed:

$$\text{average speed}, v = \frac{\text{distance moved}, s}{\text{time taken}, t}$$

$$v = \frac{s}{t}$$

The average speed of the car during the journey is the total distance travelled, divided by the time taken for the journey. If you look at the speedometer in a car you will see that the speed of the car changes from instant to instant as the accelerator or brake is used.

KEY POINT

Sometimes you may see 'd' used as the symbol for distance travelled, but in this book 's' will be used to be consistent with the symbol used in A level maths and physics.

UNITS OF SPEED

Typically the distance moved is measured in metres and time taken in seconds, so the speed is in metres per second (m/s). Other units can be used for speed, such as kilometres per hour (km/h), or centimetres per second (cm/s). In physics the units we use are **metric**, but you can measure speed in miles per hour (mph). Many cars show speed in both mph and kilometres per hour (kph or km/h). Exam questions should be in metric units, so remember that m is the abbreviation for metres (and not miles).

REARRANGING THE SPEED EQUATION

If you are given information about speed and time taken, you will be expected to rearrange the speed equation to make the distance moved the subject:

$$\text{distance moved}, s = \text{average speed}, v \times \text{time}, t$$

and to make the time taken the subject if you are given the distance moved and speed:

$$\text{time taken}, t = \frac{\text{distance moved}, s}{\text{average speed}, v}$$

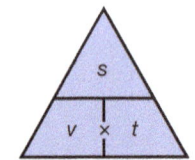

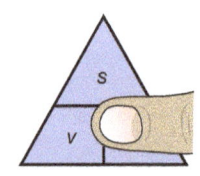

▲ Figure 1.2 You can use the triangle method for rearranging equations like $s = v \times t$.

REMINDER

To use the triangle method to rearrange an equation, cover up the part of the triangle that you want to find. For example, in **Figure 1.2**, if you want to work out how long (t) it takes to move a distance (s) at a given speed (v), covering t in **Figure 1.2** leaves $\frac{s}{v}$, or distance divided by speed. If an examination question asks you to write out the equation for calculating speed, distance or time, always give the actual equation (such as $s = v \times t$). You may not get the mark if you just draw the triangle.

SPEED TRAP!

Suppose you want to find the speed of cars driving down your road. You may have seen the police using a mobile speed camera to check that drivers are keeping to the speed limit. Speed guns use microprocessors (computers on a 'chip') to produce an instant reading of the speed of a moving vehicle, but you can conduct a very simple experiment to measure car speed.

Measure the distance between two points along a straight section of road with a tape measure or 'click' wheel. Use a stopwatch to measure the time taken for a car to travel the measured distance. **Figures 1.3** and **1.4** show you how to operate your 'speed trap'.

1 Measure 50 m from a start point along the side of the road.
2 Start a stopwatch when your partner signals that the car is passing the start point.
3 Stop the stopwatch when the car passes you at the finish point.

▲ Figure 1.3 A stopwatch will measure the time taken for the vehicle to travel the distance.

▲ Figure 1.4 How to measure the speed of cars driving on the road

Safety note: No measurements should be taken on the public road or pavement but it is possible to do so within the school boundary within sight of the road.

KEY POINT

You can convert a speed in m/s into a speed in km/h.

If the car travels 12.8 metres in one second it will travel

12.8 × 60 metres in 60 seconds (that is, one minute) and

12.8 × 60 × 60 metres in 60 minutes (that is, 1 hour), which is

46 080 metres in an hour or 46.1 km/h (to 1 decimal place).

We have multiplied by 3600 (60 × 60) to convert from m/s to m/h, then divided by 1000 to convert from m/h to km/h (as there are 1000 m in 1 km).

Rule: to convert m/s to km/h simply multiply by 3.6.

Using the measurements made with your speed trap, you can work out the speed of the car. Use the equation:

$$\text{average speed, } v = \frac{\text{distance moved, } s}{\text{time taken, } t}$$

So if the time measured is 3.9 s, the speed of the car in this experiment is:

$$\text{average speed, } v = \frac{50 \text{ m}}{3.9 \text{ s}}$$
$$= 12.8 \text{ m/s}$$

DISTANCE–TIME GRAPHS

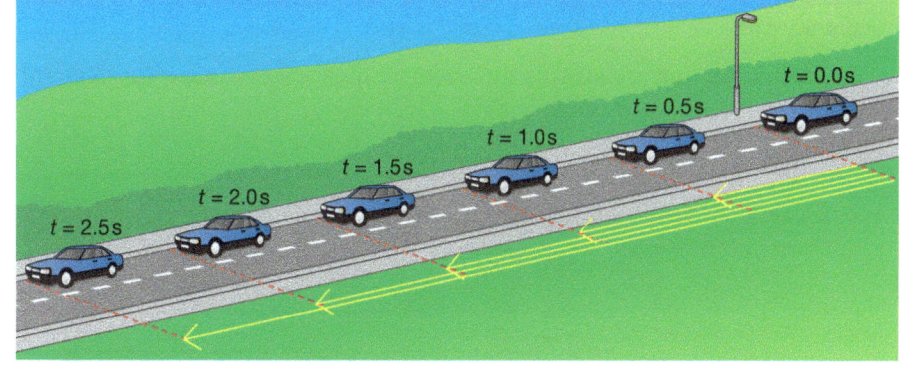

▲ Figure 1.5 A car travelling at constant speed

1 MOVEMENT AND POSITION

Figure 1.5 shows a car travelling along a road. It shows the car at 0.5 second intervals. The distances that the car has travelled from the start position after each 0.5 s time interval are marked on the picture. The picture provides a record of how far the car has travelled as time has passed. **Table 1.1** shows the data for this car. You will be expected to plot a graph of the distance travelled (**vertical** axis) against time (horizontal axis) as shown in **Figure 1.6**.

Table 1.1

Time from start / s	0.0	0.5	1.0	1.5	2.0	2.5
Distance travelled from start / m	0.0	6.0	12.0	18.0	24.0	30.0

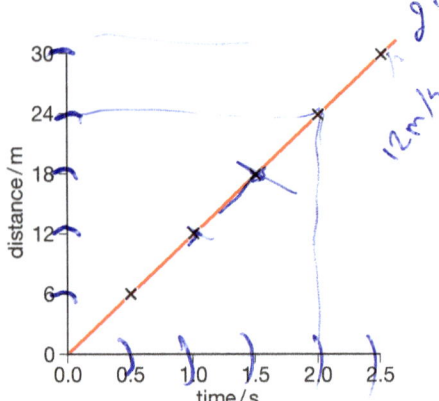

▲ Figure 1.6 Distance–time graph for the travelling car in Figure 1.5

The distance–time graph tells us about how the car is travelling in a much more convenient form than the series of drawings in **Figure 1.5**. We can see that the car is travelling equal distances in equal time intervals – it is moving at a steady or constant speed. This fact is shown immediately by the fact that the graph is a straight line. The slope or **gradient** of the line tells us the speed of the car – the steeper the line the greater the speed of the car. So in this example:

$$\text{speed} = \text{gradient} = \frac{\text{distance}}{\text{time}} = \frac{30 \text{ m}}{2.5 \text{ s}} = 12 \text{ m/s}$$

KEY POINT

A curved line on distance–time graphs means that the speed or velocity of the object is changing.

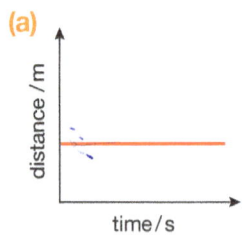

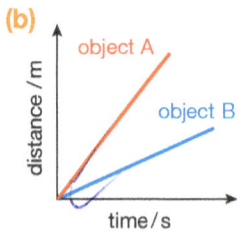

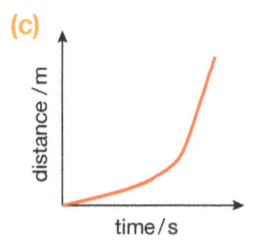

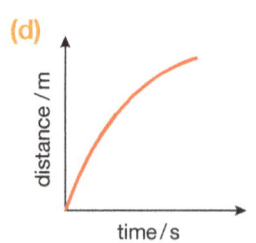

▲ Figure 1.7 Examples of distance–time graphs

In **Figure 1.7a** the distance is not changing with time – the line is horizontal. This means that the speed is zero. In **Figure 1.7b** the graph shows how two objects are moving. The red line is steeper than the blue line because object A is moving at a higher speed than object B. In **Figure 1.7c** the object is speeding up (**accelerating**) shown by the graph line getting steeper (gradient getting bigger). In **Figure 1.7d** the object is slowing down (decelerating).

ACTIVITY 1

▼ PRACTICAL: INVESTIGATE THE MOTION OF EVERYDAY OBJECTS SUCH AS TOY CARS OR TENNIS BALLS

You can use the following simple **apparatus** (**Figure 1.8**) to investigate the motion of a toy car.

You could use this to measure the average speed, v of the car for different values of h.

Safety note: Heavy wooden runways need to be stacked and moved carefully. They are best used at low level rather than being placed on benches or tables where they may fall off. If heavy trolleys are used as 'vehicles', a 'catch box' filled with bubble wrap or similar material should be placed at the end of the runway.

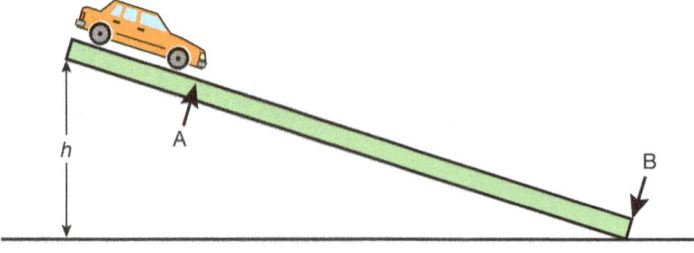

▲ Figure 1.8 Investigating how a toy car rolls down a slope

You need to measure the height, h, of the raised end of the wooden track. The track must be securely clamped at the height under test and h should be measured with a metre rule making sure that the rule is **perpendicular** to the bench surface. Make sure that you always measure to the same point or mark on the raised end of the track.

To find the average speed you will use the equation:

$$\text{average speed, } v = \frac{\text{distance moved, } s}{\text{time taken, } t}$$

so you will need to measure the distance AB with a metre rule and measure the time it takes for the car to travel this distance with a stop clock. When timing with a stop clock, human **reaction** time will introduce measurement errors. To make these smaller the time to travel distance AB should, for a given value of h, be measured at least three times and an average value found. Always start the car from the same point, A. If one value is quite different from the others it should be treated as **anomalous** (the result is not accurate) and ignored or repeated.

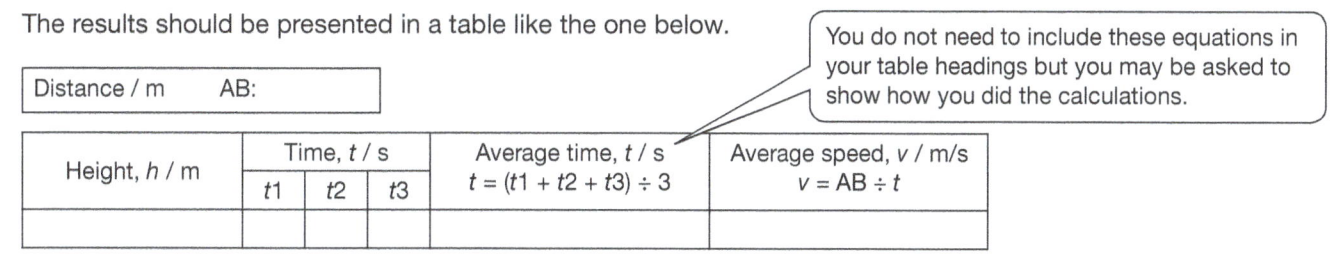

The results should be presented in a table like the one below.

> You do not need to include these equations in your table headings but you may be asked to show how you did the calculations.

Distance / m	AB:				

Height, h / m	Time, t / s			Average time, t / s $t = (t1 + t2 + t3) \div 3$	Average speed, v / m/s $v = AB \div t$
	t1	t2	t3		

In a question you may be given a complete set of results or you may be required to complete the table by doing the necessary calculations. You may be asked to plot a graph (see general notes above) and then come to a conclusion. The conclusion you make must be explained with reference to the graph, for example, if the best fit line through the plotted points is a straight line and it passes through the origin (the 0, 0 point) you can conclude that there is a **proportional** relationship between the quantities you have plotted on the graph.

SOME ALTERNATIVE METHODS

You could investigate the motion of moving objects using photographic methods either by:

- carrying out the experiment in a darkened room using a **stroboscope** to light up the object at regular known intervals (found from the **frequency** setting on the stroboscope) with the camera adjusted so that the shutter is open for the duration of the movement, or
- using a video camera and noting how far the object has travelled between each frame – the frame rate will allow you to calculate the time between each image.

In either case a clearly marked measuring scale should be visible.

Or you could use an electronically operated stop clock and electronic timing gates. This will let you measure the time that it takes for the moving object to travel over a measured distance. This has the advantage of removing timing errors produced by human reaction time.

You can also use timing gates (**Figure 1.9**) to measure how the speed of the object changes as it moves.

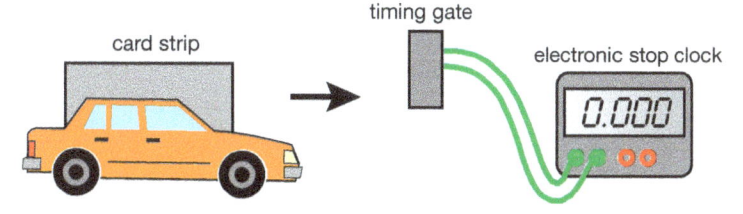

▲ Figure 1.9 Using a timing gate is a more accurate method for measuring time taken to travel a distance.

In this arrangement the stop clock will time while the card strip attached to the moving car passes through the timing gate. Measuring the length of the card strip and the time it takes for the card strip to pass through the timing gate allows you to calculate the average speed of the car as it passes through the timing gate.

ACCELERATION

Figure 1.10 shows some objects whose speed is changing. The plane must accelerate to reach take-off speed. In ice hockey, the puck (small disc that the player hits) decelerates only very slowly when it slides across the ice. When the egg hits the ground it is forced to decelerate (slow down) very rapidly. Rapid deceleration can have destructive results!

▲ Figure 1.10 Acceleration  … … constant speed  … … and deceleration

KEY POINT
Velocity has a particular meaning in physics, but, in this course take velocity as just another term for speed.

Acceleration is the rate at which objects speed up. It is defined as follows:

$$\text{acceleration, } a = \frac{\text{change in velocity}}{\text{time taken, } t} \text{ or } \frac{\text{final velocity, } v - \text{initial velocity, } u}{\text{time taken, } t}$$

$$a = \frac{(v - u)}{t}$$

Why u? Simply because it comes before v!

UNITS OF ACCELERATION

Velocity is measured in m/s, so increase in velocity is also measured in m/s. Acceleration, the rate of increase in velocity with time, is therefore measured in m/s/s (read as 'metres per second per second'). We normally write this as m/s² (read as 'metres per second **squared**'). Other units may be used – for example, cm/s².

EXAMPLE 1

A car is travelling at 20 m/s. It accelerates steadily for 5 s, after which time it is travelling at 30 m/s. Calculate its acceleration.

Write down what you know:
initial or starting velocity, u = 20 m/s
final velocity, v = 30 m/s
time taken, t = 5 s

$$a = \frac{(v - u)}{t}$$
$$= \frac{30 \text{ m/s} - 20 \text{ m/s}}{5 \text{ s}}$$
$$= \frac{10 \text{ m/s}}{5 \text{ s}}$$

The car is accelerating at 2 m/s².

EXAM HINT
It is good practice to include units in equations – this will help you to supply the answer with the correct unit.

1 FORCES AND MOTION — 1 MOVEMENT AND POSITION

DECELERATION

Deceleration means slowing down. This means that a decelerating object will have a smaller final velocity than its starting velocity. If you use the equation for finding the acceleration of an object that is slowing down, the answer will have a negative sign. A negative acceleration simply means deceleration.

EXAMPLE 2

An object hits the ground travelling at 40 m/s. It is brought to rest in 0.02 s. Calculate its acceleration.

Write down what you know:

initial velocity, u = 40 m/s
final velocity, v = 0 m/s
time taken, t = 0.02 s

$$a = \frac{(v - u)}{t}$$
$$= \frac{0 \text{ m/s} - 40 \text{ m/s}}{0.02 \text{ s}}$$
$$= \frac{-40 \text{ m/s}}{0.02 \text{ s}}$$
$$= -2000 \text{ m/s}^2$$

In **Example 2**, we would say that the object is decelerating at 2000 m/s². This is a very large deceleration. Later, in **Chapter 3**, we shall discuss the consequences of such a rapid deceleration!

MEASURING ACCELERATION

When a ball is rolled down a slope it is clear that its speed increases as it rolls – that is, it accelerates. Galileo was interested in how and why objects, like the ball rolling down a slope, speed up, and he created an interesting experiment to learn more about acceleration. A version of his experiment is shown in **Figure 1.11**.

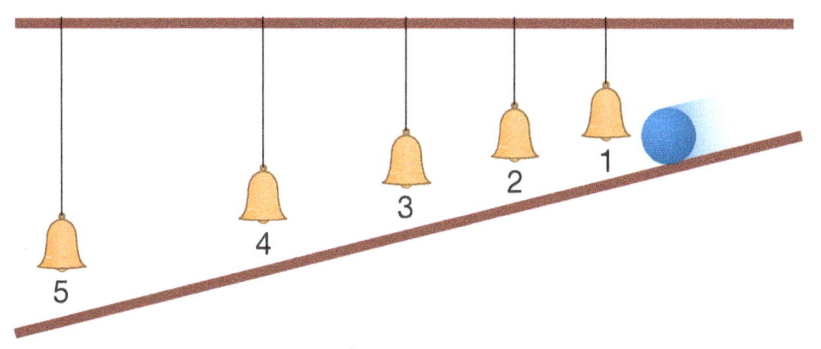

▲ Figure 1.11 Galileo's experiment. A ball rolling down a slope, hitting small bells as it rolls

Galileo wanted to find out how the distance travelled by a ball depends on the time it has been rolling. In this version of the experiment, a ball rolling down a slope strikes a series of small bells as it rolls. By adjusting the positions of the bells carefully it is possible to make the bells ring at equal intervals of time as the ball passes. Galileo noticed that the distances travelled in equal time intervals increased, showing that the ball was travelling faster as time passed. Galileo did not have an accurate way of measuring time (there were no digital stopwatches in 17th-century Italy!) but it was possible to judge equal time intervals accurately simply by listening.

EXTENSION

Galileo was an Italian scientist who was born in 1564. He developed a telescope, which he used to study the movement of the planets and stars. He also carried out many experiments on motion (movement).

Galileo also noticed that the distance travelled by the ball increased in a predictable way. He showed that the rate of increase of speed was steady or uniform. We call this uniform acceleration. Most acceleration is non-uniform – that is, it changes from instant to instant – but we shall only deal with uniformly accelerated objects in this chapter.

VELOCITY–TIME GRAPHS

Table 1.2 shows the distances between the bells in an experiment such as Galileo's.

Table 1.2

Bell	1	2	3	4	5
Time / s	0.5	1.0	1.5	2.0	2.5
Distance of bell from start / cm	3	12	27	48	75

We can calculate the average velocity of the ball between each bell by working out the distance travelled between each bell, and the time it took to travel this distance. For the first bell:

$$\text{velocity, } v = \frac{\text{distance moved, } s}{\text{time taken, } t}$$

$$= \frac{3 \text{ cm}}{0.5 \text{ s}} = 6 \text{ cm/s}$$

This is the average velocity over the 0.5 second time interval, so if we plot it on a graph we should plot it in the middle of the interval, at 0.25 seconds.

Repeating the above calculation for all the results gives us the results shown in **Table 1.3**. We can use these results to draw a graph showing how the velocity of the ball is changing with time. The graph, shown in **Figure 1.12**, is called a velocity–time graph.

Table 1.3

Time in s	0.25	0.75	1.25	1.75	2.25
Velocity in cm/s	6	18	30	42	54

The graph in **Figure 1.12** is a straight line. This tells us that the velocity of the rolling ball is increasing by equal amounts in equal time periods. We say that the acceleration is uniform in this case.

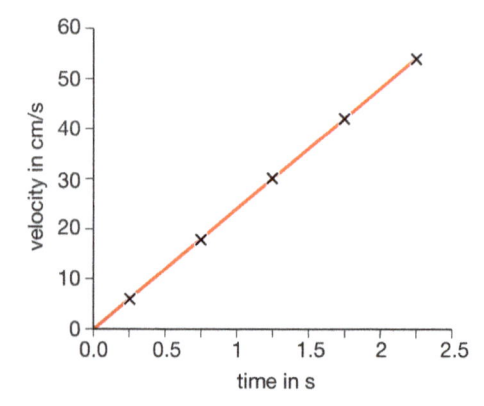

▲ Figure 1.12 Velocity–time graph for an experiment in which a ball is rolled down a slope. (Note that as we are plotting average velocity, the points are plotted in the middle of each successive 0.5 s time interval.)

1 FORCES AND MOTION 1 MOVEMENT AND POSITION 303

A MODERN VERSION OF GALILEO'S EXPERIMENT

Safety note: A cylinder vacuum cleaner (or similar) used with the air-track should be placed on the floor as it may fall off a bench or stool. Also, beware of any trailing leads.

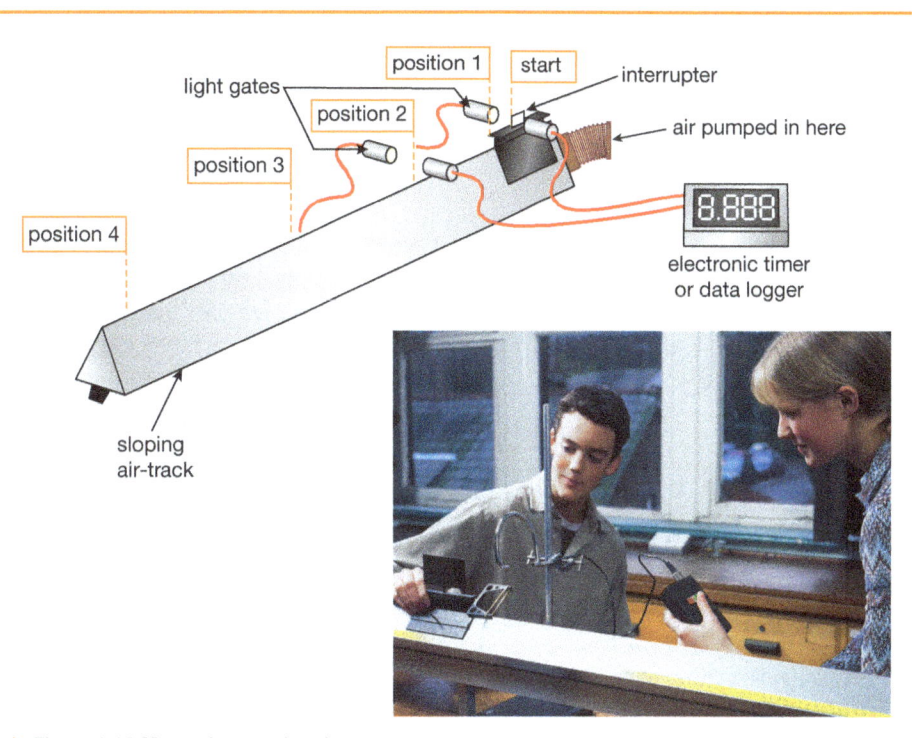

▲ Figure 1.13 Measuring acceleration

Today we can use data loggers to make accurate direct measurements that are collected and analysed by a computer. A spreadsheet program can be used to produce a velocity–time graph. **Figure 1.13** shows a glider on a slightly sloping air-track. The air-track reduces **friction** because the glider rides on a cushion of air that is pushed continuously through holes along the air-track. As the glider accelerates down the sloping track the card stuck on it breaks a light beam, and the time that the glider takes to pass is measured electronically. If the length of the card is measured, and this is entered into the spreadsheet, the velocity of the glider can be calculated by the spreadsheet program using $v = \frac{s}{t}$.

Figure 1.14 shows velocity–time graphs for two experiments done using the air-track apparatus. In each experiment the track was given a different slope. The steeper the slope of the air-track the greater the glider's acceleration. This is clear from the graphs: the greater the acceleration the steeper the gradient of the graph.

The gradient of a velocity–time graph gives the acceleration.

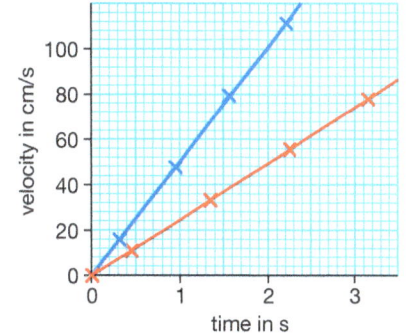

Air-track at 1.5°		Air-track at 3.0°	
Time in s	Av Vel. in cm/s	Time/s	Av Vel. in cm/s
0.00	0.0	0.00	0.0
0.45	11.1	0.32	15.9
1.35	33.3	0.95	47.6
2.25	55.6	1.56	79.4
3.15	77.8	2.21	111.1

▲ Figure 1.14 Results of two air-track experiments. (Note, once again, that because we are plotting average velocity in the velocity–time graphs, the points are plotted in the middle of each successive time interval.)

MORE ABOUT VELOCITY–TIME GRAPHS

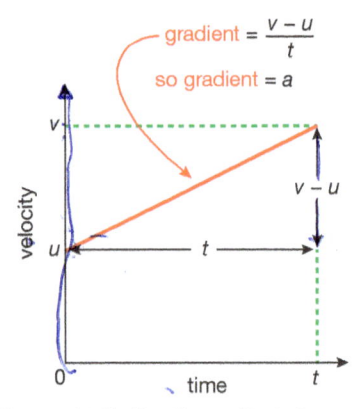

▲ Figure 1.15 Finding the gradient of a velocity–time graph

EXAM HINT

1. When finding the gradient of a graph, draw a big triangle.
2. Choose a convenient number of units for the length of the base of the triangle to make the division easier.

EXAM HINT

Find the distance travelled for more complicated velocity–time graphs by dividing the area beneath the graph line into rectangles and triangles. Take care that units on the velocity and time axes use the same units for time, for example, m/s and s, or km/h and h.

KEY POINT

This equation of motion only works for uniform (or constant) acceleration – therefore for objects with velocity–time graphs that are straight lines.

GRADIENT

The results of the air-track experiments in **Figure 1.14** show that the slope of the velocity–time graph depends on the acceleration of the glider. The slope or gradient of a velocity–time graph is found by dividing the increase in the velocity by the time taken for the increase, as shown in **Figure 1.15**. In this example an object is travelling at u m/s at the beginning and accelerates uniformly (at a constant rate) for t s. Its final velocity is v m/s. Increase in velocity divided by time is, you will recall, the definition of acceleration (see page 300), so we can measure the acceleration of an object by finding the slope of its velocity–time graph. The meaning of the slope or gradient of a velocity–time graph is summarised in **Figure 1.16**.

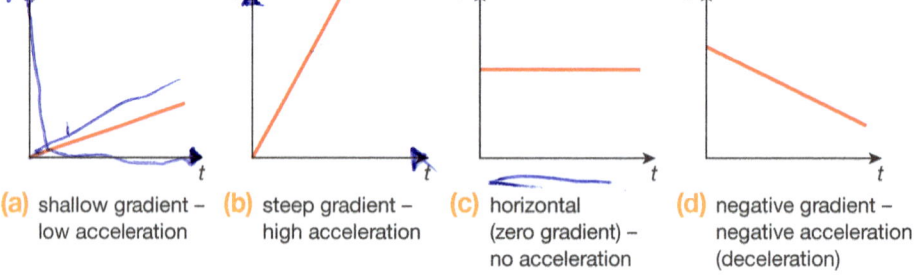

(a) shallow gradient – low acceleration
(b) steep gradient – high acceleration
(c) horizontal (zero gradient) – no acceleration
(d) negative gradient – negative acceleration (deceleration)

▲ Figure 1.16 The gradient of a velocity–time graph gives you information about the motion of an object at a glance.

AREA UNDER A VELOCITY–TIME GRAPH GIVES DISTANCE TRAVELLED

Figure 1.17a shows a velocity–time graph for an object that travels with a constant velocity of 5 m/s for 10 s. A simple calculation shows that in this time the object has travelled 50 m. This is equal to the shaded (coloured) area under the graph. **Figure 1.17b** shows a velocity–time graph for an object that has accelerated at a constant rate. Its average velocity during this time is given by:

$$\text{average velocity} = \frac{\text{initial velocity} + \text{final velocity}}{2} \text{ or } \frac{u+v}{2}$$

In this example the average velocity is, therefore:

$$\text{average velocity} = \frac{0\,\text{m/s} + 10\,\text{m/s}}{2}$$

which works out to be 5 m/s. If the object travels, on average, 5 metres in each second it will have travelled 20 metres in 4 seconds. Notice that this, too, is equal to the shaded area under the graph (given by the area equation for a triangle: area = $\frac{1}{2}$ base × height).

The area under a velocity–time graph is equal to the distance travelled by (**displacement** of) the object in a particular time interval.

(a) area = 5 m/s × 10 s = 50 m = distance travelled

(b) area of a triangle = $\frac{1}{2}$ base × height
area = 25 m = distance travelled

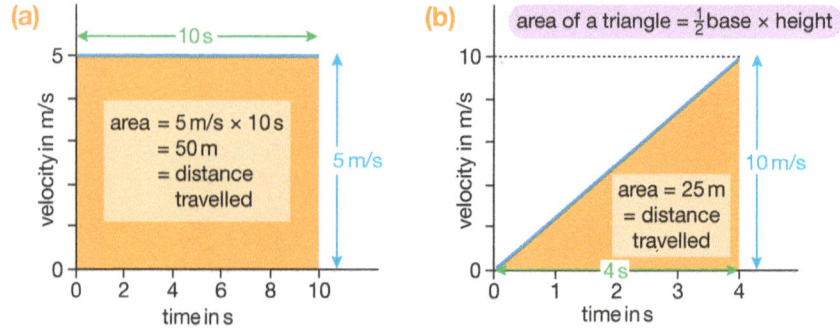

▲ Figure 1.17 (a) An object travelling at constant velocity; (b) an object accelerating at a constant rate

1 FORCES AND MOTION   1 MOVEMENT AND POSITION   305

EQUATIONS OF UNIFORMLY ACCELERATED MOTION

You must remember the equation:

$$a = \frac{v - u}{t}$$

and be able to use it to calculate the acceleration of an object.

You may need to rearrange the equation to make another term the subject (**Figure 1.18**).

EXAMPLE 3

A stone accelerates from rest uniformly at 10 m/s² when it is dropped down a deep well. It hits the water at the bottom of the well after 5 s. Calculate how fast it is travelling when it hits the water.

You will need to make *v* the subject of this equation:

$$a = \frac{v - u}{t}$$

You can use the triangle method (**Figure 1.18**) to show that $v - u = a \times t$ then add *u* to both sides of the equation to give:

$$v = u + at$$

(In words this tells you that the final velocity is the initial velocity plus the increase in velocity after accelerating for *t* seconds.)

State the things you have been told:
initial velocity, *u* = 0 m/s (It was stationary (standing still) at the start.)
acceleration, *a* = 10 m/s²
time, *t*, of the acceleration = 5 s
Substitute these into the equation: *v* = 0 m/s + (10 m/s² × 5 s)
Then calculate the result.
The stone hit the water travelling at 50 m/s (downwards).

▲ Figure 1.18 Cover *v – u* to find $v - u = a \times t$

CHAPTER QUESTIONS

Exam-style questions on movement and position can be found at the end of Unit 1 on page 322.

SKILLS PROBLEM SOLVING

1 A sprinter runs 100 metres in 12.5 seconds. Calculate the sprinter's average speed in m/s.

2 A jet can travel at 350 m/s. Calculate how far it will travel at this speed in:
   a 30 seconds
   b 5 minutes
   c half an hour.

SKILLS PROBLEM SOLVING

3 A snail crawls at a speed of 0.0004 m/s. Calculate how long it will take to climb a garden stick 1.6 m high.

SKILLS ANALYSIS

4 Look at the following distance–time graphs of moving objects.

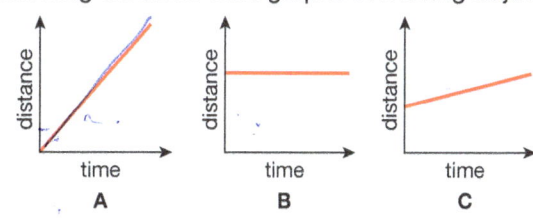

A   B   C

Identify in which graph the object is:

a moving slowly

b moving quickly

c not moving at all.

5 Sketch a distance–time graph to show the motion of a person walking quickly, stopping for a moment, then continuing to walk slowly in the same direction.

6 Plot a distance–time graph using the data in the following table. Draw a line of best fit and use your graph to find the speed of the object concerned.

Distance / m	0.00	1.60	3.25	4.80	6.35	8.00	9.60
Time / s	0.00	0.05	0.10	0.15	0.20	0.25	0.30

7 The diagram below shows a trail of oil drips made by a car as it travels along a road. The oil is dripping from the car at a steady rate of one drip every 2.5 seconds.

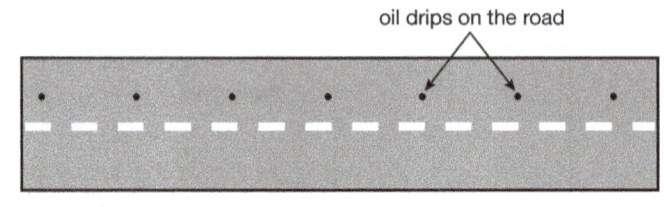

a Describe the way the car is moving.

b The distance between the first and the seventh drip is 135 metres. Determine the average speed of the car.

8 A car is travelling at 20 m/s. It accelerates uniformly at 3 m/s² for 5 s.

a Sketch a velocity–time graph for the car during the period that it is accelerating. Include numerical detail on the axes of your graph.

b Calculate the distance the car travels while it is accelerating.

9 A sports car accelerates uniformly from rest to 24 m/s in 6 s. Calculate the acceleration of the car.

10 Sketch velocity–time graphs for an object:

a moving with a constant velocity of 6 m/s

b accelerating uniformly from rest at 2 m/s² for 10 s.

Include numbers and units on the velocity and time axes in each case.

11 A plane starting from rest accelerates at 3 m/s² for 25 s. Calculate the increase in velocity after:

a 1 s

b 5 s

c 25 s.

12 Look at the following sketches of velocity–time graphs of moving objects.

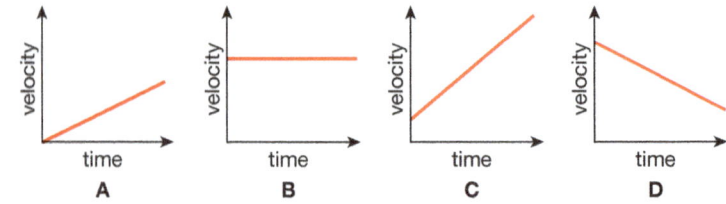

In which graph is the object:
a not accelerating
b accelerating from rest
c decelerating
d accelerating at the greatest rate?

13 Sketch a velocity–time graph to show how the velocity of a car travelling along a straight road changes if it accelerates uniformly from rest for 5 s, travels at a constant velocity for 10 s, then brakes hard to come to rest in 2 s.

14 a Plot a velocity–time graph using the data in the following table:

Velocity in m/s	0.0	2.5	5.0	7.5	10.0	10.0	10.0	10.0	10.0	10.0
Time in s	0.0	1.0	2.0	3.0	4.0	5.0	6.0	7.0	8.0	9.0

Draw a line of best fit and use your graph to find:
b the acceleration during the first 4 s
c the distance travelled in:
   i the first 4 s of the motion shown
   ii the last 5 s of the motion shown
d the average speed during the 9 seconds of motion shown.

15 The dripping car from question 7 is still on the road! It is still dripping oil but now at a rate of one drop per second. The trail of drips is shown on the diagram below as the car travels from left to right.

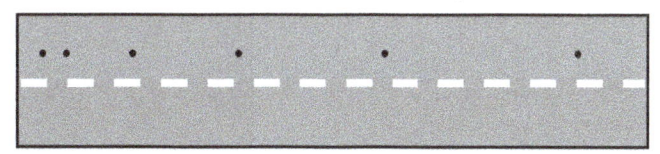

Describe the motion (the way the car is moving) using the information in this diagram.

16 A student is investigating the rate of acceleration of a tennis ball rolling down a gently sloping ramp that is 5 metres long. The student has a stopwatch and a metre rule.

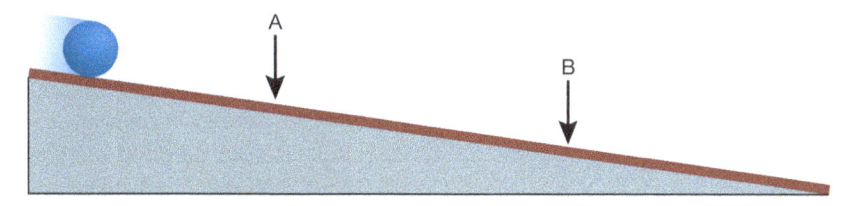

The student decides to measure the average velocity of the tennis ball in two places, A and B, as it rolls down the slope.

a Describe the measurements that the student must make to find the velocity in each place, and how these will be used to find the average velocity in each place.

b State what other measurement the student must make to find the acceleration of the ball. Explain how the student can then calculate the acceleration.

c How can the student improve the accuracy of the measurements?

d The investigation is more difficult to carry out if the slope is too steep. Explain why this is so.

2 FORCES AND SHAPE

SPECIFICATION REFERENCES: 1.11, 1.12, 1.16

Forces are acting on us, and on objects all around us, all the time. In this chapter you will learn about different kinds of forces, how they may change the speed and direction of objects and how they can affect the shape of objects.

▲ Figure 2.1 Forces include pulling, falling due to gravity and squashing

LEARNING OBJECTIVES

- Describe the effects of forces between bodies such as changes in speed, shape or direction.
- Identify different types of force such as gravitational or electrostatic.
- Know that friction is a force that opposes motion.

Forces are simply pushes and pulls of one thing on another. Sometimes we can see their effects quite clearly. In **Figure 2.1**, the tug is pulling the tanker; the bungee jumper is being pulled to Earth by the force of **gravity**, and then (hopefully before meeting the ground) being pulled back up by the stretched elastic rope; the force applied by the crusher permanently changes the shape of the cars. In this chapter we will discuss different types of forces and look at their effects on the way that objects move.

ALL SORTS OF FORCES

If you are to study forces, first you need to notice them! As we have already said, sometimes they are easy to see and their effect is obvious. Look at **Figure 2.2** and try to identify any forces that you think are involved.

You will immediately see that the man is applying a force to the car – he is pushing it. But there are quite a few more forces in the picture. To make the task a little easier we will limit our search to just those forces acting on the car. We will also ignore forces that are very small and therefore have little effect.

▲ Figure 2.2 What forces do you think are working here?

| 1 FORCES AND MOTION | 2 FORCES AND SHAPE | 309 |

The man is clearly struggling to make the car move. This is because there is a force acting on the car trying to stop it moving. This is the force of friction between the moving parts in the car engine, gears, wheel axles and so on. This unhelpful force opposes the motion that the man is trying to achieve. However, when the car engine is doing the work to make the car go, the friction between the tyres and the road surface is vital. On an icy road even powerful cars may not move forward because there is not enough friction between the tyres and the ice.

Another force that acts on the car is the pull of the Earth. We call this a gravitational force or simply **weight**. If the car were to be pushed over the edge of a cliff, the effect of the gravitational force would be very clear as the car fell towards the sea. This leads us to realise that yet another force is acting on the car in **Figure 2.2** – the road must be stopping the car from being pulled into the Earth. This force, which acts in an upward direction (going up) on the car, is called the reaction force. (A more complete name is **normal** reaction force. Here the word 'normal' means acting at 90° to the road surface.) All four forces that act on the car are shown in **Figure 2.3**.

push on the car by the man

normal reaction forces at the wheels, the upward push on the car from the ground

friction opposing the motion

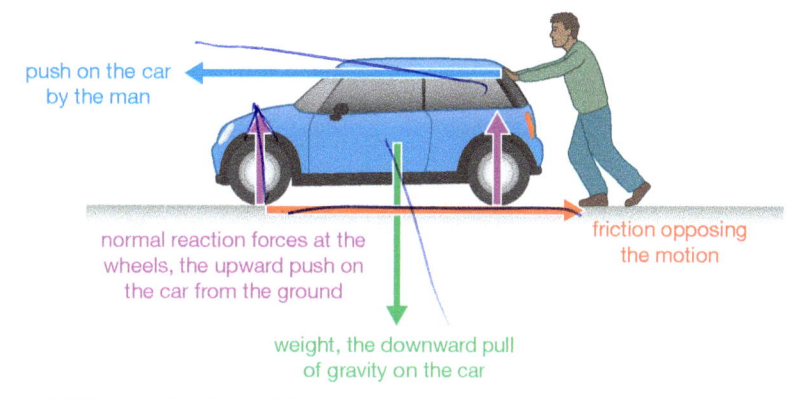

weight, the downward pull of gravity on the car

▲ Figure 2.3 There are four types of force at work.

You will have realised by now that it is not just the size of the force that is important – the direction in which the force is acting is important, too.

UNITS OF FORCE

(a)

The unit used to measure force is the newton (N), named after Sir Isaac Newton. Newton's study of forces is vital to our understanding of them today.

A force of one newton will make a **mass** of one kilogram accelerate at one metre per second squared.

This is explained more fully later (see **Chapter 3**). To give you an idea of the size of the newton, the force of gravity on a kilogram bag of sugar (its weight) is about 10 N; an average-sized apple weighs 1 N.

(b)

SOME OTHER EXAMPLES OF FORCES

It is not always easy to spot forces acting on objects. The compass needle in **Figure 2.4a**, which is a magnet, is affected by the magnetic force between it and the other magnet.

If you comb your hair, you sometimes find that some of your hair sticks to the comb as shown in **Figure 2.4b**. This happens because of an **electrostatic force** between your hair and the comb. You can see a similar effect using a Van de Graaff **generator**.

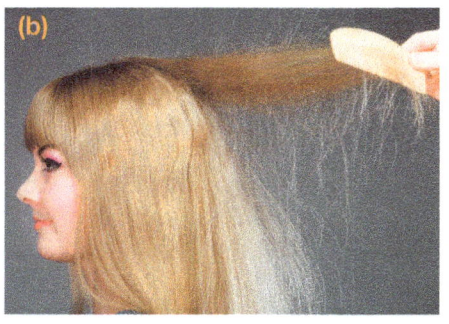

▲ Figure 2.4 More forces!

A parachute causes the parachutist to descend more slowly because an upward force acts on the parachute called air resistance or drag. Air resistance is like friction – it tries to oppose movement of objects through the air. Designers of cars, high-speed trains and other fast-moving objects try to reduce the effects of this force. Objects moving through liquids also experience a drag force – fast-moving animals that live in water have streamlined (smooth and efficient) shapes to reduce this force.

Hot air balloons are carried upwards in spite of the pull of gravity on them because of a force called **upthrust**. This is the upward push of the surrounding air on the balloon. An upthrust force also acts on objects in liquids.

More types of force, such as electric and **nuclear** forces, are mentioned in other chapters of this book. The rest of this chapter will look at the effects of forces.

BALANCED AND UNBALANCED FORCES

As we saw earlier, in most situations there will be more than just one force acting on an object. Look at the man trying to push the car, shown in **Figure 2.5**. The man pushes on the car in one direction and friction acts to stop the car moving. If these forces are balanced the car will not start to move or, if it is moving, it will not speed up.

> **KEY POINT**
> If the forces acting on an object are balanced it will either remain at rest or keep moving at the same speed in the same direction.

▲ Figure 2.5 The **resultant force** is zero because the two forces are balanced.

▲ Figure 2.6 The total pushing force is the **sum** of the two individual forces.

If the man gets someone to help him push the car (**Figure 2.6**), the pushing force is bigger. Now the pushing force may be bigger than the force of friction acting on the car. The forces are **unbalanced** so the car will start to move, or it will accelerate if it is already moving.

> **KEY POINT**
> If the forces acting on an object are unbalanced the result is a change in the way the object is moving: it might speed up, slow down or change direction.

FRICTION

Friction is the force that causes moving objects to slow down and finally stop. The **kinetic energy** of the moving object is transferred to heat as work is done by the friction force. For the ice skater in **Figure 2.7** the force of friction is very small so she is able to glide for long distances without having to do any work. It is also the force that allows a car's wheels to grip the road and make it accelerate – very quickly in the case of the racing cars in **Figure 2.7**.

1 FORCES AND MOTION   2 FORCES AND SHAPE

Scientists have worked hard for many years to develop some materials that reduce friction and others that increase friction. Reducing friction means that machines work more efficiently (wasting less energy) and do not wear out so quickly. Increasing friction can help to make tyres that grip the road better and to make more effective brakes.

▲ Figure 2.7 The ice skater can glide because friction is low. The cars need friction to grip the road.

Friction occurs when solid objects rub against other solid objects and also when objects move through fluids (liquids and gases). Sprint cyclists and Olympic swimmers now wear special materials to reduce the effects of fluid friction so they can achieve faster times in their races. Sometimes fluid friction is very desirable – for example, when someone uses a parachute after jumping from a plane!

INVESTIGATING FRICTION

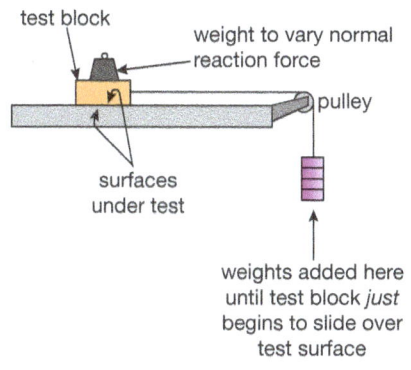

▲ Figure 2.8 This apparatus can be used to investigate friction.

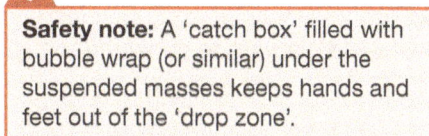

Safety note: A 'catch box' filled with bubble wrap (or similar) under the suspended masses keeps hands and feet out of the 'drop zone'.

The simple apparatus shown in **Figure 2.8** can be used to discover some basic facts about friction. The weight force on the line running over the pulley pulls the block horizontally along the track and friction acts on the block to oppose this force. The weight is increased until the block just starts to move; this happens when the pull of the weight force just overcomes the friction force. The friction force between the block and the track has maximum value.

The apparatus can be used to test different factors that may affect the size of the friction force, such as the surfaces in contact – the bottom of the block and the surface of the track. If the track surface is replaced with a rough surface, like a sheet of sandpaper, the force required to overcome friction will be greater.

It is important to remember friction when you are investigating forces and motion. Friction affects almost every form of motion on Earth. However it is possible to do experiments in the science laboratory in which the friction force on a moving object is reduced to a very low value. Such an object can be set in motion with a small push and it will continue to move at a constant speed even when the force is no longer acting on it.

You may also have seen scientists working in space demonstrating that objects keep moving in a straight line at constant speed, once set in motion. They do this in space because the objects are **weightless** and the force of air resistance acting on them is very small.

CHANGING SHAPES

We have seen that forces can make things start to move, accelerate or decelerate. The examples in **Figure 2.9** show another effect that forces can have – they can change the shape of an object.

Sometimes the shape of the object is permanently changed, like a crushed can or a car that has collided with another object. A spring or a ball can be an energy store when their shapes are changed. A force can do work on these and the energy store can then transfer the energy back to movement energy. We see this happening in clock springs and trampolines (**Figure 2.9**).

▲ Figure 2.9 Energy stores; temporary change of shape.

CHAPTER QUESTIONS

Exam-style questions on forces and shape can be found at the end of Unit 1 on page 322.

SKILLS — CRITICAL THINKING

1 Name the force that:
   a causes objects to fall towards the Earth
   b makes a ball rolled across level ground eventually stop
   c stops a car sinking into the road surface
   d makes the needle on a compass move
   e makes a rubbed balloon stick to a wall.

2 Name two types of force that oppose motion.

SKILLS — PROBLEM SOLVING

3 The drawing shows two tug-of-war teams. Each person in the red team is pulling with a force of 250 N. Each person in the blue team is pulling with a force of 200 N.

   a Calculate the total force exerted by the blue team.
   b Calculate the total force exerted by the red team.
   c Calculate the resultant (unbalanced) force on the rope.
   d State which team will win.

SKILLS — CRITICAL THINKING

4 A car is travelling along a level road at constant velocity (that is, its speed and direction are not changing). Draw a labelled diagram to show the forces that act on the car.

SKILLS — INTERPRETATION

5 Copy the diagrams below and label the direction in which friction is acting on the objects.

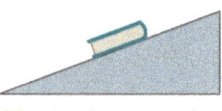

(a) a book on a sloping surface

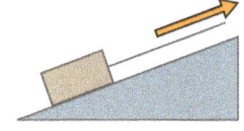

(b) a block of wood being pulled up a slope

| 1 FORCES AND MOTION | 2 FORCES AND SHAPE |

SKILLS ANALYSIS

6 This question is about friction.

A student places a toy car on a sloping wooden plank and conducts some experiment with the plank at different angles. The student notices the following.
   a With the plank at one degree of slope the car rolls a little way down the slope when given a short push then comes to rest.
   b When the slope is changed the car continues to roll down the slope but gets faster.
   c After some experimenting the car, once started by the short push, keeps on moving down the slope but without getting any faster.

Explain these observations mentioning what the student must have done to the angle of slope and whether an unbalanced force acts on the car after it has been given the short starting push.

SKILLS CRITICAL THINKING

7 State the three possible effects that an unbalanced force acting on a body may have.

3 FORCES AND MOVEMENT

SPECIFICATION REFERENCES: 1.17–1.20

The way an object moves depends upon its mass and the unbalanced force acting upon it. In this chapter you will find out how forces affect the way an object will move, particularly in the context of car safety.

▲ Figure 3.1 (a) This aircraft has only a short distance to travel before taking off and (b) a very short distance to land back on the aircraft carrier.

LEARNING OBJECTIVES

- Know and use the relationship between unbalanced force, mass and acceleration:

  force = mass × acceleration

  $F = m \times a$

- Know and use the relationship between weight, mass and gravitational field strength:

  weight = mass × gravitational field strength

  $W = m \times g$

- Know that the stopping distance of a vehicle is made up of the sum of the thinking distance and the braking distance.

- Describe the factors affecting vehicle stopping distance, including speed, mass, road condition and reaction time.

The aircraft in **Figure 3.1a** must accelerate to a very high speed in a very short time when taking off and decelerate quickly when landing back on the aircraft carrier. The unbalanced force on the plane causes the acceleration. The forces that act horizontally on the aircraft are the friction force between the wheels and the flight deck (where planes land on a ship), and air resistance, when the aircraft starts to move. At the start, the forward **thrust** of the aircraft engines is much greater than air resistance and friction, so there is a large unbalanced force to cause the acceleration. When the aircraft lands on the flight deck (**Figure 3.1b**) it must decelerate to stop in a short distance. Parachutes and drag wires are used to provide a large unbalanced force acting in the opposite direction to reduce the aircraft's movement. An unbalanced force is sometimes referred to as a resultant force. In this chapter we look at how acceleration is related to the force acting on an object.

FORCE, MASS AND ACCELERATION

An object will not change its velocity (accelerate) unless there is an unbalanced force acting on it. For example, a car travelling along a motorway at a constant speed is being pushed along by a force from its engine, but this force is needed to balance the forces of friction and air resistance acting on the car. At a constant speed, the unbalanced force on the car is zero.

1 FORCES AND MOTION 3 FORCES AND MOVEMENT 315

If there are unbalanced forces acting on an object, the object may accelerate or decelerate depending on the direction of the unbalanced force. The acceleration depends on the size of the unbalanced force and the mass of the object (**Figure 3.2**).

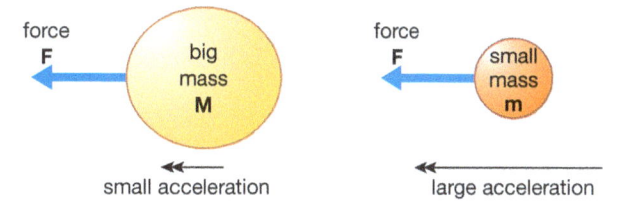

(a) When the same force is applied to objects with different mass, the smaller mass will experience a greater acceleration.

(b) Different-sized forces are applied to objects with the same mass. The small force produces a smaller acceleration than the large force.

▲ Figure 3.2 The acceleration of an object is affected by both its mass and the force applied to it.

INVESTIGATING FORCE, MASS AND ACCELERATION

The experiment shown in **Figure 3.3** shows how the relationship between force, mass and acceleration can be investigated. It uses a trolley on a slightly sloping ramp. The slope of the ramp is adjusted so that the trolley keeps moving down the slope without speeding up if you push it gently to get it started. The slope is intended to overcome the friction in the trolley's wheels that could affect the results.

Safety note: Heavy wooden runways need to be stacked and moved carefully. They are best used at low level rather than being placed on benches or tables where they may fall off. If heavy trolleys are used as 'vehicles', a 'catch box' filled with bubble wrap or similar material should be placed at the end of the runway.

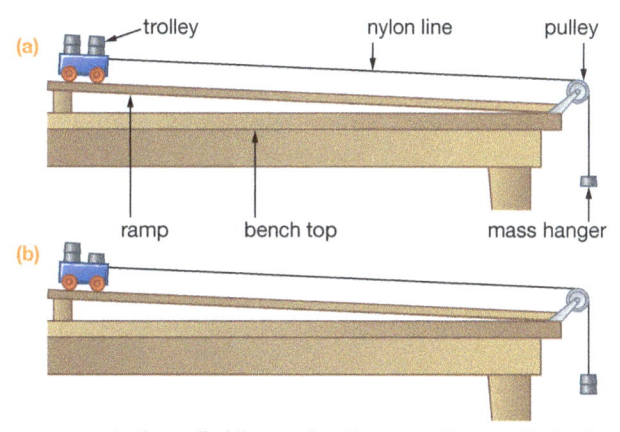

▲ Figure 3.3 You can use a trolley to find the acceleration caused by a particular force.

The force acting on the trolley is provided by the masses on the end of the nylon line. These masses accelerate as well as the trolley, so the force is increased by transferring one of the masses from the trolley to the mass hanger (**Figure 3.3b**). This increases the pulling force (explained later in this chapter) on the trolley, while keeping the total mass of the system the same.

The acceleration of the trolley can be measured by taking a series of pictures at equal time intervals using a digital video camera. Alternatively, a pair of **light gates** and a data logger can be used to find the speed of the trolley near the start of the ramp and near the end. The equation on page 300 can then be used to work out the acceleration.

Force is measured in newtons (N), mass is measured in kilograms (kg), and acceleration is measured in metres per second squared (m/s²). From this we see that:

One newton is the force needed to make a mass of one kilogram accelerate at one metre per second squared.

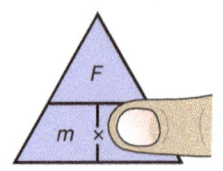

▲ Figure 3.4 The equation can be rearranged using the triangle method. If you need to find the acceleration that results when a known force acts on an object of known mass, cover up a; you can see that $a = \frac{F}{m}$.

EXAM HINT

If an examination question asks you to write out the equation for calculating force, mass or acceleration, always give the actual equation (such as $F = m \times a$). You may not get the mark if you just draw the triangle.

DECELERATION IN A COLLISION

REMINDER

v is the final velocity, u is the initial velocity and t is the time for the change in velocity to take place.

REMINDER

The minus sign in **Example 1** for velocity change indicates that the velocity has decreased.

If you are designing a car for high acceleration, the equation $F = ma$ tells you that the car should have low mass and the engine must provide a high accelerating force. You must also consider the force needed to stop the car.

When a moving object is stopped, it decelerates.

A negative acceleration is a deceleration.

If a large deceleration is needed then the force causing the deceleration must be large, too. Usually a car is stopped by using the brakes in a controlled way so that the deceleration is not excessive (too much). In an accident the car may collide with another vehicle or obstacle, causing a very rapid deceleration.

EXAMPLE 1

A car travelling at 20 m/s collides with a stationary lorry and stops completely in just 0.02 s. Calculate the deceleration of the car.

$$\text{acceleration} = \frac{\text{change in velocity}}{\text{time taken}} \text{ (see page 300)}$$

$$a = \frac{v - u}{t}$$

$$= \frac{0 \, \text{m/s} - 20 \, \text{m/s}}{0.02 \, \text{s}}$$

$$= \frac{-20 \, \text{m/s}}{0.02 \, \text{s}}$$

$$= -1000 \, \text{m/s}^2$$

A person of mass 50 kg in the car experiences the same deceleration when she comes into contact with a hard surface in the car. This could be the dashboard or the windscreen. Calculate the force that the person experiences.

$$F = m \times a$$
$$= 50 \, \text{kg} \times 1000 \, \text{m/s}^2$$
$$= 50\,000 \, \text{N}$$

1 FORCES AND MOTION · 3 FORCES AND MOVEMENT

FRICTION AND BRAKING

▲ Figure 3.5 Motorcycle disc brakes work using friction. Friction is necessary if we want things to stop.

The 'tread' of a tyre is the grooved pattern moulded into the rubber surface. It is designed to keep the rubber surface in contact with the road by throwing water away from the tyre surface.

Brakes on cars and bicycles work by increasing the friction between the rotating wheels and the body of the vehicle, as shown in **Figure 3.5**.

The friction force between the tyres and the road depends on the condition of the tyres and the surface of the road. It also depends on the weight of the vehicle. If the tyres have a good tread, are properly inflated (filled with air) and the road is dry, the friction force between the road and the tyres will be at its maximum.

Unfortunately, we do not always travel in ideal conditions. If the road is wet or the tyres are in bad condition the friction force will be smaller. If the brakes are applied too hard, the tyres will not grip the road surface and the car will skid (slide out of control). Once the car is skidding the driver no longer has control and it will take longer to stop. Skidding can be avoided by applying the brakes in the correct way, so that the wheels do not lock. Most modern cars are fitted with ABS (anti-lock braking system) to reduce the chance of a skid occurring. ABS is a computer-controlled system that senses when the car is about to skid and releases the brakes for a very short time.

SAFE STOPPING DISTANCE

KEY POINT

Stopping distance = thinking distance + braking distance

The Highway Code used in the United Kingdom gives stopping distances for cars travelling at various speeds. The **stopping distance** is the sum of the thinking distance and the braking distance. The faster the car is travelling the greater the stopping distance will be (**Figure 3.6**).

THINKING DISTANCE

When a driver suddenly sees an object blocking the way ahead, it takes time for him or her to respond to the new situation before taking any action, such as braking. This time is called reaction time and will depend on the person driving the car. It will also depend on a number of other factors including factors that might slow reaction times such as being tired. Poor visibility (for example, fog) may also make it difficult for a driver to identify a danger and so cause him or her to take longer to respond. Clearly, the longer the driver takes to react, the further the car will travel before braking even starts – that is, the longer the thinking distance will be. Equally clear is the fact that the higher the car's speed, the further the car will travel during this 'thinking time'. If the distance between two cars is not at least the thinking distance then, in the event of an emergency stop by the vehicle in front, a violent accident is inevitable.

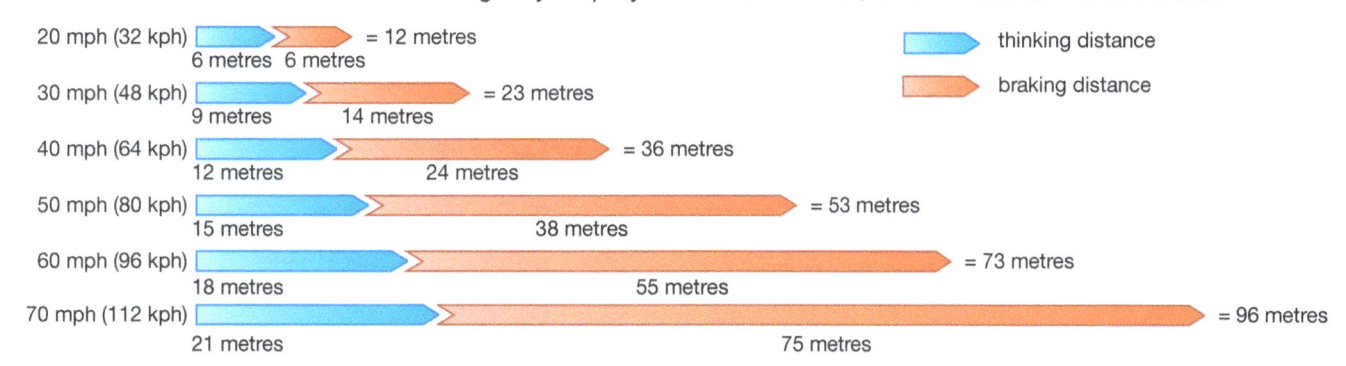

Speed	Thinking distance	Braking distance	Total
20 mph (32 kph)	6 metres	6 metres	= 12 metres
30 mph (48 kph)	9 metres	14 metres	= 23 metres
40 mph (64 kph)	12 metres	24 metres	= 36 metres
50 mph (80 kph)	15 metres	38 metres	= 53 metres
60 mph (96 kph)	18 metres	55 metres	= 73 metres
70 mph (112 kph)	21 metres	75 metres	= 96 metres

▲ Figure 3.6 The stopping distance is the distance the car covers from the moment the driver is aware of the need to stop to the point at which the vehicle comes to a complete stop.

BRAKING DISTANCE

With ABS (anti-lock braking system) braking, in an emergency you brake as hard as you can. This means that the braking force will be a maximum and we can work out the deceleration using the equation below.

$F = m \times a$, rearranged to give:

$a = \dfrac{F}{m}$ (shown in **Figure 3.4**)

It is worth pointing out here that vehicles with large masses, like lorries, will have smaller rates of deceleration for a given braking force – they will, therefore, travel further while braking.

Chapter 1 shows that the distance travelled by a moving object can be found from its velocity–time graph. The area under the graph gives the distance travelled. Look at the velocity–time graphs in **Figures 3.7** and **3.8** of four cars A, B, C and D, which all have the same mass.

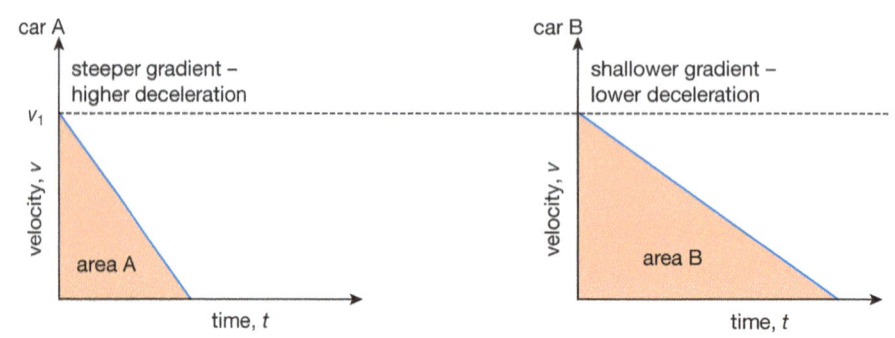

▲ Figure 3.7 Velocity–time graphs for two cars braking at different rates from the same speed, v_1, to rest.

Figure 3.7 shows two cars, A and B, braking from the same velocity. Car A is braking harder than car B and comes to rest in a shorter time. Car B travels further before stopping, as you can see from the larger area under the graph. Remember that the maximum rate of deceleration depends on how hard you can brake without skidding – in poor conditions the braking force will be lower.

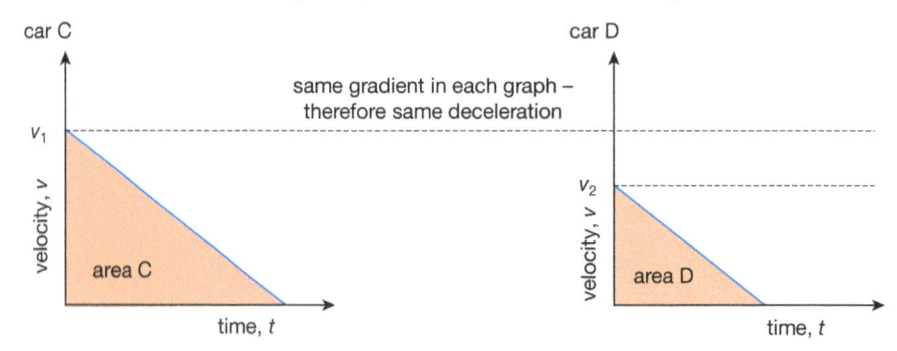

▲ Figure 3.8 Velocity–time graphs for two cars braking at the same rate to rest, from different speeds, v_1 and v_2.

Figure 3.8 shows two cars, C and D, braking at the same rate, as you can see from the gradients. Car C is braking from a higher velocity and so takes longer to stop. Again, the greater area under the graph for car C shows that it travels further while stopping than car D.

Vehicles cannot stop instantly! Remember also that the chart in **Figure 3.6** shows stopping distances in ideal conditions. If the car tyres or brakes are in poor condition, or if the road surface is wet, icy or slippery, then the car will travel further before stopping.

1 FORCES AND MOTION 3 FORCES AND MOVEMENT

KEY POINT

The force on a mass of 1 kg in the Earth's gravitational field is 10 N/kg. Using $F = ma$ we can find the acceleration of a 1 kg mass when it is dropped on Earth: it is 10 m/s^2.

WEIGHT

The weight of an object is the force that acts on it because of gravity. The weight of an object depends on its mass and the strength of gravity. The **gravitational field strength** (*g*) is the force that acts on each kilogram of mass. We can work out the weight of an object by using this equation:

weight, *W* (N) = mass, *m* (kg) × gravitational field strength, *g* (N/kg)

$$W = m \times g$$

You can use the triangle method (**Figure 3.9**) to rearrange this equation.

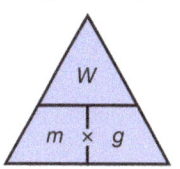

▲ Figure 3.9 Rearranging $W = m \times g$ using the triangle method

Near and on the Earth's surface the gravitational field strength is approximately 9.8 N/kg, but we often use 10 N/kg to make calculations easier. The gravitational field strength on the Moon is about 1.6 N/kg, so an object taken from the Earth to the Moon will have less weight even though it has the same mass (**Figure 3.10**).

▲ Figure 3.10 An astronaut jumping on the Moon enjoying the effect of low gravity

EXAMPLE 2

An astronaut in a space suit with a complete life support pack has a mass of 140 kg. Calculate how much the astronaut will weigh **a** on the Earth, and **b** on Mars where the gravitational field strength is about one third of that on Earth. (Take the strength of the Earth's gravitational field as 10 N/kg.)

The force of gravity or weight of an object is given by:

weight, *W* = mass, *m* × gravitational field strength, *g*

a weight on Earth = 140 kg × 10 N/kg

= 1400 N

b *g* on Mars = $\frac{10 \text{ N/kg}}{3}$ = 3.34 N/kg

weight on Mars = 140 kg × 3.34 N/kg

= 468 N

CHAPTER QUESTIONS

Exam-style questions on forces and movement can be found at the end of Unit 1 on page 322.

SKILLS CRITICAL THINKING

1. Explain what is meant by an unbalanced force. Illustrate your answer with an example.

SKILLS REASONING

2. Rockets burn fuel to give them the thrust needed to accelerate. As the fuel burns the mass of the rocket gets smaller. Assuming that the rocket motors provide a constant thrust force, explain what will happen to the acceleration of the rocket as it burns its fuel.

SKILLS PROBLEM SOLVING

3.
   a. Calculate the force required to make an object of mass 500 g accelerate at 4 m/s². (Take care with the units!)
   b. An object accelerates at 0.8 m/s² when a resultant force of 200 N acts upon it. Calculate the mass of the object.
   c. Calculate the acceleration that is produced by a force of 250 N acting on a mass of 25 kg.

SKILLS CRITICAL THINKING

4. Explain the meaning of the following terms used to describe stopping vehicles in an emergency:
   a. thinking distance
   b. braking distance
   c. overall stopping distance.

SKILLS ANALYSIS

5. State the factors that affect the braking distance of a vehicle.

SKILLS PROBLEM SOLVING

6. The diagram below shows the velocity–time graph for a car travelling from the moment that the driver sees an object blocking the road ahead.

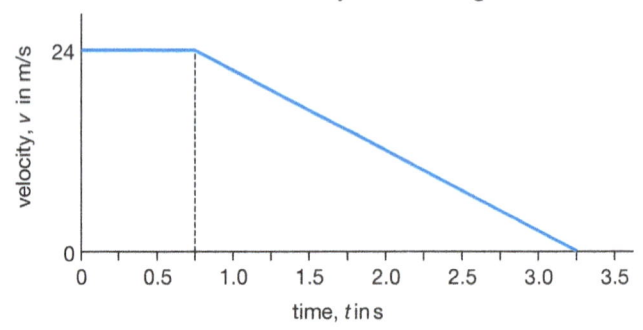

Use the graph to find out:
   a. how long the driver takes to react to seeing the obstacle (reaction time)
   b. how far the car travels in this reaction time
   c. how long it takes to bring the car to a halt once the driver starts braking
   d. the total distance the car travels before stopping.

SKILLS PROBLEM SOLVING

7. Calculate the weight of an apple of mass 100 grams:
   a. on the Earth (g = 10 N/kg)
   b. on the Moon (g = 1.6 N/kg).

SKILLS PROBLEM SOLVING

8. At a science fair teams of students are set the challenge of protecting an (uncooked) egg from being broken when it is dropped from the top of a tall flight of stairs. It is understood that if an egg or any breakable item is subjected to a force that is too large the result will be messy.

The teams are provided with a selection of simple materials like paper, cardboard, foam rubber string and cloth, sticky tape and glue and are given an hour to come up with a good solution to the problem.

The starting point is a knowledge of how force and acceleration or, in this case, deceleration are related.

Explain how understanding the physics will guide the teams to a solution, that is, to make sure that the force that acts on the egg when it hits the ground is not large enough to break it. Then use this understanding to suggest how the egg can be protected.

EXAM PRACTICE

SKILLS CRITICAL THINKING

1 Take the acceleration due to gravity, $g = 10$ m/s^2. Identify which of the following statements about the motion of an object on which unbalanced forces act is *false*.

A The object could continue moving at constant speed in a straight line.

B The object could accelerate.

C The object could slow down.

D The object could change the direction in which it is moving.

(Total 1 mark)

SKILLS CRITICAL THINKING

2 Take the acceleration due to gravity, $g = 10$ m/s^2. A ball is thrown vertically upwards in the air. Identify which of the following statements about the motion of the ball is *false*.

A The ball will be travelling as fast as it was when it gets back to the ground as it was when first thrown upwards.

B The ball will be stationary for an instant at the highest point in its flight.

C The direction of the force on the ball changes so the ball falls back to the ground.

D The direction of the acceleration is always downwards.

(Total 1 mark)

SKILLS ANALYSIS

3 Take the acceleration due to gravity, $g = 10$ m/s^2. A tennis ball is dropped from a height of 3 m and bounces back to a height of 1 m after hitting the ground ($s = 0$).

Identify which of the following distance–time graphs shows this motion correctly.

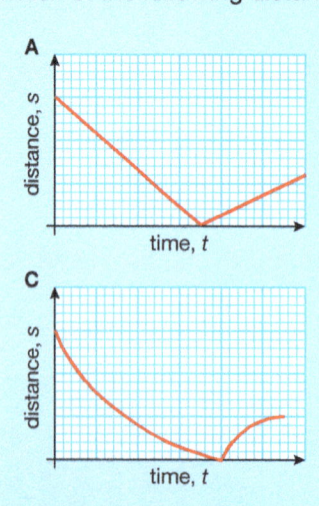

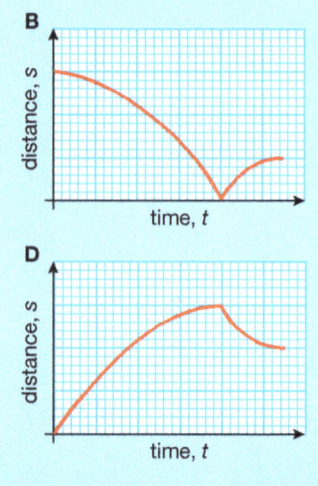

(Total 1 mark)

1 FORCES AND MOTION — EXAM PRACTICE

SKILLS PROBLEM SOLVING

4 Take the acceleration due to gravity, $g = 10$ m/s^2. A stone is dropped down a well and it takes 3 seconds to reach the water at the bottom.

a Calculate the speed of the stone when it reaches the water. (2)

b Use the answer to **a** and the fact that the stone started with velocity = 0 m/s (it was released from rest) to calculate the average velocity of the stone during its fall. (2)

c Use your answer to **b** to calculate the depth of the well. (2)

(Total 6 marks)

SKILLS PROBLEM SOLVING

5 Take the acceleration due to gravity, $g = 10$ m/s^2. A large cruise liner has a mass of 10^8 kg.

a Calculate unbalanced force needed to make the cruise liner accelerate at 0.2 m/s^2. (2)

b If it accelerates at this rate determine how long will it take to reach its cruising speed of 5 m/s. (2)

(Total 4 marks)

SKILLS CRITICAL THINKING

6 Take the acceleration due to gravity, $g = 10$ m/s^2. Here is part of a velocity–time graph for a ball that is dropped from a height of 20 m onto a hard surface. The graph shows it rebounding once. (It would be likely to rebound several times before coming to rest.)

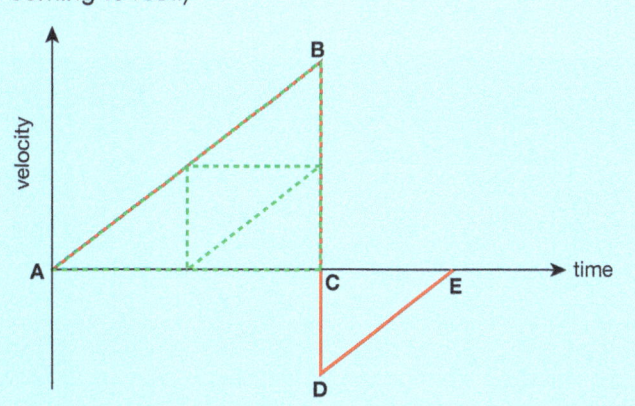

State at which point or points on the graph

a the ball is stationary (3)

b the ball is moving at its highest speed (1)

c the ball is accelerating at 10 m/s^2 (2)

d the ball is 20 m above the ground (1)

e the ball is in contact with the ground (1)

f the velocity is at its maximum downward value (1)

g the velocity is at its maximum upward value (1)

h the ball is about 5 m above the ground (1)

i the largest unbalanced force is acting on the ball. (1)

(Total 12 marks)

4 MAINS ELECTRICITY 325   5 CURRENT AND VOLTAGE IN CIRCUITS 328   6 ELECTRICAL RESISTANCE 334

PHYSICS UNIT 2
ELECTRICITY

It is sometimes really difficult to imagine how we could live without electricity. As we move around we use electricity from batteries and cells for our mobile phones, mp3 players and other mobile devices. In our homes and other buildings we use electricity from the mains for heating, lighting and providing the energy for household appliances such as televisions, radios, computers and their printers. Understanding what electricity is, where it comes from and how we can control it is vital if we are to make maximum use of this important source of energy.

4 MAINS ELECTRICITY

SPECIFICATION REFERENCES: 2.1, 2.4, 2.6

The electricity that we use for heating, lighting and air conditioning in our homes is called mains electricity and is supplied to us by power stations.

This electrical energy usually enters our homes through an underground cable. The cable is connected to an electricity meter, which measures the amount of electrical energy used. From here, the cable is connected to a consumer unit or a fuse box.

Most of the wires that leave the fuse box are connected to ring main circuits that are hidden in the walls or floors around each room. Individual pieces of electrical equipment are connected to these circuits using plugs.

UNITS

In this unit, you will need to use ampere (A) as the unit of current, coulomb (C) as the unit of charge, joule (J) as the unit of energy, ohm (Ω) as the unit of resistance, second (s) as the unit of time, volt (V) as the unit of voltage and watt (W) as the unit of power.

▲ Figure 4.1 Most household appliances use mains electricity as their source of energy.

LEARNING OBJECTIVES

- Know and use the relationship between power, current and voltage:

  power = current × voltage

  $P = I \times V$

- Know the difference between mains electricity being alternating current (a.c.) and direct current (d.c.) being supplied by a cell or battery.

▲ Figure 4.2 The wires inside a toaster have a high resistance. They become very hot when a current passes through them.

THE HEATING EFFECT OF CURRENT

The wiring in a house is designed to let current pass through it easily. As a result, the wires do not become warm when appliances are being used. We say that the wires have a low **resistance**. However, in some appliances, for example, kettles or toasters (**Figure 4.2**), we want wires (more usually called **heating elements**) to become warm. The wires of a heating element are designed to have a high resistance so that as the current passes through them energy is transferred and the element heats up. We use this heating effect of current in many different ways in our homes.

When current passes through the very thin wire (**filament**) of a traditional light bulb it becomes very hot and **glows** (shines) white (see **Figure 4.3**). The bulb is transferring electrical energy to heat and light energy.

Figure 4.3 It is the heating effect of a current that is causing this bulb to glow. Incandescent bulbs like these are very inefficient. Often more than 90% of the energy transferred is lost to the surroundings as heat. As a result they are rapidly being replaced by modern halogen bulbs and LEDs, which give off much less heat and therefore waste less energy.

ELECTRICAL POWER

Figure 4.4 shows a 50 W **halogen light bulb**. You can also buy 70 W light bulbs. Both bulbs transfer electrical energy to heat and light. The 70 W bulb will be brighter because it transfers 70 J of electrical energy every second. The dimmer 50 W halogen bulb shown transfers only 50 J of energy every second. A 70 W bulb has a higher power rating.

Power is measured in joules per second or watts (W).

Devices that transfer lots of energy very quickly have their power rating expressed in kilowatts (kW).

1 kW = 1000 W

The power (P) of an appliance is related to the **voltage** (V) across it and the current (I) flowing through it.

The equation (see also **Figure 4.5**) is:

power, P (watts) = current, I (amps) × voltage, V (volts)

$$P = I \times V$$

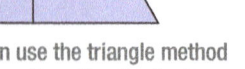

Figure 4.4 The dimmer 50 W bulb transfers less electrical energy to heat and light energy every second.

Figure 4.5 You can use the triangle method for rearranging equations like $P = I \times V$.

EXAMPLE 1

A 230 V television takes a current of 3 A. Calculate the power of the television.

$P = I \times V$
$= 3 \text{ A} \times 230 \text{ V}$
$= 690 \text{ W}$

EXAMPLE 2

Calculate the current that flows in a 230 V, 1 kW electric hairdryer.

$I = \dfrac{P}{V}$
$= \dfrac{1000 \text{ W}}{230 \text{ V}}$
$= 4.35 \text{ A}$

ALTERNATING CURRENT AND DIRECT CURRENT

If we could see the current or voltage from the mains it would appear to be very strange. Its value increases and then decreases and then does the same again but in the opposite direction. If we could draw these changes as a graph they would look like a wave.

This happens because of the way in which the electricity is generated at the power station. A current or voltage that behaves like this is called an alternating current (a.c.) or **alternating voltage**. This is very different to the currents and voltages we get from batteries and **cells**.

Cells and batteries provide currents and voltages that are always in the same direction and have the same value. This is called direct current (d.c.) or direct voltage. If we drew this as a graph it would be a straight horizontal line.

Figure 4.6 shows how the voltage of an a.c. supply compares with the voltage of a d.c. supply.

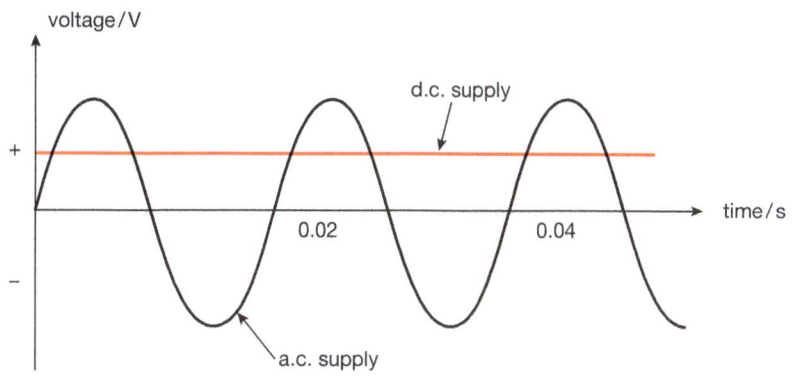

▲ Figure 4.6 How the voltage of an a.c. supply compares with that of a d.c. supply

CHAPTER QUESTIONS

Exam-style questions on mains electricity can be found at the end of Unit 2 on page 341.

SKILLS PROBLEM SOLVING

1 a There is a current of 0.25 A in a bulb when a voltage of 12 V is applied across it. Calculate the power of the bulb.
   b Calculate the voltage that is being applied across a 10 W bulb with a current of 0.2 A.
   c Calculate the current in a 60 W bulb if the voltage across it is 230 V.

SKILLS CRITICAL THINKING

2 An electric kettle is marked '230 V, 1.5 kW'.
   a Explain what these numbers mean.

SKILLS PROBLEM SOLVING

   b Calculate the current that flows through it when the kettle is turned on.

SKILLS REASONING

   c Explain why a 230 V, 100 W bulb glows more brightly than a 230 V, 60 W bulb when both are connected to the mains supply.

SKILLS CRITICAL THINKING

3 a Draw
      i a graph that shows how the voltage of the mains supply changes with time
      ii a graph that shows how the voltage from a cell or battery changes with time.
   b Explain in words the differences between the two graphs you have drawn.

SKILLS DECISION MAKING, CREATIVITY

4 Think of a room in your house where there are lots of electrical appliances. Make a list of them. Now organise your list so that the appliances that you think have the highest power rating are at the top of your list and those with the lowest are at the bottom. How could you discover if your guesses are correct?

5 CURRENT AND VOLTAGE IN CIRCUITS

SPECIFICATION REFERENCES: 2.8, 2.14, 2.16

We rely on electricity in many areas of our lives. This chapter looks at what electric current is. You will learn what happens to electric current in different circuits, and what effect it has.

Look around the room you are in. If you are at home, you will probably be able to see a television, a radio or a computer. If you are in a science laboratory, you may be able to see a projector, a power supply or lights in the ceiling. These and many other everyday objects need electric currents if they are to work. But what are electric currents?

▲ Figure 5.1 These televisions only work if there are currents flowing through their circuits.

LEARNING OBJECTIVES

- Know that electric current in solid metallic conductors is a flow of negatively charged electrons.
- Know that current is the rate of flow of charge.
- Know that lamps and LEDs can be used to indicate the presence of a current in a circuit.

CONDUCTORS, INSULATORS AND ELECTRIC CURRENT

An electric current is a flow of charge. In metal wires the charges are carried by small **negatively charged** particles called electrons.

Electrons flow easily through all metals. We therefore describe metals as being good **conductors** of electricity. Electrons do not flow easily through plastics – they are poor conductors of electricity. A very poor conductor is known as an **insulator** and is often used in situations where we want to prevent the flow of charge – for example, in the casing of a plug.

In metals, some electrons are free to move between the **atoms**. Under normal circumstances this movement is random – that is, the number of electrons flowing in any one direction is roughly equal to the number flowing in the opposite direction. There is therefore no overall flow of charge (**Figure 5.2a**).

▲ Figure 5.2 (a) With no voltage there is an equal flow of electrons in all directions.

If, however, a cell or battery is connected across the conductor, more of the electrons now flow in the direction away from the negative terminal and towards the positive terminal than in the opposite direction (**Figure 5.2b**). We say 'there is now a net flow of charge'. This flow of charge is what we call an electric current.

EXTENSION

When scientists first experimented with charges flowing through wires, they assumed that it was positive charges that were moving and that current travels from the positive to the negative. We now know that this is incorrect and that when an electric current passes through a wire it is the negative charges or electrons that move. Nevertheless when dealing with topics such as circuits and motors, it is still considered that current flows from positive to negative. This is called conventional current.

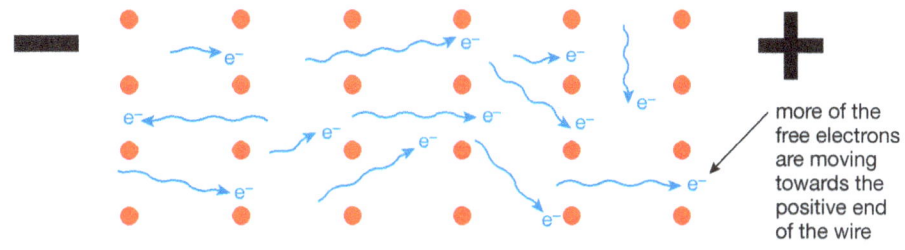

▲ Figure 5.2 (b) When a voltage is applied more electrons will move towards the positive.

In insulators, all the electrons are held tightly in position and are unable to move from atom to atom. Charges are therefore unable to move through insulators.

MEASURING CURRENT

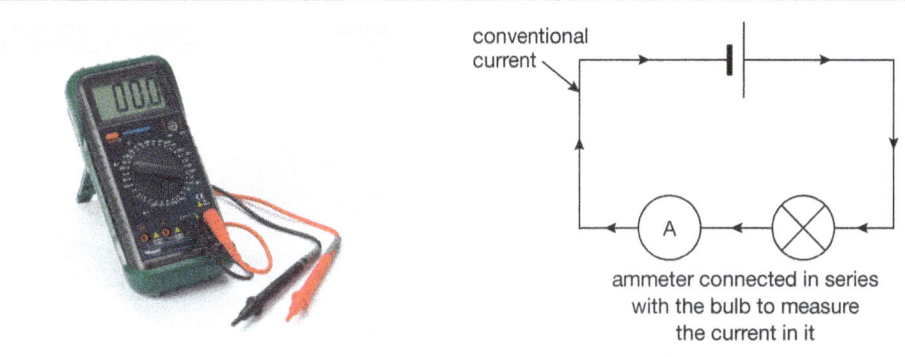

▲ Figure 5.3 An ammeter is used to measure current in a circuit. It has a very low resistance and so has almost no effect on the current.

We measure the size of the current in a **circuit** using an ammeter (**Figure 5.3**). The ammeter is connected in series (see page 332) with the part of the circuit we are interested in.

The size of an electric current indicates the rate at which the charge flows.

The charge carried by one electron is very small and would not be a very useful measure of charge in everyday life. It would be a little like asking how far away the Moon is from the Earth … and getting the answer in mm!

To avoid this problem we measure electric charge (Q) in much bigger units called coulombs (C). One coulomb of charge is equal to the charge carried by approximately six million, million, million (6×10^{18}) electrons.

We measure electric current (*I*) in amperes or amps (A). If there is a current of 1 A in a wire it means that 1 C of charge is passing along the wire each second (**Figure 5.4**).

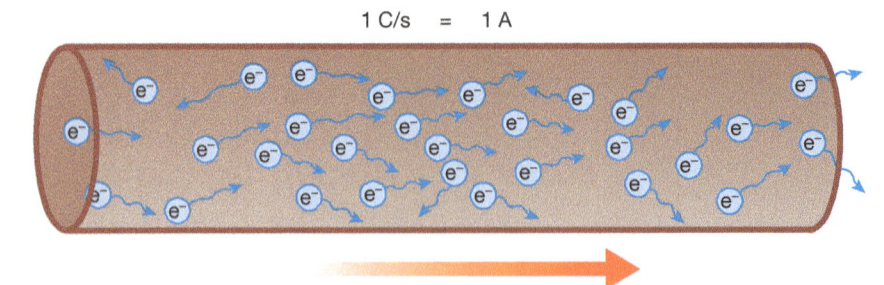

▲ Figure 5.4 One coulomb of charge flowing each second is one amp.

VOLTAGE

We often use cells or batteries to move charges around circuits. We can imagine them as being 'electron pumps'. They transfer energy to the charges. The amount of energy given to each coulomb of charge by a cell or battery is measured in volts (V) and is usually indicated on the side of the battery or cell.

If we connect a 1.5 V cell into a circuit and current flows, 1.5 J of energy is given to each coulomb of charge that passes through the cell.

If two 1.5 V cells are connected in series (**Figure 5.5**) so that they are pumping (pushing) in the same direction, each coulomb of charge will receive 3 J of energy.

▲ Figure 5.5 When several cells are connected together it is called a battery.

KEY POINT

Cells and batteries provide current which moves in one direction. This is known as direct current (d.c.).

As the charges flow around a circuit the energy they carry is transferred by the components they pass through. For example, when current passes through a bulb, energy is transferred to the surroundings as heat and light. When a current passes through the speaker of a radio, most of the energy is transferred as sound.

MEASURING VOLTAGES

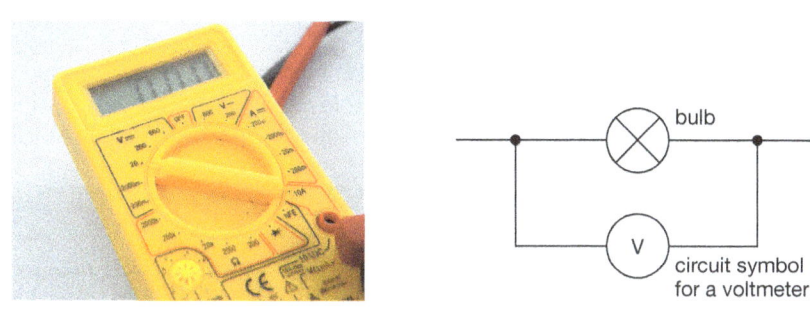

▲ Figure 5.6 A voltmeter measures voltages across a component.

We measure voltages using a voltmeter (**Figure 5.6**). This is connected across (in parallel with) the component we are investigating. A voltmeter connected across a cell or battery will measure the energy given to each coulomb of charge that passes through it. A voltmeter connected across a component will measure the electrical energy transferred when each coulomb of charge passes through it.

KEY POINT

A voltmeter has a very high resistance, so very little current flows through it.

ELECTRICAL CIRCUITS

When the button on the torch shown in **Figure 5.7** is pressed, the circuit is complete – that is, there are no gaps. Charges are able to flow around the circuit and the torch bulb glows. When the button is released the circuit becomes incomplete. Charges cease to flow and the bulb goes out.

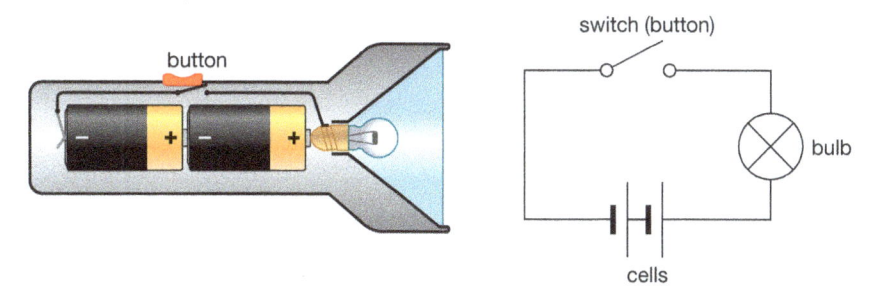

▲ Figure 5.7 A torch contains a simple electrical circuit – a series circuit.

KEY POINT

Drawing diagrams of the actual components in a circuit is a very time-consuming and skilful task. It is much easier to use symbols for each of the components. Diagrams drawn in this way are called circuit diagrams. **Figure 5.8** shows common circuit components and their symbols. You should know the common symbols but the less common ones will be given to you in the exam if you need them. Do not waste time memorising the less common ones.

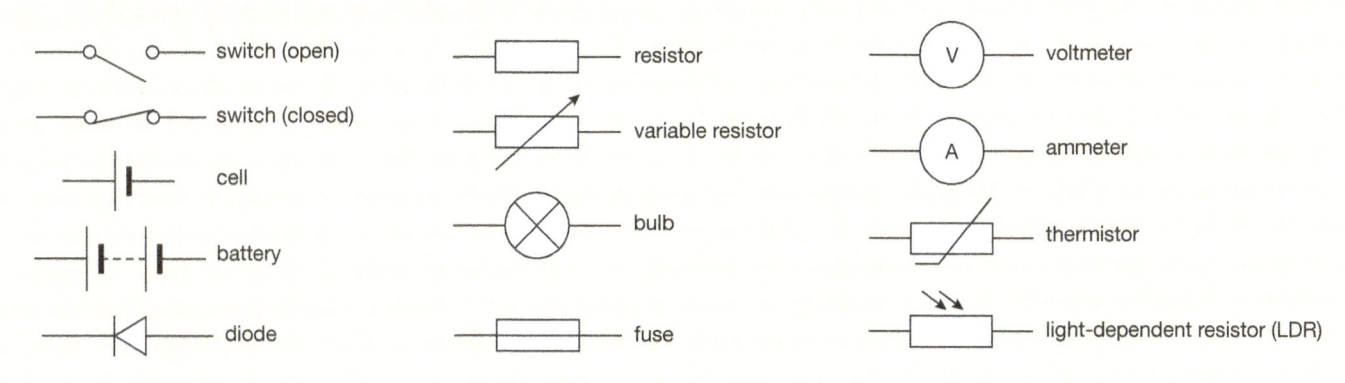

▲ Figure 5.8 Circuit symbols

2 ELECTRICITY

5 CURRENT AND VOLTAGE IN CIRCUITS

IS IT ON?

We sometimes put a small bulb or lamp in a circuit to show us if a circuit is 'turned on'. When there is a current in the circuit the bulb glows or shines. **Light emitting diodes (LEDs)** also glow when there is a current in a circuit but they require far less energy than bulbs. This is why many appliances such as televisions, DVD players and routers use small LEDs to show when the appliance is working or on standby (**Figure 5.9**).

▲ Figure 5.9 Glowing LEDs indicate which circuits are working

SERIES CIRCUITS

There are two main types of electrical circuit. There are those circuits where there are no branches or junctions and there is only one path the current can follow. These simple 'single loop' circuits are called series circuits (**Figure 5.10**).

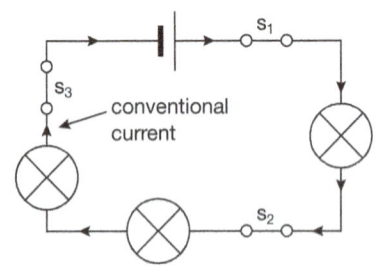

Circuits that have branches or junctions and more than one path that the current can follow are called parallel circuits, but for your examination you only need to know about series circuits.

In a series circuit containing bulbs:

- One switch placed anywhere in the circuit can be used to turn all the bulbs on and off.
- If any one of the bulbs breaks, it causes a gap in the circuit and all of the other bulbs will 'stop working'.
- The energy supplied by the cell is 'shared' between all the bulbs, so the more bulbs you add to a series circuit the less bright they all become (**Figure 5.11**).

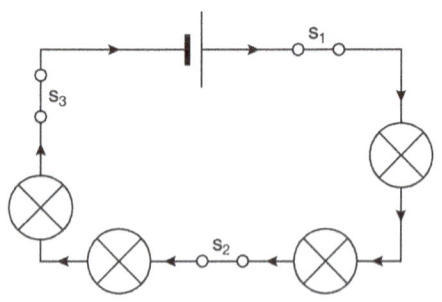

▲ Figure 5.10 A typical series circuit. Opening any one of these switches will turn all three bulbs off.

▲ Figure 5.11 Adding an extra bulb in series will result in the bulbs shining less brightly.

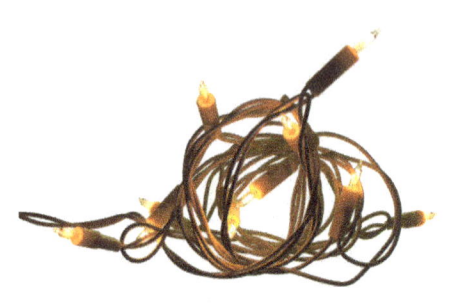

Decorative lights (**Figure 5.12**) used to be wired in series. Each bulb only needs a low voltage, so even when the voltage from the mains supply is 'shared' out between them each bulb still gets enough energy to produce light. Unfortunately, if the filament in one of the bulbs breaks then all the other bulbs will go out.

▲ Figure 5.12 Decorative lights used to be connected in series.

CURRENT IN A SERIES CIRCUIT

In a series circuit the current is the same in all parts; current is not used up (**Figure 5.13a**).

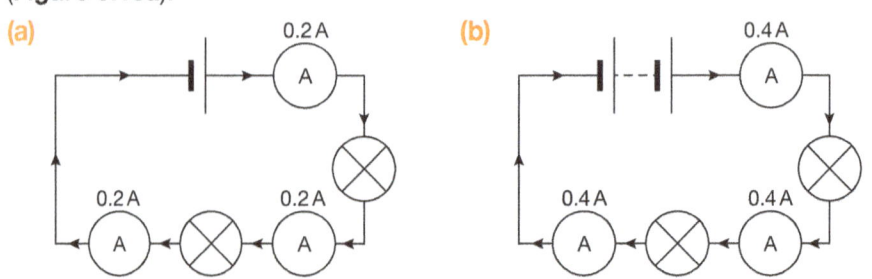

▲ Figure 5.13 (a) In a series circuit the current does not vary. (b) The addition of a second cell doubles the voltage applied to the circuit so the current will also double.

The size of the current in a series circuit depends on the voltage supplied to it, and the number and type of the other components in the circuit. If a second identical cell is added in series the voltage will double and so the current will also double (**Figure 5.13b**).

CHAPTER QUESTIONS

Exam-style questions on current and voltage in circuits can be found at the end of Unit 2 on page 341.

SKILLS CRITICAL THINKING

1 Current is a flow of charge.
   a What are the charge carriers in metals?
   b Explain why charges are able to flow through metals but not through a plastic.

SKILLS CRITICAL THINKING

2 a i Explain the difference between a complete circuit and an incomplete circuit.
     ii Draw an example of
        ■ a complete circuit and
        ■ an incomplete circuit.

SKILLS ANALYSIS

   b Look carefully at the circuit shown below. Assuming that all switches are initially closed, decide which of the bulbs go out when each of the switches is opened in turn.

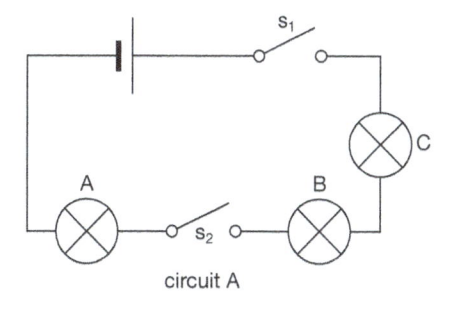

circuit A

   c In circuit A, which bulb(s) glow the brightest when all the switches in the circuit are closed?

SKILLS CRITICAL THINKING

   d Explain your answer to part c.
   e What happens to the brightness of the bulbs if a fourth bulb is added in series to circuit A?
   f Explain your answer to part e.

SKILLS INTERPRETATION

3 The voltage between two points in a circuit is measured using a voltmeter. Draw a circuit diagram to show how a voltmeter should be connected to measure:
   a the voltage across a bulb
   b the voltage of a cell.

SKILLS CRITICAL THINKING

4 a Name *three* electrical devices in your house which use LEDs to indicate if the device is turned on or not.
   b Some years ago small electrical bulbs were used to show if a device was turned on. Why are LEDs now used to do this and not bulbs?

SKILLS CRITICAL THINKING

5 Why would it not be a good idea to connect all the different parts of an electric cooker (oven, grill, heating plates) in series?

6 ELECTRICAL RESISTANCE

SPECIFICATION REFERENCES: 2.9, 2.10, 2.13, 2.19

In this chapter you will learn what resistance is and how it can be useful in electrical appliances. You will learn what factors affect resistance and how to work out the resistance of a component by measuring the current in it and the voltage across it (Ohm's law). You will also read about some special resistors, and their uses.

It is likely that almost every day of your life you will make some adjustments to at least one electrical appliance. You may turn up the volume of your radio or change the brightness of a light. In each of these examples your adjustments are changing the currents and the voltages in the circuits of your appliance. You are doing this by altering the resistance of the circuits. This chapter will help you understand the meaning and importance of resistance and how we make use of it.

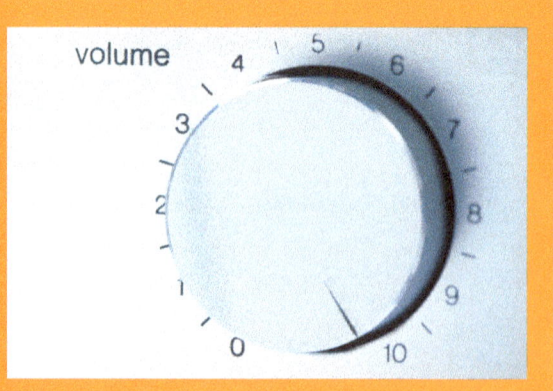

▲ Figure 6.1 Turning this dial alters the resistance in the circuit which changes the volume of the sound.

LEARNING OBJECTIVES

- Understand how the current in a series circuit depends on the applied voltage and the number and nature of other components.
- Describe how current varies with voltage in wires, resistors, metal filament lamps and diodes, and how to investigate this experimentally.
- Describe the qualitative effect of changing resistance on the current in a circuit.
- Calculate the currents, voltages and resistances of two resistive components connected in a series circuit.
- Know and use the relationship between voltage, current and resistance:

  voltage = current × resistance

  $V = I \times R$

REMINDER
We normally assume that connecting wires have zero resistance.

RESISTANCE

All components in a circuit offer some resistance to the flow of charge. Some (for example, connecting wires) allow charges to pass through very easily losing very little of their energy. We describe connecting wires as having very low resistance. The flow of charge through some components is not so easy and a large amount of energy may be used to move the charges through them. This energy is transferred, usually as heat. Components like these are said to have a high resistance.

We measure the resistance (R) of a component by comparing the size of the current (I) in that component and the voltage (V) applied across its ends. Voltage, current and resistance are related as follows:

voltage, V (volts) = current, I (amps) × resistance, R (ohms)

$V = I \times R$

We measure resistance in units called ohms (Ω).

HINT

If an examination question asks you to write out the equation for calculating resistance, current or voltage, always give the actual equation such as $V = I \times R$. You will not get the mark if you just draw the triangle.

EXAMPLE 1

When a voltage of 12 V is applied across a doorbell there is a current of 0.1 A. Calculate the resistance of the doorbell.

$V = I \times R$

Rearrange the equation (see **Figure 6.2**).

$R = \dfrac{V}{I}$

$= \dfrac{12\,V}{0.1\,A}$

$= 120\,\Omega$

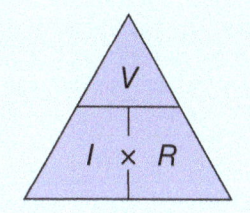

▲ Figure 6.2 You can use the triangle method for rearranging equations like $V = I \times R$.

If there are two or more resistors connected in series in a circuit, their total resistance is found by simply adding the individual resistances together. (This is not true for parallel circuits. You do not need to know how to do this.)

EXAMPLE 2

The circuit in **Figure 6.3** contains a 12 V battery and two resistors connected in series.

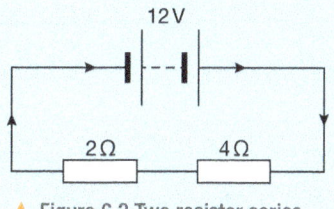

▲ Figure 6.3 Two resistor series circuit

Calculate:

a the current in each of the resistors

b the voltage across each resistor.

a The total resistance the current must pass through is $2\,\Omega + 4\,\Omega = 6\,\Omega$

The current in the circuit (*I*) is therefore:

$I = \dfrac{V}{R}$

$= \dfrac{12\,V}{6\,\Omega}$

$= 2\,A$

The current in a series circuit is the same everywhere. So the current in both resistors is 2 A.

b Using $V = I \times R$

for the $2\,\Omega$ resistor: $V = 2\,A \times 2\,\Omega = 4\,V$

for the $4\,\Omega$ resistor: $V = 2\,A \times 4\,\Omega = 8\,V$

Safety note: The resistance wire in the circuit may get hot enough to burn skin if the current/voltage is increased too much.

EXPERIMENT TO INVESTIGATE HOW CURRENT VARIES WITH VOLTAGE FOR DIFFERENT COMPONENTS

1 Set up the circuit shown in **Figure 6.4**.
2 Turn the variable resistor to its maximum value.
3 Close the switch and take the readings from the ammeter and the voltmeter.
4 Alter the value of the variable resistor again and take a new pair of readings from the meters.
5 Repeat the whole process at least six times.
6 Place the results in a table (see **Table 6.1** below) and draw a graph of current (*I*) against voltage (*V*).

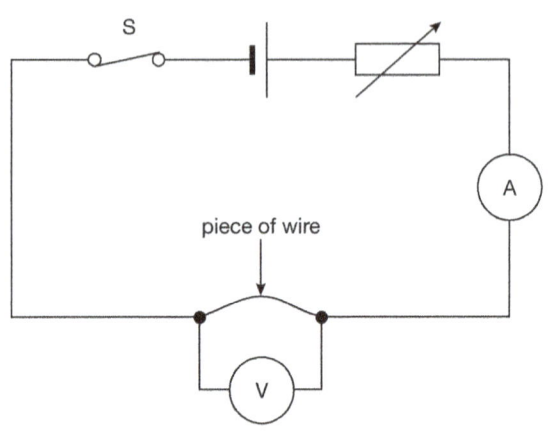

▲ Figure 6.4 This circuit can be used to investigate the relationship between current and voltage.

Table 6.1 Typical results table

Current / amps	Voltage / volts
0.0	0.0
0.1	0.4
0.2	0.8
0.3	1.2
0.4	1.6
0.5	2.0

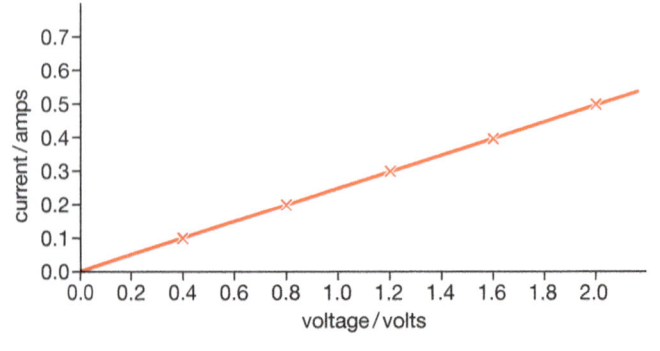

▲ Figure 6.5 Graph of results

The graph in **Figure 6.5** is a straight line graph passing through the origin. The slope of the graph tells us about the resistance of the wire. The steeper the slope the smaller the resistance of the wire.

If we repeat this experiment for other components, such as a resistor, a filament bulb and a diode, the shapes of the graphs we obtain are often very different from that shown in **Figure 6.5**. By looking very carefully at these shapes we can see how they behave.

CURRENT/VOLTAGE GRAPH FOR A WIRE OR A RESISTOR

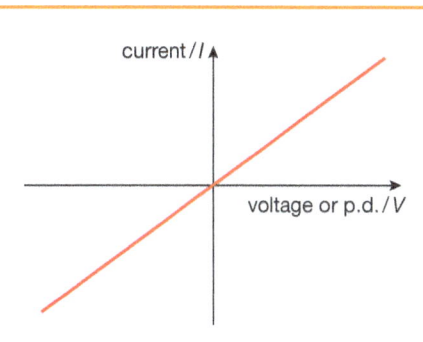

▲ Figure 6.6

The graph in **Figure 6.6** is a straight line. It has a constant slope. So the resistance of this component does not change.

CURRENT/VOLTAGE GRAPH FOR A FILAMENT BULB

> **HINT**
> The flatter the slope the higher the resistance.

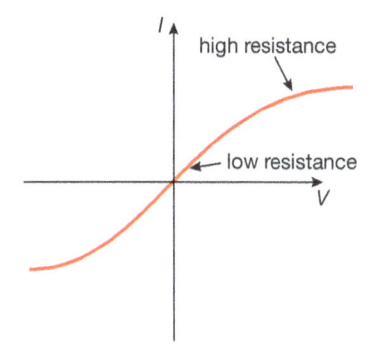

▲ Figure 6.7

The graph in **Figure 6.7** is not a straight line. The resistance of the bulb changes as the currents and voltages change. At higher currents and voltages the bulb gets hotter and the slope of the graph shows us that the resistance of the filament bulb increases.

USING RESISTANCE

FIXED RESISTORS

In many circuits you will find components similar to those shown in **Figure 6.8**. They are called fixed resistors. They are included in circuits in order to control the sizes of currents and voltages. The resistor in the circuit in **Figure 6.9** is included so that both the current in the bulb and the voltage applied across it are correct. Without the resistor the voltage across the bulb may cause too large a current and the bulb may 'blow' or break.

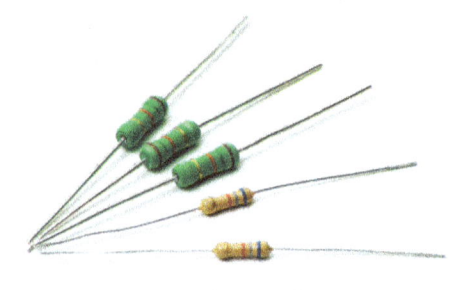

▲ Figure 6.8 A selection of resistors

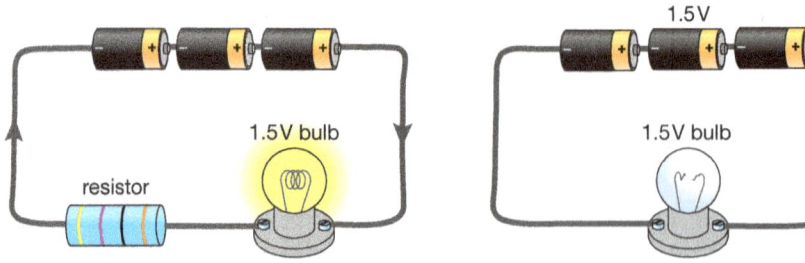

▲ Figure 6.9 The resistor in the first circuit limits the size of the current. Without the resistor the current in the second circuit is too high and the bulb breaks.

VARIABLE RESISTORS

Figure 6.10 shows examples of a different kind of resistor. They are called variable resistors as it is possible to alter their resistance. If you alter the volume of your radio using a knob you are using a variable resistor to do this.

▲ Figure 6.10 Variable resistors and their symbol

In the circuit in **Figure 6.11** a variable resistor is being used to control the size of the current in a bulb. If the resistance is decreased there will be a larger current and the bulb shines more brightly. If the resistance is increased the current will be smaller and the bulb will glow less brightly or not at all. The variable resistor is behaving in this circuit as a **dimmer switch**. In circuits containing electric motors, variable resistors can be used to control the speed of the motor.

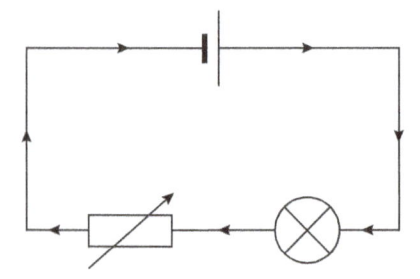

▲ Figure 6.11 Circuit with a variable resistor being used as a dimmer switch

EXTENSION

The relationship between the voltage across a component and its current is described by Ohm's law, which states:

The current in a conductor is directly proportional to the potential difference across its ends, provided its temperature remains constant.

So the resistance of a wire can be found by measuring the voltage (*V*) across it and the current (*I*) in it when this voltage is applied to the wire and then calculating a value for the **ratio** $\frac{V}{I}$ (see page 334). But the law also states that the temperature of the wire must be constant. This is because if the temperature of the wire changes, its resistance also changes.

This happens because at higher temperatures the atoms in the wire **vibrate** more vigorously, making it more difficult for the electrons to flow between them (**Figure 6.12**).

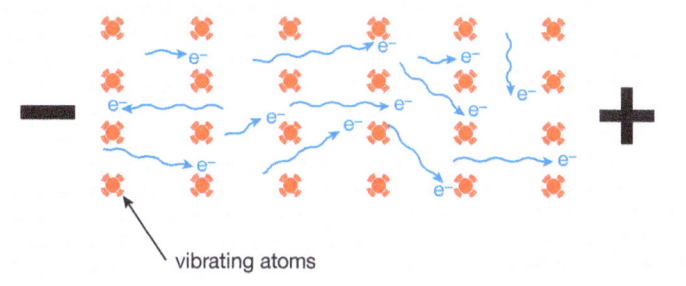

▲ Figure 6.12 At higher temperatures the increased vibration of the atoms makes it more difficult for charges to flow.

If a wire or conductor is cooled the vibration of its atoms decreases and so its resistance decreases. At very low temperatures, close to absolute zero (−273 °C), these vibrations stop and the conductor offers no resistance to the flow of charge. This event is called superconductivity and could be extremely useful (see **Figure 6.13**). For example, when electricity flows through a superconductor there is no loss of energy. This means that by using superconductivity we could transmit electrical energy from power stations without losses. Scientists around the world are now searching for materials that are superconductors at temperatures well above absolute zero.

▲ Figure 6.13 Maglev trains use superconducting electromagnets to help them hover above the tracks.

CHAPTER QUESTIONS

Exam-style questions on electrical resistance can be found at the end of Unit 2 on page 341.

1 Which of the following could be used to change the speed of an electric motor?
   A inductor
   B fixed resistor
   C variable resistor
   D capacitor

SKILLS — CRITICAL THINKING

2 a Describe how the current in a wire changes as the voltage across the wire increases.

SKILLS — INTERPRETATION

   b Draw a diagram of the circuit you would use to confirm your answer to part a.

SKILLS — DECISION MAKING

   c Describe how you would use the apparatus and what readings you would take.

SKILLS — INTERPRETATION

   d Draw an I–V graph for
      i a piece of wire at room temperature
      ii a filament bulb.
      Explain the main features of each of these graphs.

SKILLS — PROBLEM SOLVING

3 a There is a current of 5 A when a voltage of 20 V is applied across a resistor. Calculate the resistance of the resistor.
   b Calculate the current when a voltage of 12 V is applied across a piece of wire of resistance 50 Ω.
   c Calculate the voltage that must be applied across a wire of resistance 10 Ω if the current is to be 3 A.

> **HINT**
> Remember when doing calculations like these to show all your working out and include units with your answer.

SKILLS — INTERPRETATION

4 a Draw a simple series circuit which contains a battery, an open switch a bulb a variable resistor.

SKILLS — CRITICAL THINKING

   b Explain what happens when the switch is closed and the resistance of the variable is changed.

SKILLS — REASONING

   c Suggest one practical use for a circuit like this.

EXAM PRACTICE

SKILLS CRITICAL THINKING

1
a Which of the following particles carries charge through a wire?
  A neutrons
  B electrons
  C protons
  D ions (1)

b Which of the following is true for all series circuits?
  A Parts of the circuit can be turned off while other parts remain on.
  B The current is the same in all parts of the circuit.
  C The current decreases as it goes around the circuit.
  D There are junctions or branches. (1)

SKILLS PROBLEM SOLVING

c When a voltage of 6 V is applied across a resistor there is a current of 0.1 A. The value of the resistor is
  A 6 Ω
  B 60 Ω
  C 16.6 Ω
  D 0.6 Ω (1)

(Total 3 marks)

SKILLS ANALYSIS

2 Asma set up the circuit shown below to investigate how the resistance of a bulb changes as the current in it changes.

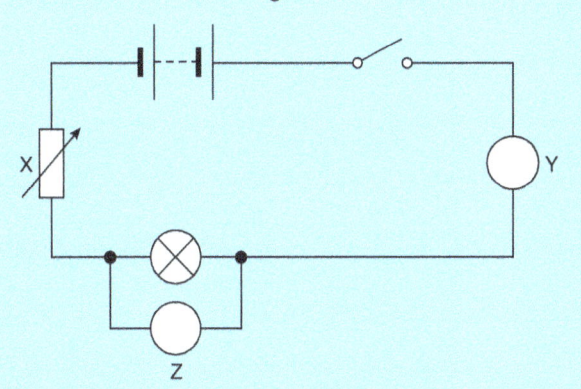

a Name the instruments labelled Y and Z. (2)
b Name the component labelled X. (1)
c State the purpose of X in this circuit. (1)

Asma takes a series of readings. She measures the voltage across the bulb and the current in it. She then plots the graph shown below.

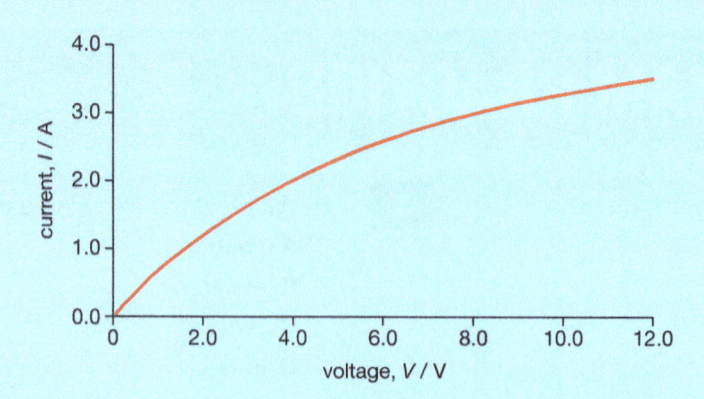

d Determine the current in the bulb when a voltage of 6 V is applied across it. (1)

e Determine the voltage applied across the bulb when there is a current of 2 A. (1)

f Calculate the resistance of the bulb when there is a current of 2 A. (2)

g Describe what happens to the resistance of the bulb as the current increases. (1)

(Total 9 marks)

3 A simple series circuit containing a 12 V battery and a 10 Ω resistor was constructed as shown below.

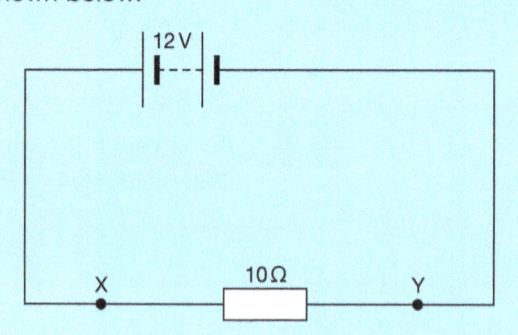

a Calculate the current between points X and Y. (2)

b Calculate the current which will flow between points X and Y if a second 10 ohm resistor is added to the circuit, immediately next to the battery. (2)

(Total 4 marks)

4 An electric kettle is rated at 2 kW when connected to a 230 V electrical supply.

a Calculate the current when the kettle is turned on. (3)

b Calculate the resistance of the heating element of the kettle. (3)

(Total 6 marks)

2 ELECTRICITY — **EXAM PRACTICE**

SKILLS PROBLEM SOLVING

5 Calculate:

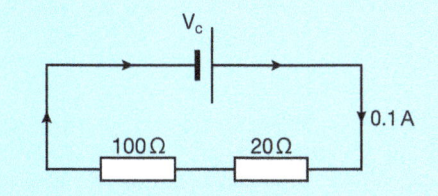

(circuit: cell V_c, 100 Ω and 20 Ω resistors in series, current 0.1 A)

a the voltage across the 20 Ω resistor (2)

b the voltage across the 100 Ω resistor (2)

c the voltage of the cell (V_c). (1)

(Total 5 marks)

| 7 PROPERTIES OF WAVES 345 | 8 THE ELECTROMAGNET SPECTRUM 352 | 9 LIGHT AND SOUND WAVES 359 |

PHYSICS UNIT 3
WAVES

There are many different types of waves. They affect all of our lives. Sometimes they are useful and can be a tremendous benefit to the way we live. Sometimes they can be dangerous and pose a real risk to life. It is therefore very important that we understand the main features and properties of waves.

7 PROPERTIES OF WAVES

SPECIFICATION REFERENCES: 3.1, 3.3–3.5, 3.7, 3.9

Talking to someone using a mobile phone is something most of us do several times a day. The technology that had to be developed for this to happen was based on a thorough understanding of the properties of waves.

In this chapter you will learn about different types of waves and their properties (characteristics).

▲ Figure 7.1 Using microwaves to communicate

LEARNING OBJECTIVES

- Know the definitions of amplitude, wavefront, frequency, wavelength and period of a wave.
- Know that waves transfer energy and information without transferring matter.
- Know and use the relationship between the speed, frequency and wavelength of a wave:

  wave speed = frequency × wavelength

  $v = f \times \lambda$

- Use the above relationships in different contexts including sound waves and electromagnetic waves.
- Explain that all waves can be reflected and refracted.

UNITS

In this unit, you will need to use degrees (°) as the unit of angle, hertz (Hz) as the unit of frequency, metre (m) as the unit of length, metre per second (m/s) as the unit of speed and second (s) as the unit of time.

WHAT ARE WAVES?

Waves are a way of transferring energy from place to place. As we can see in **Figure 7.1** we often use them to transfer information. All these transfers take place with no matter being transferred (see also **Figure 7.2**).

▲ Figure 7.2 Waves are produced if we drop a stone into a pond. The circular wavefronts spread out from the point of impact, carrying energy in all directions, but the water in the pond does not move from the centre to the edges.

WHAT ARE WAVEFRONTS?

Wavefronts are created by overlapping lots of different waves (**Figure 7.3**).

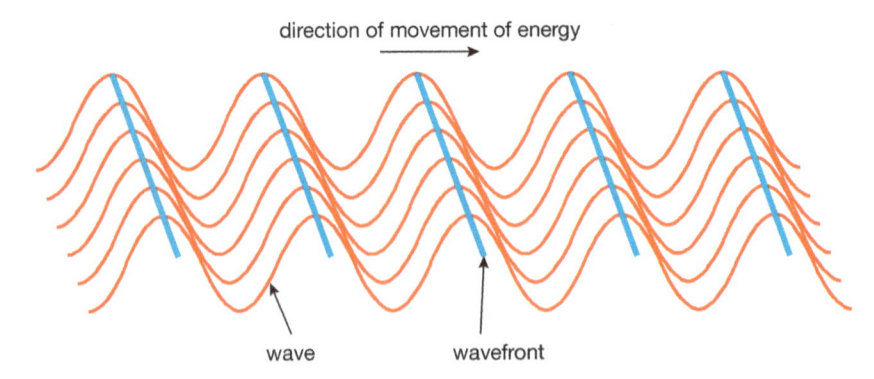

▲ Figure 7.3 A wavefront is a line where all the vibrations are in phase and the same distance from the source.

DESCRIBING WAVES

When a wave moves through a substance, its particles will move from their equilibrium (resting position). The maximum movement of particles from their resting or equilibrium position is called its **amplitude** (A) (**Figure 7.4**).

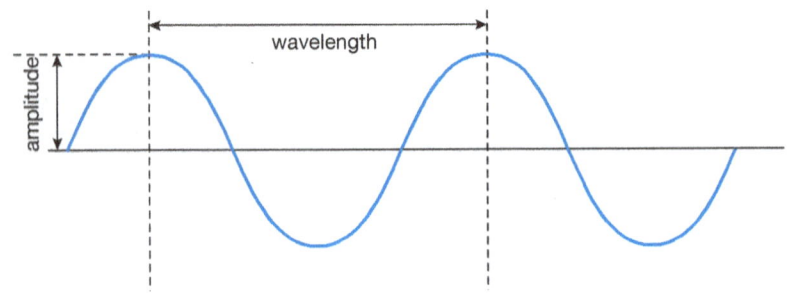

▲ Figure 7.4 A wave has amplitude and wavelength.

KEY POINT

λ is the Greek letter lambda and is the usual symbol for wavelength.

The distance between a particular point on a wave and the same point on the next wave (for example, from crest to crest) is called the **wavelength** (λ).

If the source that is creating a wave vibrates quickly it will produce a large number of waves each second. If it vibrates more slowly it will produce fewer waves each second. The number of waves produced each second by a source, or the number passing a particular point each second, is called the frequency of the wave (*f*). Frequency is measured in hertz (Hz). A wave source that produces five complete waves each second has a frequency of 5 Hz.

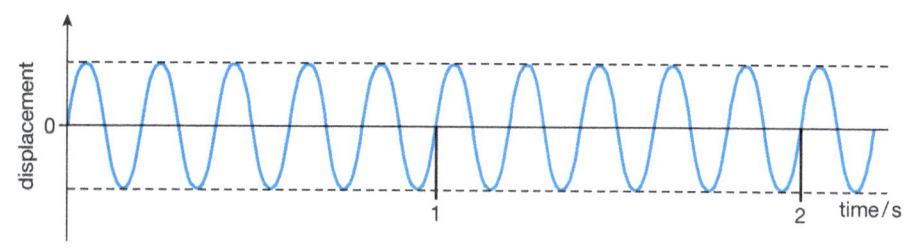

▲ Figure 7.5 This graph shows a wave with a frequency of 5 Hz.

The time it takes for a source to produce one wave is called the **time period** of the wave (*T*). In **Figure 7.5**, we can see that there are 5 waves produced each second. That means the period of this wave is 1/5 second or 0.2 s.

THE WAVE EQUATION

There is a relationship between the wavelength (λ), the frequency (*f*) and the wave speed (*v*) that is true for all waves (see **Figure 7.6**):

wave speed, *v* (m/s) = frequency, *f* (Hz) × wavelength, λ (m)

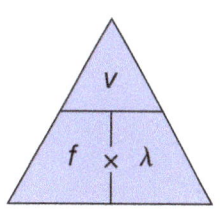

$$v = f \times \lambda$$

▲ Figure 7.6 You can use the triangle method for rearranging equations like $v = f \times \lambda$.

HINT

If an examination question asks you to write out the equation for calculating wave speed, wavelength or frequency, always give the actual equation such as $v = f \times \lambda$. You may not be awarded a mark if you just draw the triangle.

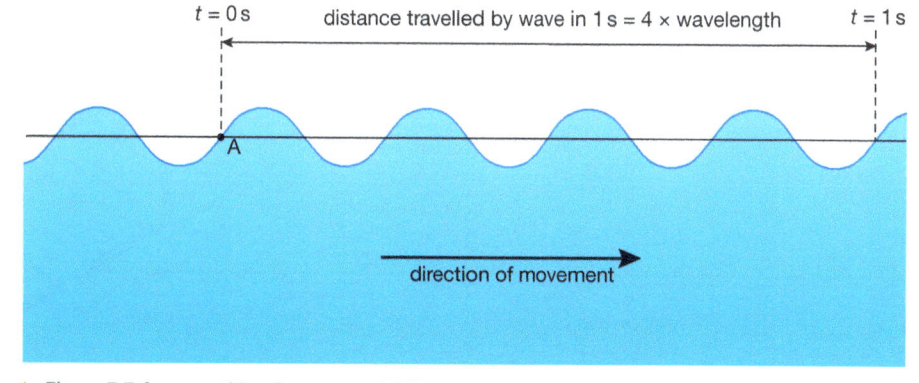

▲ Figure 7.7 A wave with a frequency of 4 Hz

Imagine that you have created water waves with a frequency of 4 Hz. This means that four waves will pass a particular point each second (See **Figure 7.7**). If the wavelength of the waves is 3 m, then the waves travel 12 m each second. The speed of the waves is therefore 12 m/s.

$v = f \times \lambda$
= 4 Hz × 3 m
= 12 m/s

EXAMPLE 1

A **tuning fork** (**Figure 7.8**) creates sound waves with a frequency of 170 Hz. If the speed of sound in air is 340 m/s, calculate the wavelength of the sound waves.

$$v = f \times \lambda$$

So $\lambda = \dfrac{v}{f}$

$= \dfrac{340 \text{ m/s}}{170 \text{ Hz}}$

$= 2 \text{ m}$

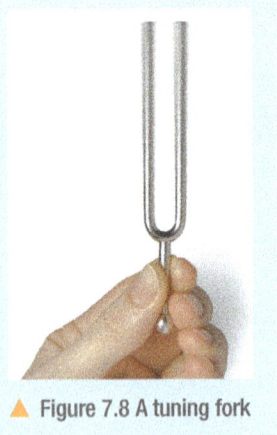

▲ Figure 7.8 A tuning fork

THE RIPPLE TANK

We can study the behaviour of water waves using a ripple tank (**Figure 7.9**).

When the motor is turned on, the wooden bar vibrates creating a series of ripples or wavefronts on the surface of the water. A light placed above the tank creates patterns of the water waves on the floor. By observing the patterns we can see how the water waves are behaving.

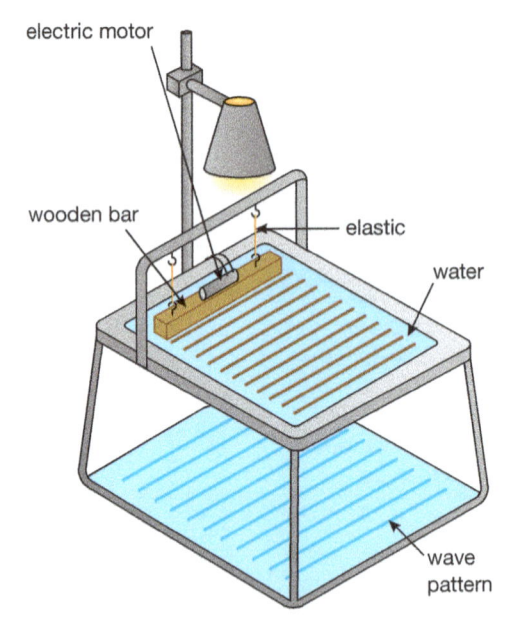

▲ Figure 7.9 The light shines through the water and we can see the patterns of the waves.

WAVELENGTH AND FREQUENCY

The motor can be adjusted to produce a small number of waves each second. The frequency of the waves is small and the pattern shows that the waves have a long wavelength (**Figure 7.10a**).

At higher frequencies, the water waves have shorter wavelengths (**Figure 7.10b**). The speed of the waves does not change.

3 WAVES | 7 PROPERTIES OF WAVES | 349

(a) low frequency

(b) higher frequency

side view

longer wavelength

shorter wavelength

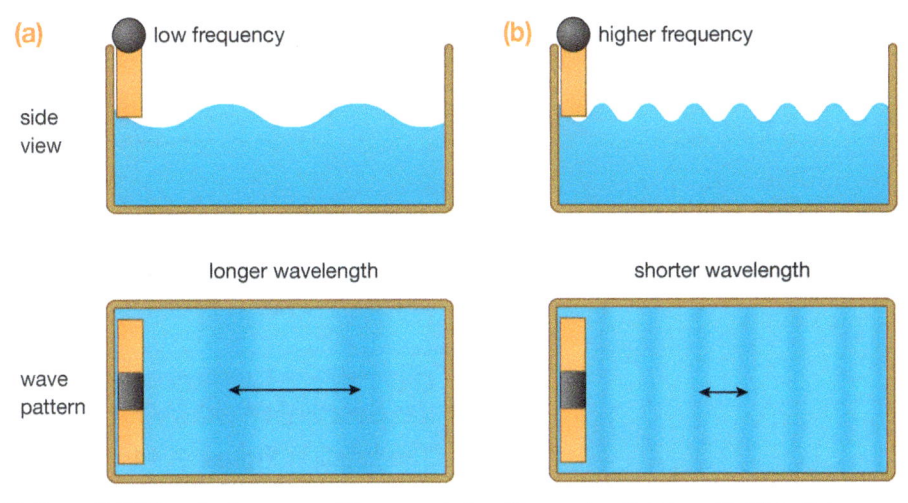

wave pattern

▲ Figure 7.10 When the frequency of the waves is low, the wavelength is long (a). When the frequency is higher, the wavelength is shorter (b).

REFLECTION

All waves can be reflected. If they hit a straight or flat barrier, the angle at which they leave the barrier surface is equal to the angle at which they meet the surface – that is, the waves are reflected from the barrier at the same angle as they strike it. This is described by the 'Law of Reflection' which states that:

The *angle of incidence* is equal to the *angle of reflection* (**Figure 7.11**).

KEY POINT

A normal is a line drawn at right angles to a surface.

The angle of incidence is the angle between the direction of the waves as they approach the barrier and the normal.

The angle of reflection is the angle between the direction of the waves after striking the barrier and the normal.

▲ Figure 7.11 Waves striking a flat barrier are reflected. The angle at which they strike the barrier is the same as the angle at which they are reflected.

EXTENSION

Although you will not be asked this in your exam, it is interesting to see how waves are reflected from curved surfaces (**Figures 7.12** and **7.13**).

When the waves strike a concave barrier, they are made to converge (come together).

When waves are reflected by a surface that is curved outwards (convex), they diverge (spread out).

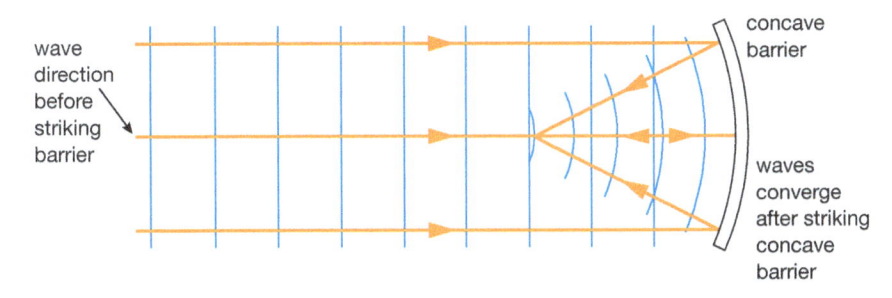

▲ Figure 7.12 Waves striking a concave barrier are reflected and converge.

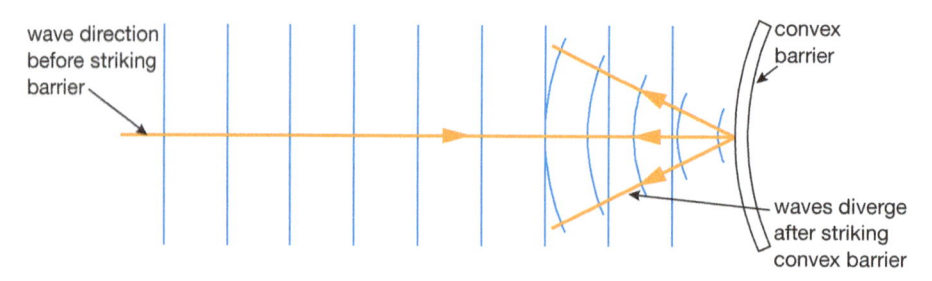

▲ Figure 7.13 Waves striking a convex barrier are reflected backwards and spread out.

REFRACTION

The pencil in **Figure 7.14a** is straight but it seems to bend at the surface of the water. This happens because light waves in water travel more slowly than light waves in air. This change in speed as they leave the water causes the light waves to change direction. This change in direction is called refraction. All waves – light waves, sound waves, water waves – can be refracted.

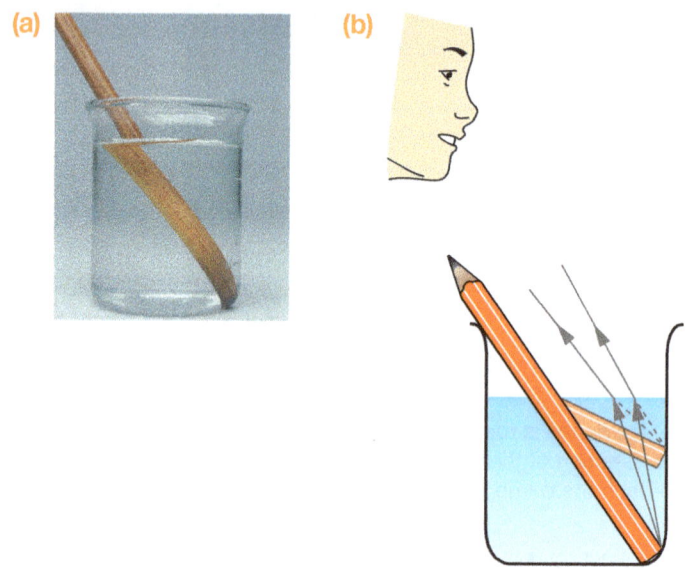

▲ Figure 7.14 (a) The pencil seems to bend at the air/water boundary. (b) This ray diagram shows why the pencil appears to be bent. Rays of light are refracted at the water surface.

EXTENSION

Many optical instruments such as microscopes, telescopes and cameras (**Figure 7.15**) use specially shaped pieces of glass or plastic (called lenses) to bend or refract light waves in a useful way.

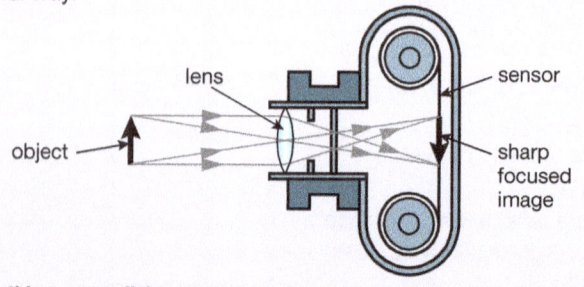

▲ Figure 7.15 In this camera, light waves are refracted by a glass lens to create a sharp image on the sensor or film. Refraction occurs because light travels more slowly in glass than in air.

CHAPTER QUESTIONS

Exam-style questions on properties of waves can be found at the end of Unit 3 on page 370.

1 Which of the following is *not* a property of *all* waves?
   A colour
   B frequency
   C period
   D wavelength

SKILLS CRITICAL THINKING

2 a What do waves carry from place to place?
  b Draw two waves, one with a long wavelength and the other with a short wavelength.
  c Draw two waves, one of which has a large amplitude and the other a small amplitude.

SKILLS INTERPRETATION

SKILLS ANALYSIS, PROBLEM SOLVING

3 The diagram below shows the displacement of water as a wave travels through it.

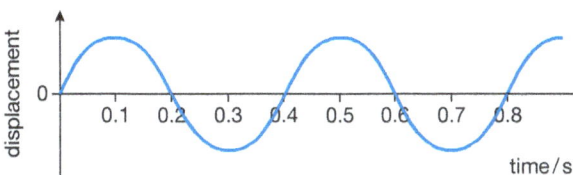

From the diagram calculate:
  a the period of the wave
  b the frequency of the wave.

SKILLS PROBLEM SOLVING

4 The speed of sound in water is approximately 1500 m/s.
  What is the frequency of a sound wave with a wavelength of 1.5 m?

SKILLS CRITICAL THINKING

5 The speed of sound in air is 340 m/s. What is the wavelength of a sound wave which has a frequency of 500 Hz?

6 Explain why this hunter should not aim at the fish he can see.

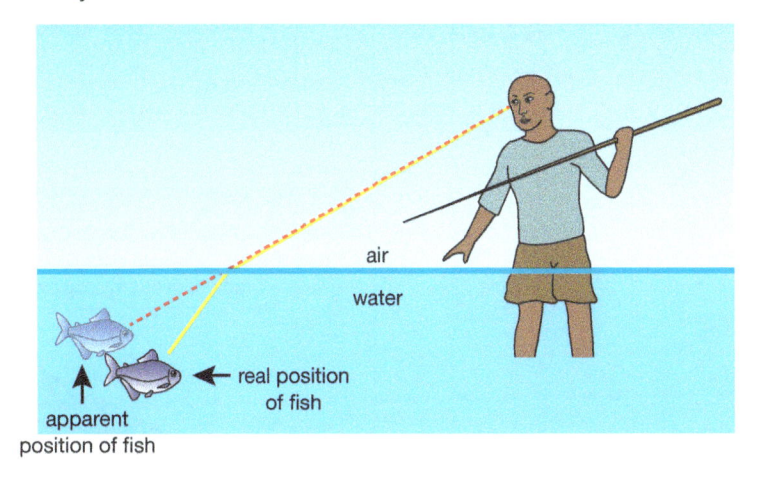

8 THE ELECTROMAGNETIC SPECTRUM

SPECIFICATION REFERENCES: 3.10–3.14

The electromagnetic spectrum is a family of waves, varying in wavelength and frequency. Although it is continuous, it is helpful to consider smaller groups of waves within the spectrum. These groups have distinct properties. As we will see in this chapter, understanding the different properties allows us to use these waves in many situations including cooking and communication.

▶ Figure 8.1 When we shine white light through a prism it splits up forming a band of colours. This band is one small part of the electromagnetic spectrum.

LEARNING OBJECTIVES

- Know that light is part of a continuous electromagnetic spectrum that includes radio, microwave, infrared, visible, ultraviolet, x-ray and gamma ray radiations and that all these waves travel at the same speed in free space.

- Know the order of the electromagnetic spectrum in terms of decreasing wavelength and increasing frequency, including the colours of the visible spectrum.

- Explain some of the uses of electromagnetic radiations, including:
  - radio waves: broadcasting and communications
  - microwaves: cooking and satellite transmissions
  - infrared: heaters and night vision equipment
  - visible light: optical fibres and photography
  - ultraviolet: fluorescent lamps
  - x-rays: observing the internal structure of objects and materials, including for medical applications
  - gamma rays: sterilising food and medical equipment.

- Explain the detrimental effects of excessive exposure of the human body to electromagnetic waves, including:
  - microwaves: internal heating of body tissue
  - infrared: skin burns
  - ultraviolet: damage to surface cells and blindness
  - gamma rays: cancer, mutation

  and describe simple protective measures against the risks.

THE ELECTROMAGNETIC SPECTRUM

| radio waves | microwave | infrared | ultraviolet | x-rays | gamma rays |

visible light

| red | orange | yellow | green | blue | indigo | violet |
| 700 nm | 650 nm | 570 nm | 510 nm | 475 nm | 445 nm | 400 nm |

typical wavelengths in nanometres (1 nm = 1 × 10^{-9} m)

▲ Figure 8.2 The complete electromagnetic spectrum

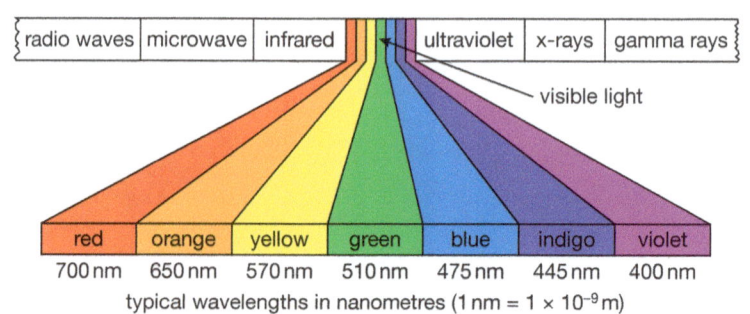

The **electromagnetic spectrum** (EM spectrum; **Figure 8.2**) is a continuous spectrum of waves, which includes the visible spectrum. At one end of the spectrum the waves have a very long wavelength and low frequency, while at the other end the waves have a very short wavelength and high frequency. All the waves have the following properties:

- They all transfer energy.
- They are all transverse waves.
- They all travel at 300 000 000 m/s, the speed of light in a **vacuum** (free space).
- They can all be reflected and refracted.

Remember that the wave equations we met in the previous chapter can be applied to any member of the electromagnetic spectrum.

> **EXAMPLE 1**
>
> Yellow light has a wavelength of 5.7×10^{-7} m. What is the frequency of yellow light waves?
>
> $$v = f \times \lambda$$
>
> So $f = \dfrac{v}{\lambda}$
>
> $= \dfrac{3 \times 10^8 \text{ m/s}}{5.7 \times 10^{-7} \text{ m}}$
>
> $= 5.26 \times 10^{14}$ Hz

Table 8.1 shows the different groups of waves, including **visible light**, in order and gives some of their uses.

Table 8.1

	Typical frequency / Hz	Typical wavelength / m	Sources	Detectors	Uses
Radio waves	$10^5 – 10^{10}$	$10^3 – 10^{-2}$	radio transmitters, TV transmitters	radio and TV aerials	long-, medium- and short-wave radio, TV (UHF)
Microwaves	$10^{10} – 10^{11}$	$10^{-2} – 10^{-3}$	microwave transmitters and ovens	microwave receivers	mobile phone and satellite communication, cooking
Infrared (IR)	$10^{11} – 10^{14}$	$10^{-3} – 10^{-6}$	hot objects	skin, blackened thermometer, special photographic film	infrared cookers and heaters, TV and stereo remote controls, night vision
Visible light	$10^{14} – 10^{15}$	$10^{-6} – 10^{-7}$	luminous objects	the eye, photographic film, light-dependent resistors	seeing, communication (optical fibres), photography
Ultraviolet (UV)	$10^{15} – 10^{16}$	$10^{-7} – 10^{-8}$	UV lamps and the Sun	skin, photographic film and some fluorescent chemicals	fluorescent tubes and UV tanning lamps
X-rays	$10^{16} – 10^{18}$	$10^{-8} – 10^{-10}$	x-ray tubes	photographic film	x-radiography to observe the internal structure of objects, including human bodies
Gamma rays	$10^{18} – 10^{21}$	$10^{-10} – 10^{-14}$	radioactive materials	Geiger–Müller tube	sterilising equipment and food, radiotherapy

3 WAVES — 8 THE ELECTROMAGNETIC SPECTRUM

> **HINT**
>
> To remember the order of the waves in the electromagnetic spectrum try using **G**raham's **X**ylophone **U**ses **V**ery **I**nteresting **M**usical **R**hythms.

You do not need to remember the values of frequency and wavelength given in the table but you do need to know the order of the groups and which has the highest frequency or longest wavelengths. Most importantly, you need to realise that it is these differences in wavelength and frequency that give the groups their different properties – for example, gamma rays have the shortest wavelengths and highest frequencies, and carry the most energy.

RADIO WAVES

Radio waves have the longest wavelengths in the electromagnetic spectrum. They are used mainly for communication (**Figure 8.3**).

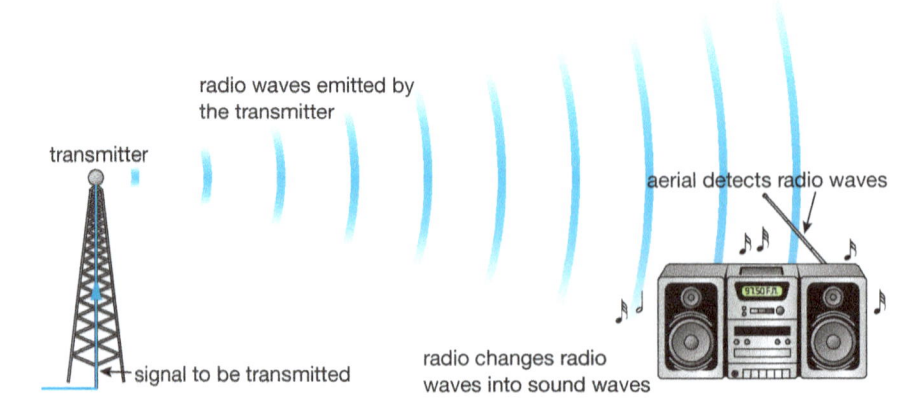

▲ Figure 8.3 Radio waves are emitted by a transmitter and detected by an aerial.

Radio waves are given out (**emitted**) by a transmitter. As they arrive at an aerial, they are detected and the information they carry can be received. Televisions and FM radios use radio waves with the shorter wavelengths to carry their signals.

MICROWAVES

Microwaves (**Figure 8.4**) are used for communications, radar and cooking foods. Radar uses waves to find the position of things.

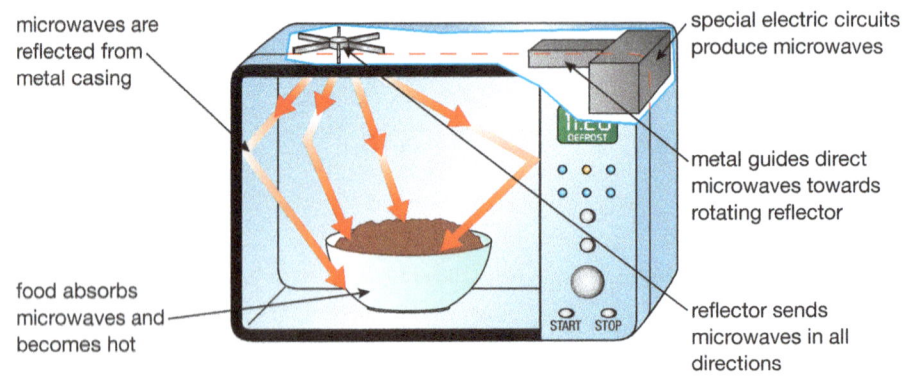

▲ Figure 8.4 Food cooks quickly in a microwave oven because water molecules in the food absorb the microwaves.

Food placed in a microwave oven cooks more quickly than in a normal oven. This is because water **molecules** in the food absorb the microwaves and become very hot. The food therefore cooks throughout rather than just from the outside.

Microwave ovens have metal screens that reflect microwaves and keep them inside the oven. This is necessary because if microwaves can cook food, they can also heat human body tissue! The microwaves used by mobile phones transmit much less energy than those used in a microwave oven, so they do not cook your brain when you use the phone.

Microwaves are used in communications. The waves pass easily through the Earth's atmosphere and so are used to carry signals to orbiting satellites. From here, the signals are passed on to their destination or to other orbiting satellites. Messages sent to and from mobile phones are also carried by microwaves. The fact that we are able to use mobile phones almost anywhere in the home and at work confirms that microwaves can pass through glass, brick, concrete, wood, and so on.

INFRARED

All objects, including your body, emit infrared (IR) radiation. The hotter an object is, the more energy it will emit as infrared. Energy is transferred by infrared radiation to bread in a toaster or food under a grill. Electric fires also transfer heat energy by infrared.

Special cameras designed to detect infrared waves can be used to create images even when there is no visible light (**Figure 8.5**). These cameras have many uses, including searching for people trapped in collapsed buildings, searching for criminals and checking for heat loss from buildings.

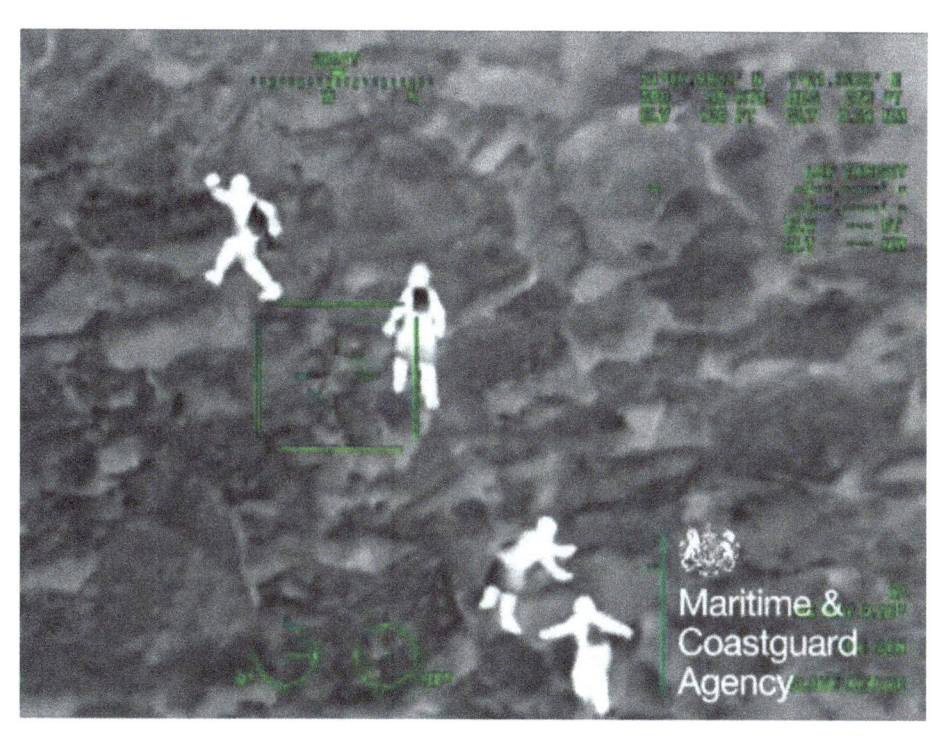

▲ Figure 8.5 It is not possible to see these people trapped at the bottom of a cliff using normal visible light. By using infrared detectors they can be found easily and rescued.

Infrared radiation is also used in remote controls for televisions, DVD players and stereo systems (**Figure 8.6**). It is very convenient for this purpose because the waves are not harmful. They have a low **penetrating power** and will therefore operate only over small distances, so they are unlikely to interfere with other signals or waves.

The human body can be harmed by too much infrared radiation, which can cause skin burns.

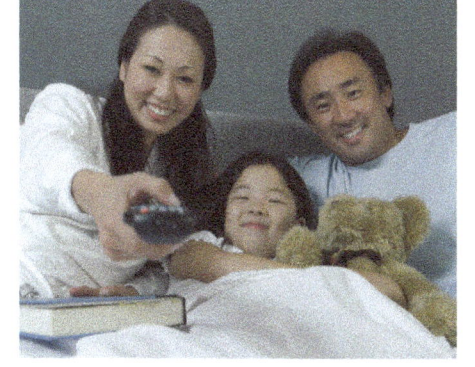

▲ Figure 8.6 Signals are carried from this remote control to a TV by infrared waves.

VISIBLE LIGHT

EXTENSION

When talking about light and colour, we often refer to the seven colours in the visible spectrum. These colours are red, orange, yellow, green, blue, indigo and violet; red light has the longest wavelength and lowest frequency. If you look back at **Figure 8.1**, you may only be able to make out six colours – most people have difficulty separating indigo and violet (two types of purple). Sir Isaac Newton (1642–1727) discovered that 'white' light can be split up into different colours. He believed that the number seven had magical significance, and so he decided there were seven colours in the spectrum!

▲ Figure 8.7 Using visible light

This is the part of the electromagnetic spectrum that is visible to the human eye. We use it to see. Visible light from lasers is used to read compact discs and barcodes (**Figure 8.7**). It can also be sent along optical fibres, so it can be used for communication or for looking into hard-to-reach places such as inside the body of a patient (see page 366). Visible light can be detected by the sensors in digital cameras, and used to take still photographs or videos. Information stored on DVDs is also read using visible light.

ULTRAVIOLET LIGHT

Part of the light emitted by the Sun is ultraviolet (UV) light. UV radiation is harmful to human eyes and can damage the skin (**Figure 8.8**).

UV light causes the skin to tan, but overexposure (too much) will lead to sunburn and blistering. Ultraviolet radiation can also cause skin cancer and blindness. Protective goggles or glasses and skin creams can block the UV rays and will reduce the harmful effects of this radiation.

The **ozone layer** in the Earth's atmosphere absorbs large quantities of the Sun's UV radiation. In recent years there was real concern that the amount of ozone in the atmosphere was decreasing due to pollution, which would increase numbers of skin cancer. However, there is now evidence to show that the ozone layer is recovering.

Some chemicals glow (shine), or fluoresce, when under UV light. This property of UV light is used in security marker pens. The special ink is invisible in normal light but becomes visible in UV light (**Figure 8.9**).

▲ Figure 8.8 UV light can cause sunburn so we need to protect our skin.

▲ Figure 8.9 This red code is only visible under UV light.

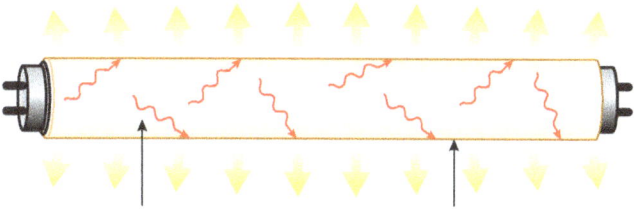

mercury vapour inside the tube gives off UV rays when a current is passed through it

when the UV light strikes the fluorescent powder coating the tube, white light is given out

▲ Figure 8.10 Fluorescent tubes glow when UV light hits the fluorescent coating in the tube.

Fluorescent tubes glow (shine) because the UV light they produce strikes a special coating (covering) on the inside of the tube, which then emits visible light (**Figure 8.10**).

X-RAYS

X-rays pass easily through soft body tissue but cannot pass through bones. As a result, radiographs or x-ray pictures can be taken to check a patient's bones (**Figure 8.11**).

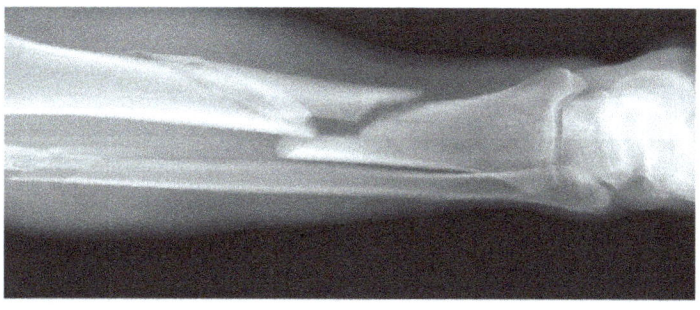

▲ Figure 8.11 X-ray of a broken leg

Working with x-rays can cause cancer. Radiographers, who take x-rays, are at risk and have to stand behind lead screens or wear protective clothing.

X-rays are also used in industry to check the internal structures of objects – for example, to look for cracks and faults in buildings or machinery – and at airports as part of the security checking procedure (**Figure 8.12**).

▲ Figure 8.12 X-rays were used to see what was in this suitcase.

GAMMA RAYS

Gamma rays, like x-rays, are highly penetrating rays and can cause damage to living cells. The damage can cause mutations (negative changes), which can lead to cancer. They are used to **sterilise** medical instruments, to kill micro-organisms so that food will keep for longer and to treat cancer using radiotherapy. Gamma rays can both cause and cure cancer. Large doses of gamma rays targeted directly at a cancerous growth can be used to kill the cancer cells completely (**Figure 8.13**).

Like x-rays the use of lead screens, boxes and aprons can prevent the damage caused by gamma rays (overexposure).

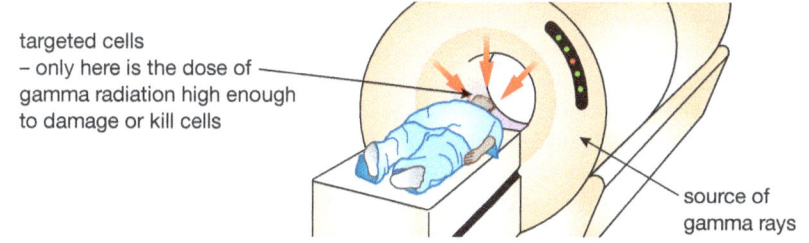

targeted cells – only here is the dose of gamma radiation high enough to damage or kill cells

source of gamma rays

▲ Figure 8.13 The gamma rays are aimed carefully so that they cross at the exact location of the cancerous cells.

CHAPTER QUESTIONS

Exam-style questions on using waves can be found at the end of Unit 3 on page 370.

SKILLS   CRITICAL THINKING

1   a   Name four wave properties that are common to all members of the electromagnetic spectrum.
    b   Name three types of wave that can be used for communicating.
    c   Name two types of wave that can be used for cooking.
    d   Name one type of wave that is used to treat cancer.
    e   Name one type of wave that might be used to 'see' people in the dark.
    f   Name one type of wave that is used for radar.

SKILLS   REASONING

2   Explain why:
    a   microwave ovens cook food much more quickly than normal ovens
    b   x-rays are used to check for broken bones
    c   it is important not to damage the ozone layer around the Earth
    d   food stays fresher for longer after it has been exposed to gamma radiation.

3   a   Explain one way in which you could prevent overexposure (damage) by the following waves:
        i   x-rays
        ii ultraviolet waves.

SKILLS   CRITICAL THINKING

    b   Select one of the above waves and then describe one consequence of overexposure.

SKILLS   INTERPRETATION

4   Copy and complete the table below for four more different wave groups within the electromagnetic spectrum.

Type of radiation	Possible harm	Precautions
x-rays	cancer	lead screening

9 LIGHT AND SOUND WAVES

SPECIFICATION REFERENCES: 3.14, 3.15, 3.17, 3.20, 3.21, 3.23

We see objects because they emit or reflect light. In this chapter you will learn how light behaves when it reflects from different surfaces, and what happens when light travels from one transparent material to another. Sound waves can be reflected and refracted in just the same way. In this chapter you will learn about the nature and behaviour of sound waves, and how we make use of them in our everyday lives.

▲ Figure 9.1 In the Hall of Mirrors at the fairground the reflection of light can be very confusing!

LEARNING OBJECTIVES

- Know that light waves can be reflected and refracted.
- Use the law of reflection (the angle of incidence equals the angle of reflection).
- Practical: Investigate the refraction of light, using rectangular blocks, semi-circular blocks and triangular prisms.
- Describe the role of total internal reflection in transmitting information along optical fibres and in prisms.
- Know what is meant by the critical angle c.
- Know that sound waves can be reflected and refracted.

SEEING THE LIGHT

The patient shown in **Figure 9.2** has a cataract. The front of one of his eyes has become so cloudy that he is unable to see. Nowadays it is possible to remove this damaged part of the eye and replace it with a clear plastic that will allow light to enter the eye again.

There are many sources of light, including the Sun, the stars, fires, light bulbs and so on. Objects such as these that emit their own light are called luminous objects. When the emitted light enters our eyes we see the object. Most objects, however, are non-luminous. They do not emit light. We see these non-luminous objects because of the light they reflect (**Figure 9.3**).

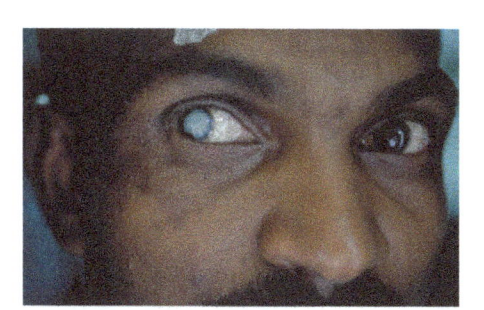

▲ Figure 9.2 Cataracts mean that light cannot enter the eye correctly.

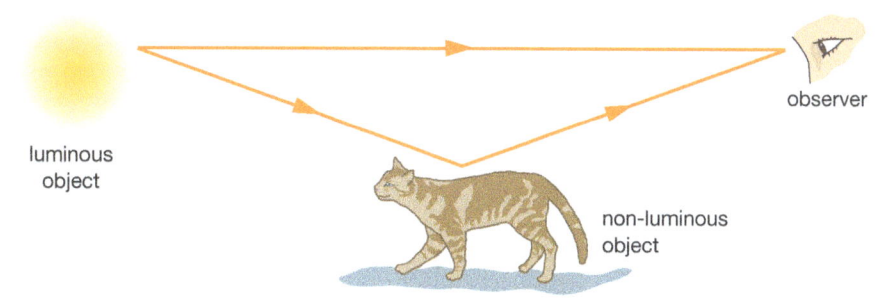

▲ Figure 9.3 Luminous objects, such as the Sun, give out light. Non-luminous objects only reflect light.

REFLECTION

When a ray of light strikes a plane (flat) mirror, it is reflected so that the angle of incidence (*i*) is equal to the angle of reflection (*r*) (**Figure 9.4**).

> **KEY POINT**
>
> The angle of incidence is the angle between the incident ray and the normal.
>
> The angle of reflection is the angle between the reflected ray and the normal.

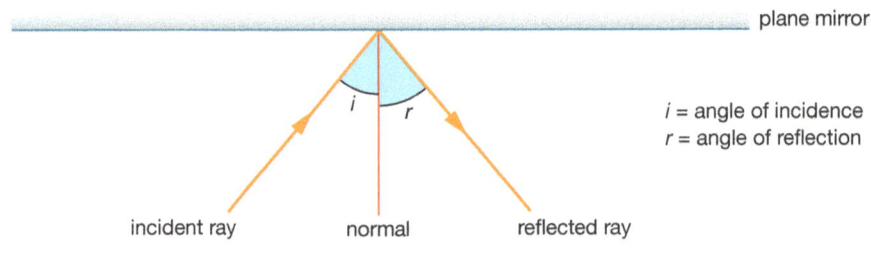

▲ Figure 9.4 Light is reflected from a plane mirror. The angle of incidence is equal to the angle of reflection. The normal is a line at right angles to the mirror.

Mirrors are often used to change the direction of a ray of light. One example of this is the simple **periscope**, which uses two mirrors to change the direction of rays of light.

Rays from the object strike the first mirror at an angle of 45° to the normal. The rays are reflected at 45° to the normal and so are turned through an angle of 90° by the mirror. At the second mirror the rays are again turned through 90°. Changing the direction of rays of light in this way allows an observer to use a periscope to see over or around objects (**Figure 9.5**).

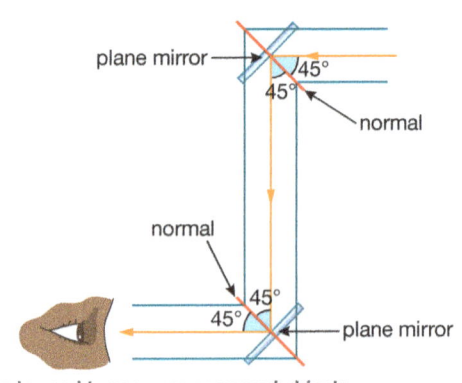

▲ Figure 9.5 A periscope is used to see over or around objects.

▲ Figure 9.6 This rainbow is caused by refraction.

> **KEY POINT**
>
> A medium is a material, such as glass or water, through which light can travel. The plural of medium is media.

> **KEY POINT**
>
> Light does travel more slowly in air than in a vacuum but the difference is tiny.

REFRACTION

Rays of light can travel through many different transparent media, including air, water and glass. Light can also travel through a vacuum. In a vacuum and in air, light travels at a speed of 300 000 000 m/s. In other media it travels more slowly. For example, the speed of light in glass is approximately 200 000 000 m/s. When a ray of light travels from air into glass or water it slows down as it crosses the border between the two media (see **Figure 9.6**). This change in speed may cause the ray to change direction. This change in direction of a ray is called refraction (**Figure 9.7**).

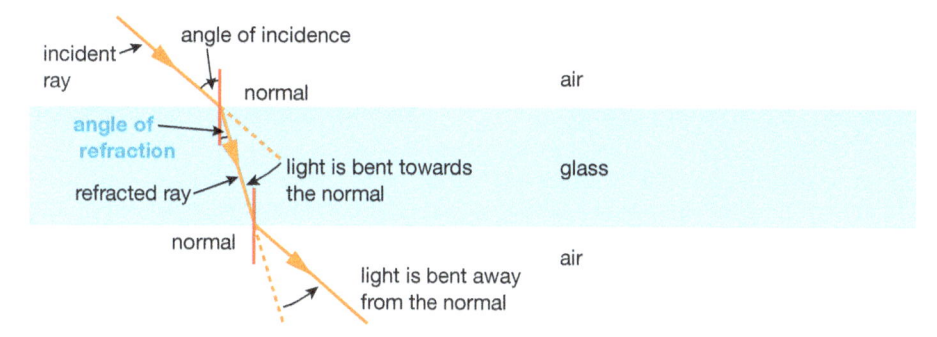

▲ Figure 9.7 This light ray is being refracted twice – once as it travels from air into glass and then again as it travels from glass to air.

As a ray enters a glass block, it slows down and is refracted towards the normal. As the ray leaves the block it speeds up and is refracted away from the normal.

If the ray strikes the boundary between the two media at 90°, the ray continues without change of direction (**Figure 9.8**).

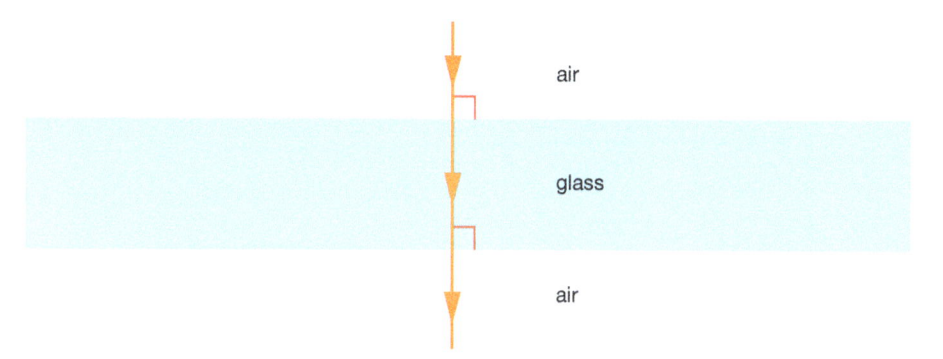

▲ Figure 9.8 If the light hits the boundary at 90° the ray does not bend.

REFRACTIVE INDEX AND OPTICAL DENSITY

Different materials can bend rays of light by different amounts. We describe this by using a number called the **refractive index** (n). The refractive index of glass is about 1.5 and water is 1.3. This tells us that under similar circumstances glass (which is optically more dense than water) will bend the light more than water. Another way of saying this is to say that glass is optically more dense than water.

9 LIGHT AND SOUND WAVES

Safety note: Ray box lamps get hot enough to burn skin and char paper. Glass blocks and prisms should be handled carefully and not knocked together – they can splinter or shatter.

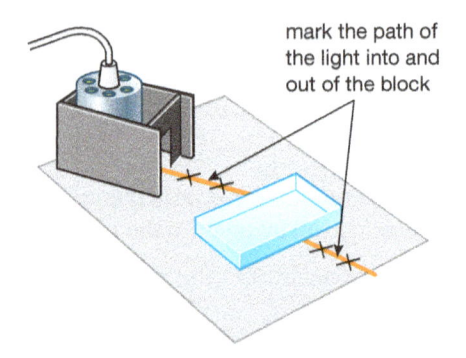

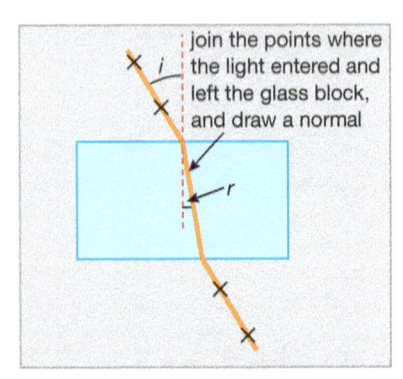

▲ Figure 9.9 How to investigate refraction using a rectangular glass block

KEY POINT
Be careful, the symbol '*r*' is used for both the angle of reflection and the angle of refraction.

ACTIVITY 1

▼ PRACTICAL: INVESTIGATE REFRACTION IN A GLASS BLOCK

You can investigate refraction using a ray box and a rectangular glass block.

- Shine a ray of light onto one of the sides of the glass block, so that the ray emerges on the opposite side of the block. Mark the directions of both of these rays with crosses.
- Draw around the glass block before removing it.
- Using the crosses, draw in the direction of both rays.
- Draw in the direction of the ray that travelled inside the glass block.
- Draw a normal (a line at 90° to the glass surface) where the ray enters the block.
- Measure the angles of incidence (*i*) and refraction (*r*) (see **Figure 9.9**).

What happens to the angle of refraction as you increase the angle of incidence?

TOTAL INTERNAL REFLECTION

When a ray of light with a small angle of incidence passes from glass into air, most of the light is refracted away from the normal but if we look carefully we can see that there is a small amount that is reflected from the boundary (**Figure 9.10**).

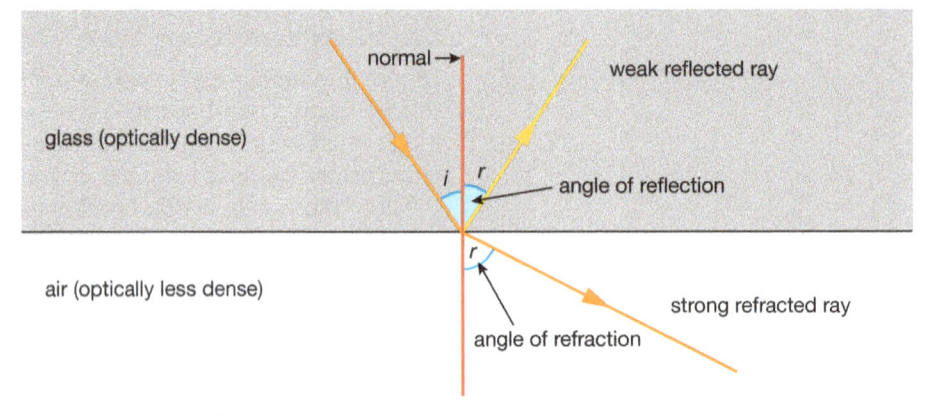

▲ Figure 9.10 A ray of light travelling from glass to air

But as the angle of incidence in the glass increases, the angle of refraction also increases until it reaches a special angle called the critical angle (c). The angle of refraction now is 90° (**Figure 9.11a**).

KEY POINT

The critical angle is the smallest possible angle of incidence at which light rays are totally internally reflected.

(a)

i is equal to the critical angle, *c*

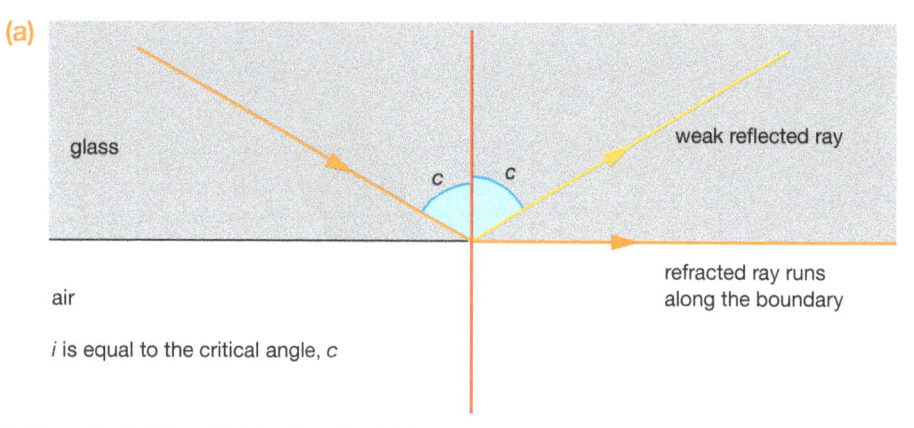

▲ Figure 9.11(a) Ray of light strikes glass/air boundary at the critical angle

When *i* is greater than the critical angle, all the light is reflected at the boundary. No light is refracted. The light is totally internally reflected (**Figure 9.11b**).

KEY POINT

Total internal reflection only occurs when rays of light are travelling towards a boundary with a less optically dense medium (e.g. from glass to air or water to air).

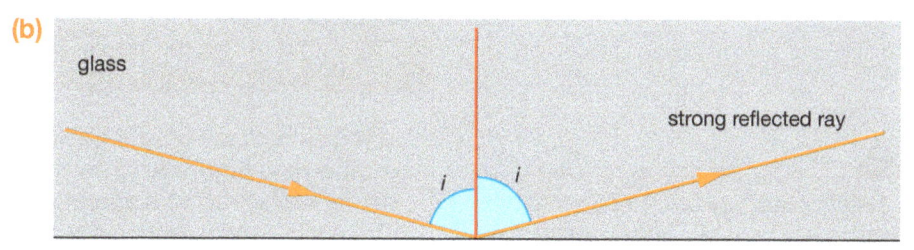

(b)

▲ Figure 9.11(b) When *i* is greater than *c* total internal reflection occurs.

ACTIVITY 2

▼ PRACTICAL: INVESTIGATE TOTAL INTERNAL REFLECTION

You can investigate total internal reflection in the laboratory using a semi-circular glass block and a ray box. As shown in **Figure 9.12a**, a ray of light is directed at the centre of the straight side of the block through the curved side. (We do this because the incident ray will then always hit the edge of the glass block at 90°, so there are no refraction effects to take into account as the light goes into the block.)

Now by carefully increasing and decreasing the angle at which the ray strikes the flat edge of the glass block, we can discover the smallest angle at which most of the light is refracted along the edge of the glass block (see **Figure 9.12b**). This angle is the critical angle.

Safety note: Ray box lamps get hot enough to burn skin and char paper. Glass blocks and prisms should be handled carefully and not knocked together – they can splinter or shatter.

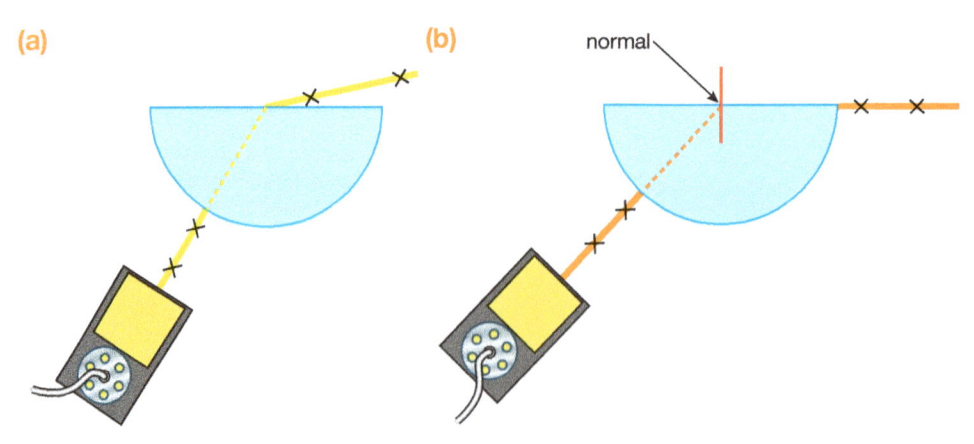

▲ Figure 9.12 (a) A semi-circular glass block used to demonstrate total internal reflection (b) Light striking the edge of the glass block at the critical angle

For light passing from glass to air, the critical angle is typically 42° and the critical angle for light passing from water to air is 49°.

We sometimes use **prisms** rather than mirrors to reflect light. The light is totally internally reflected by the prism.

ACTIVITY 3

▼ PRACTICAL: INVESTIGATE TOTAL INTERNAL REFLECTION IN PRISMS

If you shine a ray of light into a prism as shown in **Figure 9.13** it will strike the far surface at an angle of 45°. The critical angle for glass is about 42° so the ray will be totally internally reflected. You will see therefore that the ray will be reflected through an angle of 90° (45 + 45).

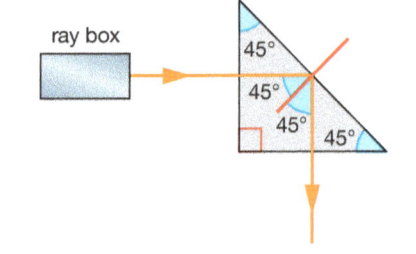

▲ Figure 9.13 Turning through 90° using total internal reflection

If you shine a ray into the prism as shown in **Figure 9.14** the ray will be reflected through an angle of 180° – that is, it will go back in the direction from which it came.

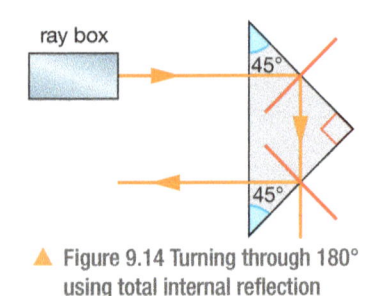

▲ Figure 9.14 Turning through 180° using total internal reflection

Safety note: Ray box lamps get hot enough to burn skin and char paper. Glass blocks and prisms should be handled carefully and not knocked together – they can splinter or shatter.

USING TOTAL INTERNAL REFLECTION

THE PRISMATIC PERISCOPE

The images produced by prisms are often brighter and clearer than those produced by mirrors. A periscope that uses prisms to reflect the light is called a prismatic periscope. Light passes through the surface AB of the first prism at 90° and so does not change direction (it is undeviated). It then strikes the surface AC of the prism at an angle of 45°. The critical angle for glass is 42°

so the ray is totally internally reflected and is turned through 90°. When it leaves the first prism the light travels to a second prism. The second prism is positioned so that the ray is again totally internally reflected. The ray emerges parallel to the direction in which it was originally travelling (**Figure 9.15**).

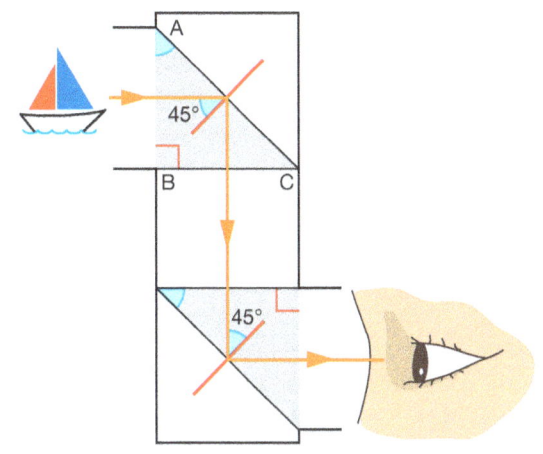

▲ Figure 9.15 Total internal reflection in a prismatic periscope

BICYCLE AND CAR REFLECTORS

Light entering the prism in **Figure 9.16** is totally internally reflected twice. It emerges from the prism travelling back in the direction from which it originally came. This arrangement is used in bicycle or car reflectors (**Figure 9.17**).

Binoculars also make use of total internal reflection within prisms (**Figure 9.18** and **9.19**).

Each side of a pair of binoculars contains two prisms to totally internally reflect the incoming light. Without the prisms, binoculars would have to be very long to obtain large magnifications and would look like a pair of telescopes.

(a)

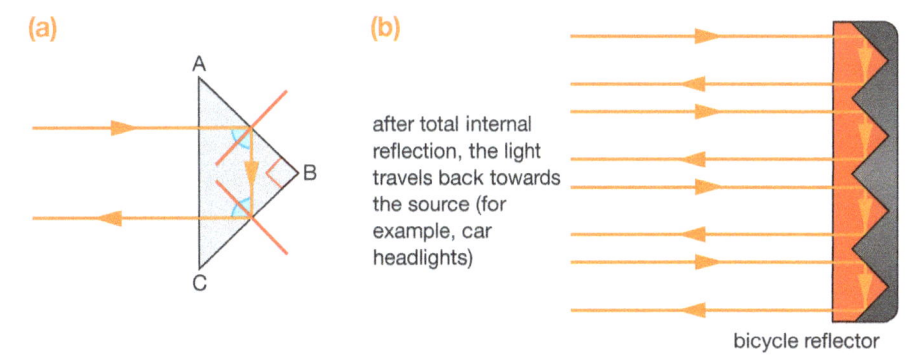

(b) after total internal reflection, the light travels back towards the source (for example, car headlights)

bicycle reflector

▲ Figure 9.16 Prisms can also be used as reflectors.

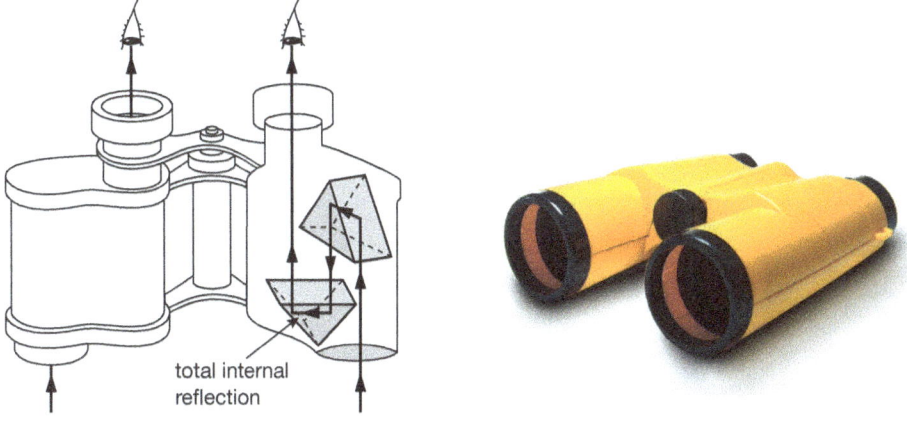

▲ Figure 9.17 Reflectors like these can save lives.

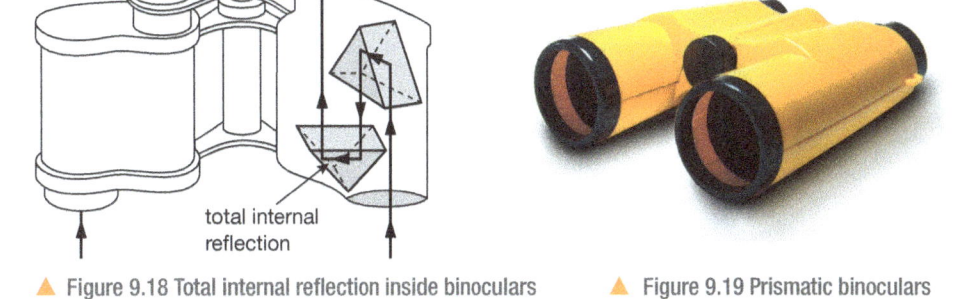

total internal reflection

▲ Figure 9.18 Total internal reflection inside binoculars

▲ Figure 9.19 Prismatic binoculars

OPTICAL FIBRES

One of the most important **applications** for total internal reflection is the optical fibre (**Figure 9.20**). This is a very thin piece of fibre composed of two different types of glass. The centre is made of an optically dense glass surrounded by a different type of glass that has a lower optical density.

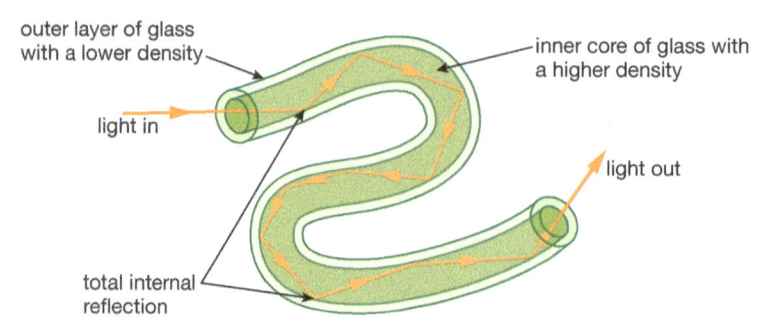

▲ Figure 9.20 In an optical fibre, light undergoes total internal reflection.

As the fibres are very narrow, light entering the inner **core** always strikes the boundary of the two glasses at an angle that is greater than the critical angle. No light escapes across this boundary. The fibre therefore acts as a 'light pipe' providing a path that the light follows even when the fibre is curved.

Large numbers of these fibres fixed together form a bundle (**Figure 9.21**). Bundles can carry sufficient light for images of objects to be seen through them. If the fibres are tapered (narrower at one end) it is also possible to produce a magnified image.

Figure 9.22 shows optical fibres in an **endoscope**. The endoscope is used by doctors to see the inside the body – for example, to examine the inside of the stomach. Endoscopes can also be used by engineers to see hard-to-reach parts of machinery.

Light travels down one bundle of fibres and shines on the object to be viewed. Light reflected by the object travels up a second bundle of fibres. An image of the object is created by the eyepiece.

▲ Figure 9.21 Optical fibres

THE ENDOSCOPE

By using optical fibres to see what they are doing, doctors can carry out operations through small holes made in the body, rather than through large cuts. This is called 'keyhole surgery'. This is less stressful for patients and usually leads to a more rapid recovery.

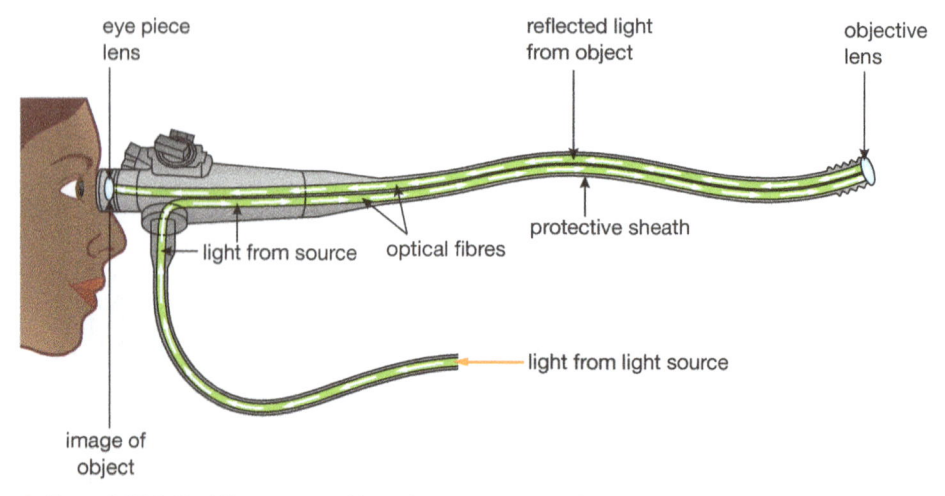

▲ Figure 9.22 Optical fibres are used in endoscopes to see inside the body.

| **OPTICAL FIBRES IN TELECOMMUNICATIONS** | Modern telecommunications systems use optical fibres rather than copper wires to transmit messages as less energy is lost. Electrical signals from a telephone are converted into light energy produced by tiny lasers, which send pulses (small amounts) of light into the ends of optical fibres. A light-sensitive detector at the other end changes the pulses back into electrical signals, which then flow into a telephone receiver (ear piece). |

SOUND WAVES

Figure 9.23 shows part of the sound system used by a band playing at a concert. This equipment must produce sounds that are loud enough to be heard by all the audience and the sound quality must be good enough for the music to be appreciated. We are going to look at how sounds are made and how they travel as waves.

▲ Figure 9.23 The sound produced by the speakers must be loud but also of good quality.

Sounds are produced by objects that are vibrating. We hear sounds when these vibrations, travelling as sound waves, reach our ears (**Figure 9.24**).

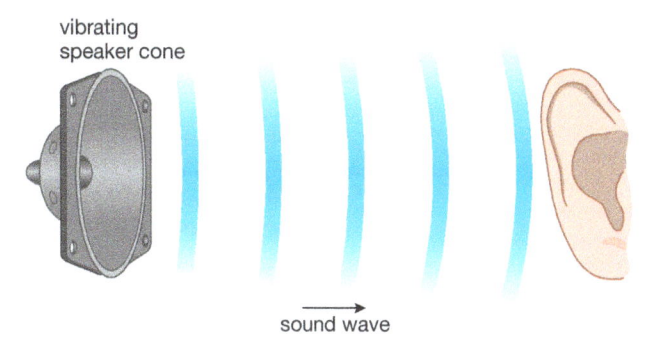

▲ Figure 9.24 The loudspeaker vibrates and produces sound waves.

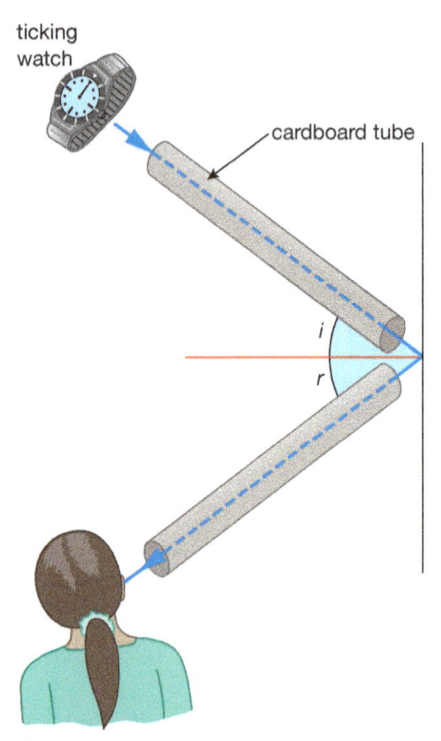

▲ Figure 9.25 Sound waves are reflected in the same way that light rays are reflected.

REFLECTION

Sound waves behave in the same way as any other wave.

When a sound wave strikes a surface it may be reflected. Like light waves, sound waves are reflected from a flat surface so that the angle of incidence is equal to the angle of reflection (see **Figure 9.25**).

Ships often use echoes to discover the depth of the water beneath them. This is called echo sounding.

1. Sound waves are emitted from the ship and travel to the seabed (sea floor).
2. Some of these waves are reflected from the seabed back up to the ship.
3. Equipment on the ship detects these sound waves.
4. The time it takes the waves to make this journey is measured.
5. Knowing this time, the depth of the sea below the ship can be calculated.

The system of using echoes in this way is called **sonar** (Sound, Navigation And Ranging; **Figure 9.26**).

▲ Figure 9.26 Reflected sound can be used to tell ships about the depth of the sea beneath them.

REFRACTION OF SOUND

All waves can be refracted, even sound waves! For example, if some parts of a sound wave are travelling through warm air, they will travel more quickly than those parts travelling through cooler air. As a result the direction of the sound wave will change. It will be refracted.

Although it is not possible to see sound waves being refracted, we can sometimes hear its effect. Standing at the edge of a large pond or lake we can sometimes hear sounds from things on the other side of the water much more clearly than we would expect. This is due to refraction. **Figure 9.27** explains how this happens.

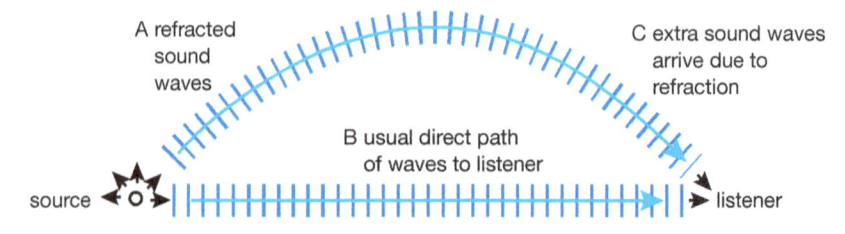

▲ Figure 9.27 Why sometimes sounds travelling across water are louder than we expect

3 WAVES   9 LIGHT AND SOUND WAVES   369

1 Most of the sound we hear travels to us in a straight line (Path B).

2 But some sound travels upwards (Path A).

3 If the temperature conditions are right, then as the sound waves travel through air of different densities they are refracted and follow a curved path downwards (Path C).

4 We now receive two sets of sound waves.

5 So the sound we hear seems louder and clearer.

CHAPTER QUESTIONS

Exam-style questions on light and sound waves can be found at the end of Unit 3 on page 370.

SKILLS INTERPRETATION, PROBLEM SOLVING

1 Draw a ray diagram to show how a ray of light can be turned through 180° using two plane mirrors. Mark on your diagram a value for the angle of incidence at each of the mirrors.

SKILLS INTERPRETATION

2 a Draw a diagram to show the path of a ray of light travelling from air into a rectangular glass block at an angle of about 45°.

b Show the path of the ray as it emerges from the block.

SKILLS CRITICAL THINKING

c Explain why the ray changes direction each time it crosses the air/glass boundary.

SKILLS INTERPRETATION

d Draw a second diagram showing a ray that travels through the block without its direction changing.

3 Explain how sound waves can be used to discover the depth of the sea below a ship.

SKILLS INTERPRETATION

4 Draw three ray diagrams to show what happens to a ray of light travelling in a glass block in the following situations. It hits a face of the block at an angle:

a less than the critical angle

b equal to the critical angle

c greater than the critical angle.

SKILLS CRITICAL THINKING

5 a What is meant by 'total internal reflection of light' and under what conditions does it occur?

SKILLS INTERPRETATION

b Draw a diagram to show how total internal reflection takes place in a prismatic periscope.

SKILLS REASONING

c Give one advantage of using prisms in a periscope rather than plane mirrors.

SKILLS INTERPRETATION

d Draw a second diagram to show how a prism could be used to turn a ray of light through 180°. Give one application of a prism used in this way.

SKILLS INTERPRETATION, CRITICAL THINKING

6 a Explain why a ray of light entering an optical fibre is unable to escape through the sides of the fibre. Include a ray diagram in your explanation.

SKILLS CRITICAL THINKING

b Explain how doctors use optical fibres to see inside the body.

c Name one other use of optical fibres.

EXAM PRACTICE

SKILLS CRITICAL THINKING

1 a Which of these waves has the smallest wavelength?
   A ultraviolet light
   B sound wave
   C surface water wave
   D microwave (1)

b Which of these best describes what is happening to a light wave as it travels through an optical fibre?
   A total internal reflection
   B refraction
   C reflection
   D diffraction (1)

(Total 2 marks)

SKILLS INTERPRETATION

2 The diagram below shows the cross-section of a water wave.

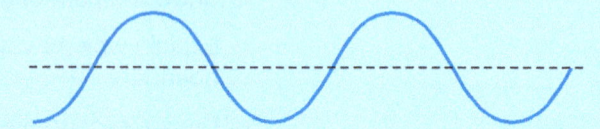

a Copy this diagram and mark on it:
   i the wavelength of the wave (λ) (1)
   ii the amplitude of the wave (A). (1)

SKILLS PROBLEM SOLVING

b A water wave travelling at 20 m/s has a wavelength of 2.5 m. Calculate the frequency of the wave. (3)

(Total 5 marks)

SKILLS ANALYSIS

3 The diagram below shows a ray of light travelling down an optical fibre.

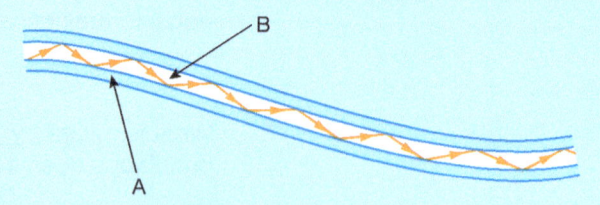

SKILLS ANALYSIS

a Identify the type of glass labelled A. (1)
b Identify the type of glass labelled B. (1)
c Explain why light is reflected from the boundary between A and B. (2)

SKILLS CRITICAL THINKING

d Describe one medical use for optical fibres. (1)

(Total 5 marks)

4 A girl stands 500 m from a tall building and bangs two pieces of wood together. At the same moment her friend starts a stopwatch. The sound waves created by the two pieces of wood hit the building and are reflected. When the two girls hear the echo they stop the stopwatch and note the time. The girls repeat the experiment four more times. The results are shown in the table below.

Experiment	Time / seconds
1	2.95
2	3.00
3	2.90
4	3.20
5	2.95

SKILLS EXECUTIVE FUNCTION
   a Explain why the girls repeated the experiment five times. (1)

SKILLS PROBLEM SOLVING
   b Calculate the speed of sound using the results. (6)

SKILLS EXECUTIVE FUNCTION
   c One of the girls thought that their answer might be affected by wind. Was she correct? Explain your answer. (2)

(Total 9 marks)

SKILLS CRITICAL THINKING

5 The electromagnetic spectrum contains the following groups of waves: infrared, ultraviolet, x-rays, radio waves, microwaves, visible spectrum and gamma rays.

   a Put these groups of waves in the order they appear in the electromagnetic spectrum starting with the group that has the longest wavelength. (2)

   b Write down four properties that all of these waves have in common. (4)

   c Write down one use for each group of waves. (7)

   d Identify which three groups of waves could cause cancer. (3)

   e Identify which three groups of waves can be used to communicate. (3)

(Total 19 marks)

SKILLS CRITICAL THINKING

6 Give one use of total internal reflection in the following situations:

   a in a submarine (1)

   b birdwatching (1)

   c keyhole surgery (1)

   d cars (1)

(Total 4 marks)

| 10 ENERGY TRANSFERS 373 | 11 WORK AND POWER 379 |

PHYSICS UNIT 4
ENERGY RESOURCES AND ENERGY TRANSFER

Energy, energy stores and the energy transfers! These are all vital to modern life.

The photo shows energy produced from a wind farm. We also obtain energy by burning fossil fuels like coal and oil, directly from the Sun in the form of heat, from hydroelectric power and nuclear power, and from many other resources.

We need to understand how to transfer energy from one store to another, to use it efficiently and to conserve resources that cannot be replaced. We also need to be aware of the advantages and disadvantages of different energy resources.

Physics is about energy!

4 ENERGY RESOURCES AND ENERGY TRANSFER | 10 ENERGY TRANSFERS

10 ENERGY TRANSFERS

SPECIFICATION REFERENCES: 4.1–4.5

Whenever anything happens, energy is transferred from one store to another – indeed, without energy things simply cannot happen! In this chapter, you will learn that energy can be transferred in a number of different ways from one type of energy store to another. You will also find out that, although energy is never destroyed, in every energy transfer some energy is transferred to the surroundings, often as thermal energy.

▲ Figure 10.1(a) Here energy is being transferred from the band as light and heat radiation. (b) The bikers store kinetic energy and gravitational energy. (c) Energy is transferred electrically to the advertising display in this street and the energy is then transferred to the surroundings as light radiation.

LEARNING OBJECTIVES

- Describe energy transfers involving energy stores:
    - energy stores: chemical, kinetic, gravitational, elastic, thermal, magnetic, electrostatic, nuclear
    - energy transfers: mechanically, electrically, by heating, by radiation (light and sound).
- Use the principle of conservation of energy.

- Know and use the relationship between efficiency, useful energy output and total energy output:

$$\text{efficiency} = \frac{\text{useful energy output}}{\text{total energy output}} \times 100\%$$

- Describe a variety of everyday and scientific devices and situations, explaining the transfer of the input energy in terms of the above relationship, including their representation by Sankey diagrams.

For things to happen we need energy! Energy is used to produce sound. Energy is used to transport people and goods from place to place, whether it is by train, boat or plane or on the backs of animals or even by bicycles. Energy is needed to lift objects, make machinery work and run all the electrical and electronic equipment we have in our modern world. Energy is transferred by heating and as light radiation. The demand for energy increases every day because the world's population is increasing. People consume energy in the form of food and need energy for the basics of life, like warmth and light. As people become wealthier they demand much more than the basics, so the need for energy grows!

ENERGY STORES

Energy is found in many different stores:

- We need energy to keep our bodies warm, to be able to move and to talk. We get this energy from a chemical store, the food we eat. Fuels like gas, oil and coal are also chemical energy stores.

- Moving objects store kinetic energy. Moving water in a stream is a kinetic energy store. The Moon orbiting the Earth is a kinetic energy store.

> **EXTENSION**
> Sound energy can be used to break up small stones that can form inside a person's body, without the need for an operation. Sound energy is also used in medicine to examine the inside of the body, as an alternative to x-rays.

- Objects in gravitational fields store gravitational energy. The water in a reservoir in mountains is a gravitational energy store. The weights in a grandfather clock are a gravitational energy store.
- Stretched or **compressed** (squashed) springs are elastic energy stores. Clockwork toys store elastic energy in springs.
- Hot objects are **thermal** energy stores. Some electric heaters use special bricks that are heated during the night so that the thermal energy stored in them can be used in the daytime. Countries like Iceland make use of the natural thermal energy stored in hot rocks beneath the ground.
- The Earth has a magnetic energy store, thunder clouds are dramatic examples of electrostatic energy stores, and nuclear energy stores are used in nuclear power stations.

ENERGY TRANSFERS

Energy can be transferred to an object mechanically. If we lift an object above our heads, we transfer some of our stored energy to the object by doing mechanical work on it.

Energy can be transferred electrically. When we turn on a light the energy from the power station is transferred to the light bulb electrically. In the light bulb energy is transferred by heating to its surroundings. Energy is also transferred by light radiation to the surroundings.

Energy can also be transferred by sound radiation.

> **HINT**
> You may meet the following abbreviations: KE – kinetic energy; GPE – gravitational potential energy; EPE – elastic potential energy.

'WASTED' ENERGY TRANSFERS

For energy to be useful, we need to be able to transfer it from one store into whichever store we require. Unfortunately, when we try to do this there is usually some energy transferred to unwanted stores. We often refer to these energy transfers to unwanted stores as 'wasted' energy because it is not being used for a useful purpose.

Here are some examples of wasted energy:

- Energy can be transferred electrically to hot water in a tank (a thermal energy store) in a house to be used when needed. Although the tank may be well insulated, some energy will be transferred from the water in the hot water tank by heating other objects like the metal tank and then the surrounding air. These are unwanted energy stores.
- We provide our cars with an energy store, the tank of petrol (gas). We want energy from this store to be transferred to the kinetic energy of the moving car, and to gravitational energy if we are driving up a hill – both transfers are useful. Heating will also transfer thermal energy to the surroundings, sound will radiate energy to the surroundings, and friction between moving parts and the air will cause mechanical work to be done making things get hot therefore transferring thermal energy to the surroundings. These are examples of chemical energy stored in the fuel being transferred to unwanted energy stores.

Unwanted energy transfers reduce efficiency. This problem is the same whether the system is a small one, like a car, or a large system, like the nationwide electricity generation and distribution industry. We need to be aware of where our energy is transferring to if we are to find ways of using it well.

SOME ENERGY TRANSFERS

We have many ways of transferring energy from one store to another.

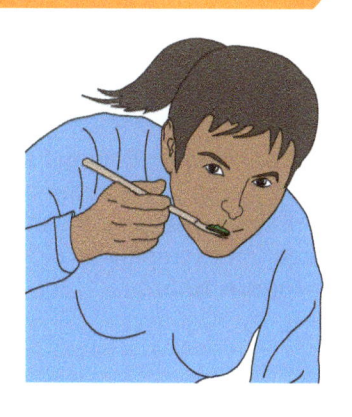

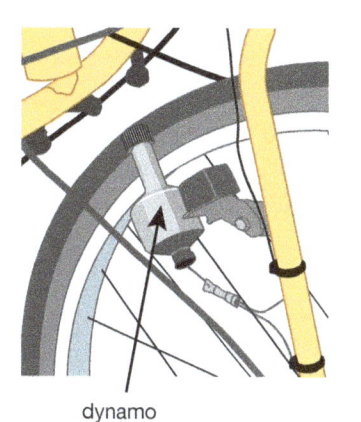

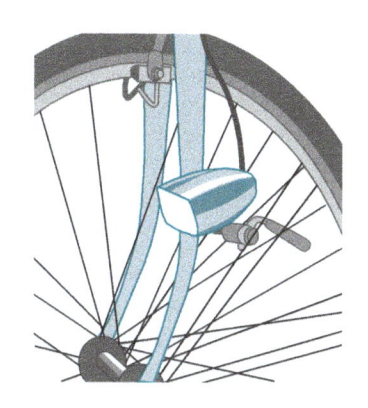

▲ Figure 10.2 Energy is transferred from one store to another, and to another, and so on.

In **Figure 10.2**, stored chemical energy in the food is needed to help our bodies make a range of other chemicals. Some of these – like carbohydrates – are used to produce heat to maintain our body temperature and energy for movement through muscle activity. Having eaten a meal, the cyclist in **Figure 10.2** is transferring the chemical energy stored in her body mechanically to movement energy. The movement is in the cyclist's legs and in the machine (the bicycle). The cyclist is transferring additional energy by heating the surroundings. Friction in various parts of the bicycle will also result in energy being transferred mechanically to heat and sound.

The movement energy of the wheel is transferred mechanically to the dynamo. The dynamo transfers energy electrically to the the lamp. The lamp radiates the energy to the surroundings as light and by heating.

Examples of other energy transfers are given in the questions at the end of the chapter.

CONSERVATION OF ENERGY

The principle of conservation of energy is a very important rule. It states that:

Energy is not created or destroyed in any process.

(It is just transferred from one store to another.)

We often hear about the energy crisis: as our demand for more energy increases our reserves of energy in the form of fuels like oil and gas (chemical stores) are rapidly being used up. The principle of conservation of energy makes it seem as if there is no real problem – that energy can never run out. We need to understand what the principle really means.

Physicists believe that the amount of energy in the Universe is constant – energy can be transferred from one store to another but there is never any more or any less of it. This means we cannot use energy up. However, if we consider our little piece of the Universe, the problem becomes more obvious. As we make energy do useful things – for example, transferring energy from the chemical store of petrol to the kinetic energy store of a moving car – some of it will be transferred to heat in the surroundings. Some of this thermal energy stored will be transferred by radiation into space. This energy is not available for us on the Earth to use any more.

> **EXTENSION**
>
> Even though the amount of energy in the Universe is constant, it is becoming more spread out and so less available for use. Some scientists think that all the energy in the Universe will eventually be transferred to heat and that everywhere in the Universe will end up at the same very low temperature. This possible 'end of the world' is sometimes referred to by the dramatic name of 'heat death'. If the Universe does end up this way, it is not expected to do so for some time yet, so carry on working for those exams!

This is just like a badly insulated house; if heat energy escapes, it is transferred away from the system we call our home, and is no longer available to keep us warm.

SANKEY DIAGRAMS

We use different ways to show how energy is transferred. Energy transfer diagrams show the energy input (contribution), the energy transfer process and the energy output (production). The system may be a very simple one with just one main energy transfer process taking place. An example of a simple system with its energy transfer diagram is shown in **Figure 10.3**.

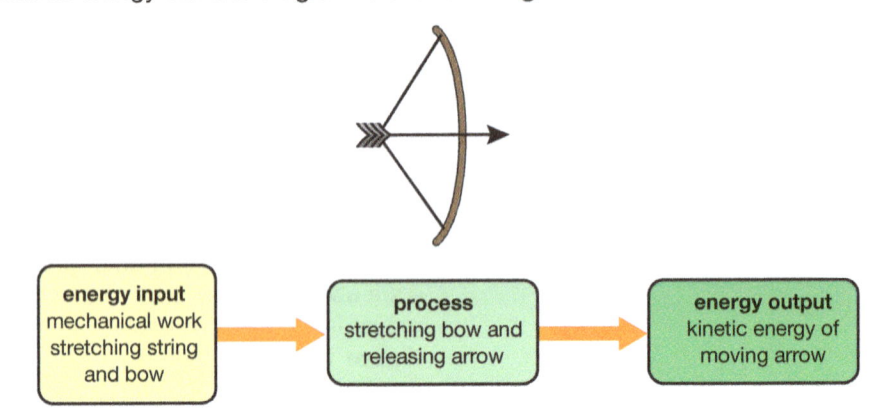

▲ Figure 10.3 Energy transfer diagram for an arrow being fired from a bow

Sankey diagrams are a simpler and clearer way of showing what happens to an energy input into a system. The energy flow is shown by arrows whose width is proportional to the amount of energy involved. Wide arrows show large energy flows, narrow arrows show small energy flows.

Figure 10.4 shows a Sankey diagram for a complex system – the energy flow for a car. Chemical energy in the form of petrol is the input to the car. The energy outputs from the car are:

- electrical energy to drive lights, radio and so on, to charge the battery (transferred to chemical energy) and allow the car to switch on
- movement (kinetic) energy from the car engine
- wasted energy as electrical heating in wiring and lamp filaments, as frictional heating in various parts of the engine and alternator, and as noise.

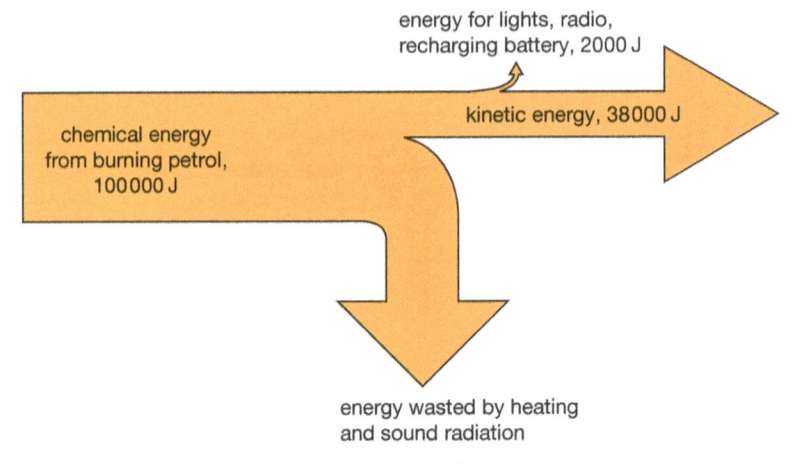

▲ Figure 10.4 Sankey diagram showing the energy flow in a typical car

Here the 100 000 J of chemical energy input might be shown by an arrow 20 mm wide, so the 60 000 J of energy wasted (60% of the input) would then be shown by an arrow that is 12 mm wide (60% of 20 mm). It is difficult to draw the 2% arrow for the energy output to scale; it is enough to show it as very small. In an examination question you will not be required to draw the Sankey diagram accurately to scale, but the relative sizes of the arrows should show the relative sizes of the output energy stores.

EFFICIENCY

Whenever we are considering energy transfers, we have to remember that a proportion of the energy input is wasted. Remember that wasted means transferred into stores other than the useful store required. We would like our energy transfer systems to be perfect with all the output energy being in the store that we want. For example, not all the output energy for an electric lamp is light (the useful energy output), some of the output energy is thermal energy (not useful when what we want is light).

Real systems always have an unwanted energy output so can never have 100% efficiency.

The efficiency of an energy conversion system is defined as:

$$\text{efficiency} = \frac{\text{useful energy output}}{\text{total energy output}} \times 100\%$$

Efficiency does not have a unit because it is a ratio. Sometimes efficiency is shown as a **fraction** of the energy output that is in the wanted or useful store. In real energy transfers this fraction will always be less than 1 because some of the total output energy will be in an unwanted store.

EXAM HINT

If you calculate the efficiency of a system and get an answer bigger than 100% then you have put the numbers into the equation the wrong way round!

EXAMPLE 1

A 60 W tungsten filament bulb uses 60 J of energy every second. It is 5% efficient. Calculate how much of the total energy output per second is useful light radiation.

$$\text{efficiency} = \frac{\text{useful energy output}}{\text{total energy output}} \times 100\%$$

$$5\% = \frac{\text{useful energy output}}{60 \text{ J}} \times 100\%$$

$$\frac{5}{100} = \frac{\text{useful energy output}}{60 \text{ J}}$$

So useful (light) energy from bulb = $\frac{5 \times 60 \text{ J}}{100}$ = 3 J each second.

CHAPTER QUESTIONS

SKILLS CREATIVITY

Exam-style questions on energy transfers can be found at the end of Unit 4 on page 387.

1 Describe the main energy transfers taking place in the following situations:
   a turning on a torch
   b lighting a candle
   c rubbing your hands to keep them warm
   d bouncing on a trampoline.

2. Copy and complete the following Sankey diagrams. Remember that the width of the arrows must be proportional to the amount of energy involved. This has been done for you in part a.

   a for an electric lamp

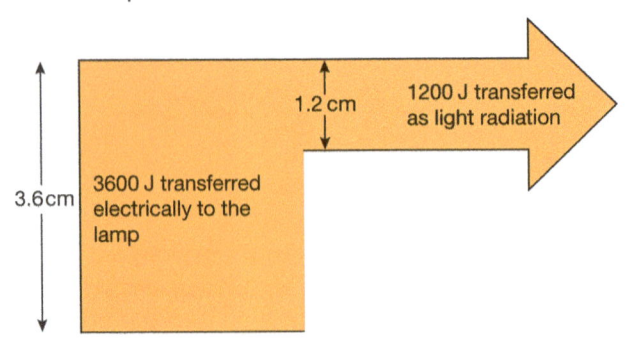

   b In a typical wash in a washing machine 1.2 MJ is transferred to the kinetic energy of the rotating drum, 6 MJ of energy is transferred to heat the water and 0.8 MJ is wasted as heat transferred to the surroundings and sound.

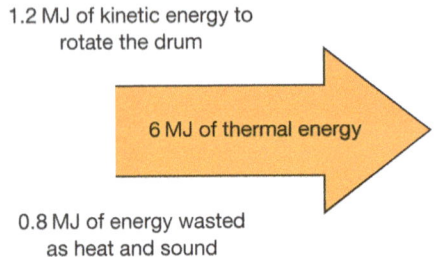

3. a Draw a Sankey diagram for the following situation. An electric kettle is used to heat some water. 350 kJ of energy is used to heat the water, 10 kJ to raise the temperature of the kettle and 40 kJ escapes to heat the surroundings.

   b Calculate the efficiency of the kettle.

4. A ball is dropped. It hits the ground with 10 J of kinetic energy and bounces with 4 J of kinetic energy.

   a State what happens to 6 J of the energy during the bounce.

   b Draw a Sankey diagram for the energy flow that takes place during the bounce.

11 WORK AND POWER

SPECIFICATION REFERENCES: 4.11–4.17

Work is calculated by multiplying the force applied by the distance through which the force moves – the bigger the force, or the longer the distance through which it moves, the more work is done. Work always involves an energy transfer. Power is the rate at which energy is transferred, and efficiency is a measure of how much of the input energy to a system is converted to useful output energy. In this chapter you will learn how to calculate the work done in a system and its power as energy is transferred.

▶ Figure 11.1 James Joule (1818–1889) was the son of a wealthy Manchester brewer. He was tutored by James Dalton and carried out scientific research in his own laboratory, built in the basement of his father's home.

LEARNING OBJECTIVES

- Know and use the relationship between work done, force and distance moved in the direction of the force:

  work done = force × distance moved

  $W = F \times d$

- Know that work done is equal to energy transferred.

- Know and use the relationship between gravitational potential energy, mass, gravitational field strength and height:

  gravitational potential energy = mass × gravitational field strength × height

  $GPE = m \times g \times h$

- Know and use the relationship:

  kinetic energy = ½ × mass × speed squared

  $KE = \frac{1}{2} \times m \times v^2$

- Understand how conservation of energy produces a link between gravitational potential energy, kinetic energy and work.

- Describe power as the rate of transfer of energy or the rate of doing work.

- Use the relationship between power, work done (energy transferred) and time taken:

  $power = \frac{work\ done}{time\ taken}$ $power = \frac{energy\ transferred}{time\ taken}$

  $P = \frac{W}{t}$

The unit of energy is named after James Joule. It was Joule who realised that heat was a store of energy. He showed that kinetic energy could be transferred to heat. At that time heat was measured in calories.

ENERGY AND WORK

Energy is the ability to do work.

This statement tells us what energy does rather than what energy is. We know that energy is found in a wide variety of different stores but we are really interested in what energy can do – the answer is that energy does work.

We need to define work in a way that is measurable. Some types of work are not easy to calculate the value of. Mechanical work, like lifting heavy objects, is easy to measure: if you lift a heavier object, you do more work; if you lift an object through a greater distance, again, you do more work. The definition of work in physics is:

work done, W (joules) = force, F (newtons) × distance moved, d (metres)

$$W = F \times d$$

If the force is measured in newtons and the distance through which the force is applied is measured in metres then the work done will be in joules.

Work done is equal to the amount of energy transferred.

1 J of work done is transferred when a force of 1 N is applied through a distance of 1 m in the direction of the force.

EXAMPLE 1

Figure 11.2 shows a weightlifter raising an object that weighs 500 N through a distance of 2 m. To calculate the work done we use:

$$W = F \times d$$
$$= 500 \text{ N} \times 2 \text{ m}$$
$$= 1000 \text{ J}$$

▲ Figure 11.2 Doing work by lifting a weight

This work done on the weight has increased its energy. This is explained in the section on gravitational potential energy (page 381).

EXAMPLE 2

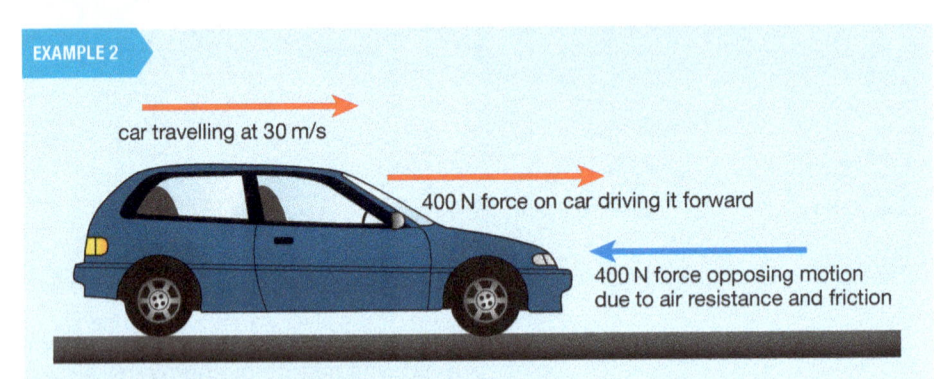

▲ Figure 11.3 A car travelling at a constant speed doing work

In the example shown in **Figure 11.3** the force acting on the car is not accelerating it – instead, it is being used to balance the forces opposing its movement. The resultant force on the car is zero, so it keeps moving in a straight line at constant speed. To work out the work done on the car in one second we substitute the force required, 400 N, and the distance through which it acts in one second, 30 m, in the equation:

$$W = F \times d$$
$$= 400 \text{ N} \times 30 \text{ m}$$
$$= 12\,000 \text{ J or } 12 \text{ kJ}$$

4 ENERGY RESOURCES AND ENERGY TRANSFER   11 WORK AND POWER

GRAVITATIONAL POTENTIAL ENERGY (GPE)

The gravitational potential energy of an object that has been raised to a height, *h*, above the ground is given by:

gravitational potential energy, *GPE* (joules) = mass of object, *m* (kilograms)

× gravitational field strength, *g* (newtons per kilogram) × height, *h* (metres)

$$GPE = m \times g \times h$$

The change in the GPE of an object will be an increase if we apply a force on it in the opposite direction to the pull of gravity – that is, if we lift it off the ground. When an object falls it loses GPE. To keep things simple, we usually assume that an object has no GPE before we do work on it.

In the weightlifting example given on page 380, the weightlifter has used some chemical energy to do the work. We know that energy is conserved so what has happened to the chemical energy that the weightlifter used? Some has been transferred to heat in the weightlifter's body. The remainder has been transferred to the weight because he has increased its height in the gravitational field of the Earth. The energy that the weight has gained is called gravitational potential energy or GPE (see **Figure 11.4**).

work done = *F* × *d*
        = *mg* × *h*

so, lifting the object through a distance of *h* m involves doing *mgh* J of work

force = *mg* N

mass = *m* kg
weight = *mg* N

force required to lift object = *mg* N

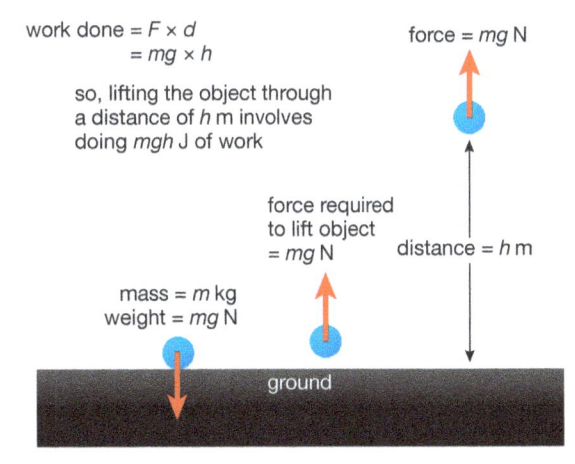

distance = *h* m

ground

▲ Figure 11.4 The work done to lift an object is equal to the GPE the object has at its new height.

(a) held above the ground
GPE maximum
KE zero

(b) released
GPE decreasing
KE increasing

(c) about to hit the ground
GPE zero
KE maximum

(d) on hitting the ground all the KE is transferred to heat, sound and deforming the object and the ground

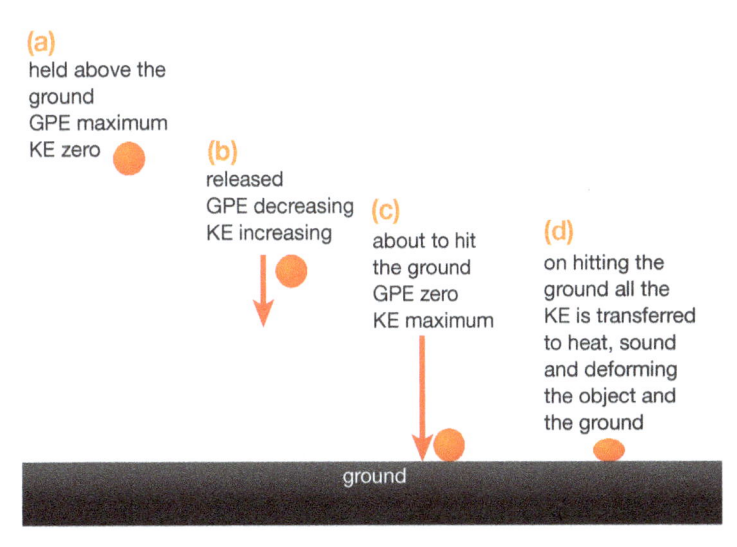

ground

▲ Figure 11.5 When a raised object falls, its gravitational potential energy is transferred first to kinetic energy and then to heat and sound.

REMINDER

Gravitational field strength is the force acting per kilogram on a mass in a gravitational field. The gravitational field strength, *g*, on the surface of the Earth is approximately 10 N/kg. Since the weight of an object is *mg*, increase in GPE is a special version of the equation $W = F \times d$, with $F = mg$ and $d = h$.

> **KEY POINT**
> Kinetic energy (KE) is the energy stored by moving objects.

In **Figure 11.5**, we can see the GPE stored by the weight is being transferred to other stores as the weight falls. The weight accelerates because of the force of gravity acting on it, so it gains kinetic energy. When it reaches the ground all the initial GPE is transferred to kinetic energy. When it hits the ground all the movement energy is then transferred to other stores, mainly heat and sound.

KINETIC ENERGY, KE

The kinetic energy of a moving object is calculated using the equation:

kinetic energy, *KE* (joules) = mass, *m* (kilograms) × speed squared, v^2 (metres squared per seconds squared)

$$KE = \frac{1}{2}mv^2$$

We see that the amount of kinetic energy stored by a moving object depends on its speed and its mass. As the Earth travels through space, orbiting the Sun, it runs the risk of colliding with chunks of matter that are drawn into the gravitational field of the Solar System. In fact, this is very common. If you have ever seen a shooting star – or, to give it its proper name, a meteor – you have seen the line of light produced as a small piece of space debris (waste) burns up on entering our atmosphere (see **Figure 11.6**). This is an example of kinetic energy being transferred to heat and light by the friction produced between the air and the object passing through it.

▲ Figure 11.6 Meteors burn up on entering our atmosphere – we see them as 'shooting stars'.

▲ Figure 11.7 This crater was created when a meteorite collided with Earth in Arizona.

HIGH ENERGY COLLISION!

The meteorite that caused the Arizona crater (**Figure 11.7**) is thought to have hit the Earth travelling at 11 000 m/s and to have had a mass of 109 kilograms. It hit the ground with an energy equivalent to a 15 megaton hydrogen bomb, 1000 times greater than the atomic bomb dropped on Hiroshima at the end of the Second World War.

EXAMPLE 3

Calculate the kinetic energy carried by a meteorite of mass 500 kg (less than that of an average-sized car) hitting the Earth at a speed of 1000 m/s.

$$KE = \tfrac{1}{2}mv^2$$
$$= \tfrac{1}{2} \times 500 \text{ kg} \times (1000 \text{ m/s})^2$$
$$= 250\,000\,000 \text{ J (or 250 MJ)}$$

CALCULATIONS USING WORK, GPE AND KE

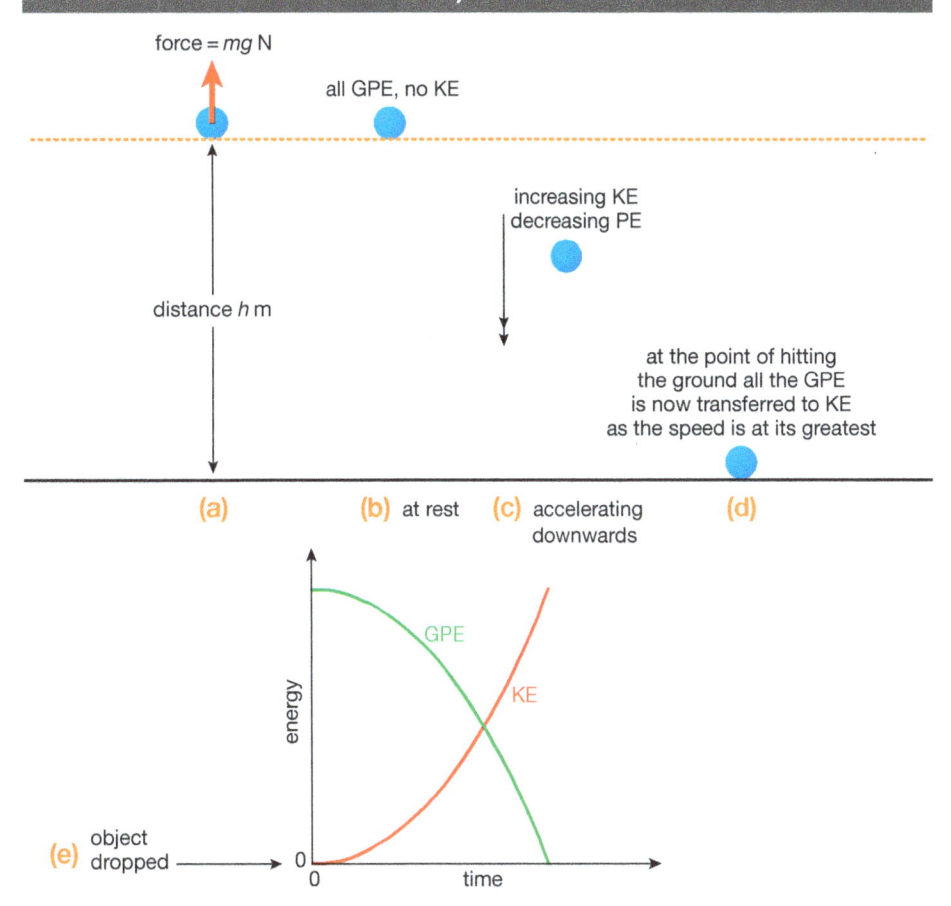

▲ Figure 11.8 GPE and KE of a falling object: **(a)** doing work to lift an object; **(b)** all GPE; **(c)** GPE transferring to KE during fall; **(d)** all KE at end of fall; **(e)** graph showing relationship between GPE and KE as the object falls

Work transfers energy to an object: $W = Fd$. An object of mass, m, weighs ($m \times g$) newtons so the force, F, needed to lift it is mg (**Figure 11.8**). If we raise the object through a distance h, the work done on the object is $mg \times h$. This is also the gain in GPE.

When the object is released, it falls – and its GPE is transferred to KE. At the end of the fall, all the initial GPE of the stationary (not moving) object has been transferred to the KE of the moving object. The graphs in **Figure 11.8** show how the GPE of the object is changing into KE as it falls. The sum of the two graphs is always the same. Energy is conserved, so the loss of GPE is equal to the gain in KE.

work done lifting object = gain in GPE = gain in KE of the object just before hitting the ground

EXAMPLE 4

In a rollercoaster ride (**Figure 11.9**) the truck falls through a height of 17 m. Calculate the truck's speed at the bottom of this fall. (Take g = 10 N/kg)

If we assume that all the GPE of the truck at the top of the ride is transferred to KE at the bottom we can use the equation:

$$GPE = KE$$
$$mgh = \tfrac{1}{2}mv^2$$

▲ Figure 11.9 A rollercoaster ride

The mass, m, of the truck appears on both sides of the equation, so it cancels out:

$$gh = \tfrac{1}{2}v^2$$

Substituting h = 17 m and g = 10 N/kg:

$$17 \text{ m} \times 10 \text{ N/kg} = \tfrac{1}{2}v^2$$
$$v^2 = 2 \times 17 \text{ m} \times 10 \text{ N/kg}$$
$$v = \sqrt{(2 \times 17 \text{ m} \times 10 \text{ N/kg})}$$
$$= 18.44 \text{ m/s (about 66 kph)}$$

Some of the GPE the truck had at the start will be transferred to heat and sound, so the speed at the bottom of the fall will be a little slower than this.

POWER

Power is the rate of transfer of energy or the rate of doing work.

James Watt (**Figure 11.10a**) is remembered as the inventor of the steam engine and is said to have been inspired by watching the lid on a kettle being forced up by the pressure of the steam forming inside. Neither story is accurate, but what is true is that Watt, working in partnership with Matthew Boulton, developed improvements to the steam engine that made it a commercial product and completely changed industry and transport.

The SI unit of power is named in honour of James Watt. The watt (W) is the rate of transfer or conversion of energy of one joule per second (1 J/s).

$$\text{power, } P \text{ (watts)} = \frac{\text{work done, } W \text{ (joules)}}{\text{time taken, } t \text{ (seconds)}}$$

$$P = \frac{W}{t}$$

▲ Figure 11.10 (a) James Watt (1736–1819) was a Scottish engineer who improved the performance of the steam engine and can be said to have started the Industrial Revolution – the beginning of the machine age. (b) A model of a steam engine that transfers the heat energy of steam to movement. Watt's engines were used to pump water out of mines.

4 ENERGY RESOURCES AND ENERGY TRANSFER | 11 WORK AND POWER

ACTIVITY 1

▼ PRACTICAL: INVESTIGATE YOUR POWER OUTPUT

You may have done a simple experiment involving running upstairs to measure your output power. You do work as you raise your GPE, and to find your power output in watts you divide the work done by the time taken. The experiment is shown in **Figure 11.11**. Notice that calculating the work you do against gravity using force × distance works just as well as using the equation for *GPE* (mass × gravitational field strength × height).

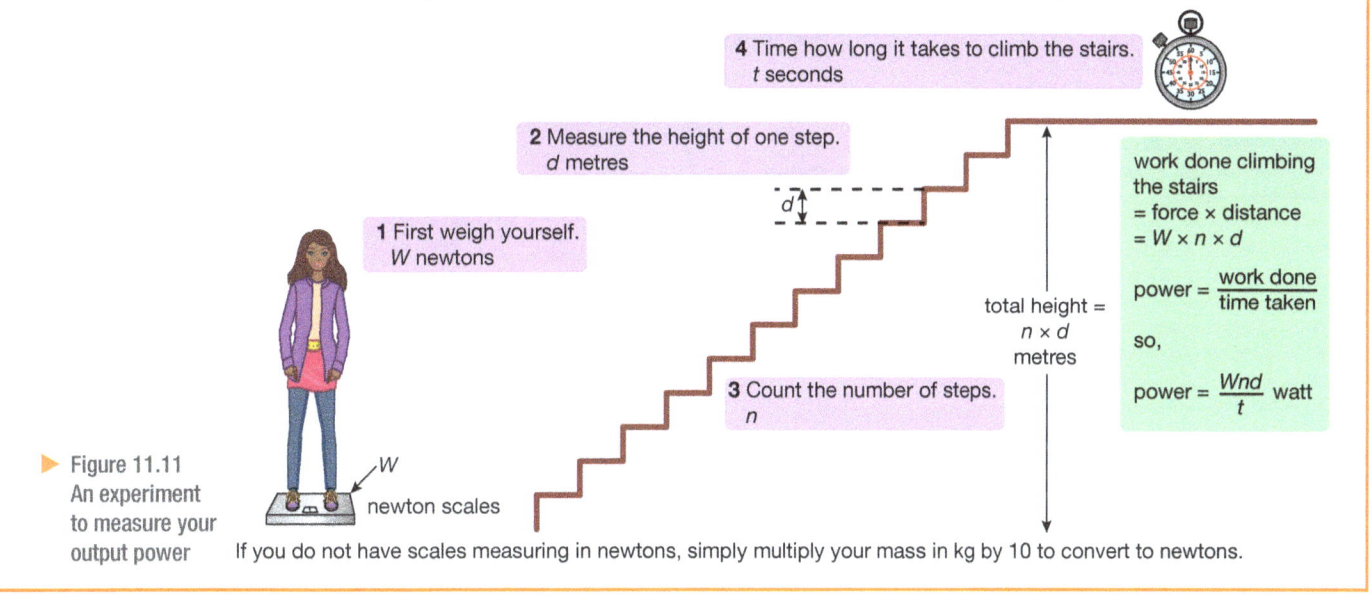

1 First weigh yourself. *W* newtons

2 Measure the height of one step. *d* metres

3 Count the number of steps. *n*

4 Time how long it takes to climb the stairs. *t* seconds

total height = $n \times d$ metres

work done climbing the stairs
= force × distance
= $W \times n \times d$

$$\text{power} = \frac{\text{work done}}{\text{time taken}}$$

so,

$$\text{power} = \frac{Wnd}{t} \text{ watt}$$

▶ Figure 11.11 An experiment to measure your output power

If you do not have scales measuring in newtons, simply multiply your mass in kg by 10 to convert to newtons.

Safety note: Wear suitable footwear and only allow one person at a time on the staircase. Ensure the stairs are dry, in good condition and free of any obstacles.

A more convenient way of raising your GPE and getting to a higher floor in a building is to take a lift. The lift will transfer its energy input, usually electrical, to kinetic energy and then, if you are going up, to GPE. As usual, unwanted energy transfers are inevitable – sound and heat will be produced. If we know the weight of the lift and its contents and the height through which it moves, we can calculate the work done in the usual way. If we measure the time that the lift journey takes we can then calculate the power output of the lift motor. (Strictly this will be the useful power output – it will not take account of the wasted power due to unwanted energy transfers.)

EXAMPLE 5

If a lift and passengers have a combined weight of 4000 N and the lift moves upwards with an average speed of 3 m/s (see **Figure 11.12**) find the useful power output of the lift motor.

To keep the lift moving upwards at a steady speed, the lift motor must provide an upward force to balance the weight of the lift. This is 4000 N. In each second, this force is applied through a vertical distance of 3 m, so:

work done per second = 4000 N × 3 m/s

= 12 000 J/s

= 12 000 W

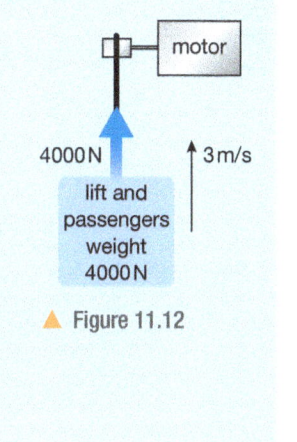

▲ Figure 11.12

CHAPTER QUESTIONS

Exam-style questions on work and power can be found at the end of Unit 4 on page 387.

In the questions below, where necessary, take the strength of the Earth's gravity to be 10 N/kg.

SKILLS CRITICAL THINKING

1 James Joule showed that heat is a store of energy. He did this by showing that heat can be produced by using mechanical energy.
   a Give an example of a process in which kinetic energy is transferred to heat.
   b Describe how heat energy can be transferred to either kinetic energy or gravitational potential energy.

SKILLS CRITICAL THINKING

SKILLS PROBLEM SOLVING

2 a State the SI unit of work.
   b Define the unit of work.
   c Calculate how much work is done in each of the following situations.
      i A bag of six apples each weighing 1 N is lifted through 80 cm.
      ii A rocket with a thrust of 100 kN travels to a height of 200 m.
      iii A weightlifter raises a mass of 60 kg through a height of 2.8 m.
      iv A lift of mass 200 kg lifts three people of mass 50 kg each through a distance of 45 m.

SKILLS PROBLEM SOLVING

3 Water from a **hydroelectric power** station reservoir is taken from a reservoir (artificial lake) at a height of 800 m above sea level to turbines (engines) in the power station itself. The power station is at sea level. The reservoir holds 200 million (2×10^8) litres of water. If a litre of water has a mass of 1 kg, find how much gravitational potential energy is stored in the water in the reservoir.

SKILLS CRITICAL THINKING

SKILLS PROBLEM SOLVING

4 a State how to calculate the kinetic energy stored by a moving object.
   b Calculate the kinetic energy of the following:
      i a man of mass 80 kg running at 9 m/s
      ii an air rifle pellet of mass 0.2 g travelling at 50 m/s
      iii a ball of mass 60 g travelling at 24 m/s.

SKILLS PROBLEM SOLVING

5 A catapult fires a stone of mass 0.04 kg vertically upwards. If the stone has an initial kinetic energy of 48 J, calculate how high will it travel before it starts to fall back to the ground.

SKILLS PROBLEM SOLVING
CRITICAL THINKING

6 If a coin is dropped from a height of 80 m, how fast will it be travelling when it hits the ground? State any assumptions you may need to make.

SKILLS CRITICAL THINKING

7 Define power and state its unit.

SKILLS PROBLEM SOLVING

8 A person with a mass of 40 kg runs upstairs in 12 s. The stairs have 20 steps and the height of each step is 20 cm.
   a Find the weight of the person, in newtons.
   b Find the total height that the person has climbed.
   c Calculate how much work is done in climbing the stairs.
   d Now work out the power output of the person running up the stairs.

9 A drag car, of mass 500 kg, accelerates from rest to a speed of 144 km/h in 5 s.
   a What is its final speed in:
      i m/h (metres per hour)
      ii m/s?
   b Calculate the increase in KE of the drag car.
   c Find the average power developed by the drag car's engine.

EXAM PRACTICE

SKILLS PROBLEM SOLVING

1 A fluorescent lamp is 25% efficient. Choose the statement that correctly describes how the lamp performs.

　　A the lamp only works for a quarter of the time

　　B 25% of the energy transferred to the lamp is wasted

　　C the lamp does not work properly

　　D 25% of the energy supplied to the lamp is transferred to light

(Total 1 mark)

SKILLS CRITICAL THINKING

2 A car uses energy stored in chemical form in petrol. When the engine is running this energy is transferred to other types of stored energy. Select, from the following list, energy store(s) that are useful.

　　A noise

　　B heat

　　C movement

　　D hot exhaust gases

(Total 1 mark)

SKILLS PROBLEM SOLVING

3 Four students, A, B, C and D, measure their power output by running upstairs and timing how long it takes. Calculate which student has the greatest power output.

　　A mass of 50 kg, takes 20 s to gain a height of 10 m

　　B mass of 40 kg, takes 30 s to gain a height of 15 m

　　C mass of 45 kg, takes 10 s to gain a height of 5 m

　　D mass of 55 kg, takes 25 s to gain a height of 15 m

(Total 1 mark)

SKILLS PROBLEM SOLVING

4 An electric motor is used to raise a load that weighs 800 N through a distance of 30 m.

　a Determine how much work the electric motor does in raising the load. **(3)**

　b Calculate the power output of the motor if it takes 16 s to raise the load. **(2)**

　c The motor is 75% efficient.

SKILLS CRITICAL THINKING

　　i Explain what this means. **(2)**

SKILLS PROBLEM SOLVING

　　ii Calculate the electrical power that must be supplied to the motor to raise this load in the time stated. Give your answer in kW. **(2)**

SKILLS INTERPRETATION

　d Draw a labelled Sankey diagram to represent the energy transfers that take place as the motor raises the load. **(3)**

(Total 12 marks)

SKILLS ANALYSIS, REASONING

5 The diagram shows a toy rocket launcher that uses a spring in a tube.

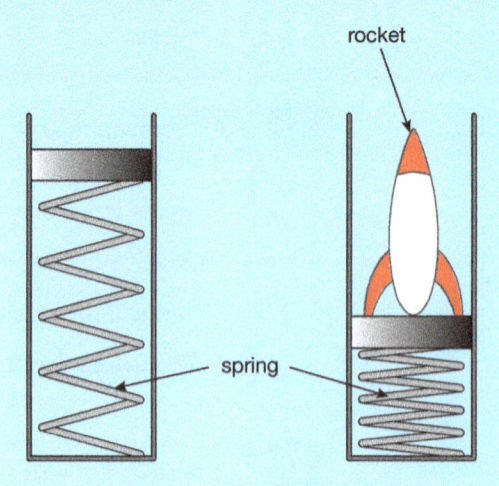

a Here are statements that describe the events leading to the launch of the toy rocket:

1 spring released
2 rocket leaves launcher
3 rocket gains kinetic energy
4 spring stores elastic potential energy
5 child does work squashing the spring
6 spring transfers stored energy to rocket

Choose from the following list the letter that describes the events in the order that they must happen. (1)

A 1 5 6 3 2 4   **B** 5 4 1 6 3 2   **C** 1 5 4 6 3 2   **D** 5 4 1 6 2 3

SKILLS CRITICAL THINKING

b Describe the energy transfers that take place after the rocket leaves the launcher, up to and including when it hits the ground. (4)

(Total 5 marks)

6 This question is about PV (photovoltaic) cells. A student wanted find the best angle to set up a PV cell to get the maximum amount of energy transferred from the Sun's rays to electrical energy. Here is the apparatus she set up and the results she obtained.

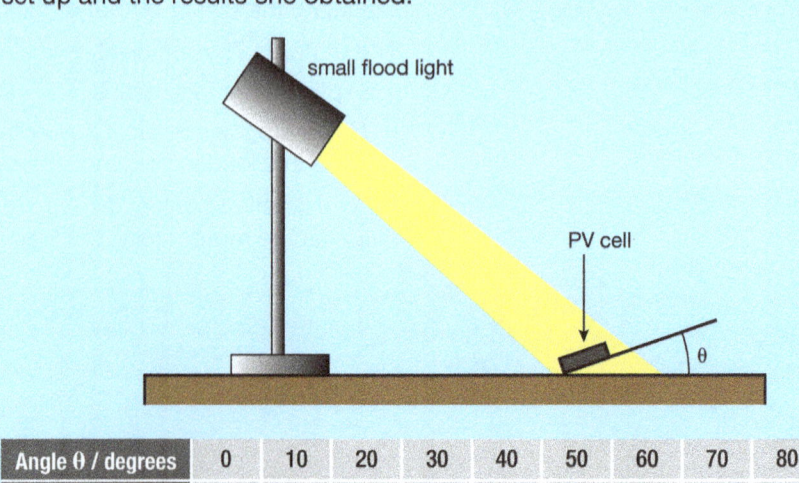

Angle θ / degrees	0	10	20	30	40	50	60	70	80	90
Current / mA	117	144	155	189	202	208	210	204	191	172

4 ENERGY RESOURCES AND ENERGY TRANSFER | EXAM PRACTICE

SKILLS CRITICAL THINKING

The PV cell was connected to a load and she measured the current, I, produced by the cell with the cell at different angles, θ, to the horizontal.

a State:
  i the dependent variable (1)
  ii the independent variable (1)
  iii a control variable. (1)

SKILLS INTERPRETATION

b On a graph grid, 18 cm by 22 cm, plot a graph of the current produced by the PV cell against the angle of the cell to the horizontal. (5)

SKILLS PROBLEM SOLVING

c Use the graph to find:
  i any anomalous result (1)
  ii the angle to get the maximum output from the PV cell in the set-up shown. (1)

SKILLS EXECUTIVE FUNCTION

d When installing PV panels it is important to have them pointing towards the Sun as you would expect. In the experimental set-up shown, the lamp is modelling conditions in the UK in early March at midday (when the Sun reaches its highest position in the sky).

  i Describe how the experiment could be set up to model different positions of the Sun. (1)

SKILLS INTERPRETATION

  ii The experiment is repeated by another student at a time and place when the Sun is directly overhead at midday. Sketch a line on your graph to show how this student's results might appear. Label this line 'Sun overhead'. (3)

(Total 14 marks)

SKILLS PROBLEM SOLVING, REASONING

7 An electric kettle has a power rating of 2.4 kW. It should take 300 kJ to heat 0.9 litres of water to 100 °C.

a Calculate how long it takes to boil the water in the kettle. (3)

In practice it takes 2½ minutes to bring the water to boiling point.

b Suggest a reason for this. (2)

c Calculate the efficiency of the kettle. (4)

(Total 9 marks)

12 PRESSURE 391   13 SOLIDS, LIQUIDS AND GASES 395

PHYSICS UNIT 5
SOLIDS, LIQUIDS AND GASES

Matter can exist in three basic forms: as a solid, a liquid or a gas. In this photo all three are present, though we can only see the solid iceberg and the liquid ocean. Fortunately the iceberg is surrounded by gas, the mixture of oxygen and nitrogen that makes up our atmosphere. Our atmosphere usually contains some water in gas form, which we cannot see. When gaseous water in the atmosphere condenses into tiny water droplets we can see these as clouds.

12 PRESSURE

SPECIFICATION REFERENCES: 5.1, 5.5, 5.6

One way of characterising materials is by their density. This chapter looks at density and at how materials can affect things around them by exerting pressure.

▲ Figure 12.1 Some effects of pressure

LEARNING OBJECTIVES

- Know and use the relationship between pressure, force and area:
  $$\text{pressure} = \frac{\text{force}}{\text{area}} \qquad p = \frac{F}{A}$$

- Understand how the pressure at a point in a gas or liquid at rest acts equally in all directions.

UNITS

In this section you need to use degree Celsius (°C) and Kelvin (K) as the units of temperature (these units both represent the same change in temperature but the Kelvin scale starts from absolute zero, as explained later), cubic metre (m³) as the unit of volume, pascal (Pa) as the unit of pressure and square metre (m²) as the unit of area, as well as other units you have met in earlier units.
It is important to remember
1 m³ = 1 000 000 cm³ (a cubic metre is 1 million cubic centimetres) and
1 m² = 10 000 cm² (a square metre is 10 thousand square centimetres).

The properties of a material affect how it behaves, and how it affects other materials around it. Weather balloons get bigger and bigger as they rise as air pressure gets smaller and smaller. The skis spread the weight of the skier over the snow so she does not sink into it. The submersible is designed to explore the seabed – it has a very strong hull to withstand the high pressure from water deep in the oceans.

PRESSURE UNDER A SOLID

You can push a drawing pin into a piece of wood quite easily, but you cannot make a hole in the wood with your thumb, no matter how hard you push! The small point of the drawing pin concentrates all your pushing force into a tiny area, so the pin goes into the wood easily. Similarly, it is easier to cut things with a sharp knife than a blunt one, because with a sharp knife all the force is concentrated into a much smaller area.

Pressure is defined as the force per unit area. Force is measured in newtons (N) and area is measured in square metres (m²). The units for pressure are pascals (Pa), where 1 Pa is equivalent to 1 N/m².

HINT
Check the units when you are working out pressure – do not mix up cm² and m², for example.
To convert cm² to m², divide by 10 000.
1 m² = 10 000 cm²
If the question asks for the answer in Pascals then you must use the area in square metres.

REMINDER
When answering questions, start with the equation you need to use in words or recognised symbols.

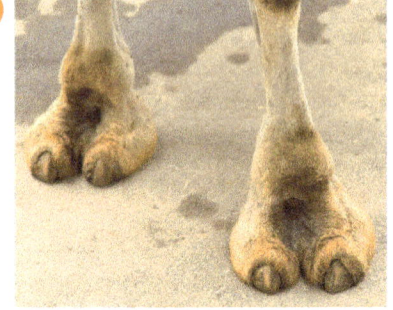

▲ Figure 12.3 (a) The caterpillar tracks on this vehicle spread its weight over a large area. (b) Camels have large feet so they are less likely to sink into loose sand.

Pressure (p), force (F) and area (A) are linked by the following equation (**Figure 12.2**):

$$\text{pressure, } p \text{ (pascals)} = \frac{\text{force, } F \text{ (newtons)}}{\text{area, } A \text{ (square metres)}}$$

$$p = \frac{F}{A}$$

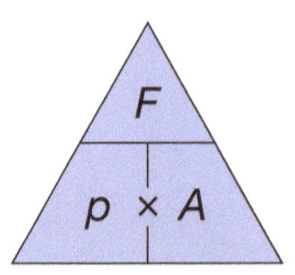

▲ Figure 12.2 The equation for pressure can be rearranged using the triangle method.

EXAMPLE 1

An elephant has a weight of 40 000 N, and her feet cover a total area of 0.1 m².

A woman weighs 600 N and the total area of her shoes in contact with the ground is 0.0015 m². Who exerts the greatest pressure on the ground?

Elephant:

$$p = \frac{F}{A}$$

$$= \frac{40\,000 \text{ N}}{0.1 \text{ m}^2}$$

$$= 400\,000 \text{ Pa (or 400 kPa)}$$

Woman:

$$p = \frac{F}{A}$$

$$= \frac{600 \text{ N}}{0.0015 \text{ m}^2}$$

$$= 400\,000 \text{ Pa (or 400 kPa)}$$

They both exert an equal pressure.

Some machines, including cutting tools like scissors, bolt cutters and knives, need to exert a high pressure to work well. In other applications, a low pressure is important. Tractors and other vehicles designed to move over mud have large tyres that spread the vehicle's weight. The pressure under the tyres is relatively low, so the vehicle is less likely to sink into the mud. Caterpillar tracks used on bulldozers and other earth-moving equipment serve a similar purpose. (In **Figure 12.3a** the caterpillar tracks are very large.)

PRESSURE IN LIQUIDS AND GASES

The submersible shown in **Figure 12.4a** has a very strong hull to withstand the high pressure **exerted** on it by seawater. Pressure in liquids acts equally in all directions, as long as the liquid is not moving. You can easily demonstrate this using a can with holes punched around the bottom, as shown in **Figure 12.4b**. When the can is filled with water, the water is forced out equally in all directions.

Gases also exert pressure on things around them. The pressure exerted by the atmosphere on your body is about 100 000 Pa (although the pressure varies slightly from day to day). However, the pressure inside our bodies is similar, so we do not notice the pressure of the air.

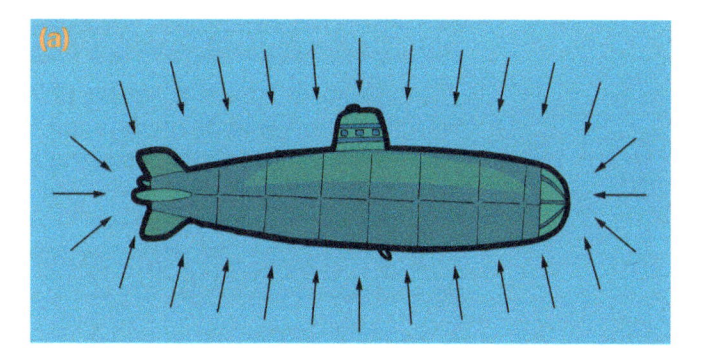

▲ Figure 12.4 **(a)** Pressure in liquids acts equally in all directions. **(b)** A can of water with holes can be used to demonstrate this.

One of the first demonstrations of the effects of air pressure was carried out by Otto van Guericke in 1654, in Magdeburg, Germany. Van Guericke had two large metal bowls made, put them together and then pumped the air out. The bowls could not be pulled apart, even when he attached two teams of horses to the bowls (see **Figure 12.5**).

▲ Figure 12.5 Van Guericke's experiment at Magdeburg

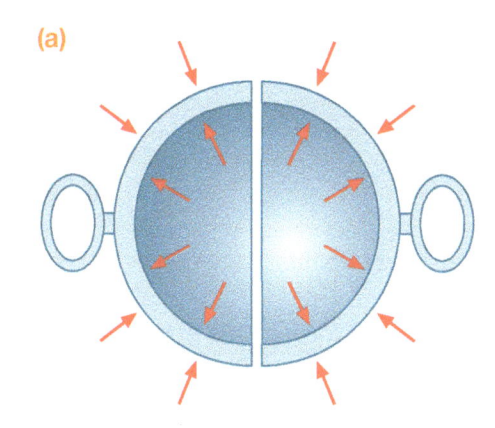

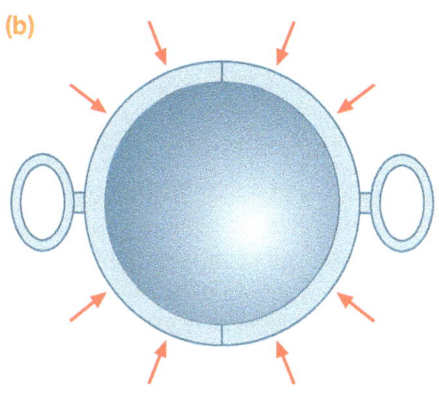

▲ Figure 12.6 **(a)** When the hemispheres are full of air, the forces are the same inside and outside. **(b)** When the air is taken out, there is only a force on the outside of the hemispheres.

You can do the same experiment in the laboratory, using much smaller bowls called Magdeburg **hemispheres**. When air is inside the spheres, the pressure is the same inside and outside. If the air is sucked out, pressure is only acting from the outside. The hemispheres cannot be pulled apart until air is let back into them (see **Figure 12.6**).

EXAMPLE 2

A laboratory set of Magdeburg hemispheres has a surface area of 0.045 m². What is the total force on the outside of the hemispheres?

$F = p \times A$
$= 100\,000 \text{ Pa} \times 0.045 \text{ m}^2$
$= 4500 \text{ N}$

PRESSURE AND DEPTH

The experiment shown in **Figure 12.7** demonstrates that the pressure in a liquid increases with depth. The water trickles out of the hole near the top of the can full of water; it comes out at a much greater rate from the hole at the bottom, furthest from the water level in the can.

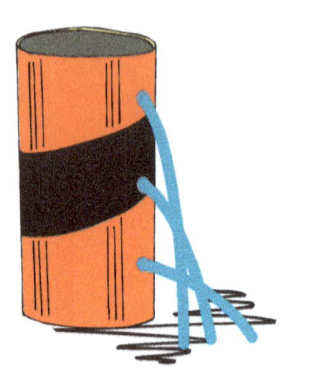

▲ Figure 12.7 Pressure in a liquid increases with depth.

THE UNIT OF PRESSURE

The unit for pressure is named after Blaise Pascal (1623–1662). He was the first person to demonstrate that air pressure decreases with height.

CHAPTER QUESTIONS

Exam-style questions on pressure can be found at the end of Unit 5 on page 400.

SKILLS — REASONING

1. People working on the roofs of buildings often lay a ladder or plank of wood on the roof. They walk on the ladder rather than the roof itself.

   a. Explain why using a ladder or plank will help to prevent damage to the roof.

SKILLS — PROBLEM SOLVING

   b. A worker's weight is 850 N, and each of his boots has an area of 210 cm². Calculate the maximum pressure under his feet when he is walking. Give your answer in pascals.

SKILLS — PROBLEM SOLVING

   c. The worker lays a plank on the roof. The plank has an area of 0.3 m² and a weight of 70 N. Calculate the pressure under the plank when the worker is standing on it. (You can imagine that the mass of the plank is not significant.)

HINT

Remember that all your weight is on one foot at some point while you are walking. To convert cm² to m², divide by 10 000 or 10⁴.

SKILLS — REASONING

2. a. Describe how the pressure exerted on the walls of a container by a gas is explained in terms of the motion of the particles (molecules).

   b. If some of the air in the container was pumped out of the container what would happen to the pressure inside the container and how is this explained in terms of the movement of the particles in the air?

SKILLS — CRITICAL THINKING

3. Rubber suckers are sometimes used to fix things to smooth surfaces like the windscreens of cars. Explain, with the aid of a diagrams, how a sucker sticks to a smooth surface.

13 SOLIDS, LIQUIDS AND GASES

SPECIFICATION REFERENCES: 5.15–5.20

All matter is made up of particles that are continuously moving. The arrangement and movement of the particles determine the properties of the material. In gases, scientists have discovered laws that describe the relationship between pressure, temperature and volume. In this chapter, you will learn what these laws are and how this relationship can be explained in terms of the behaviour of the particles.

▶ Figure 13.1 The botanist Robert Brown (1773–1858) made an observation while studying pollen grains under a microscope that has become known as Brownian motion in his honour. The observation led to the kinetic theory of matter that we use to explain the behaviour of solids, liquids and gases.

LEARNING OBJECTIVES

- Explain how molecules in a gas have random motion and that they exert a force and hence a pressure on the walls of a container.
- Understand why there is an absolute zero of temperature which is −273 °C.
- Describe the Kelvin scale of temperature and be able to convert between the Kelvin and Celsius scales.
- Understand why an increase in temperature results in an increase in the average speed of gas molecules.
- Know that the Kelvin temperature of a gas is proportional to the average kinetic energy of its molecules.
- Explain, for a fixed amount of gas, the qualitative relationship between:
  - pressure and volume at constant temperature
  - pressure and Kelvin temperature at constant volume.

GAS LAWS

We are now going to focus our attention on the properties of gases. We shall explain the different properties in terms of the movement of particles.

We have already said that gases are made up of particles called molecules that are moving. We believe that the particles in gases are spread out and constantly moving in a random, haphazard way.

When the molecules hit the walls of a container they exert a force. The combined effect of the huge number of **collisions** results in the pressure that is exerted on the walls of the container.

> **KEY POINT**
>
> Gases exert a pressure on the walls of a container because the molecules are continuously bumping into the walls. The molecules move randomly in all directions so the pressure on all of the walls is the same.

BOYLE'S LAW

The scientist Robert Boyle (**Figure 13.2**) discovered something that you have probably noticed if you have ever used a bicycle pump: air is squashy! He noticed that you can squeeze air in a cylinder and that it springs back to its original volume when you release it. You can try this for yourself with a plastic syringe (**Figure 13.3**).

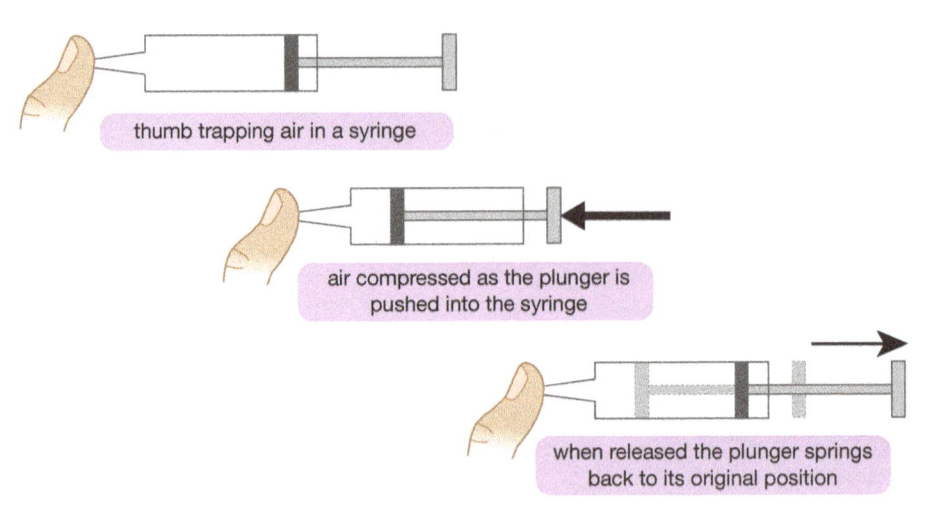

▲ Figure 13.2 Robert Boyle (1627–1691) was an Anglo-Irish chemist and philosopher. As well as discovering the law that bears his name, he worked with Robert Hooke at Oxford developing the air pump.

thumb trapping air in a syringe

air compressed as the plunger is pushed into the syringe

when released the plunger springs back to its original position

▲ Figure 13.3 Air is squashy and springy!

Boyle devised an experiment to see how the volume occupied by a gas depends on the pressure exerted on it. Pressure is the force acting per unit area. This is measured in N/m^2. One N/m^2 is called a pascal (Pa). A version of Boyle's experiment is shown in **Figure 13.4**.

Boyle took care to make sure that the trapped gas he was studying stayed at the same temperature. These are the control variables in this experiment. He increased the pressure on the gas and made a note of the new volume. His results looked like the graph shown in **Figure 13.5**.

Safety note: Eye protection is needed in case any tubing leaks or detaches, which will cause gas under high pressure to be ejected.

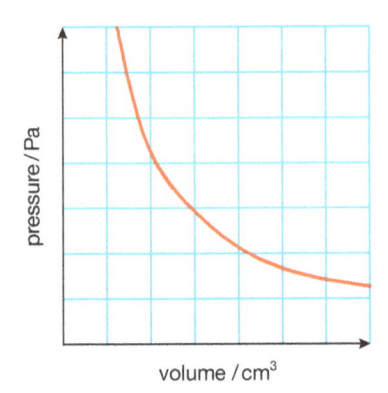

▲ Figure 13.5 Graph to show how the pressure of a gas at constant temperature varies with the volume.

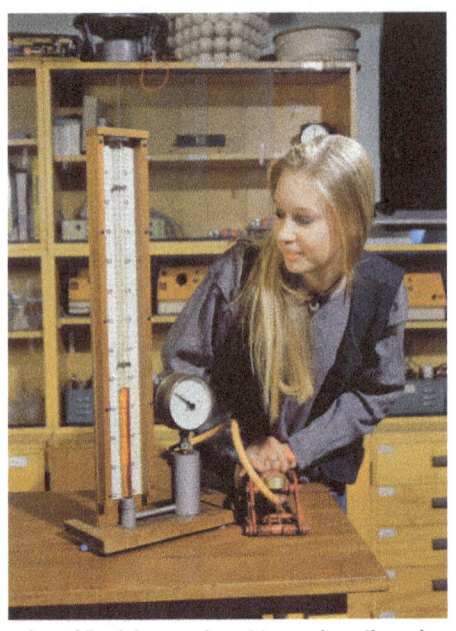

▲ Figure 13.4 A school version of Boyle's experiment to see how the volume of a gas depends on the pressure exerted on it.

Boyle noticed that when he doubled the pressure on the trapped gas, the volume of the gas halved. This is what you notice when you trap air in a bicycle pump, you can squash the air into a smaller space but you must push harder (increasing the pressure on the air) to squash it into a still smaller space.

Gases can be compressed because the gas molecules are very spread out. When a gas is squashed into a smaller container it presses on the walls of the container with a greater pressure. This is explained in terms of particle theory as follows.

If the gas is kept at the same temperature, the average speed of the particles stays the same. (Remember that temperature is an indication of the kinetic energy of the particles.) If the same number of particles is squeezed into a smaller volume, they will hit the container walls more often. Each particle exerts a tiny force on the wall with which it collides. More collisions per second means a greater average force on the wall and, therefore, a greater pressure.

ABSOLUTE ZERO

Boyle took care to conduct his experiment at constant temperature. He was aware that temperature also had an effect on the pressure of a gas.

If we want to investigate how temperature affects (changes) the pressure of a gas we need to trap a fixed amount of the gas and keep the volume it takes up constant (control variables). Then we would need to measure the pressure of the gas at different temperatures.

Here is a simple experiment that shows the effect of temperature on the pressure of a gas (see **Figure 13.6**). Take a empty tin with a metal lid.

Trap some air in the tin by pushing the lid on – but not too tightly! Now gently heat the tin with a Bunsen burner. As the air is heated up the air molecules move faster and so collide with the walls and lid of the tin faster and more often – the pressure of the trapped air increases and eventually the lid is pushed off.

As we cool the gas, the pressure keeps decreasing because the average speed of the gas molecules decreases. The pressure of the gas cannot become less than zero. This suggests that there is a temperature below which it is not possible to cool the gas further. This temperature is called absolute zero. Experiments show that absolute zero is approximately −273 °C.

The Kelvin temperature scale starts from absolute zero. The Kelvin temperature of a gas is proportional to the average kinetic energy of its molecules.

To convert a temperature on the Celsius scale (in °C) to a Kelvin scale temperature (in K), add 273 to the Celsius scale temperature:

- temperature in K = temperature in °C + 273
- temperature in °C = temperature in K − 273

▲ Figure 13.6 Heating an empty metal tin

KEY POINT

When we transfer energy to a gas by heating its store of thermal energy increases. This means that the average speed of the gas particles increases. Kelvin temperature is proportional to the average KE of the gas particles.

KEY POINT

We often use the symbol θ for temperature in °C. For temperature in K we always use the symbol T.

EXAMPLE 1

a At what temperature does water freeze, in Kelvin?

Water freezes at 0 °C. To convert 0 °C to Kelvin:

T = (0 °C + 273) K
= 273 K

b What is room temperature, in Kelvin?

Typical room temperature is 20 °C, so:

T = (20 °C + 273) K
= 293 K

c What temperature is 400 K on the Celsius scale?

θ = (400 K − 273) °C
= 127 °C

The relationship between the pressure of a gas and its temperature is explained as follows.

The number of gas particles and the space, or volume, they occupy remain constant. When we heat the gas the particles continue to move randomly, but with a higher average speed. This means that their collisions with the walls of the container are harder and happen more often. This results in the average pressure exerted by the particles increasing.

When we cool a gas the kinetic energy of its particles decreases. The lower the temperature of a gas the less kinetic energy its particles have – they move more slowly. At absolute zero the particles have no thermal or movement energy, so they cannot exert a pressure.

CHAPTER QUESTIONS

Exam-style questions on solids, liquids and gases can be found at the end of Unit 5 on page 400.

SKILLS CRITICAL THINKING

1 Explain how ideas about particles can account for the absolute zero of temperature.

SKILLS PROBLEM SOLVING

2 a Convert the following Celsius temperatures to Kelvin temperatures.
  i 0 °C   ii 100 °C   iii 20 °C

 b Convert the following Kelvin temperatures to Celsius temperatures.
  i 250 K   ii 269 K   iii 305 K

SKILLS ANALYSIS

3 State what happens in the situations shown in the diagrams. Explain your answers using ideas about particles.

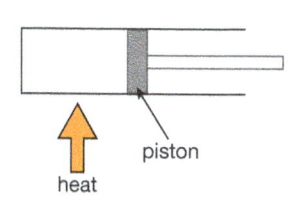

(a) Some air, trapped in a cylinder by a low friction piston, is heated.

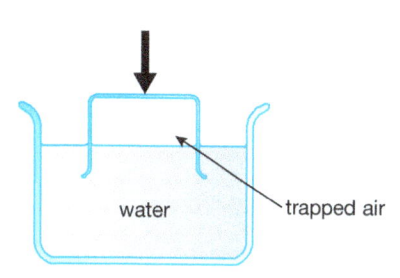

(b) A small beaker with some air trapped inside it is pushed down into a larger beaker of water.

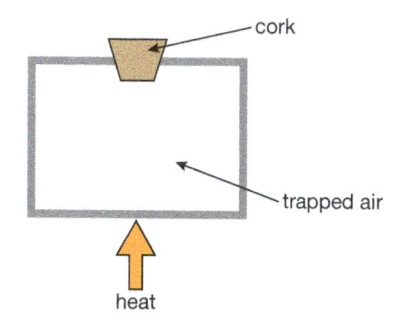

(c) A rigid container with a cork stopping its opening is heated.

EXAM PRACTICE

SKILLS — PROBLEM SOLVING

1
 a State which of the following will exert the greatest pressure when standing on the ground.

    A an elephant: weight 50 000 N, area of one foot 0.2 m^2

    B atmospheric pressure: 10^5 Pa

    C ballerina: weight 450 N, on one point, area 0.0015 m^2

    D man: weight 800 N, area of one foot 0.025 m^2 (1)

SKILLS — CRITICAL THINKING

 b Select which of the following descriptions most accurately describes a gas.

    A very low density, easily compressed, cannot flow

    B high density, cannot be compressed, definite shape

    C very low density, easily compressed, expands to fill available space

    D high density, difficult to compress, can flow (1)

SKILLS — CRITICAL THINKING

 c From the following statements choose which accurately describes the effect of pressure on the volume occupied by a fixed amount of air provided its temperature stays the same.

    A if you double the pressure on a gas its volume doubles

    B if you double the pressure on a gas its temperature halves

    C if you double the pressure on a gas its volume doubles provided its temperature is constant

    D if you double the pressure on a gas its volume halves provided its temperature is constant (1)

(Total 3 marks)

2 Look at the diagram below showing a small gas bubble in a glass of fizzy drink, like cola.

SKILLS — INTERPRETATION

 a Copy the diagram and use eight arrows to shows how the pressure of the liquid acts on the gas bubble. (2)

SKILLS — REASONING

 b Describe what happens to the bubble as it floats up towards the top of the drink and explain the reason for your answer (assume that the amount of gas in the bubble does not change as the bubble rises up through the cola). (3)

(Total 5 marks)

5 SOLIDS, LIQUIDS AND GASES — EXAM PRACTICE

SKILLS CRITICAL THINKING

3 a Explain how the temperature of a gas affects the behaviour of the particles (molecules) that make up the gas. (2)

SKILLS REASONING

b Explain how this helps us to understand that there is an absolute zero temperature. (4)

(Total 6 marks)

4 The temperature of a fixed amount of gas held at constant volume in a rigid container is increased from −73°C to 127°C.

SKILLS PROBLEM SOLVING

a Convert these temperatures to their equivalent on the Kelvin or absolute temperature scale. (2)

SKILLS REASONING

b Describe what will happen to the pressure of the gas trapped in the container as a result of this rise in temperature. (2)

SKILLS REASONING

c State the effect of allowing the container to expand when it was at this higher temperature would have on the pressure of the gas inside it. (3)

(Total 7 marks)

SKILLS REASONING

5 Explain how the idea that gases are made up of many fast-moving particles accounts for the change in the pressure in a bicycle tyre when we pump more air into the tyre.

(Total 4 marks)

| 14 MAGNETISM AND ELECTROMAGNETISM 403 | 15 ELECTRIC MOTORS 408 |

PHYSICS UNIT 6
MAGNETISM AND ELECTROMAGNETISM

In Norse (Norwegian) mythology the spectacular light display we call the aurora borealis was seen as a bridge of fire that connected the Earth to the sky. Nowadays we know it is caused by charged particles, emitted by the Sun, interacting with the Earth's magnetic field and atmosphere. In this section we will be looking at magnetism and the crucial role it plays in our everyday lives.

14 MAGNETISM AND ELECTROMAGNETISM

SPECIFICATION REFERENCES: 6.1, 6.4, 6.6–6.8

There are two types of magnets that we use in our everyday lives. These are permanent magnets and electromagnets. A permanent magnet has a magnetic field around it all the time. An electromagnet only has a magnetic field around when it is turned on and a current is flowing through it.

▲ Figure 14.1 Electromagnets can be used to lift iron or steel objects.

The huge electromagnet in **Figure 14.1** is being used in a scrapyard to pick up large objects that contain iron or steel. When the objects have been moved to their new position the electromagnet is turned off and the objects fall, its magnetic field disappears.

LEARNING OBJECTIVES

- Practical: Investigate the magnetic field pattern for a permanent bar magnet and between two bar magnets.
- Understand the term magnetic field line.
- Describe how to use two permanent magnets to produce a uniform magnetic field pattern.
- Know that an electric current in a conductor produces a magnetic field around it.

UNITS

In this section you will need to use ampere (A) as the unit of current, volt (V) as the unit of voltage and watt (W) as the unit of power.

REMINDER

Magnets are able to **attract** objects made from magnetic materials such as iron, steel, nickel and cobalt (**Figure 14.2**). Magnets cannot attract objects made from materials such as plastic, wood, paper or rubber. These are non-magnetic materials.

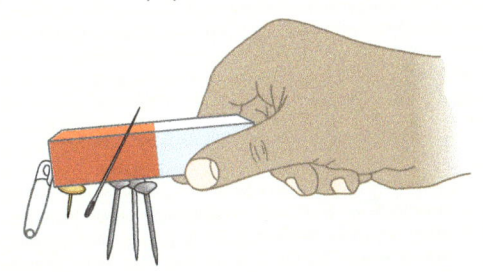

▲ Figure 14.2 The magnetic field around this magnet is attracting objects made from magnetic materials such as iron and steel.

6 MAGNETISM AND ELECTROMAGNETISM | 14 MAGNETISM AND ELECTROMAGNETISM

REMINDER

The strongest parts of a magnet are called its poles. Most magnets have two poles. These are called the north pole and the south pole.

MAGNETIC FIELDS

Around every magnet there is a volume of space where we can detect magnetism. This volume of space is called a **magnetic field**. Normally a magnetic field cannot be seen but we can use iron filings or plotting compasses to show its shape and discover something about its strength and direction.

ACTIVITY 1

▼ PRACTICAL: INVESTIGATE THE MAGNETIC FIELD PATTERNS OF BAR MAGNETS

- Place a bar magnet between two books and place a sheet of paper or thin card over it.
- Sprinkle some iron filings on the paper above the magnet.
- Tap the paper very gently.
- The iron filings will move to show the magnetic field pattern (**Figure 14.3**).

OR

- Place a bar magnet on a piece of paper.
- Place a large number of small compasses on the paper near the magnet.
- Look carefully at the pattern shown by the needles of the compasses.

Repeat the same experiment using two bar magnets, placing them about 5 cm apart.

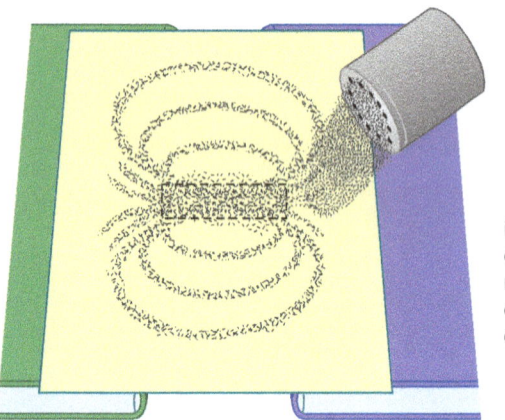

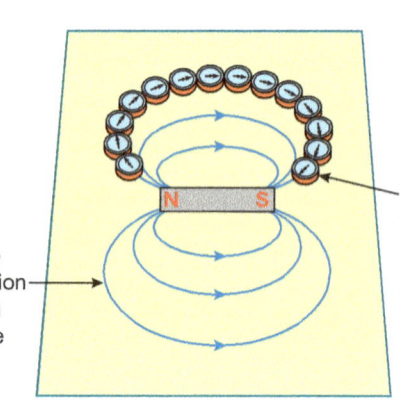

Safety note: Avoid skin contact with iron filings, since they irritate the skin. Do not blow them off the paper, because they may get into the eyes, which is very painful.

▲ Figure 14.3 We can see the shape of the magnetic field around a magnet by using iron filings or plotting compasses.

We draw magnetic fields like that in **Figure 14.4** using magnetic field lines. Magnetic field lines do not really exist but they help us to visualise the main features of a magnetic field.

The magnetic field lines:

- show the shape of the magnetic field
- show the direction of the **magnetic force** – the field lines 'travel' from north to south
- show the strength of the magnetic field – the field lines are closest together where the magnetic field is strongest.

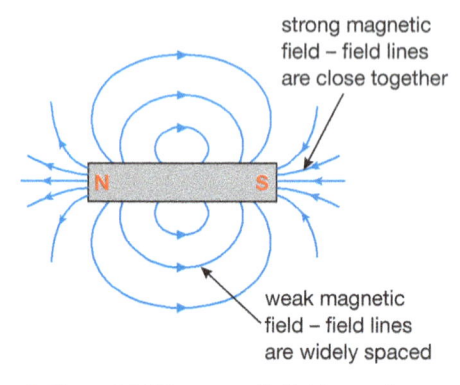

▲ Figure 14.4 The magnetic field around a bar magnet follows a pattern like this.

OVERLAPPING MAGNETIC FIELDS

If two magnets are placed near each other, their magnetic fields overlap and affect each other. We can investigate this using iron filings or plotting compasses. **Figure 14.5** shows the different field patterns we would see.

EXTENSION

Point X in **Figure 14.5** is called a neutral point. It is a position where the effects of the two magnetic fields have cancelled each other out, meaning that there is no resultant magnetic field here. Can you find any other neutral points in these magnetic field patterns?

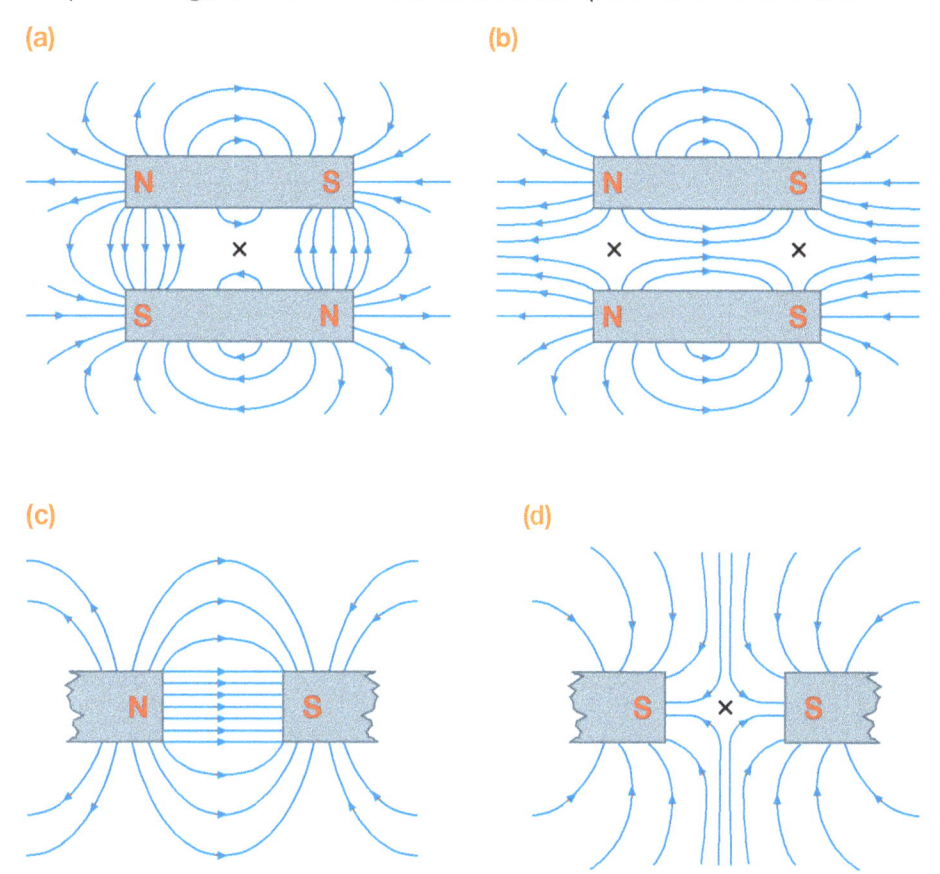

(a) (b) (c) (d)

▲ Figure 14.5 Magnetic fields around pairs of magnets

CREATING A UNIFORM MAGNETIC FIELD

If we look very carefully at the magnetic field created between the north pole of one magnet and the south pole of a different magnet we will see that the field is shown as a series of straight field lines that are evenly spaced. A field like this is described as a uniform magnetic field – that is, its strength and direction is the same everywhere (**Figure 14.6**). Creating a uniform field like this is extremely useful as we will see later in this chapter and in the next chapter.

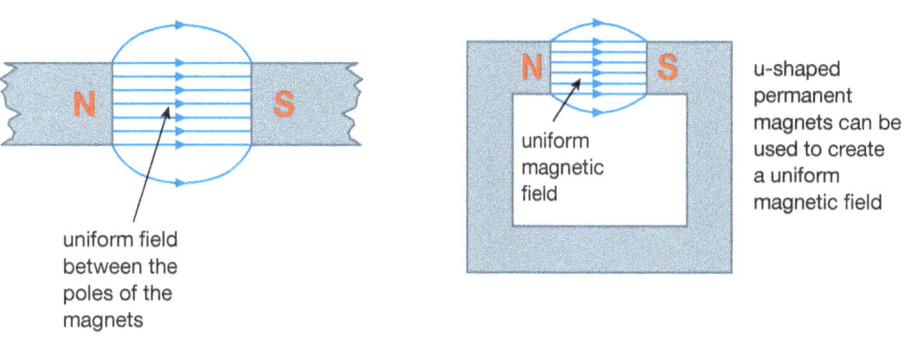

uniform field between the poles of the magnets

uniform magnetic field

u-shaped permanent magnets can be used to create a uniform magnetic field

▲ Figure 14.6 Two examples of uniform magnetic fields

ELECTROMAGNETISM

When a current flows through a wire a magnetic field is created around it. This is called electromagnetism. We investigate the field around a wire which has a current flowing through it using iron filings and plotting compasses. We discover that

- the magnetic field is quite weak (and gets weaker as we move away from the wire),
- it is circular in shape and
- if we change the direction of the current in the wire, the direction of the magnetic field changes (**Figure 14.7**).

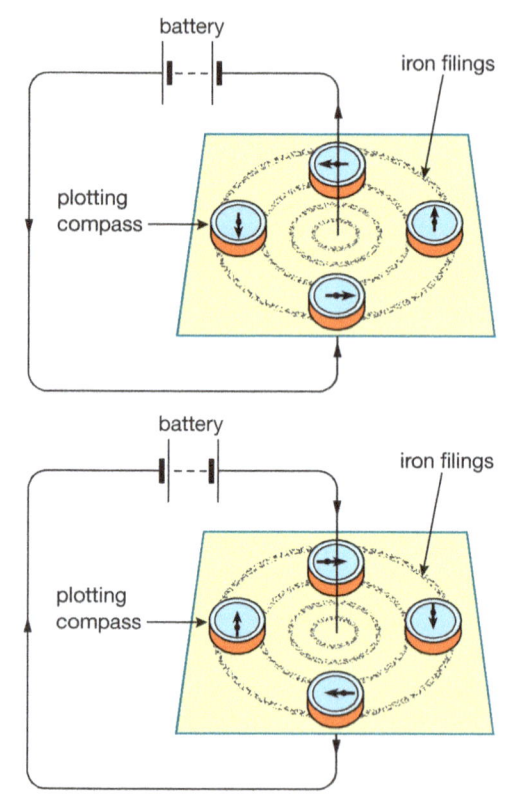

▲ Figure 14.7 Changing the direction of the current in the wire changes the direction of the magnetic field.

CHAPTER QUESTIONS

Exam-style questions on electromagnetism can be found at the end of Unit 6 on page 412.

1 What is a uniform magnetic field?

    A a magnetic field which gradually increases in strength

    B a magnetic field where the strength is the same everywhere within it

    C a vertical magnetic field

    D a horizontal magnetic field

SKILLS CRITICAL THINKING

2 You want to draw a magnetic field which is strong. Do you draw it with field lines which are

   A far apart

   B vertical

   C horizontal or

   D close together?

SKILLS INTERPRETATION, REASONING

3 Why do the shapes of the magnetic fields around two bar magnets change if they are brought close together?

SKILLS CRITICAL THINKING

4 a What three features of a magnetic field do field lines show?

   b What is a uniform magnetic field?

SKILLS INTERPRETATION

   c Draw a diagram of a uniform field between two bar magnets.

   d Draw a second diagram showing a uniform magnetic field which is stronger than the one you drew for part c.

SKILLS INTERPRETATION

5 Draw a diagram to show the magnetic field between two bar magnets if the poles of the magnets which are next to each other are

   a both north poles

SKILLS REASONING

   b a north pole and a south pole.

6 In 1819 a scientist named Hans Christian Oersted was using a cell to produce a current in a wire. Close to the wire there was a compass. When there was a current in the wire, Oersted noticed – much to his surprise – that the compass needle moved.

   a Why did the compass needle move?

   b When there is a current in a horizontal wire, the needle of a compass placed beneath the wire comes to rest at right angles to the wire, pointing from left to right. In which direction will the compass needle point if it is held above the wire? Explain your answer.

   c Would your answer to part b still be correct if the direction of the current in the wire was changed? Explain your answer.

15 ELECTRIC MOTORS

SPECIFICATION REFERENCES: 6.12–6.14

Trains in many cities use electric motors to transport millions of people to and from work each day. In this chapter, we are going to look at how an electric motor works. An electric motor creates motion from an electric current.

▲ Figure 15.1 Electric train in Bangkok (the Skytrain)

LEARNING OBJECTIVES

- Understand why a force is exerted on a current-carrying wire in a magnetic field, and how this effect is applied in simple d.c. electric motors and loudspeakers.
- Use the left-hand rule to predict the direction of the resulting force when a wire carries a current perpendicular to a magnetic field.
- Describe how the force on a current-carrying conductor in a magnetic field changes with the magnitude and direction of the field and current.

MOVEMENT FROM ELECTRICITY

If a wire carrying a current is placed in a magnetic field, it may experience a force. We can demonstrate this as shown in **Figure 15.2**. When the switch is closed and current flows, the wire will try to move upwards.

OVERLAPPING MAGNETIC FIELDS

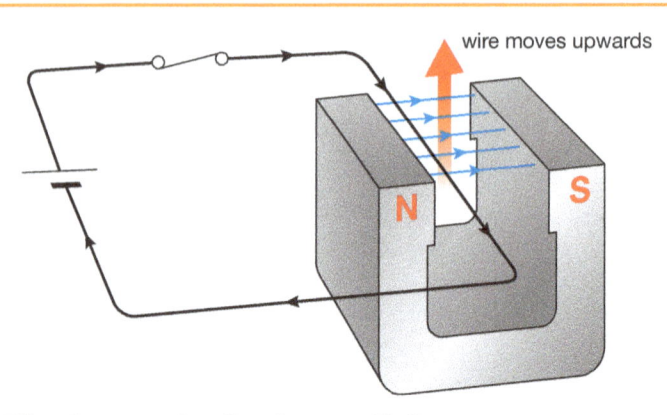

▲ Figure 15.2 The wire moves where there is a current in it.

6 MAGNETISM AND ELECTROMAGNETISM 15 ELECTRIC MOTORS

(a)

uniform field of magnet

(b)

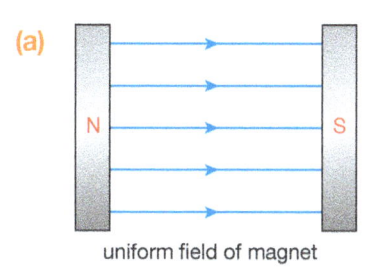

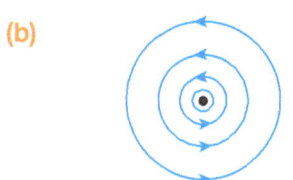

cylindrical field due to current in wire

▲ Figure 15.3 (a) Magnet's uniform magnetic field (b) Magnetic field around a current carrying wire

wire moves in this direction

strong field   weaker field

resultant field due to overlapping

▲ Figure 15.4 The new magnetic field created by overlapping

KEY POINT

We can predict the direction of the force or movement of the wire using Fleming's left-hand rule.

We can explain this motion by looking at what happens when the switch is closed and the two magnetic fields overlap.

The two diagrams in **Figure 15.3** show the shapes and directions of the magnetic fields **a** across the poles of the magnet, and **b** around the current-carrying wire before they overlap.

If the wire is placed between the poles of the magnet, the two fields overlap.

In certain places, for example, below the wire, the fields are in the same direction and so reinforce each other. A strong magnetic field is produced here. In other places, for example, above the wire, the fields are in opposite directions. A weaker field is produced here (**Figure 15.4**). Because the fields are of different strengths the wire 'feels' a force, pushing it from the stronger part of the field to the weaker part – that is, in this case, upwards. The overlapping of the two magnetic fields has produced motion. This is called the motor effect.

A stronger force will be produced if the magnetic field is stronger or if the current is increased.

If we change the direction of the current or the magnet's field, a different overlapping pattern is created and we will see the wire move in the opposite direction (**Figure 15.5**).

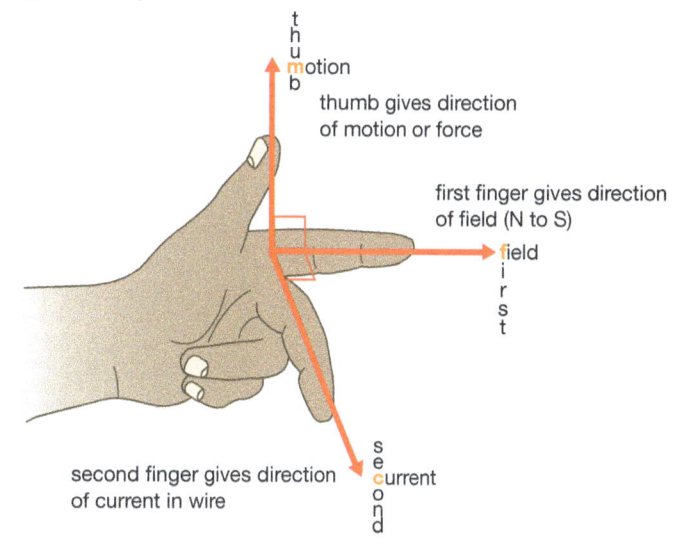

thumb gives direction of motion or force

first finger gives direction of field (N to S)

second finger gives direction of current in wire

▲ Figure 15.5 Fleming's left-hand rule helps you to work out the direction of the force.

THE LOUDSPEAKER

Loudspeakers change electric currents into sounds (see **Figure 15.6**).

- Electric currents from a source, such as a microphone or radio, pass through the coils of a speaker.
- These currents, which represent sounds, are always changing in size and direction, like vibrating sound waves.
- The magnetic fields of the coil and the permanent magnet are therefore creating new magnetic field patterns which are also always changing in strength and direction.
- These fields in turn apply rapidly changing forces to the wires of the coil, which cause the speaker cone to vibrate.
- These vibrations create the sound waves we hear.

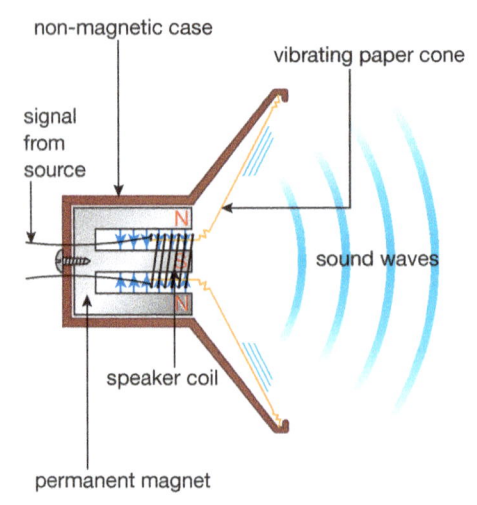

▲ Figure 15.6 A loudspeaker transfers energy to create sound.

THE ELECTRIC MOTOR

The electric motor is one of the most important uses of the motor effect. **Figure 15.7** shows the most important features of a simple d.c. electric motor.

HINT

Carbon brushes are two pieces of carbon which are pushed against the split ring by two small springs. The split ring can still rotate because the springs are weak and electricity can flow through them and around the rotating coil.

EXTENSION

Although you will not be asked this in your exam it is interesting to know how commercial motors like the one used in the electric drill in **Figure 15.8** differ from the simple motor described in **Figure 15.7**.

- The permanent magnets are replaced with curved electromagnets capable of producing very strong magnetic fields.
- The single loop of wire is replaced with several coils of wire wrapped on the same axis. This makes the motor more powerful and allows it to run more smoothly.
- The coils are wrapped on a soft iron core that has been covered by a thin layer of plastic. This makes the motor more efficient and more powerful.

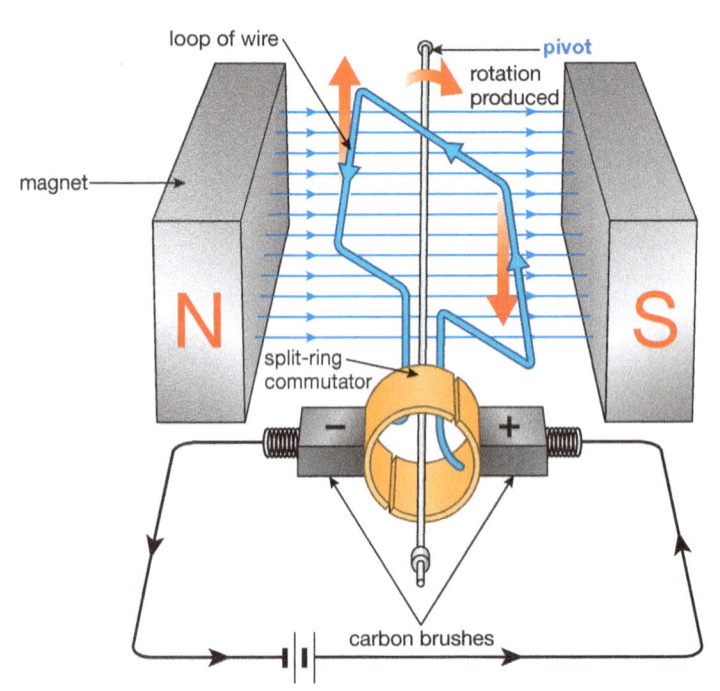

▲ Figure 15.7 A simple electric motor

When there is current in the loop of wire, one side of it will experience a force pushing it upwards. The other side will feel a force pushing it downwards, so the loop will begin to **rotate** (turn).

As the loop reaches the vertical position, its momentum takes it past the vertical. If the rotation is to continue the forces on the wires must now be reversed so that the wire at the top is now pushed down and the bottom one is pushed up.

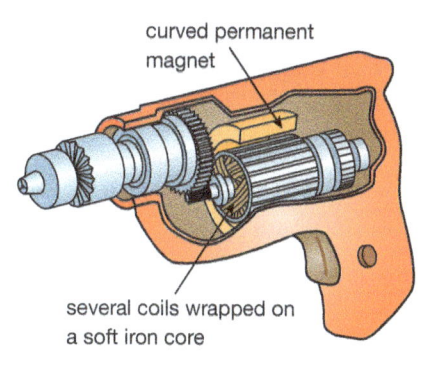

6 MAGNETISM AND ELECTROMAGNETISM   15 ELECTRIC MOTORS

curved permanent magnet

several coils wrapped on a soft iron core

▲ Figure 15.8 A real electric motor

This can be done easily by using a split ring to connect the loop of wire to the electrical supply. Now each time the loop of wire passes the vertical position, the connections change, the direction of the current changes, and the forces on the different sides of the loop change direction. The loop will rotate continuously.

To increase the rate at which the motor turns we can:

- increase the number of turns or loops of wire, making a coil
- increase the strength of the magnetic field
- increase the current in the loop of wire.

CHAPTER QUESTIONS

Exam-style questions on electric motors can be found at the end of Unit 6 on page 412.

SKILLS ANALYSIS, REASONING

1 The diagram below shows a long wire placed between the poles of a magnet.

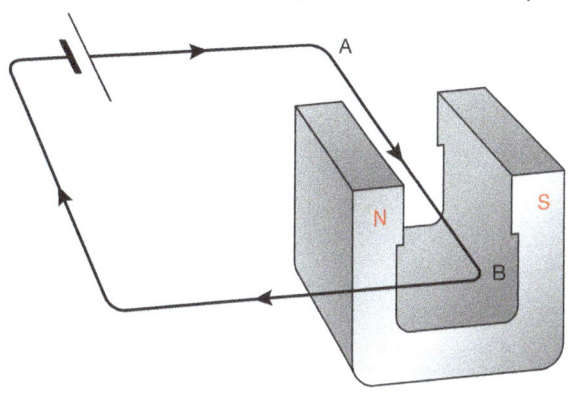

Describe what happens when:

   a there is current in the wire from A to B

   b the direction of the current is reversed – that is, from B to A

   c with the current from B to A, the poles of the magnet are reversed

   d there is a larger current in the wire.

2 Draw a diagram to show:

   a the uniform magnetic field between the poles of a U-shaped magnet

   b the magnetic field around a current carrying wire

   c the new field which is created when the fields in **a** and **b** overlap. In which direction will the wire move?

3 Describe two ways you could increase the speed at which an electric motor is turning.

SKILLS INTERPRETATION
SKILLS CRITICAL THINKING

4 a Draw a simple labelled diagram of a moving-coil loudspeaker.

   b Explain how sound waves are made by the speaker when a signal is passed through its coil.

EXAM PRACTICE

1 Which of the following does *not* make use of electromagnetism?

   A loudspeaker

   B electric light bulb

   C electric motor

   D electromagnet (Total 1 mark)

2 Copy this diagram showing the magnetic field created when two magnets are placed next to each other.

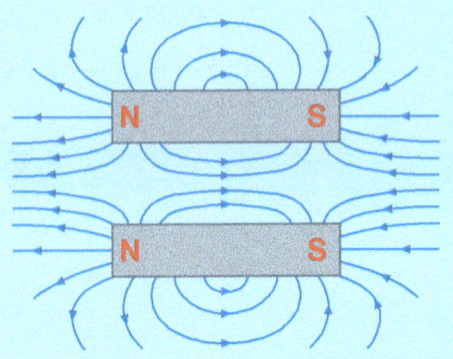

   a On your diagram mark with a letter S two places where the magnetic field is strong. (2)

   b On your diagram mark with a letter W two places where the magnetic field is very weak. (2)

   (Total 4 marks)

3 a Describe the strength of the magnetic field as we move from place to place between the poles of the magnets. (1)

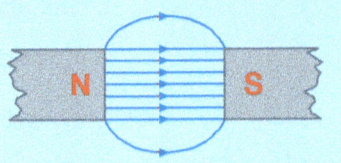

   b State the name used to describe a magnetic field like the one drawn here. (1)

   (Total 2 marks)

4 Copy and complete the following passage, filling in the blanks.

   When current _____ through a wire, a _____ field is created around it. The field is _____ in shape. If the direction of the current is changed the _____ of the field _____ . If the battery connected to the wire is removed _____ _____ _____ and the field _____ .

   (Total 9 marks)

5 The diagram below shows a wire, which is carrying a current, placed between the poles of a magnet.

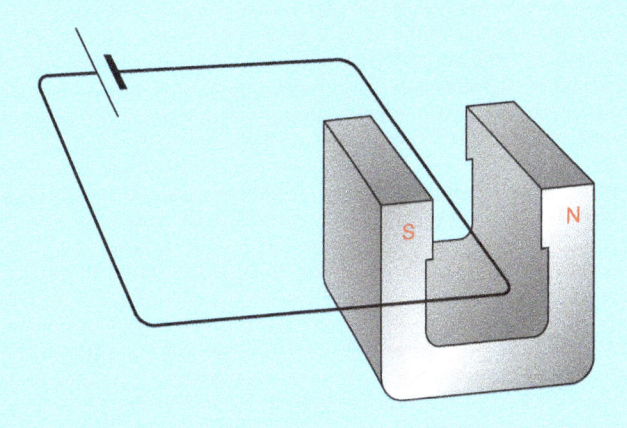

Copy this diagram then

a add arrows to the circuit to show the direction in which the current is flowing (1)

b add field lines to show the shape and direction of the magnetic field between the poles of the magnet (2)

c add an arrow to your diagram to show the direction in which the wire will try to move. (1)

d Suggest one way in which to make the wire move in the opposite direction. (1)

e Suggest one way in which to increase the force on the wire. (1)

(Total 6 marks)

| 16 ATOMS AND RADIOACTIVITY 415 | 17 RADIATION AND HALF-LIFE 422 | 18 APPLICATIONS OF RADIOACTIVITY 427 |

| 19 FISSION AND FUSION 433 |

PHYSICS UNIT 7
RADIOACTIVITY AND PARTICLES

Henri Becquerel was a scientist whose pioneering work led to the discovery of radioactivity and set other scientists on a path of research that continues today.

Using radioactivity has enabled us to learn about the structure of matter, to develop new sources of energy and to understand a new force of nature: nuclear forces, which bind matter together, control the processes that fuel stars and formed all the elements that we and the Universe are made of.

16 ATOMS AND RADIOACTIVITY

SPECIFICATION REFERENCES: 7.1–7.6

Atoms are made up of subatomic particles called neutrons, protons and electrons. It is the numbers of these particles that give each element its unique properties. In this chapter you will find out how atoms can break up and become transformed into different elements, and about the different types of radiation they give out.

LEARNING OBJECTIVES

- Describe the structure of an atom in terms of protons, neutrons and electrons and use symbols such as $^{14}_{6}C$ to describe particular nuclei.
- Know the terms atomic (proton) number, mass (nucleon) number and isotope.
- Know that alpha (α) particles, beta (β−) particles, and gamma (γ) rays are ionising radiations emitted from unstable nuclei in a random process.
- Describe the nature of alpha (α) particles, beta (β−) particles, and gamma (γ) rays, and recall that they may be distinguished in terms of penetrating power and ability to ionise.
- Investigate the penetration powers of different types of radiation using either radioactive sources or simulations.

UNITS

In this section you will need to use becquerel (Bq) as the unit of activity of a radioactive source, centimetre (cm) as the unit of length, and minute (min) and second (s) as the units of time.

ELECTRONS, PROTONS AND NEUTRONS

Atoms are made up of electrons, protons and neutrons. **Figure 16.1** shows a simple model of how these particles are arranged.

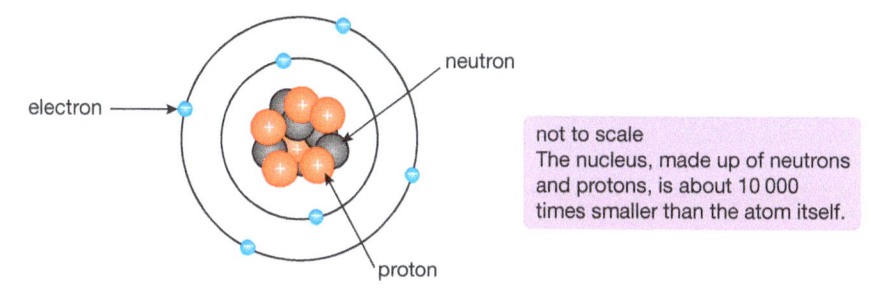

not to scale
The nucleus, made up of neutrons and protons, is about 10 000 times smaller than the atom itself.

▲ Figure 16.1 A simple model with protons and neutrons in the nucleus of the atom and electrons in orbits around the outside

The electron is a very small particle with very little mass. It has a negative electric charge. Electrons orbit the nucleus of the atom. The nucleus is very small compared with the size of the atom itself. If the nucleus of an atom were enlarged to the size of a full stop on this page, the atom would have a **diameter** of around 2.5 metres.

The nucleus is made up of protons and neutrons. Protons and neutrons have almost exactly the same mass. Protons and neutrons are nearly 2000 times heavier than electrons. Protons carry positive electric charge but neutrons, as the name suggests, are electrically neutral or uncharged. The amount of charge on a proton is equal to that on an electron but opposite in sign.

The properties of these three atomic particles are summarised in **Table 16.1**. Protons and neutrons are also called nucleons because they are found in the nucleus of the atom.

Table 16.1

Atomic particle	Relative mass of particle	Relative charge of particle
electron	1	−1
proton	2000	+1
neutron	2000	0

THE ATOM

KEY POINT

An atom has the same number of electrons as the number of protons in its nucleus.

The nucleus of an atom is surrounded by electrons. We sometimes think of electrons as orbiting the nucleus in a way similar to the planets orbiting the Sun. It is more accurate to think of the electrons as moving rapidly around the nucleus in a cloud or shell.

An atom is electrically neutral. This is because the number of positive charges carried by the protons in its nucleus is balanced by the number of negative charges on the electrons in the electron 'cloud' around the nucleus.

ATOMIC NUMBER, Z

The chemical behaviour and properties of a particular element depend upon how the atoms combine with other atoms. This is determined by the number of electrons in the atom. Although atoms may gain or lose electrons, sometimes quite easily, the number of protons in atoms of a particular element is always the same. The atomic number of an element tells us how many protons each of its atoms contains. For example, carbon has six protons in its nucleus – the atomic number of carbon is, therefore, 6. The symbol we use for atomic number is Z. Each element has its own unique atomic number. The atomic number is sometimes called the proton number.

ATOMIC MASS, A

The total number of protons and neutrons in the nucleus of an atom determines its atomic mass. The mass of the electrons that make up an atom is tiny and can usually be ignored. The mass of a proton is approximately 1.7×10^{-27} kg. To save writing this down we usually refer to the mass of an atom by its mass number or nucleon number. This number is the total number of protons and neutrons in the atom. The mass number of an element is given the symbol A.

ATOMIC NOTATION – THE RECIPE FOR AN ATOM

Each particular type of atom will have its own atomic number, which identifies the element, and a mass number that depends on the total number of nucleons, or particles, in the nucleus. **Figure 16.2** shows the way we represent an atom of an element whose chemical symbol is X, showing the atomic number and the mass number.

So, using this notation, an atom of oxygen is represented by:

$$^{16}_{8}O$$

The chemical symbol for oxygen is O. The atomic number is 8 – this tells us that the nucleus contains eight protons. The mass number is 16, so there are 16 nucleons (protons and neutrons) in the nucleus. Since eight of these are protons, the remaining eight must be neutrons. The atom is electrically neutral overall, so the +8 charge of the nucleus is balanced by the eight orbiting electrons, each with charge −1.

KEY POINT

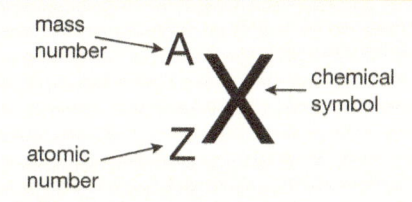

▲ Figure 16.2 Atomic notation

mass number, A = number of neutrons + number of protons, Z = number of nucleons

so

number of neutrons = number of nucleons − number of protons = A − Z

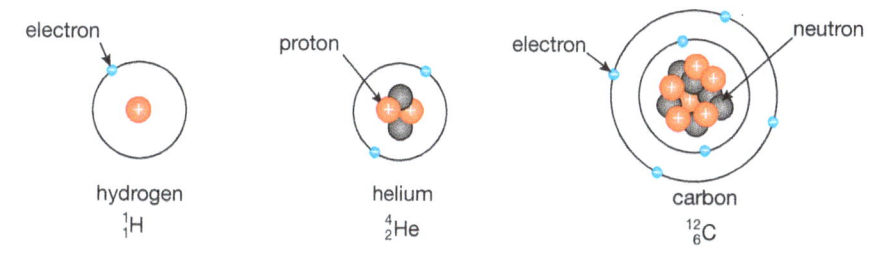

▲ Figure 16.3 The hydrogen atom has one proton in its nucleus and no neutrons, so the mass number A = 1 + 0 = 1. As it has one proton, its atomic number, Z = 1. For helium, A = 4 (2 protons + 2 neutrons) and Z = 2 (2 protons). For carbon, A = 12 (6 protons + 6 neutrons) while Z = 6 (6 protons).

Figure 16.3 shows some examples of the use of this notation for hydrogen, helium and carbon, together with a simple indication of the structure of an atom of each of these elements. In each case the number of orbiting electrons is equal to the number of protons in the nucleus, so the atoms are electrically neutral.

ISOTOPES

The number of protons in an atom identifies the element. The chemical behaviour of an element depends on the number of electrons it has and, as we have seen, this always balances the number of protons in the nucleus. However, the number of neutrons in the nucleus can vary slightly. Atoms of an element with different numbers of neutrons are called isotopes of the element. The number of neutrons in a nucleus affects the mass of the atom. Different isotopes of an element will all have the same atomic number, Z, but different mass numbers, A. **Figures 16.4** and **16.5** show some examples of isotopes.

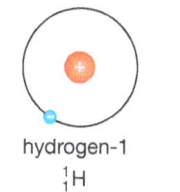

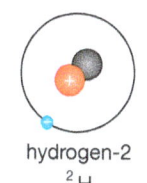

▲ Figure 16.4 Isotopes of hydrogen – they all have the same atomic number, 1, and the same chemical symbol, H.

EXTENSION

Hydrogen-2 is also called heavy hydrogen or deuterium. Hydrogen-3 is called tritium.

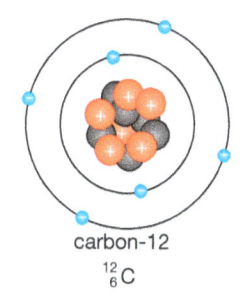

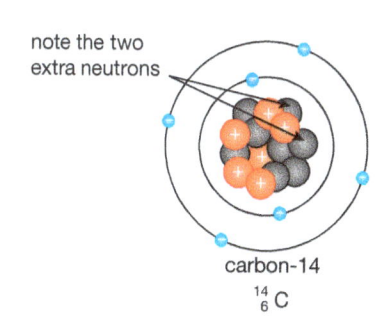

▲ Figure 16.5 Two isotopes of carbon – they are referred to as carbon-12 and carbon-14 to distinguish between them.

THE STABILITY OF ISOTOPES

Isotopes of an element have different physical properties from other isotopes of the same element. One obvious difference is the mass. Another difference is the stability of the nucleus.

The protons are held in the nucleus by the nuclear force. This force is very strong and acts over a very small distance. It is strong enough to hold the nucleus together against the electric force repelling the protons away from each other. (Remember that protons carry positive charge and like charges **repel**.) The presence of neutrons in the nucleus affects the balance between these forces. Too many or too few neutrons will make the nucleus **unstable**. An unstable nucleus will eventually decay. When the nucleus of an atom decays it gives out energy and may also give out alpha or beta particles.

IONISING RADIATION

When unstable nuclei decay they give out ionising radiation. Ionising radiation causes atoms to gain or lose electric charge, forming ions (see **Figure 16.6**). Unstable nuclei decay at random. This means that it is not possible to predict which unstable nucleus in a piece of **radioactive** material will decay, or when decay will happen. We shall see that we can make measurements that will enable us to predict the probability that a certain proportion of a radioactive material will decay in a given time.

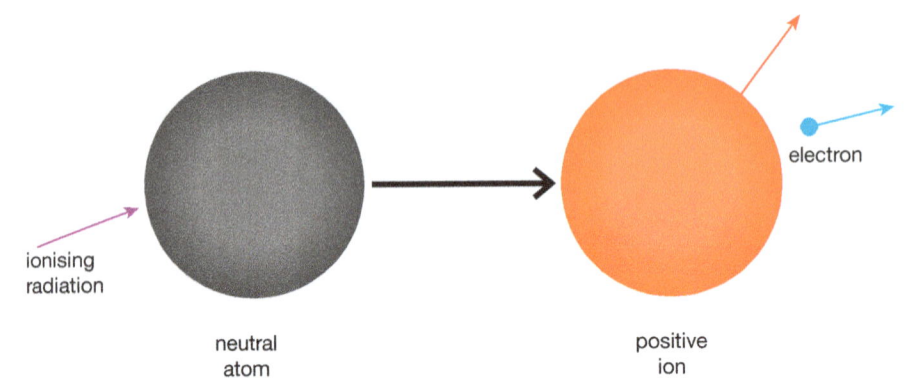

▲ Figure 16.6 When a neutral atom (or molecule) is hit by ionising radiation it loses an electron and becomes a positively charged ion.

There are three basic types of ionising radiation. They are: alpha (α), beta (β) and gamma (γ) radiation.

ALPHA (α) RADIATION

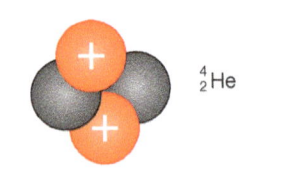

$^{4}_{2}He$

▲ Figure 16.7 An alpha particle (α particle)

Alpha radiation consists of fast-moving particles that are thrown out of unstable nuclei when they decay. These are called alpha particles. Alpha particles are helium nuclei – helium atoms without their orbiting electrons. **Figure 16.7** shows an alpha particle and the notation that is used to denote it in equations.

Alpha particles have a relatively large mass. They are made up of four nucleons and so have a mass number of 4. They are also charged because of the two protons that they carry. The **relative charge** of an alpha particle is +2.

Alpha particles have a short range. The range of ionising radiation is the distance it can travel through matter. Alpha particles can only travel a few centimetres in air and cannot penetrate more than a few millimetres of paper. They have a limited range because they interact with atoms along their paths, causing ions to form. This means that they rapidly give up the energy that they had when they were ejected from the unstable nucleus.

BETA RADIATION (β−)

Beta minus particles (β−) are very fast-moving electrons that are ejected by a decaying nucleus. The nucleus of an atom contains protons and neutrons, so where does the electron come from? The stability of a nucleus depends on the proportion of protons and neutrons it contains. The result of radioactive decay is to change the balance of protons and neutrons in the nucleus to make it more stable. Beta minus decay involves a neutron in the nucleus splitting into a proton and an electron. The proton remains in the nucleus and the electron is ejected at high speed as a beta minus particle.

Beta particles are very light – almost nothing compared with the mass of an alpha particle. The relative charge of a β⁻ is −1.

Beta particles interact with matter in their paths less often than alpha particles. This is because they are smaller and carry less charge. This means that beta particles have a greater range than alpha particles. Beta particles can travel long distances through air, pass through paper easily and are only absorbed by denser materials like aluminium. A millimetre or two of aluminium foil will stop all but the most energetic beta particles.

GAMMA RAYS (γ)

Gamma rays are electromagnetic waves (see page 352) with very short wavelengths. As they are waves, they have no mass and no charge. They are weakly ionising and interact only occasionally with atoms in their paths. They are extremely penetrating and pass through all but the very densest materials with ease. It takes several centimetres thickness of lead, or a metre or so of concrete, to stop gamma radiation.

KEY POINT

As neutrons are not electrically charged they do not directly cause ionisation. They are absorbed by nuclei of other atoms and can cause them to become radioactive. The radioactive nuclei formed in this way will then decay emitting ionising radiation. Neutrons are the only type of radiation to cause other atoms to become radioactive. We shall see later (**Chapter 19**) that neutron radiation plays an important part in the process of fission used in nuclear reactors.

SUMMARY OF THE PROPERTIES OF IONISING RADIATION

We have said that ionising radiation causes uncharged atoms to lose electrons. An atom that has lost (or gained) electrons has an overall charge. It is called an ion. The three types of radioactive emission can all form ions.

As ionising radiation passes through matter, its energy is absorbed. This means that radiation can only penetrate matter up to a certain thickness. This depends on the type of radiation and the density of the material that it is passing through.

The ionising and penetrating powers of alpha, beta and gamma radiation are compared in **Table 16.2**. Note that the ranges given in the table are typical but they do depend on the energy of the radiation. For example, more energetic alpha particles will have a greater range than those with lower energy.

Table 16.2

Radiation	Ionising power	Penetrating power	Example of range in air	Radiation stopped by
alpha, α	strong	weak	5–8 cm	paper
beta, β	medium	medium	500–1000 cm	thin aluminium
gamma, γ	weak	strong	100s of metres	thick lead sheet

7 RADIOACTIVITY AND PARTICLES
16 ATOMS AND RADIOACTIVITY

ACTIVITY 1

▼ PRACTICAL: INVESTIGATE THE PENETRATING POWERS OF DIFFERENT KINDS OF RADIATION

Safety note: All work with radioactive sources must be closely supervised by qualified science staff and no sources must be touched or pointed towards any part of the body. Source usage must be logged and they must be returned to their secure storage immediately after use. In the UK, students under 16 years are not permitted to handle sources; over 16, they are allowed to do this with close supervision.

KEY POINT

The Geiger–Müller (GM) tube is a detector of radiation.

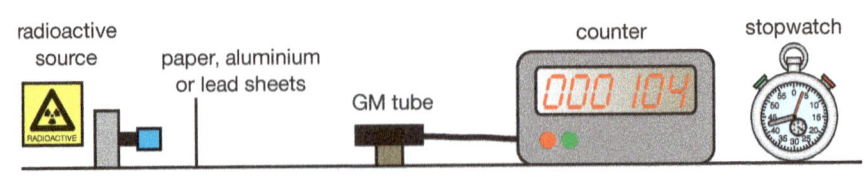

▲ Figure 16.8 Measuring the penetrating power of different types of radiation

Radioactive sources must be stored in lead-lined boxes and kept in a metal cupboard with a radiation warning label. The source must be handled with tongs away from the body. (See **Chapter 18** page 431 and the safety note on this page for more details of safe practice with radioactive materials.)

- Before the source is removed from its storage container, measure the background radiation count by connecting a Geiger–Müller (GM) tube to a counter (see **Figure 16.8**). Write down the number of counts after 5 minutes. Repeat this three times and find the average background radiation count. Background radiation comes from radioactive material in the Earth, the atmosphere and from space.
- Take a source of alpha radiation and set it up at a measured distance (between 2 and 4 cm) from the GM tube. Keep the distance between the radiation source and the GM tube the same throughout these experiments.
- Measure the counts detected in a 5 minute period. Repeat the count with a sheet of thick paper in front of the source. You should find that the counts have dropped to the background radiation count. This shows that alpha radiation does not pass through paper.
- Now replace the alpha source with a beta source. After measuring the new count for 5 minutes place thin sheets of aluminium between the source and detector. When the thickness of the aluminium sheet is 1–2 mm thick you will find that the count has dropped to the background radiation level. This shows that beta radiation is blocked by just a few millimetres of aluminium.
- Finally carry out the same steps using a gamma radiation source. Now you will find that gamma radiation is only blocked when a few centimetres of lead are placed between the source and the detector.

CHAPTER QUESTIONS

SKILLS CRITICAL THINKING

Exam-style questions on atoms and radioactivity can be found at the end of Unit 7 on page 438.

1 Copy and complete the table below. Identify the particles and complete the missing data.

Atomic particle	Relative mass of particle	Relative charge of particle
	1	−1
		+1
	2000	0

2 Identify the following atomic particles from their descriptions.
   a an uncharged nucleon
   b the particle with the least mass
   c the particle with the same mass as a neutron
   d the particle with the same amount of charge as an electron
   e a particle that is negatively charged

3 Explain the following terms used to describe the structure of an atom.
   a atomic number
   b mass number

4 Copy and complete the table below, describing the structures of the different atoms in terms of numbers of protons, neutrons and electrons.

	$^{3}_{2}$He	$^{13}_{6}$C	$^{23}_{11}$N
protons			
neutrons			
electrons			

5 Copy and complete the following sentences:
   a An alpha particle consists of four _____. Two of these are _____ and two are _____. An alpha particle carries a charge of _____.
   b A beta minus particle is a fast-moving _____ that is emitted from the nucleus. It is created when a _____ in the nucleus decays to form a _____ and the beta particle.
   c A third type of ionising radiation has no mass. It is called _____ radiation. This type of radiation is a type of wave with a very _____ wavelength.
   d Gamma radiation is part of the _____ spectrum.

6 A certain radioactive source emits different types of radiation. The sample is tested using a Geiger counter. When a piece of card is placed between the source and the counter, there is a noticeable drop in the radiation. When a thin sheet of aluminium is added to the card between the source and the counter, the count rate is unchanged. A thick block of lead, however, causes the count to fall to the background level.

Explain what type (or types) of ionising radiation the source is emitting.

HINT
Look at **Table 16.2**.

17 RADIATION AND HALF-LIFE

SPECIFICATION REFERENCES: 7.10, 7.12

In this chapter you will learn about ways of detecting radiation, and where some of the radiation around us comes from. You will also learn why we use a value called half-life to describe the activity of radioactive isotopes.

LEARNING OBJECTIVES

- Explain the sources of background (ionising) radiation from Earth and space.
- Know the definition of the term half-life and understand that it is different for different radioactive isotopes.

BACKGROUND RADIATION

Background radiation is low-level ionising radiation that is produced all the time. This background radiation has a number of sources (**Figure 17.1**). Some of these are natural and some are artificial.

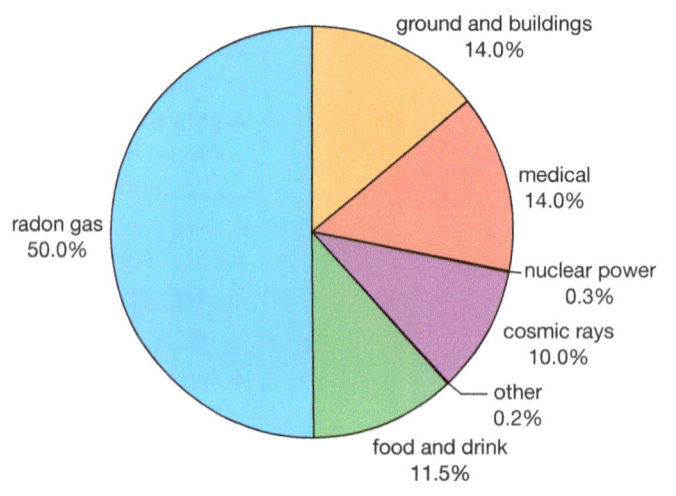

▲ Figure 17.1 Sources of background radiation in the UK. These are the average values – the true amounts and proportions vary from place to place.

Pie chart values:
- radon gas 50.0%
- ground and buildings 14.0%
- medical 14.0%
- nuclear power 0.3%
- cosmic rays 10.0%
- other 0.2%
- food and drink 11.5%

NATURAL BACKGROUND RADIATION FROM THE EARTH

KEY POINT

When an atom of a radioactive element decays it gives out radiation and changes to an atom of another element. This may also be radioactive, and decay to form an atom of yet another element. The elements formed as a result of a radioactive element experiencing a series of decays are called decay products.

Some of the radiation we receive comes from rocks in the Earth's crust (hard outer layer). When the Earth was formed, around 4.5 billion years ago, it contained many radioactive isotopes. Some decayed very quickly but others are still producing radiation. Some of the decay products of these long-lived radioactive materials are also radioactive, so there are radioactive isotopes with much shorter half-lives (see **Table 17.2** on page 425) still present in the Earth's crust.

One form of uranium is a radioactive element that decays very slowly. Two of its decay products are gases. These are the radioactive gases radon and thoron. Radon-222 is a highly radioactive gas produced by the decay of radium-226. Thoron, or radium-220, is an isotope of radium formed by the decay of a radioactive isotope of thorium (thorium-232).

As these decay products are gases, they come out of radioactive rocks. They are dense gases so they build up in the basements of buildings. Some parts of the Earth's crust have higher amounts of radioactive material so the amount of background radiation produced in this way varies from place to place.

NATURAL BACKGROUND RADIATION FROM SPACE

Violent nuclear reactions in stars and exploding stars called supernovae produce cosmic rays (very energetic particles) that continuously hit the Earth. Lower energy cosmic rays are given out by the Sun. Our atmosphere gives us fairly good protection from cosmic rays but some still reach the Earth's surface.

RADIATION IN LIVING THINGS

The atoms that make up our bodies were formed in the violent reactions that take place in stars that exploded (supernovae) billions of years ago. Some of these atoms are radioactive so we carry our own personal source of radiation around with us. Also, as we breathe we take in tiny amounts of the radioactive isotope of carbon, carbon-14. Because carbon-14 behaves chemically just like the stable isotope, carbon-12, we continuously renew the amount of the radioactive carbon in our bodies.

Carbon-14 and other radioactive isotopes are eaten by humans (and animals which are in turn eaten by humans) because they are present in all living things.

ARTIFICIAL RADIATION

We use radioactive materials for many purposes. Generating electricity in nuclear power stations has been responsible for the leaking of radioactive material into the environment. The levels are usually small, but there have been a number of major incidents around the world, especially at Three Mile Island in the USA in 1979 and at Chernobyl in the Ukraine in 1986. The tsunami and earthquake that caused major damage and loss of life in Japan in 2011 also damaged the Fukoshima nuclear power station resulting in the release of radioactive materials into the air and the ocean as well as making a large area of land around the damaged power station unsafe for humans to live there.

Testing nuclear weapons in the atmosphere has also increased the amounts of radioactive isotopes on the Earth.

Radioactive **tracers** are used in industry and medicine. Radioactive materials are also used to treat certain forms of cancer. However, the majority of background radiation is natural – the amount produced from medical use in industry is very small indeed.

RADIOACTIVE DECAY

Radioactive decay is a random (unpredictable) process, just like throwing a coin. If we throw a coin we cannot say with certainty whether it will come down heads or tails. If we throw a thousand coins we cannot predict which will land heads and which will land tails. The same is true for radioactive nuclei. It is impossible to tell which nuclei will disintegrate (break down) at any particular time. However, if we threw a thousand coins we would be surprised if the number that landed as heads was not around 500. We know that a normal coin has an equal chance of landing as a head or a tail, so if we got 600 heads we would think it was unusual. If the proportion of heads were much greater than this we would be right to think that the coin was not fair.

EXPERIMENTAL SIMULATION OF NUCLEAR DECAY

We could, if we had the time, take 1000 coins and throw them (**Figure 17.2**). We could then remove all the coins that came down heads, note the number of coins remaining and then repeat the process. If we did this for, say, six trials we would begin to see the trend (see **Table 17.1**). A set of typical results is shown in the following table and in **Figure 17.3**.

▲ Figure 17.2 Throwing a coin

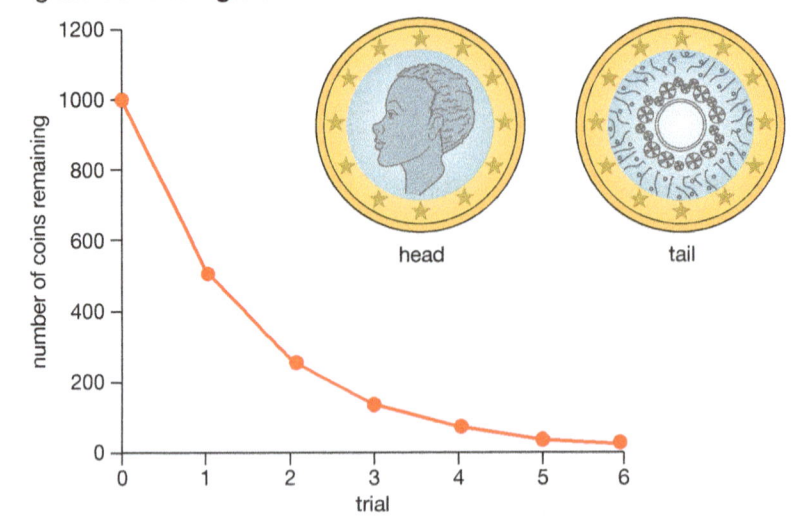

▲ Figure 17.3 Coin-throwing experiment. Each time the coins are thrown about 50% of them land as 'heads' and are removed from the pile. The graph decreases steeply at first but then does so more and more slowly.

Table 17.1

Trial	Number of coins remaining
0	1000
1	519
2	264
3	140
4	72
5	33
6	19

Notice that the graph in **Figure 17.3** falls steeply at first and more slowly after each throw. How quickly the graph falls depends on how many heads occur on each throw. But as the number of coins decreases, the number of coins that come up heads also gets smaller. This graph follows a rule: the smaller the quantity, the more slowly the quantity decreases. The quantity here is the number of coins still in the experiment. The name for this kind of decrease proportional to size is called exponential decay.

If we have a sample of a radioactive material, it will contain millions of atoms. The process of decay is random, so we do not know when an atom will decay but there will be a probability that a certain fraction of them will disintegrate in a particular time. This is the same as in the coin toss – there was a 50%

probability that the coins would land heads each time we conducted a trial. Once an unstable nucleus has disintegrated, it is out of the game – it will not be around to disintegrate during the next period of time. If we plot a graph of number of disintegrations per second against time for a radioactive isotope we would, therefore, expect the rate of decay to fall as time passes because there are fewer nuclei to decay.

HALF-LIFE

Our coin-tossing model of radioactive decay shows a graph that approaches the horizontal axis more and more slowly as time passes. The model will produce a number of throws after which all the coins have been taken out of the game. The number is likely to vary from trial to trial because the model becomes less and less reliable as the number of coins becomes smaller. With real radioactive decay we use a measure of activity called the **half-life**. This is defined as follows.

The half-life of a radioactive sample is the average time taken for half the original mass of the sample to decay. If the amount of radioactive matter has halved then the activity of the decay halves – this activity is what is measured in finding the half-life of an isotope. The half-life is different for different radioactive isotopes.

Figure 17.4 shows what this means. After one half-life period, $t_{\frac{1}{2}}$, the amount of the original unstable element has halved. After a second period of time, $2t_{\frac{1}{2}}$, the amount has halved again, and so on.

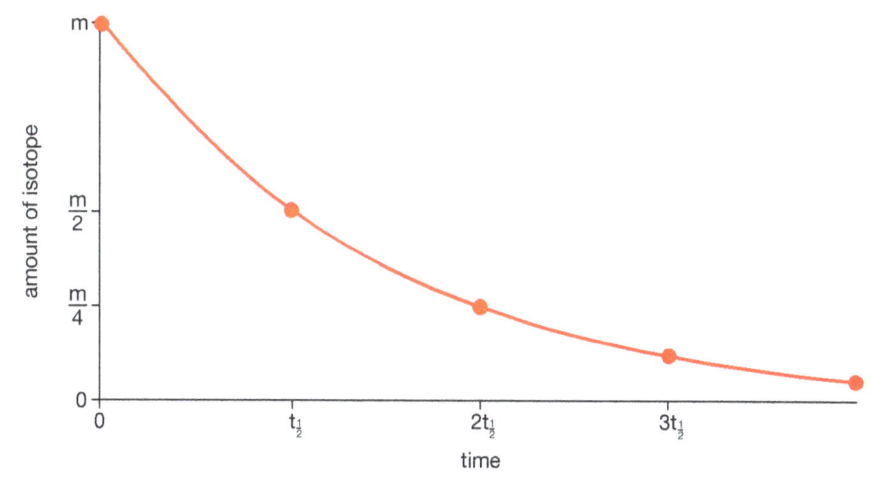

▲ Figure 17.4 Graph showing the half-life period for a radioactive isotope

As we have already mentioned, different isotopes can have very different half-lives. Some examples of different half-lives are shown in **Table 17.2**.

Table 17.2

Isotope	Half-life	Decay process
uranium-238	4.5 billion years	α particle emission
radium-226	1590 years	α particle emission, γ ray emission
radon-222	3.825 days	α particle emission

Isotopes with short half-lives are suited to medical use (see page 427). This is because the activity of a source will rapidly become very small as the isotope decays quickly.

Isotopes used for dating samples of organic material need to have very long half-lives. This is because the activity will become difficult to measure accurately if it drops below a certain level. In **Chapter 18**, we shall see that there are suitable isotopes for these different applications.

CHAPTER QUESTIONS

Exam-style questions on radiation and half-life can be found at the end of Unit 7 on page 438.

SKILLS CRITICAL THINKING

1 a Explain what is meant by background radiation.
   b Explain the difference between natural background radiation and artificial background radiation.

SKILLS CRITICAL THINKING

2 a Define what is meant by the half-life of a radioactive material.
   b Radioactive decay is a random process. Explain what this means.

SKILLS PROBLEM SOLVING

3 The activity of a radioactive sample is measured. The activity, corrected for background radiation, is found to be 240 Bq. If the half-life of the radioactive material is 8 hours state the value of the count rate after 8 hours.

SKILLS PROBLEM SOLVING

4 In a model of radioactive decay, a student fills a burette with water, as shown in the diagram, and starts a timer at the instant the tap at the bottom is opened. She notes the height of the column of water at regular intervals. It takes 35 seconds to empty from 50 ml to 25 ml. Assuming that the arrangement provides a good model of radioactive decay:
   a Calculate the time it would take for three-quarters of the water in the burette to drain away.
   b Calculate the amount of water you would expect to find in the burette after 1¾ minutes.

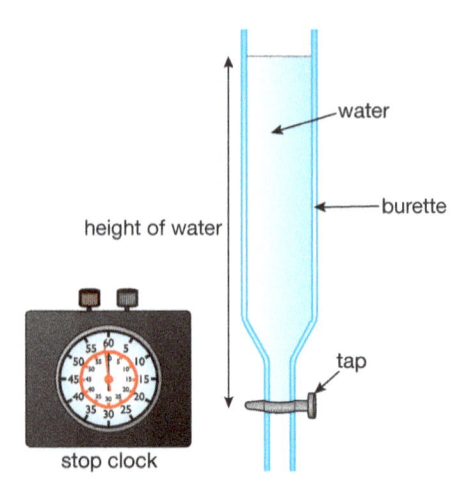

18 APPLICATIONS OF RADIOACTIVITY

SPECIFICATION REFERENCES: 7.14–7.16

Radioactivity has a wide variety of uses, including medicine, industry and power generation. In this chapter, you will read about these uses and also learn about the dangers associated with the use of radioactivity.

LEARNING OBJECTIVES

- Describe uses of radioactivity in industry and medicine.
- Describe the difference between contamination and irradiation.
- Be able to describe the dangers of ionising radiations including:
- that radiation can cause mutations in living organisms
- that radiation can damage cells and tissue
- the problems arising from the disposal of radioactive waste and how the associated risks can be reduced.

THE USE OF RADIOACTIVITY IN MEDICINE

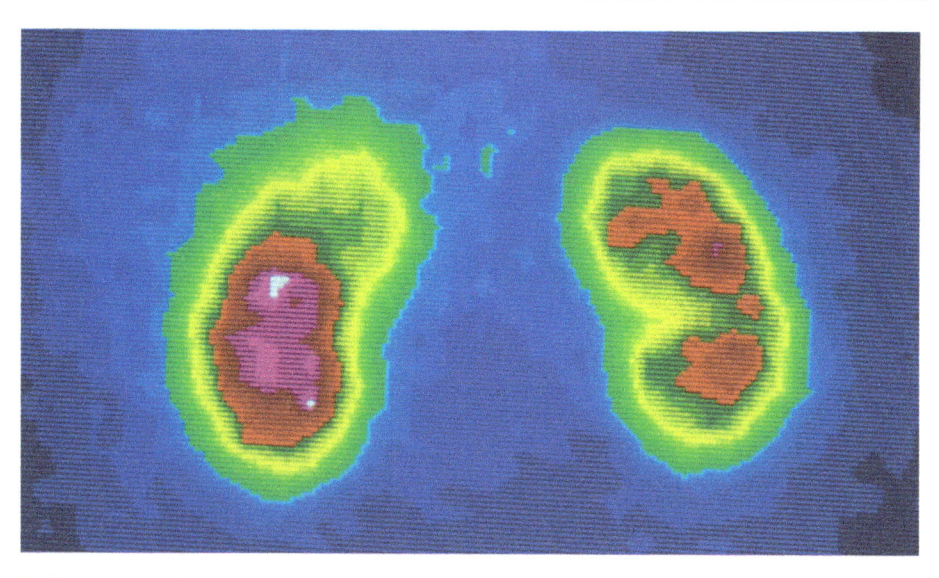

▲ Figure 18.1 This scan shows the kidneys in a patient's body.

USING TRACERS IN DIAGNOSIS

Radioactive isotopes are used as tracers to help doctors identify diseased organs (like the kidneys or the liver). A radioactive tracer is a chemical compound that emits gamma radiation. The tracer is taken orally (swallowed) by the patient or injected. Its journey around the body can then be traced (followed) using a gamma ray camera.

Different compounds are chosen for different diagnostic tasks. For example, the isotope iodine-123 is absorbed by the thyroid gland (a part of the body found in the neck that controls growth) in the same way as the stable form of iodine. The isotope decays and emits gamma radiation. A gamma ray camera can then be used to form a clear image of the thyroid gland.

The half-life of iodine-123 is about 13 hours. A short half-life is important as this means that the activity of the tracer decreases to a very low level in a few days.

Other isotopes are used to image specific parts of the body. Technetium-99 is the most widely used isotope in medical imaging. It is used to help identify medical problems that affect many parts of the body. **Figure 18.1** shows a scan of a patient's kidneys. It shows clearly that one of the kidneys is not working properly.

> **KEY POINT**
>
> Radiologists and doctors have to take care to avoid exposure to ionising radiation produced by materials used in the diagnosis and treatment of illnesses.

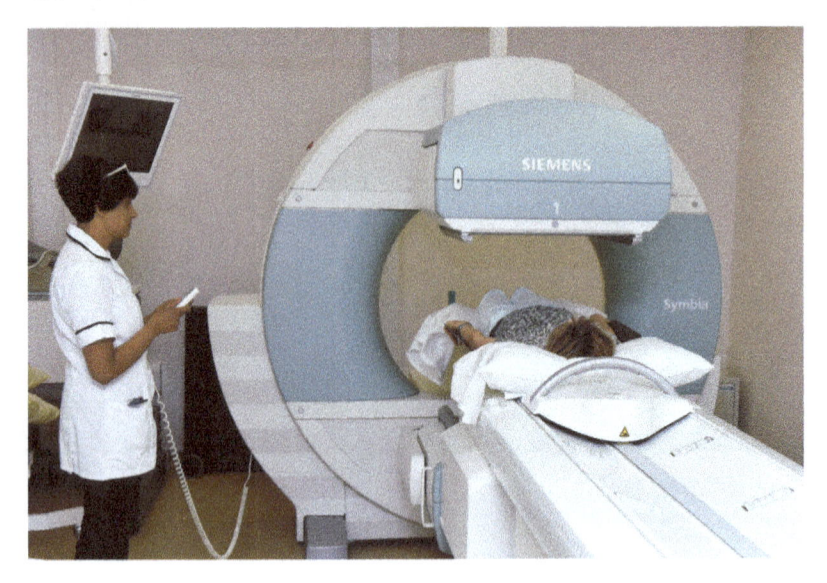

▲ Figure 18.2 Scanner used to provide 3D images of a patient's body

Imaging techniques enable doctors to produce three-dimensional (3D) computer images of parts of a patient's body. These are of great value in diagnosis. **Figure 18.2** shows the kind of equipment used for three-dimensional imaging.

TREATMENT

Radiation from isotopes can have various effects on the cells that make up our bodies. Low doses of radiation may have no lasting effect. Higher doses may cause the cells to stop working properly as the radiation damages the DNA in the cells. This can lead to abnormal growth and cancer. Very high doses will kill living cells.

Cancer can be treated by surgery that involves cutting out cancerous cells. Another way of treating cancer is to kill the cancer cells inside the body. This can be done with chemicals containing radioactive isotopes. Unfortunately, the radiation kills healthy cells as well as diseased ones. To reduce the damage to healthy tissue, chemicals are used to target the location of the cancer in the body. They may emit either alpha or beta radiation. Both these types of radiation have a short range in the body, so they will affect only a small volume of tissue close to the target.

The **radioisotope** iodine-131 is used in the treatment of various diseases of the thyroid gland. It has a half-life of about eight days and decays by beta particle emission.

STERILISATION USING RADIATION

Gamma radiation can kill **bacteria** and viruses. It is therefore used to kill these micro-organisms on surgical instruments and other medical equipment. The technique is called irradiation. The items to be **sterilised** are placed in secure bags to ensure that they cannot be re-contaminated before use (see **Figure 18.3**). The gamma radiation will pass through the packaging and destroy bacteria without damaging the item.

KEY POINT

Irradiation will not destroy any poisons that bacteria may have already produced in the food before it is treated.
Irradiation does not destroy vitamins in the food like other means of killing bacteria, such as high-temperature treatment.

KEY POINT

You will be expected to explain the difference between irradiation and contamination. Irradiation is a deliberate process whereas contamination is usually accidental.

Some food products are treated in a similar way to make sure that they are free from any bacteria that will cause the food to rot or will cause food poisoning. The irradiation of food is an issue that causes concern among the public and is not a widely used procedure at the present time.

Irradiation such as the deliberate exposure of food products and surgical instruments to controlled amounts of radiation should not be confused with radioactive contamination. If radioactive waste is accidentally released either into the air or the sea it could result in fish, animals or agricultural crops being contaminated with radioactive material.

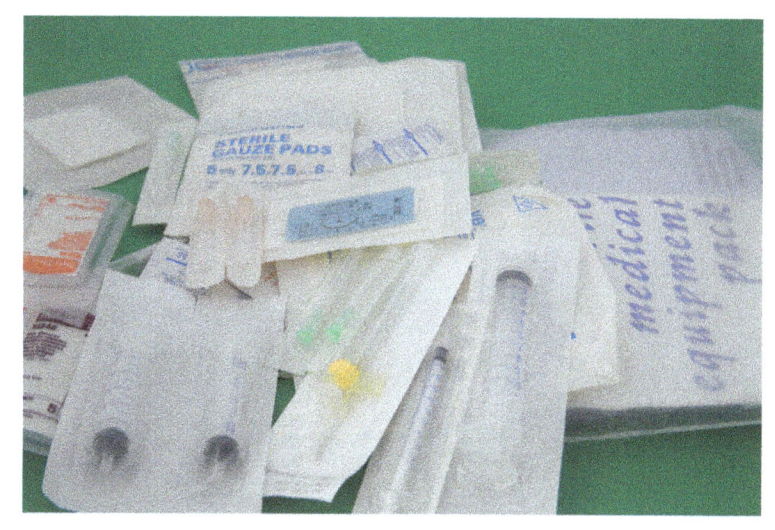

▲ Figure 18.3 Gamma radiation is used to sterilise medical equipment.

THE USE OF RADIOACTIVITY IN INDUSTRY

GAMMA RADIOGRAPHY

A gamma ray camera is like the x-ray cameras used to examine the contents of your luggage at airports. A source of gamma radiation is placed on one side of the object to be scanned and a gamma camera is placed on the other. Gamma rays pass through more objects than x-rays. They can be used to check for faults in casting (making things out of metal) or welding (joining metal objects together). Without the technique of gamma radiography, neither problem could be detected unless the welding or casting were cut through. An additional advantage of gamma radiography over the use of x-rays for this purpose is that gamma sources can be small and do not require a power source or large equipment.

TRACING AND MEASURING THE FLOW OF LIQUIDS AND GASES

Radioisotopes are used to check the flow of liquids in industrial processes. Very tiny amounts of radiation can easily be detected. Complex piping systems, like those used in in power stations, can be monitored for leaks. Radioactive tracers are even used to measure the rate of spread of sewage (human waste) (**Figure 18.4**)!

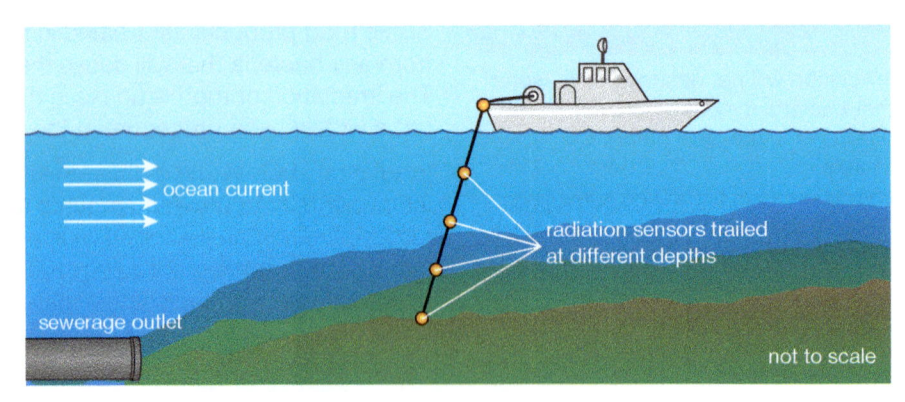

▲ Figure 18.4 Radioactive tracers released with the sewage allow its spread to be monitored to make sure the concentration does not reach harmful levels in any area.

RADIOACTIVE DATING

A variety of different methods involving radioisotopes are used to date minerals and organic matter. The most widely known method is radiocarbon dating. This is used to find the age of organic matter – for example, from trees and animals – that was once living.

THE DANGERS TO HEALTH OF IONISING RADIATION

Ionising radiation can damage the molecules that make up the cells of living tissue. Cells suffer this kind of damage all the time for many different reasons. Fortunately, cells can repair or replace themselves given time so, usually, no permanent damage results. However, if cells suffer repeated damage because of ionising radiation, the cell may be killed. Alternatively the cell may start to behave in an unexpected way because it has been damaged. We call this effect cell mutation. Some types of cancer happen because damaged cells start to divide uncontrollably and no longer perform their correct function.

Different types of ionising radiation present different risks. Alpha particles have the greatest ionising effect, but they cannot pass through many materials. This means that an alpha source presents little risk, as alpha particles do not penetrate (pass through) the skin. The problem of alpha radiation is much greater if the source of alpha particles is taken into the body. Here the radiation will be very close to many different types of cells and they may be damaged if the exposure is prolonged. Alpha emitters can be breathed in or taken in through eating food. Radon gas is a decay product of radium and is an alpha emitter. It therefore presents a real risk to health. Smokers greatly increase their exposure to this kind of damage as they draw the radiation source right into their lungs (cigarette smoke contains radon).

Beta and gamma radiation do provide a serious health risk when outside the body. Both can penetrate skin and flesh (body) and can cause cell damage by ionisation. Gamma radiation, as we have mentioned earlier, is the most penetrating. The damage caused by gamma rays will depend on how much of their energy is absorbed by ionising atoms along their path. Beta and gamma emitters that are absorbed by the body present less risk than alpha emitters, because of their lower ionising power.

In all cases, the longer the period of exposure to radiation the greater the risk of serious cell damage. Workers in the nuclear industry wear badges to indicate their level of exposure.

7 RADIOACTIVITY AND PARTICLES 18 APPLICATIONS OF RADIOACTIVITY

SAFE HANDLING OF RADIOACTIVE MATERIALS

Samples of radioactive isotopes used in schools and colleges are very small. This is to limit the risk to users, particularly those who use them regularly – the teachers! Although the risk is small, certain precautions must be followed. The samples are stored in lead-lined containers to block even the most penetrating form of radiation, gamma rays (see **Figures 18.5** and **18.6**). The containers are clearly labelled as a radiation hazard (danger) and must be stored in a locked metal cabinet. The samples are handled using tongs and are kept as far from the body as possible.

In the nuclear industry and research laboratories, much larger amounts of radioactive material are used. These have to be handled with great care. Very energetic sources will be handled remotely by operators who are protected by lead shields, concrete and thick glass viewing panels (**Figure 18.7**).

▲ Figure 18.5 The hazard symbol for radioactivity.

▲ Figure 18.6 Radioactive samples are stored in lead-lined containers and are handled with tongs or protected fingers.

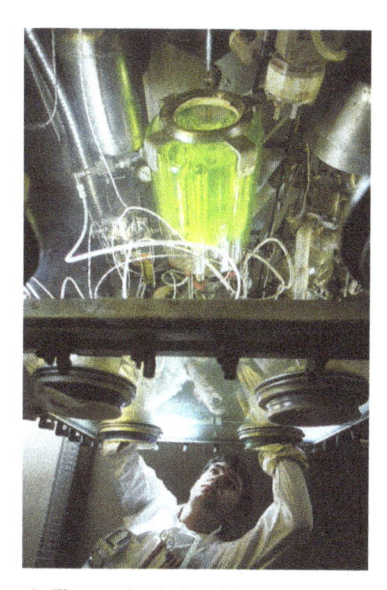

▲ Figure 18.7 Industrial sources of radioactivity must be handed with a lot of care.

The major problem with nuclear materials is long-term storage. Some materials have extremely long half-lives so they remain active for thousands and sometimes tens of thousands of years. Nuclear waste must be stored in sealed containers that must be capable of containing the radioactivity for enormously long periods of time.

CHAPTER QUESTIONS

Exam-style questions on applications of radioactivity can be found at the end of Unit 7 on page 438.

SKILLS REASONING

1 The most widely used isotope in medicine is technetium-99m. It has a half-life of six hours and decays by the emission of low-energy gamma rays and beta particles.

   a Explain why it is important that the half-life of materials that are used in medicine is short.

SKILLS CREATIVITY, REASONING

   b Technetium-99m emits gamma radiation. Explain why an alpha emitter would be unsuitable as a tracer in diagnosis of illness.

SKILLS CREATIVITY, REASONING

2 A radioactive isotope of iodine is used in both the diagnosis and treatment of a condition of the thyroid gland. This gland naturally takes up ordinary iodine as part of its function. If a patient has an overactive thyroid it concentrates too much iodine in the gland and this has serious effects on the patient's health.

Explain how the radioisotope iodine-131 may be used to:

a identify an overactive thyroid gland

b treat an overactive thyroid.

(Iodine-131 has a half-life of eight days and is a high-energy beta emitter.)

SKILLS CRITICAL THINKING

3 a Explain the difference between radioactive contamination and irradiation.

b Give an example of a use of irradiation.

SKILLS CREATIVITY, REASONING

4 Paper is made in a variety of different 'weights', with different thicknesses. Explain how ionising radiation could be used to check the thickness of paper during production. You should consider the following:

a the type of radiation to be used

b how it will be used to measure the paper thickness

c what checks should be made to ensure that the measurements are accurate

d safety procedures.

SKILLS REASONING

5 An isotope that decays by alpha emission is relatively safe when outside the body but very dangerous if absorbed by the body, either through breathing or eating.

a Explain why this is so.

b Explain why radon-220 is a particularly dangerous isotope.

SKILLS CRITICAL THINKING

6 Radioactivity is used in measurement in many manufacturing processes. One example is measuring and controlling the thickness of paper. Paper is rolled through heavy rollers to compress it to the required thickness.

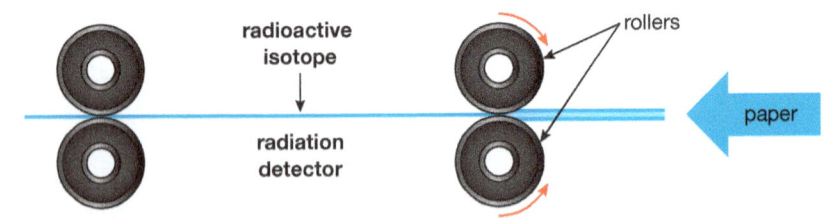

The thickness of the paper is gauged (measured) and the spacing of the rollers is automatically adjusted to keep the paper at the required thickness.

a Choose the type of radiation, alpha, beta or gamma, that should be used in this process. Give reasons for your choice.

b Ideally the radioactive isotope used should have a very long half-life. Explain why a short half-life, measured in days rather than centuries, would be unsuitable.

7 RADIOACTIVITY AND PARTICLES — 19 FISSION AND FUSION

19 FISSION AND FUSION

SPECIFICATION REFERENCES: 7.17–7.19, 7.22, 7.25

Scientists have speculated about the nature of the atom for thousands of years, but it is only relatively recently that our current ideas were developed. In this chapter you will read about how our ideas about the structure of the atom have developed over the centuries and how we use nuclear energy to produce electricity.

LEARNING OBJECTIVES

- Know that nuclear reactions, including fission, fusion and radioactive decay, can be a source of energy.
- Understand how a nucleus of U-235 can be split (the process of fission) by collision with a neutron, and that this process releases energy as kinetic energy of the fission products.
- Know that the fission of U-235 produces two radioactive daughter nuclei and a small number of neutrons.
- Understand the role of shielding around a nuclear reactor.
- Know that fusion is the energy source for stars.

KEY POINT
Fission is splitting apart, fusion is joining together.

NUCLEAR REACTIONS AS A SOURCE OF ENERGY

Nuclear reactions involve a change in the qualities of atoms. Heavy atoms may split into lighter atoms and other pieces in a process called **fission**. Lighter atoms may be forced to join together to make heavier atoms in a process called fusion. In either process, the mass of the starting atoms is greater than the mass of the products. This missing mass has been converted into energy.

Within the core of the Earth, radioactive isotopes of elements like uranium, thorium and potassium provide a large proportion of the heat within the Earth itself through radioactive decay.

In the Sun, hydrogen is converted into helium in a **fusion reaction** providing us with a continuous supply of energy in the form of heat and other electromagnetic radiation.

NUCLEAR FISSION

Uranium-235 is used as fuel in a nuclear reactor. It is used because its nuclei can be split by a neutron. The process of splitting an atom is called fission.

Uranium-235 is called a fissile material because it goes through the splitting process easily. The fission process is shown in **Figure 19.1**.

In the fission reaction, a slow-moving neutron is absorbed by a nucleus of uranium-235.

KEY POINT
You do not need to know this equation for the exam. You need to know that a neutron can trigger a break up of a U-235 atom and this releases some neutrons that can go on to split other atoms.

The resulting nucleus of uranium-236 is unstable and splits apart. The fragments of this decay are the two daughter nuclei of barium-144 and krypton-89. The decay also produces gamma radiation and three more neutrons. The equation for this decay is:

$$^{236}_{92}U \rightarrow \ ^{144}_{56}Ba + \ ^{89}_{36}Kr + 3\ ^{1}_{0}n + \gamma \text{ radiation}$$

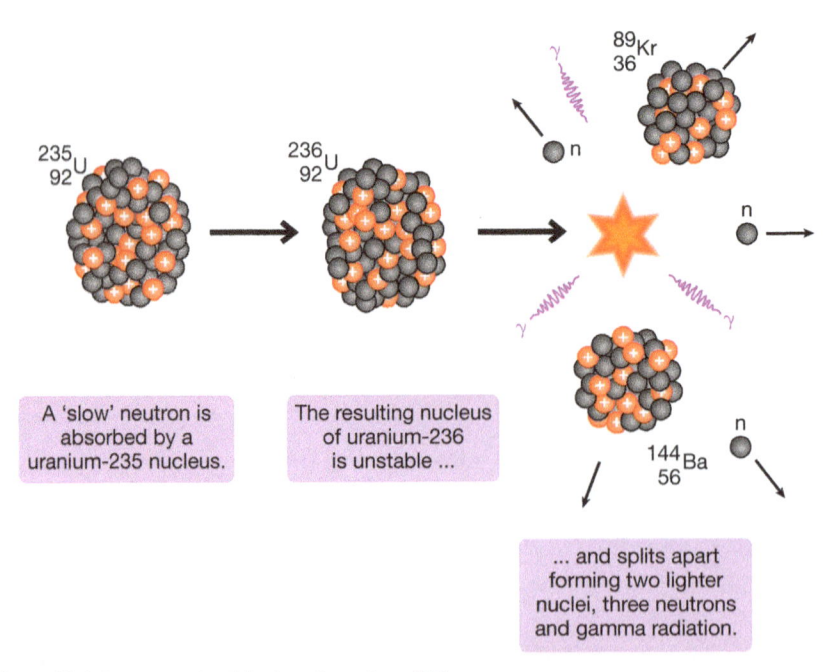

▲ Figure 19.1 One example of fission of uranium-235

The fission reaction produces a huge amount of energy. This is because the mass of the products, the barium and krypton nuclei and the three neutrons, is slightly less than that of the original uranium-236 nuclei. This lost mass is converted to energy. Most of the energy is carried away as the kinetic energy of the two lighter nuclei. Some is emitted as gamma radiation. The three neutrons produced by the fission may hit other nuclei of uranium-235, so causing the process to repeat, as shown in **Figure 19.2**. If one neutron from each fission causes one nearby uranium-235 to split, then the fission reaction will keep going. If more than one neutron from each fission causes fission in surrounding nuclei, then the reaction gets faster and faster – a bit like an avalanche.

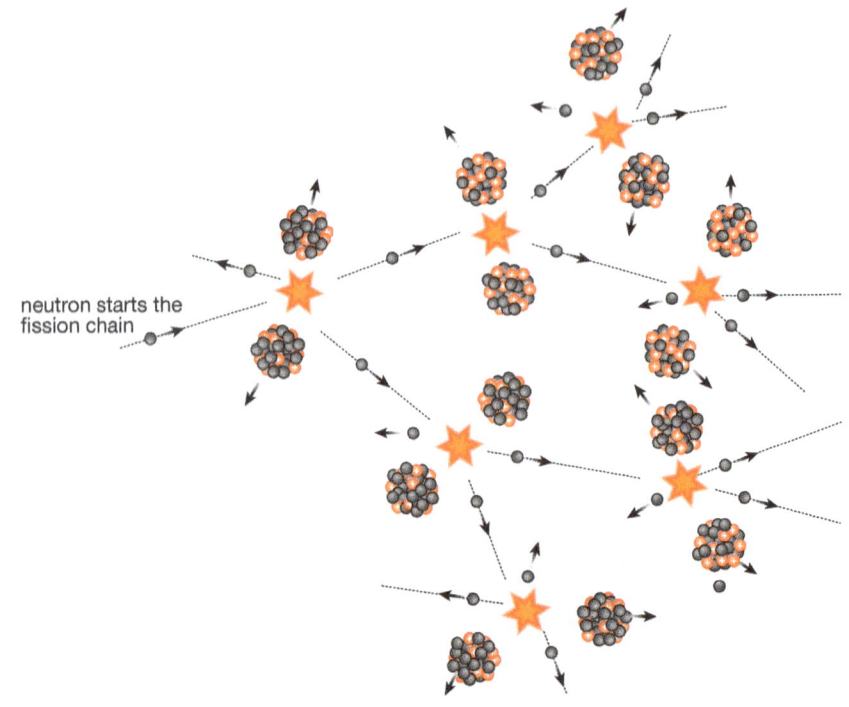

▲ Figure 19.2 A chain reaction in uranium-235

This is called a chain reaction. Each fission results in more nuclei splitting apart. If the amount of uranium-235 is small, many of the neutrons released do not hit other uranium nuclei and the reaction does not get faster and faster. For a chain reaction to happen there must be a minimum amount of the uranium-235. This minimum amount is called the critical mass.

In an atomic bomb two pieces of fissile material (isotopes that can be triggered into splitting apart) that are smaller than the critical mass are forced together under high pressure to form a mass greater than the critical mass. The result is a chain reaction with the rapid and uncontrolled release of huge amounts of energy.

If this is allowed to take place in a nuclear reactor, the reactor core overheats, resulting in a nuclear explosion with the sudden release of enormous amounts of heat energy and radiation. In a nuclear reactor the process is controlled so that the heat energy is released over a longer period of time. The heat produced in the core or heart of the reactor is used to heat water. The steam produced then drives turbines (engines) to turn generators. The basic parts of a nuclear reactor are shown in **Figure 19.3**.

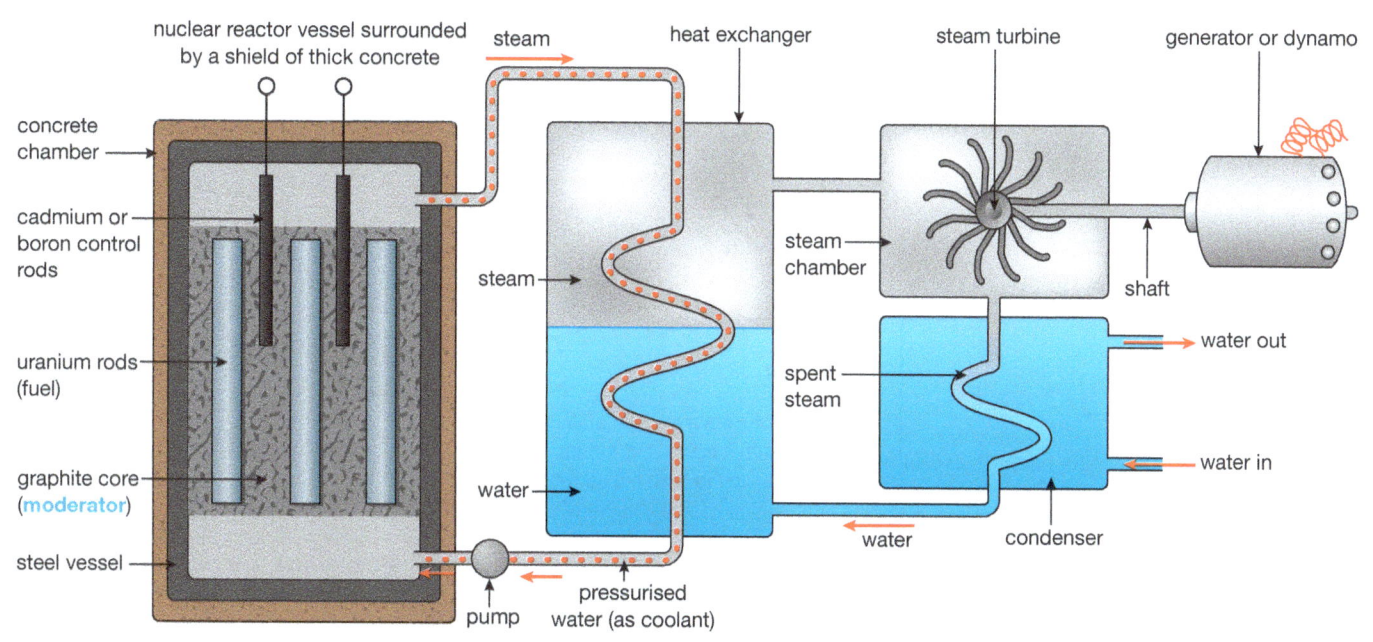

▲ Figure 19.3 A nuclear reactor controls a chain reaction so that heat energy is released slowly.

The reactor core contains fuel rods of enriched uranium. Enriched uranium is uranium-238 with a higher proportion of uranium-235 than is found in natural reserves of uranium.

In the nuclear reactor there are also **control rods**, made of boron or cadmium. These are used to slow down or stop the nuclear fission process.

The reactor vessel is made of steel and surrounded by a concrete layer about 5 metres in thickness. This prevents any radiation escaping and endangering life around the reactor.

KEY POINT

You **do not** need to know what the purpose of the moderator or the control rods is. You **do** need to know why shielding is important.

The nuclear process in a reactor produces a variety of different types of radioactive material. Some have relatively short half-lives and decay rapidly. These soon become safe to handle and do not present problems of long-term storage. Other materials have extremely long half-lives. These will continue to produce dangerous levels of ionising radiation for thousands of years. These waste products present a serious problem for long-term storage. They are usually sealed (closed) in containers which are then buried deep underground. The sites for underground storage have to be carefully selected. The rock must be water resistant and the geology of the site must be stable – storing waste in earthquake zones or areas of volcanic activity would not be sensible.

Some reactors are designed to produce plutonium. Plutonium is a very radioactive artificial element. Small amounts of plutonium represent a serious danger to health. Plutonium is another fissile material. If a large enough mass of plutonium is brought together a chain reaction will start. Plutonium can be used in the production of nuclear weapons.

Nuclear power stations do not produce carbon dioxide or acidic gases as fossil fuel power stations do. This means that nuclear power does not contribute to global warming or acid rain. Only small amounts of uranium are needed for a chain reaction and the supply of nuclear fuel will last many hundreds of years – unlike some **fossil fuels** that could run out in the next fifty years.

NUCLEAR FUSION

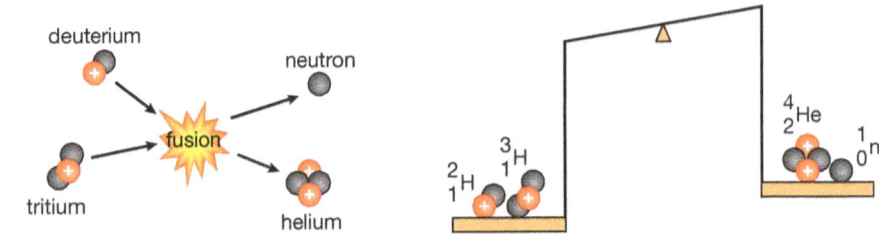

▲ Figure 19.4 Here a nucleus of deuterium collides with a nucleus of tritium. They undergo fusion to form the nucleus of helium, a neutron and a large amount of energy.

▲ Figure 19.5 The mass of the products of fusion is smaller than the two hydrogen nuclei.

Figure 19.4 shows a fusion process that is being used in projects to develop nuclear fusion reactors. Two isotopes of hydrogen, deuterium (H-2) and tritium (H-3), collide at very high speed. The result is the formation of a helium nucleus, a neutron and a large amount of energy. The fusion process is the energy source of our Sun and all stars.

7 RADIOACTIVITY AND PARTICLES
19 FISSION AND FUSION

CHAPTER QUESTIONS

Exam-style questions on fission and fusion can be found at the end of Unit 7 on page 438.

SKILLS — CRITICAL THINKING

1. a Uranium-235 (U-235) is a fissile material. Explain the meaning of the term *fissile*.
   b If there is a large enough mass of U-235, it may cause a chain reaction. (This is called the critical mass for the isotope.)
   Describe how a chain reaction may take place when a U-235 nucleus splits apart.

SKILLS — CRITICAL THINKING

2. List two advantages and two disadvantages of nuclear fission as a way of producing energy.

SKILLS — REASONING

3. An important part of a nuclear reactor is its shielding. Explain
   a why it is needed
   b what it is made of.

SKILLS — CRITICAL THINKING

4. Describe the differences between nuclear fission and nuclear fusion.

EXAM PRACTICE

SKILLS PROBLEM SOLVING

1 Select the particle, from the list below, which has the smallest atomic mass.

A alpha

B neutron

C proton

D electron

(Total 1 mark)

SKILLS CRITICAL THINKING

2 A radioactive isotope has an activity of 1000 Bq; after 5 hours its activity has fallen to 500 Bq. This period of time is called

A the shelf-life of the isotope

B the useful life of the isotope

C the half-life of the isotope

D the life time of the isotope

(Total 1 mark)

SKILLS CRITICAL THINKING

3 State which of the following types of radiation that may be emitted during radioactive decay is not ionising.

A alpha

B beta

C neutron

D gamma

(Total 1 mark)

SKILLS ANALYSIS

4 Here are descriptions of some nuclear particles:

- particle A has 0 mass and a charge +1
- particle B has 1 mass and a charge 0
- particle C has 1 mass and a charge +1
- particle D has 0 mass and a charge −1
- particle E has 4 mass and a charge +2

a State which particle is an alpha. (1)

b State which particle is a beta. (1)

c State which particle is a proton. (1)

d State which particle is a neutron. (1)

(Total 4 marks)

SKILLS CRITICAL THINKING

5 Two types of nuclear reactor are used to produce energy. Fission reactors are already in use in nuclear power plants around the world. Fusion reactors are still at the experimental stage.

a Explain what is meant by:

i nuclear fission (4)

ii nuclear fusion. (4)

b In a fission reactor the process of generating energy is a chain reaction using a suitable fissile fuel like uranium-235.

Explain what a chain reaction is. (4)

(Total 12 marks)

6 a Explain what the letters A and Z tell us about the structure (make up) of the nucleus of any element X.

$^A_Z X$ (2)

b Here is a list of the type of radiation that may be emitted (given out) by an unstable nucleus:

A alpha   **B** beta   **C** gamma   **D** neutron

  i State which type affects A but not Z. (1)
  ii State which type affects Z but not A. (1)
  iii State which type affects both A and Z. (1)
  iv State which type affects neither A nor Z. (1)

(Total 6 marks)

7 Identify the type of ionising radiations below from the following descriptions:

This type of radiation

a is in the form of an electromagnetic wave (1)

b is a fast-moving electron that is emitted from the nucleus of an unstable atom (1)

c is made up of the same particles as a helium nucleus (1)

d can only be blocked by several metres of concrete or several centimetres of lead (1)

e is strongly ionising (1)

f is blocked by a few millimetres of aluminium foil (1)

g is a negatively charged particle. (1)

(Total 7 marks)

| 20 MOTION IN THE UNIVERSE 441 | 21 STELLAR EVOLUTION 446 |

PHYSICS UNIT 8
ASTROPHYSICS

A supernova is an exploding star. The explosion occurs when the gravitational forces within a star are so great that its core collapses releasing huge amounts of energy. It is the largest explosion to take place in space. In this section we will see how important gravitational forces are in our Universe.

8 ASTROPHYSICS

20 MOTION IN THE UNIVERSE

SPECIFICATION REFERENCES: 8.1, 8.3–8.5

We live on a planet called Earth. It is one of many planets that, together with their moons, form our Solar System. Gravitational forces hold our Solar System together. These forces cause the planets, asteroids and comets to orbit the Sun, and moons and artificial satellites to orbit the planets. In this chapter we will look at the key role played by gravitational forces in controlling these movements.

UNITS

In this unit you will need to use kilogram (kg) as the unit of mass, metre (m) as the unit of length, metre/second (m/s) as the unit of speed, metre/second^2 (m/s^2) as the unit of acceleration, newton (N) as the unit of force, second (s) as the unit of time and newton/kilogram (N/kg) as the unit of gravitational field strength.

▲ Figure 20.1 The force of gravity keeps these moons in orbit around Jupiter.

LEARNING OBJECTIVES

- Explain that gravitational force causes moons to orbit planets; causes the planets and comets to orbit the Sun; causes artificial satellites to orbit the Earth.

- Understand why gravitational field strength, g, varies and know that it is different on other planets and the Moon from that on the Earth.

- Describe the differences in the orbits of comets, moons and planets.

THE SOLAR SYSTEM

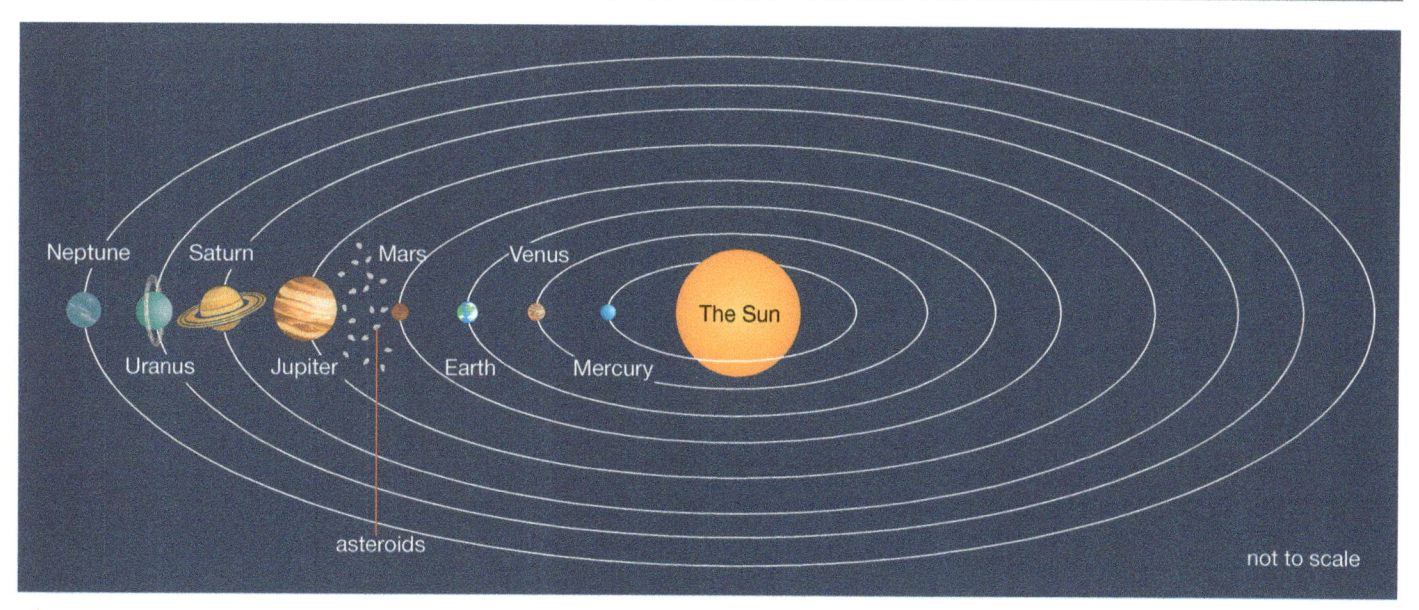

▲ Figure 20.2 The Earth is one of eight planets that orbit the Sun. The orbits of the planets are elliptical (an oval shape) with the Sun close to the centre.

WHY DO OBJECTS MOVE IN A CIRCLE?

Figure 20.3 shows a boy swinging a heavy ball around on a wire. To make this ball travel in a circle he needs to spin around and at the same time pull on the wire. Without this continuous pulling force the ball will not travel in a circle.

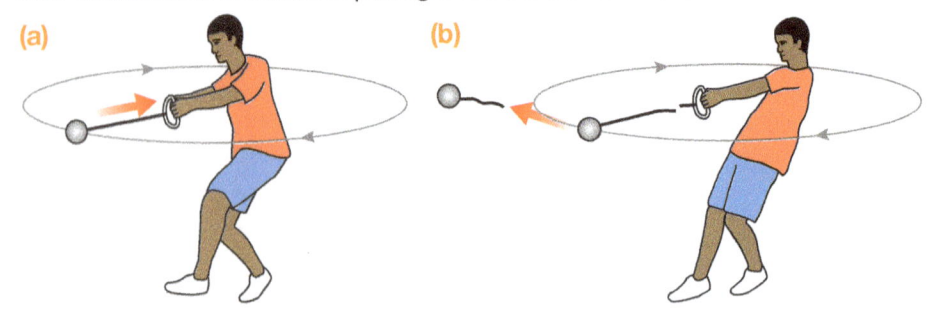

▲ Figure 20.3 **(a)** A 'pulling' force has to be applied to the ball to make it travel in a circle. **(b)** If the wire breaks or the boy releases the handle the ball flies away.

Planets, **asteroids** and **comets** travel around the Sun. Moons and satellites travel around the planets. For this to happen there must be forces being applied to them. There is no string or wire to pull on as in the example above, so where do these forces come from? In 1687, Isaac Newton suggested his theory of gravity to explain these movements.

Newton suggested that between any two objects there is always a force of attraction. This attraction is due to the masses of the objects. He called this force gravitational force.

He suggested that the size of this force depends on the:

- masses of the two objects
- distance between the masses (**Figure 20.4**).

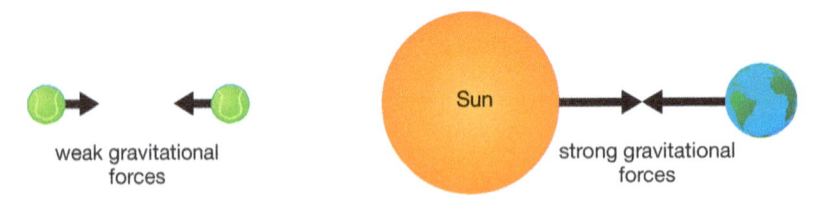

The greater the masses of the two objects the stronger the attractive forces between them.
If the distance between the masses is increased the forces between them decrease.

attractive gravitational force = F

attractive gravitational force = $\frac{1}{4}F$

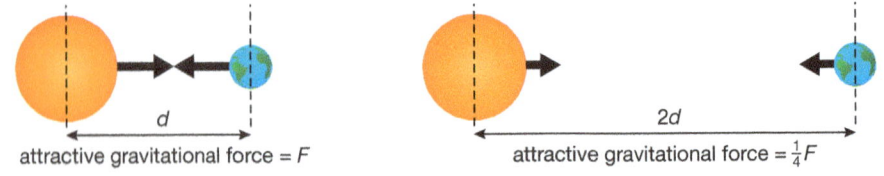

▲ Figure 20.4 Gravitational forces obey an inverse square law – that is, if the distance between the masses is doubled, the forces between them are **quartered**; if the distance between them is **trebled**, the forces become one-ninth of what they were.

The gravitational attraction between two objects with small masses is tiny. Only when one or both of the objects has a very large mass – for example, a moon or a planet – is the force of attraction obvious.

Our Sun is massive. It contains over 99% of the mass of the Solar System. It is the gravitational attraction between this mass and each of the planets that holds the Solar System together and causes the planets to follow their curved paths (**Figure 20.5**).

8 ASTROPHYSICS   20 MOTION IN THE UNIVERSE   443

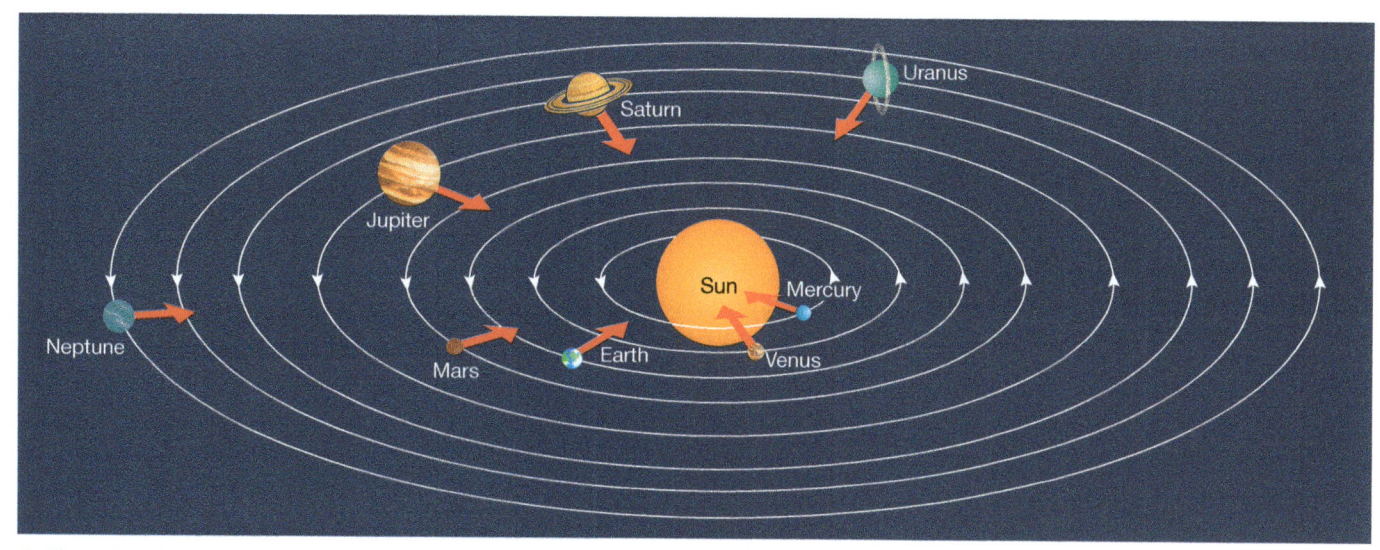

▲ Figure 20.5 Gravitational forces make the planets follow nearly circular paths.

Those planets that are closest to the Sun feel the greatest attraction and so follow the most curved paths. Planets that are the furthest from the Sun feel the weakest pull and follow the least curved path.

EXTENSION

The planet Neptune is a very long way from the Sun so the gravitational force between them is very small. This means that the orbit of Neptune is not very curved and it takes a very long time for it to complete one orbit.

Table 20.1

Planet	Average distance from Sun compared with the Earth	Time for one orbit of the Sun in Earth years
Mercury	0.4	0.2
Venus	0.7	0.6
Earth	1.0	1.0
Mars	1.5	1.9
Jupiter	5.0	12
Saturn	9.5	30
Uranus	19	84
Neptune	30	165

SATELLITES AND MOONS

A satellite is an object that orbits a planet. There are two types of satellite: natural and artificial (human-made).

Natural satellites are called moons. The Earth has just one moon. It is the fifth largest moon in our Solar System, approximately 340 000 km from Earth, and takes just over 27 days to complete one orbit. Although we call our moon 'The Moon' it is not unique. Many planets have moons. Some have more than one, for example, Mars has two moons while Jupiter and Saturn (**Figure 20.6**) have more than 60 each. All moons have circular orbits because of the gravitational forces between them and their planet.

▲ Figure 20.6 Some of the many moons of Saturn.

Since the late 1950s humans have been able to launch, and to put into orbit around the Earth, objects like the one seen in **Figure 20.7**. These are known as artificial satellites and are extremely useful. Some satellites are put into a very high orbit above the Earth and are used to help us communicate over large distances, for example, for international phone calls or video links, the internet and so on. Some satellites are put into a much lower orbit and are used to monitor in detail the Earth's surface, such as the temperature of the world's oceans or the progress of forest fires.

▲ Figure 20.7 This satellite is held in orbit by the gravitational attraction between it and the Earth.

COMETS

Comets are large rock-like pieces of ice that orbit the Sun. They have very elliptical (elongated) orbits which at times take them very close to the Sun. At other times they travel close to the very edge of our Solar System (**Figures 20.8** and **20.9**).

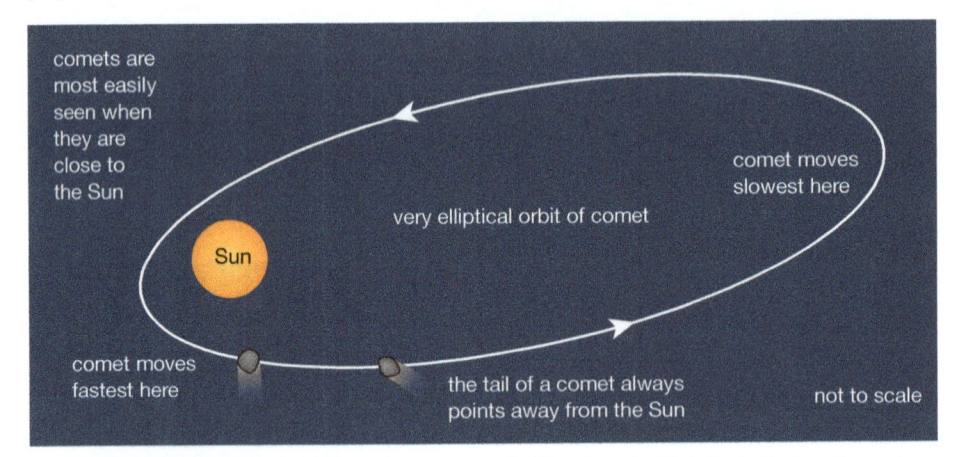

▲ Figure 20.8 The speed of a comet varies enormously. They travel at their fastest when they are very close to the Sun.

EXTENSION

Although you will not be asked in your exam about the 'tails of comets' it is interesting to know that, close to the Sun, some of a comet's frozen gases evaporate to become gases again, forming a long tail that shines in the sunlight. These tails can be millions of kilometres in length. Perhaps the most famous of the comets is Halley's Comet, which visits our part of the Solar System every 76 years. It was last visible from Earth in 1986.

▲ Figure 20.9 Halley's comet could be last seen from Earth in 1986.

GRAVITATIONAL FIELD STRENGTH

The strength of gravity on a planet or moon is called its gravitational field strength, and given the symbol *g*. Different planets have different masses and different radii – both of these will affect their gravitational field strengths.

- The larger the mass of a planet the greater its gravitational field strength.
- The larger the radius of a planet the smaller the gravitational field strength at its surface.

The gravitational field strength on the Earth is approximately 10 N/kg whereas on the Moon it is approximately 1.6 N/kg.

Table 20.2

Planet	Diameter compared with the Earth	Mass compared with the Earth	Gravitational field strength / N/kg
Mercury	0.4	0.06	4
Venus	0.9	0.38	9
Earth	1.0	1.0	10
Mars	0.5	0.10	4
Jupiter	11	320	23
Saturn	9	95	9
Uranus	4	15	9
Neptune	4	17.0	11

On the Moon, the gravitational field strength is only one-sixth that of the Earth's. This means that on the Moon you would weigh six times less. If however you visited Jupiter you would weigh almost 2½ times more (**Figure 20.10**)!

▲ Figure 20.10 The difference in one person's weight on the Moon and on Jupiter

CHAPTER QUESTIONS

Exam-style questions on motion in the Universe can be found at the end of Unit 8 on page 450.

SKILLS CRITICAL THINKING

1   a What is the name of the force that keeps all the planets of the Solar System in orbit around the Sun?
    b What two factors determine the size of this force on the surface of a planet?
    c Describe one difference between the orbits of Mercury and Neptune. Give one reason for this difference.
    d Describe how the speed of a comet changes as it orbits the Sun.

SKILLS CRITICAL THINKING

2 Describe the differences between the orbits of a moon, a planet and a comet.

3 Give one example of:
    a a natural satellite
    b an artificial satellite.

SKILLS ANALYSIS

4 Look at **Table 20.2**, then answer the following questions.
    a Which planet has the greatest mass?
    b Which planet has the strongest gravitational field?
    c Which planet has almost the same mass and gravitational field strength as the Earth?

21 STELLAR EVOLUTION

SPECIFICATION REFERENCES: 8.2, 8.7–8.9

The Universe is mainly empty space within which are scattered large numbers of galaxies. Astronomers (scientists who study space and the Universe) believe that there are billions of galaxies in the Universe. The distances between galaxies are millions of times greater than the distances between stars within a galaxy. The distances between the stars in a galaxy are millions of times greater than the distances between planets and the Sun.

▲ Figure 21.1 Photograph of galaxies of the Universe taken by the Hubble space telescope

LEARNING OBJECTIVES

- Know that the Sun is a star at the centre of our Solar System.
- Know that the Universe is a large collection of billions of galaxies; galaxies are a large collection of billions of stars; our Solar System is in the Milky Way galaxy.
- Understand how stars can be classified according to their colour.
- Know that a star's colour is related to its surface temperature.

- Describe the evolution of stars of similar mass to the Sun through the following stages:
  - nebula
  - star (main sequence)
  - red giant
  - white dwarf.

8 ASTROPHYSICS 21 STELLAR EVOLUTION

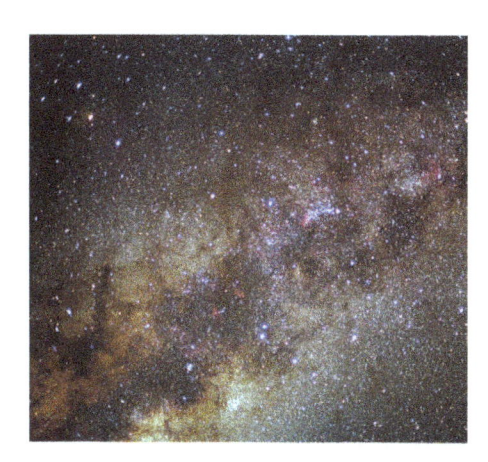

▲ Figure 21.2 Our galaxy, the Milky Way

▲ Figure 21.3 Our galaxy takes the shape of a spiral, like the one shown here.

▲ Figure 21.4 The colour of the light emitted by this piece of iron tells us how hot it is.

THE MILKY WAY

Our nearest star is the Sun. It is approximately 150 million kilometres from the Earth. Its surface temperature is approximately 6000 °C and temperatures within its core are about 15 000 000 °C. Attractive gravitational forces between stars cause them to group together in enormous groups called galaxies. Galaxies consist of billions of stars. Our galaxy is a **spiral galaxy** called the Milky Way. We are approximately two-thirds of the way out from the centre of our galaxy along one of the arms of the spiral.

CLASSIFYING STARS

Even within our galaxy we can see a wide variety of stars (**Figures 21.2** and **21.3**).

Looking up into a clear night sky, especially if we use a telescope, we can see that stars are not all identical. They have different colours, different levels of brightness and appear to be different sizes. Scientists who study the stars in detail have created classes or star groups based upon these similarities and differences.

Why are some stars white, some red and others yellow? Surprisingly we can find the answer to this question in a traditional blacksmiths. To shape a piece of iron without it breaking the iron must be very hot. A skilled blacksmith will know when the temperature of the iron is high enough simply by taking it out of the furnace (very hot oven) and looking at its colour (**Figure 21.4**). If it is glowing white or bright orange it is very hot. If it is a dull red it is much cooler and not ready to be shaped.

In a similar way the colours of stars tell us about their temperatures. A very hot star emits more blue in its spectrum and therefore looks blue, a medium star like our Sun looks yellow and cooler stars appear red.

Using the colours of stars and their surface temperatures, scientists have created seven different groups of stars. These groups are called O, B, A, F, G, K, M. O and B are the hottest stars and K and M the coolest.

Table 21.1

Star classification	Surface temperature / K	Colour
O	more than 33 000	blue
B	33 000–10 000	blue–white
A	10 000–7500	white
F	7500–6000	yellow–white
G	6000–5200	yellow
K	5200–3700	orange
M	3700–2000	red

REMINDER

The brightness of a star depends on:
- the distance the star is from the Earth
- the luminosity of the star – that is, how much energy is being emitted from the star each second.

THE BIRTH OF A STAR

dust and gas particles are drawn together by gravitational forces

compression (pulling together) of particles causes increases in temperature and nuclear reactions begin

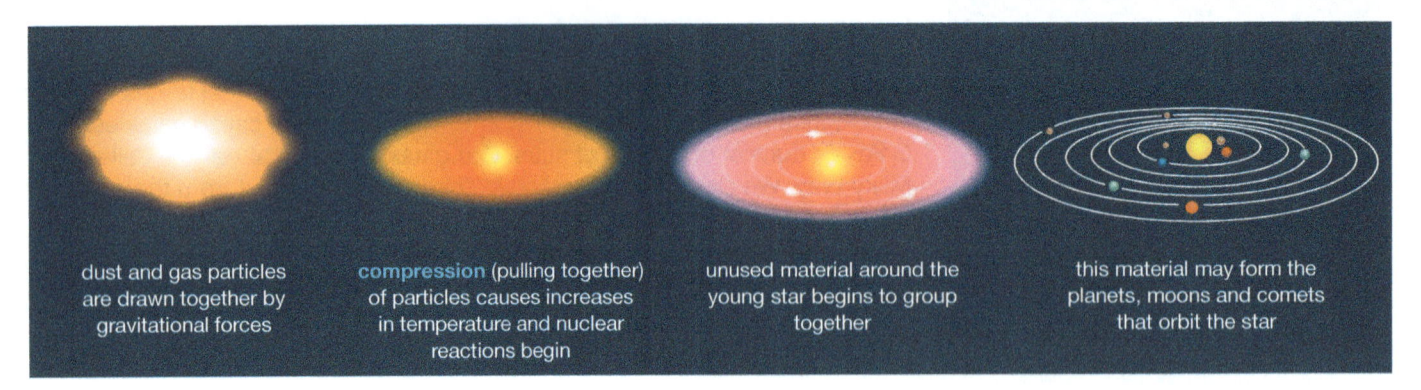

unused material around the young star begins to group together

this material may form the planets, moons and comets that orbit the star

▲ Figure 21.5 Birth of a solar system

Stars like our Sun are formed from large clouds of dust and gas particles we call **nebulae** or stellar nebulae. These particles are drawn together over a very long period of time by gravitational forces. The particles are pulled together so tightly that there is a very large increase in temperature and pressure. As a result of this nuclear fusion reactions begin. Hydrogen nuclei join together to make larger nuclei and huge amounts of energy are emitted as heat and light. This incredibly hot ball of gas is a very young star (**Figure 21.5**).

THE LIFE OF A STAR

The appearance of a star changes gradually with time. These changes follow a pattern.

When a star first forms, gravitational forces are pulling particles together. Then when nuclear reactions begin, the high temperatures create forces that try to push the particles apart – that is, make the gases expand. When these two forces are balanced, the star is said to be in its main stable period. A star in this main stable period is referred to as a main sequence star. This period can last for many millions of years. At the moment our Sun is in this stable period.

Towards the end of this stable period, there are fewer hydrogen nuclei and eventually the hydrogen fusion reactions stop. Gravitational forces are now the largest forces and compress the star. As the star shrinks in size there is a large increase in temperature. So high that fusion reactions between helium nuclei begin. The energy released by these reactions causes the star to expand to many times its original size. As it expands it becomes a little cooler and more of its light energy is emitted in the red part of the spectrum. The star is changing into a **red giant**.

Sometime later when most of the helium nuclei have fused (joined) together, new nuclear reactions begin, but now the compressive or squashing forces are larger and the star begins to get smaller or contract. This contraction causes an increase in temperature so the star again changes colour. It now emits more blue and white light. It has changed into a **white dwarf** star (**Figure 21.6**). The matter from which white dwarf stars are made is millions of times more dense than any matter found on the Earth.

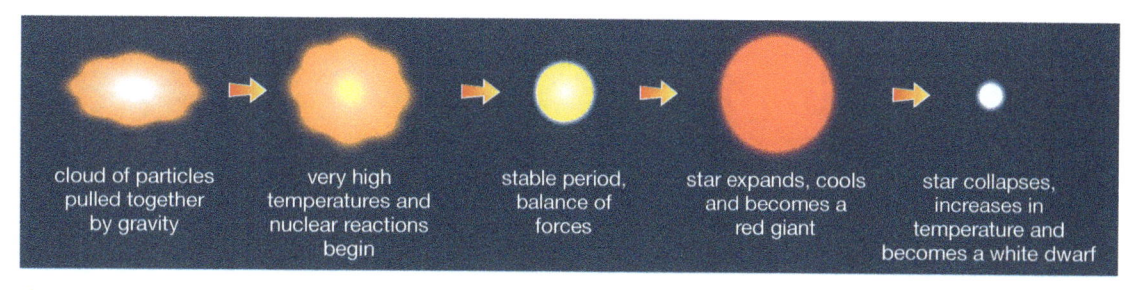

cloud of particles pulled together by gravity → very high temperatures and nuclear reactions begin → stable period, balance of forces → star expands, cools and becomes a red giant → star collapses, increases in temperature and becomes a white dwarf

▲ Figure 21.6 The life-cycle of stars with a mass similar to that of our Sun

CHAPTER QUESTIONS

Exam-style questions on stars and their life cycles can be found at the end of Unit 8 on page 450.

1 A star which is much cooler than our Sun emits most of its light from which part of the electromagnetic spectrum?

   A red

   B white

   C blue

   D yellow

SKILLS CRITICAL THINKING

2 a What do we call a large group of stars?

   b Why do these groups form?

   c What is the name of the group where we live?

   d How many other groups of stars do we think exist in the Universe?

SKILLS ANALYSIS

3 Using **Table 21.1** on page 447 answer the following questions.

   a Describe two properties of stars that belong in classes B and K.

   b To which group does a star belong if its surface temperature is 2500 K?

   c To which two groups might a star belong if it is emitting a lot of yellow light?

   d What range of surface temperatures might this star have?

SKILLS CRITICAL THINKING

4 What are the two factors which will affect how brightly we see a star in the night sky?

5 Describe the different stages of a life of a star that has the same mass as our Sun.

SKILLS CRITICAL THINKING

6 a What kinds of reactions begin in a very young star when dust and gas particles are pulled together strongly by gravitational forces?

   b What is released when these reactions take place?

EXAM PRACTICE

1 a Which of the following statements is *incorrect*?
   A Gravitational forces keep our Moon in orbit around the Earth.
   B Comets and moons orbit planets.
   C Planets orbit the Sun.
   D Artificial satellites orbit a planet. (1)

b Which of the following sequences might be followed by a star that has a mass similar to our Sun?
   A main sequence, stellar nebula, red giant, white dwarf
   B stellar nebula, main sequence, red giant, white dwarf
   C stellar nebula, main sequence, white dwarf, black hole
   D main sequence, red giant, neutron star, white dwarf (1)

c What kinds of forces pull dust and gas particles together to form a stellar nebula?
   A electrical forces
   B magnetic forces
   C electrostatic forces
   D gravitational forces (1)

(Total 3 marks)

2 Copy and complete the following passage about gravitational forces, filling in the spaces.

Gravitational forces cause planets and _____ to _____ the Sun. The planets _____ to the Sun, for example, _____ and _____, experience the _____ forces and so have the most _____ orbits. The planets _____ from the Sun, for example, _____ and _____, experience the _____ forces and so have the least _____ orbits. The shape of a planet's orbit is not quite _____. It is _____.

All objects that orbit a planet are called _____ but natural ones are called _____.

(Total 16 marks)

3 A man has a mass of 80 kg. On the Earth he weighs 800 N. Using **Table 20.2** on page 445 calculate the weight of this man on the surface of:
   a Venus (3)
   b Mars (3)
   c Neptune. (3)

(Total 9 marks)

SKILLS ANALYSIS

4 The table below contains information about some of the planets in our Solar System.

Planet	Surface gravity compared with the Earth	Distance from Sun compared with the Earth	Period / Earth years
Mercury	0.4	0.4	0.2
Venus	0.9	0.7	0.6
Mars	0.4	1.5	1.9
Jupiter	2.6	5.0	12
Saturn	1.1	9.5	30

HINT

circumference of a circle = 2π*r*

SKILLS PROBLEM SOLVING

a Name three planets that have a weaker gravitational pull on their surface than there is on Earth. (1)

b State how long a year is on Saturn. (1)

c If the distance from the Earth to the Sun is 150 million kilometres, calculate the distance of Jupiter from the Sun. (2)

(Total 4 marks)

SKILLS INTERPRETATION

SKILLS REASONING

5 a Draw a diagram to show the shape of the orbit of a comet around the Sun. (2)

b Describe and explain how the speed of a comet changes as it travels around its orbit. (4)

(Total 6 marks)

APPENDIX A: PERIODIC TABLE

Period	Group 1	Group 2		Group 3	Group 4	Group 5	Group 6	Group 7	Group 0
1	1 H Hydrogen 1								4 He Helium 2
2	7 Li Lithium 3	9 Be Beryllium 4		11 B Boron 5	12 C Carbon 6	14 N Nitrogen 7	16 O Oxygen 8	19 F Fluorine 9	20 Ne Neon 10
3	23 Na Sodium 11	24 Mg Magnesium 12		27 Al Aluminium 13	28 Si Silicon 14	31 P Phosphorus 15	32 S Sulfur 16	35.5 Cl Chlorine 17	40 Ar Argon 18
4	39 K Potassium 19	40 Ca Calcium 20	45 Sc Scandium 21; 48 Ti Titanium 22; 51 V Vanadium 23; 52 Cr Chromium 24; 55 Mn Manganese 25; 56 Fe Iron 26; 59 Co Cobalt 27; 59 Ni Nickel 28; 63.5 Cu Copper 29; 65 Zn Zinc 30	70 Ga Gallium 31	73 Ge Germanium 32	75 As Arsenic 33	79 Se Selenium 34	80 Br Bromine 35	84 Kr Krypton 36
5	85 Rb Rubidium 37	88 Sr Strontium 38	89 Y Yttrium 39; 91 Zr Zirconium 40; 93 Nb Niobium 41; 96 Mo Molybdenum 42; (98) Tc Technetium 43; 101 Ru Ruthenium 44; 103 Rh Rhodium 45; 106 Pd Palladium 46; 108 Ag Silver 47; 112 Cd Cadmium 48	115 In Indium 49	119 Sn Tin 50	122 Sb Antimony 51	128 Te Tellurium 52	127 I Iodine 53	131 Xe Xenon 54
6	133 Cs Caesium 55	137 Ba Barium 56	178 Hf Hafnium 72; 181 Ta Tantalum 73; 184 W Tungsten 74; 186 Re Rhenium 75; 190 Os Osmium 76; 192 Ir Iridium 77; 195 Pt Platinum 78; 197 Au Gold 79; 201 Hg Mercury 80	204 Tl Thallium 81	207 Pb Lead 82	209 Bi Bismuth 83	(209) Po Polonium 84	(210) At Astatine 85	(222) Rn Radon 86
7	(223) Fr Francium 87	(226) Ra Radium 88	(267) Rf Rutherfordium 104; (268) Db Dubnium 105; (269) Sg Seaborgium 106; (270) Bh Bohrium 107; (277) Hs Hassium 108; (278) Mt Meitnerium 109; (281) Ds Darmstadtium 110; (282) Rg Roentgenium 111; (285) Cn Copernicium 112	(286) Nh Nihonium 113	(289) Fl Flerovium 114	(290) Mc Moscovium 115	(293) Lv Livermorium 116	(294) Ts Tennessine 117	(294) Og Oganesson 118

Lanthanides: 139 La Lanthanum 57; 140 Ce Cerium 58; 141 Pr Praseodymium 59; 144 Nd Neodymium 60; (145) Pm Promethium 61; 150 Sm Samarium 62; 152 Eu Europium 63; 157 Gd Gadolinium 64; 159 Tb Terbium 65; 163 Dy Dysprosium 66; 165 Ho Holmium 67; 167 Er Erbium 68; 169 Tm Thulium 69; 173 Yb Ytterbium 70; 175 Lu Lutetium 71

Actinides: (227) Ac Actinium 89; 232 Th Thorium 90; 231 Pa Protactinium 91; 238 U Uranium 92; (237) Np Neptunium 93; (244) Pu Plutonium 94; (243) Am Americium 95; (247) Cm Curium 96; (247) Bk Berkelium 97; (251) Cf Californium 98; (252) Es Einsteinium 99; (257) Fm Fermium 100; (258) Md Mendelevium 101; (259) No Nobelium 102; (266) Lr Lawrencium 103

Key:
a = relative atomic mass
X = atomic symbol
b = atomic number

a
X
Name
b

(Masses in brackets are the mass numbers of the longest-lived isotope)

APPENDIX B: COMMAND WORDS

Command word	Definition
Add/Label	Requires the addition or labelling of a stimulus material given in the question, for example labelling a diagram or adding units to a table.
Calculate	Obtain a numerical answer, showing relevant working.
Comment on	Requires the synthesis of a number of variables from data/information to form a judgement.
Complete	Requires the completion of a table/diagram.
Deduce	Draw/reach conclusion(s) from the information provided.
Describe	To give an account of something. Statements in the response need to be developed, as they are often linked but do not need to include a justification or reason.
Design	Plan or invent a procedure from existing principles/ideas.
Determine	The answer must have an element that is quantitative from the stimulus provided, or must show how the answer can be reached quantitatively. To gain maximum marks, there must be a quantitative element to the answer.
Discuss	Identify the issue/situation/problem/argument that is being assessed within the question. Explore all aspects of an issue/situation/problem/argument. Investigate the issue/situation etc. by reasoning or argument.
Draw	Produce a diagram either using a ruler or freehand.
Estimate	Find an approximate value, number or quantity from a diagram/given data or through a calculation.
Evaluate	Review information (for example, data, methods) then bring it together to form a conclusion, drawing on evidence including strengths, weaknesses, alternative actions, relevant data or information. Come to a supported judgement of a subject's quality and relate it to its context.

Command word	Definition
Explain	An explanation requires a justification/exemplification of a point. The answer must contain some element of reasoning/justification – this can include mathematical explanations.
Give/State/Name	All of these command words are really synonyms. They generally all require recall of one or more pieces of information.
Give a reason/reasons	When a statement has been made and the requirement is only to give the reason(s) why.
Identify	Usually requires some key information to be selected from a given stimulus/resource.
Justify	Give evidence to support (either the statement given in the question or an earlier answer).
Plot	Produce a graph by marking points accurately on a grid from data that is provided and then draw a line of best fit through these points. A suitable scale and appropriately labelled axes must be included if these are not provided in the question.
Predict	Give an expected result.
Show that	Verify the statement given in the question.
Sketch	Produce a freehand drawing. For a graph, this would need a line and labelled axes with important features indicated. The axes are not scaled.
State what is meant by	When the meaning of a term is expected but there are different ways for how these can be described.
Suggest	Use your knowledge to propose a solution to a problem in a novel context.
Verb proceeding a command word	
Analyse the data/graph to explain	Examine the data/graph in detail to provide an explanation.
Multiple-choice questions	
What, Why	Direct command words used for multiple-choice questions.

INDEX

A

abiotic components, ecosystems 102
abiotic factors, ecosystems 105, 106
absolute zero 397, 398
acceleration 296, 298, 300, 306, 315–316
   measuring 301–304
acid rain 272
acid tests 222
acids 214–217
   formulae 216
   questions 217–218
   reactions with metals 209–210
acquired immune deficiency syndrome (AIDS) 9
actinoids 159
active sites, enzymes 23
active transport 32, 33
adaptations 93
addition polymerisation 284, 286, 288
adenosine diphosphate (ADP) 48
adenosine triphosphate (ATP) 32, 47, 48, 49
adrenaline 58
aerobic respiration 32, 47–48, 49, 50
   yeast 121
Agrobacterium 128–129
AIDS (acquired immune deficiency syndrome) 9
air, composition 199
alcohols, combustion 234–237
algae 7
alimentary canal 40
alkali metals 159, 189–193
   questions 194–195
alkalis 214–217
   questions 217–218
alkanes 264, 274–278
   questions 278–279
alkenes 264, 280–282
   questions 282–283

alleles 82
alpha radiation 418
alternating current 327
aluminium, reaction with dilute acids 209–210, 212–213
aluminium sulfate 174
alveoli 50, 53–54
amino acids 21
ammeter 329
ammonia 139
   solution 216, 218
   test 220
ammonium chloride 178
amplitude 346
amylase 42
   effect of temperature 25–27
anaerobic respiration 48–49, 49
   yeast 121–123
anhydrous copper sulfate 221
animals 5
   cells 17, 19
anions 170
anthers 74
antibodies 56, 59–60
antigens 59
anus 43
aorta 61
arteries 61, 63–64, 65
asexual reproduction 73–74, 74, 78
astatine 196–197, 198
asteroids 442
astrophysics
   motion 441–445
   questions 445, 449
   stellar evolution 446–449
atmospheric gases 199–203
   questions 203–205
atomic mass 416
atomic notation 416–417
atomic nucleus 152, 415–416
   unstable 418
atomic numbers 142, 152–153, 160–161, 416

atomic structure 151–155
   diagram 155
   questions 155–157
atomic weapons 435–436
atoms 151, 415–416
   number in formulae 163
ATP (adenosine triphosphate) 32, 47, 48, 49
atria 62, 63
average speed 296, 299, 305
average velocity 304, 307

B

background radiation 422–423, 426
bacteria 7–8
   genetically modified 126–128, 130
bacteriophages 127–128
balanced chemical equations 163–165
balanced forces 310
barium nitrate 174
batteries 330
Benedict's solution 22, 27
beta radiation 418–419
bile 42
binoculars 365
biological catalysts 23
biological fitness 91, 94
biological molecules 20
   carbohydrates 20
   enzymes 23–27
   lipids 21–22
   proteins 21
   questions 27
biomass 109
biomes 105
biotic components 102
biotic factors, ecosystems 105, 106
bitumen 271
blood
   cells 31, 58, 59–60, 65
   composition 58–60, 65, 66
   vessels 61, 64, 65

INDEX

boiling points 137, 138, 141, 183
   alkanes 277
     giant covalent structures 182
     ionic compounds 176
     simple molecular structures 181
bombardier beetles 251
Boyle's law 396
braking 317–318, 320
branched chain molecules 276
breadmaking 121–123
breathing see respiration
bromine 196–197, 198
   reaction with alkenes 282
bronchial tree 50, 54
bronchioles 50
butane 265, 274
but-1-ene 280

C

caesium 191
calcium
   reaction with dilute acids 209
   reaction with water 207–208
calcium carbonate 222
   reaction with hydrochloric acid 244–251
calcium chloride 174
calcium oxide 175
calories 379
calorimetry experiments 234–237
capillaries 54, 61, 64, 65
carbohydrases 41
carbohydrates 4, 5, 20
carbon cycle 111–112, 113
carbon dioxide 111, 120, 202–203
   atmospheric 199, 203, 205
   effect on photosynthesis 39, 120–121
   formula 164
   respiration 28
   sublimation 138
   test 220
carbon isotopes 166, 417, 423
carbon monoxide 270
carbonates 222
carbon-carbon double bond 280–281
carnivores 107

cartilage 50
catalase 251
catalysts 251–252, 253, 254
   biological see enzymes
catalytic converters 272
cataracts 359
cations 170
cell membranes 7, 17–18, 19
cell structure 15–18
   questions 19
cell walls 19
   bacteria 7
   plant 4, 18
cells 15, 28; see also movement, intercellular
   active transport 32
   animal 17, 19
   diffusion 28–29
   metabolism 23
   osmosis 29–32
   plant 17, 18, 19
   questions 33
cellulose 4, 18, 19, 20, 27
chain reaction 434–435
changing states of matter 136–138
charges on ions 172–173
chemical energy 373, 375
chemical formulae 143, 162–163, 168
   equations 162–167
   ionic compounds 174–175, 176–177
   questions 168–169
chemical reactions see reactions
chemical tests 219–222
   questions 222–223
chitin 5
chlorine 196–197, 198
   test 220
chloroethene, polymerisation 287
chlorophyll 8, 18, 36–37
chloroplasts 4, 7, 18
chromatogram 148
chromatography, paper 147–149, 150
chromosomes 7, 17, 76, 81, 82
   sex 88
cilia 51

circuit diagrams 331
circuits, electrical 329–330, 331–332, 334–335
circulatory systems 16, 56–57
   arteries, veins and capillaries 63–64
   composition of blood 58–60
   heart 61–63
   questions 64–66
climate change 202–203, 205, 271
climate, ecosystems 105
clones 74
coefficients, chemical equations 163
colon 43
combustion
   alkanes 278
   alkenes 282
   chemical equation 165
   incomplete 270
   reactions 201, 232, 234–237
comets 442, 444
communities, ecosystems 102, 106
complete combustion 236
compounds 143
   covalent 178
   ionic 170, 172
concentration, effect on reaction rates 248–249, 253, 254
concentration gradient 28, 32
   diffusion rates 29
condensation 137
condensation point 269
conductors 328–329
conservation of energy 375
consumers, ecosystems 101, 107
control rods, nuclear reactor 435
copper
   reaction with oxygen 204–205
   reactivity series 207
coronary arteries and veins 63
covalent bonding 178–182
   diagrams 179
   questions 182–183
cross-pollination 74
crude oil 267–272
   questions 272–273

456 INDEX

crystals/crystallisation 145, 175
   water 221
current
   alternating/direct 327
   heating effect 325
   measuring 329–330
   questions 333
   series circuit 332–333
   and voltage 328–333
cuticle 37
cytoplasm 6, 17

D

Darwin's theory of evolution 90–92
decay, radioactive 423–425, 426
deceleration 296, 301, 316, 320–321
decomposition/decomposers 8, 102, 108–109
denaturing 24
deoxyribonucleic acid see DNA
deposition 137
depth, pressure 394
development 3
diamonds 181–182
diaphragm 50, 52
diatomic molecules 196
diesel 271
diffusion 28–29, 33
   gases 138–139, 141
   liquids 140, 141
digestion 40–43, 44
   enzymes 6, 40, 42, 46
   system 16, 40–41, 46
direct current 327
disaccharides 20
displacement reactions 237–239
displayed formulae, organic chemistry 265, 266
distance-time graphs 297–298, 305–306
distillation
   fractional 146–147
   simple 146
DNA 7, 81
   mutations 92, 93
   viruses 9
dominant alleles 82–83, 86, 94
dot-and-cross diagrams 180

double circulation 60
double covalent bonds 180
double helix see DNA
dry ice 138
ductility 160
duodenum 41, 42

E

ecological pyramids 109–110
ecosystems 101–103
   biotic/abiotic factors 105
   carbon cycle 111–112
   energy flow 110–111
   feeding relationships 107–112
   interactions 104
   questions 106
efficiency, energy transfers 377
ejaculation 77
elastic energy 374
electric motors 408–411
   questions 411
electrical circuits 329–330, 331–332, 334–335
electrical energy 376
electrical power 326
electricity; see also mains electricity
   current and voltage 328–333
   mains electricity 325–327
   resistance 334–339
electromagnetic spectrum 352–357, 358
electromagnetism 406
electrons 152, 154, 415–416
   electric current 328–329
   shared pair 178
electrostatic attraction 175
electrostatic force 309
elements 142–143, 417
embryos 73, 77
emissions, radioactive 419
endocrine system 16
endoscope 366
endothermic reactions 233
energetics
   endothermic reactions 233
   exothermic reactions 231–232
   heat energy measurements 233–241
   questions 241–243

energy flow, ecosystems 110–111
energy stores 373–374
energy transfers 373–377
   questions 377–378
environment 102; see also ecosystems
environment vs. genes 89
environmental problems, fossil fuels 271–272
enzymes 23–27, 27
   catalase 251
   digestive 6, 40, 42
   extracellular 6, 23
   genetic engineering 127
   intracellular 23
epidermis, leaf 37
equations
   chemical 162–167, 169
   ionic 217, 218
   symbol 163
   uniformly accelerated motion 305
   wave 347
essential amino acids 21
ethane 274, 277
ethanol 121
ethene 280
   polymerisation 284
eukaryotic organisms 7, 15
evaporation 137
evolution 90–93
excretion 3
excretory system 16
exhalation 52
exothermic reactions 210, 231–232
extracellular enzymes 6, 23

F

F_1 generation, genetics 84
F_2 generation, genetics 84
faeces 41, 43
family trees 86–87
fatty acids 21
feeding relationships 105, 107–108
   decomposition 108–109
   ecological pyramids 109–110
   questions 112–114
female human reproductive system 76, 80
fertilisation 73, 75–76

INDEX

fetus 77
filaments (light bulb) 325
filtration 145
fission, nuclear 433–436
fitness, biological 91, 94
fixed resistors 338
flaccidity, cells 32
flagella 8
flame tests 221, 223
flowering plants 4
fluorescent tubes 357
fluorine 196–197, 198
food chains 107, 113
food production 119
    breadmaking 121–123
    glasshouses and polytunnels 119–121
    questions 123–124
food tests 22
food webs 108, 112, 113; see also feeding relationships
forces and movement 314–319
    questions 320–321
forces and shape 308–312
    questions 312–313
formula types, organic chemistry 264–266
formulae, chemical see chemical formulae
fossil fuels 111, 202–203, 271
fossils 91
fractional distillation 146–147
    crude oil 268–271
fractionating columns 146–147, 269
francium 193
freezing point 136, 138
frequency, wavelength 348–349
friction 309, 310–311, 313
    braking 317
fructose 20
fuel oil 271
fuels, hydrocarbons 269
fungi 5–6
fusion, nuclear 433, 436, 448

G

galaxies 447
galvanised iron 211
gametes 73, 74, 83, 89
gamma radiation 357, 419, 433–434
gamma radiography 427–429
gas exchange system 16, 50–51
    questions 54–55
    ventilation of lungs 51–54
gases 135–140, 140, 395–398
    atmosphere 199–203
    noble 159
    pressure 392–394, 395, 398
    tests 219–220
gasoline (petrol) 270
Geiger–Müller (GM) tube 420
gene gun 129–130
general formulae, organic chemistry 264, 281
genes 74, 81, 82
genes vs. environment 89
genetic crosses 83–87, 95
genetic modification 125
    bacteria 126–128
    plants 128–130
    questions 130–131
    recombinant DNA 125
genetic variation 73, 79, 89–90
genetics 81
    chromosomes and genes 81
    Darwin's theory of evolution 90–92
    genes and alleles 82
    natural selection examples 92–93
    questions 94–96
    sex determination 88
genotypes 83–84, 86–87
giant covalent structures 181–182
    vs. simple molecular structures 182
giant ionic lattices 175–176
glasshouses 119–121, 123
global heating 202–203
glucose 20, 48, 121
    product of photosynthesis 34
    test for 22
glycerol 21
glycogen 5, 20, 27
golden rice 130
grass 107
grasshoppers 107
gravitational energy 374
gravitational field strength 319, 444–445
gravitational force 442
gravitational potential energy (GPE) 381–384, 385
gravity 308
greenhouse effect 119, 202–203
greenhouse gases 203, 205, 271
greenhouses 39, 119–121, 123
groups, elements 158–159
guard cells 37
guinea pigs 83–84, 94

H

habitats 102, 106
haemoglobin 59
half-life 425, 426
halogen light bulbs 326
halogens 159, 196–197
    questions 198
health dangers, radioactivity 430–431
heart 61–62, 66
heart cycle 62, 65
heat death, universe 376
heat energy measurements 233–241
    questions 241–243
heating elements 325
herbicides 129
herbivores 107
heterozygous genes 83–84, 86–87, 94
high-density polythene (HDPE) 285
HIV (human immunodeficiency virus) 9
homozygous genes 83, 85, 86–87
hormones 56, 58
host cells 8
hoverflies 92
human immunodeficiency virus (HIV) 9
human insulin, transgenic bacteria 126, 130, 131
human reproductive systems 76–78
hydra 74

hydrocarbons 202–203, 264, 266, 268
  saturated 274, 277
  unsaturated 281
hydrochloric acid 139, 197, 210
  reaction with calcium carbonate 244–251
hydroelectric power 386
hydrogen
  isotopes 417, 436
  reaction with oxygen 202, 204
  test 219
hydrogen chloride 139, 179, 197
hydrogen halides 197
hydrogen peroxide 251–252, 254
hydroponics 120
hyphae 6, 11

I

identical twins 90
ileum 41, 43
immune response 59–60
immune system 9
immunity 60
incomplete combustion 236, 270, 278
indicators, pH 215
industrial catalysts 252
infrared radiation 355
inhalation 51, 52, 54
inheritance see genetics
insect pollination 75, 79
insulators 328–329
insulin 126
interactions, ecosystems 104
intercostal muscles 50, 52
intermolecular forces 180–181
  alkanes 277
  hydrocarbons 268
internal control 3
intestines 41, 42–43
intracellular enzymes 23
invertebrates 5
iodine 196–197, 198
  isotope 427–428
  solution 35, 43
ionic bonding 170–176
  questions 176–177

ionic compounds 140, 182
ionic equations 217, 218
ionic salts 197
ionising radiation 418–419; see also radioactivity
  health dangers 430–431
  penetration 419–420
ions 170, 171
  testing 221
iron
  reaction with dilute acids 209–210
  reaction with oxygen 200, 203–204
  reaction with water 208
  reactivity series 207
  rusting 200, 211, 213
irradiation, sterilisation 428–429
isomers 275
isotopes 153, 156, 157, 166–167, 417–418, 427–428
  half-life 425–426

J

joules 379

K

kerosene 270
kidney dialysis 29
kinetic energy 310–311, 373, 376, 378, 382–384, 386

L

lactate 48–49
Lactobacillus bulgaricus 8
lanthanoids 159
lattices, giant ionic 175–176
leavened bread 121
leaves, structure 37–38, 44
lenses 350
life processes 3
ligases 125
light 356
light bulbs 326
light emitting diodes (LEDs) 332
light intensity, effect on photosynthesis 38, 120–121
light waves 359–367
  questions 369

limiting factors 38–39
lipases 41
lipids 21–22, 27
  test for 22
liquids 135–140, 140
  pressure 392–393
liquified petroleum gas (LPG) 270, 274
lithium 189, 194
  reaction with air 192
  reaction with dilute acids 209
  reaction with water 191, 207
litmus 215, 217, 218
lizards 107
lock and key model, enzymes 23
low-density polythene (LDPE) 285
lungs 50–54, 55; see also respiration
lymphocytes 58, 59

M

Magdeburg hemispheres 393–394
magnesium
  reaction with dilute acids 209–210
  reaction with oxygen 202, 204
  reaction with water 208
magnesium ions 171
magnetic energy 374
magnetic fields 404–405
magnetic force 309
magnetism 403–406
  questions 406–407
magnification 365
mains electricity
  alternating/direct current 327
  current, heating effect 325
  electrical power 326
  questions 327
malleability 160
manganese oxide 251–252, 254
mangrove swamps 101
mass numbers 152–153, 156, 159
matter, states see states of matter
medical imaging 427–428
melting points 136, 138, 141, 183
  giant covalent structures 182
  ionic compounds 176, 177
  simple molecular structures 181

membranes, partially permeable 18, 29–31
memory cells 60
mesophyll 38
metabolism, cell 23
metals
   and non-metals 160, 177
   reactivity series 205–209
   reactivity series, questions 210–213
meteorites 382–383
meteors 382
methane 270, 274, 277
   covalent bonding 179
microwaves 354–355
milky way 447
mimicry 92
mitochondria 7, 18, 33
   aerobic respiration 32
mixtures 143–144, 147–149
molecular formulae, organic chemistry 264
molecular structures 180
molecules
   biological *see* biological molecules
   branched chain 276
   chemical 151
   covalent 179
   diatomic 196
   straight chain 276
monohybrid crosses 83
monomers 284, 288
monosaccharides 20
moons 443–444
motion in the universe 441–445
moulds 6
movement 3
movement, intercellular
   active transport 32
   diffusion 28–29
   osmosis 29–32
   questions 33
movement and forces 314–319
   questions 320–321
movement and position 295–305
   questions 305–307
mucus 51

multicellular organisms 4, 5, 15
muscles 15, 19
   intercostal 50
mutations 92, 93
mycelium 6

N

naming conventions, compounds 173
natural selection 96
   Darwin's theory of evolution 90–92
   examples 92–93
nebulae 448
nectaries 75
negative ions 170, 171
nematode worms 109
nervous system 16
neutralisation reactions 217, 232
   measuring heat energy 240–241
neutrons 152–153, 159, 415–416, 419
newton, unit of force 309, 316
Newton's theory of gravity 441
nitric acid 272
nitrogen
   atmospheric 199, 203
   triple bond 180
noble gases 159
non-flowering plants 4
normal reaction force 309
nuclear energy 433, 435–436
nuclear force 417–418
nuclear power stations 423
nuclear reactions 433–436
   questions 437
   stars 448
nuclear waste, long-term storage 431
nuclear weapons 423, 435–436
nucleus, atomic 152, 415–416
   unstable 418
nucleus, cell 7, 17
nutrition 3, 34
   human digestion 40–43
   photosynthesis 34–40
   questions 43–45

O

oak trees 109
octane 270
oesophagus 42
oestrogen 78
ohms 334
Ohm's law 339
optical density 361
optical fibres 366–367
optimum pH, enzymes 25
optimum temperature, enzymes 24, 27
orbits 296, 443–444, 445
organ systems 16
organelles 7, 15, 17, 19
organic chemistry 263
   alkanes 274–278
   alkenes 280–282
   crude oil 267–272
   hydrocarbons 264
   questions 266
   synthetic polymers 284–289
   types of formula 264–266
organic compounds 111
   naming conventions 275
   structural variations 275, 281
organisms
   characteristics 3
   groups 4–9, 10
   questions 10–11
organs 15
   human 16
osmosis 29–32, 33
ova 73
ovaries 74, 76
oviduct 77
ovulation 77
ovules 73, 74
oxide ions 171
oxygen 36, 53–54
   atmospheric 199, 199–201, 203
   double bond 180
   product of photosynthesis 34
   respiration 28
   test 220
oxygen debt 49
oxyhaemoglobin 59
ozone layer 356

P

palisade mesophyll 38
pancreas 41, 42
paper chromatography 147–149, 150
parasites 8, 105
partially permeable membranes 18, 29–31
particles, atomic 415–420
   questions 421
particles, states of matter 136
pascals 391, 396
pathogens 8, 59–60
pea plants 84–86, 89–90, 94, 95
penetration, ionising radiation 419–420
pentane 274, 275–276
pepsin 42
peptidoglycan 7
periodic table 143, 154, 155, 158–160
   group 1 elements 189–193, 194–195
   group 7 elements 196–197, 198
   questions 160–161
periods, elements 159
periscope 360
petrol 270
pH scale 214–215, 217
   effect on enzymes 25
phagocytes 58, 59
phagocytosis 59, 60
phenotypes 83–84, 86, 95
phloem 38
phosphorus, reaction with oxygen 201
photosynthesis 4, 18, 34–40, 44, 45, 110
   glasshouses 120–121
placenta 77
planets 442–443, 445
plants 4
   cells 17, 18, 19
   characteristics 10
   genetically modified 128–130, 131
plasma, blood 58, 59
plasmids 8, 125, 126, 128–129, 131

Plasmodium 7, 8
plasmolysis 32
plastics
   disposal 288–289
   environmental problems 288
platelets 58
pleural cavity 50, 55
pleural fluid 51
pleural membranes 50
plutonium 436
pneumothorax 55
polar bears 93
poles, magnetic 404
pollen grains 73, 74, 75–76, 79
pollen tubes 75–76
pollination 74–76, 79
pollution 105
polychloroethene 287
polydactyly 86–87
polyethene 285
polymerisation
   alkenes 286
   ethene 284
polymers 20
polymers, synthetic 282, 284–289
   questions 289
polypropene 286–287
polysaccharides 20
polystyrene 288
polytetrafluoroethene (PTFE) 287–288
polytunnels 119–121, 123
polyvinylchloride (PVC, now polychloroethene) 287
ponds 101, 102
populations, species 102–103, 106
position and movement 295–305
   questions 305–307
positive ions 170, 171
potassium 189, 194
   reaction with air 192
   reaction with dilute acids 209
   reaction with water 191, 207
potassium bromide 198
potassium carbonate 216
potassium hydroxide 216
potassium manganate 140

potassium nitrate 223
power 384–385
   questions 386
predation 105
pressure 391–394, 395
   effect on rate of reaction 250–251
   questions 394
   temperature 397–398
primary consumers 107
prisms 364–365
producers, ecosystems 101, 107
prokaryotic organisms 7, 10, 11
propane 266, 274, 277, 278
propene 280
   polymerisation 286–287
proteases 41, 42
proteins 21, 27
   test for 22
protoctists 7, 10
protons 152–153, 415–416
protozoa 7
PTFE (polytetrafluoroethene) 287–288
puberty 78
pulmonary arteries 60
pulmonary circulation 60
pulmonary veins 60
Punnett squares 84
pure breeding 85
PVC (polyvinylchloride, now polychloroethene) 287
pyramids of biomass/numbers 109–110, 113–114

Q

quadrats 102–104, 106

R

rabbits 110
radiation
   artificial 423
   living things 423
   from rocks 422–423
   from space 423
radiation, ionising *see* ionising radiation
radio waves 354

INDEX

radioactive elements 193
radioactivity 415–420, 422–426
   questions 421, 426
radioactivity, applications
   dating 430
   medicine 427–428
   questions 431–432
   scanning 429
   sterilisation 428–429
   tracers 428
radiotherapy 428
radium 422
radon 422
random sampling 103, 106
rate of diffusion 29, 33
rate of osmosis 32
rate of reaction 244–252
   questions 253–255
reaction force 309
reactions
   combustion 232, 234–237
   displacement 237–239
   endothermic 233
   exothermic 231–232
   metals 205–209
   metals, questions 210–213
   metals with acids 232
   neutralisation 232, 240–241
   rate *see* rate of reaction
recessive alleles 82–83, 86
recombinant DNA 125, 131
rectum 43
red blood cells 31, 58, 59, 65
red giants 448
refinery gases 270
reflection 349–350
   light 360
   sound 368
   total internal 362–366
reflectors 365
refractive index 361
refraction 350
   light 360–362
   sound 368–369
relative atomic mass 153–154, 156, 159, 166–167
relative formula mass 167, 169

reproduction 3, 73
   plants, sexual reproduction 74–76
   questions 78–80
   reproductive systems 16, 76–78
   sexual vs. asexual 73–74
residues 145
resistance 325, 334–339
   questions 340
respiration 3, 18, 28, 47, 111
   aerobic 32, 47–48, 50
   anaerobic 48–49
   questions 49
restriction enzymes 125, 126
retardation factor 148–149, 150
rice, genetically modified 130
ripple tank 348
RNA (ribonucleic acid) 9
rock salt 145
rods, bacteria 8
rubidium 191, 194
rusting, iron 200, 211, 213

S

saliva 42
salmon 108
salt 145, 170
salts 217, 218
   heat energy in dissolving 239–240
Sankey diagrams 376–377, 378
saprotrophic nutrition 6, 10, 11
satellites 443–444
saturated hydrocarbons 274, 277
scrotum 77
scrubbing, power station gases 272
secondary consumers 107
secondary immune response 60
secondary sexual characteristics 77–78
selection pressures 92, 93
selective advantages 92
self-pollination 74
semen 77
semilunar valves 63–64
sensitivity 3
separation, mixtures 143–149, 150

series circuits 332–333
sex determination 88
sexual intercourse 77
sexual reproduction 73–74, 89
   plants 74–76
shape and forces 308–312
   questions 312–313
shared pair, electrons 178–179
silicon dioxide 182
simple distillation 146
simple molecular structures 181
   vs. giant covalent structures 182
single-celled organisms *see* unicellular organisms
small intestine 41
sodium 189, 194
   ions 171
   reaction with air 192
   reaction with dilute acids 209
   reaction with water 190–191, 207
sodium carbonate 216
sodium chloride 170, 171–172, 217
   structure 175, 177
sodium hydroxide 216, 217
sodium oxide 174
Solar System 441
solids 135–138, 140
   pressure 391–392
soluble carbonates 216
solutions 145
solvents 145, 147–149
sonar 368
sound waves 367–368
species 4
specific heat capacity 234
speed 296
   measuring 298–299
speed trap 297
sperm 73, 77, 78
sperm count 80
spheres, bacteria 8
sphincter muscle 42
spiral galaxies 447
spirals, bacteria 8
spongy mesophyll 38
squeaky pop test 202, 219
stamens 74, 75

starch 4, 44
   test for 22, 35–36, 43
stars
   classification 447
   formation 448
   life-cycle 448–449
states of matter 135–140
   questions 140–141
   symbols 166, 169
stellar evolution 446–449
sterilisation 357
   radiation 428–429
sticky ends 126
stigmas 74, 75–76
stomach 42
stomata 37
stonefly nymphs 108
stop clock 299
stopping distance 317
straight chain molecules 276
stroboscope 299
structural formulae, organic chemistry 265–266
styles 75
subatomic particles 152, 155, 156
sublimation 137–138
subscripts, chemical formulae 162
substances, chemical 142–149
   questions 149–150
substrates 23
sucrose 4, 20, 30–31
sugars 4, 20, 38, 123
sulfur
   reaction with oxygen 202, 204
sulfur dioxide 272
sulfuric acid 272
sulfurous acid 272
superconductivity 339
surface area, effect on rate of reaction 247–248, 253
surface area to volume ratio, organisms 57
survival of the fittest 91, 92; see also natural selection
symbol equations 163
synthetic polymers 284–289
   questions 289
systemic circulation 61

T

technetium, isotope 428
Teflon 287–288
telecommunications, optical fibres 367
temperature 27
   effect on enzymes 24, 25–26
   effect on photosynthesis 39
   effect on rate of reaction 250, 253
   pressure 397–398
   rate of diffusion 29
   state of matter 138
tennessine 198
tertiary consumers 107
testes 76–77
testosterone 78
tests, chemical 219–222
tetrafluoroethene, polymerisation 287–288
thermal decomposition 164, 233
thermal energy 374
thorax 50
thrust 314
time period, wave 347
tissues 15
titanium, reactivity 213
tobacco mosaic virus 9
total internal reflection 362–366
tracers, radioactive 423
trachea 50
transgenic bacteria 126
transgenic organisms 125
transmitters, radio 354
triple covalent bonds 180
trophic levels 107, 109, 111
tropical rainforests 105
tuning fork 348
turgidity, cells 31
twins, identical 90

U

ultraviolet (UV) light 356–357
unbalanced forces 310, 313, 314–315, 320
unicellular organisms 5, 7, 56–57
uniform magnetic fields 404
uniformly accelerated motion, equations 305
units 330
   acceleration 300, 441
   electric charge 329
   electric current 330
   energy 379
   force 309, 441
   gravitational field strength 441
   length 441
   mass 441
   physics 295
   power 326, 384
   pressure 391, 394
   resistance 334
   speed 296, 441
   temperature 391, 397
   time 441
universal indicators, pH 215
unleavened bread 121
unsaturated hydrocarbons 281, 282
upthrust 310
uranium, nuclear fission 433–435
urea 56, 59
UV (ultraviolet) light 356–357

V

vacuoles 18, 59–60
variable resistors 338
variations, within species 90–91, 95–96
vectors (plasmids) 126, 128–129
vectors (viruses) 127
veins 61, 63–64, 65
velocity-time graphs 302–304, 306–307, 318, 320
vena cava 61
ventilation of lungs 51–54, 55; see also respiration
ventricles 62, 63
vertebrates 5
viruses 8–9, 10, 11
   vectors 127
viscosity, hydrocarbons 268
visible light 356
Visking tubing 29–31, 45–46
volatility, hydrocarbons 268
volume to surface area, organisms 57

voltage 326, 330
    alternating 327
    measuring 331
voltmeter 331

W

wasps 92
wasted energy 374, 376
water
    covalent bonding 180
    formula 164
    intermolecular forces 180–181
    reaction with alkali metals 190–191
    reaction with metals 207–208
    test 221, 223

watts 384
wave equation 347
wavefronts 346
wavelength 346–347
    frequency 348–349
    light 353
waves 345–350
    questions 351
weight 309, 319, 320
white blood cells 58, 59–60
white dwarfs 448
wind pollination 75, 79
windpipe 50
work 379–384
    questions 386

X

x-rays 357
xylem 38

Y

yeasts 5, 48
    breadmaking 121–123

Z

zinc
    galvanised iron 211
    reaction with dilute acids 209–210
    reaction with water 208
    reactivity series 207
zygotes 73, 76, 82, 89

(Continued from imprint page ii)

Cordelia Molloy/Science Photo Library 330, Tony & Daphne Hallas/Science Photo Library 382T, David Parker/Science Photo Library 382B, Andrew Lambert Photography/Science Photo Library 396, Cnri/Science Photo Library 427, Dr P.Marazzi/Science Photo Library 428, Patrick Landmann/Science Photo Library 431BR, Martyn F Chillmaid/Science Photo Library FM(007); **SHUTTERSTOCK:** Kateryna Kon/Shutterstock 8C, Ktsdesign/Shutterstock 8B, JONG 16899/Shutterstock 82, 279photo Studio/Shutterstock 119TL, Digieva/Shutterstock 5, Resul Muslu/Shutterstock 122TL, Arka38/Shutterstock 122TR, Jiang Hongyan/Shutterstock 130, Benson HE/Shutterstock 135TL, VanHart/Shuttertstock 135TR, Dencg/Shuttertstock 142TL, Mylisa/Shutterstock 142TR, Zakharchuk/Shutterstock 151TL, Romanova Natali/Shutterstock 151TR, Pavlo Loushkin/ Shutterstock 162TL, Chris Lenfert/Shutterstock 162TR, Peter Hermes Furian/Shutterstock 175, KDEdesign/Shutterstock 182, Anastasios71/Shutterstock 199, JJSINA/Shutterstock 206, Ron Zmiri/Shutterstock 211T, Saoirse2013/Shutterstock 230, Titi-kako/Shutterstock 244TC2, Sherri R. Camp/Shutterstock 244TL, Jeff Schultes/Shutterstock 244TR, Dr.Oga/Shutterstock 263TC, Sam Strickler/Shutterstock 263TR, Dashu/Shutterstock 267, Anan Kaewkhammul/Shutterstock 268, Sinisa Botas/Shutterstock 270T, Best images/Shutterstock 270B, Werayuth Piriyapornprapa/Shutterstock 271T, Federico Rostagno/Shutterstock 271C, Vadim Ratnikov/Shutterstock 271B, XXLPhoto/Shutterstock 272T, Mary Terribery/Shutterstock 272B, Bitt24/Shutterstock 280, Daizuoxin/Shutterstock 285, Marian Paluszkiewicz/Shutterstock 483, YanLev/Shutterstock 297, Steve Photography/Shutterstock 300TL, Voyagerix/Shutterstock 309, Tooykrub/Shutterstock 328, Norman Chan/Shutterstock 332, EpicStockMedia/Shutterstock 344, Olga Selyutina/Shutterstock 345, Smileus/Shutterstock 348, Sirtravelalot/Shutterstock 355, Anatoly Vartanov/Shutterstock 356TL, Itsmejust/Shutterstock 357T, Pavel L Photo and Video/Shutterstock 359T, Przemyslaw Skibinski/Shutterstock 360, MidoSemsem/Shutterstock 365, Joanne Harris and Daniel Bubnich/Shutterstock 366, Morchella/Shutterstock 367, Rudmer Zwerver/Shutterstock 372, V_E/Shutterstock 384T, Volodymyr Goinyk/Shutterstock 390, Karrapavan/Shutterstock 402,Viktorija Reuta/Shutterstock 431, Cardens Design/Shutterstock 440, Sander van Sinttruye/Shutterstock 447T, Wolfgang Kloehr/Shutterstock 447C, Valeriy Lebedev/Shutterstock 447B, Olga Selyutina/Shutterstock FM (006B); **Sozaijiten:** Sozaijiten/Pearson Education Ltd 005TR.

All other images © Pearson Education

Disclaimer: neither Pearson, Edexcel nor the authors take responsibility for the safety of any activity. Before doing any practical activity you are legally required to carry out your own risk assessment. In particular, any local rules issued by your employer must be obeyed, regardless of what is recommended in this resource. Where students are required to write their own risk assessments, they must always be checked by the teacher and revised, as necessary, to cover any issues the students may have overlooked. The teacher should always have the final control as to how the practical is conducted.